EXPLORING MASCULINITIES

EXPLORING MASCULINITIES

IDENTITY, INEQUALITY, CONTINUITY, AND CHANGE

C. J. Pascoe and Tristan Bridges

NEW YORK   OXFORD
OXFORD UNIVERSITY PRESS

Oxford University Press is a department of the University of Oxford.
It furthers the University's objective of excellence in research,
scholarship, and education by publishing worldwide.

Oxford   New York
Auckland   Cape Town   Dar es Salaam   Hong Kong   Karachi
Kuala Lumpur   Madrid   Melbourne   Mexico City   Nairobi
New Delhi   Shanghai   Taipei   Toronto

With offices in
Argentina   Austria   Brazil   Chile   Czech Republic   France   Greece
Guatemala   Hungary   Italy   Japan   Poland   Portugal   Singapore
South Korea   Switzerland   Thailand   Turkey   Ukraine   Vietnam

For titles covered by Section 112 of the US Higher Education
Opportunity Act, please visit www.oup.com/us/he for the
latest information about pricing and alternate formats.

Published by Oxford University Press
198 Madison Avenue, New York, NY 10016
http://www.oup.com

Oxford is a registered trademark of Oxford University Press

Library of Congress Cataloging-in-Publication Data
Exploring masculinities : identity, inequality, continuity and change / [edited by]
C.J. Pascoe and Tristan Bridges.
      pages cm
   Includes bibliographical references.
   ISBN 978-0-19-931567-3 (pbk. : alk. paper) 1. Masculinity. 2. Men--Identity.
 I. Pascoe, C. J., 1974- II. Bridges, Tristan.
   HQ1090.E924 2016
   305.31--dc23
                                                        2015001211

Printing number: 9 8 7 6 5 4 3 2

Printed in the United States of America
on acid-free paper

For

Desmond, Parker, Emerson, Ciaran, and Spencer

&

Raewyn, Mike, and Michael

CONTENTS

ACKNOWLEDGMENTS *xi*

INTRODUCTION—EXPLORING MASCULINITIES:
HISTORY, REPRODUCTION, HEGEMONY, AND DISLOCATION *1*

PART I   HISTORICIZING MASCULINITIES 35

CHAPTER **1** Historicizing Masculinities—An Introduction *37*

   1. **Remaking Manhood through Race and "Civilization"** *50*
      Gail Bederman

   2. **Houdini, Tarzan, and the Perfect Man—Introduction** *67*
      John F. Kasson

   3. **Romantic Friendship: Male Intimacy and Middle-Class Youth
      in the Northern United States, 1800–1900** *75*
      E. Anthony Rotundo

   4. **Clothing and Gender in America: Children's Fashions,
      1890–1920** *89*
      Jo B. Paoletti

   5. **Shell-Shock as a Social Disease** *94*
      George L. Mosse

   6. **Breadwinners and Losers: Sanctions Against Male Deviance** *100*
      Barbara Ehrenreich

   7. **Guyland: Gendering the Transition to Adulthood** *107*
      Michael Kimmel

PART II   MULTIPLYING MASCULINITIES *121*

CHAPTER 2   Multiplying Masculinities—An Introduction   *123*

   8. The Social Organization of Masculinity   *136*
       Raewyn Connell

   9. Retrofitting Frontier Masculinity for Alaska's War
       against Wolves   *145*
       Sine Anahita and Tamara L. Mix

   10. Manhood Over Easy: Reflections on Hegemonic, Soft-Boiled,
       and Multiple Masculinities   *155*
       Melanie Heath

   11. Synthesized Masculinities: The Mechanics of Manhood
       among Delinquent Boys   *166*
       Victor Rios and Rachel Sarabia

   12. Inclusive Masculinities   *178*
       Eric Anderson

   13. Healthy for Whom?—Males, Men, and Masculinity:
       A Reflection on the Doing (and Study) of Dominance   *188*
       Matthew B. Ezzell

   14. On Patriarchs and Losers: Rethinking Men's Interests   *198*
       Michael A. Messner

   15. Masculinities as Structured Action   *207*
       James W. Messerschmidt

PART III   NAVIGATING MASCULINITIES *221*

CHAPTER 3   Navigating Masculinities—An Introduction   *223*

   16. Latino Boys, Masculinity, and Puberty   *235*
       Richard Mora

   17. "My Passport Says Shawn": Toward a Hip-Hop
       Cosmopolitanism   *245*
       Mark Anthony Neal

   18. Masculinity Dilemmas: Sexuality and Intimacy Talk
       among Christians and Goths   *258*
       Amy C. Wilkins

   19. Styled Masculinity: Men's Consumption of Salon Hair Care
       and the Construction of Difference   *269*
       Kristen Barber

   20. Becoming a Firefighter   *280*
       Matthew Desmond

21. **Can Bourdieu Help Us Understand Masculinity, and Can Masculinity Help Us Understand Bourdieu?** *291*
Adam Reich

22. **"Manning Up to Being Gay": Minority Masculinities in the Community and at the Club** *301*
Anthony C. Ocampo

23. **Negotiating the Field of Masculinity: The Production and Reproduction of Multiple Dominant Masculinities** *311*
Tony Coles

PART IV DISLOCATING MASCULINITIES *323*

CHAPTER 4 Dislocating Masculinities—An Introduction *325*

24. **Research on Men and Masculinities: Some Implications of Recent Theory for Future Work** *337*
Alan Petersen

25. **An Introduction to Female Masculinity: Masculinity without Men** *348*
J. Jack Halberstam

26. **Gosh, Boy George, You Must Be Awfully Secure in Your Masculinity!** *359*
Eve Kosofsky Sedgwick

27. **Midwest or Lesbian?: Gender, Rurality, and Sexuality** *364*
Emily Kazyak

28. **William's Doll and Me** *376*
Karl Bryant

29. **Penis Panics: Biological Maleness, Social Masculinity, and the Matrix of Perceived Sexual Threat** *382*
Laurel Westbrook and Kristen Schilt

30. **Negotiating Vulnerability and Fear: Rethinking the Relationship between Violence and Contemporary Masculinity** *394*
Miriam J. Abelson

31. **Dude-Sex: White Masculinities and 'Authentic' Heterosexual among Dudes Who Have Sex with Dudes** *402*
Jane Ward

32. **Masculinities and Post-Homophobias?** *412*
Tristan Bridges and C. J. Pascoe

CONCLUSION—HISTORICIZING, MULTIPLYING, NAVIGATING, AND DISLOCATING: LOOKING TO THE FUTURE OF GENDER THEORY *425*

ACKNOWLEDGMENTS

It takes a village, and more than a bit of luck, to write a book like this. We were interested in crafting a book that could be used in classrooms, but also wanted to organize the field of masculinity studies in new ways. Our editor, Sherith Pankratz at Oxford University Press, guided us patiently through several iterations of this text. In addition to Sherith, we received incredible feedback from a number of reviewers of early drafts of the Table of Contents. Most specifically, we'd like to thank Freeden Oeur for such incredible feedback on an early draft that dramatically shifted our organization of the book. The whole process helped us to consider what was new about this book and how we were building on and connecting diverse bodies of existing research.

Additionally, we have both benefitted from incredible mentorship from masculinities scholars more generally. Michael Messner and Michael Kimmel in particular were so helpful in the early stages of this project. As we worked through edits and suggestions, we carefully talked through suggestions and advice from "West Coast Michael" and "East Coast Michael" and the book is so much stronger as a result. We also received feedback from Raewyn Connell and James Messerschmidt in the early stages of this project and were so grateful for their time and attention. Perhaps the earliest kernel of the manuscript emerged out of discussions C. J. had with Barrie Thorne about frustrations she had with the current state of the field as she was writing what would become the text of *Dude, You're a Fag.*

As we developed a new framework building on Connell's theory of gender relations to consider how all of the work we think of as masculinities studies can be connected, we were also incredibly fortunate to receive original contributions from a number of scholars in the field. We were both completely honored to be able to include original work by (in the order they appear in the volume) Melanie Heath, Victor Rios, Rachel Sarabia, Eric Anderson, Matthew Ezzell, James Messerschmidt, Richard Mora, Kristen Barber, Adam Reich, Anthony Ocampo, Laurel Westbrook, Kristen Schilt, and Miriam Abelson. We also want to thank John Ibson for allowing us to publish a picture from his personal collection of early U.S. photographs depicting men together.

We've also benefited from the incredible feedback we've received less formally as we discuss the book with others. Among the many who deserve recognition for these conversations, and whose ideas, we hope, are reflected in these pages are Tara Tober, Megan Sheppard, Sarah Diefendorf, Sarah Mosseri, Jaime Hartless, Lauren Stewart, and D'Lane Compton, as well as several iterations of C. J.'s *Contested Masculinities* classes at Colorado College and Tristan's *Men and Masculinities* courses at both the University of Virginia and The College at Brockport, State University of New York.

We are *deeply* indebted to our incredible research assistant, Andrea Herrera. She kept us organized and on task and, quite frankly, made the production of this book possible. We also benefited from the careful attention of Katy Albis at Oxford University Press, particularly in helping us organize the manuscript and helping us with all of the copyright issues that are a bit outside either of our expertise.

We are both also thankful for the support of our families. It is obvious that we wrote a lot for this text; what is less obvious is that we have also, between the two of us, had four babies during the period of time we were working on this book. Countless chapters have been written or reviewed holding babies, washing bottles, or with bleary eyes left over from sleepless nights. Our partners, Megan Sheppard and Tara Tober, have done that extra, often unacknowledged, labor that makes a book like this possible on top of the conversations about the book, reading over drafts, and discussions about all of the joys and struggles involved in collecting work from so many authors. To both of you we say thank you.

We have also been working on this book for a couple years now. It all started with an email between two scholars, strangers to one another. That email led not only to a close friendship, but also to generative and exciting discussions that resulted in this text. This project has led us to feel reinvigorated about the field, our research, and the future of sociology of gender. So, as cheesy as it is to "acknowledge" each other, we'd be remiss not to mention this and the importance of our hard work and friendship to this project.

EXPLORING MASCULINITIES
History, Reproduction, Hegemony, and Dislocation

"The closer we come to uncovering some form of exemplary masculinity, a masculinity which is solid and sure of itself, the clearer it becomes that masculinity is structured through contradiction: the more it asserts itself, the more it calls itself into question."

—SEGAL 1990: 123

"Manhood is not bestowed at the outset; it must be constructed, or let us say 'manufactured.' A man is therefore a sort of *artifact*, and as such he always runs the risk of being found defective."

—BADINTER 1995: 2

WHAT IS MASCULINITY?

During Super Bowl XLIV, "Dove for Men" (2010) aired a commercial entitled "You are a Man!" Against background music of the *William Tell Overture*, the commercial followed a man's life from conception through childhood through adulthood narrated by the following lyrics:

> Get born. Get slapped. Now get to school. Be good in sports. Always look cool. Lift weights. Be strong. Know how to fight. Stay out late. But be polite. And find a nice girl that will say "I Do," and have three kids that look just like you. Rake leaves from the hedge and mow the yard. Honey can you open this jar? If you hear a noise in the middle of the night, go check it out with a flashlight. You reached a stage where you feel at ease. You've come this far and it wasn't a breeze. You can take on anything. Of course you can, because you are a man!

"You are a Man!" indeed. This short, entertaining ad transmits a lesson in masculinity, telling us exactly what society expects of men. In this ad Dove presents masculinity as something men possess simply by virtue of being born male. Dove tells men they "can take on anything" *because* they are men. Masculinity messages like this are everywhere—in the music videos we watch, the books we read, the history we are taught, the advertisements at which we laugh, and more. Indeed, advertisements like this one are part of a society-wide process through which behaviors, identities, embodiments, and dispositions we come to think of as "masculine" are constructed.

Although the Dove ad situates men as unproblematically masculine (i.e., "You are a man, so these are all the things you *can* and *should* do"), a great deal of popular culture situates masculinity as something to which men must lay claim (rather than passively possess) lest they risk somehow losing it. For instance, during the same Super Bowl (XLIV), a separate commercial framed masculinity as a much more tenuous—not to mention onerous—achievement. This commercial, advertising the Dodge Charger, featured no music. It presented a series of men, looking straight-faced and somewhat defeated into the camera. Some aren't shaved, some are in pajamas, but they all look deadly serious as the camera pans closer to each man's face and then cuts to another, accompanied by the following message:

> I will get up and walk the dog at 6:30 AM. I will eat some fruit as part of my breakfast. I will shave. I will clean the sink after I shave. I will be at work at 8:00 AM. I will sit through two-hour meetings. I will say yes, when you want me to say yes. I will be quiet when you don't want me to say no. I will take your call. I will listen to your opinion of my friends. I will listen to your friends' opinions of my friends. I will be civil to your mother. I will put the seat down. I will separate the recycling. I will carry your lip-balm. I will watch your vampire TV shows with you. I will take my socks off before getting into bed. I will put my underwear in the basket. And because I do this, I will drive the car I want to drive. Charger. Man's Last Stand!

Unlike the Dove ad, this ad tells men they are *not* masculine. In fact, we are told that the requirements of modern society (being a good worker and a healthy adult) and heterosexual relationships (overbearing and demanding female partners) actually *emasculate* men. This commercial tells men they have a problem while simultaneously offering the solution (e.g., Messner and de Oca 2005; Bridges and Kimmel 2009). Their "problem," according to the commercial, is that they are fighting an endless barrage of internal urges on a moment-by-moment basis to suppress the wild man who lives inside them. The solution is purchasing the thing that will express this inner masculinity—a Dodge Charger. "Release your inner man," the commercial seems to say.

Dove portrays men as in control; Dodge situates men as controlled by others. Who's right? That is a more difficult question to answer than it might at first appear. For instance, although these two ads seem like they are talking about masculinity in completely different ways, they also rely on a great deal of common ground. Both commercials present masculinity as a natural property of men. Whereas Dove presents men as unproblematically embracing their gender through various tasks throughout life and around the house, Dodge situates these same sorts of obligations as attempts to subdue men's "natural" inclinations. Both commercials rely on us understanding masculinity as some kind of inherent property of men. But what, exactly, they each situate as "inherent" is vastly different.

The reason these seemingly contradictory advertisements resonate with viewers is that when discussing masculinity, we have learned to embrace contradictions embedded in understandings of masculinity. And we can casually ignore these contradictions most of the time because most of us proceed from the notion that everyone knows exactly what we mean when we address the topic. For instance, when we ask students to define masculinity, their answers commonly refer to specific objects (e.g., guns, beer, neck ties, tools, beef), practices (e.g., chopping wood, lifting weights, buying and selling stocks), or bodily features (e.g., facial stubble, musculature, weathered skin). Like the Dove commercial, students typically get around actually defining masculinity by instead offering a list of potential ingredients—as though one could combine many of them, bake at 350 degrees for 30 minutes, and out pops a man.

Thus, asking "What is masculinity?" often elicits smiles and knowing smirks because the question—on the surface—seems so self-evident as to not require an answer. As such, a book on masculinity might seem unnecessary. Men are studied all the time, aren't they? Isn't history the history of men? Aren't politics the politics of men? Medicine, the medicine of men? As feminist analyses have shown, academic inquiry has often taken men for granted as nongendered subjects. But this book is not addressing men per se. Instead it examines *masculinity*.

What, then, is the difference between men and masculinity? Why use these two different terms? "Man" refers to a state of being; "masculinity" refers to much more: identity, performance, power, privilege, relations, styles, and structure. In other words, masculinity is what makes one a man. But once we try to articulate exactly what makes a man, we find that it is often much more difficult than we might have anticipated. Most of us casually use a sort of "I know it when I see it" approach or think of masculinity as a series of "nots" (e.g., not feminine, not "gay," not interested in interior design, cooking, or clothing).

Whereas we often easily recognize women's lives as gendered (in fact we have established entire classes, departments, and bodies of scholarship around women's studies), masculinity is less easy to recognize and often seems invisible. Men's lives, however, are just as organized by gender as are women's. We too often fail to appreciate this. Why? Because power renders certain identities and structures less visible than others. The mechanisms that afford privilege are often invisible to those on the receiving end of that privilege; meanwhile what makes people marginal is all too apparent to the marginalized. As Michael Kimmel writes, "Marginality is visible and painfully visceral. Privilege is invisible and painlessly pleasant" (1990: 94). When privilege is "working," those most advantaged by systems of power and inequality are relatively unaware of their advantages (e.g., McIntosh 1988).

So why is it so important to recognize men as gendered? Because gender is one of the major ways through which power structures, privilege, and inequality are reproduced—in addition to (and in combination with) race and class. Therefore, it is important to see men as *gendered* because masculinity replicates power and affords power to those with that identity. It is important to investigate masculinity to understand the ways in which politics, the state, institutions of school and work, religion, family, and nationality are infused with, and themselves shape, masculinity.

This book is premised on an understanding that masculinity (as well as femininity, and gender more generally) is "socially constructed." That is, the readings in this text do not assume that masculinity is biologically determined.[1] Rather, this text operates on a social constructionist perspective—emphasizing varying definitions of masculinity, the role of individuals in contesting and enforcing these definitions, the patterning of masculinity, the role of various social institutions in sustaining and organizing masculinity, and the ways in which power is reproduced, embodied, and contested regarding masculinity. This means that three things are going to be highlighted in this text. *First*, masculinity is socially constructed. As such, meanings of masculinity are not transhistorical or universal. *Second*, variations among men are important in terms of understanding masculinity. Not all men are beholden to or enact the same masculinity. Additionally, not all men have the same privileges by virtue of being male as all other men. As such, we might begin to think of *masculinities* in the plural. *Third*, masculinity may or may not be related to a male body. That is, although some of the sociology of masculinity has assumed a male body—such as Whitehead and Barrett do in arguing that masculinity is best understood as "what men do" (2001: 15-16)—our understanding of masculinity is broadened when we understand it as something women can "do" too.

Although masculinity is a term most of us use with a certain kind of casual confidence, there are really few aspects of masculinity that we can define conclusively. There is a general agreement that masculinity has something to do with men and that it is associated with a set of approved behaviors and activities. But the image we get is vague and the details can change a great deal depending on when, where, and who we ask. Masculinity has a slippery quality to defining and understanding it: the more precisely we attempt to define the term, the more likely it becomes that we are simply defining it in a single moment, context, historical period, or culture and for a particular group. Indeed, as Segal writes in one of the quotes at the outset of this introduction, "the more it asserts itself, the more it calls itself into question" (1990: 123). For the purposes of this volume, we define **masculinity** as *the practices, behaviors, attitudes, sexualities, emotions, positions, bodies, organizations, institutions, and all manner of expectations culturally associated with (though not limited to) people understood to be male.* One thing to note about our definition is that it is *descriptive*, not *prescriptive*. By this, we mean that masculinity is a description given to all manner of cultural roles, institutions, practices, and processes. *Prescriptive* accounts of masculinity focus primarily on what men *should* be like, rather than what they *are* like.[2]

This essay addresses different explorations into masculinity, from prescriptive to descriptive approaches. Biological and early sociological approaches tend to be prescriptive, whereas later sociological, specifically social constructionist approaches, tend to be descriptive. This essay outlines these approaches, describes the shift to a social constructionist approach, highlights important concepts, and suggests four contemporary approaches that characterize contemporary explorations of masculinity: historicizing, multiplying, navigating, and dislocating masculinity.

BIOLOGICAL EXPLORATIONS

A social constructionist approach to gender contradicts many of the common-sense understandings we have of masculinity. People use phrases like "raging hormones" to explain all manner of men's (often bad) behavior. After all, men, on average, have higher levels of testosterone than women. And testosterone makes men aggressive and hypersexual, right?

Well, yes and no. There's actually a lot of evidence indicating that what we think of as masculine behavior *produces* spikes in testosterone rather than the reverse (e.g., Sapolsky 1997; Mazur and Booth 1998; Booth et al. 2006). For instance, testosterone is often hailed as a magical elixir that makes men violent, prohibits them from falling in love, and provides a biological foundation for social hierarchies. But it turns out that a much more biologically accurate understanding of testosterone is that it is a biological *response* to (rather than *causal* mechanism of) aggression, love, and social status.

These claims about testosterone are an example of biological explanations of gender inequality and, specifically, masculinity. These types of explanations focus on how innate biological differences between males and females work in ways that program them for different social behaviors. This programming is said to take several forms: endocrine functioning (testosterone = aggression and estrogen = nurturing and teamwork); number of eggs female bodies produce versus the number of sperm male bodies produce as leading to different mating behaviors; chromosomal diversity (e.g., XX, XY, XO, XXY, XYY); and sex differences in brain structure and function, for example.

Although biological sex is often treated as unproblematic, like masculinity, once we get down to the nitty-gritty, it is more complicated than many assume. One method of "sexing" the body is to ask about chromosomes. Male sperm come in two types: one carrying an X chromosome and one carrying a Y. Female eggs come in one variety: they all carry X chromosomes.[3] Usually, fetuses are born with either two X chromosomes (female) or one X and one Y (male). Some individuals, however, do not "fit" in either of these types. Some individuals, for instance, are born with two X chromosomes and one Y—XXY (a genetic condition referred to as Klinefelter's syndrome) or two Y chromosomes and one X—XYY. And there are equally diverse combinations of sex markers[4] (like testes and a vagina, ovaries and a penis, or having a chromosomal type—like XX—that does not "match" external genitalia).[5] Indeed, there are a variety of sex markers one can use to determine sex: fetal sex, gonadal sex, hormonal sex, genital sex, fetal internal reproductive sex, brain dimorphism, juvenile gender identity, pubertal hormonal sex, and more (e.g., Money and Ehrhardt 1972). Many of us are used to all of the markers "agreeing" with one another (i.e., all pointing toward either "male" or "female"). But the significant fact is that they do not always agree (e.g., Fausto-Sterling 2000, 2012; Gilbert 2010; Money and Ehrhardt 1972); we simply treat them as if they do or should.

Additionally, many tend to think of sex as incredibly inflexible (i.e., you're *either* male *or* female and whichever you "are" does not change). Interestingly, however, we *learn* from others how to think of sex as inflexible. Consider an experience Tristan had in the grocery store as an example. Tristan's one-year-old child was dressed in a light-yellow onesie, a pair of light gray cotton pants, and without anything that might definitively indicate gender identity. A precocious young girl came skipping along with her mom in tow, walked up to Tristan, pointed at his child, looked at her mom, and asked, "Mommy, is that a boy or a girl?" Her mother looked back and forth among the child, Tristan, and her daughter and tentatively offered, "That's . . . um . . . a boy, honey." "Why?" her daughter quickly shot back. Perhaps not wanting to talk about penises and vaginas in public and possibly exasperated with the "Why?" stage of toddlerhood, the mother simply said, "Because!" Still not satisfied, the young girl continued, "Will he always be a boy?" The mother awkwardly chuckled, shrugging her shoulders, grinning, and shaking her head at Tristan. "Yes, honey," she laughed, "He'll always be a boy." And with that, they moved on.

The question about the future of Tristan's child's gender seemed odd to this girl's mother. But the girl was not joking when she asked. The mother's answer conveyed significant information about our cultural understandings of gender. Like this one, some of the most important lessons we teach children are probably not on purpose—like showing them what's worthy of attention, what to ignore, what should be noticed but not discussed, and more. This little girl learned one of the ways that many people think about gender—a part of one's identity that is unchangeable, permanent. To think otherwise, she learned, is laughable. Treating the gendering process as inevitable and permanent disguises the fact that . . . well . . . it's not. It is so important to our society that we think of gender as stable that psychologists have even made it a stage in our psychological development, something they refer to as "gender constancy" (e.g., Slaby and Frey 1975; Ruble et al. 2006; Fausto-Sterling 2012)—an understanding of gender as a permanent state of being. Between the ages of three and five (in the United States), children absorb the message that gender is something that tends to remain stable over time.[6]

In other words, what that example indicates is that much of what we take for granted about gender as biological truth is actually socially taught. Thus, treating masculinity as predetermined fails to acknowledge the impact of our social environments. Science textbooks, for instance, even "gender" biological functions themselves. In Emily Martin's (1991) content analysis of descriptions of eggs and sperm in medical textbooks, she discovered that gender stereotypes pervade the biological sciences in how the behavior of sex cells is understood and explained. Martin discovered that there is a clear "importation of cultural ideas about passive females and heroic males into the 'personalities' of gametes" (1991: 500). Research like this indicates that we ought to remain skeptical of biologically deterministic explorations of masculinity, but also illustrates that we are clearly collectively preoccupied with biological frameworks for understanding masculinity (see also McCaughey 2008). What all of this research agrees on is the idea that whereas people may be *born* male or female (although some defy such classifications), all of us are socialized to *become* men and women, masculine and feminine. When we look at biological understandings of sex and gender from this perspective it becomes clear that this sort of approach is not just descriptive of some sort of natural reality; it is actually prescriptive in the way we describe and understand the diversity of seemingly natural bodies.

SOCIAL EXPLORATIONS

If masculinity (and femininity for that matter) is not dictated by biological functions, how might we begin to understand it? How is it, in other words, that we might *theorize* about it? Considerations of gender as socially and culturally constructed go back (at least) to the beginning of the 20th century with the anthropologist Margaret Mead's cross-cultural research. Mead was fascinated by varying definitions of what was considered masculine or "feminine" in different cultures around the world. One of her most famous studies on this issue—*Sex and Temperament in Three Primitive Societies* (1963 [1935])—describes three tribes in New Guinea that have understandings of gender that are dramatically at odds with one another. Not only do the three groups of people have competing understandings of masculinity and femininity (i.e., what some cultures define as masculine others define as feminine), but also two of them do not believe that men and women have meaningfully different personalities at all.

Mead's research calls into question two central assumptions about masculinity (and femininity, and gender more generally): (1) that there are certain inherent properties that every culture on earth recognizes as masculine (and feminine); and (2) that there are meaningful differences between people born with vaginas and those born with penises. Mead is widely credited as one of a group of academic pioneers who began a scholarly dialogue that challenged the "naturalness" of gender as a central organizing framework of social life.[7] This book is a small piece of this larger theoretical exploration, focusing on contemporary explorations of masculinities as socially constructed. As we describe below, the first attempt at a social theory of masculinity (and gender more broadly) is called "sex role theory." Later investigations pointed out the shortcomings in this theory and attempted to provide a more satisfactory theory of masculinity—by focusing on "gender relations" instead of "sex roles." This latter investigation into gender relations lays the groundwork for the explorations in the rest of this book.

SEX ROLE THEORY

Although it may seem surprising now, early sociological analyses of gender were not necessarily feminist. The first systematic attempt to theorize and address gender by sociologists was undertaken by an American scholar named Talcott Parsons. During the 1950s, Parsons was among the most influential sociologists in the United States. Parsons (1954) suggested that social order was possible (despite the omnipresence of conflicts or the potential for conflict in any social system) because of a social process he referred to as "functionalism." A functionalist approach to society argues that everything in society has a purpose, a role to play in the reproduction of the social system—*everything*.

The concepts of "socialization" and "roles" are key parts of functionalist framework for understanding society. Socialization *functions* to ensure that everyone understands the "dos" and "don'ts" of the society in which they live, including what roles they should perform. Roles are practices and identities into which people are socialized. They have elaborate sets of actions tied to them. Although functionalists were interested in all sorts of roles and social processes in society, the most important social roles for Parsons are what he called sex roles.

Through the concept of sex roles Parsons attempted to address the *social* organization of masculinity and femininity. Metaphorically relying on a bit of language from theater—role—allowed Parsons to draw a distinction between the role being played and the actual person playing the role. Being a man or a woman, sex role theory suggested, meant enacting a role that was understood to be definitive of one's sex. Correspondingly, sex role theorists understood there to be two sex roles in any given context: a "male sex role" and a "female sex role." Significantly, although Parsons (1954) understood these roles to be different, he emphatically did not believe them to be unequal. Parsons referred to the male sex role as "instrumental" and the female sex role as "expressive" (Parsons and Bales 1953)—and you can probably imagine the kinds of justifications for the division of labor, the public and private spheres, and more implicit in this framework. So, there's a "separate, but equal" philosophy embedded in the functionalist framework for thinking about gender.

Role theory was an impressive first attempt to talk about something as *social* that we tend to think of as natural. Like the work of Margaret Mead, sex role theory invites us to shift our attention away from cultural assumptions about biological differences between men and women. For instance, differences between men's and women's behavior—within this framework—are understood as socialized responses to different sets of social expectations, not as hardwired. In so doing, sex role theory sought to directly connect social structure with the formation of personality, human action, interaction, and identity.

Scholars built on and refined sex role theory in the subsequent decades. Some suggested that analysts might think more productively about *roles* in the plural, rather than *role* (Brannon 1976). For instance, psychologist Robert Brannon asked, if the male sex role really is one thing, then how can a football player, a jet-set playboy, a blue-collar brawler, a big-shot businessman, simply working men, Don Juan–type smoldering "studs," politicians and statesmen, and others all be living up to *it*? If the male sex role is one thing, how can all of these different men be understood as fulfilling it? To solve this problem Brannon suggested that the male sex role be understood as a role with four dimensions:

- *No Sissy Stuff*—Masculinity is the persistent repudiation of anything and everything feminine. This, for Brannon, is the most important dimension of masculinity.
- *The Big Wheel*—This dimension of masculinity is measured by success, status, power, and wealth and by occupying visible positions of leadership.
- *The Sturdy Oak*—Brannon created this dimension to address the fact that some men that we culturally identify as masculine conspicuously *lack* social status. Despite variation, common elements associated with this dimension of masculinity are self-reliance, confidence, emotional stoicism, and an ability to remain calm and composed in moments of pain, anger, danger, etc.
- *Give 'Em Hell*—Whereas Brannon argues that "the big wheel" and "the sturdy oak" are not inherently bad qualities, "give 'em hell" is a dimension that is much less benign. This dimension of masculinity is measured by an aura of aggression and violence and the participation in daring and dangerous behavior.

Brannon suggested that recognizing multiple dimensions associated with the male sex role would allow us to recognize the different ways that different groups of men fulfill the social expectations associated with men and masculinity.[8]

However, once tested empirically, the sex role model was less useful than it initially seemed (Pleck 1981). In *The Myth of Masculinity* (1981), Joseph Pleck distilled the empirical claims embedded in sex role theory and systematically evaluated whether they were supported by existing research. Pleck identified eleven central claims associated with sex role theory—claims that can be assessed by research. Below are a few from his list:

- Empirical tests can be designed to empirically "prove" who is masculine, feminine, or neither.
- The internalization of the masculine sex role through watching role models is more important for boys than for girls.
- Sex role identification—particularly for boys—is extremely complex and prone to failure.
- Homosexuality results from failed sex role identification.
- Socially "appropriate" sex role identification is necessary for psychological health.

Perhaps not surprisingly, Pleck's review of the empirical research testing these claims (among others) indicated that arguments based in sex role theory often involved selectively reinterpreting data in ways that confirmed hypotheses (Pleck 1981). The evidence, in other words, did not support the theory. Social problems did not result from men and women who were not embracing their sex roles (as role theory claimed) but because of the rigid nature and understanding of sex roles themselves (Pleck 1981).

In shifting the attention from the failure of individuals to the problems with sex roles themselves, Pleck played a crucial role in laying the groundwork for the demise of the sex role paradigm. Although it is no longer a popular theoretical approach, sex role theory forged a conversation about gender that sought to understand masculinity and femininity as features of societies and social structures rather than inherent properties associated with biological differences between male and female bodies.

We suggest that if it is possible to claim a precise date on which sex role theory was officially discredited, it occurred sometime between April and May of 1985. If that seems oddly specific, it is. Judith Stacey and Barrie Thorne (1985) published "The Missing Feminist Revolution in Sociology," and on the other side of the world, Raewyn Connell published a short article—"Theorising Gender" (1985)—that collectively spelled out the failings of sex role theory as a *social* theory of gender. Together they critique sex role theory for the fact that it was tautological, teleological, and ahistorical, and it ignored diversity and inequality (see also Connell 1979).

To say that a theory is "tautological" means that it involves a circular form of reasoning. In other words, the premise of the argument is simply a restatement of the argument's conclusion. A central premise of sex role theory is that people play the various sex roles they are socially assigned because of social expectations. But the argument can quickly dissolve into infinite regress once we ask, "Why do others apply these social expectations?" Within this framework the only logical response is, "People are expected to apply these social expectations to others," and so on. Sex role theory implicitly assumes an incredible amount of voluntarism on the part of everyone. We all—according to sex role theory—voluntarily apply sets of social expectations about masculinity and femininity to everyone around us.

Teleological arguments rely on some grand design in which we are assumed to place our faith. In the case of sex role theory, a biologically deterministic theory about sex and gender actually lurks behind what initially appeared to be a *social* theory of gender. For instance, sex role theory has no easy explanation for why men would all seamlessly take up the male sex role (nor would any empirical investigation of men be able to demonstrate this). There's a kind of false universalism implicit in the sex role framework. By a metaphorical sleight of hand, sex role theory is able to casually rely on what is ultimately biological reductionism. Connell (1985) points out that this is even apparent in the name of the theory, which awkwardly pairs a biological term—sex—with a sociological one—role. As Connell writes, "This is why discussion of sex roles constantly slides into discussion of sex differences" (1987: 50).

Sex role theory was *ahistorical.* When sex role theory really "hit its stride" among scholars, it was the 1950s. Talcott Parsons wrote a great deal about U.S. families and family life in his work. Indeed, we've been teaching about 1950s families in the United States since they existed. In fact, when we talk about the "traditional family," we're invoking some idea of what families looked like during this period of U.S. history. As far as traditions go, however, the families that we think of as characterizing the 1950s were unimpressive. The family form was far from universal even during the period it is popularly understood to characterize (Coontz 1992). And the traditional family had terrible staying power—it just was not around for all that long. There are a variety of reasons that account for its emergence during that period—an economy capable of providing a "family wage," processes of suburbanization on an unprecedented scale, etc. It was also the period when televisions became a stable feature in family homes and when we saw the emergence of family sitcoms like "I Love Lucy" and "Leave It to Beaver" that celebrated a particular family form—one with clearly delineated roles for men and women. This was also the time when Parsons was writing and he seems to have mistakenly assumed that the family forms that became prevalent during that period would stick around. Ahistorical arguments mistakenly assume that the way things are today are the way they have always been and always will be.

Because of its lack of historical context, sex role theory also lacks a theoretical mechanism to adequately explain change in gender relations (in part, because the theory did not really acknowledge change). The framework attempts to get around this by situating itself as timeless. When social definitions of masculinity (or femininity for that matter) change, sex role theory has no way of explaining precisely how or why the change occurred. Sociological theory and scholarship on gender have heavily criticized this aspect of sex role theory, framing gender both as a structure (e.g., Hearn 1987; Lorber 1994; Risman 2004) and as an institution (e.g., Martin 2004) in its own right.

Sex role theory was incapable of accounting for *diversity*; it presumed universal participation in the enactment of sex roles. Yet, any serious look at society tells us that not all men can, do, or even try to fulfill what sex role theory presented as a series of obligations for anyone belonging to the social category, "man." The issue is subtle, but significant: sex role theory implicitly mistakes what is culturally *normative* for what is *normal*. Although the male sex role and the female sex role may have been (and may continue to be) regarded as the *right* or *proper* way of doing gender—how people might think others *should* be doing gender—certainly not everyone lives up to these cultural stereotypes and ideals. It was a prescriptive theory of gender parading around as though it were descriptive. Sex role theory has no way of making sense of anyone who might deviate from the expectations associated with the role that this framework situated them as socially obligated to play.

Similarly, the sex role theoretical model also explicitly understands masculinity as one "thing" (and femininity as well). In every conceivable situation, Parsons argued that there is a male sex role and a female sex role. Yet, even the most superficial understanding of masculinity acknowledges that there is likely widespread disagreement about what "counts." It does not make sense to consider masculinity singularly in the way sex role theory treats the concept. Masculinities are *plural* (e.g., Connell 1995). Different historical periods have distinct conceptualizations of masculinity; understandings of masculinity are different in different cultures around the world; our understandings of what it means to "be a man" change over the life course; different groups might have different understandings, and we often employ different conceptualizations of masculinity in different contexts. For instance, we often casually presume that masculinity looks a little different inside men's sports team locker rooms. The idea is that certain behaviors that might label someone "lewd" in one context are openly acknowledged and celebrated in another. So, masculinities are plural and sex role theory had no way of accounting for this fact.

Finally, and most problematically, sex role theory did not address *inequality*. Although Parsons (1954) understood masculinity and femininity to be dramatically different from each other, he did not believe they were unequal in any way—just different. Betty Friedan (1963) famously referred to this strategy as "the functionalist freeze," a feature of functionalist theories of gender that implicitly naturalized the subordination of women and their relationship with "the family." Sex role theory was able to obscure issues of power and inequality by focusing more heavily on individuals than on social structures, contending that the male and female sex roles were naturally complimentary. As Stacey and Thorne write,

> The terms are depoliticizing; they strip experience from its historical and political context and neglect questions of power and conflict. It is significant than sociologists do not speak of "class roles" or "race roles." Functionalist assumptions linger more deeply in sociological conceptualizations of gender than of other forms of inequality. (1985: 307)

Shining a light on the inadequacy of sex role theory to deal with power and inequality—issues central to scholarship on gender today—produced a feminist revolution in sociological theorizing on gender.

If gender inequality does exist, the sex role theoretical framework implicitly suggests, the only way to make sense of inequality is to say that it results from differences. And if the differences are (implicitly) understood as natural, then any inequality that results from them can only logically be understood as natural as well. Gender inequality, within sex role theory, appears inevitable.[9] Subsequent theorizing about gender reveals that there is far more evidence to suggest that the relationship between gender difference and gender inequality flows in the opposite direction. Societies with understandings of masculinity and femininity as dramatically opposed have higher levels of gender inequality (e.g., Sanday 1981; Gilmore 1990). Simply put, *collective investments in ideologies of gender difference are associated with higher levels of gender inequality.*

Together, these critiques boil down to one more general critique of sex role theory: *things are just more complicated than that!* The simplicity of sex role theory is one clue that it presents society as far less complex that it actually is. Today, social theorists embrace the complexity of societies as an integral component of societies. For gender, this means that things are more complicated than saying there are instrumental and expressive roles in every imaginable situation, that men (naturally) fulfill the former, whereas women (inevitably) satisfy the latter. Social explorations of men and masculinities grew out of this frustration with sex role theory as an inadequate theoretical framework for studying masculinity (and gender more broadly). Indeed, it is not an exaggeration to suggest that studies on men and masculinities—as a subfield within gender studies—emerged out of a critique of sex role theory. And every attempt to theorize about masculinity that came after had to address some of the shortcomings associated with sex role theory. Although scholars no longer address this explicitly, each of the explorations of masculinity in this book is implicitly involved in building on this critique.

EXPLORING GENDER RELATIONS

Raewyn Connell's influential theory of gender relations provides a satisfying way for social analysts to address the fact that "things are just more complicated than that." Connell is one of the most widely read and cited gender scholars alive today. Although her theorization of masculinities is only one piece of a much larger theory of gender in social life, it has become most famous for the conceptualization of "hegemonic masculinity." Connell's theory of *gender relations* shifted the sociological discussion of gender and masculinity and her concepts provide the foundation on which each of the four trajectories of exploration we describe in this book builds.

In contrast to earlier approaches, a gender relations approach acknowledges the importance of biology without relying on it as a causal explanation for gender. Connell accomplished this by theorizing what she refers to as the "reproductive arena." When scholars say that masculinity is socially constructed, they are not saying that penises do not *actually* exist or that human reproduction does not *actually* require eggs and sperm. Rather, when we say that masculinity is socially constructed, what we are challenging is the significance of these biological facts for the rest of social life. As Connell writes, "we are talking about a historical process involving the body, not a fixed set of biological determinants. Gender is social practice that constantly refers to bodies and what bodies do, it is not social practice reduced to the body" (1995: 71). As such, the term *reproductive arena* refers to the various practices, performances, and social processes that get culturally attached to reproductive differences.

Just by way of example, consider something like lactation and breastfeeding. Women's bodies lactate; men's bodies do not. Lactation is a completely *natural* process. Right? Well, yes and no. It is true that women's bodies lactate; well, *most* women's bodies. But, breastfeeding is far from the straightforward natural process you might be thinking of it as. If it were so natural and preprogrammed, why would we need breastfeeding classes? Why would we require "lactation consultants," "nursing coaches," and all manner of breastfeeding professionals? After having children, both of us can tell you that breastfeeding is not quite the seamless natural process you may have been led to believe. Women learn to nurse children not through biological programming, but through social interactions, mediated (in many societies) by a vast array of social institutions. Indeed, if we only understand breastfeeding biologically, our understanding will always be incomplete. Breastfeeding is a biological process heavily shaped by political, cultural, and economic institutions that structure the practice of breastfeeding and the meanings associated with that practice (e.g., Schmied and Lupton 2001; Stearns 1999).

The capacity of (many) female bodies to lactate and nurse infants is often used as a justification for a wide variety of social practices. For instance, the fact that (most) women can lactate is often used to suggest that women are "natural caregivers." Implicit in this argument—and sometimes made explicit—is what this means for men. Although it is biologically possible for males to lactate (e.g., Diamond 1995), most men do not. But, what this *means* for men is a social—not a biological—matter. The fact that (most) men do not lactate is often used as an explanation for their lack of natural caregiving qualities. Caregiving and care work, however, are socially, not biologically, organized. In the United States—and many other societies around the world—we think of breastfeeding as connected with care work and the capacity to nurture. Using Connell's language, this means that we think of care work as part of the reproductive arena. Just to be clear, although lactation is a *biological* process, our collective belief and investment in the notion that lactation is justification for the gendered organization of care work is a *social* process. When we think about care work as a natural outcome of lactation, we enter the reproductive arena. The reproductive arena refers to all of those aspects of social life that we think of as inherently connected to reproductive differences between male and female bodies that are not, in fact, inherently connected to reproductive differences between male and female bodies.

This can be a tough pill to swallow. Gender may *feel* natural. Recall, however, that we wrote earlier that calling masculinity a social construction is not denying the reality of masculinity. Rather, discussing the social construction of masculinity is merely challenging the stability and origin of that reality. Connell's theory understands masculinity as inherently unstable, with its origins in the social structure and organization of society. Biologically deterministic theories of gender, in other words, consider gender as coming from *within*—as though gender is expressed from some internal, biological essence. Connell's theory, and the theorizing in this book, understands gender as coming from *without*—as socially organized and embedded in social institutions and interactions. This small change gave rise to an entirely new way of thinking about, studying, and exploring masculinity.

GENDER RELATIONS

Rather than focusing on sex or gender roles, this new way of thinking focuses on gender relations. Gender relations are understood, in this approach, as "the relationships arising in and around the reproductive arena" (Connell 2002: 73). Such relationships constitute "one of the major *structures* of all documented societies" (Connell 1995: 72, emphasis ours). This transformation in language is significant for a number of reasons, not least of which is that it allows us to go from understanding gender as a product of other social structures and institutions to considering the ways social structures and institutions are *produced by* gender. It allows us not only to consider the ways that gender is structured by society, but also the manner by which gender participates in the structuring. It also enables us to move beyond a discussion of *individuals* to *institutions* in understanding who or what is considered masculine. The state, the military, and schools, for instance, can be understood as masculine within this framework. It is for this reason that Connell theorized masculinities as "**configu-rations of practice**" rather than social roles. Configurations of practice can be mobilized by individual men, but can be understood as institutionalized as well.[10]

These configurations of gender practice take place in a particular **gender order**, in which one might find more specific **gender regimes**. The term *gender order* refers to overarching patterns in gender arrangements and relations. Although not only women are nurses, for instance, women dominate the field. Although some heterosexual married men stay home with their children while their wives work, the opposite scenario is significantly more common. Indeed, society is structured in ways that make these gender arrangements and relations likely—not inevitable, but certainly more convenient. Connell refers to aspects of social life like this as small parts of an overarching *gender order* that structures our under-standings of gender and relations of power and inequality. Yet, gender relations are—at certain moments and in certain contexts—at odds with the gender order as well. Connell uses the concept *gender regimes* to make sense of this fact. The gender arrangements of a particular institution or in a specific organization or context can be referred to as a "gender regime."[11] Connell puts it this way:

> The gender regimes of . . . particular organizations, [institutions, or social contexts,] then, are part of wider patterns, which also endure over time. I call these wider patterns the *gender order* of a society. . . . Gender regimes . . . usually correspond to the overall gender order, but may depart from it. Change often starts in one sector of society and takes time to seep through into others. (2002: 73)

Although a great deal of scholarship and theory considers institutions, organizations, and settings that sometimes appear to challenge the gender order, Connell's theory ought to caution us to examine these challenges carefully.

Thinking of gender in terms of relations, rather than roles, that are found in particular gender orders, as well as more specific regimes, allows us to more clearly understand com-plicated gendered practices, identities, and representations. Consider the iconic image of the Marlboro man: a lone cowboy, working the land, shaving once a week, smoking while leaning on fence posts in wide-open American expanses. He may be one of the most rec-ognizable images of masculinity in American advertising. The Marlboro man appeared to live by himself, for himself. We learn a bit about what he does for work or for fun in the images in the advertisements. He's running his ranch, sitting on wooden fences, lighting up with a lasso at hand, camping out for the night with his head on his saddle, and always with his cowboy hat on (or close by). But, we learn relatively little of the complete man in these images. Is he married? Is he heterosexual? Does he have children? Does he have sib-lings? Is he living on his parents' ranch or is he "on his own"? Does he have health prob-lems? Does he have a day job that allows him enough free time to ride and rope in the afternoons as the sun sets? Or is he being portrayed "at work"? If we knew all of this, we might decide that he is less masculine than we may have thought he was—or, at the very least, that he does not live up to his own image and reputation.

And these different aspects of the Marlboro man's gender identity as a masculine man might be on different historical paths. For instance, as the economy shifts and small farms struggle to survive, the Marlboro man might not be as economically "at ease" as he was made to appear. Will he have to sell the farm? If that happens, will he have to relocate— move to a more densely populated urban setting to find work and support himself? This change will certainly require new kinds of interactions with new groups of people and kinds of interactional and emotional exchange he might be ill-prepared to undertake. What will become of his iconic status? The Marlboro man was the most successful advertising image of the 20th century. As the lifestyle he was depicted as living becomes less feasible for more and more people, however, what will become of these ads as symbols of masculinity? Will future generations cease to recognize the images as masculine? Or might these images retain symbolic masculine credibility despite depicting (or perhaps because they depict) lives less possible today?[12]

By focusing on gender relations rather than roles, it becomes clear that the gender order is composed of various dimensions capable of simultaneously moving in different directions. "We often experience disparities in gender relations, as if part of our lives were working on one gender logic, and another part on a different gender logic" (Connell 2002: 75). Connell suggests that we can understand these contradictions, disparities, and the tug and pull of gender relations by considering four distinct dimensions of gender relations: **power relations, production relations, emotional relations, and symbolic relations** (Connell 2002). These dimensions are best understood as interconnected and mutually reinforcing. Examples from any one dimension necessarily bleed into the others. They work together, even as they are often working toward different ends or the same ends in different ways.[13]

Emphasizing the dimension of *power relations* enabled Connell's theory to directly challenge the way in which role theory ignored gender inequality. Instead, in Connell's model, power is central to understanding gender. The primary axis of power in Connell's theory is "the overall subordination of women and dominance of men" (1995: 74). This is what organizes gender relations on a global scale. These power relations can operate directly (as in the deployment or threat of physical violence) or symbolically (as illustrated by referring to a father as the "head of the household"). In this approach power relations are understood as simultaneously interpersonal and institutional.[14]

Focusing on the dimension of *production relations* incorporates gendered divisions of labor into her analysis of gender. As Connell writes, "The division of labour itself is only part of a larger pattern. In an industrial economy, the shared work of women and men is embodied in every major product, and every major service. Yet women and men are differently located in the economic process" (2002: 80). In most societies around the world, men perform certain tasks and women perform others. Although the specific tasks assigned to men or women vary by society and historical period, the division itself is ubiquitous (e.g., Charles and Gruski 2004). It might be tempting to think that perhaps men are doing the more important work or work that has a larger impact on a society because men control a great deal of the world's resources. But historical data suggest an alternative explanation. Men are not rewarded more for their work because they are doing work that is "more important." Rather, we tend to think of the work men do—whatever it happens to be—as more important and deserving more pay *because* it is men who happen to be doing it.[15]

Attending to *emotional relations* focuses attention on the significance of emotional attachments and the way these arrangements may feel idiosyncratic and personal, but are deeply patterned by gender. Indeed, part of the reason gender inequality is difficult to spot in our lives is the result of our emotional commitments and relationships. Conceptualizing emotional relations as a distinct dimension of gender relations enables Connell's theory to get at this powerful paradox embedded within gender relations that helps us simultaneously desire to promote change *and* cling to what we know and, sometimes, love. We may think of emotional commitments primarily as positive (think of love and romance). Yet Connell understands emotional commitments as capable of being negative and hostile as well. Prejudice, for instance, may be understood as an emotional relationship. Therefore, misogyny and homophobia can both be analyzed by attending to this dimension of gender relations.

More recently, Connell added *symbolic relations* to her theory to refer to the ways in which gender is embedded in cultural symbols. We are symbol-using creatures who communicate through symbolic systems (a single word is a symbol standing in for a whole set of meanings, for instance). Gender is deeply embedded in this symbolic system. "Though language—speech and writing—is the most analyzed site of symbolic gender relations, it is not the only one. Gender symbolism also operates in dress, make-up, gesture, in photography and film, and in more impersonal forms of culture such as the built environment" (Connell 2002: 84). Events, acts, and objects are all cultural symbols that can convey gendered meanings and are embedded in gender relations.

The fact that we tend to think of kitchens as feminine spaces in the home, whereas basements and garages have a masculine air about them, is one way to consider this. Kitchens, interestingly, have undergone a shift in symbolic meaning. In U.S. homes, kitchens are, by far, the most remodeled room in the house (Arnold et al. 2012), in part because they occupy a different place in family life today than they did when a great deal of the houses in the United States were built. People are not just putting in new stoves and refrigerators; they are breaking down walls, removing doors, and generally opening kitchens up. The kitchen might once have been a small room inhabited primarily (and possibly, in extreme cases, only) by women. But today, kitchens are the room in the house in which most families spend most of their time. Kitchens went from being a room to collect and prepare food to "command central" in most American family homes. This transformation speaks to the ways that objects (in this case kitchens) come to take on symbolic gendered meaning and how that meaning can change. Gender is, quite literally, a part of the architecture. Similarly, whereas one-bathroom homes might have worked for families of four in the 1950s with one "breadwinner," today's families require more. The rhythms of family life have transformed as more women entered the workplace, and the transformations that followed in our built environments illustrate just how pervasive symbolic gender relations are.

Importantly, Connell's theory can be used to think about these types of historical changes in the home. Remember that sex role theory was criticized as ahistorical and incapable of accounting for change. Connell suggests that these sorts of changes actually constitute gender relations. Connell considers each of the dimensions of gender relations historically unstable, prone to crisis. Connell addresses this by theorizing what she refers to as **"crisis tendencies"** as a historically constant process within gender relations.[16] Thus, "the analysis of crisis tendencies is a question of identifying dynamics which have the potential to transform [these four dimensions], and thus change in fundamental ways the conditions of future social practice" (Connell 1987: 159). But crisis tendencies are uneven, often affecting gender relations incompletely. And although Connell argues that the gender order continually tends toward crisis, she also suggests that this tendency may have intensified in recent history. This has produced "a major loss of legitimacy for patriarchy," and Connell suggests that "different groups of men are now negotiating this loss in very different ways" (1995: 202). As relations of power, production, emotions, and symbols change and adapt to changing circumstances, this inevitably involves reverberations throughout gender relations.

Conceptualizing crisis tendencies as an integral feature of gender relations allows Connell's understanding of gender relations to make sense of historical change. But it does so by considering the diverse potential embedded within any historical transformation in gender relations. Crisis tendencies enable Connell's theory to make sense of moves toward and away from gender inequality and simultaneously speak to the flexibility of systems and structures of power and inequality. They illustrate that masculinity is, in some ways, in a state of continuous crisis. Speaking of masculinity as "in crisis" at any point in time makes little sense from this perspective, "other than to say that masculinity is perhaps partially constituted *as* crisis" (Edwards 2006: 24). The history of gender inequality is often casually presented as a slow but steady march toward equality. But, this casual observation often presumes that inequality will not transform—that patriarchies are not, to use Johnson's (2005) term, "flexible." Connell's theory makes possible an understanding of "progress" and contextualizes this potential with a conceptualization of inequality as flexible, adaptive, and on the move.[17]

FROM MASCULINITY TO MASCULINITIES

Moving beyond sex role theory also involved moving beyond the language that posited *one* male or *one* female role. To do this Connell suggested that we begin to talk about *masculinities*, rather than the singular *masculinity*. Pluralizing masculinity allows us to think about relationships between men and women as well as *among* men and *among* women. Whereas masculinity—as an ideology and configuration of practice—affords men power, Connell wanted a theory capable of accounting for the fact that not all men benefit from gender inequality in the same way. As such, Connell conceptualized four configurations of masculinity, defined by status and power—**hegemonic masculinity**, **subordinated masculinity**, **complicit masculinity**, and **marginalized masculinity**. To properly understand these various configurations of masculinity, however, it is important to remember that, for Connell, what is thought to comprise normative masculinity is embattled terrain.

Significant for Connell, however, was the notion that not all men benefited from gender inequality in precisely the same ways. Some groups of men benefit a great deal, but some might seem to benefit little from men's collective advantages. To address this, Connell introduced the term "patriarchal dividend," referring to things like the gender wage gap (in which men make more on average than woman), feelings of safety, authority, respect, and bodily integrity. Connell emphasizes the centrality of power and inequality through the concept of the patriarchal dividend and situates it as "the main stake in contemporary gender politics.

Its scale makes patriarchy worth defending" (2002: 142). Different configurations of masculinity are positioned differently with respect to the patriarchal dividend—some masculinities collect more (or different aspects) of the patriarchal dividend than others.

Hegemonic masculinity[18] is one of the most used terms from Connell's theory. Of all of the work that relies on Connell's theory, an incredible share draws solely on this concept. It is a sexy concept that provided scholars a way out of the many dead ends offered by role theory. Connell defines hegemonic masculinity as "not a fixed character type, always and everywhere the same. It is, rather the masculinity that occupies the hegemonic position in a given pattern of gender relations, a position always contestable. . . . It is the successful claim to authority, more than direct violence, that is the mark of hegemony" (1995: 76–77). Although the concept has sustained critique (e.g., Donaldson 1993; Demetriou 2001; Schippers 2007) and reformulation (Connell and Messerschmidt 2005), its central premise has not changed.[19] That premise is that hegemonic masculinity is "the configuration of practice which embodies the currently accepted answer to the problem of the legitimacy of patriarchy, which guarantees (or is taken to guarantee) the dominant position of men and the subordination of women" (Connell 1995: 77).[20] Connell makes no mention of specific traits or behaviors here—although a great deal of scholarship making use of the term often artificially flattens it by misinterpreting it to suggest that it has a specific performance and applies to a specific group of men or historical period.

Most simply, hegemonic masculinity refers to the most culturally exalted forms of masculinity—configurations that justify dominance and inequality. Whereas we tend to think of masculine icons as deserving to be held up, conceptualizing them as "hegemonic" offers a different explanation. As Bridges writes, "we do not exalt hegemonic masculinities because they are hegemonic; they are hegemonic because we exalt them" (2009: 91). Hegemonic masculinity is historically and contextually mobile. Indeed, given this definition, we might even discuss hegemonic *masculinities* because the same configurations are not exalted everywhere (at least not necessarily in the same ways or to the same degree). And although few—if any—people may embody these forms, they play a critical role in justifying gender inequality and dominance. Precisely as the term *hegemonic* indicates, these forms of masculinity are seen as ideologically legitimate even by those whose practices would not be characterized as hegemonically masculine.

Subordinated masculinity refers to configurations of masculinity with the least cultural status, power, and influence. Connell initially used gay men as the key example here. She writes, "Oppression positions homosexual masculinities at the bottom of a gender hierarchy among men. Gayness, in the patriarchal ideology, is the repository of whatever is symbolically expelled from hegemonic masculinity, the items ranging from fastidious taste in home decoration to receptive anal pleasure" (Connell 1995: 78; see also Connell 1992). We have an elaborate language to symbolically expel people from occupying masculine statuses (often, although not always, feminizing them in the process):

> sissy, fag, homo, nerd, dork, pussy, mama's boy, girl, girly, baby, apron strings, wuss, wussy
> boy, wimp, turkey, pussy, pussy whipped, whipped, homo, twat, baby, little girl, queer,
> punk, dickwad, cock, cocksucker, cock gobbler, pecker, puff, dandy, fopp, weenie, weiner,

fuck hole, fudge packer, bitch, lil' bitch, bitch ass, bitch nigga, son, kid, poof, poofter, puffta, queen, fairy, batty boy, gay lord, cunt, cunt licker, clown, ass clown, tool, tool bag, wife, dickless, Nancy, Nancy-boy, Nelly, Mary, Sally, deadbeat, scrub, scumbag, fruit, milquetoast, fruitcake, pretty boy, punk, douche, douchebag, ladyfinger, lady/ladies, pantywaist, pansy, cream puff, maricon, puta, joto, pato . . .

And on and on and on. As these terms indicate, masculinities may be subordinated in more ways than one. For instance, subordination may include political and cultural exclusion and segregation, violence (symbolic, legal, and physical), economic discrimination, and more. So, subordinated masculinities are best understood as subordinated within each of the dimensions of gender relations Connell defines.

Connell theorizes the term *complicit masculinity* to refer to configurations of masculinity that benefit from the overall subordination of women, but do not appear to be actively involved in the subordination. "Masculinities constructed in ways that realize the patriarchal dividend, without the tensions or risks of being the frontline troops of patriarchy, are complicit in this sense" (Connell 1995: 79). Complicit masculinity enables Connell's theory to conceptualize configurations of gender practice and identity that benefit from gender power and inequality although they appear to play no role (or a small role) in shoring up systems of gendered power and inequality. An example might be the way in which a husband who endorses an egalitarian relationship with his wife may still benefit from making more money for performing the same job she does. Or if they have children and he is an involved father, he may receive surplus credit for parenting in ways his wife's parenting contributions are not afforded the same attention, recognition, or status.

Marginalized masculinity refers to "the interplay of gender with other structures such as class and race" (Connell 1995: 80). This enables Connell to illustrate how different masculinities can share some ground with hegemonic configurations, but simultaneously exist as marginalized by and to these forms. It also provides the possibility for conceptualizing the ways in which dominant masculinities can reproduce other forms of inequality alongside gender inequality. For instance, Connell writes, "In a white-supremacist context, black masculinities play symbolic roles for white gender construction. For instance, black sporting stars become exemplars for masculine toughness" (1995: 80). Thus, stereotypes of black masculinity can work in ways that shore up hegemonic masculine forms without necessarily occupying the same practical terrain—marginalized by the same construct they symbolically participate in defining. The tensions that are ever-present between, on the one hand, marginalized and subordinated masculinities and, on the other, hegemonic masculinities produce a system of relationships in which disruptions and transformations are in a state of continuous play.

Although the concept has received far less attention, Connell initially theorized hegemonic masculinity in relation to a configuration of femininity she termed "**emphasized femininity**." As a result of the "global domination of women," Connell suggests that a "hegemonic femininity" does not exist.[21] Connell suggests that the highest status masculinities, those most culturally exalted, are also forms associated with the greatest power. Yet, she argues that—as a result of gender inequality—the relationship works differently for femininities. Although she did not define configurations of femininity in the way she does for masculinities, she does suggest that the most culturally dominant femininity achieves power and status through its connection with hegemonic masculinity. Connell defines *emphasized femininity* as "defined around compliance with . . . subordination and . . . oriented to accommodating the interests and desires of men" (1987: 183). Thus, for Connell the highest status form of masculinity is the least culturally subordinated, but the highest status configuration of femininity remains subordinate to hegemonic masculinity. Significant here is that Connell does begin to theorize *femininities* as well as *masculinities*, although less attention was given to feminine configurations of practice in the theory (see Schippers 2007). What is significant is that emphasized femininities receive status and power through their association with hegemonic masculinity. Indeed, along with other configurations of masculinity, emphasized femininity plays a key role in propping hegemonic masculinities up—and as such, emphasized femininities also can be understood as benefitting in some ways from the patriarchal dividend. Other femininities, however, do not.

The vast majority of scholarship on masculinities has primarily utilized Connell's theory by exporting her concept—hegemonic masculinity—to different settings, to make sense of various individuals and groups. We detail the main strand of analyses that emerged from her theorizing in the "Multiplying Masculinities" section. A great deal of scholarship, however, exports this concept without a complete understanding (or often with an inaccurate understanding) of the theoretical framework within which it is situated. And as a result, hegemonic masculinity is often inaccurately (or, more mildly, imprecisely) deployed. Work citing the term often considers it solely alongside other configurations of masculinity, but fails to situate these forms within any of the dimensions of gender relations Connell outlined. As such, hegemonic masculinity is often depicted as a specific "type" of man rather than a configuration of gendered practice within a system of gender relations that is internally contradictory and rife with conflict. It is a configuration of practice that Connell understands as always capable of transforming (despite not always being depicted this way in research relying on the term).

CONTEMPORARY EXPLORATIONS: HISTORICIZING, MULTIPLYING, NAVIGATING, AND DISLOCATING

When Connell produced her theory of gender relations, she cautioned readers at the outset not to consider her theory (or any other, for that matter) as outside of the social relations it sought to explore. In the preface to *Gender and Power*, she wrote, "theories don't grow on trees; theorizing is itself a social practice with a politics" (Connell 1987: xi). This admonition inspired and has continued to shape her theory and research. As two scholars who were keenly interested in masculinity, both of us did what graduate students are supposed to do when positioning your research in the existing literature. We took our empirical data and tried to place it in a theoretical tradition of analyzing masculinities. Unfortunately, what we found was ONE theoretical tradition. It is not that there is anything wrong with this particular theoretical tradition or that there has not been research on men and masculinities across the social sciences and in other disciplinary traditions. Most of what we found in the social science literature, however, was dominated by a single theoretical framework. We did not find the animating questions, discussions, and tensions that so enliven the feminist literature on gender inequality.

Of course, none of this is to say that this particular approach is incorrect or that there are not other approaches that can engender these sorts of discussions. Indeed, that is what this book aims to do—to bring a variety of approaches to exploring masculinities into dialogue with one another. What we found is that when analyses of masculinity from a social scientific perspective did not engage with a particular approach and theoretical framework, they were often not seen as a part of "Masculinities Studies" proper. The animating discussions that would enliven both perspectives failed to happen (at least to the extent we expected) because the studies were categorized as not of a particular sort. The dominance of the single approach has—we suggest—produced a field of inquiry that has become overly segregated from gender studies, writ large. No single scholar is to blame for this segregation. Indeed, it speaks volumes to the power, omnirelevance, and interdisciplinary relevance of Connell's framework, in addition to that of a number of other scholars who provided a foundation for research and theory on masculinities when the field of inquiry didn't quite exist. Building on insights from groundbreaking feminist scholarship within and out of sociology, scholars like Raewyn Connell, Michael Kimmel, Michael Messner, Jeff Hearn, Michael Schwalbe, Barrie Thorne, Nancy Chodorow, Michael Kaufman, Patricia Yancey Martin, Arthur Brittan, Victor Seidler, James Messerschmidt, Joseph Pleck, Elizabeth Badinter, Harry Brod, Helen Hacker, Scott Coltrane, David Morgan, Mairtin Mac An Ghaill, Oystein Gullvag Holter, Alan Petersen, Kenneth Clatterbaugh, Matthew Gutmann, Tim Edwards, Robert Staples, Alan Johnson, Judith Kegan Gardiner, Wayne Martino, Debbie Epstein, Ann Ferguson, Isaac Julian, Kobena Mercer, Mary Jane Kehily, Peter Lyman, Richard Majors, Karin Martin, Jennifer Pierce, Christine Williams, Marlon Ross, Paul Willis, Julian Wood, and Maxine Baca Zinn, among others, produced a field of inquiry that enabled us to study masculinities and ask questions not previously possible.

With this volume, we are endeavoring to do two things simultaneously. First, we hope to continue to celebrate and examine the incredible work being produced by scholars who situate their work directly within masculinities studies. Second, we seek to cultivate what we understand as incredibly fertile ground at the outskirts of masculinities studies. Collecting research and theory widely acknowledged in the field alongside explorations of masculinity that rarely receive citation by "masculinities scholars," we attempt to highlight some of the common ground between these approaches. But we are equally interested in the tensions that exist as we recognize diverse approaches, theoretical models, concepts, and more. Indeed, we suggest that the field is becoming defined by four separate but related trajectories of scholarship. Each stresses different aspects of social life and, given this fact, may come to different conclusions about any number of social phenomena. We outline the approaches themselves (historicizing, multiplying, navigating, and dislocating) and elaborate on the assumptions, methods, and general approaches associated with each. We have also endeavored to put these bodies of scholarship into dialogue with one another in this volume in ways not currently recognized.

With this volume, we suggest continuing to mine Connell's research and theory for more ideas. But, rather than suggesting that there are no other ways of studying masculinities, we suggest that Connell's theory be understood as an organizing framework within which we can connect these diverse bodies of scholarship. Indeed, Connell's theoretical framework for understanding gender relations (and masculinities within those relations) offers us potential areas for dialogue, disagreement, and more by incorporating research on and theoretical explorations of masculinities that continue to push the boundaries of the field to more fully realize the potential of both Connell's theory and the field of study more generally. Below, we briefly introduce the four trajectories we see as organizing contemporary scholarly explorations into masculinities along with how each can be understood as connected by Connell's theoretical framework. We introduce each trajectory of exploration in more detail prior to each of the four sections that organize the book.

HISTORICIZING MASCULINITIES

Considering masculinity within a historical perspective is one of the most basic building blocks that scholars initially used to critique the sex role theoretical framework. Research within this theoretical trajectory is primarily concerned with historical transformations in the meanings, social status, power arrangements, and even the look and feel of masculinities throughout time. What masculinity has been called, of what it was thought to be composed, and what it has been hailed as entailing have all varied throughout time. It might seem like a simple point—masculinity varies historically—but it is one with enormous implications for studying the topic. Indeed, the types of things we consider as comprising masculinity today have not been regarded as masculine throughout time. Conversely, many things that may have once been understood as primary features of masculinity may have nothing to do with masculinity today.

Two examples from Western and U.S. culture are the historical transformation of high heels and changes in androgynous names. In the 17th and 18th centuries, high heels were understood as a masculine shoe and men were, largely, the group wearing them. Like plump bodies and pale skin, wearing high heels (the impractical shoe that they are) symbolized an individual's wealth, his lack of a need to work. In fact, women initially wore heels in an attempt to appropriate some of the power associated with men (Wade and Ferree 2014). Less affluent groups adopted the fashion hoping to obtain social status. Perhaps surprisingly, given modern understandings of beauty, men's legs also symbolized masculinity during this time period. Men wore tights to display the shapeliness of their legs. It goes without saying that male legs, much less those atop a pair of high heels, are not widely embraced as key markers of masculinity today. Indeed, as high heels were gradually worn more and more by women, they eventually lost their status as masculine.

The gendering of names over time also illustrates historical changes in masculinity. At one point, parents in the United States named their sons Kim, Cary, or Robin without thinking twice about it—or Shannon, Riley, or Casey more recently. Think of Cary Grant—a masculine icon on the silver screen, to be sure. The name Kim was popularized as a name for boys after Rudyard Kipling published *Kim* (1901)—a story of a poor orphaned *boy*. Both of these names likely strike contemporary readers as feminine or—at the very least—not masculine. Names that were at one point in time androgynous (like Kim or Cary a half-century ago or perhaps Cameron, Bailey, or Hunter today) follow a specific pattern—not so different from high heels, as it turns out. As androgynous names become more popular and a critical mass of girls receive them, the number of boys receiving those names drops precipitously (Lieberson, Dumais, and Baumann 2000). This is how Kim, Cary, Dana, Robin, and Casey have come to be understood as "girl" names. Like high heels, this belies a more general finding in historical analyses of masculinity: changes in masculinity most often occur as *reactions* to changes in femininity (Kimmel 1987).

What both of these examples have in common is that masculinity, studied over time, is often (re)situated as "not feminine." As gender relations transform, what we understand as masculine will necessarily transform to adapt. These periods of change are often associated with claims that masculinity is in crisis. Although masculinities scholars are largely critical of the "crisis of masculinity" thesis for reasons we address in more detail in the "Historicizing Masculinities" section introduction, a great deal of this work examines historical periods during which masculinity was understood as in crisis. Although often not explicitly in conversation with Connell's work, this trajectory of masculinities scholarship is usefully understood as implicitly relying and building on four ideas within Connell's theory: power relations, production relations, hegemonic masculinity, and, perhaps most significantly, crisis tendencies.

This trajectory in masculinities scholarship is structured by four dominant themes that we articulate in greater detail in the section introduction. But, as a whole, historicizing masculinities scholarship is interested in the historical form and maintenance of gender and power relations. Many scholars in this vein are interested in historical challenges to power relations (and transformations in production relations often play a large role in this research). Changes in production relations, for instance, produced by mass industrialization at the turn of the 20th century, echoed throughout gender relations and are a powerful illustration of what Connell refers to as crisis tendencies. Conceptualizations of hegemonic masculinity shift and transform at these moments as new masculinities historically emerge and others decline. Historicizing masculinities scholarship traces these shifts across time and builds on Connell's framework, providing examples of these transformations as they take place. In the section introduction, we spell out four dominant themes that structure historical research on masculinity and provide a selection of readings in this section that exemplify these themes.

MULTIPLYING MASCULINITIES

The emergence of what we refer to as the *multiple masculinities* perspective is most clearly attributable to Connell's (1995) research and theory. Her initial insight, building on her dissatisfaction with sex role theory, is that masculinity is not one *thing*—it is not one identity, role, practice, whatever. Although the term is often used in ways that imply that masculinity is an "it," Connell's understanding of masculinities situated what was thought of an it rather as a "they," "them," or "those." She argues that research on masculinity could only adequately overcome the pitfalls associated with sex role theory by pluralizing the term: *masculinities*.

But beyond suggesting that we need to be studying masculinities (rather than masculinity), Connell created a framework within which we could make sense of the fact that not all masculinities are created equal and posited that masculinity is better understood as social "practice" than as a social role. As a practice, Connell does not mean to suggest that masculinities are purely voluntary—that we can simply do masculinity however we please. Rather, the multiple masculinities framework offered a new model for understanding gender practice as structured by four separate dimensions of gender relations: power relations, production relations, emotional relations, and symbolic relations. So, the multiple masculinities perspective understands masculinity as plural and frames gender as a configuration of practice rather than as a role.

A great deal of the research within the multiple masculinities perspective does not apply the full potential of Connell's theoretical framework. Rather, as Pascoe (2003) argues, the framework is more often reified. Although the vast majority of scholarship within this perspective relies on Connell's conceptualization of masculinities, sometimes research stops here and creates new typologies of masculinity that are then applied to individual men (although Connell's conceptualization of masculinities referred to diverse social practices—rather than different kinds of men). This framework still has extraordinary power, but the majority of scholarship within the framework uses a small piece of Connell's overall theoretical perspective, situating individual men or groups of men relative to hegemonic masculinity with less of a consideration on how this concept fits within the larger multiple masculinities model and approach. In the introduction to this section, we articulate these pitfalls in greater detail and discuss how the research and theory in this section attempts to build on this model and to avoid the shortcomings associated with a great deal of the scholarship seeking to apply Connell's model (not with the model itself). The research that we include in this section is representative of the scholarship that deals more critically with the approach and builds on Connell's original conceptualization.

NAVIGATING MASCULINITIES

Navigating masculinities scholarship is also best understood as an extension of Connell's theory, but stressing, extending, and building on slightly different elements of the framework than the previous two trajectories in masculinities scholarship. Research within this trajectory in the field often focuses on configurations of gender practice that Connell discussed as "marginalized masculinity" and "subordinated masculinity." The work here takes Connell's conceptualization of the patriarchal dividend seriously and is interested in the ways that different configurations of masculinity receive more and less of it in different ways and in distinct contexts.

Not all of the research and theory that we recognize within this trajectory of masculinities studies explicitly cites and connects with Connell's theory. But we suggest that this body of work is building on her theoretical apparatus nevertheless. This is an approach that utilizes tools from feminist intersectional theories of interconnections between different systems of inequality (e.g., inequalities based on race, class, education, sexuality, age, ability, and more). This body of scholarship and the theory that it has produced brings fresh insights, concepts, theoretical models, and tools to the study of masculinities.

In the introduction to this section, we more fully explain what it means to look at gender and inequality "intersectionally," where this perspective comes from, and how these tools build on concepts, relationships, and ideas within Connell's theoretical model. We explain some of the central issues dealt with in scholarship within what we refer to as the navigating masculinities perspective. Unlike the multiple masculinities perspective, the scholarship here is not united around a key set of texts. Rather, we suggest that this body of scholarship can be understood as building on key elements associated with intersectionality within Connell's theoretical framework—marginality and the unevenness of the patriarchal dividend—while maintaining an interest in fundamental aspects of Connell's theory of gender relations (like power and production relations).

The scholarship represented in the navigating masculinities section expands the dialogue of scholars studying masculinities. Indeed, some of the scholarship represented here (and in the following section) has not historically been understood as part of the canon of research and theory within masculinities studies. But by extending our definition of what qualifies as masculinities scholarship, we suggest that a great many masculinities scholars have much to learn from explorations of masculinity by scholars outside of the field (narrowly defined) who are building on core aspects of the theoretical framework that continues to define the field.

DISLOCATING MASCULINITIES

Similar to the navigating masculinities framework, the work within the trajectory of masculinities research and theory we call *dislocating masculinities* does not rely on a common theorist or set of concepts. Indeed, many of these scholars likely to do not recognize themselves as in conversation with one another or with masculinities studies, per se. What unites the theory and research within this perspective is a set of common concerns that are best summarized as building on three separate aspects of Connell's theory. This framework continues to highlight "power relations," a significant element uniting all four of these approaches. But what we refer to as dislocating masculinities scholarship also builds on two central aspects of Connell's theory.

First, dislocating masculinities scholarship is critically concerned with the dimension of gender relations that Connell refers to as "symbolic relations." How discourses, ideologies, and more support certain configurations of practice as masculine and specific gendered relations of power and inequality is a central question for these scholars. Just as navigating masculinities scholarship brought in new theoretical tools from intersectional theory and research, dislocating masculinities scholarship engages more critically with postmodern theories of gender, poststructuralism, and queer theory. It is significant that each of these theoretical perspectives emerged outside of the social sciences. The work here is interdisciplinary (like Connell's theory) and, collectively, dislocating masculinities scholarship helps to operationalize elements of theories developed in diverse fields to make sense of important configurations of gender and practice less studied by scholars within masculinities studies more narrowly defined.

Second, and perhaps most significantly, dislocating masculinities scholarship is noteworthy in that it detaches studies of masculinities from studies of people with male bodies.

Whereas Connell conceptualized the reproductive arena to help detach understandings of masculinity from biological imperatives and male bodies, a great deal of scholarship often implicitly (and sometimes explicitly) considers masculinity as anything and everything people with male bodies do and configurations of practice only available to male-bodied persons. But, like sex role theory, this is a casual form of biological reductionism, and Connell was interested in developing a theoretical framework capable of moving beyond it. So, this body of scholarship focuses on the boundaries between masculinities and femininities, often interrogating these boundaries with research on populations that call the very boundaries themselves into question: transgender men, drag kings, and all manner of what Halberstam (1998) refers to as "female masculinities."

Dislocating masculinities scholarship is best understood as critically highlighting and building on elements of Connell's theory less often deployed by scholars who we situate within the previous three trajectories of theory and research. This scholarship—and we count our theory and research with this trajectory—presents exciting opportunities to more fully realize the mission of Connell's theory and the full potential of her framework.

Significant here is that there is a great deal of scholarship (even represented among the contributions to this volume) that might be understood as belonging to more than one trajectory of exploration. So, it is important to acknowledge that the framework we present here is a way of thinking about the field that allows us to highlight the diverse ways that illustrate both the continued endurance and the power of Connell's theory of gender relations and masculinities. Rather than thinking of a given scholar as only occupying one of these four trajectories, we suggest that it is much more useful to consider how and in what ways different aspects of their work can be situated within this framework for thinking about masculinities scholarship. Indeed, considering how research might fit within more than one of the four trajectories we outline here allows us to more carefully consider different aspects of the research and emergent theories and concepts in the field. Below, we offer a set of questions to consider as readers approach each of the contributions to this volume, followed by a brief overview of the organization of the remainder of the book.

EXPLORATORY QUESTIONS

As you read the work that we have collected for this volume, it is important to consider how this work builds on the theoretical traditions that structure social constructivist investigations of masculinity. Below is a list of questions we invite you to consider throughout the volume.

- How is masculinity defined? Does it have clear or contextual boundaries? Is it related to sex? And if so, how? Different answers to these questions allow scholars to highlight distinct aspects of the social world.
- Where is masculinity "located" in the theory? Does the perspective situate masculinity as a property of individuals? Does the perspective discuss masculinity as a property of interactions or systems of social relations? Is masculinity explained as a feature of social institutions or as "institutionalized"? How do you know? What is it about the treatment of the topic that leads you to classify it this way?

- Does this perspective explain some of the variation in masculinities that we know exists? How?
- Does this perspective acknowledge other theoretical perspectives as important as well? Or does the perspective necessitate understanding other perspectives as inaccurate or as no longer useful?
- What are the theory's implications? Another way of thinking about this is as follows: If this theory is correct, what are some of the consequences of this fact? For instance, how might it help or hinder different understandings of gender inequality?
- How is power understood in the theory? Is it understood as something held by a relatively small group of people and wielded over others? Is it understood as more diffuse, structuring all of our identities and interactions? Can it be understood in both ways?
- Can you recognize elements of Connell's theory in the research? Are elements from Connell's theory missing that might provide a different perspective?
- How does the perspective respond to some of the early problems with sex role theory?

Remember that every perspective does not necessarily have to resolve *all* of the issues associated with sex role theory to be a powerful perspective. Sometimes, for example, a concept might prove incredibly useful in dealing with one of the shortcomings of sex role theory in an incredibly effective way. Any framework for analyzing masculinity and gender inequality can be looked at in two ways. We can consider what it *can* do and we can consider what it *cannot* do. Keeping both in mind can help you recognize the significance of each of the contributions to this volume, even those that might fail to acknowledge everything. Although sex role theory is widely discredited in the social sciences today, it is important to remember that it opened doors to new ways of understanding and studying gender that enabled subsequent theory and scholarship. When sex role theory is discussed today, it is most often discussed, as we address it here, for what it *failed* to do. But, sometimes, we need new theories to attempt to shift the conversation—even if done so imperfectly—in ways that help us realize we can ask questions we might never have seen. Consider each of the readings in this light. Yet, it is equally important to recognize how far we have come from sex role theory and how much this new work has to offer.

At the outset of this introduction, we offered two quotes that structure the explorations of masculinity in this book. Both Segal (1990) and Badinter (1995) agree that masculinities are constructed. But they are also both keen to recognize the ways in which contradictions are embedded within constructions of masculinity. As such, as objects of research and theory, masculinities are best understood as moving targets. We often treat masculinity as though it is a stable, transhistorical, cross-cultural, objective thing. Yet, as the readings in this volume attest, masculinities are anything but natural or stable. It is only through recognizing and understanding that masculinities can, do, and will change that we can better understand them. And once we do, they are sure to change again. The framework offered in this book provides a way of contextualizing these changes, seeking to better understand where and how they emerge, what they mean, and how power and inequality are challenged and reproduced. The diverse strands of scholarship within this book are connected by a common interest in exploring masculinities. Built into our understanding of the four trajectories shaping contemporary explorations of masculinities is the possibility for new interdisciplinary dialogue and debate. We invite you to participate as we continue to explore continuity and change in masculinities as well as social systems of power and inequality.

REFERENCES

Anderson, Eric. 2009. *Inclusive Masculinity*. New York: Routledge.

Arnold, Jeanne E., Anthony P. Graesch, Enzo Ragazzini, and Elinor Ochs. 2012. *Life at Home in the Twenty-First Century*. Los Angeles: Cotsen Institute of Archaeology Press.

Badinter, Elisabeth. 1995. *XY: On Masculine Identity*. Ithaca, NY: Columbia University Press.

Booth, Alan, Douglas A. Granger, Allan Mazur, and Katie T. Kivlighan. 2006. "Testosterone and Social Behavior." *Social Forces* 85 (1): 167–91.

Bourdieu, Pierre. 1984. *Distinction: A Social Critique of the Judgement of Taste*. Cambridge: Harvard University Press.

Brannon, Robert. 1976. *The Forty-Nine Percent Majority: The Male Sex Role*. New York: Random House.

Bridges, Tristan. 2009. "Gender Capital and Male Bodybuilders." *Body & Society* 15 (1): 83–107.

Bridges, Tristan. 2010. "Men Just Weren't Made To Do This: Performances of Drag at 'Walk a Mile in Her Shoes' Marches." *Gender & Society* 24 (1): 5–30.

Bridges, Tristan. 2014. "A Very 'Gay' Straight? Hybrid Masculinities, Sexual Aesthetics, and the Changing Relationship between Masculinity and Homophobia." *Gender & Society* 28 (1): 58–82.

Bridges, Tristan, and Michael Kimmel. 2009. "Book Review: Buchanan, Andrea J., and Miriam Peskowitz. 2007. *The Daring Book for Girls*. New York: Collins. Iggulden, Conn, and Hal Iggulden. 2007. *The Dangerous Book for Boys*. New York: Collins." *Men and Masculinities* 12 (1): 141–44.

Bridges, Tristan, and C. J. Pascoe. 2014. "Hybrid Masculinities: New Directions in the Sociology of Men and Masculinities." *Sociology Compass* 8 (3): 246–58.

Buss, David M. 1995. "Psychological Sex Differences: Origins through Sexual Selection." *American Psychologist* 50 (3): 164–68.

Charles, Maria, and David B. Grusky. 2004. *Occupational Ghettos: The Worldwide Segregation of Women and Men*. Stanford, CA: Stanford University Press.

Connell, Raewyn. 1979. "The Concept of Role and What to Do with It." *Australia and New Zealand Journal of Sociology* 15 (3): 7–17.

Connell, Raewyn. 1985. "Theorising Gender." *Sociology* 19: 260–72.

Connell, Raewyn. 1987. *Gender and Power: Society, the Person and Sexual Politics*. Stanford, CA: Stanford University Press.

Connell, Raewyn. 1990. "An Iron Man: The Body and Some Contradictions of Hegemonic Masculinity." In *Sport, Men, and the Gender Order*, edited by Michael A. Messner and Donald F. Sabo, 83–95. Champaign, IL: Human Kinetic Books.

Connell, Raewyn. 1992. "A Very Straight Gay: Masculinity, Homosexual Experience, and the Dynamics of Gender." *American Sociological Review* 57 (6): 735–51.

Connell, Raewyn. 1995. *Masculinities*. Berkeley: University of California Press.

Connell, Raewyn. 2002. *Gender: Short Introductions*. London: Polity Press.

Connell, Raewyn, and James W. Messerschmidt. 2005. "Hegemonic Masculinity: Rethinking the Concept." *Gender & Society* 19 (6): 829–59.

Coontz, Stephanie. 1992. *The Way We Never Were: American Families and the Nostalgia Trap*. New York: Basic Books.

De Boise, Sam. 2014. "I'm Not Homophobic, 'I've Got Gay Friends': Evaluating the Validity of Inclusive Masculinity." *Men and Masculinities*, published online ahead of print 16 October 2014.

Demetriou, Demetrakis. 2001. "Connell's Concept of Hegemonic Masculinity: A Critique." *Theory and Society* 30 (3): 337–61.

Diamond, Jared. 1995. "Father's Milk." *Discover* 16 (2): 82–87.

Donaldson, Mike. 1993. "What Is Hegemonic Masculinity?" *Theory and Society* 22 (5): 643–57.

Dreger, Alice Domurat. 1998. *Hermaphrodites and the Medical Invention of Sex*. Cambridge, MA: Harvard University Press.

Edwards, Tim. 2006. *Cultures of Masculinity*. New York: Routledge.

Fausto-Sterling, Anne. 2000. *Sexing the Body: Gender Politics and the Construction of Sexuality*. New York: Basic Books.

Fausto-Sterling, Anne. 2012. *Sex/Gender: Biology in a Social World*. New York: Routledge.

Friedan, Betty. 1963. *The Feminine Mystique*. New York: Norton.

Gilbert, Scott F. 2010. *Developmental Biology*. Sunderland, MA: Sinauer.

Gilmore, David D. 1990. *Manhood in the Making: Cultural Concepts of Masculinity*. New Haven, CT: Yale University Press.

Gramsci, Antonio. 1971. *Selections from the Prison Notebooks*. London: Lawrence & Wishart.

Habermas, Jürgen. 1975. *Legitimation Crisis*. Boston: Beacon Press.

Halberstam, Judith. 1998. *Female Masculinity*. Durham, NC: Duke University Press.

Hearn, Jeff. 1987. *The Gender of Oppression: Men, Masculinity and the Critique of Marxism*. New York: St. Martin's Press.

Hearn, Jeff. 2004. "From Hegemonic Masculinity to the Hegemony of Men." *Feminist Theory* 5 (1): 49–72.

Heilman, Madeline E. 2001. "Description and Prescription: How Gender Stereotypes Prevent Women's Ascent up the Organizational Ladder." *Journal of Social Issues* 57 (4): 657–74.

Johnson, Alan. 2005. *The Gender Knot*, rev. and updated ed. Philadelphia: Temple University Press.

Kessler, Suzanne J. 1998. *Lessons from the Intersexed*. New Brunswick, NJ: Rutgers University Press.

Kimmel, Michael. 1987. "The Contemporary 'Crisis' of Masculinity in Historical Perspective." In *The Making of Masculinities: The New Men's Studies*, edited by Harry Brod, 121–53. Boston: Allen & Unwin.

Kimmel, Michael. 1990. "After Fifteen Years: The Impact of the Sociology of Masculinity on the Masculinity of Sociology." In *Men, Masculinities and Social Theory*, edited by Harry Brod and David Morgan, 93–109. London: Unwin Hyman.

Kimmel, Michael. 1994. "Masculinity as Homophobia." In *Theorizing Masculinities*, edited by Harry Brod and Michael Kaufman, 119–41. Thousand Oaks, CA: Sage.

Kipling, Rudyard. 1901. *Kim*. New York: Macmillan.

Lieberson, Stanley, Susan Dumais, and Shyon Baumann. 2000. "The Instability of Androgynous Names: The Symbolic Maintenance of Gender Boundaries." *American Journal of Sociology* 105 (5): 1249–87.

Lorber, Judith. 1994. *Paradoxes of Gender*. New Haven, CT: Yale University Press.

Martin, Emily. 1991. "The Egg and the Sperm: How Science Has Constructed a Romance Based on Stereotypical Male–Female Roles." *Signs* 16 (3): 485–501.

Martin, Patricia Yancey. 2004. "Gender as Social Institution." *Social Forces* 82: 1249–73.

Matthews, Richard. 1662. *The Unlearned Alchemist*. London: Joseph Leigh.

Mazur, Allan, and Alan Booth. 1998. "Testosterone and Dominance in Men." *Behavioral and Brain Sciences* 21 (3): 353–63.

McCaughey, Martha. 2008. *The Caveman Mystique: Pop-Darwinism and the Debates over Sex, Violence, and Science.* London: Routledge.

McIntosh, Peggy. 1988. "White Privilege and Male Privilege: A Personal Account of Coming to See Correspondences through Work in Women's Studies." Working Paper No. 189. Wellesley, MA.

McNay, Lois. 1999. "Gender, Habitus and the Field: Pierre Bourdieu and the Limits of Reflexivity." *Theory, Culture & Society* 16 (1): 95–117.

Mead, Margaret. 1963 [1935]. *Sex and Temperament in Three Primitive Societies.* New York: Morrow.

Meadow, Tey. 2011. "'Deep Down Where the Music Plays': How Parents Account for Childhood Gender Variance." *Sexualities* 14 (6): 725–47.

Meadow, Tey. 2014. "The Child." *Transgender Studies Quarterly* 1 (1–2): 57–59.

Messner, Michael A. 1992. *Power at Play: Sports and the Problem of Masculinity.* Boston: Beacon Press.

Messner, Michael A., and Jeffrey Montez de Oca. 2005. "The Male Consumer as Loser: Beer and Liquor Ads in Mega Sports Media Events." *Signs* 30 (3): 1879–909.

Money, John, and Anke A. Ehrhardt. 1972. *Man and Woman, Boy and Girl: Differentiation and Dimorphism of Gender Identity from Conception to Maturity.* Oxford: Johns Hopkins University Press.

Oakley, Ann. 1972. *Sex, Gender and Society.* London: Gower.

Padavic, Irene, and Barbara F. Reskin. 2002. *Women and Men at Work.* Thousand Oaks, CA: Pine Forge Press.

Parsons, Talcott. 1954. *Essays in Sociological Theory.* New York: Free Press.

Parsons, Talcott, and Robert Bales. 1953. *Family, Socialization and Interaction Process.* London: Routledge & Kegan Paul.

Pascoe, C. J. 2003. "Multiple Masculinities?: Teenage Boys Talk about Jocks and Gender." *American Behavioral Scientist* 46 (10): 1423–38.

Pascoe, C. J. 2007. *"Dude, You're a Fag": Masculinity and Sexuality in High School.* Berkeley: University of California Press.

Pleck, Joseph H. 1981. *The Myth of Masculinity.* Cambridge, MA: MIT Press.

Preves, Sharon E. 2003. *Intersex and Identity: The Contested Self.* New Brunswick, NJ: Rutgers University Press.

Risman, Barbara. 2004. "Gender as a Social Structure: Theory Wrestling with Activism." *Gender & Society* 18 (4): 429–50.

Ruble, Diane N., Carol L. Martin, and Sheri A. Berenbaum, eds. 2006. *Gender Development.* Hoboken, NJ: Wiley.

Sanday, Peggy Reeves. 1981. "The Socio-Cultural Context of Rape: A Cross-Cultural Study." *Journal of Social Issues* 37 (4): 5–27.

Sapolsky, Robert. 1997. "Testosterone Rules." *Discover,* March 1, 1997.

Schippers, Mimi. 2007. "Recovering the Feminine Other: Masculinity, Femininity, and Gender Hegemony." *Theory and Society* 36 (1): 85–102.

Schmied, Virginia, and Deborah Lupton. 2001. "Blurring the Boundaries: Breastfeeding and Maternal Subjectivity." *Sociology of Health & Illness* 23 (2): 234–50.

Segal, Lynne. 1990. *Slow Motion: Changing Masculinities, Changing Men.* New Brunswick, NJ: Rutgers University Press.

Slaby, Ronald G., and Karin S. Frey. 1975. "Development of Gender Constancy and Selective Attention to Same-Sex Models." *Child Development* 46 (4): 849–56.

Stacey, Judith, and Barrie Thorne. 1985. "The Missing Feminist Revolution in Sociology." *Social Problems* 32 (4): 301–16.

Stearns, Cindy A. 1999. "Breastfeeding and the Good Maternal Body." *Gender & Society* 13 (3): 308–25.

Stoller, Robert J. 1994 [1968]. *Sex and Gender: The Development of Masculinity and Femininity.* London: Hogarth Press.

Wade, Lisa, and Myra Marx Ferree. 2014. *Gender: Ideas, Interactions, Institutions.* New York: Norton.

West, Candace, and Don Zimmerman. 1987. "Doing Gender." *Gender & Society* 1 (2): 125–51.

Whitehead, Steven M., and Frank J. Barrett. 2001. *The Masculinities Reader.* London: Polity Press.

NOTES

1. An important point to stress here is the distinction between "biology" and "biological determinism." Sociologists and other scholars disagreeing with biological determinist theories of gender are not denying that biological differences exist between male and female bodies. Rather, we are challenging a group of biological scientists who suggest that the biological differences we know exist "determine" things about the way we act, think, love, and more. "Biological determinism" is a term scholars use for an array of theories and ideologies that attempts to reduce types of behavior to unchanging biological roots—considering human behavior as biologically predetermined. So, just to be clear, this means that we are not denying the existence of things like penises and vaginas or biological processes like lactation—we are challenging the significance of these differences in determining other aspects of social life.

2. See Heilman (2001) for an account of how "descriptive" and "prescriptive" gender stereotypes perpetuate gender inequality in the workplace.

3. This treatment is leaving out a discussion of autosomes for the sake of simplicity. For a more engaged discussion of the significance of autosomes in the process of chromosomal sex, see Fausto-Sterling (2012).

4. "Sex markers" is a term scholars use to discuss those aspects of human physiology that we rely on when making distinctions between males and females (penises, vaginas, ovaries, testicles, chromosomes, etc.).

5. On the social significance of intersexed individuals, see also Kessler (1998), Dreger (1998), Fausto-Sterling (2000), and Preves (2003).

6. This, of course, does not account for transgender children or children who regularly encounter openly transgender children or adults—processes that understandably complicate this process. See Meadow (2011, 2014) for work on transgender children.

7. It's worth noting that Margaret Mead uses the awkward language of "sex temperament" to address what we might write about as "gender" today. The reason for this is that the term "gender" did not mean then what we use it to mean today. For instance, for much of the 17th century, gender was used to distinguish between classes of things that have something in common with one another. For instance, in Richard Matthews' (1662) *Unlearned Alchemist*, he writes, "Diseases of this gender are for the most part incurable." When Matthews was writing, gender could be used to discuss differences between men and women, but these differences were not a special use of the term and were treated in the same way differences of any other class of objects or things would have been treated using the word.

   During the 18th, 19th, and 20th centuries, gender began to acquire a new meaning. As "sex" started to increasingly mean "sexual intercourse," gender began to be used primarily to refer to the biological grouping of males and females. Sometime in the mid-20th century—after Margaret Mead was writing—gender started to refer to the social and cultural distinctions between men and women (as opposed to biological differences). Although many credit the British sociologist, Ann Oakley, with drawing this distinction formally between sex and gender in *Sex, Gender, and Society* (1972), others suggest that Robert Stoller made this distinction formalized in the social science literature earlier in his book, *Sex and Gender: The Development of Masculinity and Femininity* (1994 [1968]) or that the distinction emerged with John Money's research on the diversity of bodies and sex characteristics (e.g., Money and Ehrhardt 1972). Either way, gender acquired a new meaning during the latter half of the 20th century, in part because of some of the revolutions in thinking Margaret Mead produced by writing about "sex temperaments" in different cultures.

8. Subsequently, sociologist Michael Kimmel (1994) relied on Brannon's framework to theorize the relationship between masculinity and homophobia, suggesting that homophobia and fear are fundamental elements of Brannon's "No Sissy Stuff" as well. Scholars continue to theorize acts of repudiating femininity as a central aspect of public demonstrations and declarations of masculinity (e.g., Pascoe 2007; Bridges 2010).

9. This technique of ignoring power and inequality survives in a great deal of scholarship on gender, even today. It is probably most recognizable in evolutionary psychology, a new discipline that purports to examine the evolutionary history of psychological and behavioral traits. The field has received sharp criticism because it often relies on inaccurate, unscientific, and sexist stereotypes about early humans. Yet, one of the central scholars in the field, David Buss, characterizes the field as free of "values" (and, presumably, more "scientific" as a result). Similar to sex role theory, evolutionary psychologists argue that "neither women nor men can be considered 'superior' or 'inferior' to the other, any more than a bird's wing can be considered superior or inferior to a fish's fin or a kangaroo's legs. . . . Notions of superiority and inferiority are logically incoherent from the vantage point of evolutionary psychology. The meta-theory of evolutionary psychology is descriptive, not prescriptive—it carries no values in its teeth" (Buss 1995: 167). By this, Buss argues that evolutionary psychology seeks to explain why and how men and women are the way they are, but avoids making claims about how they *should* be. Yet, similar to sex role theory, gendered characterizations produced by evolutionary psychologists present power and inequality as natural, biological features of social life despite great evidence to the contrary (e.g., McCaughey 2008). Cross-cultural and historical variation in understandings of masculine and feminine alone ought to give us serious pause when considering arguments about gender attempting to generalize to the entire human race throughout all of human history. Variation is the rule, not the exception.

10. It is worth noting that Connell's theory emerged alongside West and Zimmerman's (1987) classic article, "Doing Gender." The theories share a number of similarities and both critique and build on sex role theory.

11. Connell's use of the concept of gender regime bears a great deal of similarity to Pierre Bourdieu's (1984) conceptualization of "fields." Bridges's (2009) research on male bodybuilders explores this connection in greater detail and is a useful example of how scholars might make better use of Connell's conceptualization of gender regimes in ways that causes us to be more critical of how masculinities are performed and evaluated differently (sometimes subtly, sometimes substantially) in distinct gender regimes. Lois McNay's (1999) theorization of gender within Bourdieu's framework addresses a similar use of Bourdieu's conceptualization of "field" as well.

12. For an example of this, consider Connell's (1990) analysis of Steve Donoghue, a national competitor in Australian "iron man" competitions. Although Steve might seem to embody the most culturally exalted forms of masculinity—as, perhaps, the Marlboro man does as well—as we learn more about Steve's life, we learn that living up to this ideal involves a host of contradictions. "Being an exemplar of masculinity actually forbids Steve to do many things that his peer group and culture define as masculine . . . [For instance,] sustaining the training regime that yields the bodily supremacy, giving him his status as a champion, is incompatible with the kind of sexual and social life that is expected of affluent young men" (Connell 1990: 94). For more on this, see Messner's (1992) analysis of the relationship between sports and masculinity over the life course.

13. Significantly, it was here that Connell bluntly conceptualizes her theory as "open" in a way that structural functionalism and sex role theory were not. When she initially conceptualized three dimensions of gender relations (power, production, and cathexis), she began by stating, "The argument does not assume that they are the only discoverable structures, that they exhaust the field. Nor does it claim that they are necessary structures. . . . The argument rests on a gentler, more pragmatic but perhaps more demonstrable claim that with a framework like this we can come to a serviceable understanding of current history" (Connell 1987: 97).

14. "Power relations" is the term that Connell uses in her theory to get at what many feminist theorists refer to as "patriarchy"—or the notion that men are the dominant sex class, the various origins of this notion, the diverse individual and institutional support for this notion, and the diverse consequences of continuing to uphold this notion.

15. We know this interesting fact by tracing the history of occupations that have undergone gender transformations. Occupations that were, for instance, once dominated by women that are now dominated by men or vice versa can tell us a great deal of how we think about a particular occupation. The pay and status of occupations follow the gender of the primary occupants of the job—not the reverse (e.g., Padavic and Reskin 2002).

16. Connell borrows this term from another social theorist, Jürgen Habermas. Habermas (1975) initially used the term to address class dynamics in late capitalist societies. In *Legitimation Crisis* (1975), Habermas theorized capitalism as replete with internal contradictions. To get at these contradictions, Habermas analyzes four separate crisis tendencies embedded within the structure and action of late capitalist societies. According to Habermas, this dynamic quality of late capitalist societies means that the threat of change is ever-present, looming just below the surface. Connell examines gender relations in a similar way. Rather than considering gender relations as orderly and organized, Connell's theory situates gender as internally contradictory and messy.

17. See Bridges and Pascoe (2014) for some examples of how flexible systems of inequality structure the masculinities available to and desired by contemporary, young, straight, white men.

18. Borrowing Antonio Gramsci's (1971) conceptualization of "hegemony," Connell's understanding of power and inequality is historically mobile and flexible. This may be one of the most significant aspects of Connell's theory—one that is, in our reading of the research, too often ignored. Gramsci was interested in class inequality and his central argument was that the ruling elite retained power by legitimating their dominance primarily through ideological persuasion rather than brute physical force. As we mentioned earlier, privilege works best when it goes unrecognized as "privilege"—when it is understood as deserved. According to Gramsci, ideological hegemony is achieved via an intricate process of gaining ideological dominance through symbolic struggles with competing groups. Gramsci was primarily

interested in how ideology operated in ways that justified class inequality, and his theory helped to situate *ideology* as an important site of political struggle.

19.   There have been a number of critiques of hegemonic masculinity. Some challenge the meaning of the concept itself (e.g., Donaldson 1993), others challenge its utility (e.g., Hearn 2004) or enduring relevance (e.g., Anderson 2009), and some scholars have done less to critique the term than to consider expanding its scope (e.g., Demetriou 2001; Schippers 2007; Bridges 2009; Bridges and Pascoe 2014). Connell and Messerschmidt (2005) responded to a number of these challenges with an exploration of the use and meaning of the term and offer useful suggestions for future research. Although we do not address all of these issues here, we mention them to let readers understand that we are on controversial ground even when we attempt to define the term.

20.   It significant that Connell is explicitly relying on Habermas's (1975) theory of late capitalism here when she argues that hegemonic masculinity is best understood as the "currently accepted answer to the problem of the legitimacy of patriarchy." As Habermas understood late capitalist societies as inherently unstable, Connell too understands gender relations in this way. Habermas argued that late capitalist societies suffer a "legitimacy crisis" when citizens perceive their demands to be unmet to a significant degree. As societies transform, powerful groups and ideologies require new strategies of legitimation. Connell argues that movements for women's and gay men's liberation called patriarchy into question in historically new ways. Ideas about things like domestic violence, men's presumed inherent aggression, and women's sexuality and sexual desires were openly challenged in new ways. Thus, as Demetriou writes, "Patriarchy was in need of new legitimatory strategies and many men were asked to renegotiate their positions in patriarchal societies, their power, and their masculine identities" (2001: 349). With crisis, in other words, comes the possibility of change. But, in being careful to assess social transformations, Connell's theory provides for an understanding of patriarchy as a social structure equally capable of adaptation and flexibility (see also Bridges and Pascoe 2014; Bridges 2014; de Boise 2014). As Gramsci's (1971) theory of power suggests, hegemonies are so powerful precisely because of their ability to react to changing circumstances and challenges from below.

21.   Mimi Schippers (2007) challenges this claim and suggests that we can, in fact, theorize hegemonic femininity and that it is best juxtaposed to what she refers to as "pariah femininities." This intersectional framework merits much more attention from masculinities scholars. Indeed, Connell and Messerschmidt (2005) consider Schippers' claim critically in their retheorization of hegemonic masculinity.

1

HISTORICIZING MASCULINITIES

CHAPTER 1

HISTORICIZING MASCULINITIES

An Introduction

"Manhood is neither static nor timeless. Manhood is not the manifestation of an inner essence; it's socially constructed. Manhood does not bubble up to consciousness from our biological constitution; it is created in our culture. In fact, the search for a transcendent, timeless definition of manhood is itself a sociological phenomenon—we tend to search for the timeless and eternal during moments of crisis, those points of transition when the old definitions no longer work and the new definitions are yet to be firmly established."

—MICHAEL KIMMEL, 2012 [1996],
Manhood in America: A Cultural History, p. 4[1]

What masculinity has been thought to be has changed over time. It's a simple point. But it has incredible implications. The reasons why we would consider someone "manly," "macho," "butch," or "masculine," for instance, are not historically constant. Different groups have collectively answered the question "What does it mean to be a man?" in different ways at different points in time.

Scholarship on gender and inequality is critically concerned with historical changes in the cultural definitions of masculinity (and femininity). The fact that *gender varies* is one of the most basic building blocks of understanding what it means to discuss and analyze gender as socially constructed. Simply put, this means that what we consider masculine and feminine has changed over time. Masculinity is not, in other words, historically constant (and neither is femininity). What it means to "be a man" has changed, and this is one of the ways that scholars of gender have been able to prove that gender is socially constructed—rather than an inherent property. Although gender varies in more ways than one, examining historical variation provides new insight into the development gender theory.[2]

To think of masculinity as a description of cultural practices enacted by or prescribed to individuals or groups rather than having a specific (and universal) definition alters the parameters of academic discussion surrounding the topic. In a basic way, "masculinities" refer to all of the social roles, obligations, behaviors, meanings, and all manner of actions, objects, and emotions prescribed for men within a given society or social context at a given point in time. Scholars who examine variation in masculinity do so with the understanding that what is considered masculine and masculinity has been—and will continue to be—subject to change. Historical research on masculinities charts these changes and seeks to attribute transformations in masculine enactments, understandings, meanings, and more to aspects of the organization and structure of the societies in which they emerge.

The fact that gender has varied throughout history is one way of illustrating that what we recognize as masculine or feminine is not built into our biology, it is constructed in our culture. And although this might seem like a small discovery, the consequences of this argument are much farther reaching than you might imagine. For instance, demonstrating that gender is not naturally occurring opened the door to a consideration of the ways that inequalities between men and women are not natural either. The idea that some of our most intimate behaviors and beliefs about what we think of as masculine and feminine are social (or cultural) rather than natural is, for many people, a challenging idea. Pioneering historical research and theory empirically demonstrates that our understandings of gender are, in many ways, unique not only to our culture, but also to the historical periods we happen to occupy. In this introduction, we provide a framework to make sense of the different ways scholars have uncovered some of the diverse meanings of masculinity throughout time—a tradition we refer to as *historicizing masculinities*. Although we will not provide exhaustive references here, our aim here is to provide readers with a toolkit for making sense of historical research on masculinity, its significance, and the various ways scholars study and make sense of historical transformations in masculinity.

FROM MANLINESS TO MASCULINITY

Historical scholarship on masculinities has uncovered an incredible diversity of masculinities among different historical periods. Indeed, we didn't always even use the terms masculine or masculinity. Masculinity only emerged in the past 100 years or so (at least in terms of the meaning we associate with it today). For a long time, "manly" and "manliness" were the popular terms used to denote something similar to what we mean today. The term "masculinity" started to be used around the turn of the 20th century. Indeed, right around the same time, manliness—which had been an incredibly common term throughout the 19th century—began to lose favor. It was not until around 1940, however, that masculinity eclipsed manliness (see Figure 1). It turns out that it was much more than just a new word. The switch from manliness to masculinity is part of a larger story about the historical emergence of new understandings of what it meant to be a man, how to demonstrate that quality to others, and newly minted anxieties around the turn of the 20th century surrounding the possibility of "failing" to demonstrate these qualities.

As you'll read in the excerpt from Gail Bederman's (1995) *Manliness & Civilization* (Reading 1), manliness referred to a subset of qualities to which not all men had equal access. Thus, embedded in a history of masculinity are questions of access, power, and inequality. Things like sexual restraint, a powerful will, and strong character situated Victorian middle- and upper-class men as comfortably "manly." But these were qualities that became less secure, less assured, with the social and economic transformations underway at the close of the 19th century. At the time, masculinity was a fairly vacuous term by

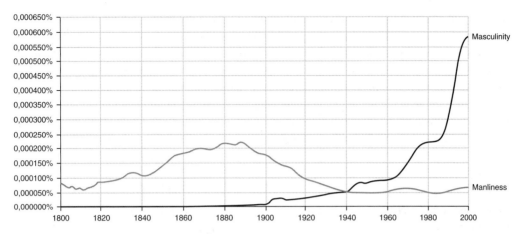

FIGURE 1 Google Books NGram Graph—Mentions of "manliness" and "masculinity" in published work, 1800–2000.[3]

comparison. Rather than describing a particular kind of man, masculine was primarily used to distinguish things that defined men collectively from women. This new term—masculinity—provided greater access than manliness and seems to have been created at a moment when men's collective power was in question. It might be understood as part of a larger move to symbolically "circle the wagons" when men's ability to demonstrate manliness was made more difficult for social and historical reasons you'll read about in more detail throughout this section. Some scholars discuss masculinity as "in crisis" at different periods of time—and the turn of the 20th century is just such a historical moment.

ON THE "CRISIS OF MASCULINITY"

One of the interesting insights in historical research on masculinity is that, although men have historically been the group in power, changes in definitions of masculinity often follow (rather than precede) transformations in femininity. As Michael Kimmel writes, "The historical evidence suggests that while both masculinity and femininity are socially constructed within [the] historical context of gender relations, definitions of masculinity are historically *reactive* to changing definitions of femininity" (1987: 123). Kimmel's research on historical transformations in masculinities in late 17th- and early 18th-century England paralleled later patterns in the United States in the late 19th and early 20th century. As the group in power, Kimmel explains why men might be best understood as unlikely to initiate change in gender relations. The periods during which societal understandings of masculinity changed are a popular topic of research.

Thus, a great deal of historical research on masculinity has sought to ask whether masculinity was (or is) "in crisis" in specific historical periods. During these periods, everyday enactments might shift, masculine archetypes are sometimes questioned or openly challenged, and new masculine entrepreneurs often emerge. The context of the United States at the turn of the 20th century is one such period and the one we primarily focus on in this section. The discourse of crisis continues to be used today. Books abound in the popular press claiming that men no longer understand what it means to be a man, and claims about the implications of this enter policy discussions about the family, education, the workplace, and—for some—the demise of our civilization. Considering so-called crises of masculinity in historical perspective, however, sheds light on the fact that the discourse relies on an inaccurate understanding of masculinity.

First, to claim that something is in crisis relies on an understanding that it had been a unified, coherent "thing" in the first place. Certainly, on some level, to be in crisis means that prior to this time, stability must have been the norm. Crisis requires a previous state of permanence, stability, or stasis. As Raewyn Connell explains, "As a theoretical term 'crisis' presupposes a coherent system of some kind, which is destroyed or restored by the outcome of the crisis. Masculinity . . . is not a system in that sense" (1995: 84). Indeed, some suggest that transformations in late modernity have so profoundly altered sexual divisions of labor and patriarchal belief systems that we are no longer witnessing a crisis of masculinity so much as what John MacInnes (1998) refers to as "the end of masculinity." As the essays in this section indicate, masculinity is in a state of change, it is "on the move," shifting and reacting to social and historical forces that transform the texture, shape, and meaning of masculinity. But this state of change is what has been historically constant.

What these crises in masculinity might actually be about are challenges to inequitable gendered arrangements of power. Although groups in power do not always individually recognize their interests in maintaining inequitable arrangements, this does not mean they do not have collective interests. As Raewyn Connell writes, "Inequalities construct interests (whether or not those interests are articulated). Those benefitting from inequalities have an interest in defending them. Those who bear the costs have an interest in ending them" (2002: 141).

Although there has been a great deal of change throughout time in the vestigial aspects associated with masculinity, historicizing masculinities can also help us keep these transformations in perspective. Change in the superficial features of masculinity has been the historical rule, not the exception. But how these changes are related to structures of power and inequality is also important to consider. And often, changes that appear to be completely transformative are more superficial when we investigate them more closely. Arthur Brittan (1989) draws a useful distinction between masculinity and what he refers to as "masculinism." Whereas he refers to masculinity as "those aspects of men's behaviour that fluctuate over time" (things like hairstyles, clothing, all manner of self-presentation, but also shifts in men's behaviors as parents and more), masculinism refers to "the ideology that justifies and naturalizes male domination." And, significant for Brittan is the notion that masculinism "is not subject to the vagaries of fashion—it tends to be relatively resistant to change" (1989: 3–4). In other words, *masculinity has been shown to be much more historically flexible than masculinism.*

Challenges to masculinist ideologies often come from structurally disadvantaged groups. When women organized to fight for the right to vote, for instance, they were challenging more than a set of voting rights and restrictions; they were challenging gendered ideologies of citizenship that bolstered systems of men's collective power and privilege (one of many different pillars propping up masculinism in the early 20th century). But, challenges to masculinism can also come from social, structural, and historical locations. Indeed, Connell (1987, 1995) suggests that such challenges are near-constant features of gender relations.

> [Masculinity] is . . . a configuration of practice within a system of gender relations. We cannot logically speak of a crisis of configuration; rather we might speak of its disruption or transformation. We can, however, logically speak of the crisis of the gender order as a whole, and of its tendencies toward crisis. (Connell 1995: 84)

Transformations in the economy, the political system, and forces of globalization can impact gender relations at the micro-level. Indeed, historical research and theory on transformations in masculinities situate a changing economy as having reverberations into some of the most intimate spheres of our lives (e.g., Blumberg and Coleman 1989; Segal 1990). And although certain historical moments seem rife with conflict and change, scholars of masculinities largely oppose the language of crisis because it (implicitly) presumes a state of uniformity and agreement about masculinity prior to such a period. Such a state, however, did not historically exist—at least not in the way the language of crisis suggests.

In perhaps the most exhaustive history of masculinity in the United States—*Manhood in America* (2012 [1996])—Michael Kimmel frames economic factors as the key variables motivating conflict and change in cultural conceptions of masculinity in the United States. Kimmel argues that throughout the 18th and 19th centuries, two different (although perfectly compatible) definitions of masculinity coexisted, ideal types he refers to as "the genteel patriarch" and "the heroic artisan." He documents how the emergence of a capitalist economy changed the relationship between these two symbols of masculinity, in which both gave way to the "self-made man," a masculinity Kimmel argues continues to govern contemporary gender relations.

Economic transformations fundamentally shaped the gender relations in and the gender of home and work—as work was separated from the domestic sphere, the home became feminized and work became masculinized (e.g., Rosenberg 1982; Cowan 1983; Hansen 1996). Indeed, it was in reference to this period that Christopher Lasch (1977) famously referred to the home as "a haven in a heartless world." The processes at work that made the public world of work more "heartless," and the private sphere of the home more of a "haven," were buttressed by changing meanings of masculinity and femininity, new obligations for women and men, and new types of relationships between and among men and women as well. It is important to note, however, that this model was much less prevalent in reality than it tends to be in our imaginations surrounding early to mid-20th-century family life (e.g., Coontz 1992). Despite this, this period underwent a historical revolution in relations between men and women that produced effects we still feel today. And although these changes had dramatic implications for the ways men and women understood themselves and their respective "roles" in society, they also had implications for relationships among men and among women.

For instance, John D'Emilio (1993) discusses the ways in which capitalism in the United States provided the social infrastructure wherein men were able to engage in same-sex intimacy in ways not possible in previous historical periods (see also Adam 1996). They left their families and went off to work in impersonal public spaces with large groups of other men. This meant that men were increasingly in homosocial settings (only around other men) in which many of the men were strangers to one another. This type of anonymity provided new kinds of possibilities for men. And all of this happened quite suddenly, historically speaking (see also Greenberg, 1988). Women faced conditions that mirrored men's—but women's homosocial worlds were not composed of strangers. Lillian Faderman's (1991) *Odd Girls and Twilight Lovers* explores the emergence of lesbian identities and a history of same-sex intimacy in 20th-century America as well. These structural differences in how men and women encountered same-sex intimacy in early 20th-century American society provided the foundation for different kinds of encounters and sexual cultures to emerge.

Historical research addresses these changes in different ways. In the following, we provide a roadmap to consider different types of historical research. Rather than concentrating solely on key contributors (although we include some here as well), our larger goal is to provide a framework to consider the different ways scholars make claims about transformations and look for clues that might help us better understand the origins and meanings of such changes. This will help provide readers with tools to consider the work in this section in a new light.

MASCULINE ARCHETYPES, COUNTERTYPES, ENTREPRENEURS, AND EVERYDAY ENACTMENTS

Historical research on masculinity comes from diverse disciplinary and theoretical traditions. Some of it is based in the humanities and offers a kind of textual analysis.[4] Other research relies on more formal historical or social scientific methods of inquiry. Rather than attempting to distill key figures in this section, we focus on the four dominant themes that structure historical research on masculinity. We refer to these as: (1) masculine archetypes, (2) masculine countertypes, (3) masculine entrepreneurs, and (4) everyday enactments. Although in practice, a great deal of research fits into multiple categories here, we think of these as ideal types, meant to provide a structure to consider historical research and theory on masculinities. So, we'll focus on aspects of specific research that exemplify each type, but much research fits into more than a single classification.

One way that historical research has sought to investigate the meanings of manliness throughout time is to focus on key figures, who seem to exemplify elements of what it meant to be a man at particular points in history—"*masculine archetypes*" of a particular time and place. For instance, historical research on the United States often focuses on key figures who embodied particular forms of masculine identity at a specific point in history—who would have been widely recognized as manly men. Thus, as Michael Kimmel (2012 [1996]) charts the transformation in the meanings associated with manhood over the course of U.S. history, Thomas Jefferson and Paul Revere are used as key figures—masculine archetypes—who exemplify different modes of masculinity. Like Kimmel, research focusing on masculine archetypes focuses on the qualities of these figures to uncover some of the historical dynamics of what it meant to be a man throughout time. It asks questions about the archetypal features of masculinity at different points in history—those elements thought to be typical of men or for which certain men were idealized.

Another way that historical scholarship has uncovered masculine archetypes associated with manhood for different periods is through a study of the artifacts produced that might have outlined those archetypes in fine detail. Judy Hilkey's (1997) analysis of success manuals produced in America during end of the 19th and beginning of the 20th century is a great example of analyzing masculine archetypes in this way. A great deal of the information within those pages directly addresses some of the normative ideals surrounding masculinity during that era. As Hilkey writes, "A close reading of [success manuals] shows that the concept of manhood and manliness was used as a way to make distinctions among men, to identify a particular type of man with success in the new order, and to promote a particular set of behaviors as appropriate for the new age" (1997: 9). Success manuals allowed Hilkey to uncover information on archetypes for masculine behavior, dress, demeanor, and more—things that would likely not have been spelled out in as fine detail in other artifacts. Hilkey's work builds on Kimmel's (2012 [1996]) and Rotundo's (1993) historical analysis that charts the progression of more competitive ideals associated with masculinity. This was a subtle change, but it affected men's understandings of their role in society, their relationships with women and other men, and it produced new forms of inequality (both among men and between men and women more generally).

Research also focuses on what George Mosse (1996) refers to as *masculine "countertypes."* Conceptions of ideal masculinities need, according to Mosse, images and identities against which they can be defined. Like many privileged categories, masculinity has throughout history often been defined more by what it is *not* than by what it is. And historical research considers masculinities that have been historically cast as "unmasculine" for one reason or another for clues about historical meanings of manhood and the systems of power and inequality that structured those meanings. So, for instance, Mosse addresses the various ways that Jews and homosexuals were portrayed as "unmanly" in all manner of historical media at various points throughout history (Mosse 1996). Medicine and medical professionals have also played a key role in constructing masculine countertypes. As an example, in Mosse's essay (Reading 5), he addresses the ways that World War I soldiers experiencing "shell shock" ceased to be seen as "real men." Medical professionals participated in constructing an understanding of psychologically traumatized soldiers returning from battle as "weak" and "unmanly."[5] But countertypes can also be constructed in court proceedings, legislation, and popular culture more generally.

Historical research can also focus on what we call *masculine entrepreneurs*: individuals who—either by accident or by design—became incredibly well known for and associated with transformations in masculinity. So, if we think of masculine archetypes as individuals who embodied a normative model of manhood for a specific time, masculinity entrepreneurs are individuals who forged new models. For instance, historians have made a great deal out of the model of manhood that Theodore Roosevelt became associated with at the turn of the 20th century (e.g., Kimmel 2012 [1996]; Kasson 2001). Roosevelt "built" his body, was fascinated by his muscles, and prominently displayed them in pictures of himself as a young man. Roosevelt became associated with new forms of masculine embodiment and self-surveillance, along with others (like the originator of modern bodybuilding, Eugen Sandow, or figures like Charles Atlas). Masculine entrepreneurs are interesting to study because they provide important information about transformations and periods of history in which the meanings of masculinity were in flux. Rather than illustrating the masculine status quo, these figures emerge (or perhaps it would be more accurate to say they gain prominence) at historical moments when masculine archetypes are being questioned or are less easy to live up to than they may have been for previous generations.

Finally, a great deal of historical scholarship also considers what we refer to as *everyday enactments* of masculinity. So, rather than only focusing on key figures who may have been known to many, historical research also attempts to interrogate the more taken-for-granted elements of manhood in everyday life—through personal objects like diaries, pictures, or other personal items. This research relies on a terrific array of evidence to make claims about how individuals and groups from long ago understood masculinity in their day-to-day lives in ways that differ (sometimes subtly, sometimes significantly) from many of our own understandings today. Historicizing manhood is difficult, in part, because many aspects of manhood were not necessarily seen as in need of explanation. So, for instance, in John Tosh's history of middle-class manhood and the relationship between masculinity and domesticity in mid- to late 19th-century England—*A Man's Place: Masculinity and the Middle-Class Home in Victorian England* (1999)—he relies on, among other things, personal diaries and correspondence to get at some of these hidden meanings.

Similarly, Judith Flanders (2003) relies on information embedded in Victorian novels to learn more about the Victorian household and people's behavior within it. Flanders looks for the information in novels that would have been regarded as background information for readers at the time of publication—information about the use of rooms, behaviors of individuals within them, duties of various persons throughout the household, etc. She then attempts to balance this information by corroborating it with more conventional sources of documentation. Scholars focusing on everyday enactments of masculinity face a difficult task in figuring out precisely how to study them. Much of what these scholars uncover would have been largely taken for granted by the people in the historical periods they dissect. And the thing about what we take for granted is that we tend not to talk about it, write about it, or document it carefully.

Another interesting study relying on what we're calling "everyday enactments" of masculinity is John Ibson's pioneering study of masculinity. In *Picturing Men: A Century of Male Relationships in Everyday American Photography* (2002), Ibson considers historical transformations in masculinity by relying on everyday photographs of men depicted with other men. Many of these photographs depict relationships between men that might seem odd by modern standards. Indeed, in many of the photographs, men are depicted in a warm embrace, or with one on another's lap, sometimes gazing adoringly at one another, holding hands, or hugging. Ibson is much less interested in whether these men were actually sexually intimate with one another. What he finds fascinating is that there is no evidence of whether they were in the photographs. As Ibson writes of this photograph (see Image 1), "In spite of today's homophobic equation of same-sex affection with sexual interest, affection between men need not involve sex any more than sex between them is necessarily a sign of affection. Indeed what actually constitutes 'intimacy' may vary across time" (2002: xiii). And, as you will read more of in Reading 3 by E. Anthony Rotundo, boys

(From John Ibson, *Picturing Men: A Century of Male Relationships in Everyday American Photographs.*)

and men used to be more intimate with each other than they are today. In his analysis of personal correspondence between men in the 19th century, Rotundo traces the contours of relationships between heterosexual young men that might be difficult to imagine today. Similarly, in *We Boys Together: Teenagers in Love before Girl-Craziness*, Jeffery Dennis (2007) documents this shift in popular culture. Although we tend to (heteronormatively) think of teenage boys as inherently preoccupied with teenage girls today, Dennis traces the cultural history of this belief. In the beginning of the 20th century, teenage boys romantically or sexually interested in teenage girls were most commonly depicted as deviant in popular culture. Affection and even romance between teenage boys was not exceptional, it was normative.

Ibson's photographs provide some pictorial evidence of this shift—evidence that suggests these relationships were not just depicted on screens and in novels, but were an important part of the lives of boys and men as well. One of the largest shifts Ibson documents in his study is a gradual decrease in what he refers to as "homotactility" (same-sex touching) (Ibson 2002). It might be difficult to actually measure intimacy, but Ibson's pictures provide us an avenue for glimpsing pieces of what was lost—relationships we can only guess at from these images, but ones that look qualitatively different from those that followed. Collections of personal photographs from the turn of the 20th century forward depict a transformation in tactility and "touch taboos" among boys and men. Ibson documents the ways men used to physically embrace one another in photographs and the emotional and physical distancing that ensued, providing a unique and powerful kind of historical evidence not only of changing definitions of manhood, but also of transformations in relationships between boys and men that resulted from this shift.

As these examples all illustrate, historicizing masculinity is tricky business. The scholars associated with this tradition find creative kinds of data to draw conclusions about historical transformations in the content, form, performance, and meaning associated with masculinity. As you read the selections in this section, consider the ways that scholars rely on masculine archetypes, masculine countertypes, masculine entrepreneurs, and everyday enactments to make their claims. Below, we briefly summarize some of the key contributions of scholars in the historicizing masculinities tradition.

SECTION SUMMARY

We begin this section with Gail Bederman's analysis of the ways that race and the idea of "civilization" played key roles in the construction of new models of manhood at the turn of the 20th century in the United States (Reading 1). What makes Bederman's contribution so intriguing and important for scholars studying masculinities to consider is her treatment of masculinity as what she refers to as a "historical, ideological process." As Bederman writes, "To study the history of manhood . . . is to unmask this process and study the historical ways different ideologies about manhood develop, change, are combined, amended, contested—and gain the status of 'truth'" (Reading 1, page 53). Bederman's treatment of masculinity as a historical discourse is a dominant framework within the tradition of historicizing masculinities. And, like others, Bederman analyzes competing discourses in addition to the various ways that different groups participate in constructing and are simultaneously constructed by historical, ideological processes of masculinity—or what might be more aptly called "masculinization." Her treatment of intersecting discourses of race and "civilization" in her dissection of this period is unique among historicizing masculinities scholars. Bederman considers masculine archetypes, countertypes, and emerging entrepreneurs during this period and focuses on key events that provoked national anxiety surrounding masculinity.

During a similar historical period, John Kasson considers a number of masculine entrepreneurs in Reading 2. Like Bederman, Kasson is also interested in intersections in historical processes of masculine construction with race. But he is also fascinated by emerging embodiments of masculinity—how men sought to embody masculinity in historically novel ways. Relying on Theodore Roosevelt, among others, Kasson provides a dynamic way of considering processes of transformation in masculinity and the attendant anxieties associated with the periods during which change seems to have been immanent. As previously mentioned, E. Anthony Rotundo (Reading 3) relies on personal correspondence between men to chart some of the intimacy that was lost during this period as the transformations that Bederman and Kasson discuss take hold. Rotundo's research is an incredible portrayal of what we refer to as "everyday enactments" within the historicizing masculinities tradition. Rotundo is interested not only in historicizing masculinity, but also in paying specific attention to men's relationships with one another and how these relationships changed. Next, Jo B. Paoletti looks at children's fashion at the turn of the 20th century in the United States as a window into transformations in the meanings of masculinity (Reading 4). Paoletti's research relies on an incredibly clever use of historical data to attempt to understand what masculinity (and gender more broadly) meant to people in different historical periods. And, as Paoletti's research demonstrates, the masculinities that emerged in this period demonstrate the anxieties documented by other scholars as well.[6]

George Mosse's essay on the medical classification of shell shock in Reading 5 is an important illustration of the ways that social institutions play a role in shoring up particular social definitions of masculinity. As we discussed earlier, Mosse documents the ways medical professionals dealt with men experiencing extreme psychological trauma after coming back from World War I. When we consider what the soldiers endured during World War I, we often consider what the bodies of soldiers had to endure and the extreme conditions men encountered in trench warfare. Mosse's essay is an important articulation of how psychological states of being become gendered as well. Men suffering from shell shock were relied on as *countertypes*—important examples of *failed* masculinity. In a different way, Barbara Ehrenreich considers the role of the "male breadwinner" in the United States in the middle of the 20th century (Reading 6). She considers this role in historical context, framing it as a masculine archetype and paying specific attention to men's failure to fulfill the role as important countertypes. She offers an important consideration of the ways that failure to approximate masculinities within historical periods is often the norm because many men are quite simply unable or unwilling. Ehrenreich's reading encourages readers to remember to differentiate what was culturally normative from what was actually normal.

We conclude this section with a historicization of the present. Michael Kimmel's essay considers transformations in contemporary masculinity in historical perspective (Reading 7). Although Kimmel is best known within the historicizing masculinities tradition for his book—*Manhood in America: A Cultural History* (2012 [1996])—this new research puts contemporary conceptualizations of masculinity among young men into historical perspective in new ways. Kimmel addresses the ways that the "failure to launch" phenomenon is bolstered by structural and cultural forces that have framed new configurations of masculinity in the contemporary United States—a cultural landscape he refers to as "Guyland." Like other essays in this section, historicizing masculinities is about distilling powerful historical, ideological processes of masculinization that frame our understandings of masculinity, gender, power, and inequality. Collectively, the essays in this section show how historicizing masculinities scholarship is an important illustration of the social construction of masculinity and how the social, historical, cultural, political, and economic processes of power and inequality frame transformations in what we understand as masculine in the first place.

REFERENCES

Adam, Barry D. 1996. "Structural Foundations of the Gay World." In *Queer Theory/Sociology*, edited by Steven Seidman, 111–26. Malden, MA: Blackwell.
Blumberg, Rae Lesser, and Marion Tolbert Coleman. 1989. "A Theoretical Look at the Gender Balance of Power in the American Couple." *Journal of Family Issues* 10 (2): 225–50.
Brittan, Arthur. 1989. *Masculinity and Power.* New York: Basil Blackwell.

Connell, Raewyn. 1987. *Gender and Power: Society, the Person and Sexual Politics*. Stanford: Stanford University Press.

Connell, Raewyn. 1995. *Masculinities*. Berkeley: University of California Press.

Connell, Raewyn. 2002. *Gender: Short Introductions*. Cambridge, UK: Polity.

Coontz, Stephanie. 1992. *The Way We Never Were: American Families and the Nostalgia Trap*. New York: Basic Books.

Cowan, Ruth Schwartz. 1983. *More Work for Mother: The Ironies of Household Technology from the Open Hearth to the Microwave*. New York: Basic Books.

D'Emilio, John. 1993. "Capitalism and Gay Identity." In *The Lesbian and Gay Studies Reader*, edited by Henry Abelove, Michele Aina Barale, and David Halperin, 467–76. London: Routledge.

Dennis, Jeffery P. 2007. *We Boys Together: Teenagers in Love before Girl-Craziness*. Nashville, TN: Vanderbilt University Press.

Faderman, Lillian. 1991. *Odd Girls and Twilight Lovers: A History of Lesbian Life in Twentieth-Century America*. New York: Columbia University Press.

Flanders, Judith. 2003. *Inside the Victorian Home: A Portrait of Domestic Life in Victorian England*, reprint ed. New York and London: Norton.

Greenberg, David F. 1988. *The Construction of Homosexuality*. Chicago: University of Chicago Press.

Hansen, Karen. 1996. *A Very Social Time: Crafting Community in Antebellum New England*. Berkeley: University of California Press.

Hilkey, Judy. 1997. *Character Is Capital: Success Manuals and Manhood in Gilded Age America*. Chapel Hill: University of North Carolina Press.

Ibson, John. 2002. *Picturing Men: A Century of Male Relationships in Everyday American Photography*. Washington, D.C., and London: Smithsonian Institution Press.

Kasson, John F. 2001. *Houdini, Tarzan, and the Perfect Man: The White Male Body and the Challenge of Modernity in America*. New York: Hill and Wang.

Kimmel, Michael. 1987. "The Contemporary 'Crisis' of Masculinity in Historical Perspective." In *The Making of Masculinities: The New Men's Studies*, edited by Harry Brod, 121–53. Boston: Allen & Unwin.

Kimmel, Michael. 2012 [1996]. *Manhood in America: A Cultural History*, 3rd ed. New York: Oxford University Press.

Lasch, Christopher. 1977. *Haven in a Heartless World: The Family Besieged*. New York: Basic Books.

MacInnes, John. 1998. *The End of Masculinity: The Confusion of Sexual Genesis and Sexual Difference in Modern Society*. Buckingham, UK, and Philadelphia: Open University Press.

Martin, Emily. 1991. "The Egg and the Sperm: How Science Constructed a Romance Based on Stereotypical Male–Female Roles. *Signs* 16 (3): 485–501.

Mosse, George L. 1996. *The Image of Man: The Creation of Modern Masculinity*. New York: Oxford University Press.

Paoletti, Jo B. 2012. *Pink and Blue: Telling the Boys from the Girls in America*. Bloomington: Indiana University Press.

Rosenberg, Rosalind. 1982. *Beyond Separate Spheres: Intellectual Roots of Modern Feminism*. New Haven, CT: Yale University Press.

Rotundo, E. Anthony. 1993. *American Manhood: Transformations in Masculinity from the Revolution to the Modern Era*. New York: Basic Books.

Segal, Lynne. 1990. *Slow Motion: Changing Masculinities, Changing Men*. New Brunswick, NJ: Rutgers University Press.

Tosh, John. 1999. *A Man's Place: Masculinity and the Middle-Class Home in Victorian England*. New Haven, CT: Yale University Press.

NOTES

1. Reprinted by permission of Oxford University Press, USA.
2. Gender varies along many different axes—historical variation is only one. And variation is key to any understanding of gender as socially constructed. Gender also varies cross-culturally. Although we don't consider this dimension of variation in much detail in this collection, masculinities are constructed differently in different cultures around the world. Masculinities also vary contextually within a single culture. This means two things. First, it means that what it means to be masculine in Los Angeles might be something dramatically different from what it means to be a man in rural Arkansas. But it also means that performances of masculinity shift contextually as well. Just think about how someone might perform masculinity in a college classroom versus at a college party, at work versus at home, etc. Finally, masculinity also varies over the life course. So, what it means to be a man is age specific.
3. Google Books NGram Viewer enables users to chart the relative prevalence of a word or phrase in published work. The tool graphs the annual count of selected "n-grams" (letter combinations) found in Google's digitized collection of books (their collection is over 5.2 million and spans a huge period of time). The data you see illustrate how common the n-gram was over the period of time specified—and is normalized to take into account the number of published works in each given year. The tool is free and available online here: https://books.google.com/ngrams/.
4. Textual analysis is a cultural studies method that differs significantly from other social scientific and historical methods. The primary focus of textual analysis is to convincingly trace narratives across different kinds of cultural and historical "texts" (broadly interpreted). This method allows scholars to tell a particular story about masculinity in a specific period, but it is more difficult to use this method to make claims about how representative that story is or was for the historical period in question.
5. Social scientists sometimes refer to these processes as "medicalization," a term used to refer to the processes by which social behaviors, identities, problems, and more come to be defined as medical conditions in ways that they then become amenable to medical study, diagnosis, treatment, and prevention. The medicalization of gender is the topic of a considerable amount of research, referring to the ways that masculinity and femininity come to be seen as biological realities, rather than social ones. Perhaps the most famous study associated with this is Emily Martin's (1991) influential article on medical descriptions of eggs and sperm in medical textbooks and how these descriptions create a discourse within which gender difference and stereotypes of masculinity and femininity come to appear inherent, inevitable, and timeless.
6. Readers interested in this approach should consider Paoletti's book, which addresses clothing as a window into understanding transformations in gender in U.S. history—*Pink and Blue: Telling the Boys from the Girls in America* (2012).

GAIL BEDERMAN

1. REMAKING MANHOOD THROUGH RACE AND "CIVILIZATION"

At 2:30 P.M. on July 4, 1910, in Reno, Nevada, as the band played "All Coons Look Alike to Me," Jack Johnson climbed into the ring to defend his title against Jim Jeffries. Johnson was the first African American world heavyweight boxing champion. Jeffries was a popular white former heavyweight champion who had retired undefeated six years before. Although it promised to be a fine match, more than mere pugilism was at stake. [. . .] Twenty thousand men from across the nation had traveled to Reno to sit in the broiling desert sun and watch the prizefight. Five hundred journalists had been dispatched to Reno to cover it. Every day during the week before the fight, they had wired between 100,000 and 150,000 words of reportage about it to their home offices. Most had assured their white readership that Jeffries would win. On the day of the fight, American men deserted their families' holiday picnics. All across America, they gathered in ballparks, theaters, and auditoriums to hear the wire services' round-by-round reports of the contest. Over thirty thousand men stood outside the *New York Times* offices straining to hear the results; ten thousand men gathered outside the *Atlanta Constitution*. It was, quite simply, a national sensation (Gilmore 1975: 41; Roberts 1983: 99).

Ever since 1899, when Jeffries first won the heavyweight championship, he had refused to fight any Negro challengers. Jack Johnson first challenged him as early as 1903. Jeffries replied, "When there are no white men left to fight, I will quit the business. I am determined not to take a chance of losing the championship to a negro" (Roberts 1983: 31). Jeffries' adherence to the color line was not unique. Ever since 1882, when John L. Sullivan had won the title, no white heavyweight champion had fought a black challenger,

even though black and white heavyweights had previously competed freely (Gilmore 1975: 25–26). Sullivan had announced he would fight all contenders—except black ones. [. . .] It was in this context that Jack Johnson began his career, and eventually defeated every fighter, black or white, who faced him.

For two years, Jeffries refused to fight Johnson, but when Jeffries retired in 1905, the remaining field of white contenders was so poor that the public temporarily lost interest in prizefighting. Finally in 1908, the reigning white champion, Tommy Burns, agreed to fight Johnson. By accepting Johnson's challenge, Burns hoped to raise both interest and prize money. Johnson promptly and decisively thrashed Burns, however, and won the title. Faced with the unthinkable—a black man had been crowned the most powerful man in the world!—interest in pugilism rebounded. [. . .] Across America, white newspapers pleaded with Jeffries to vindicate Anglo-Saxon manhood and save civilization by vanquishing the upstart "Negro."

Eventually the aging, reluctant Jeffries agreed to fight, reportedly explaining, "I am going into this fight for the sole purpose of proving that a white man is better than a negro" (*Literary Digest* 1910: 85). From its inception, then, the Johnson–Jeffries fight was framed as a contest to see which race had produced the most powerful, virile man. [. . .] With few exceptions, predictions of the fight's outcome focused on the relative manliness of the white and the black races. For example, *Current Literature* predicted Jeffries would win because "the black man . . . fights emotionally, whereas the white man can use his brain after twenty rounds" (*Current Literature* 1910: 57).

Thus, when Johnson trounced Jeffries—and it was a bloody rout—the defenders of white male supremacy

This reading is an excerpt from Gail Bederman's *Manliness & Civilization: A Cultural History of Gender and Race in the United States, 1880–1917* (Chicago: University of Chicago Press, 1995), 1–44. © 1995 by The University of Chicago.

were very publicly hoist by their own petards. They had insisted upon framing the fight as a contest to demonstrate which race could produce the superior specimen of virile manhood. Johnson's victory was so lopsided that the answer was unwelcome but unmistakable. After the fight, the black *Chicago Defender* exulted that Johnson was "the first negro to be admitted the best man in the world" (Roberts 1983: 114).

[. . .] Race riots broke out in every Southern state, as well as in Illinois, Missouri, New York, Ohio, Pennsylvania, Colorado, and the District of Columbia. Occasionally, black men attacked white men who were belittling Johnson. In most of the incidents, however, rampaging white men attacked black men who were celebrating Johnson's victory (Roberts 1983: 59–73, 108–109). In Manhattan, the *New York Herald* reported, "One negro was rescued by the police from white men who had a rope around his neck. . . . On Eighth Avenue, between Thirty-Seventh and Thirty-Ninth Streets, more than three thousand whites gathered, and all the negroes that appeared were kicked and beaten, some of them into insensibility. . . . Three thousand white men took possession of Eighth Avenue and held against police as they attacked every negro that came into sight" (quoted in Roberts 1983: 65–66). [. . .]

Even the United States Congress reacted to the implicit aspersions Johnson's victory cast on white manhood. Before the Johnson–Jeffries fight, Congress had refused even to consider a bill suppressing motion picture films of prizefights. The prospect of the filmic reenactment of the "Negroes' Deliverer" thrashing the "White Hope" in hundreds of movie theaters across the nation was too much for them, however. Within three weeks, a bill suppressing fight films had passed both houses and was soon signed into law (Gilmore 1975: 75–93).

Soon after Johnson won the championship, an even more scandalous public controversy arose: the "Negroes' Deliverer" was making no secret of his taste for the company of white women. [. . .] The spectacle of dozens of white women in pursuit of Johnson's favor pleased Johnson and infuriated many whites. These women were mostly prostitutes, but racial etiquette held all white women were too "pure" for liaisons with black men (Gilmore 1975: 14; Roberts 1983: 74–75). It seemed bad enough that Johnson's first wife

was white, although antimiscegenist doomsayers felt smugly vindicated when she committed suicide in 1912 (*New York Times* 1912a: 12). But when authorities discovered Johnson was having an affair with an eighteen-year-old blond from Minnesota, Lucille Cameron, they charged him with violating the Mann Act—that is, with engaging in white slavery. [. . .] Effigies of Johnson were hung from trolley and electric poles around the city. Wherever Johnson went he was greeted with cries of "Lynch him! Lynch the nigger!" (Roberts 1983: 146; *New York Times* 1912b: 12). It didn't matter that Lucille Cameron insisted she was in love with Johnson and soon married him. It made no difference that she turned out to have been an established prostitute, not a seduced virgin. It didn't even matter that no violations of the Mann Act had occurred, and the original charges had to be dropped. By winning the heavyweight championship and by flaunting his success with white women, Johnson had crossed the line, and the white public demanded punishment (Gilmore 1975: 95–116; Roberts 1983: 138–154).

The national Bureau of Investigation was ordered to conduct a massive search to find *something* to pin on Johnson. After an expensive and exhaustive inquiry, it dredged up some old incidents in which Johnson had crossed state lines with a long time white mistress. Although the government usually invoked the Mann Act only to combat white slavery and commercial prostitution, officials made an exception for Johnson. He was convicted of crossing state lines with his mistress and of giving her money and presents. For most American men, these were perfectly legal activities. Johnson, however, was sentenced to a year in prison and a thousand-dollar fine. Hoping to get rid of him, government employees tacitly encouraged him to jump bail and leave the country, which he did. For the next seven years, all Johnson's efforts to make a bargain and turn himself in were rebuffed. Only in 1920 was Johnson allowed to return to the United States to serve his sentence, an impoverished and greatly humbled former champion (Gilmore 1975: 117–133; Roberts 1983: 158–219). The photograph of him losing his last championship bout to white fighter Jess Willard in Havana in 1915 was a standard feature in white bars and speakeasies for many years thereafter (Gilmore 1975: 148).

By any standard, white Americans' response to Jack Johnson was excessive. Why should a mere prize-fight result in riots and death? What was it about Jack Johnson that inspired the federal government to use the Bureau of Investigation to conduct a vendetta against him? That moved Congress to pass federal legislation to mitigate his impact? That impelled prominent leaders like former President Theodore Roosevelt to condemn him in print (Roosevelt 1910: 550–551)? That caused so many respected Americans to describe Johnson's activities as "a blot on our 20th century American Civilization"? (Gilmore 1975: 81, 108). That caused American men to celebrate his ultimate defeat in their saloons for decades?

The furor over Jack Johnson was excessive, yet it was not unique. During the decades around the turn of the century, Americans were obsessed with the connection between manhood and racial dominance. This obsession was expressed in a profusion of issues, from debates over lynching, to concern about the white man's imperialistic burden overseas, to discussions of childrearing. The Jack Johnson controversy, then, was only one of a multitude of ways middle-class Americans found to explain male supremacy in terms of white racial dominance and conversely, to explain white supremacy in terms of male power.

[. . .] [B]etween 1890 and 1917, as white middle-class men actively worked to reinforce male power, their race became a factor which was crucial to their gender. In ways which have not been well understood, whiteness was both a palpable fact and a manly ideal for these men. During these years, a variety of social and cultural factors encouraged white middle-class men to develop new explanations of why they, as men, ought to wield power and authority. In this context, [. . .] Johnson's championship, as well as his self-consciously flamboyant, sexual public persona, was an intolerable—and intentional—challenge to white Americans' widespread beliefs that male power stemmed from white supremacy. [. . .]

In order to understand why turn-of-the-century middle-class Americans were so interested in using race to remake manhood, we need to outline a larger historical and analytical context. Thus, the rest of this chapter will consider three points. First, it will consider [. . .] what do we mean by "manhood," and how do we study its history. Second, it will outline what was happening to middle-class manhood at the turn of the century [. . .] Finally, it will introduce a central set of ideas that turn-of-the-century Americans frequently used to tie male power to racial dominance—the discourse of "civilization."

"MANHOOD": WHAT IS IT, AND HOW DOES IT WORK?

What do we mean by manhood? This question is not as simpleminded as it appears. Although most people can easily identify certain human beings as men, manhood has been defined quite differently in different times, places, and contexts (Gilmore, D. 1990). [. . .] (I am purposely using the term "manhood" instead of "masculinity" here because, as we will see, the noun "masculinity" was only beginning to be widely adopted by 1890 and had very specific connotations which have been largely forgotten today.)

Many historians have simply assumed that manhood is an unproblematic identity—an unchanging essence—inherent in all male-bodied humans. These historians see manhood as a normal aspect of human nature, transparent and self-evident, which simply needs to be expressed without inhibiting factors like "anxiety." Although they recognize that manhood might be expressed differently at different times, they nonetheless assume that its underlying meaning remains basically the same. Historians using this sort of theoretical approach have tended to write about what men have done, historically, to express their manhood. [. . .] Their approach has the drawback of *assuming* what it ought to *investigate*. What did "masculinity" mean to men [. . .]? Why was it so important to them? Why would its presumed loss be painful enough to cause a "crisis"? Does power of authority have anything to do with manhood? By ignoring these historically important questions, this approach leaves the impression that manhood is a transhistorical essence, substantially unchanging over time, rooted in biology, and therefore not amenable to historical analysis—or to human efforts to change gender relations (Carnes 1989; Hantover 1980).

Other historians have seen manhood as a culturally defined collection of traits, attributes, or sex roles. [. . .]

These historians often analyze how the traits or occupations which are seen as masculine change from period to period or class to class. For example, colonial American men were socialized to be strong patriarchal fathers, while nineteenth-century middle-class men were shunted off to a "separate sphere" to be competitive businessmen. By investigating how manhood changes over time, historians using this approach encourage readers to see gender relations as mutable and improvable. Yet this approach, too, has its limitations. Attempting to define manhood as a coherent set of prescriptive ideals, traits, or sex roles obscures the complexities and contradictions of any historical moment. [. . .] Envisioning manhood as a unified set of traits gives us no way to consider the relations between [. . .] contradictory aspects of [. . .] manhood, nor does it give us a way to understand how men themselves negotiated the contradictions (Adams 1990; Filene 1975: 69–93; Griffen 1990; Kimmel 1987; Marsh 1988).

This study is based on the premise that gender— whether manhood or womanhood—is a *historical, ideological process* (e.g., Haraway 1989; Poovey 1988). Through that process, individuals are positioned and position themselves as men or as women. Thus, I don't see manhood as either an intrinsic essence or a collection of traits, attributes, or sex roles. Manhood— or "masculinity," as it is commonly termed today—is a continual, dynamic process. Through that process, men claim certain kinds of authority, based upon their particular type of bodies. At any time in history, many contradictory ideas about manhood are available to explain what men are, how they ought to behave, and what sorts of powers and authorities they may claim, as men. Part of the way gender functions is to hide these contradictions and to camouflage the fact that gender is dynamic and always changing. Instead, gender is constructed as a fact of nature, and manhood is assumed to be an unchanging, transhistorical essence, consisting of fixed, naturally occurring traits. To study the history of manhood, I would argue, is to unmask this process and study the historical ways different ideologies about manhood develop, change, are combined, amended, contested—and gain the status of "truth" (e.g., Butler 1990; de Lauretis 1987; Foucault 1978; Riley 1988; Scott 1988, 1992).

To define manhood as an ideological process is not to say that it deals only with intellectuals or ideas. It is, rather, to say that manhood or masculinity is the cultural process whereby concrete individuals are constituted as members of a preexisting social category— as men. The ideological process of gender—whether manhood or womanhood—works through a complex political technology composed of a variety of institutions, ideas, and daily practices. Combined, these processes produce a set of truths about who an individual is and what he or she can do, based upon his or her body. Individuals are positioned through that process of gender, whether they choose to be or not. [. . .] And with that positioning as "man" or "woman" inevitably comes a host of other social meanings, expectations, and identities. Individuals have no choice but to act upon these meanings—to accept or reject them, adopt or adapt them [. . .].

Another way to say this is to define manhood as the process which creates "men" by linking male genital anatomy to a male identity, and linking both anatomy and identity to particular arrangements of authority and power. Logically, this is an entirely arbitrary process. Anatomy, identity, and authority have no intrinsic relationship. Only the process of manhood—of the gender system—allows each to stand for the others.

We can see more concretely how this cultural process works by returning to our discussion of Jack Johnson and considering how Johnson's championship was construed by his culture's historically specific way of linking male anatomy, identity, and authority. Late Victorian culture had identified the powerful, large male body of the heavyweight prizefighter [. . .] as the epitome of manhood. The heavyweight's male body was so equated with male identity and power that American whites rigidly prevented all men they deemed unable to wield political and social power from asserting any claim to the heavyweight championship. Logically, there was no reason to see a heavyweight fighter's claim to bodily strength as a claim to public power. Yet the metonymic process of turn-of-the-century manhood constructed bodily strength and social authority as identical. [. . .]

Yet Johnson was not only positioned by these cultural constructs—he also actively used them to position himself. Embittered by years of vainly seeking a title bout, Johnson consciously played upon white Americans' fears of threatened manhood by laying public claim to all three of the metonymic facets of manhood—body, identity, and authority. During his public sparring matches, Johnson actually wrapped his penis in gauze to enhance its size. Clad only in his boxing shorts, he would stroll the ring, flaunting his genital endowments for all to admire, displaying his superior body to demonstrate his superior manhood (Gilmore 1975: 14; Roberts 1983: 74). In his private life, Johnson also took great pleasure in assuming a more conventional middle-class manly identity, sometimes taking on the persona of a successful self-made man. In 1912, he publicly claimed the right to move into an exclusive white suburb until the horrified residents took steps to prevent him (Roberts 1983: 66–67, 160–161). He also dressed both his beautiful blond wives in jewels and furs and paraded them in front of the press. Johnson, who grew up in Texas, was well aware that throughout the South black men were regularly tortured and lynched for consorting with white women, and that even Northern whites feared that black men lusted irrepressibly after pure white womanhood. Therefore, he made certain the public could not view his wives as pathetic victims of Negro lust. Instead, he presented his wives as wealthy, respectable women whose husband was successful and manly enough to support them in comfort and luxury.

Johnson was equally insistent upon his masculine right to wield a man's power and authority. He treated minor brushes with the law—his many speeding tickets and automobile violations—contemptuously, as mere inconveniences which he was man enough to ignore (Roberts 1983: 124–126). [. . .] On a more sinister note, he physically beat and emotionally maltreated his wives and mistresses, implicitly claiming a man's right to dominate women (Roberts 1983: 54–67, 122). In short he recognized that dominant white usage prevented him from being treated as the epitome of manhood, as a white heavyweight champion would be treated. Nevertheless he scornfully refused to accept this racial slight. Defiantly, Johnson positioned himself as a real man by laying ostentatious claim to a male body, male identity, and male power.

As Jack Johnson's example suggests, then, gender ideology, although coercive, does not preclude human agency. Numerous ideological strands of gender, class, and race position Johnson in a web which he could not entirely escape. He was inescapably a man, a black man, the son of a freed slave brought up in poverty, and so on. Yet although these discourses inescapably defined him, Johnson was able to take advantage of the contradictions within and between these ideologies in order to assert himself as a man and a pro-active historical agent. Recognizing that "Negroes" were considered less than men, he sometimes asserted his manliness in a race-neutral context, as a champion, a self-made man, and a world-famous hero. In other situations, he played upon his blackness, using his champion's body to present himself as an embodiment of highly sexed Negro masculinity. [. . .]

In other words, ideologies of gender are not totalizing. Like all ideologies, they are internally contradictory. Because of these internal contradictions, and because ideologies come into conflict with other ideologies, men and women are able to influence the ongoing ideological processes of gender, even though they cannot escape them. Men and women cannot invent completely new formations of gender, but they can adapt old ones. They can combine and recombine them, exploit the contradictions between them, and work to modify them. They can also alter their own position in relation to those ideologies [. . .]. Thus, looking at manhood as an ongoing ideological process—instead of as an inherent essence, or a set of traits or sex roles—allows historians to study the ways people have been historical agents of change (e.g., Poovey 1988).

CLASS, GENDER, AND THE IMPULSE TO REMAKE MANHOOD

Historians have long been aware that turn-of-the-century middle-class men seem to have been unusually interested in—even obsessed with—manhood. They have spoken of a "virility impulse" among the Progressives, a cult of the "strenuous life," and, most frequently, a "masculinity crisis" among American men, pointing to the popularity of cowboy novels, the craze for hunting and fishing, and the profusion of "he-man" rhetoric (Dubbert 1980; Filene 1975;

Higham 1978; Kimmel 1989; McGovern 1966). Other historians have denied such a "masculinity crisis" existed, correctly noting that despite virile, chest-thumping rhetoric, most middle-class men did not flee to the Western frontier but remained devoted to hearth and home (Marsh 1988; Griffen 1990).

Both positions have merit. Middle-class men were unusually obsessed with manhood at the turn of the century; yet I would hesitate to call this obsession a "crisis." For one thing, there is no evidence that most turn-of-the-century men ever lost confidence in the belief that people with male bodies naturally possessed both a man's identity and a man's right to wield power. They might not have been entirely certain *how* these three factors were related, but few seem to have lost confidence *that* they were related. Moreover, to imply that masculinity was in crisis suggests that manhood is a transhistorical category or fixed essence that has its good moments as well as its bad, rather than an ideological construct which is constantly being remade. [. . .] Thus, change in the gender system—even extensive change—doesn't necessarily imply a "crisis." In any event, by 1890 a number of social, economic, and cultural changes were converging to make the ongoing gender process especially active for the American middle class. [. . .]

Class issues underlay many of these changes. [. . .] Ever since the middle class had begun to define itself as a class in the early nineteenth century, ideals of gender and of "manliness" had been central to middle-class consciousness (Davidoff and Hall 1987; Ryan 1981). Between 1820 and 1860, as increasing numbers of men had begun to earn comfortable livings as entrepreneurs, professionals, and managers, the middle class had begun to differentiate itself from other classes by stressing its gentility and respectability (Blumin 1989; Johnson 1978). Gender was central to this self-definition [. . .]. [. . .] Middle-class parents taught their sons to build a strong, manly "character" as they would build a muscle, through repetitive exercises of control over impulse (e.g., Susman 1984; Macleod 1983). The middle class saw this ability to control powerful masculine passions through a strong character and a powerful will as a primary source of men's strength and authority over both women and the lower classes. [. . .]

The mingled honor, high-mindedness, and strength stemming from this powerful self-mastery were encapsulated in the term "manliness" (e.g., Davidoff and Hall 1987: 108–113; Filene 1975: 70–71; Mangan and Walvin 1987; Rosenberg 1973; Vance 1985). [. . .] In the context of the market economy's unpredictability, a manly character built on high-minded self-restraint was seen as the rock on which middle-class men could build their fortunes. Middle-class men were awarded (or denied) credit based on others' assessment of the manliness of their characters. [. . .] Manly control over impulse also helped the middle class develop their distinctive family practices. Celebrations of manly self-restraint encouraged young men to postpone marriage until they could support a family in proper middle-class style, to work hard and live abstemiously so that they could amass the capital to go into business for themselves (Ryan 1981: 165–185). In short, by the end of the century, a discourse of manliness stressing self-mastery and restraint expressed and shaped middle-class identity.

By the 1890s, however, both "manliness" and middle-class identity seemed to falter, partly because economic changes had rendered earlier ideologies of middle-class manhood less plausible. Middle-class manliness had been created in the context of a small-scale, competitive capitalism which had all but disappeared by 1910. Between 1870 and 1910, the proportion of middle-class men who were self-employed dropped from 67 percent to 37 percent (Filene 1975: 73; Hofstadter 1955: 218). At the same time, the rapid expansion of low-level clerical work in stores and offices meant that young men beginning their careers as clerks were unlikely to gain promotion [. . .] as their fathers had (Blumin 1989: 290–295; Filene 1975: 70–73). Moreover, between 1873 and 1896, a recurring round of severe economic depressions resulted in tens of thousands of bankruptcies and drove home the reality that even a successful, self-denying small businessman might lose everything, unexpectedly and through no fault of his own. Under these conditions, the sons of the middle class faced the real possibility that traditional sources of male power and status would remain closed to them forever—that they would become failures instead of self-made men.

[. . .] In this context, Victorian codes of manly self-restraint began to seem less relevant. Increasingly, middle-class men were attracted to new ideals—ideals at odds with older codes of manliness.

Concurrent with middle-class men's narrowing career opportunities came new opportunities for commercial leisure. The growth of a consumer culture encouraged many middle-class men, faced with lowered career expectations, to find identity in leisure instead of in work (Erenberg 1981: 33–59; Kasson 1978). Yet codes of manliness dictated they must work hard and become economically independent. The consumer culture's ethos of pleasure and frivolity clashed with ideals of manly self-restraint, further undermining the potency of middle-class manliness (Bederman 1989). Economically based changes in middle-class culture were thus eroding the sense of manliness which remained so essential to nineteenth-century men's identity.

At the same time middle-class ideals of manliness were eroding from within, middle-class men's social authority faced an onslaught from without—from working-class men, competing with them for control over the masculine arena of politics. During the nineteenth century, electoral politics had been viewed as part of the male sphere [. . .]. [. . .] Political campaigns were male rituals celebrating participants' identities both as party members and as men. At the same time, electoral politics dramatized and reinforced men's connection, as men, to the very real power of the government (Baker 1984, 1991: 24–55). Men objected so strenuously to woman suffrage precisely because male power and male identity were both so central to nineteenth-century electoral politics. In this light, immigrant men's contestation for control of city governments can be seen, in a very real sense, as a contestation of manhood. As immigrants wrested political control from middle-class men in one city after another, a very real basis of urban middle-class men's manhood received both symbolic and material blows. Immigrant men's efforts to control urban politics were, in a very real sense, contests of manhood—contests which the immigrants frequently won (e.g., Gossett 1963: 287–309; Higham 1971).

While immigrant working men were challenging middle-class men's manly power to govern the cities, other laboring men were challenging their manly

power to control the nation. [. . .] Between 1881 and 1905 there were nearly thirty-seven thousand strikes, often violent, involving seven million workers—an impressive number in a nation whose total work force in 1900 numbered only twenty-nine million (Trachtenberg 1982: 80; [. . .]). Middle-class men worried that they were losing control of the country. [. . .]

Immigrant and working-class men were not the only ones challenging middle-class men's claims on public power and authority. Concurrently, the middle-class woman's movement was challenging past constructions of manhood by agitating for woman's advancement. "Advancement," as these New Women understood it, meant granting women access to activities which had previously been reserved for men. Small but increasing numbers of middle-class women were claiming the right to a college education, to become clergymen, social scientists, and physicians, and even to vote. Men reacted passionately by ridiculing these New Women, prophesying that they would make themselves ill and destroy national life, insisting that they were rebelling against nature. [. . .] The woman's movement thus increased the pressure on middle-class men to reformulate manhood (e.g., Buhle 1981: 49–103; Cott 1987; Filene 1975: 3–68).

These challenges from women, workers, and the changing economy not only affected men's sense of identity and authority, they even affected men's view of the male body. White middle-class men now learned that they were threatened by a newly discovered disease, "neurasthenia." According to doctors, neurasthenia was spreading throughout the middle class, due to the excessive brain work and nervous strain which professionals and businessmen endured as they struggled for success in an increasingly challenging economy (Beard 1881; Lears 1981: 49–57; Rotundo 1993: 185–193 [. . .]). This discovery of neurasthenia led many to fear that middle-class men as a sex had grown decadent. Working class and immigrant men, with their strikes and their "primitive" customs, seemed to possess a virility and vitality which decadent white middle-class men had lost.

Not coincidentally, while some doctors were focusing their attention on the neurasthenic male body, other physicians and medical investigators began to pay a great deal of attention to male homosexuals. After the 1880s, medical experts ceased to see homosexuality as a punishable act, and began to see it as an aberrant and deficient male identity, a case of the male body gone wrong through disease or congenital deformity (Chauncey 1989; D'Emilio and Freedman 1988: 225–227). [. . .]

Although some medical experts were discovering new identities and illnesses which threatened men's bodies, other middle-class men were finding new ways to celebrate men's bodies as healthy, muscular, and powerful (Green 1986; Mrozek 1983). Even the popular imagery of a perfect male body changed. In the 1860s, the middle class had seen the ideal male body as lean and wiry. By the 1890s however, an ideal male body required physical bulk and well-defined muscles. [. . .] By the 1890s, strenuous exercise and team sports had come to be seen as crucial to the development of powerful manhood. [. . .]

Between 1880 and 1910, then, middle-class men were especially interested in manhood. Economic changes were undermining Victorian ideals of self-restrained manliness. Working class and immigrant men, as well as middle-class women, were challenging white middle-class men's beliefs that they were the ones who should control the nation's destiny. Medical authorities were warning of the fragility of men's bodies, and athletes like Jim Jeffries, boxing's "White Hope," were providing new models of muscular manhood to emulate. All this activity suggests that men were actively, even enthusiastically engaging in the process of remaking manhood. Yet, although older meanings of manhood were gradually losing their persuasiveness, masculinity was hardly in crisis. Middle-class men were clearly still convinced that manhood was powerful, that it was part of their identity, and that all beings with healthy male bodies had it. [. . .]

MULTIPLE STRATEGIES TO REMAKE MANHOOD: SEX, CLASS, RACE, AND THE INVENTION OF "MASCULINITY"

Facing a variety of challenges to traditional ways of understanding male bodies, male identities, and male authority, middle-class men adopted a variety of strategies in order to remake manhood. Uncomfortable with the ways their history and culture were positioning them as men, they experimented with a host of cultural materials in order to synthesize a manhood more powerful, more to their liking. In the process, they began to formulate new ideologies of manhood—ideologies not of "manliness" but of "masculinity."

Many men tried to revitalize manhood by celebrating all things male. Millions joined fraternal orders [. . .]. Others concentrated on making boys into men through organizations like the Boy Scouts and YMCA (Hantover 1980: 285–302; Macleod 1983). Many [. . .] glorified the athletic male body through muscular sports like prizefighting, college football, and bodybuilding (Green 1986: 182–215). [. . .]

Other men believed they could revitalize manhood by opposing excessive femininity. Some focused on strong-minded women as the problem, and complained about feminism, coeducation, divorce, and the suffragists (Kimmel 1987). Others worked to safeguard little boys' masculinity by recruiting more male teachers (Brown 1990). Still others worried that Victorian culture itself was "effeminate" and insisted that men must re-virilize their society. [. . .]

Conversely, other men, perhaps feeling that women had appropriated too much of the male sphere, worked to take control of erstwhile "feminine" occupations away from women. For example, men began to take a greater interest in fatherhood and to claim an active role in raising their children (Marsh 1988). [. . .]

Class, too, provided materials to remake manhood. Just as some men were remaking middle-class manhood by appropriating activities which had been deemed feminine, others appropriated activities which had been deemed working-class. Throughout the nineteenth century, many working-class men had embraced a "rough" code of manhood formulated, in part, to resist the respectable, moralistic manliness of the middle class. This rough, working-class masculinity had celebrated institutions and values antithetical to middle-class Victorian manliness—institutions like saloons, music halls and prizefights; values like physical prowess, pugnacity, and sexuality (Gorn 1989: 129–145; Rosenzweig 1983: 57–64; Stansell 1986:

76–100; Wilentz 1984: 257–264). Since the 1820s, advocates of this rough working-class manhood had ridiculed middle-class manliness as weak and effeminate, while respectable middle-class men had derided this rough masculine ethos as coarse and backward. By the 1880s, however, as the power of Victorian manliness eroded, many middle-class men began to find this rough working-class masculinity powerfully attractive. [. . .] Boxing and prizefighting, too—long associated with the working class—became fascinating to middle- and upper-class men. Amateur sparring became popular and respectable enough for even YMCAs to offer instruction. [. . .]

As men worked to remake manhood, they adopted new words which could express their dynamic new understandings of the nature of male power. During the 1890s, they coined the new epithets "sissy," "pussy-foot," "cold feet" and "stuffed shirt" to denote behavior which had once appeared self-possessed and manly but now seemed overcivilized and effeminate (Higham 1978: 78–79). Indeed, the very word "overcivilized" was coined during these years (Rotundo 1993: 251). Most telling, however, was the increasing use of a relatively new noun to describe the essence of admirable manhood. This newly popular noun was "masculinity."

Although historians usually use the terms "manly" and "masculine" interchangeably, as if they were synonymous, the two words carried quite different connotations throughout the nineteenth century. Until about 1890, literate Victorians rarely referred to individual men as "masculine." Instead, admirable men were called "manly" (e.g., Marsh 1988: 181). After 1890, however, the words "masculine" and "masculinity" began to be used far more frequently—precisely because they could convey the new attributes of powerful manhood which middle-class men were working to synthesize.

[. . .] "[M]anliness" comprised all the worthy, moral attributes which the Victorian middle class admired in a man. Indeed, historians rightly use the term "manliness" to mean "Victorian ideals of manhood"—for example, sexual self-restraint, a powerful will, a strong character (Vance 1985; Rotundo 1993). "Manliness," in short, was precisely the sort of middle-class Victorian cultural formulation which grew shaky in the late nineteenth century. Thereafter, when men wished to invoke a different sort of male power, they would increasingly use the words "masculine " and "masculinity."

Unlike "manly," which referred to the "highest conceptions" of manhood, the adjective "masculine" was used to refer to any characteristics, good or bad, that all men had. [. . .] During the early nineteenth century, "masculine" was most frequently employed to differentiate between things pertaining to men versus women—for example, "masculine clothing," "a masculine gait," or "masculine occupations." Thus "masculine," more frequently than "manly," was applied across class or race boundaries; for, by definition, all men were masculine.

"Masculine" thus existed as a relatively empty, fluid adjective—devoid of moral or emotional meaning—when the cultural changes of the 1890s undermined the power of "manliness." This very fluidity and emotional neutrality made the word "masculine" attractive to people casting about to synthesize new explanations and descriptions of male power.

As the adjective "masculine" began to take on these new sorts of connotations, people began to need a noun to mean "masculine things in the aggregate," a word they hadn't needed before "masculine" began to carry such powerful freight. It is probably not coincidental, then, that in the mid-nineteenth century, a new English noun was adopted from the French and very slowly made its way into popular usage—"masculinity." [. . .]

As middle-class men worked to add new shades of meaning and new powers to that masculine "quality or state," the words "masculine" and "masculinity" took on increasingly definite shades of meaning. By 1930, "masculinity" had developed into the mix of "masculine" ideals more familiar to twentieth-century Americans—ideals like aggressiveness, physical force, and male sexuality. Of course, these ideals had been associated with manhood from very early times. Yet with the rise of the middle class in the early nineteenth century, new "manly" ideals of manhood had partially eclipsed these traditional male values for most "respectable" Americans, although "rough" working-class male culture had continued to celebrate them (Gorn 1989: 179–206). It took several generations for the new formulations of "masculinity" to overtake Victorian "manliness" as the primary middle-class ideology of powerful manhood. [. . .]

Thus, in 1910, when Jack Johnson stepped into the ring to challenge Jim Jeffries for the championship, he was entering a larger arena as well—an arena in which white middle-class men were casting about for new ways to explain the sources and nature of male power and authority. Men were not only flocking to entertainments which had been associated with rough working-class men, like prizefighting; they were also joining male-only institutions like The Freemasons, working to masculinize the high schools by recruiting male teachers, ridiculing woman suffrage and coeducation, and even changing the very language associated with manhood with new words like "sissy" and "masculinity." [. . .] This study, however, will focus on only one type of strategy—the ways middle-class men and women worked to redefine manhood in terms of racial dominance, especially in terms of "civilization."

CONSTRUCTING MALE DOMINANCE THROUGH RACIAL DOMINANCE: AN ONGOING STRATEGY

As the middle class worked to remake manhood, many turned from gender to a related category—one which, like gender, also linked bodies, identities, and power. That category was race.[1] In a variety of ways, Americans, who were trying to reformulate gender, explained their ideas about manhood by drawing connections between male power and white supremacy, as we have already seen with white men's hysterical response to Jack Johnson's heavyweight championship.

In itself, linking whiteness to male power was nothing new. White Americans had long associated powerful manhood with white supremacy. For example, during the first two-thirds of the nineteenth century American citizenship rights had been construed as "manhood" rights which inhered to white males, only. Framers of state constitutions in sixteen northern and western states explicitly placed African American men in the same category as women, as "dependents" (Berthoff 1989). Negro males, whether

free or slave, were forbidden to exercise "manhood" rights—forbidden to vote, hold electoral office, serve on juries, or join the military. [. . .] The conclusion was implicit but widely understood: Negro males, unlike white males, were less than men.

Conversely, African American men understood that their purported lack of manhood legitimized their social and political disfranchisement. They therefore protested that they were, indeed, men. Male slaves agitating for their freedom demanded their "manhood rights" (Horton 1986: 55; [. . .]). [. . .]

Although linking manhood to whiteness was no novelty, by the 1880s middle-class white Americans were discovering an extraordinary variety of ways to link male power to race. Sometimes they linked manly power with the racial supremacy of civilized white men. For example, popular anthropology magazines like the *National Geographic*, first published in 1889, achieved a large circulation by breathlessly depicting the heroic adventures of "civilized" white male explorers among "primitive" tribes in darkest Africa (e.g., Pauly 1979; [. . .]). [. . .] Similarly, Anglo-Saxonist imperialists insisted that civilized white men had a racial genius for self-government which necessitated the conquest of more "primitive," darker races. [. . .] In a variety of venues and contexts, white Americans contrasted civilized white men with savage dark-skinned men, depicting the former as paragons of *manly* superiority.

Yet in other contexts, middle-class white men adopted a contrasting strategy and linked powerful manhood to the "savagery" and "primitivism" of dark-skinned races, whose *masculinity* they claimed to share. According to historian E. Anthony Rotundo, by 1870 middle-class men's letters and diaries had become infused with a new sense of primal manhood very different from moral Victorian manliness. These late-nineteenth-century men—unlike their fathers' generation—believed that true manhood involved a primal virility which Rotundo has called the "masculine primitive." According to him, this masculine primitive stressed "the belief that all males—civilized or not—shared in the same primordial instincts for survival" (Rotundo 1993: 227–232; [. . .]) [. . .] Middle-class men who saw themselves in terms of this masculine primitive ethos were drawn to a variety of "savage" activities. [. . .] Interest in camping, hunting, and fishing—seen as virile survival skills of primitive man—flourished as never before. Middle-class men began to read heroic adventure stories.

"CIVILIZATION" AND IT'S MALCONTENTS: LINKING RACE TO MIDDLE-CLASS MANHOOD THROUGH THE DISCOURSE OF CIVILIZATION

How could middle-class white men simultaneously construct powerful manhood in terms of both "civilized manliness" and "primitive masculinity?" Although these strategies may seem contradictory, they appeared coherent at the time because they both drew on the powerful discourse of civilization. "Civilization," as turn-of-the-century Americans understood it, simultaneously denoted attributes of race and gender. By invoking the discourse of civilization in a variety of contradictory ways, many Americans found a powerfully effective way to link male dominance to white supremacy [. . .].

"Civilization" was protean in its applications. Different people used it to legitimize conservatism and change, male dominance and militant feminism, white racism and African American resistance. On the one hand, middle- and upper-class white men effectively mobilized "civilization" in order to maintain their class, gender, and racial autonomy, whether they invoked primitive masculinity or civilized manliness. Yet as effective as "civilization" was in its various ways of constructing male dominance, it was never totalizing. People opposed to white male dominance invoked civilization to legitimize quite different points of views. Feminists pointed to civilization to demonstrate the importance of woman's advancement. African Americans cited civilization to prove the necessity of racial egalitarianism.

Thus, the interesting thing about "civilization" is not what was meant by the term, but the multiple ways it was used to legitimize different sorts of claims to power. Therefore, [. . .] I will be discussing it as a discourse that worked, albeit unevenly, to establish (or to challenge) white male hegemony. [. . .] Rather than trying to isolate commonalities about what people meant by "civilization"—and perhaps flattening out contradictions and complexities—I will be concentrating on the different, even contradictory, ways people invoked the discourse of civilization to construct what it meant to be a man.

A brief tangent on methodology is in order. [. . .] By "discourse," I mean a set of ideas and practices which, taken together, organize both the way a society defines certain truths about itself and the way it deploys social power. This sort of methodology shifts intellectual history in three useful ways (e.g., Foucault 1978 [. . .]).

First, unlike traditional intellectual history, this methodology does not differentiate between intellectual ideas and material practices, or between superstructure and base. Discourses include both intellectual constructs and material practices. Following Foucault, historians who use this methodology presume that intellectual knowledge and concrete power relations are mutually constitutive. On the one hand, the daily practices which enforce a society's power relations—its institutions, customs, political movements—determine what sort of knowledges will appear to be true. On the other hand, ideas widely accepted as true determine what sorts of power relations people believe are desirable, as well as what sorts of political aims and strategies they can imagine. [. . .]

Second, this methodology assumes that the ideas and practices comprising any discourse will be multiple, inconsistent, and contradictory. As we've already begun to see with "civilization," discourses can be complex. Their very contradictions frequently give them a tenacious power over people's thoughts and actions. [. . .]

Finally, because it interrogates these inconsistencies, this methodology implies a particular emphasis on human agency and the possibility of intentional change. [. . .] Discourse theory does not leave open an infinite possibility for intentional change. Only certain types of truth, and therefore only certain possibilities for action, are imaginable under the terms of existing discourses. Yet because so many potential ambiguities and contradictions exist within any discourse many possibilities for dissent and resistance always remain.

[. . .] By about 1890, the discourse of civilization had taken on a very specific set of meanings which revolved around three factors: race, gender, and millennial assumptions about human evolutionary progress. [. . .]

To understand the counterhegemonic versions, we first need to understand the dominant version of civilization, and the way it interwove race, gender, and millennialism. To begin with race: In the context of the late nineteenth century's popularized Darwinism, civilization was seen as an explicitly racial concept. It meant more than simply "the west" or "industrially advanced societies." Civilization denoted a precise stage in human racial evolution—the one following the more primitive stages of "savagery" and "barbarism." Human races were assumed to evolve from simple savagery, through violent barbarism, to advanced and valuable civilization. But only white races had, as yet, evolved to the civilized stage. [. . .]

Gender, too, was an essential component of civilization. Indeed, one could identify advanced civilizations by the degree of their sexual differentiation [. . .]. Savage (that is, nonwhite) men and women were believed to be almost identical, but men and women of the civilized races had evolved pronounced sexual differences. Civilized women were womanly—delicate, spiritual, dedicated to the home. And civilized white men were the most manly ever evolved—firm of character; self-controlled; protectors of women and children. In contrast, gender differences among savages seemed to be blurred. Savage women were aggressive, carried heavy burdens, and did all sorts of "masculine" hard labor. Savage men were emotional and lacked a man's ability to restrain their passions. Savage men were creatures of whim who raped women instead of protecting them. Savage men abandoned their children instead of providing for them. Savage men even dressed like women, in skirts and jewelry. In short, the pronounced sexual differences celebrated in the middle class's doctrine of separate spheres were assumed to be absent in savagery, but to be an intrinsic and necessary aspect of higher civilization (Russett 1989: 144–148).

Finally, the discourse of civilization linked both male dominance and white supremacy to a Darwinist version of Protestant millennialism. A Christian millennialist interpretation of human progress had been rooted in American culture for centuries. According to these doctrines, ever since Adam and Eve, human history had one cosmic purpose: the millennial fight against evil. Human history was itself the battleground, as Christian men and women, directed by the hidden hand of God, struggled against evil. Each small victory brought the world closer to the millennium—the day when evil would be vanquished [. . .]. [. . .]

American Protestants who accepted Darwinism, but could not bear to jettison the belief that they were part of a cosmic plan to perfect the world, found in "civilization" a way to reconcile the seemingly contradictory implications of Darwinism and Protestant millennialism. Discourses of civilization gave millennialism a Darwinistic mechanism. Instead of God working in history to perfect the world, believers in civilization described evolution working in history to perfect the world. Instead of Christians battling infidels, they envisioned superior races out-surviving inferior races. Eventually, perfect human evolution would triumph. [. . .] And it was the duty of all civilized people to do what they could to bring about this perfect civilization, just as it had once been the duty of all Christians to take up the banner of the Lord. This millennial vision of perfected racial evolution and gender specialization was what people meant when they referred to "the advancement of civilization" (Crosby 1991).

"Civilization's" greatest cultural power, however, stemmed not from any of these elements individually but from the way the discourse interwove middle-class beliefs about race, gender, and millennialism. By harnessing male supremacy to white supremacy and celebrating both as essential to human perfection, hegemonic versions of civilization maintained the power of Victorian gender ideologies by presenting male power as natural and inevitable. [. . .]

Ideologies of "manliness," like ideologies of race, were imbued with "civilization's" millennial evolutionism. As we have seen, manliness was not something which was intrinsic to all men, as we today think of masculinity. Instead, manliness was a standard to live up to, an ideal of male perfectibility to be achieved. [. . .] Ideologies of manliness were thus similar to—and frequently linked with—ideologies of civilization. Just as manliness was the highest form of manhood, so civilization was the highest form of humanity. Manliness was the achievement of a perfect man, just as civilization was the achievement of a perfect race. (Masculinity, we should remember, was usually not associated with civilization, because it dealt with "attributes which all men had," including savages. Manliness, in contrast, dealt with moral achievements which only the most civilized men could attain.)

Scientific theories corroborated this belief that racial difference, civilization, and manliness all advanced together. Biologists believed that as human races slowly ascended the evolutionary ladder, men and women evolved increasingly differentiated lives and natures. [. . .] Civilized women were exempt from heavy labor and ensconced in the home. Civilized men provided for their families and steadfastly protected their delicate women and children from the rigors of the workaday world. [. . .] In short, as civilized races gradually evolved toward perfection, they naturally perfected and deepened the sexual specialization of the Victorian doctrine of spheres.

"Savage" (that is, nonwhite) races, on the other hand, had not yet evolved pronounced sexual differences—and, to some extent, this was precisely what made them savage. Savage men had never evolved the chivalrous instinct to protect their women and children but instead forced their women into exhausting drudgery—cultivating the fields, tending the fires, carrying heavy burdens. Overworked savage women had never evolved the refined delicacy of civilized women (Russett 1989: 143–148). [. . .] In these contexts, African Americans were depicted as unsexed primitives who had never evolved the perfect manhood or womanhood characteristic of more civilized races.

Although to twentieth-century sensibilities, "civilization" seems to confuse biology and culture, Victorian ideas of race were predicated on precisely that conflation. Historian of anthropology George Stocking has persuasively argued that Victorians understood "race" to mean a seamless mix of biology and culture. [. . .]

Lacking the conceptual framework to differentiate between physical morphology and cultural traits, educated Victorians subsumed both into a gestalt which they termed "race." Thus, white Americans' belief that primitive men were biologically incapable of achieving manliness was not a confusion between

biology and culture, as some historians have argued, but a logical, if noxious, confusion based upon their understandings of race.

Lamarckian biological theories about human heredity, too, supported "civilization's" assumption that racially primitive men lacked the biological capacity to be manly. [. . .] Until 1900, most biologists still assumed that the only way human races could evolve toward a higher civilization was for each generation to develop a bit more, and to pass these learned traits, genetically, on to their offspring. The educated public retained these beliefs decades longer than scientists. Thus, many middle-class whites felt scientifically justified in believing that no racially primitive man could possibly be as manly as a white man, no matter how hard he tried. Primitive races, lacking the biological capacity to develop racially advanced traits like manliness of character, would require many generations to slowly acquire manliness and pass these civilized capacities on to their offspring.

Civilization thus constructed manliness as simultaneously cultural and racial. White men were able to achieve perfect manliness because they had inherited that capacity from their racial forebears. Black men, in contrast, might struggle as hard as they could to be truly manly, without success. They were primitives who could never achieve true civilized manliness because their racial ancestors had never evolved that capacity.

By stressing the biological causation of race and gender, turn-of-the-century discourses of civilization tended to obscure the importance of another crucial category: class. Class issues had long been implicit in ideas of civilization, as historians have more frequently argued. [. . .]

Yet by insisting that these "civilized" tastes and customs were racial and by downplaying the importance of mores and culture, the middle class was able to obscure the continuing importance of class. In the light of civilization, the middle class could depict its own preferences and styles as biologically determined, superior racial traits. Evolution—and not financial resources—gave the middle class the ability to enjoy and create great art, classical music, and their elaborately furnished homes. Evolution—and not middle-class cultural standards—had made white, middle-class women so delicate and domestic. Evolution—and not economic self-interest—had given white middle-class men the manly self-restraint which allowed them to become self-made men. The large proportion of immigrants in the working class lent credence to these ideas. [. . .] In the light of "civilization," these class-based differences could be coded "racial."

Moreover, the evolutionary millennialism embedded in discourses of civilization provided more satisfying ways for middle-class men to contain class-based challenges to their manly social authority. For example, middle-class Americans had long believed that a man's hard work and talent would inevitably be rewarded with riches and success. Yet by 1880 an increasingly corporate economy, as well as recurring rounds of bankruptcy-spawning depressions, meant fewer middle-class men could achieve manly power as successful, independent entrepreneurs. In the light of "civilization," however, these economic setbacks could appear temporary and insignificant: Middle-class whites' racial destiny was to approach civilized perfection, so eventually they or their children would inherit the earth, anyway. Similarly, recurring and seemingly unstoppable strikes by hostile working men might seem to threaten middle-class men's control over the nation's future; yet discourses of civilization suggested these challenges were irrelevant. In the long run, middle-class men's evolutionary destiny as members of highly civilized northern European races would allow them to prevail over a predominantly immigrant, and therefore racially inferior, working class. Thus, class-based challenges to the power of middle-class manhood seemed to disappear behind civilization's promise that the hard-working, meritorious, virile Anglo-Saxon man was inexorably moving toward racial dominance and the highest evolutionary advancement. [. . .]

CONCLUSION

With this discussion of civilization in mind, let us take a final look at the Jack Johnson controversy, focusing on white journalists' reasons for expecting Jim Jeffries, the "Hope of the White Race," to prevail. Frequently, journalists predicted that Jeffries would beat Johnson because manly white civilization had long been evolving toward millennial perfection. *Collier's* magazine asserted that white men expected Jeffries to win because, unlike the primitive Negro, he was of a civilized race: "The white man has thirty centuries of traditions behind him—all the supreme efforts, the inventions and the conquests, and whether he knows it or not, Bunker Hill and Thermopylae and Hastings and Agincourt" (Ruhl 1910). The *San Francisco Examiner* agreed, predicting that the "spirit of Caesar in Jeff ought to whip the Barbarian" (quoted in Gilmore 1975: 35). Faced with rumors of a Johnson victory, the *Chicago Daily News* wailed, "What would Shakespeare think of this if he could know about it? . . . Could even Herbert Spencer extract comfort from so dread a situation?" Anglo-Saxon civilization itself might fall if Jeffries were beaten by the "gifted but non-Caucasian Mr. Johnson" (quoted in Gilmore 1975). In these reports, a Johnson victory was depicted as an affront to the millennial advancement of civilization and the power of white manliness.

Yet in other reports, Jeffries was depicted, not as an exemplar of advanced civilization and high-minded manliness, but as a paragon of violent, primitive masculinity. In this context, Jeffries' eagerly awaited victory would show that white men's capacity for masculine violence was as powerful as black men's—that civilization had not undermined whites' primal masculinity. Journalists waxed lyrical about Jeffries' primal physical attributes, his "vast hairy body, those legs like trees, the long projecting jaw, deep-set scowling eyes, and wide, thin, cruel mouth" (Ruhl 1910). They printed pictures of him training for the fight by sawing through huge tree-trunks— which, in urban, twentieth-century America, had primitive connotations redolent of log cabins and the frontier. [. . .] For these men, a Jeffries victory would prove that despite being civilized, white men had lost none of the masculine power which had made their race dominant in the primeval past.

Because both approaches drew upon the discourse of civilization, few people saw any inconsistency. Under the logic of "civilization," Jeffries could be simultaneously a manly, civilized heir to Shakespeare and a masculine, modern-day savage lifted from the forests of ancient England. The crucial point was that Jeffries' racial inheritance made him the superior man; and his superlative manhood would prove the superiority of his race. Whether manly and civilized or masculine and savage, whites were confident that Jeffries would beat Jack Johnson.

Thus, many white men panicked when the black champion thrashed the white. By annihilating Jeffries so completely, Johnson implicitly challenged the ways hegemonic discourses of civilization built powerful manhood out of race. Johnson's victory suggested that the heirs of Shakespeare were not the manly, powerful beings they had thought—that "primitive" black men were more masculine and powerful than "civilized" white men. Many white men could not bear this challenge to their manhood. [. . .]

In sum, when late nineteenth-century Americans began to synthesize new formulations of gender, hegemonic discourses of civilization explained concisely the precise relation between the male body, male identity, and male authority. White male bodies had evolved through centuries of Darwinistic survival of the fittest. They were the authors and agents of civilized advancement, the chosen people of evolution and the cutting edge of millennial progress. Who better to make decisions for the rest of humankind, whether female or men of the lower races? It was imperative to all civilization that white males assume the power to ensure the continued millennial advancement of white civilization.

REFERENCES

Adams, Michael C. 1990. *The Great Adventure: Male Desire and the Coming of World War I*. Bloomington: University of Indiana Press.

Baker, Paula. 1984. "The Domestication of Politics: Women and American Political Society, 1780–1920." *American Historical Review* 89: 620–47.

Baker, Paula. 1991. *The Moral Framework of Public Life: Gender, Politics, and the State in Rural New York, 1870–1930*. New York: Oxford University Press.

Beard, George B. 1881. *American Nervousness: Its Causes and Consequences*. New York: Putnam.

Bederman, Gail. 1989. "'The Women Have Had Charge of the Church Work Long Enough': The Men and Religion Forward Movement of 1911–1912 and the Masculinization of Middle-Class Protestantism." *American Quarterly* 41: 435–40.

Bederman, Gail. 1995. *Manliness & Civilization: A Cultural History of Gender and Race in the United States, 1880–1917*. Chicago: University of Chicago Press.

Berthoff, Rowland. 1989. "Conventional Mentality: Free Blacks, Women, and Business Corporations as Unequal Persons, 1820–1870." *Journal of American History* 76: 753–84.

Blumin, Stuart M. 1989. *The Emergence of the Middle Class: Social Experience in the American City, 1760–1900*. Cambridge, UK: Cambridge University Press.

Brown, Victoria Bissell. 1990. "The Fear of Feminization: Los Angeles High Schools in the Progressive Era." *Feminist Studies* 16: 493–518.

Buhle, Mari Jo. 1981. *Women and American Socialism, 1870–1920*. Urbana: University of Illinois Press.

Butler, Judith. 1990. *Gender Trouble: Feminism and the Subversion of Identity*. New York: Routledge.

Carnes, Mark C. 1989. *Secret Rituals and Manhood in Victorian America*. New Haven, CT: Yale University Press.

Chauncey, George Jr. 1989. "Christian Brotherhood or Sexual Perversion? Homosexual Identities and the Construction of Sexual Boundaries in the World War I Era." In *Hidden from History: Reclaiming the Gay and Lesbian Past*, edited by Martin Duberman, Martha Vicinus, and George Chauncey Jr., 313–15. Ann Arbor: University of Michigan Press.

Cott, Nancy F. 1987. *The Grounding of Modern Feminism*. New Haven, CT: Yale University Press.

Crosby, Christina. 1991. *The Ends of History: Victorians and "The Woman Question."* New York: Routledge.

Current Literature. (June 1910). "A Review of the World." 48.

Davidoff, Leonore, and Catherine Hall. 1987. *Family Fortunes: Men and Women of the English Middle Class, 1780–1850*. Chicago: University of Chicago Press.

de Lauretis, Teresa. 1987. *Technologies of Gender: Essays on Theory, Film, and Fiction*. Bloomington: Indiana University Press.

D'Emilio, John, and Estelle Freedman. 1988. *Intimate Matters: A History of Sexuality in America*. New York: Harper & Row.

Dubbert, Joe L. 1980. "Progressivism and the Masculinity Crisis." In *The American Man*, edited by Elizabeth

Pleck and Joseph Pleck, 303–20. Englewood Cliffs, NJ: Prentice Hall.

Erenberg, Lewis A. 1981. *Steppin' Out: New York Nightlife and the Transformation of American Culture, 1890–1930*. Chicago: University of Chicago Press.

Filene Peter. 1975. *Him/Her/Self: Sex Roles in Modern America*. Baltimore: Johns Hopkins University Press.

Foucault, Michel. 1978. *The History of Sexuality, vol. 1: An Introduction*. New York: Vintage.

Gates, Henry Louis Jr. 1986. *"Race," Writing, and Difference*. Chicago: University of Chicago Press.

Gilmore, Al-Tony. 1975. *Bad Nigger! The National Impact of Jack Johnson*. Port Washington, NY: Kennikat Press.

Gilmore, David. 1990. *Manhood in the Making: Cultural Concepts of Masculinity*. New Haven, CT. Yale University Press.

Gorn, Elliott J. 1989. *The Manly Art: Bare-Knuckle Prize Fighting in America*. Ithaca, NY: Cornell University Press.

Gossett, Thomas F. 1963. *Race: The History of an Idea in America*. Dallas, TX: Southern Methodist University Press.

Green, Harvey. 1986. *Fit for America: Health, Fitness, Sport, and American Society*. Baltimore: Johns Hopkins University Press.

Griffen, Clyde. 1990. "Reconstructing Masculinity the Evangelical Revival to the Waning Progressivism: A Speculative Synthesis." In *Meanings for Manhood: Constructions of Masculinity in Victorian America*, edited by Mark C. Carnes and Clyde Griffen, 183–204. Chicago: University of Chicago Press.

Hantover, Jeffrey P. 1980. "The Boys Scouts and the Validation of Masculinity." In *The American Man*, edited by Elizabeth Pleck and Joseph Pleck, 285–302. Englewood Cliffs, NJ: Prentice Hall.

Haraway, Donna. 1989. *Primate Visions: Gender, Race, and Nature in the World of Modern Science*. New York: Routledge.

Higham, John. 1971. *Strangers in the Land: Patterns of American Nativism, 1860–1925*. New York: Atheneum.

Higham, John. 1978. "The Reorientation of American Culture in the 1890s." In *Writing American History: Essays on Modern Scholarship*. Bloomington: Indiana University Press.

Hofstadter, Richard. 1955. *The Age of Reform: From Bryan to FDR*. New York: Vintage.

Horton, James Oliver. 1986. "Freedom's Yoke: Gender Conventions among Antebellum Free Blacks." *Feminist Studies* 12: 51–76.

Johnson, Paul E. 1978. *A Shopkeeper's Millennium: Society and Revivals in Rochester, New York, 1815–1837*. New York: Hill and Wang.

Kasson, John F. 1978. *Amusing the Million: Coney Island at the Turn of the Century*. New York: Hill and Wang.

Kimmel, Michael S. 1987. "Men's Responses to Feminism at the Turn of the Century." *Gender & Society* 1: 261–83.

Kimmel, Michael S. 1989. "The Contemporary 'Crisis' of Masculinity in Historical Perspective." In *The Making of Manhood*, edited by Harry Brod, 121–54. Boston: Allen & Unwin.

Lears, T. J. Jackson. 1981. *No Place of Grace: Anti-Modernism and the Transformation of American Culture, 1880–1920*. New York: Pantheon.

Literary Digest. (16 July 1910). "Is Prize-Fighting Knocked Out?" 41.

Macleod, David. 1983. *Building Character in the American Boy: The Boy Scouts, YMCA, and Their Forerunners, 1870–1920*. Madison: University of Wisconsin Press.

Mangan, J. A., and James Walvin. 1987. *Manliness and Morality: Middle-Class Masculinity in Britain and America, 1800–1940*. New York: St. Martin's Press.

Marsh, Margaret. 1988. "Suburban Men and Masculine Domesticity." *American Quarterly* 40: 165–86.

McGovern, James R. 1966. "David Graham Phillips and the Virility Impulse of the Progressives." *New England Quarterly* 39: 334–55.

Mrozek, Donald J. 1983. *Sport and American Mentality, 1880–1910*. Knoxville: University of Tennessee Press.

New York Times. (14 September 1912a). "Reflections on a Suicide." 12.

New York Times. (20 October 1912b). "Mob Threatens Johnson." 12.

Pauly, Philip J. 1979. "The World and All That Is in It: The National Geographic Society, 1888–1918." *American Quarterly* 1979: 516–32.

Poovey, Mary. 1988. *Uneven Developments: The Ideological World of Gender in Mid-Victorian England*. Chicago: University of Chicago Press.

Riley, Denise. 1988. *Am I That Name? Feminist and the Category of "Women" in History.* New York: Macmillan.

Roberts, Randy. 1983. *Papa Jack: Jack Johnson and the Era of White Hopes.* New York: Free Press.

Roosevelt, Theodore. (16 July 1910). "The Recent Prizefight." *Outlook* 95: 550–51.

Rosenberg, Charles. 1973. "Sexuality, Class and Role in Nineteenth-Century America." *American Quarterly* 35: 131–53.

Rosenzweig, Roy, 1983. *Eight Hours for What We Will: Workers and Leisure in an Industrial City, 1870–1920.* Cambridge, UK: Cambridge University Press.

Rotundo, E. Anthony. 1993. *American Manhood: Transformations in Masculinity from the Revolution to the Modern Era.* New York: Basic Books.

Ruhl, Arthur. (23 July 1910). "The Fight in the Desert." *Collier's* 45: 13.

Russett, Cynthia Eagle. 1989. *Sexual Science: The Victorian Construction of Womanhood.* Cambridge, MA: Harvard University Press.

Ryan, Mary P. 1981. *Cradle of the Middle Class: The Family in Oneida County, New York, 1790–1865.* Chicago: University of Chicago Press.

Scott, Joan W. 1988. *Gender and the Politics of History.* New York: Columbia University Press.

Scott, Joan W. 1992. "Experience." In *Feminist Theory the Political*, edited by Judith Butler and Joan W. Scott, 22–40. New York: Routledge.

Stansell, Christine. 1986. *City of Women: Sex and Class in New York, 1789–1869.* New York: Knopf.

Susman, Warren I. 1984. "Personality and the Making of Twentieth-Century Culture." In *Culture as History*, 273–277. New York: Pantheon.

Trachtenberg, Alan. 1982. *The Incorporation of America: Cultural and Politics in the Gilded Age.* New York: Hill and Wang.

Vance, Norman. 1985. *The Sinews of the Spirit: The Ideal of Christian Manliness in Victorian Literature and Religious Thought.* Cambridge, UK: Cambridge University Press.

Wilentz, Sean. 1984. *Chants Democratic: New York City and the Rise of the American Working Class, 1788–1850.* New York: Oxford University Press.

NOTE

1. A few words need to be said about the way I am using the term "race." Like gender, race is a way to metonymically link bodies, identity, and power. Its connection to bodies, however, is perhaps more tenuous than that of gender. While men's and women's reproductive systems are not as dualistically opposite as our culture represents them, at least reproductive organs do exist. Race, however, is purely a cultural sign [. . .] [(e.g., Gates, Jr. 1986)]. Most anthropologists deny that any pure racial differences or strains can even be identified. Thus, race, like gender, is a way to naturalize arrangements of power in order to depict them as unchangeable when, in fact, these arrangements of power are actually socially constructed and thus historically mutable. [. . .]

JOHN F. KASSON

2. HOUDINI, TARZAN, AND THE PERFECT MAN—INTRODUCTION

In 1904 a balding, compactly built banker in Muncie, Indiana, posed for the camera on his forty-fifth birthday. It was not a conventional birthday portrait, however. For the occasion he stripped to the waist, flexed his biceps, and had himself photographed from behind. His business life was sedentary, but during the next forty years he kept up various physical regimens, ranging from lifting light weights to deep-breathing exercises. His name was Albert G. Matthews, and he was my great-grandfather; he died nine days before I was born.

[. . .] My initial response was surprise: What was he doing? Other male relatives in photographs showed their bodies, if at all, only in swim trunks as they squinted at the camera, usually holding a fish. Later I wondered, What was his sense of his body, and how was it shaped by the technologies and culture of his time? What models of strength did he admire? What dreams and anxieties did this image contain? Family photographs were one of the earliest ways by which I learned the importance of visual evidence in history. [. . .]

Many years later, I sifted through some thirteen thousand photographs at Harvard University devoted to the most famous of all Albert Matthews's contemporaries (ten months his senior), the man who was president when his birthday portrait was made in 1904, Theodore Roosevelt. Here the sense of theatricality that I had first glimpsed with my ancestor burst forth on a colossal scale. Crucial to Roosevelt's success was his ability to turn prized characteristics of manliness into spectacle, literally to embody them. The camera and the pen were essential aids in that effort. Born in 1858 to one of the richest and most socially prominent families in New York, Roosevelt created his own stirring drama of childhood adversity overcome in an account of how he transformed his "sickly, delicate," asthmatic body into the two-hundred-pound muscular, barrel-chested figure of a supremely strong and energetic leader. His *Autobiography*, first published in 1913, included illustrations of Roosevelt in positions of executive authority (assistant secretary of the navy, governor of New York, president of the United States) carefully balanced with portraits of him active and outdoors (on horseback, returning from a bear hunt in Colorado, with hand on hip as Rough Rider colonel in the Spanish–American War, and holding a rifle "in winter riding costume").[1]

The photographic archive showed that Roosevelt had practiced such poses assiduously, and no American of his generation or president before or since—not Lincoln, not Kennedy, not Reagan—developed a broader repertoire. Once past his childhood, when he was pictured in the unisex white dress, long hair, and bonnet worn by upper-class children of the time, he seems to have determined never to appear before the camera in a pampered guise again. In a routine physical examination as a Harvard undergraduate, he learned from Dr. Dudley A. Sargent, the college physician and the nation's leading authority on physical education, that he had "heart trouble" and should lead a sedentary life, taking care not even to run up stairs. Roosevelt replied that he could not bear to live that way and intended to do precisely the opposite.[2] [. . .]

From his college days to the end of his life, Roosevelt appears to have considered no hunting trip complete without recording it either in the field or in a photographer's studio. For his first book, *Hunting Trips of a Ranchman* (1885), based on his adventures in the Dakota Territory, he struck various attitudes, holding a rifle and wearing a fringed buckskin outfit in the style of Buffalo Bill and sporting the holsters, pistols, chaps, and broad-brimmed hat of the ranchman. In 1898, upon his return from Cuba, where he had led his regiment of Rough Riders in victorious charges up Kettle Hill and San Juan Hill, he instantly memorialized his achievements in portraits that displayed a commanding martial bearing. In 1904, the year my great-grandfather posed for his birthday portrait, Roosevelt repeatedly jumped a fence on horseback until a *Harper's Weekly* photographer caught just the right dynamic image for the upcoming presidential campaign.[3] After his presidency, a stage of life in which most of his successors have done nothing more strenuous than golf, he threw himself into new activities—with photographers always at the ready. He recorded his exploits as big-game hunter and explorer (including obligatory poses with animal trophies) in Africa in 1909. Four years later, after his fiercely energetic but unsuccessful "Bull Moose" campaign against William Howard Taft and Woodrow Wilson, he headed for uncharted wilderness and big game once again, this time in Brazil, where he nearly lost his life. He spent his last years, also before the camera, stumping on behalf of the U.S. military effort during the Great War and itching to be in the thick of battle himself.

Many historians exploring manliness in this period have stopped with Roosevelt. But my pursuit has taken me further. And it has led to three immensely popular artists who entertained Americans in the two decades between 1893 and 1914: the strongman Eugen Sandow (1867–1925), the escape artist Harry Houdini (1874–1926), and the author of *Tarzan of the Apes*, Edgar Rice Burroughs (1875–1950). Sandow, Houdini, and Burroughs's Tarzan all acquired immense national and international fame. They literally became part of our language, which suggests that the cultural need for the metaphors they supplied was great, as was the power with which they entered into the lives of their audiences. Viewed in conjunction, these figures assume still greater significance: they expressed with special force and clarity important changes in the popular display of the white male body and in the challenges men faced in modern life.

Although Sandow's name is no longer a household word, he is still revered as the father of modern bodybuilding and a pioneer of physical culture. In his heyday as a vaudeville performer, his position was even more exalted. Physical-fitness experts and journalists alike hailed him as the "perfect man," and his unclad body became the most famous in the world. He established a new paradigm of muscular development and attracted countless followers, ranging from the reformed "ninety-seven-pound weakling" Charles Atlas to the poet William Butler Yeats. His significance for cultural history is still greater. His display of his physique provides a fresh point by which we can assess the changing standards of male strength and beauty that may have inspired men like Albert Matthews to inspect their own bodies in private.

Sandow's celebrity has faded, but Houdini's hold on the popular imagination remains strong even today, though the nature of his feats and the context of his career have been obscured. For the general public, his name dominates the history of magic—to the intense annoyance of many conjurers and magic historians, who rank others superior. Wildly erroneous myths about him persist, such as that he died performing his "Chinese Water Torture Cell" escape (as does Tony Curtis's character in the 1953 Paramount film *Houdini*). Meanwhile, there has been little effort to place him in full historical and cultural context as not only the most brilliant escape artist in the history of illusion but also a magus of manliness, known for some of the most audacious displays of the male body in his time.

Burroughs's fictional character Tarzan is best known of all, but, again, in ways that obscure the significance of his creation. As the subject of twenty-four books written by Burroughs over thirty-five years, and of roughly fifty films, four major television series, a radio serial, and comic books, Tarzan and his adventures have been adapted in ways that hardly resemble the original. The persistence of his popularity testifies to enduring cultural fantasies about manly freedom and wildness. And an examination of the cultural milieu at his first appearance in Frank Munsey's *All-Story* magazine in 1912 illuminates important, if forgotten, aspects of American life a century ago. It reveals why a story about an immensely strong, incomparably free, indomitably wild noble savage could so entrance men who felt locked in the "iron cage" of modern urban, corporate life.[4]

The spectacles of the male body mounted by these three figures built on values embodied in men such as Theodore Roosevelt. In fact, at various points in their careers, all three sought to associate themselves directly with Roosevelt. As a confused young man in 1898, Burroughs wrote to Roosevelt to volunteer for the Rough Riders; he received a gracious but firm refusal. In 1905, at the height of his international prestige, Sandow met with Roosevelt, then president, to discuss their mutual support of the physical-fitness cause. As for Houdini, after entertaining the ex-president on a transatlantic voyage in 1914, he eagerly distributed hundreds of copies of a photograph of himself and his new "pal," in which five other men had been carefully airbrushed away.[5]

Nonetheless, the popular spectacles created by Sandow, Houdini, and Burroughs take us far beyond Roosevelt's performances of manliness, expressing even deeper fantasies and anxieties. All three laid great stress on the unclad male body in ways that Roosevelt would have found unimaginable. This element was crucial to their novelty and impact. They contributed to a new popular interest in the male nude as a symbol of ideals in peril and a promise of their supremacy, as a monument to strength and a symbol of vulnerability, as an emblem of discipline and an invitation to erotic fantasy. In the guise of entertaining, they reasserted the primacy of the white male body against a host of challenges that might weaken, confine, or tame it. Popular spectacles of the female body in this period usually revolved around issues of subordination and transgression, but the overriding theme for these three men concerned metamorphosis. They repeatedly dramatized the transformation from weakness to supreme strength, from vulnerability to triumph, from anonymity to heroism, from the confinement of modern life to the recovery of freedom.

These images of manliness were obviously images of whiteness as well. Neither Sandow, nor Houdini, nor Burroughs was a racial extremist by the lights of his era, any more than Roosevelt himself, who famously invited Booker T. Washington to dine with him at the White House (and infamously issued dishonorable discharges to 170 African American soldiers in the "Brownsville affair"). Yet like Roosevelt, all three shared—and to various degrees contributed to—the highly racialized views that mark and mar this period. In science, popular literature, art, and daily life, the bodies of African American and Native American men had been frequently displayed, even fetishized, while their dignity and worth were denied. [. . .]

Manliness is a cultural site that is always under construction, of course, but in this period it seems to have been undermined on a number of fronts and demanded constant work in new arenas to remain strong. Many men born too late for the Civil War wondered how they would fare in a similar test of courage, and some, like Roosevelt, plunged into the Spanish–American and Philippine–American Wars as opportunities to prove themselves and to build American manhood.[6] Alarmed by the "new immigration" from southern and eastern Europe, composed principally of Catholics and Jews, some Americans worried that the "enterprising, thrifty, alert, adventurous, and courageous" immigrants of past generations were being replaced by "beaten men from beaten races; representing the worst failures in the struggle for existence."[7] At the same time, reports warned that Americans of Anglo-Saxon stock were declining markedly in physical vigor and, by failing to reproduce themselves in sufficient numbers, might ultimately commit "race suicide."[8] Keenly aware of the passing of the frontier, many Americans believed that a nation of farmers was rapidly becoming a nation of city dwellers. Roosevelt's fervent commitment to conservation represented one attempt among many to stay close to the wild lest it be extinguished. Even those such as he who occupied the most privileged positions often worried that society's comforts might weaken their bodies and their wills. Anglo-Saxon Protestants from refined and intellectually cultivated classes were thought to be especially susceptible to neurasthenia, that distinctively modern, characteristically American disease of nervous weakness and fatigue. The founder of this medical specialty, George M. Beard, placed high among its manifold causes excessive brain work, intense competition, constant hurry, rapid communications, the ubiquitous rhythm and din of technology. At the turn of the century, neurasthenia appeared to be reaching epidemic proportions.[9]

Above all, perceptions of manliness were drastically altered by the new dynamics created by vast corporate power and immense concentrations of wealth. Fundamental to traditional conceptions of American manhood had been autonomy and independence, which had to be recast in a tightly integrated economy of national and international markets. Titanic corporations arose with incredible swiftness in all areas of industry: Standard Oil, United States Steel, Pennsylvania Railroad, General Electric, Consolidated Coal, American Telephone and Telegraph, International Harvester, Weyerhaeuser Timber, U.S. Rubber, Pittsburgh Plate Glass, International Paper, Du Pont de Nemours, American Sugar Refining, Armour, United Fruit, American Can, Central Leather, and Eastman Kodak. By 1904, about three hundred industrial corporations had gained control of more than 40 percent of all manufacturing in the United States.[10]

And at the head of these new companies stood a greatly expanded, highly bureaucratized managerial class. Clerical workers, no more than 1 percent of the workforce in 1870, had swelled to no more than 3 percent by 1900 and nearly 4 percent by 1910. These nascent "organization men" (and some women) increasingly worked in large buildings where the offices were as hierarchical and rule-bound as armies. [. . .]

Factory workers, for their part, were the foot soldiers in this expanding industrial force. The period 1890–1914 was pivotal in the struggle between them and management over control of production within factories. Skilled workers had treasured a certain autonomy in setting the pace, organization, and distribution of wages for their work, an autonomy they had earned because of their superior knowledge of their craft. As Big Bill Haywood of the Industrial Workers of the World liked to boast: "The manager's brains are under the workman's cap."[11] The new corporate industrial order massively assaulted this power and the ethic of manly pride and brotherhood among workers that sustained it. Through intense mechanization, division of labor, and "scientific management," industrialists endeavored to dominate all aspects of production and to reduce the workers' bodies to components in a gigantic machine.

Americans were in the forefront of this corporate revolution. [. . .] Yet to contemporaries, this industrial growth felt not like an orderly process but like a wild, careening ride. Wall Street panics in 1873 and 1893 began two of the greatest depressions in American history, and smaller depressions in 1885 and 1907 jolted the economy. By the mid-1880s supporters of labor and capital alike had come to fear that the strains of the new industrial society might erupt in large-scale riots, even a class-based civil war.

Industrialization accelerated major demographic shifts that were also altering the arenas in which manliness might be exercised. The nation's population continued to be the fastest growing in the world, leaping from fewer than forty million in 1870 to roughly sixty-three million in 1890 and nearly ninety-two million in 1910. This increase was partly due to unprecedented numbers of immigrants, amounting to 16 percent of the population in 1881–1900 and a staggering 24 percent in 1901–1920.[12] The new arrivals clustered mostly in America's cities, particularly along the manufacturing belt from the Northeast to the upper Midwest. In 1910 in New York, Chicago, Boston, Cleveland, Detroit, and Providence, more than one in three residents was foreign-born.[13]

Yet even as the population grew, more and more men deferred marriage; in fact, one historian has called this period "the age of the bachelor." In 1890 an estimated two-thirds of all men aged fifteen to thirty-four were unmarried, a proportion that changed little through the first two decades of the twentieth century. In cities the proportion was higher still, forming the basis for a flourishing urban bachelor culture that included a growing gay subculture. In many respects, this bachelor culture represented a pocket of resistance to—or at least a refuge from—the responsibilities of family and community, the demands of women, the discipline of work, and the pressures of a more regulated society. In boisterous play and aggressive competition, bachelors could enjoy a continuity between boyhood and manhood. They played or watched sports and reveled in contests of physical skill and decisive triumph. At the beginning of this period, their great hero was no exponent of manly rectitude such as Roosevelt became, but boxing's brawling heavyweight champion John L. Sullivan. In newspapers and pulp fiction, they avidly read adventure stories about other heroic men, from Eugen Sandow to Tarzan. Many also indulged in pursuits that more respectable elements condemned: heaving drinking, swearing, gambling, engaging in casual sex with women—or other men.[14]

These urban bachelors had several female counterparts, including the working-class "tough girl," the radical needleworker, the shop clerk, the typist, and the "New Woman." The last was a capacious term for middle- and upper-class women who in various ways conducted themselves with a new independence and assertiveness, whether by shopping in department stores, smoking in public, playing tennis, expressing interest in sexuality, earning advanced degrees, entering traditionally male professions, calling for social and political reforms, or agitating for the ballot. Self-development, not self-sacrifice, was the New Woman's watchword. [...] Although neither the term "feminism" nor its full expression emerged until the end of this period, it was already clear that many women were refusing to be bound by traditional notions of women's domestic sphere.[15]

As the structure of both work and urban life changed dramatically, so too did the forms of leisure and communications by which people found release from and perspective on their worlds. Many commercial enterprises offered attractions calculated to appeal to broad popular tastes across different classes, ethnicities, and genders, and they grew into big businesses with some of the same characteristics of systematization, centralization, and managerial control that defined corporate industries. As they intersected, they created the conditions for a new society of spectacle that seemed to ease some of the deep divisions in America's new urban, industrial life. It is here that Sandow, Houdini, and Burroughs flourished.

Vaudeville theater, one of the most popular new entertainments and the springboard for both Sandow's and Houdini's careers, emerged in the 1880s. It represented an extraordinarily successful effort to unite a fragmented theatergoing public: it combined the format of the variety show with standards or morality and settings of refinement that placed it decisively apart from the concert saloons and burlesque houses where variety shows had flourished. With as many as ten or twelve acts, sometimes in continuous performance throughout the day, vaudeville triumphed by offering "something for everyone." [...] Whether in small-time houses or big-time theaters, vaudeville performers prided themselves on being able to engage diverse audiences of men, women, and children from both working-class and middle-class backgrounds in cities and towns across America. Even so, theirs was an industrialized art in which the vaudevillians worked along regional circuits that were dominated after 1900 by the United Booking Office, which spanned the continent.

Sport experienced a similar transformation into commercial entertainment. As once local, informal, and unregulated games became big business, they were systematized and put under managerial control. Yet they did not succumb to bureaucratic rationalization; the most popular sports, boxing and baseball, offered stirring dramas of individual prowess and communal aspiration that some fans treasured for their lifetimes. These professional sports, as well as college football, were heavily freighted with ambitions to revitalize American manhood. Even while seeking to reform their abuses, elite spokesmen extolled the value of these sports in instilling strength, skill, toughness, endurance, and courage. Writing in the dignified pages of *The North American Review* in 1888, Duffield Osborne simultaneously advocated replacing bare-knuckle fighting with regulated glove boxing and defended pugilism, with its "high manly qualities," as a bulwark against the emasculating tendencies of modern life. Without such antidotes to "mawkish sentimentality," he warned, civilization would degenerate into "mere womanishness."[16] Four years later, "Gentleman Jim" Corbett defeated John L. Sullivan in the first heavyweight championship bout fought with padded gloves and timed rounds under the Marquis of Queensberry Rules. When the African American Jack Johnson won the title in 1908, however, it became abundantly clear that many fans thought revitalization should be for whites only. They raised an insistent call for a "Great White Hope" who could defeat Johnson, which was finally answered by the hulking Jess Willard in 1915.[17]

The transformations in popular theater and sport were sustained by profound changes in journalism. In the country as a whole from 1892 to 1914, the number of daily newspapers rose by more than a third, from 1,650 to 2,250, an all-time high; and their size expanded and circulation doubled. In the vanguard of change marched the great metropolitan newspapers. In 1892 ten papers in four cities had circulation bases higher than 100,000; in 1914 more than thirty papers in a dozen cities could make such a claim. Publishers, led by Joseph Pulitzer and William Randolph Hearst, increasingly encouraged the practice of what was called the New Journalism, by which they hoped to attract as diverse a readership as possible. They offered at low prices a bulging combination of sensational stories (such as those about Houdini's flamboyant escapes), serious news coverage, reportorial stunts, personal interviews (often with vaudeville and sports celebrities), civic crusades, and lavish illustrations. When newspapers were organized into spaces and departments devoted to sports, fashion, Sunday magazine supplements, and special columns, they acquired a variety format that resembled a vaudeville bill. And like vaudeville, these newspapers self-consciously aspired to be the "voice of the city," speaking for as well as to its myriad residents. They expressed this ambition both in their publications and, frequently, in their very offices, exemplified by the Pulitzer Building, which, upon its completion in 1890, surpassed Trinity Church as the tallest structure in New York City.[18]

The birth of the modern metropolitan daily and Sunday newspaper was accompanied by that of the modern, low-priced, mass-circulation magazine [. . .] in which *Tarzan* first appeared. By 1903 Munsey could fairly estimate that the ten-cent magazines had gained 85 percent of the entire magazine circulation in the country. Offering a wide variety of stories and articles, abundant illustrations, and a lively tone, such magazines represented a significant cultural challenge to established competitors. The editor of *The Independent* snobbishly defended his magazine's concentration on the "comparatively cultivated class" in magazines and newspapers, saying it was "the only audience worth addressing, for it contains the thinking people." But publishers such as McClure, Munsey, Pulitzer, and Hearst, like vaudeville impresarios such as B. F. Keith and F. F. Proctor, staked their fortunes on their ability to hold a mass following by giving people plenty of varied materials at low prices.[19]

[. . .] [I]n their development, revenues from advertising were indispensable. Between 1892 and 1914 advertising in newspapers and periodicals increased by roughly 350 percent, and most of it was from local sources, especially the new department stores. Yet magazines, long the messengers for correspondence courses and patent nostrums, now were key sites for national advertising of standard brands from Victrolas to Grape-Nuts. Older "polite" magazines had once prided themselves on avoiding advertising, but for mass-circulation magazines in the early twentieth century the situation was fundamentally different. "There is still an illusion to the effect that a magazine is a periodical in which advertising is incidental," explained an advertising executive in 1907. "But we don't look at it that way. A magazine is simply a device to induce people to read advertising."[20]

Associated with these transformations in the popular theater, sports, and the press, as well as with the expansive commercial culture as a whole, was the continuing proliferation of photographic images. The passion for studio portraits, awakened with the rise of photography, not only seized people of all classes but helped to make possible a new celebrity culture. Innovations in photographic reproduction and display changed individuals' very apprehension of themselves and the world. In 1888 George Eastman introduced his Kodak camera, initially a toy for the wealthy but a device that quickly demonstrated its potential to make virtually everyone an amateur photographer. At about the same time, between 1885 and 1910, the halftone, a new, cheaper technique of photoengraving that permitted the direct reproduction of photographs in newspapers, magazines, and books, effected a visual revolution.[21] Finally, the new mass medium of the movies grew with dazzling speed from Thomas Edison's peephole kinetoscope of 1893 (in which Sandow made an appearance), to large-scale motion-picture projection in 1896 (which was frequently the concluding two-and-a-half-hour epic of white supremacy, *The Birth of a Nation*, in 1915. What had begun as a novelty became a consuming national pastime.

These popular spectacles were crucial in both maintaining and subverting gender categories. Indeed, one of the most striking elements was that men's and women's bodies were displayed and dramatized as never before in popular theater, sports, photography, fiction, film, and advertisements. [. . .] In the popular theater, [. . .] spectacle could be used to address quite different audiences for vastly different purposes. Burlesque, expelled from "legitimate" theaters and vaudeville houses, offered leg shows for working-class and lower-middle-class men. By contrast, vaudeville theaters, looking to attract middle-class families as well as members of the bachelor subculture, offered women a broader range of roles. Many of these were constraining, but others allowed for freedom, independence, and self-expression that laid the groundwork for an emergent feminism. By the second decade of the twentieth century, protesting women, including socialists, trade unionists, and suffragists, had taken this sense of theatricality from the stage to the streets to gather support for their causes.[22]

Historians have paid less attention to the importance of the *male* body in popular spectacles—and, especially, challenges to the exposed white male body—as expressing the meaning of manliness in this emergent urban, industrial order. [. . .] My approach is highly selective. I have chosen to focus on Sandow, Houdini, and Burroughs in order to see how they reveal popular aesthetic and cultural patterns. In a context dominated by the rise of corporate capitalism, the changing character of work, the advent of a skyscraper civilization, and the emergence of the New Woman, they helped to create the Revitalized Man. As a model of wholeness and strength, this figure ostensibly stood above the political conflict and class strife of the period, inviting a broad and diverse public of men and women, blue-collar and white-collar workers, to celebrate common gender ideals. [. . .]

Sandow, Houdini, and Burrough's Tarzan can thus illuminate much about the place of popular culture at the advent of modern society. They help us to understand more about how the shift to an advancing technological civilization was communicated to and apprehended by publics in North America and abroad. They tell us about how modernity was understood in terms of the body and how the white male body became a powerful symbol by which to dramatize modernity's impact and how to resist it. They reveal the degree to which thinking about masculinity in this period meant thinking about sexual and

racial dominance as well. They also tell us that hopes and fears, aspirations and anxieties are often difficult to distinguish. Perhaps every dream is the sunny side of some nightmare; perhaps every cultural wish has a dark lining of fear.

NOTES

1. Theodore Roosevelt, *An Autobiography* (New York: Charles Scribner's Sons, 1920).
2. Carleton Putnam, *Theodore Roosevelt*, vol. 1, *The Formative Years* (New York: Charles Scribner's Sons, 1958), 198; Edmund Morris, *The Rise of Theodore Roosevelt* (New York: Coward, McCann, and Geoghegan, 1979), 129; David McCullough, *Mornings on Horseback* (New York: Simon and Schuster, 1981), 229.
3. See "Snap-Shots of the Presidential Candidates," *Harper's Weekly*, July 30, 1904, 1174–75.
4. Max Weber, *The Protestant Ethic and the Spirit of Capitalism*, trans. Talcott Parsons (New York: Charles Scribner's Sons, 1958); originally published in essay form in German, 1904–1905.
5. Theodore Roosevelt to Edgar Rice Burroughs, San Antonio, Tex., May 19, 1898, Irwin Porges Papers, Edgar Rice Burroughs Memorial Collection, University of Louisville, Ky. [. . .]
6. Kristin L. Hoganson, *Fighting for American Manhood: How Gender Politics Provoked the Spanish–American and Philippine–American Wars* (New Haven, Conn.: Yale University Press, 1998).
7. Francis A. Walker, *Discussions in Economics and Statistics*, ed. Davis R. Dewey (1899; reprint, New York: Augustus M. Kelley, 1971), 2:446–47.
8. Harvey Green, *Fit for America: Health, Fitness, Sport, and American Society* (New York, Pantheon, 1986), 224–5.
9. George M. Beard, *American Nervousness, Its Consequences and Causes* (1881; reprints, New York: Arno Press, 1972), esp. 96–138.
10. See esp. Alfred D. Chandler Jr., *The Visible Hand: The Managerial Revolution in American Business* (Cambridge, Mass.: Belknap Press of Harvard University Press, 1977).
11. Olivier Zunz, *Making American Corporate, 1870–1920* (Chicago: University of Chicago Press,

1990), 126–27; "The Fate of the Salaried Man," *Independent* Aug. 20, 1903, 2002–3.

12. Reed Ueda, *Postwar Immigrant America: A Social History* (Boston: Bedford Books of St. Martin's Press, 1994), 2.

13. D. W. Meinig, *The Shaping of America*, vol. 3, *Transcontinental America, 1850–1015* (New Haven, Conn.: Yale University Press, 1998), 278.

14. Howard P. Chudacoff, *The Age of the Bachelor: Creating an American Subculture* (Princeton, N.J.: Princeton University Press, 1999), esp. 48, 217–250; George Chauncey, *Gay New York: Gender, Urban Culture, and the Making of the Gay Male World, 1890–1940* (New York: Basic Books, 1994); Elliott J. Gorn, *The Manly Art: Bare-Knuckle Prize Fighting in America* (Ithaca, N.Y.: Cornell University Press, 1986), esp. 179–247.

15. Caroline Ticknor, "The Steel-Engraving Lady and the Gibson Girl," *Atlantic Monthly*, July 1901, 106; Peter G. Filene, *Him/Her/Self: Gender Identities in Modern America*, 3rd ed. (Baltimore, Md.: Johns Hopkins University Press, 1998), 19–22; Nancy F. Cott, *The Grounding of Modern Feminism* (New Haven, Conn.: Yale University Press, 1987), esp. 9.

16. Duffield Osbourne, "A Defense of Pugilism," *North Atlantic Review*, Apr. 1888, 433–35.

17. For a cogent overview of sports in this period, see Elliott J. Gorn and Warren Goldstein, *A Brief History of American Sports* (New York: Hill and Wang, 1993), 98–182.

18. Frank Luther Mott, *American Journalism: A History, 1690–1960*, 3rd ed. (New York: Macmillan, 1962), esp. 436, 547, 549.

19. Frank Luther Mott, *A History of American Magazines, 1885–1905* (Cambridge, Mass.: Belknap Press of Harvard University Press, 1957), 5–6; John Tebbell, *The American Magazine: A Compact History* (New York: Hawthorn Books, 1969), 106–81. See Frank A. Munsey, "Impressions by the Way," *Munsey's Magazine*, Oct. 1903, 51–52; "Cheap Magazines," *Independent*, June 27, 1895, 867.

20. Mott, *American Journalism*, 593; James Collins, testimony before congressional committee, quoted in Jackson Lears, *Fables of Abundance: A Cultural History of American Advertising* (New York: Basic Books, 1994), 201.

21. Neil Harris, "Iconography and Intellectual History: The Halftone Effect," in *Cultural Excursions: Marketing Appetites and Cultural Tastes in Modern America* (Chicago: University of Chicago Press, 1990), 304–317.

22. Robert C. Allen, *Horrible Prettiness: Burlesque and American Culture* (Chapel Hill: University of North Carolina Press, 1991); Susan A. Glenn, *Female Spectacle: The Theatrical Roots of Modern Feminism* (Cambridge, Mass.: Harvard University Press, 2000).

E. ANTHONY ROTUNDO

3. ROMANTIC FRIENDSHIP: MALE INTIMACY AND MIDDLE-CLASS YOUTH IN THE NORTHERN UNITED STATES, 1800–1900

When Daniel Webster was eighteen years old, he called his best friend "the partner of my joys, griefs, and affections, the only participator of my most secret thoughts."[1] And four years later in 1804, young Daniel asked another close friend: "What is this world worth without the enjoyment of friendship, and the cultivation of the social feelings of the heart?" He answered his own question later in the same letter when he told his friend: "My heart is now so full of matters and things impatient to be whispered into the ear of a trusty friend, that I think I could pour them into yours till it ran over."[2]

In these two statements, Webster laid out a concept of friendship that differed sharply from the one that was embedded in the culture of boyhood. To boys, friendship meant a stalwart alliance and a boon companionship. It was a bond cemented by loyalty and invigorated by shared enjoyment. As boys reached their mid-teens and entered the phase of life known as youth, their notions of friendship tended to change. Daniel Webster, in his letters to his friends, expressed the essence of this contrasting idea of friendship. It was based on intimacy, on a sharing of innermost thoughts and secret emotions. In this altered conception of friendship, a friend was a partner in sentiment as well as action. [. . .]

Such changes marked a sudden shift in sensibility and self-expression—the tender (even "feminine") emotions of the heart replaced the rough aggressions of boyhood. Gentle emotions served both as the cement of male friendship in youth and as one of its chief subjects as well. More than this, many young men expressed their fondness in affectionate physical gestures. All together, these friendships inverted usual patterns of male behavior—they were intimate attachments that verged on romance.

The romantic friendships of male youth resembled in many respects the intense bonds between women first portrayed by Carroll Smith-Rosenberg in her landmark article, "The Female World of Love and Ritual."[3] This resemblance serves as a reminder that, in spite of separate spheres and separate male and female cultures, men and women of the nineteenth century continued to share basic emotional capacities, like the capacity for forming intimate same-sex bonds. And yet there were fundamental differences as well between the intimate ties that bound men and those described by Smith-Rosenberg. The most important of these differences lay in the fact that, among males, romantic friendship was a product of one distinct phase in the life cycle—youth. In analyzing male bonds of intimacy, this essay will focus on their vital role in that transitional period of life.

The intimate, romantic bonds of male youth were intense off-shoots of less remarkable friendship patterns. To start with, young men in their late teens and twenties filled their letters and diaries with the mention of a great many casual associates. These fellows—colleagues at work, occupants of the same boarding house, classmates at a college or academy—passed through young men's lives in a procession marked by good fellowship and little attachment.[4] Such friends were drawn together by the accidents of propinquity more than a deeper affinity of taste or temperament.

From among this large pool of casual companions, though, a young man chose special friends.

This essay was originally published as E. Anthony Rotundo's "Romantic Friendship: Male Intimacy and Middle Class Youth in the Northern United States, 1800–1900," *Journal of Social History* 23, no. 1 (1989): 1–25. Reprinted by permission of Oxford University Press.

Sensing a congenial spirit in a few of these fellows, the young man developed closer ties. These close friendships started, then, with good companionship but moved into deeper realms of feeling and sharing. Male friends who developed a warm bond shared youthful obsessions. They pondered their career plans, and they sifted through hopes and fears about their prospects for success. They offered—and sought—emotional support that was warm, reliable, and reassuring. These reserves of comfort and support grew out of a feeling of warmth and a trustful sense of candor.[5]

From time to time, a close male friendship in youth would blossom into something more intimate and intense. Warmth turned into tender attachment, and fondness became romance. An ardor developed between young men that would seem unusual outside of gay circles in the twentieth century. Based on available evidence, it is impossible to say precisely how often this happened or how many young middle-class men experienced romantic friendship. [. . .] Moreover, this special form of friendship evoked no apologies and elicited no condemnations; apparently, it was accepted without question among middle-class male youth. Regardless of statistical frequencies, then, romantic friendship was a normal, common form of behavior which revealed much about the phase of life in which it occurred.

What were the customary features of these ardent attachments? Since they varied a good deal in the qualities that characterized them, it makes sense to examine several of these relationships, as much for their differences as for their common traits. We have already noted one such bond, the intense friendship between Daniel Webster and James Hervey Bingham. Webster and Bingham became close friends at Dartmouth, and the warmth of their relationship continued past graduation. While they studied law, taught school, and served as law clerks, the two offered each other an intimacy which might otherwise have been lacking from their small-town bachelor's lives. Of course, their relationship encompassed many of the same qualities as a close—but less intimate—friendship. They shared dreams and doubts about their careers and they offered each other honest expressiveness and emotional support.[6]

But there were several dimensions of the friendship between Webster and Bingham that gave it an intimate, even romantic tone. First, there was the way in which Webster and Bingham addressed one another. They sometimes opened their letters with greetings like "Lovely Boy" or "Dearly Beloved," and Webster on occasion signed his letters with affectionate phrases such as, "I am, dear Hervey, your Daniel Webster," and "Accept all the tenderness I have, D. Webster." In between the salutation and the closing Webster used many other terms of endearment—"my Hervey," "my dearest J.H.B.," "dear Hervey."[7]

And the romantic tone extended beyond nicknames and salutations to the way these young men described their feelings for each other. While they were together in college, Daniel described his "dear Hervey" as "the only friend of my heart, the partner of my joys, griefs, and affections, the only participator of my most secret thoughts." Then, after they had graduated, young Webster discovered that being separated from his friend was even harder than he had expected. "I knew not," he wrote to Bingham, "how closely our feelings were interwoven; had no idea how hard it would be to live apart, when the hope of living together again no longer existed." On another occasion when Dan found that he was missing his friend, he reminisced warmly about their special talks together at the end of each day in college. Writing late at night after everyone else had gone to bed, Webster told his friend: "The hour is arrived when you and I . . . used to pile up our books and converse with a fondness I always approve . . ."[8]

The content of these intimate chats varied over a wide range of topics—daily events, career plans, college life, gossip about friends. But the topic which Daniel and Hervey discussed with the greatest fervor—and which required the most intimate trust—was the subject of women. Like other males in their late teens and early twenties, they were obsessed with the topic. Their dreams, their fears, and their puzzlements about women and romance had a stubborn hold on their attention. And again like many of their peers, Webster and Bingham needed a special friend with whom they could discuss such vexing, delicate matters.[9] So they wrote to each other constantly about "the Misses." They exchanged advice, they rhapsodized about feminine beauty, they cursed feminine wiles, and they consoled one another when romantic hopes were dashed. And when a new young woman caught the fancy of one or the other, they carried on like the future lawyers they were, sifting the fragmentary evidence of passing words, stolen glances, and idle gossip for clues to feminine intentions. Underneath it all lay a child-like anxiety that was deeply embarrassing to a young man, so embarrassing that he could reveal it only to intimate friends. [. . .]

[T]here were relationships in this phase of Dan's life which endured with the constancy and devotion of a good marriage—they were his relationships with other young men. Indeed, his bond with Hervey Bingham came to resemble a marriage in many respects. These "bosom pals" shared the joys and sorrows of life, they offered each other emotional support and revealed their deepest secrets, and they even spoke to one another in terms of endearment. At a time of great discouragement in his quest for a wife, Webster offered Bingham a vision of their common future that amounted to a marriage proposal.[10] "I don't see how I can live any longer," wrote Webster, "without having a friend near me, I mean a male friend, just such a friend as one J.H.B." And so he announced—only half-jokingly—that he would move in with Bingham: "Yes, James, I must come; we will yoke together again; your little bed is just wide enough; we will practise at the same bar, and be as friendly a pair of single fellows as ever cracked a nut." The picture that Daniel painted of their life together was modest but idyllic:

> We perhaps shall never be rich; no matter we can supply our own personal necessities. By the time we are thirty, we will put on the dress of old bachelors, a mourning suit, and having sown all our wild oats, with a round hat and a hickory staff we will march on to the end of life, whistling as merry as robins.[11]

Dan was not quite offering Hervey a romantic love nest or a vine-covered cottage, but it was a cozy, intimate image of the two men yoked together happily for life, sharing Bingham's "little bed." What Webster's feelings lacked in romance, they made up in the loving familiarity of a happily married couple. [. . .]

In his more realistic moments, Webster knew that he would marry. Yet it stands as a tribute to the power of his tie with Bingham that he saw their friendship

as occupying the same ground as marriage—to the point where the two seemed to be mutual contradictions. [. . .] Dan sensed that male intimacy and marriage were similar, perhaps to the point of mutual exclusion.

Still, for all the similarities between a marriage and the youthful male intimacy of Webster and Bingham, there was one irreducible difference. Only within marriage was sexual activity allowed. There is no evidence to indicate that Dan and Hervey ever developed a physical relationship of any sort. There were, however, intimate relationships between young men which involved touching, kissing, and caressing. In most respects, these relationships had the same emotional textures and qualities as other intimate male friendships. Yet their physical expressiveness gave them an extra blush of romance that was lacking in other fond attachments between young men.

The friendship between James Blake and Wyck Vanderhoef was certainly one that had a romantic aura. These two young men—both engineers—met in 1848, when they were in their twenties. Their friendship did not blossom immediately, but when it did, Blake wrote of the event as if he had just been engaged to be married. In his dairy, he exulted: "I have found a friend! one upon whom I can repose every trust, and when in trouble and affliction can seek relief." Blake's account of events between himself and Wyck sounds more like the choice of a wife than the start of a friendship: "After an acquaintance of nearly three years I have chosen [Wyck] as my friend, and he has reciprocated; May he live long and happy, and may the tie of pure friendship which has been formed between us, never be severed, but by the hand of death." Just as these words have the ring of marriage vows, so too Blake's description of their relationship sounds like a statement of the union of husband and wife. He prayed that God would "ever keep us as we now are in oneness, one life, one interest, one heart, one love." [. . .]

The marital overtones of James and Wyck's relationship were not confined to words and imagery, but extended as well to their actions. Like other devoted young friends of the time, they made a pact of friendship as a promise of lasting devotion. The arrangement was unusual, though, in that it also included

Wyck's fiancée, Mary, with whom James, too, enjoyed a very close relationship. The three, who were already "bound together in friendship" and "cemented by affection," now exchanged "a kiss of purity"—each with the other—as a pledge "ever to love, ever to cherish and assist each other." [. . .]

Of all the similarities to marriage in the Blake–Vanderhoef relationship, though, the most striking to the twentieth-century eye is their physical affection. For these two young men, "the embrace of friendship" was not just a figure of speech. As James noted without comment on one occasion, "We retired early and in each others arms did friendship sink peacefully to sleep."[12] In other words, the two friends not only shared a bed, but they shared embraces there as well. Apparently, this was a common occurrence for them, and James noted their nocturnal embraces in his dairy with no hint of an apology. The most revealing of these diary entries came just after Wyck and James had parted company, and James was describing their last night together:

> We retired early, but long was the time before our eyes were closed in slumber, for this was the last night we shall be together for the present, and our hearts were full of that true friendship which could not find utterance by words, we laid our heads upon each other's bosom and wept, it may be unmanly to weep, but I care not, the spirit was touched.[13]

This statement is noteworthy for its description of intimate affection between men, but it is even more noteworthy for what it reveals about the limits of acceptable male behavior. James closes his comments with an apology for his unmanly conduct, but his apology is for weeping, not for laying his head on the bosom of his intimate male friend in bed. Apparently, crying violated the norms of manliness more than the exchange of affectionate physical gestures with another man.[14]

Thus, the range of acceptable behavior in friendship did not end with the intimate bonds of youths like Webster and Bingham, but extended further to include romantic and physically affectionate relationships like that of Blake and Vanderhoef. The variety of these bonds did not stop there, either. The relationship of young Ralph Waldo Emerson and

Martin Gay, for instance, was really a romantic crush more than a personal connection, since there is no recorded evidence that Emerson and Gay ever exchanged more than a few words. Their romantic flirtation began in 1820, when Martin Gay entered Harvard where Emerson was already a student. Soon after Gay's arrival, Emerson—who was seventeen at the time—noted "a strange face in the Freshman class whom I should like to know very much." Emerson found "a great deal of character in his features" and determined "to become acquainted with him." He also mentioned "the singular sensation which [Gay's] presence produced" in him.[15] [. . .]

Having invented a personality for Gay, Emerson proceeded to construct a romance of meaningful gazes and "accidental" encounters. A few months after Gay's arrival on campus, Emerson noted that he and his mysterious stranger had "already had two or three long profound stares at each other." From there, the affair took a course which closely resembled that of a boy–girl flirtation. Emerson contrived chance encounters with Gay, and then, when they did meet, he lost his nerve and avoided his "friend." The young scholar seemed puzzled by his own behavior, writing: "All this baby play persists without any apparent design, and as soberly as if both were intent on some tremendous affair."[16]

The "affair" persisted for a year and a half until Emerson graduated from Harvard. And his interest in Gay surfaced occasionally for another year after that. Finally, when he was almost eighteen months beyond his graduation, Emerson affirmed that the "ardour of his college friendship" was "nearly extinct." And yet even then—as he began to recognize his infatuation as "a curious incident in the history of so cold a being"—Emerson mentioned that their "glance at meeting, is not that of indifferent persons."[17] Like other romantic crushes, this one was finally killed by time and a heavy dose of reality. In fact, we do not know whether Martin Gay ever shared Emerson's feelings of infatuation, for we know the affair only through Emerson's journal. In this as in other ways, the "relationship" was like a schoolboy's crush on a girl he has never met.

The contrast between the Emerson–Gay flirtation and the attachment of Blake and Vanderhoef was sharp. One was a fantasy of romance and probably quite onesided. The other was itself a romance, apparently rooted in mutual fondness. One was based on a physical attraction that was never consummated, while the other seemed independent of physical attraction but was full of physical affection. Both relationships were tinged with romance, but they were romances of very different sorts.[18]

The blush of romance was deeper still in the affairs of a Connecticut college student named Albert Dodd. Writing in his journal in the late 1830's, Albert described his intimate relationships with two other young men, John Heath and Anthony Halsey. His infatuation with John came shortly before his attachment to Anthony, and it resembled Emerson's crush on Martin Gay in that Albert never confessed his affectionate feelings. On the surface, the relationship was simply a close friendship, and Albert was left to sort out his unspoken feelings in his journal. He wrote about John in sentimental terms that were typical of exalted nineteenth-century friendship: "O yes John has an affectionate heart, a noble heart." And Albert tried to characterize his special feelings in this way: "it is not friendship merely which I feel for him, or it is friendship of the strongest kind. It is a heartfelt, a manly, a pure, deep, and fervent love." This final phrase captures some of Albert's confusion, because—for all the purity and nobility of it—he was also a "fervent lover." He wrote in his journal of John's "beloved form" and of his "deep and burning affection for him." Yet Albert's love for John remained a secret. "I love you, indeed I love you," he wrote to John in his journal. "But you are not here, you cannot hear me confess this to you, a confession which perhaps you would care not for."[19]

In his next male romance, Dodd was not at all cautious about confession. For while he poured out his feelings for Anthony Halsey in his journal [. . .] as he had for John Heath, he was willing to bare his soul to Anthony in long hours of intimate talk. Moreover, Albert's relationship with Anthony Halsey brought together the two themes of physical attachment that appeared in separate relationships earlier in this article. For just as Emerson dwelled romantically on Martin Gay's blue eyes, Albert Dodd noted eagerly in his journal that he found Anthony *"so handsome."* But, while

Emerson never acted physically on his attraction to Gay, Dodd enjoyed an erotic relationship with his "dearest Anthony." His description of their nights together resembles that of James Blake describing his loving embraces with Wyck Vanderhoef. Dodd and Halsey were apparently more intimate in their physical relationship, though: "Often too [Anthony] shared my pillow—or I his, and then how sweet to sleep with him, to hold his beloved form in my embrace, to have his arms about my neck, to imprint upon his face sweet kisses!" This description is different from Blake's accounts of his nights with Wyck, for the latter does not bear the same erotic tinge that Dodd's shows. Not only does Dodd kiss his Anthony as they embrace in bed (Blake mentions no such erotic play), but there is an undertone of passion to Albert Dodd's account in his mention of Anthony's "beloved form" and in his remembrance of the kisses—and the nights—as "sweet" ones. All these subtle differences take additional erotic force from Albert's confession that he found Anthony *"so handsome,"* a confession that has no equivalent in James Blake's journal entries about Wyck Vanderhoef. The relationships described in the journals of Blake and Dodd were very similar, but Dodd's affair with Anthony Halsey seemed to go one significant—and passionate—step beyond that of Vanderhoef and Blake. And yet, as significant as this step appears to the twentieth-century observer, it did not take Dodd and Halsey across any perilous social boundaries. Albert Dodd described their erotic encounter without a hint of self-censure or a word of apology.[20]

Another striking feature of Dodd's romantic life was that it mixed male and female love objects as if that were the most natural habit in the world. [. . .] Nor was Dodd alone in blending the love of men with the love of women. James Blake, after all, enjoyed an intense relationship with Wyck Vanderhoef's fiancée, Mary. [. . .] As we noted earlier, James, Mary, and Wyck even shared a sacred pledge "ever to love, ever to cherish and assist each other," then sealed their pledge with "a kiss of purity," each with the others. At this transitional stage in life, the distinction between love objects—and between their genders—sometimes faded to invisibility. [. . .]

Even when the experiences of young men and women in their separate social settings did not mingle or overlap, they often ran parallel to one an-other. Certainly, the experience of romantic friend-ship among males in their late teens and twenties resembled—and in some respects even duplicated—the experience of homosocial romance among women at the same age. As described by Carroll Smith-Rosenberg in her classic article, "The Female World of Love and Ritual," these powerful bonds between females shared many characteristics with the male friendships described in this essay.

To start with, Smith-Rosenberg pointed out that committed, loving ties between women were not only "socially acceptable" but were viewed as "fully compatible" with heterosexual bonds.[21] Recent re-search on romantic friendships has filled in more of the cultural context which enabled those bonds to flourish. [. . .] The culture of the educated middle-class provided a variety of models and a rich language to support romantic friendships between members of the same sex. As Smith-Rosenberg pointed out, these bonds were accepted even among the most conserva-tive and respectable families.

The romantic friendships of the two sexes were similar not only in their social acceptability, but also in their daily content of activities and pastimes. [. . .] But it is another form of resemblance that is most striking: intimate pairs of each sex often had physical relationships—relationships which might include kisses, caresses, verbal expressions of physical long-ing, and the sharing of beds. These signs of romantic love led Smith-Rosenberg to one of her most dra-matic insights. She proposed that "we view sexual and emotional impulses as part of a continuum or spectrum of affect gradations strongly affected by cultural norms and arrangements." "At one end of the continuum," she wrote, "lies committed heterosexual-ity, at the other uncompromising homosexuality; be-tween, a wide latitude of emotions and sexual feelings." Smith-Rosenberg asserted that some cultures allow a person "a great deal of freedom in moving across this spectrum," and she suggested that nineteenth-century America was one such culture.[22]

In the years since Smith-Rosenberg made this as-sertion, many scholars have explored the issue of sexual boundaries and definitions in middle-class culture of the 1800s. [. . .] These studies have, first of all,

supported Smith-Rosenberg's contention that our fore-bears did not make clear distinctions between what was "homosexual" and what was not. Perhaps the single most revealing fact about middle-class attitudes toward homosexuality in the 1800's is that there was no such term. [. . .] The lack of a *word* for homosexuality is closely tied to the fact that there was no *concept* of it, no *model* for sexuality other than heterosexuality. When middle-class Northerners wrote about homosexual acts, they did not usually treat them separately from other forms of carnality such as bestiality, prostitution, or heterosexual buggery. Here again, word usage is re-vealing. The nineteenth-century term for the legal crime of homosexual intercourse was "sodomy," but that term could also be used to indicate copulation with an animal or "unnatural" (oral or anal) intercourse with a member of the opposite sex. It is further significant that "sodomy" [. . .] referred to acts and not to types of per-sons, relationships, or personality systems. And, indeed, the one other term which loosely referred to homosexuality was the phrase "unnatural act," which again created the concept of a vaguely-defined sexual behavior, not of a person, a broader sexual orientation, or a social identity.

[. . .] And, as we shall see shortly, the fact of two men sharing a bed had fewer sexual overtones in the nineteenth century than it might today. In other words, the behavior in bed described by James Blake and Albert Dodd was far more innocent—and there-fore socially acceptable—than it would be in the late twentieth century. [. . .]

So middle-class Americans of the nineteenth cen-tury had no clear concept of homosexuality, not really differentiating it from many other forms of car-nality. To the extent that they did have ideas—and a language—about homosexuality, they thought of particular sexual acts, not of a personal disposition or social identity that produced such acts. This set of attitudes threw a blanket of ambiguity over the pri-vate acts of physical affection between men and left them, in some ways, freer to express their feelings than they would have been in the twentieth century.

The physical dimension of nineteenth-century ro-mantic friendship cannot be understood solely in terms of sexual boundary definition, though. There were other common experiences—some distinctive to males, others common to both sexes—which helped to shape patterns of physical affection between friends of the same sex. Nineteenth-century boys, for one thing, expressed their feelings for each other in physical ways much more than verbal ones. Fist fights and wrestling matches not only bespoke boyhood rivalries, but they served as a disguised channel of affection in a boy's world that forbade gestures of tenderness. So, although a boy of this era would rarely exchange a warm embrace with a pal and probably never expressed friendship through a caress, he knew the feeling of a close friend's body locked with his at a moment of high emotion. He learned the habit of physical contact with others of his sex at an early age.[23]

The heated body contact between boy friends was not the only childhood experience that affected young men's behavior in the realm of physical expressiveness. There were also long-standing customs of daily life that gave distinctive meanings to the experience of two males (or two females) sharing a bed. In our own time, the phrase "sleeping together" has become a euphemism for sexual intimacy. But we need to remember that in the nineteenth century that phrase still carried its literal meaning. Many middle-class men grew up in large families where children, of necessity, shared a bed. Boys were the natural choice as bed partners for other boys, so the habit of sleeping with one or more brothers developed early in life and continued throughout childhood.[24] [. . .]

As a boy reached his youth and left home, he lost his brothers as bed-mates but gained new ones from outside the family. At colleges, academies, and boarding schools, students often shared a mattress.[25] And young men starting out in careers found that obtaining a bed-partner was a good way to live cheaply on a limited budget. [. . .] Men slept with men that they did not know and never gave it a second thought.[26]

Nor was this a custom limited to male youth of small means. Men of business and the professions sometimes had to share beds with other men even after they were established and successful. Those who travelled stayed frequently at inns where the two sexes were separated but strangers of the same sex were thrown together with two or more in a bed. [. . .] Such commonality, when added to the sleeping arrangements that were usual in boyhood and youth,

led nineteenth-century males to think of sleeping together as a completely ordinary occurrence.

This view of the subject puts some of the evidence we have examined into a special focus. For instance, it makes Daniel Webster's suggestion that he permanently share Hervey Bingham's "little bed" seem less seductive and more commonplace. That playful statement may have been made in total innocence. The most useful means of understanding Webster's suggestion, though, is one that recognizes bed partners as a common custom of the time, even as it concedes more intimate possibilities for two men who sleep together. After all, Webster was proposing to sleep with Bingham not just as a matter of necessity but as a statement of on-going emotional preference. And, in a culture that barely recognized the existence of homosexuality, there was no need for Webster to distinguish one motive from another. [. . .]

Once we recognize that this possibility of intimacy in bed could exist in an era when men slept together as a casual occurrence, then we can see the spectrum of meanings that attached to the act of sharing a bed—a spectrum that spread out from the incidental (and often annoying) contact of strange bedfellows, to the body warmth of fond brothers, to the embraces of Wyck Vanderhoef and James Blake, and on to the loving kisses of Albert Dodd and Anthony Halsey. In a society that had no clear concept of homosexuality, young men did not need to draw a line between right and wrong forms of contact, except perhaps at genital play. And even there the line would have been drawn not so much in fear of homosexuality *per se* as in fright at the thought of any genital activity except for sexual intercourse between husband and wife. In fact, there is no evidence of genital sexuality in the sort of private relationships discussed here. That lack of evidence strongly suggests that genital play between males was proscribed—either intimate friends were not engaging in genital sexuality or they did not feel safe in writing about it. [. . .]

In many ways, then, Smith-Rosenberg's depiction of intimate friendship between females—and of the cultural norms which governed those friendships—bears a striking resemblance to the romantic male friendships described in these pages and to the rules which bounded those relationships. There were some fundamental differences, though, between these forms of male and female intimacy, differences which were closely tied to issues of continuity, independence, and relatedness in the lives of men and women. The most important difference lay in the fact that the intimacy in women's relationships, once formed, would often endure through life, while the intimacy of male friendship was largely limited to those years between boyhood and manhood which were known as youth.

The distinctive conditions of youth did much to breed romantic bonds between males, so those conditions deserve at least brief attention here. Male youth was a period of transition, whose uncertainties were increased by vague social expectations and loose definitions of boundary. It usually began sometime in the teens, and it ended as soon as the early twenties or as late as a man's thirties. Youth was essentially a time when a young male had reached physical maturity but had not yet established the two identifying marks of middle-class manhood—a career and marriage. At this time of life, a young man might be working to prepare himself for a career (through education, a clerkship, or a professional apprenticeship) or performing tasks that were recognized as ways for a youth to mark time while making middle-class career choices (school teaching, menial labor); it was common for young men to move among these activities, experimenting with their skills and interests. [. . .]

A young man had not only to cope with the vagueness and uncertainty of an experimental period in life, but he also had to face the problems that came with the transition from boyhood to manhood. That transition involved many smaller ones. A male youth was moving from a realm of impulse and play to a realm of serious work and careful plans, from the sheltering world of childhood to the responsible world of manly independence, from the love and nurture of home to the anonymity of the market place, from the security and moral rectitude of women's sphere to the freedom and competitive rigor of men's sphere. A male youth was no longer in the powerless position of a boy but he had not yet achieved the authority of manhood. [. . .] A male youth occupied a status without a status: he was neither boy nor man.

Adrift in this period of change and uncertainty, a young male cast about for whatever anchor of security he could find. The people closest to him at this time were likely to be of his own age and sex. The offices, counting houses, and classrooms where a middle-class youth spent his days were likely to be sex-segregated. The boarding houses and dormitories in which he lived away from home were all-male environments, and the literary clubs, debating societies, and fraternities where he spent his spare hours were not open to females. His relationship to his parents was in flux (even if he was living at home, he was often eager to prove his independence), and he met adults only at work, usually as his superiors. So present circumstances led a young man naturally to seek other male youth for companionship and security; then, too, he had long been accustomed to turn to friends of his sex as allies in the face of challenge. [. . .]

Romantic friendships gave young men a chance to play-act the trials and the possibilities of marriage, to test their feelings about adult intimacy in a setting where life-long commitment was not at stake. In a time when divorce was not an acceptable option, young men felt understandably insecure about what lay ahead in marriage. Intimate friendship offered them a chance for rehearsal. And more than that, it was a rehearsal with a member of the more familiar and less intimidating sex. The intimate attachments of male youth served as a testing ground for manhood even as they offered a reprise of boyhood.

In this mixture of past and future, the intense friendships of young men may not have differed so much from the loving bonds of young women. For the female sex as well as the male, close relationships could offer a substitute for nurturing bonds at home and provide a rehearsal for marriage. What made the intimate attachments of youthful men and women so different was their continuity (or lack of it) with friendship in other phases of the life cycle. [. . .]

Young men formed intimate ties which differed sharply from the relationships formed at other points in the life cycle. The tender warmth of close male bonds could not have varied more widely from the violent aggression that typified boys' play [. . .]. [. . .] There was, at the same time, a stark contrast with male relationships in manhood. The turbulent competition of the adult workplace would prove to be a harsh change from the warm mutual concern of youthful friendship, while the self-interest and calculation that crept into the relations of adult male friends were distinctly different from the romantic bonds of earliest manhood which were ends in themselves. In short, the sense of intimate connection in male friendships was largely confined to one phase in the life cycle. [. . .]

The friendships of male youth provided them with nurture, love, and intimacy; they offered a sense of safety at an uncertain time of life. And yet, even as young men were pursuing friendship eagerly (and sometimes passionately), they believed that intimate male attachment was a passing fancy. They themselves were conscious of the fact that these relationships belonged to an era in their lives which would not last. [. . .]

The self-conscious segmenting of life and of personal attachment—which would have been unthinkable to most women—was evident in many of the romantic friendships we have studied. When Daniel Webster proposed to Hervey Bingham that they should live together forever, he was expressing a strong and genuine wish, but he knew that the wish would not come true. Webster, after all, was obsessed with the pursuit of marriage, and that topic—together with career worries—formed the chief concern of Webster's letters to Bingham. He even wrote candidly about the limits of their intimate relationship. As he reflected on the pleasure he took in their confidential talks late at night, Daniel told Hervey that they "converse[d] with a fondness I always approve, though sometimes think almost childish."[27] To Daniel Webster, then, the warmest, most confiding moments of his friendships were worthy of a child but not a man.

Webster's choice of words is echoed in Ralph Waldo Emerson's journal. He understood that "by and by" he might think his obsession with Martin Gay to be a "childish sentiment," and he even referred to their flirtation as "baby play."[28] [. . .]

What was it that made the intimate friendships of youth seem childish even to their participants? By using the word "childish," young men were contrasting the qualities of their own intense attachments to the qualities of manhood. First of all, they knew that the tenderness, the dependence, and the

expressiveness which these relationships evoked in them were qualities at odds with the independence and emotional austerity expected of a grown man. It was the "fondness" of his conversations with Bingham that made them seem "childish" to Webster; and it was the contrast between Emerson's warm ardor for Gay and his coldness in the rest of life that made his romantic yearning seem like "childish sentiment." Furthermore, there was a quality of play in these relationships, something both passionate and whimsical which set them apart from manhood with its serious, determined tone. [. . .]

Why did close friends assume that their ties would be broken or drastically loosened by manhood? There were several reasons, and all of them were related to the task of assuming a man's duties. We noted earlier, for instance, that many young men thought of their intimate friendships as the functional equivalent of marriage, and they expected that wedlock would threaten those male bonds. A young artist named John Lambert told his dearest friend Sergeant Kendall that his love for him was his measure of what love for a woman should feel like; then John had to reassure Sergeant hastily that no woman had yet lived up to the standard.[29] Daniel Webster made a similar gesture of reassurance to Hervey Bingham, joking that they would exile any future wife of his who tried to take sole possession of his heart.[30] Such reassuring talk was needed because young men sensed what would happen to their attachment after one of them married.

And their fears proved accurate: of all the intimate friendships described here, not a single one maintained its former intensity after marriage. Some of them did not survive at all. One dramatic instance of this transformation was the fate of Abraham Lincoln's friendship with Joshua Speed. The two were bedmates and ardently close friends for more than three years. Lincoln and Speed—who both turned thirty during their time together—were living through a period of tentative beginnings in courtships and career. They became so close that when Speed shut down his store and moved away, Lincoln was plunged into the worst depression of his life. As he followed the subsequent triumph of his friend's courtship, though, Lincoln emerged slowly from his depression. Then, once Speed was married, their relationship suddenly lost its significance for Lincoln. His letters to Speed grew distant in tone, and soon they were corresponding only on business matters. There was little anger or bitterness at the demise of the friendship, and once or twice in later years the two men reminisced warmly during brief visits. But without doubt their intimacy had come to a sharp and sudden halt when Joshua Speed married.[31]

There came other changes in a young man's life that also worked to doom his intimate friendships. Chief among these was a strong commitment to a career. Albert Dodd, noted earlier for his passionate attachments to other youthful males, underwent a dramatic change during his time at Yale in the late 1830's. [. . .] Albert Dodd's commitment to a career played a central part in the redirection of his passions away from romantic friendship, but that commitment was clearly not the only force at work in the transformation of this young man's life. For he had also done something larger in the process of finding a calling[;] [. . .] in doing so, he had to sacrifice some of the passions and personal attachments that had given meaning to his days as a student.

The experience of Daniel Webster at this same point in life shows even more vividly how a young middle-class man achieved his manhood—and how he gave up other modes of feeling and attachment in the process. The ten years after Daniel's graduation from Dartmouth were a time of experiment and uncertainty. These were the years when he sustained and strengthened the intimate ties formed in college with Hervey Bingham. He continued several other friendships with nearly equal zeal. And, as mentioned earlier, young Dan and his friends engaged in constant exploration of their hopes and fears about marriage and work. Then, gradually, Dan started to put together the pieces of his adult life. His hesitation about a career in the law vanished. His beloved father died, leaving him free to practice law wherever he pleased. He began courting a young woman named Grace Fletcher, and, in the process of wooing her, he made a confession of faith and became a church member. Finally in 1808, nearly a full decade after his college graduation, Daniel married Grace Fletcher. A recent biographer wrote of Webster at this stage

that he "had finally taken the last step" in fitting himself for his life as a mature man. "He had committed himself to a profession, made his peace with his family and his God, and taken the kind of wife he needed. The doubting and inward looking were behind him forever."[32]

This transformation—like the one that Albert Dodd experienced—was achieved at a price. For "the doubting and inward looking" that Webster left behind had been the stuff and substance of his intimate friendship with Hervey Bingham and of many other fond attachments as well. In the absence of a wife, a settled career, or a home of his own, Webster latched onto the security of close friendship. Indeed, the uncertainty of life in a period of transition added a special strength to these bonds of friendship. But once that uncertainty was gone, the soul-searching stopped and the basis for intimacy grew suddenly narrow. [. . .]

Daniel Webster's experience, it should be stressed, was a common one among young men of the middle class. Major commitments—marriage, a settled career, a home of one's own—were the marks of a man's identity. Once these commitments were made, a male became a man, and the romance and the carefree play of boyhood and youth were set aside. And when "the sweet dreamy times of boyhood's romance" ended, so did romantic friendship.[33] There was little room for attachments to other men which were tender, intimate, dependent—in short, "childish."

Instead, the identity of a middle-class man was founded on independent action, cool detachment, and sober responsibility. [. . .] Adult male identity—so detached and independent—contrasted with that of adult females, which was built on interdependence and connection. [. . .]

Of course, it had been this way from the start for middle-class women in the nineteenth century. Growing up in a domestic world where women set the tone, girls built close expressive relationships with mothers and sisters and inherited from their mothers a network of female friends and relatives which provided personal support and a foundation for a woman's identity. According to Carroll Smith-Rosenberg, a girl developed her own network as she grew up to be a woman, but this new network meshed with the one she had inherited; it extended its reach beyond marriage, connecting a woman closely to other women and to her past.[34] For boys, it was a different matter. At age five or six, they were allowed a freedom to roam which enabled them to start building their own relationships and begin learning to make their own way early in life. For a part of the day, they were already experiencing independence and a measure of discontinuity with their personal past. The relationships which they developed with other boys had little in the way of tenderness or intimacy, and they were based on constantly shifting needs in a boy-world of ceaseless competition.[35] Then, when a youth left home to seek his own fortune in the world, he broke many of his boyhood ties and created a whole new network of peers. Thus, the romantic friendships of young manhood were an anomaly; they were not part of a life-long pattern of intimate bonding with members of the same sex. That bonding experience was unique for male youth, as it was not for females of the same age.

And yet, even though these intense attachments of male youth did not last into manhood, they did leave a legacy to men's adult lives. They had, first of all, provided a rehearsal for the marriage on which nearly every man embarked. And while friendships between men lacked the intensity of youthful bonds, they often showed a loyal, enduring fondness which must have owed something to earlier and more intimate ties. More than that, the special friendships of youth may have contributed to the cohesion of social relationships in the keenly competitive marketplace where middle-class men spent their days. As men struggled to maintain the balance between cooperation and competition in the workplace, they built on their experiences with the rivalrous comradeship of boyhood and then added to it the experience in youth of intimacy with another man. By teaching empathy and a sense of appreciation for the interior lives of other men, those youthful relationships helped to provide a readier feeling of trust when building bonds with competitors and collaborators.

This process suggests a final legacy of the intimate friendships of youth, for many of the social bonds which men did develop with their fellows in the marketplace were nurtured in men's clubs, fraternal lodges, political parties, and various formal and informal business associations. Men tied their loyalties to those groups with a passion that equaled the passion of their youthful friendships. These male institutions may, in fact, have offered their members a viable emotional compromise between connection and autonomy. [. . .] By absorbing an intense desire for male attachment and diffusing it over a broad membership, all-male clubs could provide an outlet for deep emotional needs without threatening the individual autonomy or the psychological armor that were basic parts of a man's public identity.[36] [. . .]

Just as romantic friendship entered a young man's life and then disappeared, this special kind of bond flourished temporarily on the broader historical scene and then faded. Intimacy among male youth was not, of course, a phenomenon unique to the nineteenth-century; young American men have enjoyed the embrace of close friendship at all points in the nation's history. Nor was the very special form of intimacy described in this essay limited strictly to the nineteenth century. As early as the Revolutionary War, young men of elite backgrounds expressed their friendship in the same language of romantic devotion used by intimate youths in the 1800s.[37] But this intense style of friendship did not become widespread among young men in the northern states—or, at least, did not become readily evident in their letters and diaries—until the turn of the nineteenth century.

Why did romantic friendship become more common among young men at that point in time? First of all, the male youths in question were part of a flood of young men in the 1800s seeking to gain (or hold) a place in the growing commercial and professional classes. In the previous century, most such places—distinctly limited in number—were gained through a process of apprenticeship and family patronage that kept a young man within his own web of familial connection, moving on a predictable route to a desirable status. The transition from boyhood to manhood, though not necessarily smooth, was a process of continuity.[38] But in the nineteenth century, as young men more often made their own way, the process became less predictable, more tumultuous, and more elongated. Young men had greater need of emotional security, and they were more likely to crave nurture and support from others.

The nineteenth century, much more than the eighteenth, was also an era of sharp cultural differentiation between male and female. As the distance—both symbolic and personal—grew between the sexes, a young man would be more inclined to turn to a person of his own sex for the support he needed. And at this point in the life cycle, he was physically segregated from people of other ages and sexes, thus making a powerful bond with another male youth even more likely.[39]

These factors which generated romantic friendship continued to operate through most of the nineteenth century. But in the late 1800s, a variety of cultural and social changes acted to eradicate the romantic male friendships of youth. By the turn of the century, the separation of spheres—as symbolism and as personal and physical distance in youth—was beginning to break down.[40] Young men thus felt more inclined to turn to young women for their first try at adult intimacy.

They were strongly encouraged in this inclination by new modes of thought and discourse about manliness and sexual orientation. It was in the final decades of the 1800s that the twentieth-century language of homosexuality developed. New concepts like "sexual deviance" and "perversity" took hold, and the idea emerged that such "inversions" were not the result of unnatural impulse, but of indwelling, biological urges. With these changes in thinking, homosexuality became associated not with an *act*, but with a *person* and a *social identity*. The act, the person, and the identity were all stigmatized, and most men sought to distance themselves from each one. The idea of kissing another man or sharing a bed with him became frightening, and the romantic language of male friendship evaporated.[41]

As the distinction between homosexual and heterosexual emerged, a parallel distinction appeared among the middle and upper classes, dividing men into two types—the hearty, vigorous, active man and the gentle, reflective, neurasthenic one. The former type was viewed positively and the latter was seen as unmanly and undesirable. In such an atmosphere, the cultural encouragement for vigorous exercise and athletic combat of the late nineteenth century flourished, and the tender affection and intimate talk of earlier years faded.[42]

With this change, the tone and activity of young manhood came to resemble the cultural world of boys much more closely. Such change was part of a broader trend in the late nineteenth century toward greater continuity between boyhood and manhood. The modern, rationalized, age-graded system of education grew and spread in the closing years of the 1800s; this system established a ladder of progress from boyhood to manhood. One advanced toward middle-class manhood by ascending this ladder through the grades and upward into business or a profession. This process smoothed the transition from boyhood to manhood, and it placed that transition much more closely under the supervision of concerned adults. Now there was much less need for a young man to establish a bond of security that would help him through turbulent times in his twenties.[43]

In sum, close male friendships did not end with the nineteenth century; powerful bonding between male youths did not come to a halt and neither did homosexual activity. But what did vanish at the turn of the century was the form of male relation that we have called here the romantic friendship—a friendship expressed in fond words, filled with pledges of devotion, hinting at the possibility of physical affection, and serving the needs of young men at a perilous time of transition. Romantic male friendship is an artifact of the nineteenth century.

NOTES

1. Daniel Webster to J. Hervey Bingham, *The Writings and Speeches of Daniel Webster* (National Edition, Boston, 1903), vol. 17, Feb. 11, 1800.
2. Webster to Thomas Merrill, *ibid.*, May 1, 1804.
3. Carroll Smith-Rosenberg, "The Female World of Love and Ritual: Relations between Women in Nineteenth-Century America," *Signs* 1 (1975): 1–29. [. . .]
4. See, for example, Aaron Barlow Olmstead Papers, New York Historical Society, and John Ward, Diaries and Notebooks, New York Historical Society.
5. A good illustration of this sort of relationship—close but not intimate—can be found in the

correspondence of Morton Bailey and James Cattell, collected in James Cattell Papers, Family Correspondence, Manuscript Division, Library of Congress.

6. Daniel Webster to J. Hervey Bingham, *Writings*, Feb. 11, 1800, Sept. 22, 1801, Oct. 26, 1801, and Oct. 6, 1803.

7. Daniel Webster to J. Hervey Bingham, *ibid.*, Dec. 28, 1800, Sept. 10, 1801, Oct. 26, 1801, May 18, 1802, July 22, 1802. Such words of affection were common to the correspondence of many young male intimates in the nineteenth century. [. . .]

8. Daniel Webster to J. Hervey Bingham, *Writings*, Feb. 11, 1800, Oct. 26, 1801, and Dec. 28, 1800. [. . .]

9. For the same phenomenon, see John Doane Barnard, "Journal of His Life, 1801–1858," p. 10, Essex Institute; James Barnard Blake, Diary, July 13, 1851, American Antiquarian Society. [. . .]

10. Such promises of enduring commitment were not uncommon between intimate male friends in youth. See Blake, Diary, Jan. 5, 1851; *Abzug*, p. 233; Charles B. Strozier, *Lincoln's Quest for Union: Public and Private Meanings* (New York, 1982), p. 42.

11. Daniel Webster to J. Hervey Bingham, Writings, Apr. 3, 1804.

12. Blake, Diary, Dec. 27, 1851.

13. Blake, Diary, July 10, 1851; see also Blake's entry for July 13, 1851.

14. More casual, public touching was also acceptable between young men and could have great emotional significance. See Ward, Diary, Apr. 15, 1864.

15. Ralph Waldo Emerson, *The Journals and Miscellaneous Notebooks of Ralph Waldo Emerson*, William H. Gilman, Alfred R. Ferguson, George P. Clark, and Merrell R. Davis, eds. (Cambridge, Mass., 1960), vol. 1, Aug. 8, 1820.

16. *Ibid.*, vol. 1, Oct. 24, 1820, and May 2, 1821.

17. *Ibid.*, vol. l, Nov. 29, 1822.

18. There is yet another sort of romantic bond between males, one which differs in key respects from the others discussed here. This type of attachment developed between a youth and an older man. Both participants were invariably ministers or reformers who were intensely devout Christians. The concerns which these friends shared were not ones of courtship and career choice, but rather of spiritual growth and social transformation. Their ties certainly bore the aura of a mentor–student relationship (and a father–son bond as well), but they also resembled the more widespread form of male intimacy in fundamental ways—openly affectionate letters, romantic terms of endearment, ardent emotional support, and an active language of touch. These Christian love bonds are described in Yacovone, *passim*. For a specific example, see Abzug, pp. 32–34, 168–169, 186, 190, 233.

19. Peter Gay, *The Tender Passion* (New York, 1986), pp. 207–209.

20. *Ibid.*, pp. 206–211.

21. Smith-Rosenberg, p. 59.

22. *Ibid.*, pp. 75–76.

23. E. Anthony Rotundo, "Boy Culture: Middle-Class Boyhood in Nineteenth-Century America," presented at the Conference on Masculinity in Victorian America, Barnard College, Jan. 8–9, 1988, pp. 27–28.

24. Lewis Wallace, *Lew Wallace: An Autobiography,* (New York, 1906), vol. 1, p. 19; [. . .] Claude M. Fuess, Daniel Webster (Boston, 1930), vol. 1, p. 25. [. . .]

25. Stephen Salisbury, Jr., to Stephen Salisbury, Sr., July 19, 1814, Salisbury Family Papers, Box 16, American Antiquarian Society.

26. Strozier, pp. 41–42.

27. Daniel Webster to J. Hervey Bingham, *Writings*, Dec. 28, 1800.

28. Emerson, *Journals*, vol. 1, May 2, 1821.

29. John Lambert to Sergeant Kendall, 1891.

30. Daniel Webster to J. Hervey Bingham, *Writings*, Feb. 22, 1803.

31. Strozier, pp. 41–49.

32. Irving Bardett, *Daniel Webster* (New York, 1978), p. 45.

33. The phrase about "boyhood's romance" comes from a long letter about the approach of manhood written by a young Boston lawyer, C. Theodore Russell, to his father, Charles Russell, on May 30, 1838 (Charles Russell Papers, Massachusetts Historical Society).

34. Smith-Rosenberg, p. 60–71.

35. Rotundo, "Boy Culture," *passim*.

36. It seems that nineteenth-century voluntary associations offered middle-class people a kind of sanction to set aside certain gender expectations. Just as voluntary associations gave women an opportunity for "manly" self-assertion without undermining their female identity, so, too, these organizations provided men with an outlet for "feminine" relational needs without corroding the integrity of their male identity.

37. See John C. Miller, *Alexander Hamilton: A Portrait of Paradox* (New York, 1959), pp. 21–24.

38. E. Anthony Rotundo, "Manhood in America: The Northern Middle Class, 1770–1920," Ph.D. dissertation, Brandeis University, 1982, pp. 54–58.

39. [. . .] E. Anthony Rotundo, "Male Youth Culture in Nineteenth-Century America," unpublished essay.

40. On the closing of the gap between the spheres, see Ellen Rothman, *Hands and Hearts: A History of Courtship in America* (New York, 1984), pp. 189–192, 203–211. See also Rotundo, "Manhood in America," pp. 368–378, and Peter Gabriel Filene, *Him/Her/Self: Sex Roles in Modern America* (Baltimore, Md., 1986), pp. 76–77.

41. [. . .] [F]or variations on this theme, see also Lillian Faderman, *Surpassing the Love of Men: Romantic Friendships and Love between Women from the Renaissance to the Present* (New York, 1981) and George Chauncey, Jr., "Christian Brotherhood or Sexual Perversion? Homosexual Identities and the Construction of Sexual Boundaries in the World War One Era," *Journal of Social History* 19 (Winter 1985): 203–206. The entries in the Supplement to the *Oxford English Dictionary* (in volume II of the Compact Edition [New York, 1971]) under "homosexual," "invert," and "pervert" point in the same way to the arrival of the modern language for homosexuality as a late nineteenth-century phenomenon.

42. For instance, Charles Eliot to Charles W. Eliot, ed., in *Charles Eliot, Landscape Architect*, Charles W. Eliot, ed. (Cambridge, Mass., 1924), pp. 90–91; Richard Cabot to Ella Lyman, undated, summer 1889, Ella Lyman Cabot Papers, Schlesinger Library, Radcliffe College.

43. Storm and stress certainly did not disappear from the process of growing up, but the youthful turbulence followed the descending age of puberty and the social invention of adolescence down into the mid- and early teens. [. . .]

JO B. PAOLETTI

4. CLOTHING AND GENDER IN AMERICA: CHILDREN'S FASHIONS, 1890–1920

Despite several decades of women's adopting tra-ditionally masculine garments and styling, there are still many differences between what is considered appropriate dress for men and women. These differ-ences may be obvious (women wear high-heeled shoes, men do not) or subtle (women's shirt buttons are sewn on the left, men's are sewn on the right). Children in our society begin to learn these distinc-tions before they have started school, as they begin to select their own clothing and dress themselves. Even in infancy, before the child can comprehend the meaning of such signals, pink or blue clothing identi-fies the baby's gender to all observers. All of these differences are usually described as "traditional," implying that they are long-standing cultural patterns. In the case of adult clothing, this is essentially true; most of the rules we observe today in choosing adult dress date back to the mid-nineteenth century or ear-lier. This is not the case with children's clothing. Until World War I, little boys were dressed in skirts and had long hair. Sexual "color coding" in the form of pink or blue clothing was not common in this country until the 1920s; before that time male and female infants were dressed in identical white dresses. In fact, between 1890 and 1920 the clothing of in-fants and preschoolers became more sex-typed, while adult women's clothing was beginning to look more androgynous. How did this happen?

The history of women's clothing is fairly well doc-umented, since most of the work done by costume historians concerns female dress. Beginning in the late 1880s, after centuries of superficial stylistic change, women's clothing styles became consider-ably more practical and more varied. Shorter skirts and the abandonment of corsets are but two exam-ples of the innovations of the period from 1880 to 1920. Some changes, such as shorter hair styles and the introduction of trousers and knickerbockers for casual wear, were clear adaptations of men's or boys' costumes. Motivation for these innovations came from a number of different directions: the increased number of women in the white-collar workforce, the rising popularity of sports, the influence of the dress-reform movement, and the democratizing effect of mass-produced ready-to-wear.[1] Most costume histo-rians agree that this increased freedom in dress re-flected the increasing number of social roles available to American women.

Less research has focused on men's and women's clothing, though in the last five years these areas have begun to attract interest. It is known, for example, that men's clothing styles also changed at the turn of the century, becoming less varied and less individual-istic. The boxy sack suit, once the ignominious uni-form of the middle-class businessman, became the standard costume of men regardless of class and oc-cupation. By 1900, the business suit had almost to-tally replaced older, more elaborate and expressive forms of dress. The range of colors and fabrics deemed acceptable for men narrowed as well. As with the changes in women's clothing styles, these changes are believed to be responses to a number of different forces. The shift from farm and factory to managerial positions, interest in sports and outdoor activities, ready-to-wear technology that favored simple styling, and the popularity of public figures such as Theodore Roosevelt all contributed to changes in turn-of-the-century men's clothing styles.[2]

Adult male and female dress today is essentially the result of a continuation of these trends of a century ago—women have continued to appropriate mascu-line styles for their own use, while men generally have

This reading originally appeared in *Signs* 13 (1987): 136–43. © 1987 by The University of Chicago. All rights reserved.

been reluctant to change what has become a uniform of masculinity. This is particularly true of the clothing worn by white-collar workers. It is only in the last twenty years that men's business dress has begun to show some traditionally "feminine" characteristics—more color and more variety—whereas leisure styles usually have been more flamboyant.

The net effect of these changes is that men and women today dress more similarly than did their counterparts of a century ago. Since clothing is known to be an important means by which young children learn sex roles, one might assume that these changes in adult costume were paralleled by changes in children's clothing.

This article reports the results of an extensive content analysis of over 500 illustrations and descriptions of children's clothing found in turn-of-the-century fashion magazines. The magazines used were *Godey's Ladies' Book and Magazine*, *Peterson's Magazine*, *Ladies' Home Journal*, and *Vogue*. *Godey's* and *Peterson's* ceased publication in the 1890s, about the same time the other two appeared, so the data from 1860 to 1890 are from the earlier magazines and the data from 1890 to 1910 are from *Vogue* and *Ladies' Home Journal*. All four magazines were used for one year (1892) in order to test variation between sources. No significant difference was found in the styles offered in each periodical for that year. The content-analysis instrument was designed to collect and quantify information on design characteristics such as sleeve, neckline, silhouette, fabric type, color, and trim. These data were then analyzed and tested for correlation with the age and sex of the wearer. In addition, articles on children's clothing were located in other sources using magazine and newspaper indexes. Child-care and housekeeping manuals were also consulted for advice concerning children's dress and child rearing. The four magazines used for the content analysis contain advice columns that occasionally included questions and answers regarding children's clothing.

The results of this study suggest that children's fashions were affected by adult trends, and that the changes that occurred in children's clothing were more dramatic than those that took place in adult styles.[3] Girls' clothing became more practical and

varied, just as women's fashions had, but unlike men's clothing, which was conservatively masculine to begin with and simply proceeded to become more so, boys' clothing underwent fundamental changes in style and usage between 1890 and 1920. In other words, children's clothing styles moved away from relatively subtle sex-typed characteristics and toward distinctive differences. This shift was most pronounced in boys' clothing.

Throughout most of the nineteenth century, gender distinctions in clothing did not begin at infancy but were delayed until several years later. Infants of both sexes wore long white dresses until they began to walk. Toddler boys and girls wore short, loose-fitting dresses until the age of two or three years. From then until the age of five or six, all children wore dresses or suits with short skirts, but differences in color, material, and trim were used to distinguish boys and girls. All of these skirted styles bore a strong resemblance to women's dress of the period, usually reflecting current fashions in sleeve, neckline, and so on. However, that is not to say that the boys were dressed "like girls." Descriptions of toddlers' clothing in fashion magazines make it clear that there were subtle differences between male and female styles:

> For boys of a year or a year and a half the blouse dress is worn, for morning wear confined at the waist with a belt. But little difference is noticed in the general style of their dress except the hat and less elaborate trimming on their dresses.[4]
>
> . . . little boys' dresses button up the front, those of their sisters fasten in back . . .[5]
>
> A boy of two can wear dresses made from the same pattern as for a little girl. There is little, if any, difference in the style at such an early age.[6]

The practice of putting a little boy in skirts until he was considered old enough for trousers has never been fully explained. It has been suggested that it was for ease of diaper changing and toileting, but this seems unlikely during a period when toilet training began early in infancy and supposedly was achieved within nine months, nor does it explain why little boys of five or six years old wore skirts. The tradition may have some roots in old superstitions that by dressing little boys like girls they were protecting their male children from supernatural threats, but this is difficult to substantiate. (Nor can we assume that nineteenth-century middle-class parents would have maintained this superstition.) No doubt it was easier to sew and fit dresses than to make miniature suits, and dresses also had the advantage of creating a pool of hand-me-downs for later children, regardless of sex.

Perhaps part of the explanation is that it was not considered important to differentiate boys and girls at such an early age. Instead, it seems to have been *very* important to distinguish between children and adults. A child's maturation was noted by gradual adoption of adult dress, a process usually regarded as marking important milestones in her or his development. These stages became more distinct and more celebrated for boys than for girls only after the age of five. Boys became men through a transition from dependency to mastery, while girls were said to "wear forever the baby petticoat with all its royal powers and privileges."[7] Boys acquired gender-distinct adult dress in two stages. At some point between the ages of five and seven years (sometimes coinciding with entering school), boys made the important change from skirts to short trousers and received their first short haircut. This was portrayed in the popular literature as a stressful time for mothers and sons alike—the boy's first step toward independence and the mother's loss of her genderless, innocent baby: "Mothers naturally resist breeching."[8] "It was the trousers that did it, Mary. From the moment he put on trousers he objected to being kissed."[9]

The exact timing of this stage was left to the mother's discretion. As a result, advice columns very commonly included queries from mothers wondering if their sons were ready to put away dresses. The usual advice was that a "manly" boy looked better in short trousers, while a delicate, small-for-his-age fellow should be kept in dresses a little longer. A few advised that the mother should wait for her boy to insist that he be allowed to graduate to short trousers, as proof of his increasing masculinity.[10]

Boys from five to twelve were dressed in distinctive styles worn only by boys and often bearing little resemblance to the normal dress of either men or women. Examples of these so-called "costume styles" include military uniforms such as the sailor suit, and "antique" costumes such as the velvet suit and lace-trimmed blouse associated with Little Lord Fauntleroy. After they turned twelve years of age, boys were permitted to wear long trousers and any of the other styles worn by adult men, except for formal wear.

In contrast to these distinct stages found in boys' costume, girls' clothing changed little between infancy and adolescence. Styles remained basically the same; the only change was a gradual lengthening of the skirt. At puberty, girls began to wear their hair arranged in adult fashion and wore dresses identical in style to those of adult women, except in the case of formal clothing. The accepted ages for these transitions were seldom discussed in magazine articles or advice columns, although descriptions of girls' fashions invariably included appropriate ages.

Toward the end of the nineteenth century, clothing styles for children changed in several important ways. The same factors that altered adult dress—dress reform, sports, and increasingly casual life-styles—encouraged the adoption of more practical and comfortable children's clothing. For girls, this often meant adapting styles worn by men—shirts and knickers instead of dresses with "bloomers" for sports dress and more tailored everyday clothing. By 1910, the *Ladies Home Journal* could advocate that girls as old as ten or twelve wear knickers or one-piece rompers for play.[11] Other evidence suggests that the practice more likely was limited to younger children; girls' rompers appeared in Sears Roebuck and Company catalogs during that time period but were sized only to age seven.[12]

As girls' clothing became more masculine, so did boys' clothing. This was particularly true of styles for boys two to seven years old, who were put directly into trousers rather than the usual skirted suits:

> As for little boys, they are all sailors; and contrary to what has been the fashion for many years past, it is now considered extra chic to put them early in trousers.[13]
>
> Little boys jump nowadays almost from baby clothes into trousers, the age of four or even three and a half years not being considered too early to such advancement.[14]

In this context, "trousers" usually meant short knickerbockers or pants, not full-length trousers such as men wore.

Fancy dress costumes also fell out of favor, except for military styles such as the sailor suit: "I saw a boy with a predestinate idiot of a mother, wearing a silk hat, ruffled shirt, silver-buckled shoes, kid gloves, cane, and a velvet suit with one two-inch pocket which is an insult to his sex."[15]

By the end of the 1890s, little boys wore dresses only until the age of two or three years old, rather than until five or six years old as before. This is evident not only from the advice columns, where mothers were counseled not to keep their boys in skirts too long, but also from the styles shown in the magazines. Skirted styles for boys aged four and above no longer appeared; all dresses in those sizes were clearly intended for girls. The age at which boys stopped wearing short pants and began to wear long trousers did not change; it continued to be about twelve years old. This suggests that these changes in boys' clothing were intended to differentiate boys from girls at an earlier age than before, and not simply to hurry the boy toward adulthood.

By 1910, boys' clothing had become as drab and conservative as those worn by men: "It is sometimes a relief to turn away from the fripperies that make up the sum of feminine dresses for all ages and consider the plain, substantial attire of the boy."[16]

In 1890, men and women dressed completely differently, but little boys and girls were dressed very much alike. By the 1920s, while women's styles had become progressively more androgynous, men's costume had become even more conservatively masculine. Infants' and toddlers' clothing echoed these changes, with the most extensive alteration being in boys' clothing. What, then, does this tell us about how changes in adult dress are translated into child-rearing practices?

The subject of sexual distinctions in dress was seldom broached in the turn-of-the-century sources. In the course of this research, seventy-one housekeeping manuals and mothers' guides were consulted, as well as advice columns and articles in *Godey's Ladies' Book and Magazine, Harpers' Bazaar, Ladies' Home Journal, Peterson's Magazine, Vogue,* and several other periodicals. Most barely mentioned clothing, save in the most general terms—it should be neat, clean, modest, and appropriate to the child's activities. Some delineated the transitions from infants' clothing through adolescence, and there was virtually no disagreement among them as to when these transitions occurred. But very, very few offered any rationale for these changes or even addressed the issue of sex difference in styles.

Those few articles that explicitly discuss the changing styles expressed repugnance toward early sexual distinction. As late as 1910, Charlotte Perkins Gilman adamantly maintained that no differentiation should be made until the child entered school: "The most conspicuous evil here is in the premature and unnatural differentiation in sex in the dress of little children . . . a little child should never be forced to think of this distinction. It does not exist in the child's consciousness. It is in no way called for in natural activities, but is forced into a vivid prominence by our attitude."[17] Gilman was expressing in more explicit terms what earlier authors had implied when they wrote of the innocence of childhood. The years of infancy and toddlerhood were a period of "bliss . . . before consciousness begins,"[18] prelude to "that blank wall of foregone conclusions which shuts out fairyland."[19] Gilman seems to have associated the absence of sex-distinctive dress with a state of innocence and, conversely, sex-differentiated dress with the loss of innocence.

If one were to judge only by the child-care literature, G. Stanley Hall was alone in his contention that early sexual distinction was essential to proper adult development.[20] But the manuals, guides, and advice columns do not tell the whole story; the children's fashion trends, as they appeared in the magazines surveyed, suggest that popular opinion was just the opposite of Gilman's position. It was becoming common to see distinctive styles advertised for boys and girls of younger and younger ages. Did American parents decide that they preferred their little boys to look "more masculine"? What role did clothing manufacturers play in this transition? Did they set the trends or were they changing their product to reflect their customers' changes in taste? What role did fathers' memories of their boyhoods—preserved in family photographs for all to see—play in this swift defeminization of boys' clothing? Was the masculinization of boys' and men's clothing a reaction to more androgynous styles for women and girls?

Most of these questions may be difficult to answer, particularly if the change in clothing traditions came from the public. Some mothers may have discussed their children's upbringing in letters and diaries. There are other nineteenth-century magazines that contained advice columns, and these may also contribute to an understanding of the changes that occurred in children's clothing. Comparison of the styles shown in ladies' magazines with ready-to-wear offerings, using manufacturer's and male-order catalogs, may give some sense of the manufacturer's place in this trend. Equally interesting would be styles offered by pattern companies, which might more closely reflect what children were wearing, since clothing for very young children was more likely to be made in the home than purchased ready-to-wear in most middle-class households prior to the twentieth century. Autobiographies and journals may contain useful information on children's clothing, though an individual parent's influence on clothing selection for children is hard to gauge. Oral histories of men and women now in their nineties who may have witnessed these changes could be another helpful approach.

Ongoing research on gender-specific clothing in the twentieth century suggests that by the 1920s the modern "tradition" of dressing infant boys in blue and girls in pink had just begun to be popular.[21] How did this trend respond to later forces, such as the post–World War II emphasis on sharp distinctions between masculinity and femininity? To what extent is the androgyny of contemporary American fashion reflected in the way in which we dress our own children? Though I have raised many more questions than I can answer here, it seems clear that some of our seemingly unshakable traditions were adopted in the course of a single generation—not so long ago.

NOTES

1. Claudia B. Kidwell and M. C. Christman, *Suiting Everyone: The Democratization of Clothing in America* (Washington, D.C.: Smithsonian Institution Press, 1974), 136–51.
2. Jo B. Paoletti, "Ridicule and Role Models as Factors in American Men's Fashion Change, 1880–1910," *Costume* 19 (1985): 121–34.
3. Jo B. Paoletti, "Clothes Make the Boy, 1860–1920," *Dress* 9 (1983): 16–20.
4. *Godey's Ladies' Book and Magazine* (April 1870), 398.
5. Elisabeth Robinson Scovil, "The Art of Dressing the Boy," *Ladies' Home Journal* (March 1895), 22.
6. "Questions and Answers," *Ladies' Home Journal* (August 1895), 27.
7. "Boys and Girls," *Harper's Magazine* (December 1876), 19.
8. Ibid., 24.
9. Annie H. Downell, "The Boy," *Harper's Magazine* (August 1901), 416.
10. This last suggestion was made, interestingly, only by two of the few nineteenth-century male authors on the subject of child care: Robert Tomes, *The Bazaar Book of the Household* (New York: Harper & Bros., 1875), 214, and Walter Grifflin, *The Homes of Our Country* (New York: Union Publishing House, 1882), 156–57.
11. "Clothes for Little Children," *Ladies' Home Journal* (March 1910), 104. Somewhat later, the *Harper's Bazaar* personal shopping service was advertising one-piece bloomer suits for girls three and a half to nine years old ([April 1915], 95). In 1911, Catherine Heath of *The Delineator* suggested that girls sew rompers for their "up-to-date" dolls ([March 1911], 257).
12. Sears, Roebuck & Co., catalogs 1908–1916.
13. *Godey's Ladies' Book and Magazine* (December 1890), 527.
14. "Questions and Answers," *New York Times* (July 9, 1893), sec. 3, p. 4.
15. Kate Wiggin, *Children's Rights* (1892), 12.
16. "The Younger Generation," *Vogue* (April 15, 1910), 58.
17. Charlotte Perkins Gilman, "Children's Clothing," *Harper's Bazaar* (January 1910), 24.
18. H. Spofford, *House and Hearth* (New York: Dodd, & Mead Co., 1891), 266–67.
19. M. Byron, "The Little Boy," *Living Age* (November 22, 1902), 489.
20. G. Stanley Hall, "Feminization in School and Home," *World's Work* (May 1908), 10237–44.
21. Jo B. Paoletti and Stephanie Thompson, "Gender Differences in Infants' Rompers, 1910–1930" (paper delivered at the annual symposium of the Costume Society of America, Richmond, Virginia, May 1987).

GEORGE L. MOSSE

5. SHELL-SHOCK AS A SOCIAL DISEASE

Shell-shock was one of the most widespread battlefield injuries during the first world war: it seemed unlike any of the other wounds contracted in the war, an injury without any bodily signs, a mass outbreak of mental disorder. For the cultural historian, shell-shock provides an excellent example of the fusion of medical diagnosis and social prejudice which had taken place during the previous century and a half. Shell-shock, in reality, was not as vague a disease as it seemed at the time; rather, as we look upon the phenomenon from a historical perspective, it was an injury, which, while raising disturbing medical questions, was easily co-opted by traditional cultural prejudice which, so it was thought, could provide it with a readily understood context.

The manifestations of shell-shock seemed to fit already present social stereotypes, the "unchanging representation of another," as *Webster's Dictionary* defined them. Such stereotypes could easily be used to explain so-called abnormal behavior; they had, in fact, served for nearly a century to define the outsider as over and against society's norms. Ever since the beginning of the modern age, European society had represented itself through ideal types which had come to symbolize society's values—what society thought it wanted and needed—as well as through those types which represented the enemy who was thought to threaten these values, and who through its very existence helped society to define itself more clearly.

Since the beginning of the last century the image of manliness as an ideal had taken on firm contours—there was a consensus in western and central Europe about what it meant to be a "true man"—and about the function which he fulfilled as exemplar and guardian of the society's values and coherence in an age of accelerated change. Such a true man was a man of action who controlled his passions, and who in his harmonious and well-proportioned bodily structure expressed his commitment to moderation and self-control.[1] The unity of body and mind is important, for it focused the image of man and gave it cohesion. Indeed, the effectiveness of the stereotype was that it made the abstract concrete, and the clear distinction between the appearance of the normal and the so-called abnormal had already been part of the new eighteenth-century sciences, and it was to influence the diagnosis of shell-shock as well. A discussion of the impact and perception of shell-shock would indicate that it is of major importance that a firm image of manliness not only existed, but had become a symbol through which society confirmed its strength, cohesion and dynamic.

The stereotype of those who were thought to menace society's norms, those defined as "outsiders," on the margins of established society, was in direct opposition to the ideal manhood, the foil to which such "outsiders" represented in mind and body. Such men were nervous, ill-proportioned, and, above all, constantly in motion. All those placed outside the confines of established society tended to look alike: the Jews, the habitual criminals, the gypsies, homosexuals, and the insane with their "moveable physiognomy."[2] The nerves of such outsiders were shattered and their willpower gone. The stereotype of such so-called abnormal men was a harbinger of social disintegration. This all pervasive stereotype can easily be verified by examining its popular image and caricatures from the second half of the nineteenth century onwards.

As the ideal of the true man established itself, several roads were thought to lead to manhood, which would transform boys into true men: from the beginning of the nineteenth century onwards, for example, gymnastics was one such way, and a proper moral education was another. We should not be

This reading was originally published in the *Journal of Contemporary History* 35 (2000): 101–108.

astonished, for example, to be told that in 1917 the products of English public schools were less prone to shell-shock, for they had the benefit of an atmosphere where character and manliness were developed side by side with learning.[3] At the same time, in much of Europe, war was regarded as a true test of manliness, and the military sought to make its influence felt in schools. The modern ideal of manliness, after all, had been formulated in the age of the French Revolution and the Napoleonic wars.

Thus, already in 1888 during the American Civil War, a report on soldiers' afflictions which was said to diminish their effectiveness in battle singled out those not able to adjust to the hardships of war as young men of feeble will and highly developed imaginative faculties. However, the nostalgia which in this report was said to afflict especially married men was no longer considered a serious impediment to the fighting spirit by the time of the first world war.[4] However, the reference to enfeebled manhood points forward to the diagnosis of shell-shock and was indebted to Jean-Marie Charcot's earlier discovery that men and not just women could be subject to hysteria. However, Charcot made sure to safeguard the male ideal: in the "hystérie virile" all the phenomena associated with hysteria in women were never complete; those stricken lacked all feminine traits and were to all appearances robust men.[5] When the English physician Charles S. Meyers in 1914 first encountered shell-shock in France, he saw full well its connection to hysteria, but did not want to stigmatize British soldiers as hysterical. He suggested that the shock they received was due to the proximity of an exploding shell, an explanation which endured during the first world war.[6]

Charcot and Freud regarded all mental abnormality as largely an individual matter, but nervousness and lack of will-power had already become signs of outsiderdom, and so it was only a small step to associate such absence of true manhood with specific social groups, the more so as doctors during the war had to distinguish between the truly ill and malingerers, and in specific cases, such as homosexuality and habitual criminals, used bodily signs to establish their diagnosis.

Social prejudice helped to define illness. Just as the Jews had been accused of being especially prone to hysteria,[7] so in the English army Irishmen and lowland Scots were thought especially prone to malingering, not up to manly combat, while the "Jew count" in the German army meant to determine how many Jews were not shirkers but were actually at the front, is well-known.[8] Hysteria and nervousness became racial characteristics and at times class characteristics as well;[9] those who were well adjusted and solidly integrated into normal, established society were considered the best military material.

Shattered nerves and lack of will-power were the enemies of settled society and because men so afflicted were thought to be effeminate, they endangered the clear distinction between genders which was generally regarded as an essential cement of society. This was another aspect of social disintegration which haunted the shell-shocked. Much was expected of manly will-power in time of war, thus Colonel J. F. C. Fuller believed that "the sapping of morale by sudden or prolonged fear subordinates a man's power of will to his instinct of self-preservation and ultimately reduces him to a state in which he cannot control his emotions."[10] *The Times* of London in 1922 equated the capacity to control one's emotion with character and courage. This was not as has been claimed naive when seen in the proper context;[11] instead the necessity for such control was taken for granted by respectable citizens, and not just in England.

German psychiatrists during the war equated "war neurosis," that is shell-shock, with lack of will-power rather than reaction to the fighting. The shock of war could only cripple those who were of a weak disposition, fearful and, above all, weak of will.[12] The emphasis on will-power, already important for the maintenance of respectability in peacetime, played an important role in both England and Germany in the discussion of war neurosis, though in Germany it all but dominated the debate. The emphasis upon the power of will in both nations was to counter the threat perceived by unbridled emotion which led to a hysteria of body and mind usually associated with women. The manly image already important in peacetime was thought all the more essential in time of war.

A soldier in full control of himself, of strong power of will, would be able to cope with the experience of battle and become accustomed to the terrible sights which surrounded him in the trenches, indifferent to death. Here, the well-established belief that psychogenetic disorders arise from a lack of adaptation to circumstances reinforced the belief that those who could not cope were somehow to be considered abnormal.[13] War was the supreme test of manliness, and those who were the victims of shell-shock had failed this test. But, in as much as the manly ideal reflected the norms established society had set for itself, the shell-shocked soldier bore not only the burden of his sickness; he had also left the confines of normal society and taken on the image common to outsiders. And if such soldiers could be cured, made normal again and sent back to the front, as many physicians wished, then some of those traditionally considered society's outsiders could also gain entrance to society through a supposed reform of their comportment, manners and morals.

The fears engendered by a presumed attack on the fundamental pillars of society—strong nerves, will-power and the clear separation of sexes—all relevant to the comprehension of shell-shock, were increased by the threat of degeneration which had haunted society and culture ever since the turn of the century. Degeneration for some spread outwards from the bearer of disoriented nerves.[14] Men who seemed to suffer from nervous exhaustion were incomplete men.[15] These late-nineteenth-century notions went into the construction of shell-shock, transforming it from a battlefield disease into a social indicator. Nervousness marked all outsiders, who represented the very opposite of normative manhood, in control over both body and mind. As a report to the World Health Organization put it as late as 1994, a soldier who feels in control during battle does not develop combat stress reaction, the mental condition which was the successor to the earlier shell-shock. Such loss of control could be prevented through education to manhood—the building of character typical of an upper-class education—but also through marriage as a barrier against so-called debilitating sexual perversions. But, above all, it was the unselfish service in the name of a higher ideal which helped put a man in control of himself.[16] Such a commitment had been part of the definition of masculinity ever since this stereotype took root.

Here the nation enters, and if commitment to the nation was not necessarily regarded as a cure for nervousness by the medical establishment, the war changed such an attitude. Earlier German medical books, for example, had recommended religious commitment as a cure of nervousness, but lacked an overt appeal to nationalism,[17] and even the euphoria of German unity of 1870/71 did not bring alienists to link national and personal regeneration.[18] And yet, such firm connection could hardly be avoided in the long run, during an age of increasing nationalism, and it was for the most part the manly ideal which was used to symbolize the nation as the prime opponent of unrest and nervousness.

This ideal in its harmony and rigidly controlled power stood for national strength, dynamic and purpose, and not only in Germany. As such it contained all the attributes which, as we saw, the shell-shock lacked. The social ideal, which we have emphasized, was identical to the national ideal: the nation reflected and supported the stereotypes of normative society. And yet, the nation also fulfilled a separate function, encouraged during the war, as a firm belief-system, a secular religion in whose service modern man must place himself facing an ideal which existed outside himself. Here was a test of manliness and of the willingness to sacrifice.

Shell-shock betrayed this ideal. The context in which shell-shock was placed was closely related to the image of masculinity as we have tried to sketch it, and by way of this image it reflected not only the ideals and prejudices of normative society, but also those of the nation. Shell-shock was regarded in much of the literature as a mental state which mirrored a social disease and national degeneration.

Yet, as H. C. Marr, an experienced Scottish physician, wrote in 1919, under the pressure of battle even highly moral men can be subject to shell-shock.[19] Some, like Lord Moran, a prominent physician, while at first being dismissive about the disease, became more sympathetic during the course of the war.[20] Physicians writing about shell-shock increasingly attempted to base their diagnosis upon data rather than speculation. They debated whether a pre-disposition to nervousness was a necessary prerequisite for contracting shell-shock, and some questioned in general whether the disease fitted so comfortably into already-existing prejudices. A German physician went so far as to write that the manifestations of hysteria seen in times of war did not differ from those observed in peacetime; there will always be in a certain number of men a strong tendency to react in a pathological manner to affective experiences.[21]

But perhaps the diagnosis made in 1926 by an American psychologist, Norman Fenton, was more typical of an increasing number of physicians. He stated that it was indeed traditional to connect psychoneuroses with physical stigmata, thus confirming the importance of stereotypes in the diagnosis of shell-shock. Another physician, he continued, held that the "type known as degenerate" indicated a predisposition to shell-shock, and this type could be recognized by his physical features. However, Norman Fenton disagreed with his colleague's stereotype; in his base hospital, less than a half percent of the patients possessed anomalies or stigmata such as marked facial asymmetry, female-type breasts and pubic hair.[22] These are, of course, some of the traditional marks of unmanly men.

However, Fenton admitted that the pathological inclination of a patient to nervousness might come to light under the stress of war.[23] Most men were said to have had no prior medical history which would have made them especially sensitive to this mental disease, though such a history would have made their succumbing to shell-shock more likely. Such caution was opposed to what he called the lay perception of shell-shock as a form of hereditary insanity.[24]

While physicians like Norman Fenton attempted to demythologize shell-shock, others like Mott discussed in great detail the bodily changes, contortions, twitches and tremors supposedly associated with the disease.[25] A soldier who used the excuse of shell-shock for malingering could be exposed through an examination of his face, for its shifty contours and furtive expression were said to reflect the construction of the mind and the power of will.[26] Shades of Lavater in the diagnosis of a twentieth-century physician. And yet even Fenton, despite his criticism of those who resorted to stereotypes in order to understand a so-called abnormal mental state, could not renounce stereotypes altogether when it

came to distinguishing the malingerer from a truly shell-shocked soldier.

Physicians like Fenton attempted to limit shell-shock as a social disease, but the linkage of hysteria, nervousness and masculinity which shell-shock represented always tended to lead back to the traditional perception of insiders and outsiders, the normal and the abnormal as exemplified in their stereotype. During and even after the war, it was difficult to get away from what one English Brigadier-General simply referred to as a "disgrace."[27]

The harsh treatment of those who suffered from shell-shock was meant to cure men of their weakness and send them back to the front. While in England a more humane treatment in which the shell-shocked were regarded as patients came to replace solitary confinement and painful electric shocks, Germany continued to treat such soldiers harshly. The unspoken rationale of German war psychiatrists had been described as believing that hysterical men had consciously fled from the war into their illness and therefore must be forced to escape their illness again.[28] Hospital stays must be made as unpleasant as possible so that service at the front came to look attractive. The shell-shocked soldier must be treated like a stubborn child.[29] Even the grudging admission that there were some who could not go back to war did not keep psychiatrists from treating most of the shell-shocked as if they were shirkers.

The German Emperor summed up the general feeling at the beginning of the war when he proclaimed that those people who had the strongest nerves would win. This was the same Emperor who had remarked earlier that the Russian defeat by the Japanese in 1905 was caused by alcohol and fornication.[30] The context of real or putative social decay always provided (and still provides) one of the most congenial explanations for frightening and unwelcome social or personal developments. Here, shell-shock as a social disease could easily be used as proof of such decay.

Though at the end of the war there was widespread agreement, at least among the allied armies, that shell-shock should be classified as an illness,[31] yet shell-shock as a metaphor for unmanly behavior even here held well into the second world war, despite the great medical advances in the treatment of mental disorder. General George Patton's behavior in the second world war towards soldiers who seemed to be malingering, even though they suffered from battle neurosis, reflected the cruder attitudes toward shell-shock. He cursed them as cowards and even attacked them physically.[32] And yet, General Eisenhower as commander-in-chief now expressed "disgust" at such behavior,[33] and the subsequent outcry against Patton's actions may have signaled a change in the public perception of shell-shock. But it was General Omar Bradley's order of 1943 that breakdown in combat be regarded as exhaustion, which helped to put to rest the idea that only those men who were mentally weak, "the unmanly men," collapsed under stress in combat.[34]

However, as German psychiatrists acted with even more rather than less harshness as the 1914–1918 war came to a close, the same diagnosis which had been applied to the shell-shocked was now applied to those who led the revolutions after the lost war. They, in turn, were branded of weak will (somewhat astounding for revolutionaries), as well as of a hysterical disposition.[35] Here in Germany a line can be drawn from the wartime perception of shell-shock to the postwar defamation of left-wing and racial enemies. They also were suffering from the same unpatriotic social disease, except that if they were of an inferior race there was no cure.

Just as shell-shock was the consequence of a new kind of industrial warfare, so it was thought to be a mental and bodily condition which transcended the war and its time. Public attitudes, and not just in Germany, changed slowly because a specific mental condition was perceived as a social disease. Moreover, stereotypes as lasting mental images are difficult to change, and the perception of shell-shock was based upon stereotypes of manliness, of outsider and insider, which were rooted in society long before the war, but which the conditions of modern warfare seemed to have confirmed and passed, strengthened, into the crises of the postwar world.

NOTES

1. I.e., George L. Mosse, *The Image of Man* (New York 1996), passim.
2. Sander L. Gilman, *Seeing the Insane* (New York 1982), 92.
3. Ted Bogacz, "War Neurosis and Cultural Change in England 1914–1922: The Work of the War Office Committee of Enquiry into 'Shell-Shock,'" *Journal of Contemporary History*, 24, 2 (April 1989), 231.
4. Ted Bogacz, "War Neurosis and Cultural Change in England 1914–1922: The Work of the War Office Committee of Enquiry into 'Shell-Shock,'" *Journal of Contemporary History*, 24, 2 (April 1989), 231.
5. Mosse, op. cit., 84–5.
6. Elaine Showalter, *Hystories* (New York 1997), 72.
7. Sander L. Gilman, *Freud, Race and Gender* (Princeton, NJ 1993), 87.
8. Joanna Bourke, *Dismembering the Male* (Chicago, IL 1996), 90–1.
9. Joanna Bourke, *Dismembering the Male* (Chicago, IL 1996), 112.
10. "Virginia Woolf's Septimus Smith and Contemporary Perceptions of Shell-Shock," *English Language Notes*, 25, 1 (September 1987), 52.
11. "Virginia Woolf's Septimus Smith and Contemporary Perceptions of Shell-Shock," *English Language Notes*, 25, 1 (September 1987), 52.
12. Peter Riedesser and Axel Verderber, *"Maschinengewehre hinter der Front": zur Geschichte der deutschen Militärpsychiatrie* (Frankfurt a. Main 1996), 35.
13. Chris Feudtner, "Minds the Dead have Ravished," *History of Science*, vol. 31, part 4 (1992), 401.
14. Janet Oppenheim, *Shattered Nerves* (New York 1991), 276.
15. Janet Oppenheim, *Shattered Nerves* (New York 1991), 153.
16. "Combat Stress Reactions," *World Health*, 47, 2 (1994), 24ff.
17. Joachim Radkau, *Das Zeitalter der Nervosität* (München 1998), 366.
18. Joachim Radkau, *Das Zeitalter der Nervosität* (München 1998), 335.
19. H. C. Marr, *Psychoses of the War* (London 1919), 48.
20. David Cohen, "A War of Nerves," *New Scientist* (9 March 1991), 43.
21. Edwald Stier, quoted in Fred W. Mott, *Neuroses and Shell Shock* (London 1919), 111.

22. Norman Fenton, *Shell Shock and Its Aftermath* (St. Louis 1926), 57.

23. Norman Fenton, *Shell Shock and Its Aftermath* (St. Louis 1926), 53.

24. Norman Fenton, *Shell Shock and Its Aftermath* (St. Louis 1926), 87.

25. Mott, op. cit., passim.

26. Mott, quoted in Fenton, op. cit., 217–18.

27. Cohen, op. cit., 43.

28. Riedesser and Verderber, op. cit., 44, 48.

29. Riedesser and Verderber, op. cit., 81ff.

30. Radkau, op. cit., 405.

31. Richard Holmes, *Acts of War. The Behaviour of Men in Battle* (New York 1985), 257.

32. Showalter, op. cit., 74–5.

33. Roger J. Spiller, "Shell Shock," *American Heritage,* 41, 4 (1990), 86.

34. Roger J. Spiller, "Shell Shock," *American Heritage,* 41, 4 (1990), 86.

35. Riedesser and Verderber, op. cit., 81ff.

BARBARA EHRENREICH

6. BREADWINNERS AND LOSERS: SANCTIONS AGAINST MALE DEVIANCE

[. . .]

Few men would admit to marrying for reasons other than love or domestic incompetence. Yet as late as 1966, a leading American psychoanalyst and writer, Dr. Hendrik Ruitenbeek, observed that

> Contemporary America seems to have no room for the mature bachelor. As a colleague of mine once remarked, a single man over thirty is now regarded as a pervert, a person with severe emotional problems, or a poor creature fettered to mother. (Ruitenbeek 1966: 12)

The average age of marriage for men in the late fifties was twenty-three, and according to popular wisdom, if a man held out much longer, say even to twenty-seven, "you had to wonder." Psychiatrists like Dr. Ruitenbeek and his colleagues were hardly aloof from the popular prejudice against "overaged," unmarried men, however. By the 1950s and '60s psychiatry had developed a massive weight of theory establishing that marriage—and, within that, the breadwinner role—was the only normal state for the adult male. Outside lay only a range of diagnoses, all unflattering.

On the face of it, the construction of a scientific justification for the male breadwinner role was a somewhat more challenging enterprise than explaining why little girls necessarily grew up to be wives and mothers. For women, biology was more clearly destiny, and Freudians had no trouble navigating the developmental passage from the first menses to baby showers and PTA membership. It was more difficult to trace how the possession of a penis should lead its owner into a middle-management career and Little League weekends. This was the task that psychoanalyst

Therese Benedek (1970) set for herself in her study of "Fatherhood and Providing." [. . .]

Benedek's hypothesis was that the conventional male role, like that of the female, has "instinctual roots." With women, things were straightforward, since "mothering behavior is regulated by a pituitary hormone." In the case of men, no fathering/providing hormone was, as yet, "recognizable" so she cited this exemplary behavior of male birds and certain species of fish who, unlike most male mammals, show a nurturant interest in their young. [. . .]

Furthermore, providing was linked to the male's "instinctual drive for survival," and the evidence for this was that men prefer male children; i.e., children who seem to be extensions of themselves. [. . .] As if sensing the sociological quagmire she had opened up, Benedek made a final appeal to history. "All significant cultures," she wrote, "have developed on the basis that the husband-father is the chief protector and provider of the family." [. . .]

But neither these ingrained habits nor the avian instincts were 100 percent reliable, and, in describing the male "failures" Benedek unwittingly opened the door to a more voluntaristic account of male behavior. "We know men often avoid marriage and parenthood," she wrote. [. . .] But she did not ascribe their failure—as her own theory would have required—to an insufficient nesting instinct or the heritage of an "insignificant" culture or similar accident of fate. Men who rejected the provider role were, in her final judgment, simply "afraid of the responsibilities involved" (Benedek 1970: 167).

Most psychologists and psychoanalysts rejected biology in favor of a less deterministic and more strenuous account of man's ascent to the breadwinner role. In the 1950s Erik Erikson had introduced the idea of the "life cycle," punctuated by crises and culminating, if all went well, in a state of maturity. This was a departure from Freud, who had concentrated all the critical psychological dramas in the preschool years (a choice that, incidentally, was important in reinforcing the need for full-time mothering until a woman's youngest child was at least six years old). [. . .] Erikson not only extended the psychoanalytically interesting life span, but introduced new elements of responsibility and choice. A person could perform the developmental "tasks" required to move from one stage of the life cycle to the next, or he or she could get stuck and fail to advance toward maturity. Nowhere did Erikson specify the precise content of the various stages of occupational terms (though his scheme bears a certain resemblance to the career trajectory of a successful college professor). But "maturity" and the "tasks" which led to it quickly entered the psychologists' vocabulary as professional code words for conformity.

It is difficult, in the way of the sixties' youth rebellion, to appreciate the weight and authority that once attached to the word "maturity." Looking back on his first marriage in the 1950s, A. Alvarez wrote in 1981, "I had this terrible lust for premature maturity, this irresponsible desire for responsibility, before I had any idea what maturity involved or had ever tasted the pleasures of youthful irresponsibility." Maturity was not dull, but "heroic," a measured acceptance of the limits of one's private endeavors at a time when action on a broader political scale could only seem foolish—or suspect. Novels like *The Man in the Gray Flannel Suit* and *Marjorie Morningstar* endorsed maturity, and the 1960 best seller *The Mature Mind* held it up as an evolutionary achievement. [. . .]

Maturity itself required predictable, sober ingredients of wisdom, responsibility, empathy, (mature) heterosexuality and "a sense of function," or, as a sociologist would have put it, acceptance of adult sex roles. Thus, a woman would be immature "if she wants all the advantages of marriage" but resents doing housework, and a man would be less-than-grown-up if he shirked the breadwinner role:

> . . . a man is immature if he regards the support of a family as a kind of trap in which he, an unsuspecting male, has somehow been caught. (Overstreet 1950)

How did a man attain maturity? In 1953 the psychologist R. J. Havighurst discovered eight "developmental tasks of early adulthood," the performance of which was a prerequisite for mature adulthood. The list, which was to be repeated in developmental psychology textbooks for nearly three decades, included: (1) selecting a mate, (2) learning to live with a marriage partner, (3) starting a family, (4) rearing children, (5) managing a home, (6) getting started in an occupation, (7) taking on civic responsibilities and (8) finding a congenial social group. In the developmental psychology literature of the 1950s, it would not take too much supplementary reading to figure out that tasks 4 and 5 are the special responsibility of the female marriage partner, and that 6 was the special province of the male.

The fact that the developmental tasks "discovered" by psychologists so closely paralleled the expectations one might find in the *Reader's Digest* seemed only to enhance their scientific status. One textbook in developmental psychology reassures the student that the tasks about to be listed will be no surprise, since "social expectations for the young adult in our culture are clearly defined and familiar to him even before he reaches legal maturity" (Hurlock 1975 [1959]: 209). [. . .] Others—and these are texts still widely read by social work students and others in the helping professions—offered more detailed psychological insights into challenges of adult life, such as: "The prompt payment of bills demands a degree of perspective and maturity" (Pikunus 1969: 333).

Marriage was not only a proof of maturity, it was a chance to exercise one's maturity through countless new "tasks." Men as well as women were to build a "working partnership," overcome romance for "a realistic conception of marriage" and seek a mutual state of "emotional maturity." Even love required discipline and maturity. "Love in marriage has to be worked at," counseled a 1962 marriage manual. "Both the giving part and the receiving part have to be worked at. The last part may sound strange because we ordinarily think that the receiving part will take care of itself. It doesn't though, any more than the giving part" (Baruch and Miller 1962: 12). [. . .]

Outside of their marital endeavors, men had the ongoing opportunity to demonstrate their maturity by actually working at a paid job. This is what grown men did and what social scientists and psychologists, in turn, observed them doing. "It is perhaps not too much to say," Talcott Parsons said with all the caution of a scientist who is about to reveal a startling new observation about the natural world, "that only in very exceptional cases can an adult man be genuinely self-respecting and enjoy a respected status in the eyes of others if he does not 'earn a living' in an approved occupational role" (Parsons 1949: 273). If the obligatory combination of marriage and job added up to a less-than-heroic definition of manhood, there were compensations. [. . .]

If adult masculinity was indistinguishable from the breadwinner role, then it followed that the man who failed to achieve this role was either not fully adult or not fully masculine. In the schema of male pathology developed by mid-century psychologists, immaturity shaded into infantilism, which was, in turn, a manifestation of unnatural fixation on the mother, and the entire complex of symptomatology reached its clinical climax in the diagnosis of homosexuality. Empirical findings were offered to support these judgments. In 1955 sociologist Manfred Kuhn reported eleven reasons for people's failure to marry. Some were simply misfortunes, such as "poor health or deviant physical characteristics," "unattractiveness," and extreme geographical isolation. But high on the list for men were homosexuality, emotion fixation on parent(s) and "unwillingness to assume responsibility" (Kuhn 1955). Dr. Paul Popenoe, whose suspenseful case studies entitled "Can This Marriage Be Saved?" appeared regularly in the *Ladies' Home Journal*, blamed bachelorhood on "emotional immaturity and infantile fixations." He reported that studies at his American Institute for Family Relations "bear out the popular opinion that a mother-fixation is responsible for the celibacy of many old bachelors who might otherwise have been superior husbands." [. . .]

Clinicians' reactions to men who actually cracked under the strain of breadwinning were, predictably, unsympathetic. The period immediately after the birth of a baby was especially likely to precipitate infantile and/or homosexual behavior in men who had only superficially accepted their responsibilities as breadwinners. A 1966 paper in the *American Journal of Psychiatry* presents ten case histories of men who required hospitalization for their post-partum breakdowns (Wainwright 1966: 40). The case of a twenty-nine-year-old securities analyst is presented as an illustration of how financial responsibility can be "the initial precipitant of a psychoneurotic illness, with latent homosexual features playing an important dynamic role." During his wife's pregnancy he had "expressed some doubts about the added financial burden," and

> In a group of company executives he began to experience periodic anxiety attacks characterized by tachycardia, apprehension, marked perspiration, and anal paresthesias. He functioned well, however, until his wife gave birth to a son. He then became preoccupied with rapidly falling quotations on a recent stock purchase and considered killing his wife and himself.

The possibility that he hated his job and harbored inadmissible feelings toward the company executives, rather than his baby, was not explored.

In another case, a twenty-nine-year-old mathematician, who had long been anxious about his job, collapsed after the birth of his fourth child, and was coldly labeled a "paranoid schizophreniac." Others of the unfortunate fathers studied were described as "acting out"—spending money foolishly, having affairs, drinking to excess, claiming to have developed an incurable disease or other forms of infantile and dependent behavior.

The occasional patient who found more articulate, less destructive ways to express his rebellion was not so easily labeled as "infantile." At least, not quite so easily. In a case from the above study, which is also featured in a major text on *Personality Development and Deviation*, we find a young scientist who, whenever the subject of parenthood came up

> . . . brought up his ardent wish for a racing car, which he did not need and could not afford. He brought it up each time his wife pleaded for a pregnancy. He gradually agreed that he would like to have a son, but that he would antagonize his Greek Orthodox parents by not baptizing his son and by naming him Darwin. (Jessner, Weigert, and Foy 1975: 214).

Could this clear break from his own parents be taken as a sign of mature "individuation"? No, he was actually revealing "infantile dependence," rather than the "mature dependency" which would have been evinced among other things, by promising a proper baptism. In the wisdom of mid-century psychology, "the rebellious person is also an immature person," just as certainly as was the sissified bachelor who could not part from his mother.

The difficulty in dealing with male rebelliousness, either on the scale of the individual, or as some psychiatrists feared, of the epidemic, was that it did have a certain seductive appeal. Women, too, were supposed to renounce many pleasures on the route to mature femininity—such as clitoral sexuality and petty career ambitions. No psychiatrist doubted, though, that the satisfactions of childbearing and mature vaginal sexuality would make up for these developmental sacrifices. Any lingering inconsistencies could be accounted for by the theory of female masochism, which conveniently transmuted the sufferings associated with the female sex role into pleasure. But men had no known capacity for masochism, just as they had no reliable instinctual drive to marry, hold down jobs, and acquire life insurance policies. While a woman would be driven by the hormones to plead for a baby, a man, like the scientist in the case above, could imagine the alternative of a racing car. It was hard for even a mature psychoanalyst not to show a flash of empathy for his sex. "The male in our society is essentially a lonely being," Dr. Hendrik Ruitenbeek observed in 1963, "deprived of any real goal except that of acquiring the skills needed to make money enough to 'settle down' into an existence which he accepts rather than chooses" (Ruitenbeek 1963: 80).

In an essay that must stand as a monument to psychoanalytic ambivalence, Kenneth Lynn began by indicting all the classics of American literature as tracts for male immaturity. Rip Van Winkle was not a harmless, befuddled old man; his twenty-year sleep was a deliberate escape from "the hateful responsibilities of work and marriage." Henry Thoreau was another "escapist," unable to adjust to the "quietly desperate world of work and marriage." "Almost every episode of *Walden* reveals," according to Lynn's

reading, "an astonishing immaturity." This is the basic American character defect:

> . . . psychic immaturity. I say psychic immaturity because one of the signs of an undeveloped personality is the failure to recognize that serious personal and social problems cannot be solved by running away from them. (Lynn 1976)

Only women writers had been exempt from this psychic immaturity, simply because it was so much harder for them to "throw over their responsibilities and walk out, slamming the door behind them." But when he came to explaining the childishness of America's male writers, Lynn suddenly softened. "The endless process of competing had become a wakening nightmare," he said, "why should [men] continue to carry intolerable burdens, when they could just as easily walk out the door and start life all over somewhere else?" (Lynn 1976: 237).

The ultimate reason why a man would not just "walk out the door" was the taint of homosexuality which was likely to follow him. Homosexuality, as the psychiatrists saw it, was the ultimate escapism. Asking himself what was the root problem afflicting male homosexuals, the distinguished psychoanalyst Dr. Abram Kardiner answered:

> They cannot compete. They also surrender in the face of impending combat. This has nothing to do with their actual ability, for many of them have extraordinary talent . . . These are men who are overwhelmed by the increasing demands to fulfill the specifications of masculinity. (Kardiner 1963: 80)

These "specifications" had become so detailed and so rigid that, according to Dr. Ruitenbeek, "it is not surprising to find an increasing number of men accepting homosexuality as a way out." Women were not tempted by a parallel perversion because they already had a relatively easy life: their "social-role expectations" were clearly "less demanding." (And, in case this all sounded suspiciously like an endorsement of male homosexuality, the psychiatrist hastened to add that the homosexual life was hardly a restful retreat, since it entails "compulsive sexual acting out.")

In psychiatric theory and in popular culture, the image of the irresponsible male blurred into the shadowy figure of the homosexual. Men who failed as breadwinners and husbands were "immature," while homosexuals were, in psychiatric judgment, "aspirants to perpetual adolescence." So great was the potential overlap between the sexually "normal," but not entirely successful man, and the blatant homosexual that psychoanalyst Lionel Ovesey had to create a new category—"pseudohomosexuality"—to absorb the intermediate cases. There was no "sexual component" to the pseudohomosexual's deviance, at least not if caught at an early stage. Rather, he suffered from some "adaptive failure" to meet the standards of masculine conformity, and had begun a subconscious slide toward a homosexual identity:

> . . . any adaptive failure—sexual, social, or vocational— may be perceived as a failure in the masculine role and, which is worse, may be symbolically extended through an equation that is calculated only to intensify the anxiety incident to the failure. This equation is the following: *I am a failure = I am castrated = I am not a man = I am a woman = I am a homosexual.* (Ovesey 1969: 24–25)

From here it was a short step to becoming an "overt homosexual," a man battered by so many adaptive failures that he "gives up all pretense of meeting the requirements of the masculine role."

If pseudohomosexuals could be treated by helping them overcome their adaptive failures, so could the overt homosexuals, since the two types were just at different points on the axis of masculine adaptation. Ovesey cites the case of an "overt" type whose homosexuality was just one part of a larger pattern of social deviance. The physical indications were promising; the patient was "23 years old, over six feet tall, good-looking, and completely masculine in his appearance." However,

> He lived alone and his social existence was a chaotic one, characterized by impulsive midnight swims and hitchhiking. He considered this made him quite unique and he was proud to be known as a bohemian. (1969: 137)

Furthermore, he showed no interest in a career, and supported himself as a stock clerk. The treatment (it is not told how he financed it) was both lengthy and stern. "The patient was treated twice a week, at first sitting up for 49 sessions, then on the couch for a total of 268 sessions over a 3½-year period. . . . When, early in the therapy, he hopefully suggested that his homosexuality might be inherited and hence not amenable to treatment, he was told in a forthright manner that this was not so" (Ovesey 1969: 139–140). In Ovesey's hands, the patient made speedy progress. By the end of the first year he had given up hitchhiking and midnight swims, enrolled in evening college courses and gotten a more acceptable middle-class job. Eventually he married and fathered a son. With the developmental tasks accomplished, the case could be closed, and Ovesey must have been pleased that his equation checked out in reverse: I am not a failure = I am a man = I am heterosexual.

It is hard to see whom the equation hurt more— the actual homosexual or the "failed" heterosexual. In association with "failure," the homosexual's sexual practices became admissions of defeat; while in association with homosexual sex, failure was meant to be doubly humiliating. [. . .] Fear of homosexuality kept heterosexual men in line as husbands and breadwinners; and, at the same time, the association with failure and immaturity made it almost impossible for homosexual men to assert a positive image of themselves. Underlying both sets of sanctions was, of course, contempt for women [. . .]. To be hunted by bill collectors (one consequence of adaptive failure as a breadwinner) was like being penetrated by other men's penises: both were conditions in which a man was like a woman. Since a man couldn't actually become a woman [. . .], heterosexual failures and overt homosexuals could only be understood as living in a state of constant deception. And this was perhaps the most despicable thing about them: they *looked like* men, but they weren't really men.

Near the end of *When She Was Good*, Roy Bassart finally abandons the dreary, uphill work of marriage and escapes to his parental home. Lucy now delivers her final denunciation of her feckless husband—not to him directly (he is afraid to come to the phone) but to his mother:

> But he tricked *me*, Alice! Tricked me to think he was a man, when he's a mouse, a monster! A moron! He's a pansy, that's what your son is, the worst and weakest pansy there ever was! (Ovesey 1969: 293)

In *Marjorie Morningstar*, the melodramatic best seller of the fifties, Herman Wouk passed a similar judgment on the errant male. Noel Airman is the great love of Marjorie's life and the object of her marital ambitions. He is everything that the earnest, stagestruck young woman might want, and everything her parents want her to avoid: glamorous, irreverent, vain ("Airman" is his fluffy, Anglicized version of Erhman), irresponsible and bohemian. For five hundred pages she pursues him while he dashes between Greenwich Village, Mexico, Casablanca and Paris. She is dogged; he wavers between defiance and submission, even promising at one point to settle down to a corporate job. For a while their affair blossoms; then they break up with him marveling at "the narrowness of my escape." Reunited, Marjorie continues to press for a commitment; she is, after all, pushing twenty-four, and her thin talents have gotten her nowhere on Broadway. Again Noel escapes, leaving her with a punishing twenty-page denunciation of her bourgeois ambitions and the announcement that "I will not be driven on and on to that looming goal, a love nest in the suburbs. I WANT NO PART OF IT OR OF YOU, do you understand?" But what Noel doesn't understand is that time is running out for him, too; unfulfilled developmental tasks are piling up and the chance of achieving maturity is slipping away. When Marjorie tracks him down for the last time, in an apartment on the left bank of Paris, it is already too late for Noel; irresponsibility has taken its inevitable course to emasculation.

In the scene that is the denouement of their long and one-sided affair, Noel professes to be ready at least to settle down.

> I'm ready to quit, Marjorie. That should be good news to you. All I want is to be a dull bourgeois. I've finally and irrevocably realized that nothing a man can do can make him stay twenty-two forever. But more important than that, and this is what's decisive, I've decided that twenty-two gets to be a disgustingly boring age after a while. Staying up all hours, sleeping around, guzzling champagne, being oh so crazy, oh so gay, is a damned damned damned damned BORE . . . I want to get some dull reliable job in some dull reliable advertising agency, and I want to drudge like a Boy Scout, nine to five, five days a week. (Wouk 1955: 530)

This is the good news; the bad news is the new Noel. He chatters away just a little too gayly, flitting from restaurant prices, to the lotions he uses to restore his slightly receding hairline, to the source of Marjorie's new suit. He has become suspiciously domestic. In his Greenwich Village days, "he had been a competent slapdash cook . . . with a couple of specialties like spaghetti and southern fried chicken, dished up any old way. But all that was changed." Now he dons a well-worn apron and applies himself to preparing and serving a multicourse, haute cuisine meal. "Noel made a distinctly odd figure, scrambling into the kitchen, serving the food," Marjorie notes with discomfort. "He was quick and disconcertingly smooth at serving and removing the dishes."

The reason for his new attention to culinary detail soon emerges. He is being kept, in a sexually ambiguous relationship, by a square-jawed German woman with the ominous surname of Oberman. "What's the difference," he rationalizes to Marjorie, "whether the man owns the apartment and the woman cooks or the other way around?" If he doesn't know how the answer to that one, in a novel published in 1955, he is clearly lost. Marjorie can forgive him for his domineering Aryan roommate, but not for his chicken in burgundy sauce. She rushes home, marries the first nice, stably employed Jewish man she meets and settles into New Rochelle to nurse her nostalgia. Noel, still broke and with no prospects, goes on cooking for Ms. Oberman. But even while thousands of co-eds were sighing over Noel's fate, other men were preparing to succeed where he had failed: to break with the responsibilities of breadwinning without, somehow, losing their manhood.

REFERENCES

Baruch, Ph.D., Dorothy Walter, and Hyman Miller, M.D. 1962. *Sex in Marriage*. New York: Hart Publishing Company.

Benedek, Therese. 1970. "Fatherhood and Providing." In *Parenthood: Its Psychology and Psychopathology*, edited by Anthony and Therese Benedek, 167–184. Boston: Little Brown & Co.

Ehrenreich, Barbara. 1983. *The Hearts of Men: American Dreams and the Flight from Commitment*. New York, NY: Anchor Books.

Hurlock, Elizabeth B. 1975 [1959]. *Developmental Psychology*. New York: McGraw–Hill International Book Company.

Jessner, Lucie, Edith Weigert, and James L. Foy. 1975. "The Development of Parental Attitudes during Pregnancy." In *Personality Development and Deviation: A Textbook for Social Work*, edited by George H. Weiderman, M.D. and Summer Matison. New York: International Universities Press.

Kardiner, Abram. 1963. "The Flight from Masculinity." In *The Problem of Homosexuality*, edited by Henrik M. Ruitenbeek. New York: E. P. Dutton, Inc.

Kuhn, Manfred. 1955. "How Mates Are Sorted." In *Family, Marriage and Parenthood*, edited by Howard Becker and Reuben Hill. Boston: Health Books.

Lynn, Kenneth S. 1976. "Adulthood in American Literature." In *Adulthood*, edited by Erik Erikson. New York: W. W. Norton and Company.

Overstreet, H. A. 1950. *The Mature Mind*. New York: W. W. Norton and Company.

Ovesey, M.D., Lionel. 1969. *Homosexuality and Pseudohomosexuality*. New York: Science House.

Parsons, Talcott. 1949. "Age and Sex in the Social Structure of the United States." In *Personality in Nature, Society and Culture*, edited by Clyde Kluckhohn and Henry A. Murray. New York: Alfred A. Knopf, Inc.

Pikunus, Justin. 1969. *Human Development: A Science of Growth*. New York: McGraw–Hill International Book Company.

Ruitenbeek, Hendrik M. 1963. "Men Alone: The Male Homosexual and the Disintegrated Family." In *The Problem of Homosexuality*, edited by Henrik M. Ruitenbeek. New York: E. P. Dutton, Inc.

Ruitenbeek, Dr. Hendrik M. 1966. *Psychoanalysis and Male Sexuality*. New Haven, CT: College and University Press.

Wainwright, M.D., William H. 1966. "Fatherhood as a Precipitant of Mental Illness." *American Journal of Psychiatry* 123(1): 40–44.

Wouk, Herman. 1955. *Marjorie Morningstar*. Garden City, NY: Doubleday & Company, Inc.

MICHAEL KIMMEL

7. GUYLAND: GENDERING THE TRANSITION TO ADULTHOOD

The period between childhood and adulthood has been expanding for centuries. "Our society has passed from a period which was ignorant of adolescence to a period in which adolescence is the favorite age," wrote the French historian Philippe Ariès (1962: 30).[1] "We now want to come to it early and linger in it as long as possible."

Recently a body of research has emerged that expands this stage of development beyond the boundaries of what had been considered adolescence. Drawing on current empirical research on postadolescent development, a new group of social and behavioral scientists have identified what they call the "transition to adulthood." Although this new body of research has mapped the broadest parameters of this stage of development, the initial analytic forays have been astonishingly lacking in any analysis of gender. This lacuna is more striking because it is during the transition to adulthood that gender plays perhaps its most central role. To understand this new stage and to better map its gendered topography, it makes some sense to begin by remembering how deeply gendered was the initial study of adolescence.

THE INVENTION OF ADOLESCENCE

In 1904, G. Stanley Hall published his massive two-volume tome, *Adolescence: Its Psychology and Its Relations to Physiology, Anthropology, Sociology, Sex, Crime, Religion, and Education*. Almost immediately, the word *adolescence* entered the common vocabulary to describe a stage of development poised anxiously between childhood puerility and adult virility. Hall saw adolescence, roughly coincident with the biological changes

of puberty (ages 12–15), as a time of transition—a time when boys and girls develop their adult identity, test themselves, and find out who they really are.

No one could accuse Hall of failing to pay attention to gender. He was preoccupied with it. While he was generally eager to shield adolescents from entering the adult world prematurely, his chief interest was in boys' development. Concerned that boys were becoming feminized, in part by overprotective mothers and largely because of the increasingly coeducational environment of school and church, Hall wanted to rescue boys—from both the feminizing tendencies of girls and the enervating world of work, hoping that adolescent boys could be immersed in supportive, controlled, adult-monitored homosocial environments. Hall opposed coeducation, which he believed turned boys gay as it "diluted the mystic attraction of the opposite sex," and proposed a host of masculinity-building activities like sports, vigorous exertion in the outdoors, and even fighting and bullying others. He championed the Boy Scouts (founded in 1910) and the YMCA (founded in 1844 and revamped in the early 1900s) as vehicles to stem the tide of enervation.[2]

Hall generalized to all adolescents from only a tiny fraction of America's youth. When his book was published, only 6% of American teenagers actually graduated from high school. By contrast, 18% of youth between 10 and 14 worked in factories or stores, and millions more were working on family farms. But Hall was on to something important. In the first decades of the twentieth century, the structural foundations of a prolonged adolescence were established, as an industrializing nation sought to stabilize its progress. Apprenticeships declined and child labor laws pushed young people out of the labor force. Compulsory education laws gave them someplace else to go if they couldn't work.

High school became the single defining experience for children of the middle and professional classes. While as late as 1920, only 16% of 17-year-old males had graduated from high school, by 1936 the majority of American teenagers attended high school. A new high school opened every day for the first 30 years of the century.[3]

With the increased universality of high school, a new word, "teenager," entered the American vocabulary in 1941, on the eve of our entrance into World War II. Critics worried that this "sudden and dramatic prolongation of adolescence" meant that over half of those who had "passed the terminal age of adolescence" were not acting as adults—physically, socially, economically, as E. C. Cline, the high school principal in Richmond, Indiana, worried.[4]

And Americans have been worrying about teenagers ever since. Some worried about teen sexuality, especially after the publication of the two volumes of Kinsey's studies of American sexual behavior. Some worried about "juvenile delinquency," another new term from the era—lonely disaffected boys who sought the approval of their fellows by participating in increasingly dangerous stunts and petty crime. "Let's Face It" read the cover of *Newsweek* in 1956, "Our Teenagers Are Out of Control." Many youths, the magazine reported, "got their fun" by "torturing helpless old men and horsewhipping girls they waylaid in public parks."

By the 1950s, many cultural critics followed Hall's lead and blamed mothers—works by Philip Wylie and Edward Strecker identified "momism" as the cultural illness that resulted in emasculated boys and henpecked husbands. Others blamed the absent or emasculated fathers, the men in the grey flannel suits, like Jim Backus in *Rebel without a Cause*; its author, Robert Lindner, argued that "almost every symptom that delineates the psychopath clinically is to be found increasingly in the contemporary adolescent."[5]

TWO BREAKTHROUGHS IN PSYCHOLOGY AND SOCIOLOGY

Into this cultural controversy stepped psychologist Erik H. Erikson and sociologist James Coleman.

Taken together, their writings helped to normalize adolescence, to neutralize and naturalize it. In his path-breaking book, *Childhood and Society* (1950) and later in *Identity: Youth and Crisis* (1968), Erikson identified the seven life-stages of individual psychological development that became a mantra in Developmental Psychology classes for decades. By labeling adolescence as a "moratorium"—a sort of prolonged time-out between childhood and adulthood—Erikson tamed and sanitized Hall's fears that adolescence was a maelstrom, a chaos of uncontrolled passions.

To Erikson, the moratorium of adolescence was a time for regrouping, reassessing, and regenerating oneself before undertaking the final quest for adult identity, "a vital regenerator in the process of social evolution," as he put it. Rather than rushing headlong into work and family lives, as children did in earlier societies, adolescents slow down the process to accomplish certain identity tasks. The venerable institutions that structured a young person's socialization—family, church, school—began to recede in their importance as the adolescent began to strike out on his or her own, plagued by doubts, taking tentative steps towards autonomy, and faced with a set of adult responsibilities looming ominously ahead.[6]

In his treatise, *The Adolescent Society* (1961), sociologist James Coleman had a somewhat less sanguine view of the displacement of education, religion, and family as the primary institutions of socialization. He noticed in high schools that teachers and administrators had lost most of their credibility as agents of socialization—they were more like agents of repression, as far as the kids were concerned. Parental scrutiny waned, and the influence of religion dissipated. As a result, he argued, adolescents developed a distinct peer culture, toward which they oriented their activities and from which they derived their sense of identity. Anti-intellectualism abounded, sports reigned supreme, and everyone wanted to be popular! Hardly tremulous individualists, Coleman saw adolescents as frighteningly dependent on peer culture, and boys, especially, desperate to prove their masculinity in the eyes of other boys.[7]

By the 1960s and 1970s, observers had a more optimistic view of late adolescence. While many shared Coleman's sense that peer groups had replaced parents as the primary source of socialization, they saw this simply as the attenuation of socialization, not its resolution. Indeed, Yale psychoanalyst Kenneth Keniston warned in 1971 that if the "conformity to peer group norms merely replaces conformity to parental norms . . . adolescent development is foreclosed before real self-regulation and independence are achieved." Reliance on peers was just another late hurdle on the way to autonomy and adulthood.[8]

As we will see, contemporary psychologists have tended to follow Erikson and Keniston. And, as we will see, Coleman was far more prescient.

POSTWAR ADOLESCENCE AS ANOMALY

One problem with Erikson and others' theories of adolescence was that although they insisted that they described eternal—or at least reliably consistent historical—trajectories, they were written during a period that is now understood to have been anomalous. The immediate postwar era was, in many ways, an era utterly unlike our own. It's the stuff of nostalgic longings, and the screen against which we often project our anxieties about the contemporary era.[9]

For adolescents, the period was no less anomalous. It was the only time when all the developmental markers were in perfect alignment with all the social and institutional frameworks in which development takes place. Those developmental psychological indicators—increased autonomy, the capacity for intimacy, a commitment to a career and the development of a life plan—all coincided with the social and cultural markers that have typically denoted adulthood.

How different that world seems now—and how different were the motivations of men and women who were in the 18–26 age group. For one thing, Americans had just emerged from a calamitous war, in which millions of young men had been killed or wounded. The generation of men that came of age in 1950 had just experienced the horrors of the beaches in Normandy or the South Pacific, the randomness of death and destruction as the guys next to them were gunned down. They couldn't wait to get married, settle down into stable adulthood, to forget the terrors of war, to silence their nightmares. They rushed into careers, married their high school sweethearts, moved to the suburbs, and started their families. The

housing boom spurred by rapid suburbanization was accompanied by an education boom and a baby boom. No wonder the "Greatest Generation" almost instantly morphed into the bland conformity of the "man in the gray flannel suit."

ADOLESCENCE STARTS EARLIER AND ENDS LATER

Adolescence today stretches out in both directions; it starts earlier and ends later. Children are becoming adolescents earlier and earlier, both biologically and socially. Typically we mark adolescence by the onset of puberty—which today occurs 4–5 years earlier than it did in the mid-nineteenth century. Improvements in nutrition, sanitation, and health care have lowered the average age of puberty about one year for every 25 years of development. Each generation enters puberty about a year earlier than its predecessor. In the years just before the Civil War, the average age for the onset of puberty was 16 for girls and 18 for boys; today it is about 12 for girls and 14 for boys.

Since the average age of marriage in the mid-nineteenth century was about the same—16 for girls and 18 for boys—there was really no "stage of development" during which time a youth was both single and sexually active. It wouldn't be farfetched to say that before the twentieth century, there were no "teenagers" in America.

But just as adolescence reaches us earlier and earlier, it also seems to stretch longer and longer. Biologically, just as puberty is beginning at earlier ages, full physiological maturation doesn't take place until well into our 20s. At 18, neuropsychological development is far from complete; the brain continues to grow and develop into the early 20s. In a bit of a stretch, one biologist suggests that this immature brain lacks the "wiring" for placing long-term benefits over shorter-term gains, which explains how we are "hard-wired" for high-risk behaviors like drug taking, smoking, and drinking.[10]

Young people today seem almost determined not to grow up too fast, to give the lie to George Bernard Shaw's famous dictum that "youth is wasted on the young." They may move directly from the "crisis" of adolescence to their "quarter-life crisis" and right into a "mid-life crisis" without ever having settled into a stage of life that wasn't a crisis!

Over the past two years, I interviewed about 400 college students at more than 40 colleges and universities across the United States. While in no way a nationally representative sample, my interviews provide compelling empirical evidence of the transition to adulthood as a new and previously unnoticed stage of development poised between adolescence and adulthood, and the ways that it is deeply and determinatively gendered.

"I feel like my whole life has been one long exercise in delayed gratification," says Matt, a graduate student in psychology at University of Wisconsin:

> I mean, in high school, I had to get good grades, study hard, and do a bunch of extracurricular things so I could get into a good college. OK, I did that. Went to Brown. Then, in college, I had to work really hard and get good grades so I could get into a good graduate school. OK, I did that. I'm here at Wisconsin. Now, though, I have to work really hard, publish my research, so I can get a good tenure track job somewhere. And then, I'll have to work really hard for six years just to get tenure. I mean, by the time I can exhale and have a little fun, I'll be in my mid-30s—and that's too old to have fun anymore!

When do young people become adults? How do they know? What are the markers of adulthood now? Is it when you can legally drink? Get married? Drive a car? Rent a car? Vote? Serve in the military? Have an abortion without parental consent? Consider how disparate these ages are. More than 50,000 Americans get married each year before their 18th birthday—that is, they are legally allowed to have sex before they can legally watch it on a video. We can buy cars before we are legally allowed to drive them and long before we can rent them.

MARKERS OF ADULTHOOD

Demographers today typically cite five life-stage events to mark the transition to adulthood: leaving home, completing one's education, starting work, getting married, and becoming a parent. Just about all adolescents live at home, go to high school, experience puberty, and are unmarried. "Adults," by contrast, have completed their educations, live away from home, are married, and have children and stable careers. (Of course, not all adults would actually check off all those markers, but they represent a pattern, a collection of indicators.) In 1950, when Erikson and Coleman wrote, all those markers clicked at almost exactly the same time.

Let's look at what happened to each of those markers of the transition from adolescence to adulthood. Let's begin with the narrative of one baby boomer:

> My parents married in 1948, after my father returned from the wartime Navy, and both he and my mother began their careers. At first, like so many of their generation, they lived in the bottom floor of my grandparents' home, saving their money to flee the city and buy a house in the New York suburbs—part of the great wave of suburban migration of the early to mid-1950s. My mother, and her five closest lifelong friends, all had their first children within two years of their weddings, and their second child three years later—all within five years of graduating from college. And all of their friends did the same.

That baby boomer is me. And that pattern is a distant memory today. Baby boomers began to expand the timeframe of these markers of adulthood, attenuating education, prolonging singlehood as a permanent life stage, and drifting toward settled careers. The U.S. census shows a steady and dramatic decline in the percentage of young adults, under 30, who have finished school, left home, gotten married, had a child, and entered the labor force sufficiently to develop financial independence of their parents. In 2000, 46% of women and 31% of men had reached those markers by age 30. In 1960, just forty years earlier, 77% of women and 65% of men had reached them.[11]

MARRIAGE AND FAMILY LIFE

In 1950, the average age of marriage was 20.3 for women and 22.8 for men. Close to half of all women were married by age 20. Even by 1975, the median age for marriage was 21.1 for women and 23.5 for men. The age of marriage has climbed steadily and today, the median age of marriage is 27.1 for men and 25.3 for women.[12]

And young people are having their first child four years later than they did in 1970. In 1970, the average age at which people had their first child was 21.4 years. By 2000, it was 24.9. (Massachusetts had the highest mean age for first birth; Mississippi had the lowest.)[13]

Today's young people live much less stable and settled family lives than their own parents did. They're far more likely to have been raised in a single-parent home. Their reticence is the result of high expectations for their own relationships and fears that their love lives will resemble those of their parents. Afraid to commit and desperate to do so, they make great cross-sex friends and casually hook up sexually. Their parents understand neither phenomenon.

"SERIAL JOBOGAMY"

They feel similarly about their careers. They know that their career is supposed to be more than a job, that it is supposed to be financially rewarding, be emotionally rich and satisfying, and offer them a sense of accomplishment and inner satisfaction. Work, for them, is an "identity quest." "Emerging adults want more out of work than a decent wage and a steady paycheck. They want their work to be an expression of themselves, to fit well their interests and abilities, to be something they find satisfying and enjoyable," writes Arnett.[14] And they expect that; they feel *entitled* to it. And why shouldn't they? They put up with four years of college, and maybe even some years of professional or graduate school, just to enhance their career prospects. Many have utterly unrealistic expectations about the range of jobs they might find satisfying. They all seem to want to write for television, become famous actors, or immediately become dot.com entrepreneurs. One employment recruiter calls them "the Entitlement Generation" since they have such "shockingly high expectations for salary, job flexibility, and duties but little willingness to take on grunt work or remain loyal to a company."[15]

But in a way, their bloated expectations may be a response to the very different economic climate in which they're coming of age. For one thing, the secure economic foundation on which previous generations have come of age has eroded. Globalization,

the decline in manufacturing jobs, the decline in union protections for workers, and the increase in the supply of service sector jobs has changed all that. They know that corporations are no longer loyal to their employees—just consider all those companies that picked up and moved out of towns they had helped to build, watching indifferently as entire communities unraveled. So why should they be loyal to the company?

They're lucky to find a job at all. In 2000, 72.2% of Americans aged 20–24 were employed; four years later it was barely two-thirds (67.9%). "Younger workers have just been crushed," commented Andrew Sum, the director of the Center for Labor Market Studies at Northeastern University.[16] Unlike virtually every single previous generation of Americans, the income trajectory for the current generation of young people is downwards. Between 1949 and 1973, during that postwar economic boom, men's earnings doubled and the income gap narrowed. But since the early 1970s, annual earnings for men, aged 25–34 with full-time jobs has steadily declined, dropping 17% from 1971 to 2002. Of male workers with only a high school diploma, the average wage decline from 1975 to 2002 was 11%. Only half of all Americans in their mid-20s earn enough to support a family. Two-thirds of this current generation "are not living up to their parents' standard of living," commented Professor Sum.[17]

And the gap between college-educated and non-college-educated has increased as well. In the late 1970s, male college graduates earned about 33% more than high school graduates; by the end of the 1980s, that gap had increased to 53%.[18] Nor do they have much protection. Once they're 18 or 19, young people are rarely covered as dependents on their parents' health and medical care plans. And many work at low-wage, temporary, low-benefit jobs, or remain dependent on their parents. As a result, in 1999, over half (53%) of all young adults (aged 18–21) had no health insurance at all—all the more striking when compared with those 35–44 (16.5% had no health care) and 45–54 (13.4% uninsured), according to the General Accounting Office. Another 12.9% are covered by Medicare or other public insurance. Fewer than 10% (8.8%) were covered by their employer.

This generation of young people is downwardly mobile. Gen Xers and Gen Yers will earn less than their parents did—at every single age marker. Of all age groups, the 18–25 year olds are the lowest ranked in earned income of all age groups. Their household income is the second lowest (right above 65 and older). "On most socioeconomic measures, the young were the worst off age group in 1997—and the gap has widened since," notes Tom Smith, the director of the General Social Survey.[19]

The only economic sector in which jobs are being created is entry-level service and sales. In *Generation X*, author Douglas Coupland calls it "McJob"—"low paying, low-prestige, low-dignity, no future job in the service sector. Frequently considered a satisfying career choice by people who have never held one."[20] Young people, along with immigrants, minorities, and the elderly, are the bulk of workers in the new service economy. Half of all workers in restaurants, grocery stores, and department stores are under 24. As one journalist recently put it, "hundreds of thousands of young people are spending hours making decaf lattes, folding jeans, grilling burgers or unpacking boxes of books and records for minimum wage." And their poverty rates are twice the national average.[21]

As a result, young people rarely commit to a career right out of college. They don't have their eyes on the prize; it's really more like their "eyes on the fries," as a recent documentary film put it. The increased instability of their employment prospects coupled with their sense that jobs must be emotionally and financially fulfilling leads to a volatile career trajectory. Many experience the "two-month itch" and switch jobs as casually as they change romantic partners. They take "stopgap jobs," engaging in what I like to call "serial jobogamy." Listen to Jon, a 1992 Rutgers grad, who told a journalist about his career cluelessness:

> I had absolutely no idea what I wanted to do right out of college. I was clueless and fell blindly into a couple of dead-end jobs, which were just there for me to make money and figure out what I wanted to do. When I had no idea what I wanted to do, I couldn't even picture myself doing anything because I was so clueless about what was out there. I had so little direction. I was hanging on to these completely dead-end

jobs thinking that maybe something would turn up. I was unhappy about the situation, and the only thing that made it better was that all of my friends out of college were in the same boat. We would all come home and complain about our jobs together. We were all still drunks back then.[22]

And remember, this is the kid who is moving back home after graduation!

EDUCATION FOR WHAT?

In 1900, only a small fraction of male teens attended secondary schools. About half were involved in agricultural labor and the rest were employed in resource, manufacturing, or the service sector, making nearly a living wage. Many lived with their families, and when they did, they made considerable financial contributions to family income. In fact, for many working-class families, the family's most prosperous years were the years their children were living at home with them.[23]

A century later, in most western nations, the vast majority of teens attended secondary school. In 2000, over 88% of all people aged 25–29 had completed high school and nearly 30% (29.1%) had a BA—up from 17% only thirty years ago. This is the most highly educated group of young people in history.[24]

But they're taking their time getting that education. Four years after high school, 15% of the high school graduating class of 1972 had obtained their degree. Ten years later, the percentage had been cut by more than half—less than 7% had obtained a degree. Today, it's closer to 4%.

And also the least financially independent generation. Two-thirds of all college graduates owe more than $10,000 when they graduate; the average debt is nearly $20,000 and 5% owe more than $100,000. Recent college graduates owe 85% more in student loans alone than graduates a decade ago according to the Center for Economic and Policy research. Credit card debt for the age group 18–24 more than doubled between 1992 and 2001.[25]

The twentieth century has seen these kids move from being productive citizens to dependents on their families, the educational system, and the state. Less than one-third of this age group are employed enough to make them potentially financially independent.

Those who live with their parents make virtually no contribution to family income. More than one-third of youth aged 18–34 receive cash from their parents, and nearly half (47%) receive time-help from their parents in any given year—averaging about $3,410 in cash and about 367 hours of help from their parents. At home, adolescents in many families are not treated as equal adults but as "indulged guests," writes psychologist Jeffrey Arnett. And away, young people who "swim" are able to do so "because families provide significant material and emotional support."[26]

No wonder two-thirds of all young people 18 to 24 live with their parents or other relatives and one-fifth of all 25-year-old Americans still live at home. And no wonder that 40% of all college graduates return to live with their parents for at least some period of time in that age span. Only 25% of men aged 25 live independently; 38% of women do. Eighteen million Americans between 20 and 34 live with their parents. Forget the empty nest syndrome—for one in five American families, it's still a "full nest."

And we're not the only country where this is happening. In Britain, for example, they're talking about nesters, boomerang children, co-resident adults, or "kippers"—Kids In Pockets, Eroding Retirement Savings, which pretty much sums up what their parents think of the 50% of college graduates who have returned home. In Japan, 70% of women between age 30 and 35 live with their parents, and in Australia, only 14% of people in their early 20s are independent.[27]

THE UPWARD AGE SPIRAL

These five classic demographic markers—education, marriage, parenthood, career and residential independence—have not simply shifted over the past generation. They've exploded, scattered across a time span that now stretches to more than a decade for a large swath of American youth. And they feed back on each other, reinforcing their separation and pushing the boundaries even further. "Because people are delaying marriage, they're living with their parents longer," writes Farnsworth Riche, in an article in *American Demographics*. "They are delaying marriage longer because they are going to school. They're going to school because most well-paying jobs now require a college degree." The National Marriage Project

found that 86% of 20–29 year olds agree that "it is extremely important to be economically set before you get married."

Surely, then, it makes little sense to speak of this entire period, from early teens to late 20s, as a single identifiable period called "adolescence." The developmental tasks of a 13 year old are just too different from those of a 23 year old—even if they both are single, unemployed, and live with their parents. We need to identify this new stage of development, between adolescence and adulthood, that both captures the developmental characteristics of this life stage and locates it within important social and cultural shifts in American life, including the historical decrease in the number of males under 25 who are married or fathers; the increased number of young males who are extending their educations beyond college, to professional or graduate school; and, the increased percentage of young males under 25 who are living with their parents.

We need to see the stage from 18–26 as a distinct stage of development, a unique period. We need to map its contours, explore its boundaries, and understand its meaning. "In another 10 or 20 years, we're not going to be talking about this as a delay," says Tom Smith, director of the General Social Survey. "We're going to be talking about this as a normal trajectory."[28]

THIRTY IS THE NEW TWENTY

Recently, some social scientists have begun to pay attention to this period between the end of adolescence and the beginning of adulthood. In September, 2004, a front page story in *USA Today* noticed that something was happening; a few months later, *Time* made it their cover story, calling them "twixters"—neither kids nor adults, but betwixt and between.[29]

The *Time* story, and the subsequent letters the magazine published offer a glimpse of our national confusion about this age. The twixters wrote eloquently about their situation. One moved back home after college because she couldn't find a job that paid enough to live on her own—only to find that "the majority of my high school class had done the same thing." But, she insisted, "we are not lazy. We want to work and make our way in the world." Another pointed out that her generation is "overwhelmed by indecision. We have the necessary tools, but now have too many options and not enough options at the same time. We are stuck." Another painted a nearly inspirational picture. Given that half their "parents are divorced, have financial problems or are stuck in jobs they loathe," she wrote, the twixters might instead be seen as "a generation that refuses to fall into the same archaic conventions that have led to so many dysfunctional families."

Adult letter writers were uniformly unsympathetic. They blamed the kids themselves, as if somehow the disastrous economy, sky-high housing costs, and high aspirations with no ways to fulfill them were somehow the fault of job seekers, not job suppliers—namely the adults themselves. "If only their parents had cut the golden apron strings and left them to their own devices, they would have learned to be more independent," wrote one. "There's not a single thing wrong with the young adults who live off their parents that a stint in the U.S. Marine Corps couldn't fix," wrote another. "Why do we need to come up with a new label for kids who stay home with their parents while figuring out what to do?" asked another, before reminding us that "we've had a name for that for years: moocher."[30]

Ironically, *all* of the twixter letters were from women, and *all* of the adult respondents were male. (*Time* did not seem to notice this interesting gender difference.) But it's an important element in our conversation: it is fathers—far more than mothers—who deeply resent the return of their college graduate children. The empty nest is experienced differently by fathers and mothers. Mothers may, for a time, mourn the absence of their children, as if their world has suddenly lost its center of gravity and spins aimlessly off its axis. Fathers, by contrast, often celebrate their new freedom from child-care responsibilities—they buy new golf clubs, load up on Viagra, and talk about this being, finally, their "turn." Similarly, mothers may be ambivalent about the "full nest" syndrome, but their husbands seem to be universally unhappy about it.

Developmental psychologists and sociologists have also tried to map this newly emerging stage of life. Sociologist James Cote calls the period "youthhood," while Terri Apter, a British social psychologist

calls them "thresholders," who suffer from the neglect and scorn from parents who mistake their need for support and guidance as irresponsibility and immaturity. Recently, the John D. and Catherine T. MacArthur Foundation convened an academic panel on the "Transition to Adulthood."

Perhaps the most ambitious effort to map this postadolescent terra incognita has been Jeffrey Arnett's studies of what he calls "emerging adulthood." Following Erikson, Arnett sees this developmental stage as a gradual unfolding of a life plan, a "time for more serious self-reflection, for thinking about what kind of life you want to live and what your Plan should be for your life" (p. 238).[31] It's a period of increased independence—including independence from the preordained roles that they inherited from their elders. So, "they are not constrained by gender roles that prescribe strict rules for how they may meet and get to know each other" (p. 94). They are moving deliberately if unevenly toward intimate relationships, a steady and stable career path, and family lives, and along the way they are developing closer friendships with their parents, since the old issues of adolescent rebellion have been resolved by time and experience.

Yet Arnett's view of this stage of life is so sanguine, so sanitized, it's hardly recognizable. It's hard to square becoming better friends with your parents and an increasing sense of autonomy (and a decreasing reliance on peer groups for validation) with the fraternity initiations, binge drinking, athletic hazing, and date rape and other forms of sexual predation that often fill the exposés of campus life.

It's also hard to square this gradual easing into adulthood with the observations of other cultural critics. For example, Christopher Lasch observed more than twenty years ago that college students have a "certain protective shallowness, a fear of binding commitments, a willingness to pull up roots whenever the need arises, a dislike of depending on anyone, an incapacity for loyalty or gratitude."[32]

So, what do psychologists and sociologists know about this stage of development? For one thing, it's a stage of life characterized by indeterminacy. Many young adults feel they are just treading water, waiting to find the right job, the right person, the right situation, to reveal itself. "I'm just sitting around waiting for my life to begin, while it's all just slippin' away," sings Bruce Springsteen on "Better Days."

All the established markers of adulthood feel more ephemeral, more transient, and less reliable—both as events and as markers of adulthood. They're children of divorce, of family instability or dysfunction. They're unsure what to think about their parents. Some, mostly young women, describe their parents (mothers) as their best friend, others see their parents as exactly who they don't want to end up like.

"I'm in no rush to get married, and even less in a rush to have a kid," says Jeff, a 22-year-old senior at Indiana University interviewed 2/23/05. "I watched my own parents divorce, and it became pretty clear that they got married and started having kids—namely me—before they were ready. I'm not going to make that mistake."

It's a time of perhaps the greatest mismatch between their ambitions and their accomplishments. They graduate from college filled with ideas about changing the world, making their contribution, finding their place, and they enter a job market at the bottom, where work is utterly unfulfilling, boring, and badly paid. "It concerns me that of the many gifted people I went to school with, so few of them are actually doing what they really want to do," said one.[33] They are among the most entitled and underappreciated people in America. This was a generation that was told from the get-go that each of them was special, in which their self-esteem was so inflated they became light-headed, in which they were rewarded for every normal developmental milestone as if they were Mozart.

They're extremely other-directed, taking their cues from outside. They perform to please grown-ups—parents, teachers—but exhibit little capacity for self-reflection or internal motivation. They have high self-esteem, but little self-awareness. Many suspect that their self-esteem, so disconnected from actual achievement, is a bit of a fraud. Many lack a moral compass to help negotiate their way in the world.

It's unstable and uncertain. They drink more than they think they should, take more drugs, and probably get involved in more hook ups and bad relationships than they think they should. And they also get more down on themselves, because at this stage they also think they should know better. Their suicide rate is the highest for any age group except men over 70.[34]

As a result, they're more disconnected. They are less likely to read a newspaper, attend church, belong to a religion or a union, vote for president, or identify with a political party than any other age group, according to the General Social Survey. They're more cynical or negative about other people and less trusting. They are less likely to believe that people are basically trustworthy, helpful, fair, or that human beings are naturally good.[35]

Nor do they have any particular confidence in social, economic, or political institutions. They don't trust corporations, the way their parents did, because they've seen how such loyalty is rewarded with layoffs, downsizing, outsourcing, and moving overseas. They've watched as corporate executives lined their pockets with the pension funds of their own employees. They believe the only way to get rich in this culture is not by working hard, saving, and sacrificing, but by winning the lottery. And they don't trust the government, which they believe is filled with people who are venal and self-aggrandizing, out of touch with the needs of their constituents.

On the other hand, there is plenty of good news. For one thing, they're developing friendships, especially across sex, the likes of which their parents do not understand. Young people constantly told me of trying to explain their cross-sex friendships to their parents. "My father just doesn't get it," said Kim, a 21-year-old senior at Oakland University in suburban Detroit. "I keep saying that they're my 'guy friends' and he's like, 'Wait. He's a boy and he's your friend, but he's not your boyfriend?' And I'm like 'Dad, chill. He's a boy. He's my friend. He is not my boyfriend.' And so he asks 'Does Jeff [her boyfriend] know?'"

Young adults go out in groups, hang out together, maybe even hook up. But they are friends first. And this bodes well in two ways. First, friendships are based on mutuality and equality, which assumes, at least in part, a more equal relationship between women and men than is offered either by the sexual predatory conquest model and its corollary, the passionate-swept-off-the-feet model, or even the chivalric code of gentlemen and ladies. And second, gender equality in marriage—marriages based on models of friendship and partnership—are far sturdier and more successful than those based on those other sexual passion-attractiveness models, according to psychologist John Gottman.

For some, friends are the new family. Think, actually, of the hit television sit-com *Friends*. Six friends share their mutual befuddlement about being grown-ups, relationships, careers, and life in general until they suddenly realize that everything they ever wanted in a life partner is right there next to them. And they then spend the next two seasons sorting out which one goes with whom. Or consider the HBO show, *Sex and the City*, the story of a quartet of single, sexually active women on the loose in New York City, each one hoping and struggling through relationships with the opposite sex, all the while aware that their real "family" was each other.

For others, our families become friends. Arnett suggests that some young adults become closer to their parents, and develop cross-generational friendships that surprise both parent and child. Over half of all Americans aged 18–29 talk to their parents every day, according to a January, 2005, article in *TIME*. But it is also true that the half who do speak to their parents every day are daughters—and the parents they are speaking to are their mothers.

There is more potentially good news. Students of domestic violence have recently noted a significant downward trend—lower and lower rates of domestic violence seem to be popping up in the United States, Canada, and Britain. For a long time, social scientists worried that a host of factors—increasing attention to the problem, better reporting of the crimes, better police and hospital evaluations, more stringent arrest mandates—would actually drive the rates higher, creating the irony that the more we talked about it, the more it seemed to increase. But the decrease in domestic violence seems to come less from the increased constraints placed on men, or even the increased deterrence of stronger laws, better enforced with mandatory sentencing. It seems to stem, instead, from the increased age of women entering into marriage (younger women are battered more often than older women) and the host of dramatic changes in women's lives (work outside the home leads to increased economic resources to leave a dangerous situation;

women feel entitled not to be battered; playing sports and working outside the home correlate with higher self-esteem, which leads them to put up with less, etc.). It may be that the older women are when they marry, the lower their chances of being battered when they do.

SITUATIONAL MATURITY

If the demographic markers of adulthood have scattered across a decade or more, young people today are turning to more attitudinal indicators of when they become adults. In a 1994 study, Jeffrey Arnett asked students at a large Midwestern university "Do you think you have reached adulthood?" Twenty-seven per cent said "yes," 10% said "no" and 63% said "in some respects yes, in some respects no." Interestingly, the students no longer used traditional markers to categorize themselves. Completing education, entering the labor force, marriage, and parenthood all got low ratings, from 14% for parenthood to 27% for entering the labor force. Marriage and completing education were only identified by 15%, having a child by 14% as indicators of adulthood.

On the other hand, psychological criteria received much higher endorsements. "Accept responsibility for the consequences of your actions" led the list at 93%. Being able to "decide on personal beliefs and values independently of parents or other influences" was noted by 81%, the same percentage that identified becoming "less self-oriented, develop greater consideration for others."[36]

They become adults when they *feel* like adults. They experience a "situational maturity." Sometimes they want to be treated like adults, sometimes they want to be treated like children. "You don't get lectures about what life is like after college," comments Brandon to journalist Alexandra Robbins. "You don't have a textbook that tells you what you need to do to find success." "People have to invent their own road map," commented another.[37]

And they don't experience a calamitous break with their childhoods, since there is no one time when all five transitional indicators are achieved. By spreading them out, adulthood becomes a gradual process, a series of smaller decisions. One looks back suddenly and realizes one is actually an adult. The General

Social Survey found that most people believe the transition to adulthood should be completed by age 26, a number that seems to rise every year.

THE MISSING CONVERSATION: GENDER

Perhaps one reason Arnett and his colleagues are so sanguine about emerging adulthood is because there is nary a word about gender in their work. The word *masculinity*—or, for that matter *femininity*—does not appear in his book's index; there's scant mention of gender gaps in attitudes. And that's about it.[38]

How can one possibly discuss the age group 16–26 and not talk about gender? In fact, this is perhaps the most gendered stage of a person's development—for one simple reason: It is a time that is utterly unmapped. The older institutions of socialization exert far less influence, although same-sex peers and media often pick up some of the slack. It is a time when there are no road maps, no blueprints, no primers that tell the young person what to do, how to understand this period. That's why none of the terms given to this stage of development—"emergent adulthood," "transition to adulthood," "twixters," "thresholders," and the like—have any resonance whatever to the young men and women I speak to on college campuses and in workplaces around the country.

Almost all of them call themselves—and call each other—"guys." It's both a generic catch-all term that goes beyond this age group and a specific term demarcating it from "kids" and "grown-ups." While it's gender-specific, women use it too. Watch a group of college women sitting around wondering what to do that evening: "What do you guys want to do?" "I don't know, what do you guys want to do?" One hardly needs a man around to whom the term would refer. (This "generic" term is also gender-specific, and we'll look at the ways that the term itself implies the gender inequality that characterizes this stage of life. Girls live in Guyland—*not* the other way around.)

In fact, this is a period of what sociologists James Cote and Anton Allahar call "gender intensification"—the assertion of "exaggerated notions associated with the different roles that still hold many men and women in separate spheres of endeavor."[39] It's when the struggle to prove manhood becomes even more intense—in

part because it is only peers who are watching—and judging.

That the territory remains so unmapped actually exacerbates the emphasis on gender. Part of the definition of masculinity is, after all, to act as if one knows exactly where one is going. If men have a difficult time asking for directions when they get lost driving their cars, imagine what they'll do when they feel lost and adrift on the highway of life! One acts as if one knows where one is going, even if it isn't true. And it's this posture, and the underlying sense that one is a fraud, that leaves young men most vulnerable to manipulation by the media and by their peers. If I just follow along and don't ask any questions, everyone will assume I have it all together—and I won't be exposed.

Guyland thus becomes the terrain in which young men so relentlessly seem to act out, seem to take the greatest risks, and do the stupidest things. It's also the time when they need the involvement of their parents—especially their fathers. Fathers often fade out of the picture, thinking their job of child-rearing and role-modeling is over once their offspring graduate from high school. For many guys, their fathers are a "shadowy presence."[40] Their kids have survived, so now, fathers seem to say, it's time for "us."

It's not entirely true that fathers are just selfish; they're also encouraged to think selfishly for the first time in a long time, by an advertising industry that has recently discovered empty nesters as an emerging market—they've finally shed all the financial responsibilities of child-rearing and college, giving them some disposable income for the first time in decades. And they're ready to find something other than their children to fulfill them.

All the advice books about boys' development offer little guidance here. Although they may be useful when they discuss boys' development up until they turn 16 or so, they all end just at the cusp of "guyland." It's pretty difficult to talk to a 17- or 22-year-old guy about what the books say about being a man when the books top out at 16!

And so, directionless and clueless, we come to rely increasingly on our peers. And our peers often have some interesting plans for what we have to endure to prove to them that we are real men. The "penalty for not living up to the norms of being tough, being 'cool' is severe," writes Marie Richmond-Abbott.[41] Is it "rejection or simply being ignored?"

BEYOND GUYLAND

Guyland is both a social space and a stage of life. It's unlikely to disappear. If anything, the stage of life is likely to become more firmly entrenched. There are positive reasons for delaying marriage, exploring different career paths, playing the field, traveling, hanging out, exploring one's self and who one wants to be, and become, in this lifetime. But it must be time well spent.

Most guys drift out of Guyland by their late 20s, as they commit to careers or girlfriends, and begin to enter the world of responsible adulthood. But still, they do so with few rules and fewer signposts to help them on their journeys.

Our task, as a society, is to disengage the stage of life with that social space—to enable young men to live through this stage more consciously, more honorably, and with greater resilience—to inject into that anomic and anarchic space called Guyland a code of ethics, of emotional responsiveness, and of wholesome occasional irresponsibility.

Some of Guyland's most celebrated inhabitants seem to be getting that message—and passing it on. In response to the death of Scott Krueger (a pledge at MIT) during a drinking and hazing ritual, the national office of Phi Gamma Delta has produced a well-conceived video about high-risk drinking that is required for all their chapters. The local chapter of another fraternity accepts openly gay men and then works to make other brothers' homophobia the problem to be addressed. Sigma Phi Epsilon has embraced a new "balanced man program," which the fraternity developed in the 1990s to combat a culture of "boozing, drugging and hazing." They've simply and unilaterally done away with the pledge system; new members have virtually all the rights and privileges of brothers. The brothers are *presumed* to be men when they begin; they don't have to prove their manhood to their peers. Scott Thompson, the fraternity's national spokesman, told a journalist:

> New members don't pledge for a certain period of time, get hazed, get initiated, and then show up for

parties until they graduate. In the Balanced Man Program, men join, and they are developed from the time they join until the time they graduate. Part of that development focuses on building a sound mind and sound body, a simple philosophy that we took from the ancient Greeks.[42]

Here, in the words of a former frat guy, lies the hope of guys everywhere: that the culture of entitlement can become a culture of integrity—in which guys know that each person's integrity is equal to his own. That guys can be valued for their integrity and encouraged to be good, whole human beings. That the culture of silence can become a culture of honor, in which each guy feels honor bound to speak up, to act ethically, and to defend his core beliefs with respect for the simple dignity of his friends. That the culture of protection can become a culture of love, in which each guy feels surrounded by support and care, knows that he is not alone, and that having left Guyland far behind, he has nothing left to prove.

NOTES

1. Phillipe Ariès, *Centuries of Childhood: A Social History of Family Life*, translated from the French by Robert Baldick (New York: Vintage Books, 1962).
2. G. Stanley Hall, *Adolescence: Its Psychology and Its Relations to Physiology, Anthropology, Sociology, Sex, Crime, Religion, and Education* (New York: Appleton, 1904). In an earlier essay, he explained that "the boy's bullying is the soul-germ of the man's independence." He defended one boy who was "overbearing and cruel" to his sister, whom he had "perfectly terrorized."
3. See Steven Mintz, "Adolescence's Neglected Anniversary" op-ed at Ascribe Newswire, January 10, 2005; archived at www.contemporaryfamilies .org/media/news%2099.htm.
4. E. C. Cline, "Social Implications of Modern Adolescent Problems" in *The School Review*, September 1941, p. 511–514.
5. Edward Strecker, *Their Mothers' Sons: The Psychiatrist Examines an American Problem* (Philadelphia: Lippincott, 1946) and Philip Wylie, *Generation of Vipers* (New York: Rinehart, 1942).

6. Erik Erikson, *Childhood and Society* (New York: W. W. Norton, 1950) and *Identity: Youth and Crisis* (New York: W. W. Norton, 1968).

7. James Coleman, *The Adolescent Society* (New York: The Free Press, 1961). See also James Coleman, *Adolescents and Schools* (New York: Basic Books, 1965).

8. Kenneth Keniston, *Young Radicals: Notes on a Committed Youth* (New York: Harcourt, 1968).

9. See Stephanie Coontz, *The Way We Never Were* (New York: Basic, 1992).

10. See Caroline Stanley, "Why Teens Do Dumb Things" in www.healthykids.com, accessed October 23, 2004, describing the research of Dr. James Bjork.

11. Sharon Jayson, "It's Time to Grow Up—Later" in *U.S.A. Today*, September 30, 2004, p. 1D.

12. U.S. Bureau of the Census, Table MS-2: "Estimated Median Age at First Marriage by Sex, 1890 to Present" released September 15, 2004. In the first part of the century, the median age of first marriage fluctuated as the economy expanded and contracted; now, however, the median age creeps up steadily, seemingly disconnected from and uninfluenced by external factors.

13. T. J. Mathews and Brady Hamilton, "Mean Age of Mother, 1970–2000" in *National Vital Statistics Reports*, 51 (1), December, 2002.

14. Jeffrey Jensen Arnett, *Emerging Adulthood: The Winding Road from the Late Teens through the Twenties* (New York: Oxford University Press, 2004), p. 162.

15. Martha Irvine, "Young Workers Want It All, Now" in *Seattle-Post-Intelligencer*, June 27, 2005; available at: http://seattlepi.nwsource.com/business/230177_entitlement27.html (accessed 6/28/05).

16. Bob Herbert, "The Young and the Jobless" in *New York Times*, May 12, 2005.

17. Cited in Herbert, "The Young and the Jobless," *ibid.*

18. Mary Corcoran and Jordan Matsudaira, "Is It Getting Harder to Get Ahead? Economic Attainment in Early Adulthood for Two Cohorts" in *On the Frontier of Adulthood: Theory, Research and Public Policy*, Richard Settersten, Jr., Frank F. Furstenberg, Jr., and Ruben G. Rumbaut, eds. (Chicago: University of Chicago Press, 2005), p. 357.

19. Tom Smith, "Generation Gaps in Attitudes and Values from the 1970s to the 1990s" in *On the Frontier of Adulthood: Theory, Research and Public Policy*, Richard Settersten, Jr., Frank F. Furstenberg, Jr., and Ruben G. Rumbaut, eds. (Chicago: University of Chicago Press, 2005), p. 182.

20. Douglas Coupland, *Generation X: Tales for an Accelerated Culture* (New York: St Martin's Press, 1991).

21. Elana Berkowitz, "Eyes on the Fries: Young People are Coming of Age in the Era of the McJob," published by CampusProgress.org on March 31, 2005.

22. Cited in Alexandra Robbins and Abby Wilner, *Quarterlife Crisis* (New York: Jeremy Tarcher, 2001), p. 113.

23. William Reese, *The Origins of the American High School* (New Haven: Yale University Press, 1995).

24. Elizabeth Fussell and Frank F. Furstenberg, Jr., "The Transition to Adulthood during the Twentieth Century: Race, Nativity and Gender" in *On the Frontier of Adulthood*, p. 38.

25. Lou Dobbs, "The Generation Gap" in *U.S. News and World Report*, May 23, 2005, p. 58.

26. Schoeni and Ross, 402; Settersten, 2005, p. 535; Jeffrey Jensen Arnett, "Are College Students Adults? Their Conceptions of the Transition to Adulthood" in *Journal of Adult Development* 1, 1994, p. 162.

27. Edi Smockum, "Done with College? Come back to the Fold" in *Financial Times*, September 10, 2005, p. 23.

28. As cited in Tom Smith, "Generation Gaps in Attitudes and Values from the 1970s to the 1990s" in *On the Frontier of Adulthood: Theory, Research, and Public Policy*, edited by Richard Settersten, Frank Furstenberg and Ruben Rumbaut (Chicago: University of Chicago Press, 2005), p. 182.

29. Sharon Jayson, "It's Time to Grow Up—Later" in *USA Today*, September 30, 2004, p. 1D; Lev Grossman, "Grow Up? Not So Fast" in *Time*, January 24, 2005, p. 42–54.

30. Letters, *Time*, February 14, 2005, p. 6.

31. Arnett, Jeffrey. 2014. Emerging Adulthood: The Winding Road from the Late Teens through the Twenties. New York: Oxford University Press.

32. Christopher Lasch, *Haven in a Heartless World* (New York: Basic Books, 1977). no page given.

33. In Jeffrey Arnett, *Emerging Adulthood*, p. 41.

34. James E. Cote and Anton L. Allahar, *Generation on Hold: Coming of Age in the Late Twentieth Century* (New York: New York University Press, 1996), p. 59.

35. Tom Smith, "Generation Gaps in Attitudes and Values from the 1970s to the 1990s" in *On the Frontier of Adulthood: Theory, Research, and Public Policy*, edited by Richard Settersten, Frank Furstenberg and Ruben Rumbaut (Chicago: University of Chicago Press, 2005), p. 182.

36. Jeffrey Jensen Arnett, "Are College Students Adults?"; see also Arnett, *Emerging Adulthood*, p. 210.

37. Alexandra Robbins and Amy Willner, *Quarterlife Crisis*, p. 121, 6.

38. Neither of the two major works cited here—Arnett's *Emerging Adulthood* and the MacArthur-sponsored *On the Frontier of Adulthood*—has a single reference to "masculinity," "manhood," or even "men" in the index.

39. James Cote and Anton Allahar, *Generation on Hold*, p. 84.

40. Larson and Richard, 1994, p. 164.

41. Marie Richmond-Abbott, *Masculine and Feminine: Gender Roles over the Life Cycle* (2nd ed). McGraw–Hill, 1992, p. 121.

42. Benoit Denizet-Lewis, "Ban of Brothers" in *New York Times Magazine*, January 9, 2005, p. 74.

MULTIPLYING MASCULINITIES

CHAPTER 2

MULTIPLYING MASCULINITIES
An Introduction

The move from thinking about *masculinity* to considerations of *masculinities* might seem like splitting hairs, but this transition in theorizing gender (and masculinity in particular) fundamentally altered the ways we thought about and studied the topic. For instance, when we thought about masculinity singularly, we were primarily interested in "how much" masculinity people had. The psychologist Sandra Bem (1974) conducted some incredibly important research from this perspective that helped illustrate the need for more room for complexity and nuance in measuring gendered identities and practices. Bem invented what she called the "sex role inventory" (SRI). She asked respondents a series of questions meant to assess how "masculine" or "feminine" people are—60 questions, actually. Using Bem's sex role inventory, people are asked to self-assess—to consider how well different characteristics describe them. Survey respondents rate themselves between a 1 and a 7 on characteristics like the following: "competitive," "loves children," "eager to soothe hurt feelings," "willing to take a stand." One interesting aspect of Bem's study is that it allowed people to score high or low on *both* masculinity *and* femininity.[1] But Bem's research also proceeds from the assumptions that masculinity is measured in one way—that we all know which of the characteristics are masculine and which are feminine. Yet, as we learned in the *Historicizing Masculinities* section, this is an assumption that is challenged by historical research on men and masculinity. "Masculinity" has meant different things at different times, in different cultures, to different groups, in different contexts.

Simply put, masculinity is not a stable category. Yet, most of us approach it and think about it as though it is stable. When it comes down to actually discussing what masculinity is, however, it's probably true that most of us apply a sort of "I know it when I see it" theory. But, when we get into the nitty-gritty of it, masculinity turns out to be much more complicated than that. Although most of us probably feel confident we could spot "it" if we saw it, there might be less agreement about what it actually is than is popularly assumed—certainly across cultures and in different historical periods, but even within a single society and time period. *Multiple masculinities* approaches begin with this dilemma about what it is and, in response, suggest that masculinity is an unstable object of inquiry that must always be thought of as multiple rather than singular. Thus, multiple masculinities approaches were the first to embrace the instability inherent in the category. But multiple masculinities approaches do more than consider a diversity of masculinities; they also consider masculinities relative to each other in terms of power and cultural prestige.

THE EMERGENCE OF THE MULTIPLE MASCULINITIES MODEL

Theorizing masculinity as multiple, rather than as a singular enactment, identity, or social role, emerged in an effort to capture historical and cultural variation and change. The multiple masculinities approach frames masculinity not as a unitary and stable category, role, disposition, or identity, but as a relational set of practices embedded in specific social structures and institutional arrangements (like families, education, laws, religion, and more). Indeed, in Connell's initial work (e.g., Connell 1987, 1995; Carrigan et al. 1985), she suggests that, rather than discuss masculinity (or femininity for that matter) as a role, we ought to think about masculinities as "configurations of practice." She argued that we are better off studying gender *relations* than gender *roles*. This model proved foundational across disciplinary boundaries in theorizing masculinity. Indeed, it is not an overstatement to claim that this is *the* dominant approach in contemporary interrogations of masculinity. The multiple masculinities approach developed a common language for analyzing masculinity, rendered masculinity a feasible object of study, provided a coherent definition of masculinity, and set the agenda for future theorizing.

In their seminal article, "A New Sociology of Masculinity" (1985), Tim Carrigan, Raewyn Connell, and Bob Lee first theorized what a social constructionist approach to masculinity might look like. This initial query later cohered as the multiple masculinities approach (e.g., Connell 1995). They explicitly critique the static analysis of gender roles in Parsons's structural functionalist sex role theory for an inability to address power and inequality.[2] Instead, Carrigan et al. (1985) draw from the social constructivist tradition in sociology, feminist theorizing about gender inequality, and insights about the role of sexuality in gender relations provided by the gay rights movement. This shift in focus leads them to suggest equally important variations *within* sex categories (like men) to those *between* sex categories (i.e., men vs. women). In other words, it is important to look at differences between men and between masculinities, not just between men and women and between masculinities and femininities—*intra*gender relations as well as *inter*gender relations.

This model also provides (what was) a new definition of gender, in which gender is defined as structured practice relating to a sex category. Framing gender as "practice" moves the discussion beyond a largely psychologized and implicitly biologically deterministic role theory approach in that it defines gender not as a personal trait or an expression of some innate disposition, but a "way in which social practice is ordered" (Connell 1995: 71). Framing gender as structured practice rejects essentialist, positivist, normative, and semiotic definitions of gender in claiming that attention must be paid to the "processes and relationships through which men and women conduct gendered lives . . . simultaneously a place in gender relations and the practices through which men and women engage that place in gender, and the effects of these practices in bodily experience, personality and culture"

(Connell 1995: 71). Gender, then, is composed of "social practices that constantly refer to the body" (Connell 1995: 71), but are not and cannot be reduced to the body. That is, bodies are important in this model, but are not definitive of a particular gender.

Importantly, gender is not a *voluntaristic* practice that one can improvise at will, nor is it the simple performance of a role. Rather, the multiple masculinities model suggests that gendered practice is organized by larger social structures and forms of social relations. Connell (1987, 1995, 2009) suggests that gender practice is primarily organized by four separate structures: (1) *power relations* (the social structure of patriarchy by which men are constructed as a dominant group); (2) *production relations* (gendered divisions of labor and their social and economic consequences); (3) *emotional relations* or relations of cathexis (the structure of emotional and sexual attachments and desires and how they are integrated throughout social life, from the bedroom to the board room); and (4) *symbolic relations* (gendered symbolism embedded in language, writing, dress, makeup, movement, art, architecture, and more). How labor is divided by gender privately and in the workplace both shapes and is shaped by gendered practice. The ordering of social power both contributes to and is the result of various enactments of masculinity. Emotional and sexual attachments, investments, and identities are informed by and contour gendered engagements. And finally, social life is framed by symbolic meaning. We all contribute to producing an elaborate language of gender that requires little speaking and often no words at all to communicate gendered meanings through the ways we display, adorn, and care for (or not) our bodies in ways that communicate gendered meanings. Attending to symbolism indicates that gender is also a central element of film, television, music, and all manner of consumer products as well as language.

Raewyn Connell's essay in this volume (Reading 8)—drawn from her influential book, *Masculinities* (1995)—provides an explanation of the important claim put forth by Carrigan et al. (1985) that relations *within* a sex category are as important to understanding gender inequality as are the relations between them. To this end she suggests that there are four configurations of gender practice that currently shape gendered power and masculinity—hegemony, complicity, marginalization, and subordination.

Hegemonic masculinity is the configuration of practice that is taken to guarantee the legitimacy of patriarchal power in a particular time and place, describing configurations of gender practice that are most culturally exalted. Hegemonic masculinity is largely defined in opposition to subordinated masculinities—configurations of practice that are stigmatized and subordinated to others by a diverse system of material and discursive practices. Connell discusses gay men as perhaps the best example of subordinated masculinities. Marginalized masculinities encompass forms of gendered practice belonging to those often excluded from traditional routes to masculinized power, such as working-class men or men who are racial or ethnic minorities. Last, complicit masculinity refers to configurations of gender practice that do not necessarily reflect the patriarchal investments of hegemonic masculinity, but do little to challenge it. As historian and political activist Howard Zinn (1994) once wrote about fighting for social change, "You can't be neutral on a moving train." Zinn suggests that doing nothing, even when we are opposed to inequalities we see and care about, is tantamount to endorsing inequality. Similarly, complicit masculinity actively benefits from the inequalities perpetuated by hegemonic masculinity and the inequalities produced by the current gender order—complicit masculinity benefits primarily through passive support of this inequality.

Through defining these configurations of gendered practices as "gender projects" or configurations of practice (as opposed to gendered roles), Connell highlights the importance of studying gender as a process and a set of relationships in addition to an identity, stating that "'Masculinity,' to the extent the term can be briefly defined at all, is simultaneously a place in gender relations, the practices through which men and women engage that place in gender, and the effects of these practices in bodily experience, personality and culture" (Connell 1995: 71). The multiple masculinities model has been interdisciplinarily deployed by an incredible array of scholars around the world.

DEPLOYMENT OF THE MULTIPLE MASCULINITIES APPROACH

The flexibility of the language and conceptual organization of the multiple masculinities approach quickly captured the imagination of scholars across the social sciences and humanities. This model analyzed men as gendered beings, but not sole agents of the patriarchy, for instance. As such, it enabled scholars to look at the interplay of other social positions like race, class, and sexuality with masculinity, tracing out the varied and often complex ways power and inequality work in men's lives. Connell's four configurations of masculine practice—hegemony, subordination, marginalization, and complicity—have been used to describe the relationship between men in a variety of settings (Lusher and Robins 2009), from construction sites (Iacuone 2005; Paap 2006), to the military (Barrett 1996), schools (Renold 2004; Swain 2006), sports (Messner 1992, 2002; Hirose and Pih 2010; Robinson 2010), technology (Lohan and Faulkner 2004; Mellström 2004), and more. Scholars have been especially interested in the way in which gendered hierarchies among men are organized (Collinson and Hearn 1994), as they investigate interactions between hegemonically masculine men and nonhegemonic masculinities (Renold 2004), including emergent masculinities (Inhorn and Wentzell 2011), nonsporting masculinities (Dworkin and Wachs 2000), and disabled masculinities (Gerschick and Miller 1994).

As Michael Messner (2004) points out in his essay for this volume (Reading 14), myriad masculinities have been uncovered and described in detail since the initial development of the multiple masculinities approach. Some masculinities are deployed to identify particular racial/ethnic/national groups, such as Asian (Luke 1997), Asian American (Chua and Fujino 2008), Caribbean (Gosine 2007), Chinese (Louie 2002), Chinese American (Chen 1999), Chinese Canadian (Millington et al. 2008), Irish (Gosine 2007), Massai (Hodgson 1999), Pacific (Taylor 2008), white (Robinson 2000), or simply "racialized" (Yep and Elia 2012; Price 1999) masculinities.

Other research examines masculinities by location—agriculture-based (Liepins 2000), displaced (Nayak 2006), frontier (Carrington et al. 2010), global (Haywood and Mac an Ghaill 2003), inner-city (Archer and Yamashita 2003), prison (Sabo et al. 2001), and rural masculinities (Bye 2009; Campbell and Bell 2000; Stenbacka 2011; Nusbaumer 2011; Woodward 2000), for instance. Other research has focused on subordinated masculinities, detailing an array of sexualized gendered practices and identities—consumer (Holt and Thompson 2004; Joseph and Black 2012; Thompson and Holt 2004), embodied heterosexual (Monaghan and Robertson 2012; Robertson and Monaghan 2012), fragile (Joseph and Black 2012), gay (Nardi 2000; Brown 2001; Linneman 2008), heterosexual (Redman 1996; Kehily 2001; Renold 2007), inclusive (Anderson 2009), philogynous (Groes-Green 2012), poly-hegemonic (Sheff 2006), queer (Heasley 2005; Wright 2005; Landreau and Rodriguez 2012), "bear" (Hennen 2005), and straight masculinities (Draper 2010).

Class location and dynamics have also informed a variety of masculinities such as collegiate (Kimmel and Messner 2004; Harper and Harris 2010), corporate (Mills 1998), counter-masculinity (Nonn 2007), managerial masculinity (Messerschmidt 1995; Kerfoot and Knights 1998; Pini 2004; Knoppers and Anthonissen 2005), transnational business masculinity (Connell and Wood 2005), nerd or "geek" (Bell 2013; Cooper 2000; Kendall 2000), versatile (Nonn 2007), watery (Bull 2009), and working-class masculinities (Fine et al. 1997; Heron 2006; Embrick et al. 2007; Nixon 2009), among others.

Other research focuses on the era or political system in which a particular gender configuration comes about—British military (Hale 2008), historical (Davin 1997), military (Atherton 2009), militarized (Whitworth 2008; Ashe 2012), modern (Dimova 2006; Pascoe 2003), new masculinity (Cooper 2000; Messner 1993), patriotic (Nielsen 2004), post-Soviet (Tereskinas 2009), socialist masculinities (Hunt 2004), etc.

The body, particularly gendered and aged bodies, is the locus of other considerations utilizing this perspective—adolescent (Hauge and Haavind 2011; Martino 1999; Messerschmidt 1999), contingent (Blackwood 2009; Bridges 2009), embodied (Monaghan and Malson 2013; Robertson et al. 2010), disabled (Shakespeare 1999; Shuttleworth 2004; Wilson 2004; Shuttleworth et al. 2012), female (Halberstam 1998, 2012; Francis 2010), feminine (Paechter 2006), and young masculinities (Haywood and Mac an Ghaill 2003), for instance.

Some research addresses the intersections of categories listed above: Cuban gay masculinities (Kurtz 2008), Filipino and Filipino American tomboy masculinities (Fajardo 2008), Latino feminist masculinities (Hurtado and Sinha 2008), prosthetic, white, hypermasculinities (Preston 2010), Puerto Rican gay masculinities (Asencio 2011; Kurtz 2008), violent rural masculinities (Pease 2010), white working-class masculinities (Fine et al., 1997; Reay 2002), young working-class (Roberts 2013), and youthful white (Kusz 2001).

In addition, there are myriad others: alternative (Beal 1996; Talbot and Quayle 2010), contested (Leyshon and Brace 2007), cool (Jackson and Dempster 2009), defensive (Barnes 2012), dominant (Skelton 2000), faux (Oliffe et al. 2013), flexible (Batnitzky et al. 2009), hybrid (Arxer 2011; Bridges 2014; Bridges and Pascoe 2014), massacred (Leavy 2009), muted (Chopra 2006), proper (Onoufriou 2010), strategic (Batnitzky et al. 2009), subaltern (Rogers 2008), subcultural (Mooney 1998), threatened (Wardrop 2009), traumatic (Kabachnick et al., 2013), and violent masculinities (Katz 2003; Tonso 2009).

This is by no means a comprehensive list of the array of masculinities that researchers have documented over the past several decades. The list does, however, underscore the diversity of gender practice—that there is no *one* masculine role but rather a wide variety of the ways in which (primarily) men inhabit masculine identities and selves as well as the ways in which they are rewarded and sanctioned for doing so.

SECTION OUTLINE

Beginning with Connell's elaboration of the multiple masculinities approach (Reading 8), this section traces three of the main ways this approach has appeared in the literature on masculinities and the relationships between them. The first approach primarily addresses different "types" of masculinity and positions them vis-à-vis hegemonic masculinity. The second approach critiques the uncritical deployment of the multiple masculinities model, divesting it of a focus on inequality and power. The third revisits the model itself and calls for renewed focus on intersecting forms of inequality as well as a return to framing gender as structured action, rather than an individual quality. This latter approach helped to pave the way toward *navigating masculinities* approaches (which we examine in detail in the next section).

As much of the literature inspired by the multiple masculinities approach does, the first four essays in this section look at the deployment of masculinity by a variety of men in a variety of contexts. In Reading 9, Anahita and Mix discuss "frontier masculinity" to illustrate how marginalized masculinities are mobilized to drum up political support. They also illustrate how masculinities become institutionalized, even state-sponsored. Rios and Sarabia use the multiple masculinities model to examine racial, ethnic, minority, urban young men who have been denied "respectable" routes to hegemonic masculinity, arguing that they invoke "synthetic masculinity" to inhabit a respected manhood and claim dignity in different environments (Reading 11). Heath complicates easy claims about masculinity by demonstrating that a particular form of masculinity may seem new stylistically, but it can simultaneously work in ways that reinscribe inequality. She introduces a gender practice she identifies as "soft boiled" masculinity—what might be considered a form of complicit masculinity—enacted by evangelical Christian men that reinscribes gendered and raced inequalities even as it seems to be less "patriarchal" (Reading 10). Like Heath, Anderson is interested in identifying gendered and sexualized change through gender projects (Reading 12). He, too, introduces a new form of masculinity he calls "inclusive masculinity" to rework the relationship between hegemonic and subordinated masculinities, as it was originally formulated, by arguing that homophobia no longer functions as a primary mechanism through which hegemonic masculinity is forged and calling into question the fact that masculinities are organized hierarchically.

Deployments of the multiple masculinities approach are critiqued in the essays by Ezzell and Messner. Both Ezzell and Messner call for a renewed focus on inequality and dominance in studies of masculinities. As Messner points out in his essay (Reading 14), the field may be losing its analytic power because of the limited deployment of the multiple masculinities model: "Like all such deconstructive projects, the danger inherent in the multiple masculinities discourse is that, ultimately, we risk deconstructing down to each and every man having his own distinct form of masculinity: My masculinity; your masculinity" (pp. 199 in this volume). He suggests a refocus from masculinities to "men's interests" to continue to root this discussion in social structure and inequality. Similarly, Ezzell argues that the field needs to shift from a focus on masculinities to "manhood acts" to regain a focus on dominance as a central component of masculinity (Reading 13). Doing so would reinvigorate a focus on the resources men deploy to signify a masculine self through dominance practices. Significant here is that both Ezzell and Messner retain the analytic insight of the plurality of gendered practices.

In response to the seeming loss of the model's analytic power, Messerschmidt's essay returns to the original concept of multiple masculinities, suggesting that masculinities be more explicitly framed as "structured action" (Reading 15). While reiterating the continued utility and significance of the multiple masculinities model, Messerschmidt suggests that the field must take intersecting inequalities more seriously, reinvigorating a focus on inequality rather than primarily on varieties of masculinities. Messerschmidt's call has also been taken up by another body of scholarship we refer to as *navigating masculinities* research, which we will address in more depth in the next section.

REFERENCES

Anderson, Eric. 2009. *Inclusive Masculinity: The Changing Nature of Masculinities*. London: Routledge.

Archer, Louise, and Hiromi Yamashita. 2003. "Theorising Inner-City Masculinities: 'Race', Class, Gender and Education." *Gender and Education* 15 (2): 115–32.

Arxer, Steven L. 2011. "Hybrid Masculine Power: Reconceptualizing the Relationship between Homosociality and Hegemonic Masculinity." *Humanity & Society* 35 (4): 390–422.

Asencio, Marysol. 2011. "'Locas,' Respect, and Masculinity: Gender Conformity in Migrant Puerto Rican Gay Masculinities." *Gender & Society* 25 (3): 335–54.

Ashe, Fidelma. 2012. "Gendering War and Peace Militarized Masculinities in Northern Ireland." *Men and Masculinities* 15 (3): 230–48.

Atherton, Stephen. 2009. "Domesticating Military Masculinities: Home, Performance and the Negotiation of Identity." *Social & Cultural Geography* 10 (8): 821–36.

Barnes, Cliona. 2012. "It's No Laughing Matter: Boys' Humour and the Performance of Defensive Masculinities in the Classroom." *Journal of Gender Studies* 21 (3): 239–51.

Barrett, Frank J. 1996. "The Organizational Construction of Hegemonic Masculinity: The Case of the US Navy." *Gender, Work & Organization* 3 (3): 129–42.

Batnitzky, Adina, Linda McDowell, and Sarah Dyer. 2009. "Flexible and Strategic Masculinities: The Working Lives and Gendered Identities of Male Migrants in London." *Journal of Ethnic and Migration Studies* 35 (8): 1275–93.

Beal, Becky. 1996. "Alternative Masculinity and Its Effect on Gender Relations in the Subculture of Skateboarding." *Journal of Sport Behavior* 19 (3): 204–20.

Bell, David. 2013. "Geek Myths: Technologies, Masculinities, Globalizations." In *Rethinking Transnational Men: Beyond, Between and Within Nations*, edited by Jeff Hearn, Marina Blagojević, and Katherine Harrison, 76–90. London: Routledge.

Bem, Sandra L. 1974. "The Measurement of Psychological Androgyny." *Journal of Consulting and Clinical Psychology* 42 (2): 155–62.

Blackwood, Evelyn. 2009. "Trans Identities and Contingent Masculinities: Being Tombois in Everyday Practice." *Feminist Studies* 35 (3): 454–80.

Bridges, Tristan. 2009. "Gender Capital and Male Bodybuilders." *Body & Society* 15 (1): 83–107.

Bridges, Tristan. 2014. "A Very 'Gay' Straight? Hybrid Masculinities, Sexual Aesthetics, and the Changing Relationship between Masculinity and Homophobia." *Gender & Society* 28 (1): 58–82.

Bridges, Tristan, and C. J. Pascoe. 2014. "Hybrid Masculinities: New Directions in the Sociology of Men and Masculinities." *Sociology Compass* 8 (3): 246–58.

Brown, J. Brian. 2001. "Doing Drag: A Visual Case Study of Gender Performance by Gay Masculinities." *Visual Sociology* 16 (1): 37–54.

Bull, Jacob. 2009. "Watery Masculinities: Fly-Fishing and the Angling Male in the South West of England." *Gender, Place & Culture* 16 (4): 445–65.

Bye, Linda Marie. 2009. "'How to Be a Rural Man': Young Men's Performances and Negotiations of Rural Masculinities." *Journal of Rural Studies* 25 (3): 278–88.

Campbell, Hugh, and Michael Mayerfeld Bell. 2000. "The Question of Rural Masculinities." *Rural Sociology* 65 (4): 532–46.

Carrigan, Tim, Raewyn Connell, and John Lee. 1985. "Toward a New Sociology of Masculinity." *Theory and Society* 14 (5): 551–604.

Carrington, Kerry, Alison McIntosh, and John Scott. 2010. "Globalization, Frontier Masculinities and Violence Booze, Blokes and Brawls." *British Journal of Criminology* 50 (3): 393–413.

Chen, Anthony S. 1999. "Lives at the Center of the Periphery, Lives at the Periphery of the Center: Chinese American Masculinities and Bargaining with Hegemony." *Gender & Society* 13 (5): 584–607.

Chopra, Radhika. 2006. "Invisible Men Masculinity, Sexuality, and Male Domestic Labor." *Men and Masculinities* 9 (2): 152–67.

Chua, Peter, and Diane Fujino. 2008. "Negotiating New Asian-American Masculinities: Attitudes and Gender Expectations." *The Journal of Men's Studies* 7 (3): 391–413.

Collinson, David, and Jeff Hearn. 1994. "Naming Men as Men: Implications for Work, Organization and Management." *Gender, Work & Organization* 1 (1): 2–22.

Connell, Raewyn. 1987. *Gender and Power: Society, the Person and Sexual Politics*. Stanford, CA: Stanford University Press.

Connell, Raewyn. 1995. *Masculinities*. Berkeley: University of California Press.

Connell, Raewyn. 2009. *Gender: Short Introductions*. 2nd ed. Cambridge, UK: Polity.

Connell, Raewyn, and Julian Wood. 2005. "Globalization and Business Masculinities." *Men and Masculinities* 7 (4): 347–64.

Cooper, Marianne. 2000. "Being the 'Go-To Guy': Fatherhood, Masculinity, and the Organization of Work in Silicon Valley." *Qualitative Sociology* 23 (4): 379–405.

Davin, Anna. 1997. "Historical Masculinities: Regulation, Fantasy and Empire." *Gender & History* 9 (1): 135–38.

Dimova, Rozita. 2006. "'Modern' Masculinities: Ethnicity, Education, and Gender in Macedonia." *Nationalities Papers* 34 (3): 305–20.

Draper, Jimmy. 2010. "'Gay or Not?!': Gay Men, Straight Masculinities, and the Construction of the Details Audience." *Critical Studies in Media Communication* 27 (4): 357–75.

Dworkin, Shari L., and Faye L. Wachs. 2000. "The Morality/Manhood Paradox: Masculinity, Sport, and the Media." In *Masculinities, Gender Relations, and Sport*, edited by Michael A. Messner, Don Sabo, and Jim McKay, 507–21. Thousand Oaks, CA: Sage.

Embrick, David G., Carol S. Walther, and Corrine M. Wickens. 2007. "Working Class Masculinity: Keeping Gay Men and Lesbians out of the Workplace." *Sex Roles* 56 (11–12): 757–66.

Fajardo, Kale Bantigue. 2008. "Transportation: Translating Filipino and Filipino American Tomboy Masculinities through Global Migration and Seafaring." *GLQ: A Journal of Lesbian and Gay Studies* 14 (2–3): 403–24.

Fine, Michelle, Lois Weis, Judi Addelston, and Julia Marusza. 1997. "(In)Secure Times: Constructing White Working-Class Masculinities in the Late 20th Century." *Gender & Society* 11 (1): 52–68.

Francis, Becky. 2010. "Re/theorising Gender: Female Masculinity and Male Femininity in the Classroom?" *Gender and Education* 22 (5): 477–90.

Gershick, Thomas, and Adam Miller. 1994. "Gender Identities at the Crossroads of Masculinity and Physical Disability." *Masculinities* 2 (1): 34–55.

Gosine, Andil. 2007. "Marginalization Myths and the Complexity of 'Men' Engaging Critical Conversations about Irish and Caribbean Masculinities." *Men and Masculinities* 9 (3): 337–57.

Groes-Green, Christian. 2012. "Philogynous Masculinities Contextualizing Alternative Manhood in Mozambique." *Men and Masculinities* 15 (2): 91–111.

Halberstam, Judith. 1998. *Female Masculinity*. Durham, NC: Duke University Press.

Halberstam, Judith. 2012. "Global Female Masculinities." *Sexualities* 15 (3–4): 336–54.

Hale, Hannah C. 2008. "The Development of British Military Masculinities through Symbolic Resources." *Culture & Psychology* 14 (3): 305–32.

Harper, Shaun R., and Frank Harris III. 2010. *College Men and Masculinities: Theory, Research, and Implications for Practice*. San Francisco: Wiley.

Hauge, Mona-Iren, and Hanne Haavind. 2011. "Boys' Bodies and the Constitution of Adolescent Masculinities." *Sport, Education and Society* 16 (1): 1–16.

Haywood, Chris, and Mairtin Mac an Ghaill. 2003. *Men and Masculinities*. Philadelphia: Open University Press.

Heasley, Robert. 2005. "Queer Masculinities of Straight Men: A Typology." *Men and Masculinities* 7 (3): 310–20.

Hennen, Peter. 2005. "Bear Bodies, Bear Masculinity: Recuperation, Resistance, or Retreat?" *Gender & Society* 19 (1): 25–43.

Heron, Craig. 2006. "Boys Will Be Boys: Working-Class Masculinities in the Age of Mass Production." *International Labor and Working-Class History* 69 (1): 6–34.

Hirose, Akihiko, and Kay Kei-ho Pih. 2010. "Men Who Strike and Men Who Submit: Hegemonic and Marginalized Masculinities in Mixed Martial Arts." *Men and Masculinities* 13 (2): 190–209.

Hodgson, Dorothy L. 1999. "'Once Intrepid Warriors': Modernity and the Production of Maasai Masculinities." *Ethnology* 38 (2): 121–50.

Holt, Douglas B., and Craig J. Thompson. 2004. "Man-of-Action Heroes: The Pursuit of Heroic Masculinity in Everyday Consumption." *Journal of Consumer Research* 31 (2): 425–40.

Hunt, Karen. 2004. "'Strong Minds, Great Hearts, True Faith and Ready Hands'? Exploring Socialist Masculinities before the First World War." *Labour History Review* 69 (2): 201–17.

Hurtado, Aída, and Mrinal Sinha. 2008. "More than Men: Latino Feminist Masculinities and Intersectionality." *Sex Roles* 59 (5–6): 337–49.

Iacuone, David. 2005. "'Real Men Are Tough Guys': Hegemonic Masculinity and Safety in the Construction Industry." *The Journal of Men's Studies* 13 (2): 247–66.

Inhorn, Marcia C., and Emily A. Wentzell. 2011. "Embodying Emergent Masculinities: Men Engaging with Reproductive and Sexual Health Technologies in the Middle East and Mexico." *American Ethnologist* 38 (4): 801–15.

Jackson, Carolyn, and Steven Dempster. 2009. "'I Sat Back on My Computer . . . with a Bottle of Whisky Next to Me': Constructing 'Cool' Masculinity through 'Effortless' Achievement in Secondary and Higher Education." *Journal of Gender Studies* 18 (4): 341–56.

Joseph, Lauren J., and Pamela Black. 2012. "Who's the Man? Fragile Masculinities, Consumer Masculinities, and the Profiles of Sex Work Clients." *Men and Masculinities* 15 (5): 486–506.

Kabachnick, Peter, Magdalena Grabowska, Joanna Regulska, Beth Mitchneck, and Olga V. Mayorova. 2013. "Traumatic Masculinities: The Gendered Geographies of Georgian IDPs from Abkhazia." *Gender, Place & Culture: A Journal of Feminist Geography* 20(6): 773–93.

Katz, Jackson. 2003. "Advertising and the Construction of Violent White Masculinity: From Eminem to Clinique for Men." In *Gender, Race, and Class in Media*, edited by Gail Dines and Jean M. Humez, 349–58. Thousand Oaks, CA: Sage.

Kehily, Mary. 2001. "Bodies in School Young Men, Embodiment, and Heterosexual Masculinities." *Men and Masculinities* 4 (2): 173–85.

Kendall, Lori. 2000. "'Oh No! I'm A Nerd!' Hegemonic Masculinity on an Online Forum." *Gender & Society* 14 (2): 256–74.

Kerfoot, Deborah, and David Knights. 1998. "Managing Masculinity in Contemporary Organizational Life: A Managerial Project." *Organization* 5 (1): 7–26.

Kimmel, Michael S., and Michael A. Messner. 2004. *Men's Lives*, 6th ed. Boston: Pearson.

Knoppers, Annelies, and Anton Anthonissen. 2005. "Male Athletic and Managerial Masculinities: Congruencies in Discursive Practices?" *Journal of Gender Studies* 14 (2): 123–35.

Kurtz, Steven. 2008. "Butterflies under Cover: Cuban and Puerto Rican Gay Masculinities in Miami." *The Journal of Men's Studies* 7 (3): 371–90.

Kusz, Kyle W. 2001. "'I Want to Be the Minority': The Politics of Youthful White Masculinities in Sport and Popular Culture in 1990s America." *Journal of Sport & Social Issues* 25 (4): 390–416.

Landreau, John C., and Nelson M. Rodriguez. 2012. "Queer Masculinities in Education: An Introduction." In *Queer Masculinities: A Critical Reader in Education*, edited by John C. Landreau and Nelson M. Rodriguez, 1–18. Dordrecht: Springer Netherlands.

Leavy, Patricia. 2009. "Fractured Femininities/Massacred Masculinities A Poetic Installation." *Qualitative Inquiry* 15 (9): 1439–47.

Leyshon, Michael, and Catherine Brace. 2007. "Men and the Desert: Contested Masculinities in Ice Cold in Alex." *Gender, Place & Culture* 14 (2): 163–82.

Liepins, Ruth. 2000. "Making Men: The Construction and Representation of Agriculture-Based Masculinities in Australia and New Zealand." *Rural Sociology* 65 (4): 605–20.

Linneman, Thomas J. 2008. "How Do You Solve a Problem Like Will Truman? The Feminization of Gay Masculinities on Will & Grace." *Men and Masculinities* 10 (5): 583–603.

Lohan, Maria, and Wendy Faulkner. 2004. "Masculinities and Technologies: Some Introductory Remarks." *Men and Masculinities* 6 (4): 319–29.

Louie, Kam. 2002. *Theorising Chinese Masculinity: Society and Gender in China*. Cambridge, UK: Cambridge University Press.

Luke, Allan. 1997. "Representing and Reconstructing Asian Masculinities: This Is Not a Movie Review." *Social Alternatives* 16 (31): 32–34.

Lusher, Dean, and Garry Robins. 2009. "Hegemonic and Other Masculinities in Local Social Contexts." *Men and Masculinities* 11 (4): 387–423.

Martino, Wayne. 1999. "'Cool Boys', 'Party Animals', 'Squids', and 'Poofters': Interrogating the Dynamics and Politics of Adolescent Masculinities in School." *British Journal of Sociology of Education* 20 (2): 239–63.

Mellström, Ulf. 2004. "Machines and Masculine Subjectivity Technology as an Integral Part of Men's Life Experiences." *Men and Masculinities* 6 (4): 368–82.

Messerschmidt, James W. 1995. "Managing to Kill: Masculinities and the Space Shuttle Challenger Explosion." *Masculinities* 3 (4): 1–22.

Messerschmidt, James W. 1999. "Making Bodies Matter: Adolescent Masculinities, the Body, and Varieties of Violence." *Theoretical Criminology* 3 (2): 197–220.

Messner, Michael A. 1992. *Power at Play: Sports and the Problem of Masculinity.* Boston: Beacon Press.

Messner, Michael A. 1993. "'Changing Men' and Feminist Politics in the United States." *Theory and Society* 22 (5): 723–37.

Messner, Michael A. 2002. *Taking the Field: Women, Men, and Sports.* Minneapolis: University of Minnesota Press.

Messner, Michael A. 2004. "On Patriarchs and Losers: Rethinking Men's Interests." *Berkeley Journal of Sociology* 48: 78–88.

Millington, Brad, Patricia Vertinsky, Ellexis Boyle, and Brian Wilson. 2008. "Making Chinese-Canadian Masculinities in Vancouver's Physical Education Curriculum." *Sport, Education and Society* 13 (2): 195–214.

Mills, Albert J. 1998. "Cockpits, Hangars, Boys and Galleys: Corporate Masculinities and the Development of British Airways." *Gender, Work & Organization* 5 (3): 172–88.

Monaghan, Lee F., and Helen Malson. 2013. "'It's Worse for Women and Girls': Negotiating Embodied Masculinities through Weight-Related Talk." *Critical Public Health* 23 (3): 304–19.

Monaghan, Lee F., and Steve Robertson. 2012. "Embodied Heterosexual Masculinities, Part 1: Confluent Intimacies, Emotions and Health." *Sociology Compass* 6 (2): 134–50.

Mooney, Katie. 1998. "'Ducktails, Flick-Knives and Pugnacity': Subcultural and Hegemonic Masculinities in South Africa, 1948–1960." *Journal of Southern African Studies* 24 (4): 753–74.

Nardi, Peter M. 2000. *Gay Masculinities.* Cambridge, UK: Sage.

Nayak, Anoop. 2006. "Displaced Masculinities: Chavs, Youth and Class in the Post-Industrial City." *Sociology* 40 (5): 813–31.

Nielsen, Kim E. 2004. "What's a Patriotic Man to Do? Patriotic Masculinities of the Post–WWI Red Scare." *Men and Masculinities* 6 (3): 240–53.

Nixon, Darren. 2009. "'I Can't Put a Smiley Face On': Working-Class Masculinity, Emotional Labour and Service Work in the 'New Economy.'" *Gender, Work & Organization* 16 (3): 300–22.

Nonn, Timothy. 2007. "Hitting Bottom: Homelessness, Poverty, and Masculinity." In *Understanding Inequality: The Intersection of Race/Ethnicity, Class, and Gender,* edited by Barbara A. Arrighi, 2nd ed., 281–88. Plymouth, UK: Rowman & Littlefield.

Nusbaumer, Michael R. 2011. "Rural Masculinity and Antique Tractors: Reliving the Men in the Machines." *Journal of Rural Social Sciences* 26 (2): 101–25.

Oliffe, John L., Paul M. Galdas, Christina S. E. Han, and Mary T. Kelly. 2013. "Faux Masculinities among College Men Who Experience Depression." *Health* 17 (1): 75–92.

Onoufriou, Andreas. 2010. "'Proper Masculinities' and the Fear of Feminisation in Modern Cyprus: University Students Talk about Homosexuality and Gendered Subjectivities." *Gender and Education* 22 (3): 263–77.

Paap, Kris. 2006. *Working Construction: Why White Working-Class Men Put Themselves—And the Labor Movement—In Harm's Way.* Ithaca, NY: Cornell University Press.

Paechter, Carrie. 2006. "Masculine Femininities/Feminine Masculinities: Power, Identities and Gender." *Gender and Education* 18 (3): 253–63.

Pascoe, C. J. 2003. "Multiple Masculinities?: Teenage Boys Talk about Jocks and Gender." *American Behavioral Scientist* 46 (10): 1423–38.

Pease, Bob. 2010. "Reconstructing Violent Rural Masculinities: Responding to Fractures in the Rural Gender Order in Australia." *Culture, Society and Masculinities* 2 (2): 154–64.

Pini, Barbara. 2004. "Managerial Masculinities in the Australian Sugar Industry." *Rural Society* 14 (1): 22–35.

Preston, John. 2010. "Prosthetic White Hyper-Masculinities and 'Disaster Education.'" *Ethnicities* 10 (3): 331–43.

Price, Jeremy N. 1999. "Schooling and Racialized Masculinities: The Diploma, Teachers, and Peers in the Lives of Young, African American Men." *Youth & Society* 31 (2): 224–63.

Reay, Diane. 2002. "Shaun's Story: Troubling Discourses of White Working-Class Masculinities." *Gender and Education* 14 (3): 221–34.

Redman, Peter. 1996. "Curtis Loves Ranjit: Heterosexual Masculinities, Schooling and Pupils' Sexual Cultures." *Educational Review* 48 (2): 175–82.

Renold, Emma. 2004. "'Other' Boys: Negotiating Non-hegemonic Masculinities in the Primary School." *Gender and Education* 16 (2): 247–65.

Renold, Emma. 2007. "Primary School 'Studs': (De)constructing Young Boys' Heterosexual Masculinities." *Men and Masculinities* 9 (3): 275–97.

Roberts, Steven. 2013. "Boys Will Be Boys . . . Won't They?': Change and Continuities in Contemporary Young Working-Class Masculinities." *Sociology* 47(4): 671–86.

Robertson, Steve, and Lee F. Monaghan. 2012. "Embodied Heterosexual Masculinities, Part 2: Foregrounding Men's Health and Emotions." *Sociology Compass* 6 (2): 151–65.

Robertson, Steve, Kay Sheikh, and Andrew Moore. 2010. "Embodied Masculinities in the Context of Cardiac Rehabilitation." *Sociology of Health & Illness* 32 (5): 695–710.

Robinson, Sally. 2000. *Marked Men: White Masculinity in Crisis*. New York: Columbia University Press.

Robinson, Victoria. 2010. "Researching Everyday Sporting Masculinities: Thoughts from a (Critical) Distance." *Journal of Gender Studies* 19 (3): 309–13.

Rogers, Martyn. 2008. "Modernity, 'Authenticity', and Ambivalence: Subaltern Masculinities on a South Indian College Campus." *Journal of the Royal Anthropological Institute* 14 (1): 79–95.

Sabo, Donald F., Terry Allen Kupers, and Willie London. 2001. *Prison Masculinities*. Philadelphia: Temple University Press.

Shakespeare, Tom. 1999. "The Sexual Politics of Disabled Masculinity." *Sexuality and Disability* 17 (1): 53–64.

Sheff, Elisabeth. 2006. "Poly-Hegemonic Masculinities." *Sexualities* 9 (5): 621–42.

Shuttleworth, Russell P. 2004. "Disabled Masculinity: Expanding the Masculine Repertoire." In *Gendering Disability*, edited by Bonnie G. Smith and Beth Hutchison, 166–80. New Brunswick, NJ: Rutgers University Press.

Shuttleworth, Russell, Nikki Wedgwood, and Nathan J. Wilson. 2012. "The Dilemma of Disabled Masculinity." *Men and Masculinities* 15 (2): 174–94.

Skelton, Christine. 2000. "'A Passion for Football': Dominant Masculinities and Primary Schooling." *Sport, Education and Society* 5 (1): 5–18.

Stenbacka, Susanne. 2011. "Othering the Rural: About the Construction of Rural Masculinities and the Unspoken Urban Hegemonic Ideal in Swedish Media." *Journal of Rural Studies* 27 (3): 235–44.

Swain, Jon. 2006. "Reflections on Patterns of Masculinity in School Settings." *Men and Masculinities* 8(3): 331–49.

Talbot, Kirsten, and Michael Quayle. 2010. "The Perils of Being a Nice Guy: Contextual Variation in Five Young Women's Constructions of Acceptable Hegemonic and Alternative Masculinities." *Men and Masculinities* 13 (2): 255–78.

Taylor, John P. 2008. "Changing Pacific Masculinities: The 'Problem' of Men." *The Australian Journal of Anthropology* 19 (2): 125–35.

Tereskinas, Arturas. 2009. "Social Suffering, Post-Soviet Masculinities and Working-Class Men." *Social Sciences/Socialiniai Mokslai* 64 (2): 79–86.

Thompson, Craig J., and Douglas B. Holt. 2004. "How Do Men Grab the Phallus?: Gender Tourism in Everyday Consumption." *Journal of Consumer Culture* 4 (3): 313–38.

Tonso, Karen L. 2009. "Violent Masculinities as Tropes for School Shooters: The Montréal Massacre, the Columbine Attack, and Rethinking Schools." *American Behavioral Scientist* 52 (9): 1266–85.

Wardrop, Joan. 2009. "Notes from a Tense Field: Threatened Masculinities in South Africa." *Social Identities* 15 (1): 113–30.

Whitworth, Sandra. 2008. "Militarized Masculinity and Post Traumatic Stress Disorder." In *Rethinking the Wo/man Question in International Relations*, edited by Jane Parpart and Marysia Zalewski, 109–26. London: Zed Books.

Wilson, Daniel J. 2004. "Fighting Polio Like a Man: Intersections of Masculinity, Disability, and Aging." In *Gendering Disability*, edited by Bonnie G. Smith and Beth Hutchison, 119–33. New Brunswick, NJ: Rutgers University Press.

Woodward, Rachel. 2000. "Warrior Heroes and Little Green Men: Soldiers, Military Training, and the Construction of Rural Masculinities." *Rural Sociology* 65 (4): 640–57.

Wright, Les. 2005. "Introduction to 'Queer' Masculinities." *Men and Masculinities* 7 (3): 243–47.

Yep, Gust A., and John P. Elia. 2012. "Racialized Masculinities and the New Homonormativity in LOGO's Noah's Arc." *Journal of Homosexuality* 59 (7): 890–911.

Zinn, Howard. 1994. *You Can't Be Neutral on a Moving Train: A Personal History of Our Times*. Boston: Beacon Press.

NOTES

1. Eve Kofosky Sedgwick theorizes the implications of this seeming contradiction in her essay in the *Dislocating Masculinities* section of the book (Reading 26).
2. See the introduction for a more in depth exploration of the sex role theoretical perspective.

RAEWYN CONNELL

8. THE SOCIAL ORGANIZATION OF MASCULINITY

[. . .] [T]wentieth-century research [. . .] [on gender
has] failed to produce a coherent science of masculinity. This does not reveal the failure of the scientists so
much as the impossibility of the task. "Masculinity"
is not a coherent object about which a generalizing
science can be produced. Yet we can have coherent
knowledge about the issues raised in these attempts.
If we broaden the angle of vision, we can see masculinity, not as an isolated object, but as an aspect of a
larger structure.

This demands an account of the larger structure
and how masculinities are located in it. The task of
this chapter is to set out a framework based on contemporary analyses of gender relations. This framework will provide a way of distinguishing types of
masculinity, and of understanding the dynamics of
change.

First, however, there is some ground to clear. The
definition of the basic term in the discussion has
never been wonderfully clear.

DEFINING MASCULINITY

All societies have cultural accounts of gender, but not
all have the concept "masculinity." In its modern
usage the term assumes that one's behaviour results
from the type of person one is. That is to say, an unmasculine person would behave differently: being
peaceable rather than violent, conciliatory rather
than dominating, hardly able to kick a football, uninterested in sexual conquest, and so forth.

This conception presupposes a belief in individual difference and personal agency. In that sense it is
built on the conception of individuality that developed in early-modern Europe with the growth of colonial empires and capitalist economic relations [. . .].

But the concept is also inherently relational. "Masculinity" does not exist except in contrast with "femininity." A culture which does not treat women and
men as bearers of polarized character types, at least in
principle, does not have a concept of masculinity in
the sense of modern European/American culture.

Historical research suggests that this was true of
European culture itself before the eighteenth century. Women were certainly regarded as different
from men, but different in the sense of being incomplete or inferior examples of the same character (for
instance, having less of the faculty of reason). Women
and men were not seen as bearers of qualitatively different characters; this conception accompanied the
bourgeois ideology of "separate spheres" in the nineteenth century.

In both respects our concept of masculinity seems
to be a fairly recent historical product, a few hundred
years old at most. In speaking of masculinity at all,
then, we are "doing gender" in a culturally specific
way. This should be borne in mind with any claim to
have discovered transhistorical truths about manhood and the masculine.

Definitions of masculinity have mostly taken our
cultural standpoint for granted, but have followed
different strategies to characterize the type of person
who is masculine: Four main strategies have been followed; they are easily distinguished in terms of their
logic, though often combined in practice.

Essentialist definitions usually pick a feature that
defines the core of the masculine, and hang an account
of men's lives on that. Freud flirted with an essentialist definition when he equated masculinity with activity in contrast to feminine passivity—though he
came to see that equation as oversimplified. Later authors' attempts to capture an essence of masculinity

This reading is an excerpt from Raewyn Connell's *Masculinities* (Berkeley: University of California Press, 2005). © 2005 by
Raewyn Connell. Published by the University of California Press.

have been colourfully varied: risk-taking, responsibility, irresponsibility, aggression, Zeus energy. Perhaps the finest is the sociobiologist Lionel Tiger's idea that true maleness, underlying male bonding and war, is elicited by "hard and heavy phenomena" [Tiger 1969: 211]. [. . .]

The weakness in the essentialist approach is obvious: the choice of the essence is quite arbitrary. Nothing obliges different essentialists to agree, and in fact they often do not. Claims about a universal basis of masculinity tell us more about the ethos of the claimant than about anything else.

Positivist social science, whose ethos emphasizes finding the facts, yields a simple definition of masculinity: what men actually are. This definition is the logical basis of masculinity/femininity (M/F) scales in psychology, whose items are validated by showing that they discriminate statistically between groups of men and women. It is also the basis of those ethnographic discussions of masculinity which describe the pattern of men's lives in a given culture and, whatever it is, call the pattern masculinity. [. . .]

There are three difficulties here. First, as modern epistemology recognizes, there is no description without a standpoint. The apparently neutral descriptions on which these definitions rest are themselves underpinned by assumptions about gender. Obviously enough, to start compiling an M/F scale one must have some idea of what to count or list when making up the items.

Second, to list what men and women do requires that people be already sorted into the categories "men" and "women." [. . .] Positivist procedure thus rests on the very typifications that are supposedly under investigation in gender research.

Third, to define masculinity as what-men-empirically-are is to rule out the usage in which we call some women "masculine" and some men "feminine," or some actions or attitudes "masculine" or "feminine" regardless of who displays them. [. . .]

Indeed, this usage is fundamental to gender analysis. If we spoke only of differences between men as a bloc and women as a bloc, we would not need the terms "masculine" and "feminine" at all. We could just speak of "men's" and "women's," or "male" and "female." The terms "masculine" and "feminine" point beyond categorical sex difference to the ways men differ among

themselves, and women differ among themselves, in matters of gender. [. . .]

Normative definitions recognize these differences and offer a standard: masculinity is what men ought to be. [. . .] Strict sex role theory treats masculinity precisely as a social norm for the behaviour of men. In practice, male sex role texts often blend normative with essentialist definitions [. . .].

Normative definitions allow that different men approach the standards to different degrees. [. . .] What is "normative" about a norm hardly anyone meets? Are we to say the majority of men are unmasculine? How do we assay the toughness needed to resist the norm of toughness, or the heroism needed to come out as gay? [. . .]

Semiotic approaches [. . .] define masculinity through a system of symbolic difference in which masculine and feminine places are contrasted. Masculinity is, in effect, defined as not-femininity.

This follows the formulae of structural linguistics, where elements of speech are defined by their differences from each other. [. . .] In the semiotic opposition of masculinity and femininity, masculinity is the unmarked term, the place of symbolic authority. The phallus is master-signifier, and femininity is symbolically defined by lack.

[. . .] It is, however, limited in its scope—unless one assumes, as some postmodern theorists do, that discourse is all we can talk about in social analysis. To grapple with the full range of issues about masculinity we need ways of talking about relationships of other kinds too: about gendered places in production and consumption, places in institutions and in natural environments, places in social and military struggles. [. . .]

What can be generalized is the principle of connection. The idea that one symbol can only be understood within a connected system of symbols applies equally well in other spheres. No masculinity arises except in a system of gender relations.

Rather than attempting to define masculinity as an object (a natural character type, a behavioural average, a norm), we need to focus on the processes and relationships through which men and women conduct gendered lives. "Masculinity," to the extent the term can be briefly defined at all, is simultaneously a place in gender relations, the practices through which men and women engage that place in gender, and the effects of these practices in bodily experience, personality and culture.

GENDER AS A STRUCTURE OF SOCIAL PRACTICE

[. . .] Gender is a way in which social practice is ordered. In gender processes, the everyday conduct of life is organized in relation to a reproductive arena, defined by the bodily structures and processes of human reproduction. This arena includes sexual arousal and intercourse, childbirth and infant care, bodily sex difference and similarity.

I call this a "reproductive arena" not a "biological base" to emphasize [. . .] that we are talking about a historical process involving the body, not a fixed set of biological determinants. Gender is social practice that constantly refers to bodies and what bodies do, it is not social practice reduced to the body. Indeed reductionism presents the exact reverse of the real situation. Gender exists precisely to the extent that biology does *not* determine the social. [. . .]

Social practice is creative and inventive, but not inchoate. It responds to particular situations and is generated within definite structures of social relations. Gender relations, the relations among people and groups organized through the reproductive arena, form one of the major structures of all documented societies.

Practice that relates to this structure, generated as people and groups grapple with their historical situations, does not consist of isolated acts. Actions are configured in larger units, and when we speak of masculinity and femininity we are naming configurations of gender practice.

"Configuration" is perhaps too static a term. The important thing is the *process* of configuring practice. [. . .] Taking a dynamic view of the organization of practice, we arrive at an understanding of masculinity and femininity as *gender projects*. These are processes of configuring practice through time, which transform their starting-points in gender structures. [. . .] We find the gender configuring of practice however we slice the social world, whatever unit of analysis we choose. [. . .]

[. . .] [G]ender is an internally complex structure, where a number of different logics are superimposed. This is a fact of great importance for the analysis of masculinities. Any one masculinity, as a configuration of practice, is simultaneously positioned in a number of structures of relationship, which may be following different historical trajectories. Accordingly masculinity, like femininity, is always liable to internal contradiction and historical disruption.

We need at least a three-fold model of the structure of gender, distinguishing relations of (a) power, (b) production and (c) cathexis (emotional attachment). This is a provisional model, but it gives some purchase on issues about masculinity [e.g., Mitchell 1971; Rubin 1975; Connell 1987]. [. . .]

(a) *Power relations* The main axis of power in the contemporary European/American gender order is the overall subordination of women and dominance of men—the structure Women's Liberation named "patriarchy." This general structure exists despite many local reversals (e.g., woman-headed households, female teachers with male students). It persists despite resistance of many kinds, now articulated in feminism. These reversals and resistances mean continuing difficulties for patriarchal power. They define a problem of legitimacy which has great importance for the politics of masculinity.

(b) *Production relations* Gender divisions of labour are familiar in the form of the allocation of tasks, sometimes reaching extraordinarily fine detail. (In the English village studied by the sociologist Pauline Hunt [1980], for instance, it was customary for women to wash the inside of windows, men to wash the outside.) Equal attention should be paid to the economic consequences of gender divisions of labour, the dividend accruing to men from unequal shares of the products of social labour. This is most often discussed in terms of unequal wage rates, but the gendered character of capital should also be noted. A capitalist economy working through a gender division of labour is, necessarily, a gendered accumulation process. So it is not a statistical accident, but a part of the social construction of masculinity, that men and not women control the major corporations and the great private fortunes. Implausible as it sounds, the accumulation of wealth has become firmly linked to the reproductive arena, through the social relations of gender. [. . .]

(c) *Cathexis* [. . .] [S]exual desire is so often seen as natural that it is commonly excluded from social theory. [. . .] [However,] [t]he practices that shape and realize desire are [. . .] an aspect of the gender order. Accordingly we can ask political questions about the relationships involved: whether they are consensual or coercive, whether pleasure is equally given and received. In feminist analyses of sexuality these have become sharp questions about the connection of heterosexuality with men's position of social dominance. [. . .]

Because gender is a way of structuring social practice in general, not a special type of practice, it is unavoidably involved with other social structures. It is now common to say that gender "intersects"—better, interacts—with race and class. We might add that it constantly interacts with nationality or position in the world order. [. . .]

To understand gender, then, we must constantly go beyond gender. The same applies in reverse. We cannot understand class, race or global inequality without constantly moving towards gender. Gender relations are a major component of social structure as a whole, and gender politics are among the main determinants of our collective fate.

RELATIONS AMONG MASCULINITIES: HEGEMONY, SUBORDINATION, COMPLICITY, MARGINALIZATION

With growing recognition of the interplay between gender, race and class it has become common to recognize multiple masculinities: black as well as white, working-class as well as middle-class. This is welcome, but it risks another kind of oversimplification. It is easy in this framework to think that there is *a* black masculinity or *a* working-class masculinity.

To recognize more than one kind of masculinity is only a first step. We have to examine the relations between them. Further, we have to unpack the milieux of class and race and scrutinize the gender relations operating within them. There are, after all, gay black men and effeminate factory hands, not to mention middleclass rapists and cross-dressing bourgeois.

A focus on the gender relations among men is necessary to keep the analysis dynamic, to prevent the acknowledgement of multiple masculinities collapsing into a character typology [. . .]. "Hegemonic masculinity" is not a fixed character type, always and everywhere the same. It is, rather, the masculinity that occupies the hegemonic position in a given pattern of gender relations, a position always contestable.

A focus on relations also offers a gain in realism. Recognizing multiple masculinities, especially in an individualist culture such as the United States, risks taking them for alternative lifestyles, a matter of consumer choice. A relational approach makes it easier to recognize the hard compulsions under which gender configurations are formed, the bitterness as well as the pleasure in gendered experience.

With these guidelines, let us consider the practices and relations that construct the main patterns of masculinity in the current Western gender order.

HEGEMONY

The concept of "hegemony," deriving from Antonio Gramsci's analysis of class relations, refers to the cultural dynamic by which a group claims and sustains a leading position in social life. At any given time, one form of masculinity rather than others is culturally exalted. Hegemonic masculinity can be defined as the configuration of gender practice which embodies the currently accepted answer to the problem of the legitimacy of patriarchy which guarantees (or is taken to guarantee) the dominant position of men and the subordination of women.

This is not to say that the most visible bearers of hegemonic masculinity are always the most powerful people. They may be exemplars, such as film actors, or even fantasy figures, such as film characters. Individual holders of institutional power or great wealth may be far from the hegemonic pattern in their personal lives. [. . .]

Nevertheless, hegemony is likely to be established only if there is some correspondence between cultural ideal and institutional power, collective if not individual. So the top levels of business, the military and government provide a fairly convincing corporate display of masculinity, still very little shaken by feminist women or dissenting men. It is the successful claim to authority, more than direct violence, that is the mark of hegemony (though violence often underpins or supports authority).

I stress that hegemonic masculinity embodies a "currently accepted" strategy. When conditions for the defence of patriarchy change, the bases for the dominance of a particular masculinity are eroded. New groups may challenge old solutions and construct a new hegemony. The dominance of any group of men may be challenged by women. Hegemony; then, is a historically mobile relation. Its ebb and flow is a key element of the picture of masculinity [. . .].

SUBORDINATION

Hegemony relates to cultural dominance in the society as a whole. Within that overall framework there are specific gender relations of dominance and subordination between groups of men.

The most important case in contemporary European/American society is the dominance of heterosexual men and the subordination of homosexual men. This is much more than a cultural stigmatization of homosexuality or gay identity. Gay men are subordinated to straight men by an array of quite material practices. [. . .]. [These practices] include political and cultural exclusion, cultural abuse (in the United States gay men have now become the main symbolic target of the religious right), legal violence (such as imprisonment under sodomy statutes), street violence (ranging from intimidation to murder), economic discrimination and personal boycotts. It is not surprising that an Australian working-class man, reflecting on his experience of coming out in a homophobic culture, would remark:

> "You know, I didn't totally realize what it was to be gay. I mean it's a bastard of a life." [Connell, Davis and Dowsett 1993: 122]

Oppression positions homosexuality at the bottom of a gender hierarchy among men. Gayness, in patriarchal ideology, is the repository of whatever is symbolically expelled from hegemonic masculinity, the items ranging from fastidious taste in home decoration to receptive anal pleasure. Hence, from the point of view of hegemonic masculinity, gayness is easily assimilated to femininity. And hence—in the view of

some gay theorists—the ferocity of homophobic attacks.

Gay masculinity is the most conspicuous, but it is not the only subordinated masculinity. Some heterosexual men and boys too are expelled from the circle of legitimacy. The process is marked by a rich vocabulary of abuse: wimp, milksop, nerd, turkey, sissy, lily liver, jellyfish, yellowbelly, candy ass, ladyfinger, pushover, cookie pusher, cream puff, motherfucker, pantywaist, mother's boy, four-eyes, ear-'ole, dweeb, geek, Milquetoast, Cedric, and so on. Here too the symbolic blurring with femininity is obvious.

COMPLICITY

Normative definitions of masculinity, as I have noted, face the problem that not many men actually meet the normative standards. This point applies to hegemonic masculinity. The number of men rigorously practising the hegemonic pattern in its entirety may be quite small. Yet the majority of men gain from its hegemony, since they benefit from the patriarchal dividend, the advantage men in general gain from the overall subordination of women.

[. . .] [A]ccounts of masculinity have generally concerned themselves with syndromes and types, not with numbers. Yet in thinking about the dynamics of society as a whole, numbers matter. Sexual politics is mass politics, and strategic thinking needs to be concerned with where the masses of people are. If a large number of men have some connection with the hegemonic project but do not embody hegemonic masculinity, we need a way of theorizing their specific situation.

This can be done by recognizing another relationship among groups of men, the relationship of complicity with the hegemonic project. Masculinities constructed in ways that realize the patriarchal dividend, without the tensions or risks of being the front-line troops of patriarchy, are complicit in this sense.

It is tempting to treat them simply as slacker versions of hegemonic masculinity—the difference between the men who cheer football matches on TV and those who run out into the mud and the tackles themselves. But there is often something more definite and carefully crafted than that. Marriage, fatherhood and community life often involve extensive compromises with women rather than naked domination or an uncontested display of authority. A great many men who draw the patriarchal dividend also respect their wives and mothers, are never violent towards women, do their accustomed share of the housework, bring home the family wage, and can easily convince themselves that feminists must be bra-burning extremists.

MARGINALIZATION

Hegemony, subordination and complicity, as just defined, are relations internal to the gender order. The interplay of gender with other structures such as class and race creates further relationships between masculinities.

[. . .] [For instance,] new information technology became a vehicle for redefining middle-class masculinities at a time when the meaning of labour for working-class men was in contention. This is not a question of a fixed middle-class masculinity confronting a fixed working-class masculinity. Both are being reshaped, by a social dynamic in which class and gender relations are simultaneously in play.

Race relations may also become an integral part of the dynamic between masculinities. In a white-supremacist context, black masculinities play symbolic roles for white gender construction. For instance, black sporting stars become exemplars of masculine toughness, while the fantasy figure of the black rapist plays an important role in sexual politics among whites, a role much exploited by right-wing politics in the United States. Conversely, hegemonic masculinity among whites sustains the institutional oppression and physical terror that have framed the making of masculinities in black communities.

Robert Staples's discussion of internal colonialism in *Black Masculinity* [1982] shows the effect of class and race relations at the same time. As he argues, the level of violence among black men in the United States can only be understood through the changing place of the black labour force in American capitalism and the violent means used to control it. Massive unemployment and urban poverty now powerfully interact with institutional racism in the shaping of black masculinity. [. . .]

Though the term is not ideal, I cannot improve on "marginalization" to refer to the relations between the masculinities in dominant and subordinated classes or ethnic groups. Marginalization is always relative to the authorization of the hegemonic masculinity of the dominant group. Thus, in the United States, particular black athletes may be exemplars for hegemonic masculinity. But the fame and wealth of individual stars has no trickledown effect; it does not yield social authority to black men generally.

The relation of marginalization and authorization may also exist between subordinated masculinities. A striking example is the trial and conviction of Oscar Wilde, one of the first men caught in the net of modern anti-homosexual legislation. Wilde was trapped because of his connections with homosexual working-class youths, a practice unchallenged until his legal battle with a wealthy aristocrat, the Marquess of Queensberry, made him vulnerable [Ellman 1987].

These two types of relationship—hegemony, domination/subordination and complicity on the one hand, marginalization/authorization on the other—provide a framework in which we can analyze specific masculinities. (This is a sparse framework, but social theory should be hardworking.) I emphasize that terms such as "hegemonic masculinity" and "marginalized masculinities" name not fixed character types but configurations of practice generated in particular situations in a changing structure of relationships. Any theory of masculinity worth having must give an account of this process of change.

HISTORICAL DYNAMICS, VIOLENCE AND CRISIS TENDENCIES

To recognize gender as a social pattern requires us to see it as a product of history, and also as a producer of history. [. . .] [G]ender practice [is] onto-formative[—it] constitut[es] reality, and it is a crucial part of this idea that social reality is dynamic in time. We habitually think of the social as less real than the biological, what changes as less real than what stays the same. But there is a colossal reality to history. It is the modality of human life, precisely what defines us as human. No other species produces and lives in history, replacing organic evolution with radically new determinants of change.

To recognize masculinity and femininity as historical, then, is not to suggest they are flimsy or trivial. It is to locate them firmly in the world of social agency. And it raises a string of questions about their historicity.

The structures of gender relations are formed and transformed over time. It has been common in historical writing to see this change as coming from outside gender—from technology or class dynamics, most often. But change is also generated from within gender relations. The dynamic is as old as gender relations. It has, however, become more clearly defined in the last two centuries with the emergence of a public politics of gender and sexuality.

With the women's suffrage movement and the early homophile movement, the conflict of interests embedded in gender relations became visible. Interests are formed in any structure of inequality, which necessarily defines groups that will gain and lose differently by sustaining or by changing the structure. A gender order where men dominate women cannot void constituting men as an interest group concerned with defence, and women as an interest group concerned with change. This is a structural fact, independent of whether men as individuals love or hate women, or believe in equality or abjection, and independent of whether women are currently pursuing change.

To speak of a patriarchal dividend is to raise exactly this question of interest. Men gain a dividend from patriarchy in terms of honour, prestige and the right to command. They also gain a material dividend. In the rich capitalist countries, men's average incomes are approximately double women's average incomes. (The more familiar comparisons, of wage rates for full-time employment, greatly understate gender differences in actual incomes.) Men are vastly more likely to control a major block of capital as chief executive of a major corporation, or as direct owner. [. . .]

Men are much more likely to hold state power: for instance, men are ten times more likely than women to hold office as a member of parliament (an average across all countries of the world). Perhaps men do most of the work? No: in the rich countries, time-budget studies show women and men work on average about the same number of hours in the year. (The major difference is in how much of this work gets paid.) [. . .]

Given these facts, the "battle of the sexes" is no joke. Social struggle must result from inequalities on such a scale. It follows that the politics of masculinity cannot concern only questions of personal life and identity. It must also concern questions of social justice.

A structure of inequality on this scale, involving a massive dispossession of social resources, is hard to imagine without violence. It is, overwhelmingly, the dominant gender who hold and use the means of violence. Men are armed far more often than women. Indeed under many gender regimes women have been forbidden to bear or use arms (a rule applied, astonishingly, even within armies). Patriarchal definitions of femininity (dependence, fearfulness) amount to a cultural disarmament that may be quite as effective as the physical kind. Domestic violence cases often find abused women, physically able to look after themselves, who have accepted the abusers' definitions of themselves as incompetent and helpless [i.e., Russell 1982; Connell 1985; Ptacek 1988; Smith 1989].

Two patterns of violence follow from this situation. First, many members of the privileged group use violence to sustain their dominance. Intimidation of women ranges across the spectrum from wolf-whistling in the street, to office harassment, to rape and domestic assault, to murder by a woman's patriarchal "owner," such as a separated husband. Physical attacks are commonly accompanied by verbal abuse of women (whores and bitches, in recent popular music that recommends beating women). Most men do not attack or harass women; but those who do are unlikely to think themselves deviant. On the contrary they usually feel they are entirely justified, that they are exercising a right. They are authorized by an ideology of supremacy.

Second, violence becomes important in gender politics among men. Most episodes of major violence (counting military combat, homicide and armed assault) are transactions among men. Terror is used as a means of drawing boundaries and making exclusions, for example, in heterosexual violence against gay men. Violence can become a way of claiming or asserting masculinity in group struggles. This is an explosive process when an oppressed group gains the means of violence—as witness the levels of violence among black men in contemporary South Africa and the United States. The youth gang violence of inner-city streets is a striking example of the assertion of marginalized masculinities against other men, continuous with the assertion of masculinity in sexual violence against women [Messerschmidt 1993: 105–117].

Violence can be used to enforce a reactionary gender politics, as in the recent firebombings and murders of abortion service providers in the United States. It must also be said that collective violence among men can open possibilities for progress in gender relations. The two global wars this century produced important transitions in women's employment, shook up gender ideology, and accelerated the making of homosexual communities.

Violence is part of a system of domination, but is at the same time a measure of its imperfection. A thoroughly legitimate hierarchy would have less need to intimidate. The scale of contemporary violence points to crisis tendencies (to borrow a term from Jurgen Habermas) in the modern gender order.

The concept of crisis tendencies needs to be distinguished from the colloquial sense in which people speak of a "crisis of masculinity." As a theoretical term "crisis" presupposes a coherent system of some kind, which is destroyed or restored by the outcome of the crisis. Masculinity, as the argument so far has shown, is not a system in that sense. It is, rather, a configuration of practice *within* a system of gender relations. We cannot logically speak of the crisis of a configuration; rather we might speak of its disruption or its transformation. We can, however, logically speak of the crisis of a gender order as a whole, and of its tendencies towards crisis [e.g., Habermas 1976; Connell 1987: 158–63]. [. . .]

Such crisis tendencies will always implicate masculinities, though not necessarily by disrupting them. Crisis tendencies may, for instance, provoke attempts to restore a dominant masculinity. Michael Kimmel has pointed to this dynamic in turn-of-thecentury United States society, where fear of the women's suffrage movement played into the cult of the outdoorsman. Klaus Theweleit in *Male Fantasies* traced the more savage process that produced the sexual politics of fascism in the aftermath of the suffrage movement and German defeat in the Great War. More recently, Women's Liberation and defeat in Vietnam have stirred new cults of true masculinity in the United States, from violent "adventure" movies such as the Rambo series, to the expansion of the gun cult and what William Gibson in a frightening recent study has called "paramilitary culture" [Kimmel 1987; Theweleit 1987; Gibson 1994].

To understand the making of contemporary masculinities, then, we need to map the crisis tendencies of the gender order. This is no light task! But it is possible to make a start, using as a framework the three structures of gender relations defined earlier in this chapter.

Power relations show the most visible evidence of crisis tendencies: a historic collapse of the legitimacy of patriarchal power, and a global movement for the emancipation of women. This is fuelled by an underlying contradiction between the inequality of women and men, on the one hand, and the universalizing logics of modern state structures and market relations, on the other.

The incapacity of the institutions of civil society, notably the family, to resolve this tension provokes broad but incoherent state action (from family law to population policy) which itself becomes the focus of political turbulence. Masculinities are reconfigured around this crisis tendency both through conflict over strategies of legitimation, and through men's divergent responses to feminism [. . .]. While the tension leads some men to the cults of masculinity just mentioned, it leads others to support feminist reforms [e.g., Kimmel and Mosmiller 1992].

Production relations have also been the site of massive institutional changes. Most notable are the vast postwar growth in married women's employment in rich countries, and the even vaster incorporation of women's labour into the money economy in poor countries.

There is a basic contradiction between men's and women's equal contribution to production, and the gendered appropriation of the products of social labour. Patriarchal control of wealth is sustained by inheritance mechanisms, which, however, insert some women into the property system as owners. The turbulence of the gendered accumulation process creates a series of tensions and inequalities in men's chances of benefiting from it. Some men, for instance, are excluded from its benefit by unemployment [. . .]; others are advantaged by their connection with new physical or social technologies [. . .].

Relations of cathexis have visibly changed with the stabilization of lesbian and gay sexuality as a public alternative within the heterosexual order [. . .]. This change was supported by the broad claim by women for sexual pleasure and control of their own bodies, which has affected heterosexual practice as well as homosexual.

The patriarchal order prohibits forms of emotion, attachment and pleasure that patriarchal society itself produces. Tensions develop around sexual inequality and men's rights in marriage, around the prohibition on homosexual affection (given that patriarchy constantly produces homosocial institutions) and around the threat to social order symbolized by sexual freedoms.

This sketch of crisis tendencies is a very brief account of a vast subject, but it is perhaps enough to show changes in masculinities in something like their true perspective. The canvas is much broader than images of a modem male sex role, or renewal of the deep masculine, imply. Economy, state and global relationships are involved as well as households and personal relationships.

The vast changes in gender relations around the globe produce ferociously complex changes in the conditions of practice with which men as well as women have to grapple. No one is an innocent bystander in this arena of change. We are all engaged in constructing a world of gender relations. How it is made, what strategies different groups pursue, and with what effects, are political questions. Men no more than women are chained to the gender patterns they have inherited. Men too can make political choices for a new world of gender relations. Yet those choices are always made in concrete social circumstances, which limit what can be attempted; and the outcomes are not easily controlled.

To understand a historical process of this depth and complexity is not a task for *a priori* theorizing. It requires concrete study; more exactly, a range of studies that can illuminate the larger dynamics. [. . .]

REFERENCES

Connell, Raewyn. 1985. "Masculinity, Violence and War." In *War/Masculinity*, edited by Paul Patton and Ross Poole, 4–10. Sydney: Intervention.

Connell, Raewyn. 1987. *Gender and Power: Society, the Person and Sexual Politics.* Cambridge, UK: Polity Press.

Connell, Raewyn. 1995. *Masculinities.* Stanford, CA: Stanford University Press.

Connell, Raewyn, M. Davis, and G. Dowsett. 1993. "A Bastard of a Life: Homosexual Desire and Practice among Men in Working-Class Milieux." *Australian and New Zealand Journal of Sociology* 29: 112–35.

Ellman, Richard. 1987. *Oscar Wilde.* London: Hamish Hamilton.

Gibson, James William. 1994. *Warrior Dreams: Paramilitary Culture in Post-Vietnam America.* New York: Hill & Wang.

Habermas, Jurgen. 1976. *Legitimation Crisis.* London: Heinemann.

Hunt, Pauline. 1980. *Gender and Class Consciousness.* London: Macmillan.

Kimmel, Michael S. 1987. "Rethinking 'Masculinity': New Directions in Research." In *Changing Men: New Directions in Research on Men and Masculinity,* edited by Michael S. Kimmel, 9–24. Newbury Park, CA: Sage.

Kimmel, Michael S., and Thomas E. Mosmiller, eds. 1992. *Against the Tide: Pro-Feminist Men in the United States, 1776–1990, a Documentary History.* Boston: Beacon Press.

Messerschmidt, James. 1993. *Masculinities and Crime: Critique and Reconceptualization of Theory.* Lanham, MD: Rowman & Littlefield.

Mitchell, Juliet. 1971. *Woman's Estate.* Harmondsworth: Penguin.

Ptacek, James. 1988. "Why Do Men Batter Their Wives?" In *Feminist Perspectives on Wife Abuse,* edited by Kersti Yllo and Michele Bograd, 133–57. Newbury Park, CA: Sage.

Rubin, Gayle. 1975. "The Traffic in Women: Notes on the 'Political Economy' of Sex." In *Toward an Anthropology of Women,* edited by Rayna R. Reiter, 157–210. New York: Monthly Review Press.

Russell, Diana E. H. 1982. *Rape in Marriage.* New York: Macmillan.

Smith, Joan. 1989. *Misogynies.* London: Faber & Faber.

Staples, Robert. 1982. *Black Masculinity: The Black Male's Role in American Society.* San Francisco: Black Scholar Press.

Theweleit, Klaus. 1987. *Male Fantasies.* Cambridge, UK: Polity Press.

Tiger, Lionel. 1969. *Men in Groups.* New York: Random House.

SINE ANAHITA AND TAMARA L. MIX

9. RETROFITTING FRONTIER MASCULINITY FOR ALASKA'S WAR AGAINST WOLVES

Masculinities shape relationships among people. They also shape people's relationships with nonhuman animals. In the long history of humanity's control of wolves, masculinity has determined the manner in which wolves are targeted, whether and how they are killed, and to what extent governments are involved. Alaska's recent reinstitution of aerial wolf control, in which wolves are shot from a low-flying airplane or helicopter or from aircraft that land after tracking wolves from the air, dramatically illustrates these gender issues.

In this article, we analyze news articles about wolf control published during 14 years in the *Anchorage Daily News*. We apply Connell's (1993) ideas about frontier masculinity to create an understanding of Alaska's wolf politics. Frontier masculinity centers on cultural myths about real and imagined heroic frontiersmen and cowboys. We contend that in Alaska, frontier masculinity is constructed and sustained at the state level by influential policy makers and is promulgated by the major news media. As we document, there has been significant pressure against Alaska's wolf control policies, including major challenges to the frontier masculinity that shapes and supports these policies. But rather than letting go of frontier masculinity, we claim Alaska policy makers have retrofitted it to garner public support for dominion over Alaska's wolves. [. . .]

FRONTIER MASCULINITY IN ALASKA

In the U.S. national imagination, Alaska is mythologized as exceptional and unique in multiple ways (Kollin 2001). Many state policies support mythological aspects of the state, especially the myth of Alaska's being "the last frontier." Smelser (1998)

describes how myths serve particular functions, including bonding disparate groups together in a collective denial of reality and providing narratives that can be deployed for political ends. Alaska politicians exploit the myth of the state's exceptionalism as the last frontier for political advantage to mobilize their supporters and to attack their opposition. [. . .] [A] particular form of masculinity plays a central role in the myth of Alaska as a modern-day frontier and is maintained and legitimized not only by the attitudes and actions of individual men and women but, more important for the purpose of this article, by state agencies and politicians working to maintain cultural hegemony through the regional media (Artz and Murphy 2000). Connell (1993) coined the term "frontier masculinity" to describe a form of masculinity built on the myths of the frontier, including the iconic Daniel Boone, cowboys, and Paul Bunyan. [. . .]

Like Connell's concept, Alaska's frontier masculinity is mythological and fantasy based. It is an idealized form of public masculinity, a state-level masculinity, more than it is a form of masculinity to which individual men are held accountable. Frontier masculinity as an ideal is built on romanticized understandings of wilderness (Bonnett 1996), rugged self-sufficiency, courage, masculine bodily strength (Little and Leyshon 2003), autonomous individualism (Miller 2004), and active subordination of nature (Kimmel 1987). [. . .] Throughout its history, first as a territory, and then as a state, Alaska has been defined and understood as primarily male space, especially as a playground for white adventurers (Kollin 2001, 92), treasure seekers, and sport hunters. Frontier masculinity played a central role in 1890s–1920s gold rush Alaska and, before that, in the quest for riches through the fur trade. Indeed, the grizzled fur trapper and rugged gold

This reading is an excerpt from Sine Anahita and Tamara L. Mix's article in *Gender & Society* 20 (2006): 332–53.

prospector are celebrated cultural heroes of frontier masculinity, credited with battling a hostile and hazardous climate, vast wilderness, and dangerous animals to subordinate natural forces. The thousands of immigrants who flowed to Alaska in the wake of oil exploration in the 1970s–1980s carried with them their own visions of the myths of Alaska (Mitchell 2003). Today, the heavily masculinized oil industry is seen as the ultimate site for machismo and the romanticized cowboy hero, and the myth of frontier masculinity persists in the industry (Miller 2004).

Frontier masculinity has been constructed within the context of wilderness, an especially important element of the myth of Alaska as a frontier (Kollin 2001). Rural and wilderness areas are seen as sites where men can be real, masculine men, while men in cities are overly civilized, affected, and effeminate (Bell 2000). Wilderness areas are imagined as places where men can go wild and where they can experience masculine freedoms unavailable in stifling, feminized, domesticated cities (Bell 2000; Bonnett 1996; Kimmel 1996). Wilderness occupations are considered to be particularly manly, as men overpowering natural forces in their quest to make a living is highly valued (Strate 1992). [. . .] Strength and power are central to constructions of rural masculinity (Little and Leyshon 2003) and are essential elements of frontier masculinity. Hunting prowess may be the most significant aspect of Alaska's frontier masculinity.

Hunting success is seen as necessary on an individual level, but more important for this article, masculine hunting success is a state issue and is a vital element of Alaska's myth of the frontier. Early-twentieth-century sportsmen writers helped create the myth that there is a moose behind every tree in Alaska (Kollin 2001) and that hunters barely need to aim accurately to bag a trophy bull. Hunting for sport or for food is a highly gendered activity (King 1991). Nationwide, less than 7 percent of women hunt (Luke 1998), and men are up to 20 times more likely to hunt regardless of any other demographic variable (Stedman and Heberlein 2001). [. . .] Killing animals that are especially fierce, such as wolves or bears, has long been considered an indicator of manly virility (Emel 1995). [. . .] Within hunting cultures, hunting

is valorized (Brightman 1996), and men who do not hunt, or who show sympathy for hunted animals (Emel 1995) are considered to not be "real men" (Murphy 2001, 68). In Alaska, hunting cannot be separated from the myth of frontier masculinity; indeed, hunting prowess is central to the concept.

Hunting communities justify hunting in multiple ways. They claim it as a God-given right (Kellert et al. 1996; Woods 1997), as providing sustenance for families (Luke 1998), as a duty to protect crops against pests (Milbourne 2003a, 2003b; Woods 1997), as instinctual (King 1991; Luke 1998), as a cultural imperative (Fox 2002), as the most important way men obtain prestige and authority (Brightman 1996), and as sustaining traditional rural community life (Milbourne 2003a, 2003b). These key concepts reveal how hunting is intimately connected with issues of masculinity: the discourses surrounding natural rights, family provider, paternalist duty, instinct, traditional culture, route to authority, and sustaining traditional community life are all tightly woven with concepts of masculinity. [. . .]

In Alaska, sport hunting is strongly supported by state policies. Many influential policy makers identify themselves as sport hunters, and state agencies and decision-making bodies have historically been controlled by the sport hunting lobby (Strohmeyer 2003). But here, as elsewhere, hunting is under siege, as an increasingly vocal antihunting movement exerts pressure on hunting communities and state government (Byrd 2002). We argue that because hunting and statewide hunter success are such integral parts of the myth of the frontier and of frontier masculinity, state agencies routinely intervene to sustain them.

Due to the dominance and pervasiveness of the myth of frontier masculinity in Alaska, its values are instituted into state policy on hunting and wildlife issues. In Alaska, wildlife policies, including those that address hunting, are largely set by the Alaska Board of Game. [. . .] Throughout most of Alaska's history, the board has been composed of almost exclusively men, and like other states (Pacelle 1998), the board is dominated by individuals active in the hunting industry—sport hunters, fur trappers, and professional game guides (Luke 1998; Stedman and Heberlein 2001; Strohmeyer 2003). [. . .] [T]he board works to maintain frontier masculinity through the valorization of hunting (Brightman 1996) and aggressive subordination of wildlife, including Alaska's wolves.

THE WOLF FRONTIER IN MASCULINITY

Alaska has had a complicated historical relationship with its wild wolf packs. Wolves have long functioned as scapegoats all across the world (Kellert et al. 1996; Kleese 2002; Lopez [1978] 1995; Moore 1994). As McBride (1995, 124) claims, whether the scapegoat is guilty of the accused crimes or not does not matter; it is "mythically guilty," and so it is considered unquestionably by community members to be, in fact, guilty. [. . .]

Aerial wolf control programs and on-the-ground trapping and hunting of wolves continued to be unregulated in most of Alaska until the mid-1960s, when the state legislature for the first time classified wolves as big game animals and furbearers and required a hunting license to kill wolves. The consequence of the reclassification from vermin to game meant that not only federal agents, but the general public, could shoot wolves from airplanes (Rawson 2001). In the 1970s, the burgeoning environmental movement helped pass the federal Airborne Hunting Act, claiming that killing wildlife from the air was unfair chase. The passage of the act put a stop to most of Alaska's wolf hunting by air. However, on-the-ground hunting of wolves for sport and fur continued, and wolves continued to be blamed for plummeting moose and caribou populations. In the 1980s and 1990s, public conflict about wolves escalated, both nationally and statewide, with sportsmen's groups pressuring Alaska's legislature and Board of Game to increase wolf eradication programs and with environmentalist groups working to protect the state's wolf packs. Meanwhile, elsewhere in the United States, wolves were protected under the 1966 federal Endangered Species Act (Kellert et al. 1996). Outside Alaska, in the mid-1990s, several wolf reintroduction projects and protection programs for the few wild wolf packs that survived widespread extermination earlier in the twentieth century were highly successful in reestablishing vibrant wolf populations in several states, although not without local conflict (Byrd

2002; Jones 2002). In Alaska, state policies fluctuated in the 1990s, sometimes authorizing wolf eradication programs and at other times restricting them, depending on who controlled the Alaska Board of Game, the state legislature, and the governorship.

In 2004, the state resumed its internationally controversial policy of exterminating wolves by air, and it continues to enact state policies that encourage land-based hunters and trappers to kill wolves. The result is that more than 15 percent of Alaska's wolves are killed legally each year, and influential policy makers are working to expand the state-sponsored aerial wolf extermination program. For example, in 2005, 89 percent of the wolves in one area were scheduled to be killed.

Throughout Alaska's historical relationship with its wolves, groups promoting a particular form of public, state-level masculinity—frontier masculinity (Connell 1993)—have controlled state policy through domination of the legislature and the state's wildlife management agencies. The fact that groups maintaining such ideologies have been the ones to control official policy-making institutions has meant that Alaska's wolf policies are designed to support sportsmen's and frontiersmen's values of subordination of wolves. This is in spite of marked resistance from most wildlife scientists, environmentalists, animal rights groups, and a majority of citizens in both the United States (Nie 2002; Pacelle 1998) and Alaska (Kellert 1985). Although many authors have noted the symbolic value of wolves (Byrd 2002; Jones 2002; Kellert et al. 1996; and Nie 2002), an area that is undertheorized is the gendered aspect of that symbolism.

CHALLENGES AND CHANGES TO FRONTIER MASCULINITY

Economies and political systems may collapse, but hegemonic masculinities are collectively retooled to fit new realities (Brandth 1995; Campbell and Bell 2000; Ní Laoire 2001) so that control and subordination processes remain intact (Connell 2002). For Alaska men, frontier masculinity is no longer available as it was during the halcyon sport hunting, fur trading, gold rush, or oil pipeline days. [. . .] [B]ecause of multiple factors that have exerted significant pressure on traditional frontier masculinity, Alaska policy makers have retooled it so as to restore its hegemonic power.

One of the factors exerting pressure on frontier masculinity has been economic restructuring. Downsizing in extraction industries such as the oil industry (Miller 2004), timber industry (Sherman 2004), and gold mining, and the decline in the international market for fur, has eliminated many traditional Alaskan frontiersmen occupations. [. . .] Still another factor that has exerted pressure on frontier masculinity is global climate change, which has caused shifts in migration patterns of birds, marine life, and land mammals; degraded wildlife habitat (Fox 2002); and is linked to plummeting moose populations (Alaska Regional Assessment Group 1999). For frontiersmen and sportsmen in Alaska, these changes are being experienced as declining hunter success. [. . .] The phenomenal success of sport hunters during extensive wolf-eradication programs is part of the basis on which traditional frontier masculinity was built in the twentieth century. But after extensive wolf control was cut back, and after a series of population crashes among moose and caribou due to human manipulation of their population, habitat degradation, and overhunting by humans, sportsmen's hunting success was no longer guaranteed as it had been in the mythological halcyon days of frontier masculinity.

In Alaska discourse, shifts in transnational capitalism, economic restructuring, climate change, and overhunting are not typically blamed for the pressures on men and frontier masculinity. Wolves are the ones that have been blamed. As a Midwestern rancher explained, "while international markets and corporatization can be quite complex, wolves are relatively simple and can fit straight into the scope of a rifle" (Nie 2001, 8). In Alaska, [. . .] policy makers scapegoat wolves in spite of overwhelming scientific evidence that wolves are not primarily responsible for the decline of caribou and moose populations, for which they are blamed and targeted for eradication.

Structural changes, such as those described above, have gendered implications. [. . .] Among men whose masculine identity is based on dominance over nature (Kruse 1999; Warren 1995), the inability to be successful at hunting, to dominate an animal by killing it, is a profound challenge to their masculinity (Emel 1995). [. . .] [W]hen hunting is constrained in hunting communities, men lose a primary route by which they accrue power. Men who are near the bottom of a collapsing economy feel embattled (Fine et al. 1997; Moore 1994). Because they experience the situation as their traditional masculinity being under siege, they must find other ways to be men (Fine et al. 1997). [. . .]

As men come to feel embattled, and feel their masculine identity is under siege, they turn to their communities and to male-dominated institutions like the Alaska Game Board and the state legislature to help them craft new ways to be men. This underscores the fact that creating new ways for men to be manly is not an individual pursuit but is structured at the level of the state. Franzway et al. (1989) analyze the state as a gendered institution, claiming it is best viewed as a set of practices that institutionalize power relations, largely for the benefit of men. Connell (2001) further expands the idea that gendered practices are structural, and not just the property of individual men, when he describes the crisis tendency of dominant masculinities. According to Connell, when a dominant masculinity, such as frontier masculinity, is threatened, there are structural, often national attempts to reestablish and reaffirm the threatened masculinity. [. . .]

In Alaska, the newspaper resources we analyzed demonstrate that attempts to reestablish and reaffirm frontier masculinity occurred at the state level. We claim that Alaska policy makers retooled traditional frontier masculinity so as to restore its dominance but that they did so in ways that reflect new emphases. [. . .]

METHOD

Our interest in this [chapter] is how a shifting, public, state-level masculinity has shaped the discourse and policy-making processes related to the wolf issue in Alaska. An analysis of newspaper accounts as the wolf issue unfolded during the course of 14 years provided us with rich longitudinal data. For this work, we conducted an interpretive content analysis of newspaper articles, editorials, and letters to the editor of the most influential and widely distributed paper in Alaska: the *Anchorage Daily News* (referred to hereafter as

ADN [. . .]). The *ADN* was selected for its frequent reporting of wolf control issues within a local and regional context. We examined articles during the period of 1 January 1990 to 31 May 2004. The first date was selected because it was a pivotal moment in wolf control, as we discuss. We chose the second date because it was the final date of the aerial wolf control program for the year in which data collection was undertaken. [. . .]

A conventional content analysis typically codes manifest content, which is countable and supposedly objective (Berg 1995). However, for this article, we follow Berg's (1995) recommendation to code latent content because of its revelation of symbolic meanings attached to the manifest content. Because we are interested in how public masculinities shape public discourse, we utilize feminist narrative interpretive methods (DeVault 1999), allowing us to see that some of the latent content is gendered, even when "gender," "masculinity," or similar words do not actually appear in the text. [. . .]

THE FADING FRONTIER OF MASCULINITY[1]

By the 1990s, after a century of hegemony, frontier masculinity was enduring significant challenges. An iconographic moment occurred in 1990 when a group of prominent sportsmen was arrested and charged with illegally using airplanes to harass a pack of wolves before killing them [. . .]. In the news article about the crime, the U.S. Fish and Wildlife investigator implied the men simply got carried away with the thrill of the hunt. In spite of the investigator's "boys will be boys" attitude, the men were charged with a series of crimes. The writer of the article was the outdoors editor for the *ADN*. Although ostensibly about the crime, most of the article lauded the mythological hunting reputation of Jack Frost, the ringleader arrested in the case. He noted that Frost had killed every species of large animal in the United States by bow and that he had received multiple awards from hunting organizations. The writer gave Frost esteemed status as an admired, untamed, rebellious sportsman, an "outlaw aerial wolf hunter." Throughout the article, frontier masculinity was valorized; however, evidence that this was a moment when frontier masculinity

shifted from its previous hegemonic position is that Frost received a number of anonymous, threatening phone calls. This signaled a shift in the way the anonymous public felt about harassing and killing wolves from the air and in the violent performance of frontier masculinity for the purpose of subordinating nature.

Less than one year later, the influence of frontier masculinity on state wildlife policy after nearly one hundred years of control was waning. In 1991, the Alaska Board of Game instituted a series of new policies based on the recommendations of a 16-member alliance composed of both sports hunters and pro-wolf environmentalists. The new policies included limits on wolf hunting, including restricting same-day airborne hunting tactics, which allowed hunters to track wolves from the air, land, and shoot them. Sport hunters decried the limits, with one claiming killing wolves is "an essential freedom" and another saying, "I have as much a right and privilege to shoot a wolf as someone else has to watch a wolf" [. . .]. Doug Pope, chair of the Game Board, acknowledged the past role played by frontier masculinity, saying airborne hunting is "the last sort of remnant of the cowboy mentality that used to pervade here in Alaska, the sort of outlaw mentality" [. . .]. Pope decided the new policy would restrict airborne hunting to special cases, saying, "we're on the edge of a new era."

In successive years, frontier masculinity as embodied in the state's wolf control policies was increasingly challenged. [. . .] As a result of the international pressure, Governor Hickel, an *ADN* headline proclaimed, "backed down," canceled the proposed aerial wolf control plan, and called for a Wolf Summit [. . .], an event that became notorious. The governor, the report stated, used bad judgment in approving the plan, and now he had "a political disaster on his hands" [. . .]. [. . .] Relying on the elements of frontier masculinity that had long shaped the wolf control issue, especially the taken-for-granted lethal subordination of wolves, no longer worked to justify why the state should carry on with its proposed wolf eradication plans. Governor Hickel, in response to a question from an NBC news journalist about why Alaska should institute wolf control, answered, "Well . . . you can't just let nature run wild" [. . .]. Nature must be dominated, according to Game Board policies shaped by frontier masculinity. A week later, Hickel, in a widely published letter [. . .], said folks outside Alaska misunderstood the wolf issue. In a telling tactical shift, instead of claiming sportsmen's right to kill wolves, Hickel claimed wolves were preventing Alaska family men from meeting the nutritional needs of their families. Deploying strategic bewilderment, the governor said Alaska's family providers were confused about why animal rights advocates did not want their families to have food to eat. This change from the state's formerly steadfast maintenance of sportsmen's right to dominate nature, to not allow it to "run wild," to an emphasis on men as embattled family providers unable to put food on their tables signals the shift of public policy to one shaped by what we call retro frontier masculinity.

THE EMERGENCE OF RETRO FRONTIER MASCULINITY

For many decades, the ideal of frontier masculinity, including the legacy of the mythological cowboy, framed the issue of wolf control. Emerging from the legacy of frontier masculinity are ideas about sportsmen's rights to unquestioned, total dominion over nature and wild animals. However, under the pressures of outrage over Alaska's aerial wolf control policies, the state's policy makers sought to reframe the issue. They did so by retooling and retrofitting frontier masculinity.

In the process of retrofitting frontier masculinity, policy makers continued to frame the wolf control issue as the right of sportsmen to subordinate nature but extended their frames [. . .] to include alternative, perhaps more compelling reasons for lethal wolf control. Frames are sets of interpretations of events made by a social movement to attract activists, to mobilize supporters, and to challenge the opposition (Snow et al. 1986). The new frames [. . .] included vilification of opponents as feminized, casting wolf hunters as paternalist protectors, reification of the masculine family provider role, and analysis of the issue as one fundamentally about competition. These emphases often overlap. A key part of the retrofit process is deploying values that have historical, even ancient, precedent, reframed for a new agenda.

Vilifying opponents as feminized is one of the reframed strategies undertaken as the state's policy makers sought to retrofit frontier masculinity. As Connell (2001) and Kimmel (1996) document, masculinity is constructed in opposition to anything feminine [. . .]. Previously, Alaska's policy makers had little need to vilify their opponents as feminized because the values of traditional frontier masculinity were hegemonic. Early in 1993, policy makers realized that compromise on the wolf control issue might be necessary, but they had to reassure the public that compromise did not necessarily threaten the state's traditional form of masculinity. [. . .] Michael Carey, editor of the *ADN*, sought to assure readers that being against aerial wolf control did not necessarily make one less of a real Alaska man: "The legendary game warden, Sam White of Fairbanks, hardly a posy sniffer, had no use for aerial wolf hunting" because it gives hunters an unfair, unsportsmanlike advantage over their prey [. . .]. Embodying sportsmanlike values such as giving prey a "fair chance," he claimed, does not mean that a hunter is an effete, flower-loving environmentalist.

Another example of the tactic of vilification of opponents as feminized appeared in 1992 when an opinion writer wrote an article criticizing central players. He trivialized those opposed to state employees gunning down wolves from the air as "defenders of forest creatures" and characterized activists as "little old ladies with umbrellas" [. . .]. The writer feminized those opposed to aerial wolf control as a way to delegitimate their stance. [. . .]

Another tactic that gained utility during the retrofitting of frontier masculinity was casting wolves as threatening and wolf hunters as protectors. Recalling that the hero of "Little Red Riding Hood" was the hunter who killed the wolf (Emel 1995), wolves were cast as a threat to children: "Participants talked of the danger the wolves pose for children walking to school in the dark," claimed one article [. . .]. "Wolves often are spotted from classrooms, and parents fear for their children's safety," a woman claimed [. . .]. This tactic, which played on ancient myths, raised the specter of innocent children being killed by bold, out-of-control wolves. The state's project to kill wolves was thus framed as a means to protect children. [. . .]

Related to the tactic of framing the wolf control issue as being necessary to protect children, women, and elderly people, with the emergence of retro frontier masculinity, the state's wolf policies began to emphasize the need for family men to have enough moose to hunt to provide meat for their families. Previously, this had been mostly a side issue, with sport hunters' rights to kill trophy bull moose or their right to kill wolves for sport taking discursive precedence. Part of the reframing of the wolf control issue, then, was a reification of the masculine family provider role. [. . .]

At the first Board of Game meeting after the 2002 gubernatorial election, 45 people complained about wolves. Many were hunters from an area where a study had documented not a general lack of moose but only a shortage of bull moose within a mile of town, indicating predation by humans, not wolves. However, families were said to be suffering for lack of meat, and a resident claimed, "we have so many wolves in our country that people are carrying handguns to the outhouse" [. . .]. The board acted swiftly to demonstrate its newly restored muscle. Aerial wolf control plans were instituted, and the state attorney was directed to find a way to circumvent the anti–aerial wolf hunting amendment to the state's constitution that had earlier been passed by citizens. Meanwhile, polls showed 76 percent of Alaskans were opposed to state-sponsored lethal wolf control [. . .].

The legislature also whirled into action, passing bills allowing wolf control practices that had earlier been prohibited by voters. Ralph Seekins, a first-term senator, introduced a bill allowing the Board of Game to make a "pre-emptive strike against predators" [. . .]. Passed by the legislature and signed by the new governor, the bill allowed preemptive strikes against predators even if moose or caribou populations were not threatened. [. . .]

Another reframed strategic emphasis state policy makers utilized was to consider the wolf control issue in terms of fairness and competition. There are three elements to this: structuring aerial wolf hunts as a matter of fair competition between wolves and their pursuers, questioning whether wolves deserve fair competition, and framing wolf control as necessary to limit wolves' competition with family providers seeking to put meat on their family tables. [. . .] [In 2003,] [f]raming the wolf control issue as one fundamentally about fair competition, [the new Republican governor]

Murkowski said, "Humaneness is in the eye of the beholder. If you run 'em down in a helicopter and shoot 'em, that's pretty efficient. If you run 'em down in a Super Cub, that requires a little more skill and the wolf has probably got a better chance." [. . .]

A third way that the idea of competition is utilized in retro frontier masculinity is describing wolf control projects as giving human hunters a competitive advantage against wolves in their mutual quest for meat. When, in 2003, the Board of Game announced plans to kill all wolves in a 1,700 square mile area, and to begin an equally aggressive wolf kill plan in another area, competition was a key part of the discussion. Paul Joslin of the Alaska Wildlife Alliance termed the hunt plans "a posse in the sky" [. . .]. Priscilla Feral, head of Friends of Animals, told Representative Ralph Seekins, "That's barbaric and out of touch with Alaska and the rest of the world. . . . In 2003 it really is an ethical outrage to be blasting wolves with shotguns." Seekins's response was, "We have to eliminate the competition to feed Alaskans." More fundamentally, Seekins also revealed what is now obvious to all who have studied the wolf control issue: "This isn't about wolves. This is about who gets to control Alaska. . . . They want us to compromise and compromise and compromise until there's nothing left."

REFLECTIONS

In Alaska, wolves are reprising a role they have played for centuries: They are scapegoats at the state level, where they pay for the multiple pressures against masculinity with their lives. A legitimate question might be, Why wolves? Kellert et al. (1996) document that in the Yellowstone Park area, mountain lions are the major culprits in livestock predation and are responsible for many attacks on humans. Yet there is little mention of mountain lions as a problem in the local press. At the same time, mere discussion of a wolf reintroduction program elicited much negative publicity, including dire predictions of children being killed in the park. Similarly, a scientist working in a particularly contentious area in Alaska documented that the majority of predation on moose was caused not by wolves but by bears [. . .]. In fact, in his study, wolves accounted for only 16 percent of predation on moose, while black bears and grizzly bears together accounted for 81 percent. But even though bears have recently been blamed as culprits in predation on moose in Alaska, including being targeted for lethal and nonlethal methods of control, bears cannot be scapegoats the way wolves are. The scientist who did the study acknowledged that even suggesting bears be killed like wolves would be "unimaginable. . . . [. . .] People have a lot of respect for them," he said. We claim there is more to the story of who plays the scapegoat role than respect for bears. First, because bears are among North America's most fierce animals, they are especially revered. [. . .] In contrast, wolves have long been attributed to the lowest status possible for animals, that of vermin, and killing vermin is considered socially acceptable, even desirable (Flynn 1999).

Second, Alaska inherited a culturally ingrained hatred of wolves handed down first from Europe, then from early American pioneers, then from Western expansionists (Kellert 1985). In fact, wolves were the target of the first wildlife laws passed by early American settlers, as a wolf bounty was established as early as 1630 (Kellert et al. 1996). Although it could be argued that bears have posed as many practical problems as wolves have, they are not subject to the kind of negative myths that have been foisted on wolves. Wolves have long been constructed in the popular imagination as symbolizing danger, while bears have escaped such symbolism. Evidence of this can be found in children's stories. Whereas the wolf is an evildoer blowing down houses of Little Pigs, or devouring Grandmother and attempting to eat Little Red Riding Hood, bears are benign, even if they are annoyed at Goldilocks's trespassing on their private property without their permission. In addition, they are considered cuddly, as the popular teddy bear aptly illustrates. [. . .]

There is also the mythological relationship bears share with masculinity. For example, the mythopoetic men's movement's celebration of the archetypal wild and hairy man (Bonnett 1996) seems bear-like. In contrast, labeling a man a "wolf" implies that he sexually harasses women, which is increasingly considered to be antisocial behavior. [. . .] Bears seem to have a special link with masculinity that wolves do not.

This [chapter] argues that policy makers in Alaska retrofitted an earlier form of masculinity, frontier masculinity, as a way to garner public support for their controversial wolf control projects. While traditional frontier masculinity emphasized sportsmen's rights to kill wolves, the framing of the issue utilizing retro frontier masculinity employs new strategic emphases: vilifying opponents as feminized, casting wolf hunters as paternalist protectors, reifying the masculine family provider role, and framing the issue as fundamentally about competition. Retro frontier masculinity is deployed on a statewide basis, reflecting the fact that states are gendered.

We hope this work opens another area where sociologists may examine issues of gender. In particular, this work contributes to the analysis of how the state may construct and sustain a symbolic form of masculinity as a way to manage systemic threats to public manliness. Our ideas about retro frontier masculinity further strengthen sociological understandings about how masculinity is not just a property of individuals but also is deployed at the state level by policy makers seeking political advantage. In addition, our work highlights not only how masculinity is socially constructed but also how the social construction of masculinity is inherently interwoven with the social construction of frontiers, wilderness, scapegoats, and wolves and other wildlife. Finally, this work documents how the symbolic politics of masculinity have not only human victims but nonhuman ones as well. [. . .]

REFERENCES

Alaska Regional Assessment Group. 1999. *The Potential Consequences of Climate Variability and Change.* Fairbanks: Center for Global Change and Arctic System Research, University of Alaska Fairbanks.

Artz, Lee, and Bren Ortega Murphy. 2000. *Cultural Hegemony in the United States.* Thousand Oaks, CA: Sage.

Bell, David. 2000. "Farm Boys and Wild Men: Rurality, Masculinity, and Homosexuality." *Rural Sociology* 65 (4): 547–61.

Berg, Bruce L. 1995. *Qualitative Research Methods for the Social Sciences.* 2nd ed. Boston: Allyn & Bacon.

Bonnett, Alastair. 1996. "The New Primitives: Identity, Landscape and Cultural Appropriation in the Mythopoetic Men's Movement." *Antipode* 28 (3): 273–91.

Brandth, Berit. 1995. "Rural Masculinity in Transition: Gender Images in Tractor Advertisements." *Journal of Rural Studies* 11 (2): 123–33.

Brightman, Robert. 1996. "The Sexual Division of Foraging Labor: Biology, Taboo, and Gender Politics." *Comparative Studies in Society and History* 38 (4): 687–729.

Byrd, Kimberly. 2002. "Mirrors and Metaphors: Contemporary Narratives of the Wolf in Minnesota." *Ethics, Place & Environment* 5 (1): 50–65.

Campbell, Hugh, and Michael Mayerfeld Bell. 2000. "The Question of Rural Masculinities." *Rural Sociology* 65 (4): 532–46.

Connell, Raewyn. 1993. "The Big Picture: Masculinities in Recent World History." *Theory and Society* 22:597–623.

Connell, Raewyn. 2001. "The Social Organization of Masculinity." In *The Masculinities Reader*, edited by S. M. Whitehead and F. J. Barrett. Malden, MA: Polity.

Connell, Raewyn. 2002. "Understanding Men: Gender Sociology and the New International Research on Masculinities." *Social Thought & Research* 24 (1/2): 13–31.

DeVault, Marjorie L. 1999. *Liberating Method: Feminism and Social Research*. Philadelphia: Temple University Press.

Emel, Jody. 1995. "Are You Man Enough, Big and Bad Enough? An Ecofeminist Analysis of Wolf Eradication in the United States." *Society and Space: Environment and Planning D* 13:707–34.

Fine, M., L. Weis, J. Addelston, and J. Marusza. 1997. "(In)secure Times: Constructing White Working-Class Masculinities in the Late 20th Century." *Gender & Society* 11 (1): 52–68.

Flynn, Clifton P. 1999. "Animal Abuse in Childhood and Later Support for Interpersonal Violence in Families." *Society and Animals* 7 (2): 161–72.

Fox, S. 2002. "These Are Things That Are Really Happening: Inuit Perspectives on the Evidence and Impacts of Climate Change in Nunavut." In *The Earth Is Faster Now: Indigenous Observations of Arctic Environmental Change*, edited by I. Krupnik and D. Jolly. Fairbanks, AK: Arctic Research Consortium.

Franzway, Suzanne, Dianne Court, and Raewyn Connell. 1989. *Staking a Claim: Feminism, Bureaucracy and the State*. Boston: Allen & Unwin.

Jones, Karen. 2002. "'A Fierce Green Fire'": Passionate Pleas and Wolf Ecology." *Ethics, Place & Environment* 5 (1): 35–44.

Kellert, Stephen R. 1985. "Public Perceptions of Predators, Particularly the Wolf and Coyote." *Biological Conservation* 31:167–89.

Kellert, S. R., M. Black, C. R. Rush, and A. J. Bath. 1996. "Human Culture and Large Carnivore Conservation in North America." *Conservation Biology* 10 (4): 977–90.

Kimmel, Michael S. 1987. "The Cult of Masculinity: American Social Character and the Legacy of the Cowboy." In *Beyond Patriarchy: Essays by Men on Pleasure, Power, and Change*, edited by Michael Kaufman. Toronto, Canada: Oxford University Press.

Kimmel, Michael S. 1996. *Manhood in America: A Cultural History*. New York: Free Press.

King, Roger J. H. 1991. "Environmental Ethics and the Case for Hunting." *Environmental Ethics* 13 (1): 59–85.

Kleese, Deborah. 2002. "Contested Natures: Wolves in Late Modernity." *Society and Natural Resources* 15: 313–26.

Kollin, Susan. 2001. *Nature's State: Imagining Alaska as the Last Frontier*. Chapel Hill: University of North Carolina Press.

Kruse, Corwin R. 1999. "Gender, Views of Nature, and Support for Animal Rights." *Society and Animals* 7 (3): 179–98.

Little, Jo, and Michael Leyshon. 2003. "Embodied Rural Geographies: Developing Research Agendas." *Progress in Human Geography* 27 (3): 257–72.

Lopez, Barry H. [1978] 1995. *Of Wolves and Men*. New York: Simon & Schuster.

Luke, Brian. 1998. "Violent Love: Hunting, Heterosexuality, and the Erotics of Men's Predation." *Feminist Studies* 24 (3): 627–55.

McBride, James. 1995. *War, Battering, and Other Sports: The Gulf between American Men and Women*. Atlantic Highlands, NJ: Humanities Press.

Milbourne, Paul. 2003a. "The Complexities of Hunting in Rural England and Wales." *Sociologia Ruralis* 43 (3): 289–308.

Milbourne, Paul. 2003b. "Hunting Ruralities: Nature, Society and Culture in 'Hunt Countries' of England and Wales." *Journal of Rural Studies* 19:157–71.

Miller, Gloria E. 2004. "Frontier Masculinity in the Oil Industry: The Experience of Women Engineers." *Gender, Work and Organization* 11 (1): 47–73.

Mitchell, Donald Craig. 2003. *Sold American: The Story of Alaska Natives and Their Land, 1867–1959.* Fairbanks: University of Alaska Press.

Moore, Roland S. 1994. "Metaphors of Encroachment: Hunting for Wolves on a Central Greek Mountain." *Anthropological Quarterly* 67 (2): 81–89.

Murphy, Peter F. 2001. *Studs, Tools, and the Family Jewels: Metaphors Men Live By.* Madison: University of Wisconsin Press.

Nie, Martin A. 2001. "The Sociopolitical Dimensions of Wolf Management and Restoration in the United States." *Human Ecology Review* 8 (1): 1–12.

Ní Laoire, Caitrína. 2001. "A Matter of Life and Death? Men, Masculinities, and Staying 'behind' in Rural Ireland." *Sociologia Ruralis* 41 (2): 220–36.

Pacelle, Wayne. 1998. "Forging a New Wildlife Management Paradigm: Integrating Animal Protection Values." *Human Dimensions of Wildlife* 3 (2): 42–50.

Rawson, Timothy. 2001. *Changing Tracks: Predators and Politics in Mt. McKinley National Park.* Fairbanks: University of Alaska Press.

Sherman, Jennifer. 2004. "Remaking Rural Masculinity: Fatherhood and Masculine Identity in the Spotted Owl's Shadow." Paper presented at the annual meeting of the Rural Sociological Society, Sacramento, CA, 14 August.

Smelser, Neil I. 1998. "Collective Myths and Fantasies: The Myth of the Good Life in California." In *The Social Edges of Psychoanalysis.* Berkeley: University of California Press.

Snow, David A., E. Burke Rochford Jr., Steven K. Worden, and Robert D. Benford. 1986. "Frame Alignment Processes, Micromobilization, and Movement Participation." *American Sociological Review* 51:464–81.

Stedman, Richard C., and Thomas A. Heberlein. 2001. "Hunting and Rural Socialization: Contingent Effects of the Rural Setting on Hunting Participation." *Rural Sociology* 66 (4): 599–617.

Strate, L. 1992. "Beer Commercials: A Manual on Masculinity." In *Men, Masculinity, and the Media,* edited by S. Craig. Newbury Park, CA: Sage.

Strohmeyer, John. 2003. *Extreme Conditions: Big Oil and the Transformation of Alaska.* Anchorage, AK: Cascade Press.

Warren, K. J. 1995. "The Power and the Promise of Ecological Feminism." In *Earth Ethics: Environmental Ethics, Animal Rights, and Practical Applications,* edited by J. P. Sterba. Englewood Cliffs, NJ: Prentice Hall.

Woods, Michael. 1997. "Researching Rural Conflicts: Hunting, Local Politics and Actor-Networks." *Journal of Rural Studies* 14:321–40.

NOTES

1. [In the complete article, Anahita and Mix cite the newspaper articles in an appendix. In an effort to reduce the text, we've removed citations to newspaper articles. See the complete article for full citations for the *ADN* articles.]

MELANIE HEATH

10. MANHOOD OVER EASY: REFLECTIONS ON HEGEMONIC, SOFT-BOILED, AND MULTIPLE MASCULINITIES

A "crisis of masculinity" has erupted in every period of backlash in the last century, a faithful quiet companion to the loudly voiced call for a "return to femininity." In the late 1800s, a blizzard of literature decrying the "soft male" rolled off the presses. "The whole generation is woman-ized," Henry James's protagonist Basil Ransom lamented in *The Bostonian*. "The masculine tone is passing out of the world; it's a feminine, a nervous, hysterical, chattering, canting age."

—*Susan Faludi, Backlash, 2006*

The fear that traditional forms of masculinity are being undermined in ways that are harmful to society has taken root in public consciousness since the 1990s. A recent manifestation is Hana Rosin's *The End of Men and the Rise of Women* (2012), in which she laments the decline of male dominance and the end of men's economic and social stranglehold over women. Her gleeful and often unsubstantiated claims about men's loss of power in the new economy feeds into riotous alarm bells being sounded in popular culture over the feminization of men and boys, a discourse that Susan Faludi traces back to the turn of the twentieth century. Similar to past reactions, current backlash tendencies have led to the emergence of numerous men's movements. The emergence of the "mythopoetic" men's movement in the 1990s was based on the philosophy that modernization has led to the feminization of men. To rectify this problem, the movement embraced rituals and storytelling to facilitate a reconnection to the "deep masculine" and enable the unleashing of men's animal nature (Messner 1997). Similarly, the Promise Keepers (PK) was a movement that grew in the 1990s with a goal of transforming and altering the norms of masculinity by challenging men to reestablish their leadership role in the family (Bartkowski 2004; Donovan 1998; Newton 2005; Williams 2001).

In the late 1990s, I conducted ethnographic research on the PK to examine how this movement helped men to reform or to shore up power in their families and in society (Heath 2003). PK is an all-male organization of evangelical Christians. Bill McCartney, then the head football coach at the University of Colorado at Boulder, founded the movement in 1990, inspired by his dream to fill a sports stadium with men, not to watch football, but to enact a godly man-hood. He realized his vision, as the movement grew from a small gathering in 1991 to millions of men attending stadium events nationwide, especially wit-nessed by the sea of men who gathered at the National Mall in Washington, D.C., in 1997 for the Stand in the Gap gathering. Since its peak in 1997 attendance has ebbed and flowed, but the organization has endured.

The philosophy of the PK movement has focused on the changing meaning of manhood, and a goal of the organization has been to unify men of different races and socioeconomic backgrounds under a single Christian banner. The most controversial aspect has revolved around its stated mission, "The Making of Godly Men," which includes recovering men's leader-ship positions within their families and communities (Conrad 2006; Heath 2003). In studying the PK move-ment, I sought to uncover how these men and their wives understood masculinity. Since the late 1980s, sociologists have theorized the ways that masculinity involves multiple, contextual and historically shifting configurations (Connell 1995). Theorizing gender as relational, this literature has outlined the ways that hegemonic masculinities—or dominant forms of masculinity—depend on other subordinated or mar-ginalized varieties of masculinity and femininities to be situated at the top of the gender hierarchy.

Reflecting back on my research (Heath 2003) that drew on participant observation and in-depth interviews with 20 PK husbands and their wives, this chapter analyzes the case of the PK as a way to think through the multiple masculinities approach to gender. What can this group of Christian men tell us about masculinities after a decade of research has developed? My reassessment of the PK movement indicates that the multiple masculinities approach can be enriched by the additions of Bourdieu's concept of "field" as well as insights from intersectionality theory. This chapter examines how PK men play the field to embrace a softer image of masculinity as "enlightened" but still hierarchical to maintain their position as leaders. The evangelical field allows non-privileged men to participate alongside those who are privileged in the benefits of hierarchical gender relations, while at the same time maintaining a racial hierarchy that does little to address the structural inequalities that marginalize men of color. Similarly, PK men are able to be more emotionally expressive, but only in spaces without women to ward off possible challenges to their heterosexuality. In the following, I show how these combined approaches of field theory and intersectionality offer a powerful conceptual metaphor for illuminating the structural arrangements of gender hierarchies and their intersections with race, class, and sexuality.

HEGEMONY AND PLAYING THE FIELD

Assessing two decades of research on hegemonic masculinity, Raewyn Connell and James Messerschmidt in 2005 called for a comprehensive re-examination of what they assessed to be a troubled concept, criticized for being structurally deterministic and denying agency (Whitehead 2002) and for being detached from everyday experience (Jefferson 2002; Wetherell and Edley 1999). In the past 20 years, since Connell first introduced the multiple masculinities model, scholarship on masculinities has detailed the ways that gender hierarchies differ according to the production of gender relations in particular social settings. In fact, as Connell and Messerschmidt argue, models of hegemonic masculinities do not necessarily correspond to men's lived experiences and can be more about "widespread ideals, fantasies, and desires" (2005: 838). In this chapter, I introduce Bourdieu's concept of fields as a tool to locate configurations of hegemonic

masculinities that depend on discursive ideals and fantasies, produced in specific historical processes and locations.

Bourdieu theorizes a social system of relatively autonomous fields that are founded on hierarchies and that depend on configurations of social arrangements able to sustain and reproduce them. Similar to conceptions of hegemony, Bourdieu argues that the persistence of these arrangements depends on the systematic misrecognition of their oppressive nature both by those in dominant positions and by those in subordinate ones (Bourdieu 1977). Bourdieu identifies the strong ties in a given field:

> The intellectual field, which cannot be reduced to a simple aggregate of isolated agents or to the sum of elements merely juxtaposed is, like a magnetic field, made up of a system of power lines. In other words, the constituting agents or system of agents may be described as so many forces which, by their existence, opposition or combination, determine its specific structure at a given moment in time. In return, each of these is defined by its particular position within this field from which it derives *positional properties* which cannot be assimilated to intrinsic properties. (Bourdieu 1971: 161)

Conceptualizing the hierarchical structures of masculinities in terms of fields can help to identify the multitude of fields in which masculinities operate and to specify how different versions of dominant (and subordinate) masculinities exist in each (Coles 2009). Although the concept of fields implies an enclosed and bounded space, Bourdieu envisions it as relational and elastic in a manner similar to Connell's theorization of gender relations. Accordingly, it has the ability to include a broad range of factors and to overlap with other fields in its influence on behavior (Swartz 1997).

My research on the PK offers an opportunity to consider the ways that multiple masculinities are produced in the evangelical field by analyzing the ways that the fields of race, class, and sexuality intersect with other fields in producing a hierarchy of multiple masculinities. The PK movement uncovers the importance of religion in maintaining gender hegemony; in the evangelical context, men are exhorted to reclaim their spiritual leadership roles as the heads of their families and as exemplars in their communities.

Within the field of evangelical religion, the ideal of hegemonic masculinity characterizes men as "born" leaders who are naturally assertive, confident, and able to control their emotions. The ability to act as a born leader can be attributed to "habitus," a matrix of dispositions that allows men to perform "masculine" activities as part of the cultural unconscious (Bourdieu 1984). Successful practice of leadership requires men to adjust their dispositions according to the situation in play and to act creatively based on past experiences that are developed over time (although not consciously). Thus, the habitus of practices such as male leadership mirror idealizations of hegemonic manhood and position men within the social space of the gender hierarchy as more competent and powerful than women.

Interviews with men and their wives uncovered an understanding of men's natural ability to lead in contrast to feminine traits of emotional instability. In PK movement literature, women are characterized as less able to take an objective and rational approach, as "nurturers" and "developers of life" called to be their husbands' "helpmates," and therefore not born leaders (Conrad 2006: 313). The movement calls for strong male leadership as central to bringing moral order to modern society, which lacks a strong moral compass. An advertisement for the 1999 conferences states,

> In this day of compromised values, where popular thought denies the existence of absolute truth, our world is crying out for someone to take a stand—for holiness, righteousness, family and Christ! Promise Keepers understands the urgency of our times and strongly believes that you have a critical role to play in reversing the current moral and spiritual downfall our nation is facing. (The Promise Keeper 1999: 3, quoted in Conrad 2006: 313)

Alice,[1] one of the wives in my study, summed up how PK could help men to reclaim their leadership roles in society where what it means to be a man has become problematic: "Men . . . for all these years have not had a base. They've been on their own trying to make it, trying to support their family, and they are constantly being sucked in by what the world says they ought to do. Finally, men are going to be men." In other words, PK helps Christian men see the importance of recognizing their "natural" authority to

be the spiritual beacons for their families and communities in a sinful world.

The field of evangelical Christianity, therefore, situates an ideal manhood at the top of the gender hierarchy based on a standard of strong leadership and positioned against women's "supportive" roles as men's helpers. However, there is ambiguity in the organization's interpretation of leadership, which exhorts men to lead by becoming more emotionally available to other men, to their wives and children, and by participating more in the domestic realm associated with feminine labor. In the following, I consider the ways that the evangelical field intersects with the fields of gender, race, class, and sexuality to produce contradictory gender and racial meanings among hegemonic and other multiple masculinities and the way in which these meanings support a gendered hierarchy.

INTERSECTIONALITY: TAKING IT TO THE MARGINS

A substantial literature has emerged in contemporary masculinity studies to examine the interactions of race and class in the construction of marginalized masculinities, and cutting-edge research has begun to examine transnational and global contexts (e.g., Hirose and Kei-ho Pih 2010; Hoang and Yeoh 2011; Lu and Wong 2013; Messner 1997; Montes 2013; Morrell et al. 2012; Pyke 1996; Scrinzi 2010; Ward 2008). Empirical studies of masculinities, however, still sometimes overlook race and class when analyzing privileged men, as if these two fields are not important to understanding whiteness and privilege. McCormack and Anderson (2010), for example, offer a compelling ethnographic study of the ways that high school boys adopt a pro-gay stance and eschew homophobic language but still privilege and regulate heterosexuality. Although they offer a trenchant analysis of how boys manage their heterosexual privilege, they choose not to analyze race and class and the importance of these to embracing pro-gay attitudes, arguing, "We have not focused on class and race in this article because they do not explicitly impact on these participants the way sexuality and gender do" (McCormack and Anderson 2010: 856).

As a relational category, research on masculinities must account for the social processes in which race and class privilege produce gender hegemony and multiple masculinities and femininities. In this regard, I employ an intersectional approach. Intersectionality is a concept introduced in the late 1980s to uncover the overlapping and conflicting dynamics of difference and sameness in the ways that gender, race, class, and other axes of power operate in producing and sustaining inequalities (Cho et al. 2013). My research on the PK movement uncovers two insights on how the concept of fields is important in intersectional thinking. On the one hand, the evangelical field offers marginalized men a way to participate in hegemonic practices of masculinity alongside more privileged men. On the other, it sustains a racial hierarchy by failing to address the conditions that perpetuate marginalization and racism. Here is how it works.

Research on the PK movement has found it to incorporate predominantly white, class-privileged men (Newton 2005), and the men I interviewed were predominantly middle to upper-middle class. Of the 10 couples, 14 men and women identified as white, 2 self-identified as black, and 2 were Latino/a (the latter were interracial couples—a white man married to a Latina women and a Latino man married to a white woman). In my interviews, I found that PK offers men specific tools to grapple with contradictory gender meanings, allowing them to make positive changes in their lives around issues of masculinity without challenging their position of authority in the family.

PK men and their wives, no matter their race or class backgrounds, described their ideals about familial roles that drew on the language of feminism and the importance of gender equality. All agreed that it was the man who needs to be at the helm of the household. At the same time, these couples demonstrated an awareness of the critique of the relations of domination and subordination between men and women that characterize the history of "traditional" marriage. To conceptualize equality, the couples discussed gender relations as "different but equal." For example, George, a 63-year-old white professional, emphasized the notion of teamwork in his characterization of leadership:

> We are a team. We make our decisions together. I can't state any specific thing that I've made the sole decision on. As far as knowledge about what's going

on out there I have a heavier lead on that. She's the nurse and I don't know what's going on in nursing. This is not a domineering relationship and it never has been.

George fended off criticism that he might be perceived as domineering in taking on the role of head of household. Yet, his depiction of the equality in the relationship designates his superior understanding of how the world operates and relegates his wife's knowledge to the field of nursing.

Megan, a 26-year-old, white, self-identified stay-at-home mom, offers a striking assessment of her relationship with Gary, also white, as "different but equal," using the analogy of making pie to focus on the fact that they both were busy taking care of what needed to be done for the family:

> It is equal; it's different equal but it's equal. [Gary] is the financial provider for the family and I am the housekeeper, child care giver, taxi driver, and maid, ha, ha, ha—no, I don't mean to be negative. But, I take care of the baby and the house. I think it is divided equally. I think he is making cherry pie and I am making apple pie, but we're both making pie. . . . We are both busy doing things.

The idea of "different but equal" portrays equality as equal commitment to and responsibility for gendered tasks while skirting the issue of the structural advantages involved in such a division of labor. Megan's sarcasm as she lists her duties provides a glimpse into her struggle to define her relationship as equal.

James and Linda, an African American middle-class couple in their late thirties, used similar language to describe their relationship. When I asked them about whether James is the head of the family, they both gave an emphatic yes. James explained, however, that the bible verse dealing with headship has been misunderstood. Headship, according to him, is about the man taking responsibility to ensure the needs of his family are meet. Linda offered her perspective on "different but equal":

> It's a two-way street, the husband has to do things for the wife and the wife has to do things for the husband. We even had that passage in our wedding so that people would understand my submission to him is not showing me to be weak, it is not

a weakness. It's a sign of reverence for him; I am showing reverence to him and if I'm doing that I am showing reverence to God.

Ed and Mary, a lower-class African American couple in their late twenties, echoed the words of Linda and James, saying that headship is a "two-way street" and that both of them are two individuals who have to work out how to make the best decisions together. Ed went on to explain that the relationship "is pretty fair and even. She might do more. Thinking and pursuing something to get it done, I think I do more." His words about being better at thinking and pursuing goals echo those of George, who discussed his superior knowledge of "what's going on out there."

PK discourses of leadership offered men from different race and class backgrounds the ability to perform an enlightened masculinity as leaders who are willing to share power with their wives. In this case, the field of evangelical religion interacts with that of the family to position men, regardless of race and class, superior to women. The idealized type of masculinity for Christian men rests on a notion of leadership that is often attributed to privileged men who have the power and authority to act as benevolent patriarchs. Participating in the PK movement allows men who are marginalized by race and/or class to participate in a hegemonic model of masculinity that calls them to be leaders in their communities and families.

In contrast to the homogenous understandings of leadership that PK men embraced, the men in my study differed markedly in their recognition of the issue of race. Within the PK movement, the evangelical field intersects with the racial field to strongly influence the ways that men understand and perform what evangelicals call "racial reconciliation," a central PK goal asking men to pursue better relations with believers of different races. PK speakers advocate breaking through racial barriers by recognizing the sin of segregation and creating friendships with men of different races. Patrick Glynn (1998) argues that religious groups have an important role to play in improving race relations in the United States and that evangelical approaches to racial reconciliation that involve collective apology among religious groups, such as the Southern Baptist Convention, the National Association of Evangelicals, and the PK, can

have more impact than that of secular groups, particularly the government.

I attended a PK large stadium event in Sacramento of about 50,000 men in 1998 and had the opportunity to discuss informally with a number of men their views on important issues that PK addresses. I found that a minority of white men (three of the eight) identified race as an issue that they had not considered before involvement in the PK organization. In contrast, the two men of color I informally interviewed mentioned race as a central reason for involvement.

My formal interviews similarly showed that only two of the seven self-identified white men directly addressed the problem of segregation in churches and the need for racial reconciliation. In contrast, all three of the men of color discussed race as one of the most important issues to be addressed by evangelical Christians. James, a 38-year-old black professional, discussed the importance of addressing race in the events:

> They stress racial reconciliation and it was really good to hear. A couple speakers at the event approached it from a biblical point of view, challenging men to put barriers aside and see we are all brothers in Christ and not this race or that race.

Ed, a 32-year-old black man, recounted his experience of PK events as one of brotherly love among Christian men regardless of race. He felt that being involved in PK was "a new experience where a bunch of men from all different races were together, hugging and loving." He felt supported by other PK men as he struggled to find employment.

Although PK events emphasize the need to foster racial reconciliation, the majority of the white men I interviewed did not indicate this as a central theme. Five did not mention the need for racial reconciliation at all as an important goal for the PK organization, and three only briefly mentioned the benefits of bringing men of all races together. When I pushed them on this subject, they were clearly uncomfortable and mainly repeated the idea of the need to bring men together in brotherly love. Ted, a white man in his thirties married to a Latina women, had a much more nuanced assessment of the need for racial reconciliation. When I asked him what he believed were the goals of the PK organization, he discussed the idea of keeping promises and then turned to the issue of race:

> I think the other thing that stands in my mind is that there are tremendous racial barriers that still exist in the Christian community. Now they don't have the solutions to all those yet, but I am willing to admit that this is true. And we can then do something about it. If I can get to that point, then it is a beginning.

Being married to a Latina woman gave Ted insight into the racial barriers and discrimination that people of color experience in the United States, and he was more attentive to this message of racial reconciliation in the PK events. He described one stadium event where a Korean minister recounted the fact that "Americans tend to be a little bigoted, and even if you don't think you are, that's how we tend to feel about a white person. This was quite enlightening." For Ted, PK events helped him understand the marginalization that men of color experience.

Another white man, George, a businessman in his sixties, also had a positive reaction to the idea of racial reconciliation. He discussed in detail this PK goal: "The way our society has gone, it is torn apart with segregation and hate in so many areas involving different people. One goal of PK is to heal these differences and make you more accountable in how you act with your fellow men." Although he embraced the PK message of reconciliation, George was at a loss for words when I asked him about what he had concretely done, in his own words, "to build more relationships outside my own group." In contrast to Ted and George, who appreciated being enlightened on the issue of race, Jim, a white man in his late fifties, expressed his exasperation with the recurring theme of racial reconciliation:

> I think it is one of the things they kind of overdo myself. In Oakland, [McCartney] spoke, and I felt that he was preaching to the choir. We got harangued all day from a group of speakers, and I felt they were talking to the wrong people.

Other studies have also found a range of responses to the issue of racial reconciliation from white attendees (Allen 2000; Newton 2005). Although the PK leadership promotes the idea of breaking down racial barriers, it is clear that the message of reconciliation is much more essential to the identity of men of color than to white PK men.

Thus, there are two ways that the racial field impacts the evangelical field. First, the evangelical field allows a space for men marginalized by race and class to perform masculinity in concert with non-marginalized men who maintain their status over women. Second, although marginalized men participate in the same practices around hegemonic masculinity, a racial hierarchy is still maintained as the PK organization seeks to move evangelicals in the direction where racial considerations are no longer entertained. Rather than pursuing institutional, political, or structural solutions to the problem of racism, PK focuses on spiritual solutions to purge individuals of the "sin" of racism and to build relationships with men of different racial backgrounds (Allen 2000). Although the message of reconciliation is important for white men to hear, the lack of focus on institutional racism means that there is little emphasis on the mechanisms in the church and in society that sustain racism and facilitate discrimination. If the PK movement does little to shift the racial hierarchy among hegemonic and marginalized men, what impact does it have on subordinated masculinities? To answer this question, I turn to a consideration of what it means to be soft-boiled.

BECOMING SOFT-BOILED

In the field of gender, subordinated masculinities, and most notably homosexual forms of masculinity, are organized according to patriarchal ideologies that act as "the repository of whatever is symbolically expelled from hegemonic masculinity" and can be "easily assimilated to femininity" (Connell 1995:78). Yet, it is also the case that the relationship between hegemonic and subordinated masculinities can challenge and transform gender hierarchies.

In the case of PK, the fields of evangelical religion and gender that uphold an idealized masculinity of male leadership interact with the sexual field in the negotiation of changing gender relations. In my research, I identify "soft-boiled masculinity," a type of masculinity that provides space for men to be more emotionally connected with one another and to express themselves in a manner that can challenge the norms of hegemonic masculinity and its strict boundaries surrounding the performance of heterosexual male behavior. While men are being instructed to take on spiritual leadership roles in their families and communities, the large stadium events help them to build bonds with other men and form what PK calls accountability groups. Ted, a 36-year-old manager, described the benefits of these groups:

> The men you sit with or you sleep with in the campground become your group. We started a study. And then we learned to open up and share, and that there is a true value in it. It's not just that you're doing it, but you begin to feel a longing to share. Most men long to have relationships with other men, but they don't know how to go about it and are quite frankly ashamed to admit that they need it.

His words point to a desire for intimate, emotional ties with other men outside the norm of what most heterosexual men consider "natural." Intimate and close friendships are more common among gay men who subvert the norm of masculinity by becoming emotionally involved (Nardi 1992; Weeks et al. 2001).

The field of evangelical religion opens a space for men to push the boundaries of conventional manhood and thereby shift the habitus that produces an emotionally disengaged masculinity as ideal. The men I interviewed expressed a need to challenge this hegemonic ideal. Jeff, a 39-year-old white father of three, told me about how PK events offer a way to express the fragility men feel:

> There are 50,000 guys praising the Lord, realizing that we are all fallible, we all make mistakes, and we all need Jesus as our Savior. It's singing, worshiping, hugging, and emotions—things that guys struggle with.

The men's ability to challenge masculine norms is based on their identities as Christians who are called on to live by a higher standard than non-Christian men. Jeff offered Jesus as an example of a man who had integrity and was loving and emotional, modeling a different kind of masculinity to strive for.

When I attended one of the large stadium events in Sacramento, I was struck by the level of emotion displayed: many in the crowd of more than 50,000 were dancing and singing, and some openly cried when one of the speakers discussed the pain that men carry with them, such as having an absent father. Certainly, for men, such sentimentality and display of emotion could be marked as nonmasculine, effeminate, or "gay," behaviors to be avoided at all costs. Within the field of sports, men are able to bond and express a range of emotions with their buddies but not those that would make them appear weak or effeminate (Messner 1992). Within the field of gender, hegemonic masculinity polices male relationships such that "gayness is easily assimilated to femininity" (Connell 1995:78), and these subordinated masculinities are situated at the bottom of the gender hierarchy.

Sociologist C. J. Pascoe (2007), for example, in her research at River High School, uncovers the ways that boys hurl the "fag epithet" at one another to bolster their masculinity and reject fag-like behavior or same-sex desire. In contrast to the word "gay," which is used as an insult to generally mean "lame" or "stupid," the word "fag" is a specific insult concerning gender used by and for boys. A fag refers to a failed masculinity and to a feminine man who is most likely gay. Pascoe's research demonstrates how gender hierarchies are constructed in different fields. The interaction of the education, gender, and sexual fields puts subordinated masculinities in relation to a hegemonic form that is by definition antithetical to the fag.

Do stadium events and group activities that enable PK to express homosocial bonds disrupt hegemonic masculinity by sanctioning expressive or feminized masculinities? Roger, a white man in his fifties, suggested just this kind of dislodgement: "I think that one thing about the rallies people would probably have trouble understanding or believing is that men's feelings could be shared so deeply." There was also general agreement among the wives I interviewed that their husbands and other PK men they knew were more willing to express their emotions as a result of the PK. Sally, a white educator in her early fifties, recounted to me the change in the behavior of her husband, Sam, who was now much more willing to touch and hug other men. Even more striking was her description of how Sam had never felt comfortable hugging his own father but now did so on a regular basis. This embrace of "soft masculinity" reorganizes the evangelical field to enable an expressive masculinity that is shunned or avoided in other fields where dominant conceptions of hegemonic masculinity are at play (such as in high schools or sport events).

Soft masculinity, however, is not necessarily non-hegemonic. Instead, the men and women in this study offered definitions of what it means to be expressive that incorporated a hegemonic understanding. For example, they described the importance of excluding women from rallies and accountability groups to ensure that men had a safe space where they could be emotionally available to one another *because* women were not present. PK men articulated enthusiasm that the events were held in football stadiums where they could bring their coolers, wear "team hats," and chant team slogans, facilitating sport-like rituals that reaffirmed their masculinity. The trappings of hegemonic masculinity and the absence of women made activities like hugging, crying, and holding hands palatable. Sally summed up the reasons that women needed to be excluded, stating that men would become more self-conscious and inhibited:

> I felt that going to Promise Keeper rallies would be a place where men could be themselves and do what men do without worrying about what women will think of them or making an impression. They could be emotional or cry without worrying about women seeing them or feeling like they have to take care of them.

Her words point to the way that soft masculinity interacts with a "hard" masculinity to maintain its hegemonic position.

Men can display soft masculinity only in environments where women are not present, and they don't have to worry about what women will think. Moreover, as one wife expressed, the men can sing and hold hands without anyone "looking at them funny." In this way, heteronormativity infuses the evangelical field to mark a strict boundary between homosexuality and heterosexuality. In the homosocial environment of a PK event, men can perform what some might mark as a subordinate masculinity without worrying about whether their behavior would be perceived as gay by women or by non-Christian men. Alice made it clear that women wanted men to be more emotional but "they also wanted men to be men." In other words, it would be a problem to display too many emotions in settings other than a stadium event, rendering PK men nonmasculine.

Research on masculinities has demonstrated the importance of attending to how whiteness and privilege allows men (and boys) to embrace soft or other hybrid masculinities. Messner (1993) theorizes the construction of the New Man based on the lives of white, class-privileged, heterosexual men who shift their lifestyles and behavior away from aspects of "traditional masculinity," such as being the strict father figure who is head of the household. The New Man is able to express emotion in public *and* can still practice a hegemonic masculinity. For example, commenters have remarked on the shift among political leaders in the United States in which it has become more acceptable to cry in public. Back in the 1990s, supportive depictions praised U.S. General Schwarzkopf—a highly decorated four-star general known as Stormin' Norman—for his sensitivity when he shed a tear in public for the U.S. men and women who were killed in the Gulf War. More recently, President Barack Obama broke down in tears as he thanked campaign workers for their tireless work for his re-election. Speaker of the House John Boehner cries so frequently that Twitter jokesters now call him the weeper of the house. Such public displays of emotion seem to signal a significant shift in the way that hegemonic masculinity is performed among men who hold some of the most powerful positions in the U.S. government and military. Yet, ultimately, in the field of politics white men still predominantly hold positions of power. The act of elite men crying in public can thus translate into a new hegemonic understanding.

In conceptualizing the ways that soft and hard masculinities might facilitate new hegemonic forms, Demetriou (2001) identifies two types of hegemony: an external form that institutionalizes men's dominance over women and an internal one that promotes the preeminence of one group of men over others. The two exist in a dialectical relationship where hegemonic masculinity can appropriate elements from subordinated and/or marginalized masculinities to perpetuate dominance. The result is an intertwining of multiple patterns, creating a process of negotiation and reconfiguration. For Demetriou, hegemonic masculinity is "capable of reconfiguring itself and adapting to the specificities of new historical conjunctures"

(Demetriou 2001: 355). For example, gay masculinity is increasingly visible in Western societies, making it possible to appropriate aspects of gay men's styles and behaviors into a new hybrid configuration of gender practices.

Masculinities scholars have employed the concept of hybridity as a new and productive direction for analyzing contemporary changes in gender relations. The central question that hybridity poses is whether such new configurations of masculinities challenge or preserve gender and other social inequalities (Bridges 2014). In the case of the PK, as I show above, the men incorporate aspects of subordinated and feminized masculinities to configure a hybrid form of soft masculinity that it is still able to perpetuate gender and sexual inequalities. Within the field of evangelical religion, the gender and sexual fields interact to produce a more "enlightened" manhood; yet, this hybrid manhood is one that still maintains a hierarchical relationship between hegemonic and subordinated masculinities and femininities. Thus, becoming soft-boiled can still allow "men to be men."

CONCLUSION

Critical assessments of research on hegemonic masculinity have noted that its use is often overemphasized in research as the more prominent concept (Wedgwood 2009). Although many empirical studies do explore non-hegemonic forms of masculinity in relation to hegemonic ones, there are many that still treat hegemonic masculinity as a master category without recognizing the multiple ways that it intersects with other historically situated masculinities. In contrast to this tendency to overutilize the theoretical concept of hegemonic masculinity, Connell argued for the importance of attending to gender relations among men; this interactional approach is "necessary to keep the analysis dynamic, to prevent the acknowledgement of multiple masculinities collapsing into a character typology" (1995:76).

Applying the concept of the field to gender relations can avoid this tendency to conceptualize a rigid hegemony and typology of masculinities. Instead, it can be a powerful tool to recognize the dynamic manifestations of multiple masculinities within the matrix of gender hierarchy that rely on an idealized and historically situated model of hegemonic masculinity. Identifying how different fields influence one another illuminates the possibility for social change, as hierarchical relationships are negotiated and reorganized. At the same time, an intersectional approach facilitates the recognition of the ways that privilege structures and restructures a field. Thus, what appears as social change on the local level can be reconfigured within a field to reestablish gender and other hierarchies.

The PK movement shines a stark light on the ways that privileged men are able to reshuffle the field to incorporate elements that can provide a softer image but still facilitate a gender hierarchy. PK men of all race and class backgrounds in the evangelical field benefit from embracing an "enlightened" masculinity in which they can claim their leadership roles as men willing to share their power with their wives. Likewise, PK men are able to perform a soft-boiled masculinity in spaces where women are not present and where their heterosexuality will not be called into question. The field of evangelical religion thus reinstitutes the hierarchy of men over women and of heterosexuality over homosexuality while incorporating the language of feminism and gender equality. I found that the racial hierarchy within the evangelical field was also re-institutionalized, even as the PK organization has sought to redress racial injustice within the church. Some white men on an individual basis were willing to consider and try to incorporate greater racial inclusion, but, as a strategy that only focuses on personal relationships, the PK organization easily maintains the structural inequalities that perpetuate the marginalization of men of color.

In the contemporary landscape, moral panics abound over fears concerning the end of man. These occur at the same time that new spaces are opening for men to "try on" hybrid masculinities and borrow elements of subordinated and feminized masculinities that resist a dominant construction. This chapter has considered some theoretical innovations in field theory and intersectionality that can facilitate a more nuanced analysis of such efforts. There is little doubt that future research on masculinities will need to assess new configurations of soft-boiled and other variations of masculinities to understand the ways these can shift and reproduce hierarchical gender relations.

REFERENCES

Allen, L. Dean. 2000. "Promise Keepers and Racism: Frame Resonance as an Indicator of Organizational Vitality." *Sociology of Religion* 61: 54–72.

Bartkowski, John P. 2004. *The Promise Keepers: Servants, Soldiers, and Godly Men*. Piscataway, NJ: Rutgers University Press.

Bourdieu, Pierre. 1971. "Intellectual Field and Creative Project." In *Knowledge and Control: New Directions for the Sociology of Education*, edited by M. K. D. Young, 161–88. London: Collier Macmillan.

Bourdieu, Pierre. 1977. *Outline of a Theory of Practice*. Cambridge, UK: Cambridge University Press.

Bourdieu, Pierre. 1984. *Distinction: A Social Critique of the Judgement of Taste*, translated by Richard Nice. Cambridge, MA: Harvard University Press.

Bridges, Tristan. 2014. "A Very 'Gay' Straight?: Hybrid Masculinities, Sexual Aesthetics, and the Changing Relationship between Masculinity and Homophobia." *Gender & Society* 28 (1): 58–82.

Cho, Sumi, Kimberlé Williams Crenshaw, and Leslie McCall. 2013. "Toward a Field of Intersectionality Studies: Theory, Applications, and Praxis." *Signs* 38 (4): 785–810.

Coles, Tony. 2009. "Negotiating the Field of Masculinity: The Production and Reproduction of Multiple Dominant Masculinities." *Men and Masculinities* 12 (1): 30–44.

Connell, Raewyn. 1995. *Masculinities*. Berkeley: University of California Press.

Connell, Raewyn, and James Messerschmidt. 2005. "Hegemonic Masculinity: Rethinking the Concept." *Gender & Society* 19: 829–59.

Conrad, Browyn Kara. 2006. "Neo-Institutionalism, Social Movements, and the Cultural Reproduction of a Mentalité: Promise Keepers Reconstruct the Madonna/Whore Complex." *The Sociological Quarterly* 47 (2): 305–31.

Demetriou, Demetrakis. 2001. "Connell's Concept of Hegemonic Masculinity: A Critique." *Theory and Society* 30: 337–61.

Donovan, Brian. 1998. "Political Consequences of Private Authority: Promise Keepers and the Transformation of Hegemonic Masculinity." *Theory and Society* 27: 817–43.

Faludi, Susan. 2006. *Backlash: The Undeclared War against Women*, 15th anniversary ed. New York: Three Rivers Press.

Glynn, Patrick. 1998. "Racial Reconciliation: Can Religion Work Where Politics Has Failed?" *American Behavioral Scientist* 41: 834–42.

Heath, Melanie. 2003. "Soft-Boiled Masculinity: Renegotiating Gender and Racial Ideologies in the Promise Keepers Movement." *Gender & Society* 17: 423–44.

Hirose, Akihiko, and Kay Kei-ho Pih. 2010. "Men Who Strike and Men Who Submit: Hegemonic and Marginalized Masculinities in Mixed Martial Arts." *Men and Masculinities* 13 (2): 190–209.

Hoang, Lan Anh, and Brenda S. A. Yeoh. 2011. "Breadwinning Wives and 'Left-Behind' Husbands: Men and Masculinities in the Vietnamese Transnational Family." *Gender & Society* 25 (6): 717–39.

Jefferson, Tony. 2002. "Subordinating Hegemonic Masculinity." *Theoretical Criminology* 6 (1): 63–88.

Lu, Alexander, and Y. Joel Wong. 2013. "Stressful Experiences of Masculinity among U.S.-Born and Immigrant Asian American Men." *Gender & Society* 27 (3): 345–71.

McCormack, Mike, and Eric Anderson. 2010. "'It's Just Not Acceptable Any More': The Erosion of Homophobia and the Softening of Masculinity at an English Sixth Form." *Sociology* 44 (5): 843–59.

Messner, Michael A. 1992. *Power at Play: Sports and the Problem of Masculinity*. Boston: Beacon.

Messner, Michael A. 1993. "'Changing Men' and Feminist Politics in the United States. *Theory and Society* 22: 723–37.

Messner, Michael A. 1997. *Politics of Masculinities: Men in Movements*. New York: Sage.

Montes, Veronica. 2013. "The Role of Emotions in the Construction of Masculinity: Guatemalan Migrant Men, Transnational Migration, and Family Relations." *Gender & Society* 27 (4): 469–90.

Morrell, Robert, Rachel Jewkes, and Graham Lindegger. 2012. "Hegemonic Masculinity/Masculinities in South Africa: Culture, Power, and Gender Politics." *Men and Masculinities* 15 (1): 11–30.

Nardi, Peter. 1992. "Sex, Friendship and Gender Roles among Gay Men." In *Men's Friendships*, edited by Peter Nardi, 173–85. London: Sage.

Newton, Judith. 2005. *From Panthers to Promise Keepers: Rethinking the Men's Movement*. Lanham, MD: Rowman & Littlefield.

Pascoe, C. J. 2007. *Dude, You're a Fag.* Berkeley: University of California Press.

Pyke, Karen D. 1996. "Class-Based Masculinities: The Interdependence of Gender, Class, and Interpersonal Power." *Gender & Society* 10 (5): 527–49.

Rosin, Hanna. 2012. *The End of Men: And the Rise of Women*. New York: Riverhead Books.

Scrinzi, Francesca. 2010. "Masculinities and the International Division of Care: Migrant Male Domestic Workers in Italy and France." *Men and Masculinities* 13 (1): 44–64.

Swartz, David. 1997. *Culture & Power: The Sociology of Pierre Bourdieu*. Chicago: University of Chicago Press.

Ward, Jane. 2008. "Dude-Sex: White Masculinities and 'Authentic' Heterosexuality among Dudes Who Have Sex with Dudes." *Sexualities* 11: 414–34.

Wedgwood, Nikki. 2009. "Connell's Theory of Masculinity: Its Origins and Influences on the Study of Gender." *Journal of Gender Studies* 18 (4): 329–39.

Weeks, Jeffrey, Brian Heaphy, and Catherine Donovan. 2001. *Same Sex Intimacies: Families of Choice and Other Life Experiments*. London: Routledge.

Wetherell, Margaret, and Nigel Edley. 1999. "Negotiating Hegemonic Masculinity: Imaginary Positions and Psycho-Discursive Practices." *Feminism and Psychology* 9 (3): 335–56.

Whitehead, Steele M. 2002. *Men and Masculinities: Key Themes and New Directions*. Cambridge, UK: Polity.

Williams, Rhys H. 2001. *Promise Keepers and the New Masculinity: Private Lives and Public Morality*. Lanham, MD: Lexington Books.

NOTES

1. All the names of Promise Keepers and their wives are pseudonyms. Alice is a 55-year-old white, self-identified housewife.

VICTOR RIOS AND RACHEL SARABIA

11. SYNTHESIZED MASCULINITIES: THE MECHANICS OF MANHOOD AMONG DELINQUENT BOYS

"I gotta be a man on the street, a man with the cops, a man at work, and a man with my son and my lady."

— *20-year-old Jason*

Masculinity is a central vehicle by which marginalized young men attempt to compensate for race and class subordination. Differing forms of masculinity (i.e. subordinate, street, working-class, dominant, and hyper-masculinity) are used by young men to access resources for maintaining dignity and respect, a process we refer to as "synthesized masculinities." The young men we studied synthesized masculinities to acquire social status and to contest various forms of subordination.[1] Like other forms of gender and sexuality practice, the masculinities they practiced were fluid, situated, and shifting. By uncovering the processes through which differing types of masculinity are utilized and identifying when these practices become perilous or productive in the lives of street life–oriented young men and the women in their lives, we can begin to explore ways to develop policy and programs that encourage productive forms of masculinity.

In addition to the morals and values of manhood the young men we studied learned from being on the streets, they found masculinity-making resources through the process of criminalization—specifically negative encounters with school discipline, police, juvenile hall, and probation officers. One consequence of criminalization and punitive social control for these boys was the development of a specific set of gendered practices that worked in ways that obstructed desistance, social relations, and social mobility. By analyzing the perceptions and actions of these young men, we uncover how masculinity produces and was produced by race, class, and gender subordination.

Jason's discussion of "being a man" represents how many of the boys in our studies developed *synthesized*

masculinities, a strategic and situational display of various masculinities. As of 2011, Jason was a 20-year-old young man with a criminal record.[2] He considered himself an "active gang member." We compared self-reports with a law enforcement gang database, and police, probation officers, or media accounts often confirmed these young men's assessments of themselves as gang members.

Jason garnered respect among his "homies" because he spent much of his teenage years on the streets, "putting in work" (fighting, dealing drugs, stealing, and "earning respect" within the gang). Jason explains,

> Well you have to earn respect, nobody gives it to you. If you give respect to the right people you get respect from the right people . . . you hold your ground you know, just throw down [fighting] . . . like some fool tries make you look like a bitch then you throw down [fight] and that's how they look at respect you know?

In our observations we saw Jason "calling shots" in the neighborhood, giving orders to other young men, and avoiding victimization and incarceration by having other young men look out for him when conflict arose. But we also noticed that Jason was one of the few active gang members *not* searched and harassed by police. One day, we were standing in front of Golden State Liquors (one of the local hang-out spots) with a group of six boys. Four of the boys were drinking tall cans of Arizona Iced Tea. A Gang Task Force officer pulled up to the curb, stepped out of his vehicle, and asked the boys, "What are you drinking?" Most of the boys ignored him; two shrugged their shoulders. The officer signaled to one of the boys, Julio, to come closer to him. Julio ignored him. The officer warned him, "If you don't come here, I'm gonna' make you look really bad in front of your homies." Julio walked up and the officer grabbed him by the shirt, pressuring him to sit on the curb. He lifted him up by the shirt and emptied Julio's pockets. He used his radio to gather information about Julio (whether he had a record or outstanding warrants). The officer proceeded to check the others' records, except for Jason. Before driving off, the officer looked at Jason and said, "I'll see you at the bagel shop . . . tell these boys they need to get a job like you."

Jason believed that the police gave him more respect after he acquired a job: he worked at a local bagel shop where police officers who patrolled the neighborhood stopped. "Police know I am a hard worker. That's what they expect of me. I'm a family man and I don't commit crime anymore." Jason was one of six homies who held a steady job of a gang of more than 80 young men.

Jason's four-year-old son, Junior, was often on the streets with him, hanging out at the park and in front of the liquor store. Junior often wore a blue bandana in his rear pocket, a sign representing the largest Mexican American prison and street organization in the country, the Mexican Mafia. Jason sometimes had Junior play fight with older kids in the neighborhood. He wanted Junior to learn to "be a man." This entailed introducing Junior to street life, teaching him how to protect himself, and showing him how to demand respect from others.

Although Jason believed that gang parents and older gang members sometimes played a negative role in the life of their younger kin, he did not realize that his own actions of socializing his son to be a tough man might also play a role in this process: "It's like the families and older guys force them to join [the gang], it's like a circle that can offer protection . . . well not just force them, but also they don't have the money to buy this and that so people join gangs for protection and go rob and shit." Jason wanted his son to have a bright future and was an active father. We observed him pushing his son in a stroller throughout the neighborhood, feeding, and changing him. Yet, he did not as often consider how the actions and lessons of manhood performed around his boy might encourage Junior to join a gang in the future. To Jason, Junior was partaking in "child's play." He did not understand this as part of a larger process that might

eventually help his son participate in the very behavior from which he seemed intent on protecting him.

Jason was also incredibly loyal and respectful to his girlfriend, even on the street, where other young women were called "bitches" and "hoes" by their partners or other boys and were physically or symbolically attacked. Jason developed the ability to balance various forms of masculinity, providing him diverse benefits: respect on the streets, acknowledgment from police, a "manly son," and a healthy romantic relationship. Jason's experience, however, was unique. Whereas all of the young men in this study adopted different forms of masculinity, Jason was one of the few young men who experienced positive outcomes associated with his masculine performances. A much more common outcome was being arrested for challenging and assaulting others and police officers. By understanding Jason's experience and comparing him with the other young men, we find concrete examples of the various practices of masculinity that exist in this context.[3]

Like Jason, many of the other boys relied on masculinity to obtain respect and cope with race and class marginality. However, their approaches often also led to victimization, stigmatization, and incarceration. With limited access to traditional pathways to accomplish conventional masculinity, the boys in this study sought alternative forms of achieving manhood. And what we refer to as "synthesized masculinities" allowed these young men to creatively accomplish masculinity throughout their lives. *Synthesized masculinities* address marginalized men's adoption of various forms of masculinities to access resources they perceive themselves to be lacking and to compensate for other forms of domination.

BACKGROUND

Masculinities studies inquire into the ways that "different ideologies about manhood develop, change, are combined, amended and contested" (Bederman 1995). Masculinity is dynamic, constructed and realized through interactions with others (Carrigan et al. 1985; Kimmel 2003). Kimmel (2003) argues that manhood is accomplished through cultural symbols and the subordination of women. Among American men, achieving masculinity is a "relentless test."

Failure to embody, affirm, or accomplish masculinity is a "source of men's confusion and pain" (Kimmel 2003: 58). But masculinities are also "subject positions taken up by different men in different cultural contexts" (Cooper 2009, 685). Because masculinity is always intersecting with sexuality, race, and class, there exists a plurality of masculine identities, not one form of masculine identity (Carrigan et al. 1985; Connell 1987, 1995).

Connell theorized "hegemonic masculinity" as the dominant form of masculinity, articulating a hierarchy of masculinities and a constant struggle for dominance (Connell and Messerschmidt 2005). Hegemonic masculinity refers to the historical process by which privileged males have dominated women and other marginalized men. The ability to produce wealth, to become recognized by mainstream institutions, and to demonstrate a respectable patriarchal persona are key features of hegemonic masculinity. Accomplishing hegemonic masculinity is almost impossible for less affluent men of color (e.g., Carter 2005; Lopez 2003; Rios 2009). Thus, working-class men, non-white men, or gay men may seek other avenues to achieve manhood. As Adams and Savran (2002) argue, all men attempt to accomplish masculinity. But not all men desire the same type of masculinity, nor do they accomplish it at the same rate or with the same level of ease. When marginalized men feel unable to accomplish the same forms of masculinity that privileged men acquire, they enact "compensatory masculinities" (e.g., Pyke 1996). Compensatory masculinities are attempts to compensate by participating in other—often deviant—behavior (drugs, alcohol, sexual carousing, etc.) to illustrate resistance toward, and independence from, institutions and existing power structures (Pyke 1996). Toughness, dominance, and the willingness to resort to violence to resolve interpersonal conflicts are central resources for men less able to acquire mainstream masculinity-making resources (e.g., Anderson 1999; Harris 2000; Messerschmidt 1993; Rios 2009).

Whereas some marginalized men enact compensatory forms of masculinity, however, others also embrace more conventional forms. These various types of masculinity are not fixed; rather they are "synthesized," depending heavily on context and type of interaction (i.e., peer–peer, male–female, youth–authority figure). Working-class masculinity, hypermasculinity, and street masculinity are not only compensatory behaviors; they are also components of fluid processes that street life–oriented young men draw on as they navigate across social contexts.

We examine how gang members' interactions with authorities shape a localized masculinity. But beyond the dominant–subordinate dichotomy often discussed, we provide a new framework for understanding the accomplishment of masculinity among a group of marginalized young men by complicating notions of dominant and subordinate masculinities. We theorize this framework by arguing that a dominant-synthesized interaction occurs between police and youth. These synthesized performances critically highlight the negotiation of street, working-class, dominant, and subordinate masculinity. Like Young, we argue that these men are more than just "violent-prone individuals who mindlessly lash out at the world with hostility and aggression" (2004: 5). They are complex individuals negotiating barriers and creatively exploring opportunities in the world around them. In this chapter, we examine how poor Latino youth weigh various possibilities for their futures and how they make conscious choices during this process.

LAW ENFORCEMENT, MASCULINITY ENFORCEMENT

Ninety-two of the 96 young men we studied and 22 of 35 young women we interviewed held negative worldviews about police. They all reported at least one negative interaction where they felt victimized, either through physical or through verbal abuse. In our observations on the street—and later in four months of ride-alongs with police—most of the interactions between youth and police were neutral. Often police simply questioned or cited the boys and let them go. We also observed a handful of positive interactions and many negative interactions with police as well. We witnessed police verbally degrade boys and use excessive force and illegal search tactics. The police, for many of the young men in this study, signified one of many obstacles in their development and ability to integrate into the community. In the minds of these young men, the police represented a set of social forces that grouped them into a criminal status, facilitating their criminalization by community members, potential employers, and in school.

They described the police as a force that consistently tested, challenged, and degraded their masculinity, often through instilling fear of violence and incarceration. Dreamy—a 17-year-old Latino male once arrested for being in possession of a marijuana pipe—represented the perceptions of the rest of the boys in the study:

> Cops are a bunch of bullies . . . They are always trying to act like they are bigger men then you . . . They think we are organized crime or something, and, like, damn, we are just a bunch of homies that are kicking it . . . I mean I think when you see a cop you should feel safe and, you know, kind of make you feel good, but hell no, when I see a cop I get fuckin' scared as hell, even if I'm not doing anything wrong I'm still fuckin' scared as hell!

Angel, an 18-year-old Latino male, arrested twice—once for being involved in a gang fight and a second time for violating probation—voiced similar interactions with police:

> They always say some fucked up shit to me. Once they told me, "Why don't you come work with us puta [bitch]?" And sometimes they're like, "I promise I won't take you in if you do something for me [like giving them information on criminal activity]." Pinche pendejos [fucking idiots]. It's all a trick. They are always on top of us . . . They're like "look, I know you're on probation," and they just keep talking shit, talking shit. Cops don't respect us. They laugh at us. En serio [seriously], they're just like, oh look at these fools.

Joker, a 16-year-old young man who hung out with the gang, but did well in school and avoided fighting, drinking, and being out late at night, discussed an incident where an officer used physical force on him:

> The cops do nothing but harass. I go to school. I try to stay out of trouble. Narc [undercover police] cars are always around. I see them driving back and forth on my way to school. Sometimes I think I'm just trippin. It's like, fuck, why are they stopping here?

> You always gotta look over your shoulder, dog, you know what I mean? They roll up and they just stare at us. One time, they tried to stop me. I ran. I bounced because it was curfew. I tried to hide. They found me. I tried to tell them I got a fucked up back, that I had been in a car accident. I told them not to slam me. That fool grabbed me from the neck, mother fucker, started cussing me out, fool. He fuckin slams the shit out of me dog, fuckin scraped my face, my chin and shit. And I'm just like, fuck, I got all dizzy. He was just talking shit. He was mad. He was like, "Yeah I fucked you up, mother fucker, keep running from me, you fuckin little bitch. I'm gonna fuckin bust you this time." They always mistreating us.

Even one of the young women, Jessica, reported feeling treated like one of the guys by police as a punishment for hanging out with them:

> They told me that if I was gonna' hang out with them [the guys] they were gonna' search me and disrespect me like how they do them. So they started to frisk me and feel up on me [she motions her right hand under her left armpit, above her ribcage, and around her breast] . . . then one day the cops tackled me down because they thought I was going to run after a fight that I had with some girl . . . I messed up my arm and had to go to the hospital because of the tackle. . . .

Although we do not have consistent data to confirm that this is a process that unfolds for all the young women that hang out with gang-associated boys, we believe that police utilized masculinity not only to socialize and discipline young boys but also to symbolically relegate women to the domestic sphere. When on the street with the boys, women in our study reported being treated like the boys. This might explain some of the expansion in incarceration rates for girls and young women during the era of mass incarceration.[4]

During our fieldwork, 4 of the boys in this study were arrested one afternoon in front of a community clinic. Three police officers were called to disperse a crowd of 20 suspected gang members loitering outside. Five additional officers were called in to provide backup. The local newspaper reported the incident in this way:

> One individual started taking pictures of the officers with his cell phone; a police officer noticed, and

started taking pictures of the suspected gang members. One of the individuals, Oscar, 19, tried to take the officer's cell phone away and was arrested for attempted robbery, resisting an officer, battery on a police officer, and participation in a criminal street gang. Four other boys were arrested for petty infractions. (Fernandez 2009)

We interviewed Oscar after he spent four months in jail for this incident. He told us he was tired of being photographed by police. He responded by taking a picture of the officers. "Why can't we take pictures of them, but they can take them of us? It's a bunch of bullshit. They just slap a bunch of shit on us. They always try to put us in the wrong and make it look they are the innocent ones, the good guys." The officers responded by telling him to put his phone away. Oscar claimed that he was attempting to cover his face so that the officer could not take a picture of him. The officer, according to Oscar, pretended to have been assaulted and this led to his arrest.

Police consistently challenged and mocked the boys for their way of talking, their dress, with whom they chose to hang out, and for not displaying conventional forms of masculinity. This process made many of the young men feel as though they were engaged in a battle for manhood with police. The camera incident demonstrates the sorts of masculinity battles waged between officers and the boys. Police demanded respect, and when it was not given, they reacted quickly and harshly. According to the boys, police "create bogus charges": attempted robbery, resisting an officer, battery of a police officer, or participation in a criminal street gang.

On another occasion, we witnessed a negative police encounter with three of the boys in this study:

A Sheriff's car approached with two officers. Jessie was just about to light a cigarette. He put it in his mouth and then out again because his lighter did not work. The driver from the Sheriff's car yells from the car to Jessie asking him how old he is. Jessie tells him his age, "Nineteen." The cop yells at him to wait on the corner. We all stopped . . . The officer asked, "Why are you out and about?" He approached Jessie from behind, pulled his hands behind his back and patted him down, emptying his pockets. They then started telling him to show them any tattoos he had, making him lift his shirt in front of several folks

eating on the patio of a nearby restaurant . . . The officers started asking the boys if they were on probation and put Jessie's name into the car's computer . . . They found a pocketknife in Jessie's pocket, and asked him about it while the Sheriff was checking the name . . . The sheriff came back after running Jessie's name, walked him over to the curb and told him to sit down . . . By this time two other police cars pulled up. Juan told the officer, "We're trying to do good things, we come to school." The officer pulled his hands behind him and patted him down like he did Jessie, lifted his shirt, checked for tattoos, asked if he's on probation, sat him down on the curb, then got in his face, and yelled, "I'm not going to take any shit from a 16 year old punk."

(from author's fieldnotes)

The group was allegedly stopped because one of the boys "looked suspicious" and underage to be smoking. But the situation quickly escalated to all of them being questioned, searched, and put on display as criminals. Scenes like this are one way officers "policed" this area—by reaffirming their authority and masculinity over these boys. The officers asserted dominance by raising their voices and displaying immediate distrust, suspicion, and disrespect toward the youth. The officers also tried to aggravate the boys so they would respond with anger, giving the cops a reason to take them in. They did this by making threats to send Jessie to county jail if the rest of the group did not obey: "Tell those little punks we're gonna' take you to county if they don't man up and listen to our commands."

Policing is a male-dominated and masculine field (Cooper 2009; Dodsworth 2007; Harris 2000). Machismo has also been found to be a central element of police culture (Herbert 2006). Many of the police–youth encounters we witnessed involved masculinity challenges. Police officers were "doing" gender through their performances of dominance (e.g., Martin 1999). Many police–youth interactions involved officers symbolically claiming to be the "real" men by strategically emasculating boys and young men.

Consistent with Angela Harris's (2000) findings, police in our study responded to perceived attacks on their masculine self-identity with the use of violence or threats of violence. When they felt their honor or dignity was being disrespected, they restored it by using or threatening violence. Police officers got "macho" with youth, staging masculinity contests with male youth—contests ripe with meaning in these young men's lives. Youth often interpreted such actions by police as attempts to get them mad, get them to talk back, or do something that could later be used to justify arrest (Gau and Brunson 2010; Harris 2000; Sollund 2006).

The boys recognized police officers as enforcers of masculinity. They viewed police as acting more out of a desire to preserve their authority over youth, prove their manhood, and maintain dominant status on the streets than to enforce the law (Cooper 2009; Hahn 1971). They described officers as power-hungry individuals who had something to prove to the boys: that they were "manlier" than the gang. Criticizing police for overcompensating was an integral part of the boys' performances masculinity. They believed that they were the real men and that the police were weak individuals hiding behind badges and guns. Simultaneously, police attempted to reinforce a particular form of working-class masculinity—a form less available in this context and to these young men than police often seemed to understand. They pushed the idea that "a real man gets a job and provides for his family." Yet these boys' age and education put them in the company of a 40 percent unemployment rate. Jobs might exist; but these boys are not among those getting hired.

Most of the officers in their community are white. The boys saw them as "rich" men with "good jobs" even as they despised some of the officers. When officers gave advice to the boys, they often relied on their profession. "Right now you're just on probation for small stuff. You can still clean your record and become a cop one day," one police officer told a group of four of the boys, as they loitered in front of the liquor store. Officers consistently made references to being "a real man" when giving boys advice. "Be a real man, get a job, leave the homies, go to school, and provide for your family," an officer told one boy as he stopped and searched him.

All of the boys understood what it took to "become a man," even if they had yet to acquire the resources to do so themselves. The following descriptions of normative ideals are representative of all of the interviewees' perceptions:

A man is someone that can support their family . . . even with the struggle . . . having a job . . . putting support . . . having food on the table, a roof over their head, and clothes on their backs . . . that's a man. (Raul, 14)

Knowing how to work makes you a man. Being responsible. A man is somebody that, you know, doesn't back down. To be a man, you gotta be down for whatever. You stick around, or stick to what you say you're gonna do. You don't learn this stuff overnight though; becoming a man is a process. (Tito, 17)

I would want to be successful you know, and come back and help people that need it the most, like people that were or kids that went through the same shit that I went through or something you know, just trying to give back to the community . . . I mean hopefully college can help me figure that out you know cause . . . a lot of people don't even know what they want to do you know, and when they go to college that's where they figure shit out. So that's what im'a try to do. (Jose, 16)

The boys believed that gang life was just a stage in their lives, that one day they might be able to transition. They had to wait to acquire the resources to become men capable of providing for their families by going to college or working. Although this kind of masculinity—working hard, finishing school, and providing for families—can place boys on a better trajectory and help them resist crime, the boys in this study encountered various obstacles on this path. These included a lack of entry-level jobs in Riverland, a dearth of community programs to help them transition back into school, and zero-tolerance school policies that led many to expulsion for gang activity. Many of the boys viewed school as a place where they were criminalized, not cared for. Twelve of the boys told us that they decided to drop out because they felt they did not belong, that schools did not care for them. Thirty-two (of the 57) had dropped out of school or been kicked out. On the streets, police gang units stopped, "tagged" (entered into a gang database), harassed, and arrested the boys, sometimes for something as simple as walking to the store to buy groceries.

Although the boys attempted to get jobs or complete school, their avenues for opportunities often turned out to be dead ends. They were not able to accomplish the manhood that mainstream society expected from them, and this realization was associated with stress, anger, and pain. As a result, they adopted and forged alternative forms of manhood—forms that often stressed being tough, gaining status and respect, and—like the police—demonstrating dominance over others.

SYNTHESIZED MASCULINITY

Cooper (2009) argues that men gain masculine esteem and status from other men's acknowledgment of their masculinity. With limited access to traditional avenues used to accomplish masculinity, the Latino boys in this study negotiated alternative masculinities. In police–youth interactions in particular, these young men forged what we refer to as *synthesized masculinities*. Youths' interactions with police encouraged the performance of a masculinity that involved aspects of dominant, street, working-class, and subordinate masculinity, and the boys and young men in our study were adept at navigating this complicated enactment. They practiced deviant behavior (chest bumping police officers, attempting to block police from taking pictures, protesting their potential arrests, etc.) as a response to police officers' mistreatment, symbolically claiming to not be dominated, controlled, and harassed without a fight. They defied authority to gain masculine status and esteem.

Officers used toughness, dominance, disrespect, humiliation, and aggressive force to try to control boys upon arrest—a tactic that often proved counterproductive. Youth lost respect for cops with every negative interaction and perceived wrongful conviction. Those who encountered negative police interactions reported feeling wrongfully treated through the court process; those who experienced positive or neutral interactions with police reported feeling that the courts and the rest of the justice system treated them fairly throughout the process, despite similar "juvi" or jail sentences. Although the boys aspired to acquire culturally dominant forms of masculinity, they embraced forms of synthesized masculinity. Fifteen-year-old Elias exemplifies this process. He defined being a man as follows:

> A real man is a leader, not a follower. He has backbone. He stands up for himself. He is able to protect himself. He doesn't go out and look for trouble just because. He lives for his own satisfaction and no one else's. He works when he can and when he can't find work he finds a way to make it work.

This redefinition of masculinity allowed the boys to see masculinity as within reach, as achievable. They could be leaders, they could stand up for themselves, and they could be themselves—guys who appreciated a street orientation. This synthesized masculinity allowed them to fill in the gaps—to access resources and mitigate race and class privileges/markers they perceived themselves to be lacking. The performances of synthesized masculinities differed by boy, unique to each of their situations and perceived strengths and weaknesses.

James Messerschmidt argues that men are constantly faced with "masculinity challenges," a process that can lead to crime when other "masculine resources" are in short supply:

> Masculinity challenges arise from interactional threats and insults from peers, teachers, parents, and from situationally defined masculine expectations that are not achievable. . . Masculinity challenges may motivate social action towards masculine resources (e.g., bullying, fighting) that correct the subordinating social situation, and various forms of crime can be the result. (2000: 13)

Crime is one available resource men rely on to communicate their manhood. Indeed, criminal activity constitutes a gendered practice. As such, crime is more likely when men need to prove themselves and when they are held accountable to a strict set of expectations. Furthermore, West and Zimmerman (1987) contend that accountability—the gendered actions that people develop in response to what they perceive others will expect of them—is encountered in interactions between individuals and institutions. Conceptualizing gender as structured by interactions with specific types of institutions enables an exploration of how the criminal justice system shapes the development of specific forms of masculinity.

The young men in both studies faced constant interrogation of and challenges to their manhood on the streets. Questions such as "Is he really a homey?" and "Is he really a man?," if answered in the negative, resulted in stigmatization or victimization. At the core of growing up in their community, the boys felt a constant necessity to prove their manhood. Institutions, also, often challenged their masculinity in the process of attempting to "reform" young men. Examples included being told that they were not "man enough" for having committed crime or that being in the system meant that they risked being emasculated. The boys responded to gendered institutional practices by synthesizing new gendered practices, identities, and models of masculinity.

There are a variety of underacknowledged collateral consequences of the criminalization and punitive social control of inner-city boys: constant surveillance and stigma imposed by schools, community centers, and families; permanent criminal credentials that exclude black and Latino males from the labor market; and the boys' mistrust and resentment toward police and the rest of the criminal justice system (see Rios 2011). In this study, we found that an additional consequence of enhanced policing, surveillance, and punitive treatment of marginalized boys is the development of a specific set of gendered practices, heavily influenced by interactions with police, detention facilities, and probation officers.

Encounters with white female teachers often created an "angry male of color" attacking a "white damsel in distress" phenomenon. Encounters with police were often a contest between who was a "bigger man," and probation officers interacted in either a motherly or a heavy-handed way. These patterns of punishment provided a constant backdrop against which these young men's understandings and performances of masculinity were formed.

Although race determines how a young person is treated in the criminal justice system, masculinity plays a role in how they desist or recidivate as they pass through that system. One of the outcomes of pervasive criminal justice contact for young black and Latino men is the production of a hypermasculinity. Harris (2000) defines hypermasculinity as an "exaggerated exhibition of physical strength and personal aggression," which is often responding to a gender threat "expressed through physical and sexual domination of others." Although not knowingly, we found that the criminal justice system encourages expressions of hypermasculinity by threatening and misunderstanding these young men's masculinity. This leads many boys and young men to rely on violence, crime, and a school and criminal justice counterculture. Detrimental forms of masculinity are partly developed through youths' interaction with police, juvenile hall, and probation officers. Thus, although we traditionally think of officers as *policing* these forms of behavior, we came to find that police often played a crucial role in *producing* these forms of behavior and their attendant meaning and significance.

MASCULINITY, CRIMINALIZATION, AND PUNITIVE SOCIAL CONTROL

Each of us shapes our behavior according to gendered expectations, and each of us is subject to a system of accountability that is gendered, raced, and classed (West and Fenstermaker 1995). The boys in this study were inculcated into a set of hypermasculine expectations that often encouraged behavior that conflicted with dominant institutions. On the street, they would take on a tough persona. They described these acts as a tool for survival: "You can't act weak, or you'll get taken out," Jose explained. "I can't act like a bitch. . . 'cause if I do, suckas will try to swoop up on me and take me out. So I gotta handle my business. Even if I am trying to change, I can't look weak," Tyrell explained.

In front of probation officers and police, they perceived two choices: engage in a masculinity battle or submit to their authority. The boys in our study understood this as a lose–lose predicament. If they acted tough, officers might hesitate to harass them. But, they might get arrested. If they acted passively, they risked humiliation and often took out this frustration on themselves or others through drug use or violence. Many of the boys had a "default" manhood they knew best, most involving masculine resources that had purchase on the streets.

To be assigned "real man" status by relevant others and institutions, men must pass multiple litmus tests among peers, family, and these institutions. Contemporary urban ethnographers emphasize this point. For example, Elijah Anderson (1999) describes the "young male syndrome" as the perceived, expected, and often necessary pressure to perform a tough, violent, and deviant manhood to receive and maintain respect. Sandra Pyke (1996) argues that whereas wealthy men can prove masculinity through an ability to make money and consume products, poor young men rely on toughness, violence, and survival as a means of proving masculinity. Nikki Jones (2010) has even found that lower-income young women use masculinity as a resource for protecting themselves and gaining respect. Jones finds young women in a double bind: they have to act tough on the streets while simultaneously meeting feminine gendered expectations (Jones 2009). Although they are not fighting for masculinity per se, they perceive masculinity as a primary vehicle to maintain respect. Kenya—a 19-year-old Latina previously in a gang but now trying to help some of the boys in this study—explains the toughness exhibited by the few young women visible on the streets:

V.R.: You work with these boys; they are disrespectful of women at times. How do you deal with it?

KENYA: I . . . had an understanding of feminism before I had a term for it. . . . You see young women in urban areas fighting for it in different ways, without the terms to define it, but it's still the same thing, fighting. . . . I had to fight dudes. . . . I've fought hella dudes. . . That's what made hella people scared of me. . . And, even though he won physically, the story got around that he was a punk for fighting a girl. One time, my friend got raped by this dude. So we beat the shit out of him and took a baseball bat with nails in it to his ass. . . taking justice into our own hands. I mean, not justice, 'cause beating his ass is not enough. . . . It sent a message out there that . . . that shit, it's just not acceptable.

Observing Kenya and other street-oriented young women interact with the boys made us realize that masculinity does not always correspond to biological sex; instead, it is a resource used by young people in specific settings to accomplish specific goals. Kenya took on the most masculine of boys to gain respect. Although we did not formally observe young women, we did find that masculinity was used by young women in similar ways: to survive and to resist forms of criminalization they encountered.

Toughness, dominance, and the willingness to resort to violence to resolve interpersonal conflicts are central characteristics of masculine identity. Kimmel and Mahler argue that most violent youths are not psychopaths but, rather, "overconformists to a particular normative construction of masculinity" (2003: 1440). We discovered that mainstream institutions and the criminal justice system expect a masculinity emphasizing hard work, law abidance, and an acceptance of subordinate social positions. Indeed, many of the boys were familiar with this form of masculinity from growing up with fathers or father figures who worked hard, respected authority, etc. Some of them attempted to embrace this masculinity as a means to reform. More commonly, however, when they tried to live up to this form of masculinity, to transform their lives, they found a dearth of viable jobs to "prove" they were hard workers. As Kimmel (1996) argues, an underacknowledged consequence of deindustrialization is that "proving" masculinity through success at work has become less possible for larger numbers of men.

The boys realized that embracing this "positive" working-class masculinity did not provide resources to survive on the streets, a place to which they constantly returned. In attempts to manage young men's criminality, institutions develop practices heavily influenced by masculinity. In response, the boys in this study became socialized to specific meanings of manhood at odds with those of dominant institutions of control. Gendered interactions with the criminal justice system placed the boys in a double bind. Most bought into the system's ideals of reform by attempting to become "hard-working men." However, frustration with the lack of viable employment and guidance opportunities led them right back to the seductive arms of hypermasculinity. The stories and actions of the young men in this study provide insight into how this double bind is partially generated by the criminal justice system.

Police officers are themselves embedded in a logic that embraces masculinity. For example, criminologists Prokos and Padavic (2002) found that academies train officers to practice a rogue and hostile masculinity. This training reverberates in the inner city. As Angela Harris explains, "Police officers in poor minority neighborhoods may come to see themselves as law enforcers in a community of savages, as outposts of the law in a jungle" (2002: 442). In this context, punitive police treatment of men of color is not only racial violence; it is gender violence. Young people in

Oakland encountered these forms of violence regularly from police on the street, at school, at community centers, and in front of their apartment complexes. The boys often became victims of police officers attempting to uphold the law. Many officers sought to "teach" the young men by feminizing and emasculating them: they manhandled them, called them "little bitches," humiliated them in front of female peers, challenged them to fights, and more.

CASTRO: Dude [the officer] was pointing his gun. "I give up, I give up." He hit him [Castro's friend] with a stick and broke his arm, and this other fool had his knee on my neck. All 'cause we were smoking some weed. . . They beat us down and call us "little bitches."

RAFA: They kick your ass, pistol whip you, even try to kill you. . . . Them bustas [cowards] just trying to prove themselves, you feel me? They trying to prove they are more manly than us, but if they didn't have guns or jails, they would end up being the bitches.

Gendered police interactions begin at an early age. The boys consistently reported early interactions with disciplinary authorities at school and by police. They learned that "being a man" meant not relying on the police, learning to take a beating from police, and—sometimes—desisting from committing crime and resisting the seductions of street life.

At the epicenter of the police–youth interactions we observed was a form of hypermasculinity—taught and learned, challenged and embraced. In attempting to teach the young men to be law-abiding citizens, officers helped support toughness, violence, and hypermasculinity in the boys. These forms of masculinity play a role in influencing young men toward violence and crime.

CONCLUSION

As adolescent boys practiced masculinity on the street, the institutions of control that "managed" the boys also generated meanings of manhood, informing and reinforcing the identities these youth formed on the street. In this case, the criminalization of black and Latino men and the criminal justice system's expectations of masculinity provided the young men with gender resources that limited their mobility, affected their families and relationships, and made them much more likely to end up in the criminal justice system. The gendered behavior and ideals promoted by police, probation officers, and others was often less possible for these boys than authorities seemed to imagine. In this context, hypermasculinity served both as resistance and as a resource for self-affirmation. This survival strategy impeded social mobility and created a ready-made rationalization entitling the system to further criminalize and punish them.

The boys in this study, however, did not passively submit to police officers in all of their interactions. They actively resisted police officers' challenges to their masculinity. This resistance demonstrated the boys' "synthesized masculinities"—a process that made the accomplishment of masculinity more attainable. Neither dominant masculinity nor subordinate masculinity alone helps to explain the actions and meanings that gang-involved Latino boys navigate and create. In this study, we found that Latino boys constantly negotiated between subordinate, street, working-class, and dominant masculinity. With few resources and diverse constraints placed on them by families, police, and schools, the young men in this study often perceived failure as their only option. In this context, demonstrations of masculinity were a last-resort effort to acquire social status and alleviate other forms of subordination. For these boys, masculinity (more so than race and class) was a coping mechanism they relied on to survive in a world that they believed attacked them for being poor and brown. Masculinity was utilized as a vehicle for attempting to alleviate forms of social marginalization and subordination based on their race and class.

As Latino boys developed this synthesized masculinity, however, others (women, in particular) often fell victim to their subordination. For instance, we found that when men found themselves battling institutions of control, they often responded to this emasculation by symbolically remasculinizing themselves by subjecting young women to physical and symbolic violence (Rios 2009). Synthesized masculinity became a vehicle by which lower-status Latino youth living in Riverland were able to feel accomplished and develop self-affirmation. Similar to Cooper's (2009) work, this study highlights the need to change the gender dynamics of policing and deconstruct the toxic definitions of what it means to be a man. We must move away from punitive models of policing. Some steps that can be taken to begin to eliminate the patterns of policing we observe include establishing extensive police training programs designed to challenge a macho police culture and address racial and gendered, raced, and classed stereotypes. Officers can also benefit from training that teaches them how to effectively communicate even when their authority is being challenged and to think about the consequences of prematurely presuming violence and acting upon that assumption.

REFERENCES

Adams, Rachel, and David Savran. 2002. *The Masculinity Studies Reader*. Oxford: Blackwell.

Anderson, Elijah. 1999. *Code of the Street: Decency, Violence, and Moral Life in the Inner City*. New York: Norton.

Bederman, Gail. 1995. *Manliness and Civilization: A Cultural History of Gender and Race in the United States, 1880–1917*. Chicago: University of Chicago Press.

Carrigan, Tim, R. W. Connell, and John Lee. 1985. "Toward a New Sociology of Masculinity." *Theory and Society* 14: 551–604.

Carter, Prudence L. 2005. *Keepin' it Real: School Success beyond Black and White*. New York: Oxford University Press.

Connell, R. W. 1987. *Gender and Power*. Stanford, CA: Stanford University Press.

Connell, R. W. 1995. *Masculinities*. Los Angeles: University of California Press.

Connell, R. W., and J. W. Messerschmidt. 2005. "Hegemonic Masculinity: Rethinking the Concept." *Gender & Society* 19: 829–59.

Cooper, Frank R. 2009. "'Who's the Man?': Masculinities Studies, Terry Stops, and Police Training." *Columbia Journal of Gender and Law* 18 (3): 671.

Dodsworth, Francis. 2007. "Police and the Prevention of Crime: Commerce, Temptation and the Corruption of the Body Politic, from Fielding to Colquhoun." *The British Journal of Criminology* 47 (3): 439–454.

Fernandez, Sonia. 2009. "4 Arrested in Franklin Clinic Gang Incident. Police Disperse Crowd of Suspected Gang Members Awaiting Rival Gang Members Being Treated Inside." *Noozhawk*, 7 April. http://www.noozhawk.com/noozhawk/article/040609_four_arrested_in_franklin_clinic_gang_incident/.

Gau, Jacinta M., and Rod K. Brunson. 2010. "Procedural Justice and Order Maintenance Policing: A Study of Inner-City Young Men's Perceptions of Police Legitimacy." *Justice Quarterly* 27 (2): 255–79.

Hahn, Harlan. 1971. "Ghetto Assessments of Police Protection and Authority." *Law & Society Review* 183 (6): 1971–72.

Harris, Angela P. 2000. "Gender, Violence, Race, and Criminal Justice." *Stanford Law Review* 52 (4): 777–807.

Herbert, Steve. 2006. "Tangled up in Blue: Conflicting Paths to Police Legitimacy." *Theoretical Criminology* 10 (4): 481–504.

Jones, Nikki. 2009. "'I Was Aggressive for the Streets, Pretty for the Pictures': Gender, Difference and the Inner-City Girl. *Gender & Society* 23 (1): 89–93.

Jones, Nikki. 2010. *Between Good and Ghetto: African American Girls and Inner–City Violence*. New Brunswick, NJ: Rutgers University Press.

Kimmel, Michael S. 1996. *Manhood in America: A Cultural History*. New York: Oxford University Press.

Kimmel, Michael S. 2003. "Masculinity as Homophobia: Fear, Shame, and Silence in the Construction of Gender Identity." In *Race, Class, and Gender in the United States: An Integrated Study*, edited by Paula S. Rothenberg, 6th ed., 81–93. New York: Worth.

Kimmel, Michael S. and Matthew Mahler. 2003. "Adolescent Masculinity, Homophobia, and Violence: Random School Shootings, 1982–2001. *American Behavioral Scientist* 46 (10): 1439–58.

Lopez, N. 2003. *Hopeful Girls, Troubled Boys: Race and Gender Disparity in Urban Education*. New York: Routledge.

Martin, Susan E. 1999. Police Force or Police Service? Gender and Emotional Labor. *The ANNALS of the American Academy of Political and Social Sciences* 561 (1): 111–26

Messerschmidt, James W. 1993. *Masculinities and Crime: Critique and Reconceptualization of Theory*. Lanham, MD: Rowman & Littlefield.

Messerschmidt, James W. 2000. "Becoming 'Real Men': Adolescent Masculinity Challenges and Sexual Violence." *Men and Masculinities* 2 (3): 286–307.

Prokos, Anastasia and Irene Padavic. 2002. "'There Oughtta Be a Law Against Bitches': Masculinity Lessons in Police Academy Training." *Gender, Work & Organization* 9 (4): 439–59.

Pyke, Karen D. 1996. "Class-Based Masculinities: The Interdependence of Gender, Class, and Interpersonal Power." *Gender & Society* 10: 527–49.

Rios, Victor M. 2009. "The Consequences of the Criminal Justice Pipeline on Black and Latino Masculinity." *The Annals of the American Academy of Political and Social Sciences* 623 (1): 150–62.

Rios, Victor M. 2011. *Punished: Policing the Lives of Black and Latino Boys.* New York: New York University Press.

Sollund, Ragnhild. 2006. "Racialisation in Police Stop and Search Practice—The Norwegian Case." *Critical Criminology* 14 (3): 265–92.

West, Candace and Sarah Fenstermaker. 1995. "Doing Difference." *Gender & Society* 9 (1): 8–37.

West, Candace and Don Zimmerman. 1987. "Doing Gender." *Gender & Society* 1: 125–51.

Yin, Robert K. 2002. *Case Study Research.* Thousand Oaks, CA: SAGE.

Young, Alford A., Jr. 2009. *The Minds of Margin Alized Black Men: Making Sense of Mobility, Opportunity, and Future Life Changes.* Princeton, NY: Princeton University Press.

NOTES

1. Insight for the ideas I present comes from nearly a decade of field work: a three-year ethnographic project in Northern California, 2002–2005, and a four-year ethnographic project in Southern California, 2007–2012. Both studies were designed to shadow young men who were caught up in the criminal justice system across institutional settings: at schools, parks, the streets, court, home, and community centers.

2. Youths' names and the names of places have been changed to protect subjects' safety and their confidentiality.

3. Yin argues that unique cases are a crucial area of study: "in case studies, rare situations are often precisely what the researcher wants" (Yin 2002).

4. The era of mass incarceration is the time period (circa 1970s to present) in which the United States has drastically expanded its incarceration and where a crackdown on crime, specifically among racialized and poor populations, has led to more criminal sanctions and criminalization than ever before.

ERIC ANDERSON

12. INCLUSIVE MASCULINITIES

HOW DO YOU THEORIZE THIS?

In the summer of 2013, I returned to visit a Southern California high school cross country team I had coached in 1990. Composed of 43 members, the team has Korean, Chinese, Caucasian, Mexican, Egyptian, and African American athletes alongside atheists and those of the Jewish, Christian, Buddhist, Mormon, Muslim, and Jehovah's Witness faiths. One team member wears black every day and sports half a dozen piercings, whereas another wears preppy clothes and does ballet. One was voted the school's homecoming king, several play instruments, and some maintain high GPAs, whereas others maintain grades just sufficient to compete. One was arrested for breaking into a school and stealing computers, and a few are Eagle Scouts. Some have special social, educational, and or physical needs, and others maintain high social, athletic, or sexual capital. Perhaps most significantly, there are two openly gay male athletes, and another publicly declares that he will just fall in love with whomever he falls in love with.

Despite this diversity, social groupings on the team are diverse and fluid. Not race, nor intelligence, nor religion, nor sexuality is a variable in establishing friendship patterns. No athlete on the team is bullied, on the team or in the school they attend. Yet, when I taught at this school 23 years ago, matters were different.

Back then the school was ruled by football players and this negatively impacted the school's general population. The runners, for example, feared the football team (Anderson 2000). Football players hated gays, femininity, and all other "lesser" masculine sports. Thus, when students started a Gay–Straight Alliance in 1993, football players started a heterosexual club, even picketing the gay club with homophobic signs.

But as the runners on the 2013 team run past the football players (lined up to do drills), they sometimes stop to have short conversations, discussing homework or forthcoming shared social engagements. Or, as the football players walk to water, they stop to talk to the stretching runners. It is evident that their friendship networks overlap. The two gay male athletes on the cross country team are no exception. They have friends on the football team. The openly gay freshman football player has friends on the cross country team.

As the team runs on the far side of the field, they pass the school's marching band, whose members possess less athletic capital than the runners. This is a group that, in 1990, runners marginalized. Yet today's runners do not mock band members' apparent lack of athleticism, and neither does the football team. Just as with the football players, the runners stop to chat with them.

As the team concludes their workout by stretching on the grass, a fully geared freshman football team walks by us on way to their first match. They walk side by side, holding hands with the player adjacent. When I asked one why they were holding hands, he responded that it is tradition (it's not). Another said, "It shows brotherhood." None of the runners on the cross country team commented about the hand-holding. From my perspective, this homosocial tactility was amazing; from their perspective, it was uneventful.

At a prerace spaghetti dinner the following night, two of the straight male runners stood chatting with other runners. From behind, one rested his head on the other's shoulder, wrapping his arms around the other's waist—a standing cuddle. I timed it from another table: it lasted for 11 minutes and 37 seconds. Last track season eight of the runners on this team made what can only be described as a highly provocative Harlem Shake video, which included nudity and featured one of the gay members mock-fucking one of the straight team members. At one of the runner's birthday parties, five of the athletes took a photo in which they stood behind each other, each with their hand in the front pocket of the guy in front of them. The boy in the middle is openly gay and each team member in the picture is of a different racial ethnic group. These are examples of bountiful similar occurrences for the boys on this team.

When I made my final goodbye to the team this summer, a number of the boys called out, "We love you" as I drove away. They gave me shirts for my one-year old twins as a going away gift. In rainbow colors the shirts had printed on them, "Two dads are better than one." These youth celebrated the fact they had an openly gay coach who is married to his husband and the proud father of two baby boys. "When you return next summer I will be the first to give a big hug," one straight runner messaged me on Facebook. He held true to his word.

The gendered behaviors of these young men on this high school team are radically different from that in 1990. Seeing the change in one city is powerful, but it is also what I see in my dozens of studies in both the United States and, even more so, the United Kingdom—studies that I detail in my (2014) book *21st Century Jocks: Sporting Men and Contemporary Heterosexuality*. Their attitudes toward diversity, homosexuality, femininity, same-sex touch, and the expression of love for another male are that of inclusion and plurality. In 1990, their attitude was one of exclusion of anything different from the jock-norm. But this school is no longer run by jocks. Friendship patterns today are fluid, and the gendered behaviors of the boys in the school are highly feminized, at least by 1990 standards.

The question I have for the readers of this chapter, therefore, is: How do you theorize this shift?

CHAPTER PURPOSE

There is a tendency to be somewhat passive in critical thought in the face of dominant paradigms. I and others (e.g., Moller 2007) argue that this is also the case with masculinities theory. Thus, the pedagogical task I ask you to engage with here is to consider how best to theorize the above vignette. First, I present my interpretation of how hegemonic masculinity and inclusive masculinity theory would explain the

vignette. Then, I explicate the reasons why hegemonic masculinity has resonance for many scholars, but also why inclusive masculinity theory is better suited to understanding many contemporary cultures of masculinity.

1. HEGEMONIC MASCULINITY THEORY

Devised by Raewyn Connell, the leading theorizing of masculinities has been hegemonic masculinity theory (HMT). Although some call hegemonic masculinity a concept, I refer to it as a theory because it maintains predictive power. In the 1980s, HMT replaced the then-leading heurism, sex role theory (Brannon and David 1976), with a more dynamic conceptualization of gender (Connell 1987, 1995). HMT viewed men's hierarchies as "configurations of practice" to accomplish its interrelated goals: (1) to understand the social dynamics of men (their social organization and behaviors); and (2) to understand how these dynamics reproduced patriarchy.

Connell defines hegemonic masculinity as "the configuration of gender practice which embodies the currently accepted answer to the problem of the legitimacy of patriarchy" (Connell 1995: 77). Implicit in this definition, however, is the configuration of gender practices of men. Although some scholars will argue that Connell discusses gender regimes and highlights that gender is relational and thus it is about men and women, it is notable that HMT is used overwhelmingly to understand the practices of men. Thus, a model for understanding the stratification of masculinities among men through a Gramscianesque hierarchical modeling has resulted from Connell's theory, as well as an understanding of the policing of men's individual gendered behaviors. Connell suggested that the social ordering was inscribed through physical domination (or threat thereof) and discursive marginalization (think homophobic discourse) (Connell 1995: 66–67). This was thought to ultimately produce or at least promote patriarchy.

Incorporating an understanding of the operation of power that is consistent with the notion of hegemony (Gramsci 1971), Connell (1995) designated three categories of masculinities that, by definition, emerge "under" the hegemonic form: complicit, subordinated, and marginalized. Although Connell does not herself discuss this hierarchy explicitly, she alludes to it by suggesting that complicit masculinities keep the dominant form of masculinity (hegemonic masculinity) in power because they aspire to attain or at least mimic it; the "subordination of nonhegemonic masculinities" (Connell and Messerschmidt 2005: 846) also clearly implies a hierarchical structure.

Marginalized masculinities are said to categorize men subordinated by the hegemonic form of masculinity because of their race or class, and Connell distinguished them from the "relations internal to the gender order" (1995: 80). Finally, highlighting homosexual oppression as distinct, Connell labeled the masculinities of gay men as "subordinated," suggesting they were "the most conspicuous" (1995: 79) form—"subordinated to straight men by an array of quite material practices" (1995: 78). These categories provided an effective framework for understanding the hierarchical stratification of men in Western society in the 1980s and 1990s.

Connell envisioned the social organization of these loosely defined categories of masculinity as a structural mechanism for the reproduction of patriarchy, although there exists scant empirical evidence or conceptual logic to support this position (Demetriou 2001; Grindstaff and West 2011). For example, New (2001) suggests that patriarchy is much more complicated than Connell suggests. HMT therefore offers a one-dimensional answer to a complex problem that has multiple social roots (Bourdieu 2001; Ferree and Hess 1995), and this is why almost all sociologists employing HMT have looked solely at the intra-masculine stratifications and the gendered behavior component.

So if we are to use HMT to understand the social dynamics of the running team in southern California, we must focus on the intra-masculine stratifications present among these men. We need to examine to see who has hegemonic power—not just social dominance—and how others emulate that power to be like them. We need to understand the experiences of the gay runners through a framework of subordination and oppression.

But HMT cannot explain the vignette. There is no apparent hegemonic hierarchy in popularity—it was a Korean, Buddhist, feminine cross country runner elected homecoming king (see also McCormack, 2011a); there is no discrimination according to sexual identity, with gay males socially included and their identities oftentimes celebrated; and there is no discursive marginalization of men that "subordinates nonhegemonic masculinities" (Connell and Messerschmidt 2005: 846). I thus contend that inclusive masculinity theory will be more useful for understanding the opening vignette.

2. INCLUSIVE MASCULINITY THEORY

When I developed inclusive masculinity theory from a number of research projects spanning almost 10 years, I came from the position that HMT had been a useful way of understanding masculinities in the 1980s and 1990s—including my experiences at school, first as a closeted gay student and then as a running coach (first closeted, then open). Yet in my research on gay athletes (Anderson 2002), I found their experiences to be a challenge to HMT—they were more positive than I was expecting and HMT predicted. Further research on heterosexual college athletes, years later (Anderson 2011b), confounded the assumptions of machismo and homophobia among male youth as well. I started to realize that the high levels of homophobia of that period that I suspect many scholars thought were inevitable were historically situated and contingent on a number of social factors. To understand the intersection of masculinities and homophobia, I realized we needed to account for the effect of how homophobia changes.

To understand the shifting nature of homophobia, I created the concept "homohysteria." This is a "homosexually-panicked culture in which suspicion [of homosexuality] permeates" (Anderson 2011a: 7) and has also been defined as the fear of being perceived as gay (Anderson 2009). I argue that for a culture of homohysteria to exist, three social factors must coincide: (1) a mass cultural awareness that homosexuality exists as a static sexual orientation within a significant portion of the population; (2) a cultural zeitgeist of disapproval toward homosexuality; and (3) a cultural disapproval of femininity in men or masculinity in women, as they are associated with homosexuality.

When levels of homophobia are high in a homohysteric culture, boys and men go to great lengths to demonstrate they are heterosexual. In other words, they have to prove that they are not gay. And this is done through distancing themselves from things perceived as gay or feminine (because of its conflation with homosexuality for males). Thus, boys eschew feminized terrains, behaviors, and emotional expressions (Pollack 1999); they buff up or support sport teams in lieu of their own physicality (Plummer 1999); they talk in explicitly sexual and misogynistic language (Pascoe 2007; Thurlow 2001); they avoid feminine entertainment choices, clothes, or sports (Francis 1999); and they adopt homophobic attitudes and marginalize those suspected of being gay (Kimmel 1994). It is this last characteristic that is most effective in securing masculinity because the greatest fear is being thought of as gay (the subordinated masculinity in Connell's language).

However, as homophobia declines, the stigma associated with homosexuality also reduces. This has the effect that boys and men care less about whether they are perceived as gay. And as they are less motivated to avoid a "gay" identity, homophobia loses its power to regulate masculinities. And in the absence of this policing mechanism, boys are permitted to engage in a wider range of behaviors without ridicule. This will include choices of clothes, expressions of friendship and emotional intimacy, hobbies and pastimes, and who one chooses to be friends with. And as straight boys become friends with gay peers, they further undo their homophobia. McCormack describes this as a "virtuous circle of decreasing homophobia" (2012: 63).

So, looking at the runners of 2013, we see that they have lost their homophobia: being friends with gay students, espousing pro-gay attitudes, making their gay coach a T-shirt that says "two dads are better than one." They are free to pursue their own interests and make friends with whom they like (whether it be from the band or football team). They wear pink, talk about their clothes, and cuddle with each other. Absent are physical domination and discursive marginalization (Connell 1995); present instead is a broadly horizontal ordering of masculinities where popularity is determined by a host of variables that are not prescribed by one's masculinity (McCormack 2011a).

There is not a social stratification among the groups of boys that I studied at this school; instead there exists a clustering of non–vertically arranged masculinity types, including football jocks, runners, band members, preps, goths, emos, and computer geeks. I find these groupings are composed of black, white, Asian, Mexican, and other ethnicities/races, alongside sexual minorities and heterosexuals. Although some are "cooler" than others, these popularity rankings are shorn of the dominating and damaging practices of homophobia, violence, and misogyny.

My argument is that there is little doubt that inclusive masculinity theory explains the social dynamics of these youth better than HMT. If you need to, have a think about that. But if you have any doubts, or if you wonder why there is any debate at all, let me explain why I think HMT still has resonance for some scholars.

THE ORIGINS OF A HEGEMONIC THEORY

The original power and continued endurance of HMT comes from the fact that it was an effective theory in understanding the social dynamics of men in the 1980s and early 1990s. The 1980s marked an apex of homophobic attitudes in the Western world (Loftus 2001). General Social Survey data from 1988 documents that 81.8 percent of American respondents indicated homosexual sex was always or almost always wrong, up from the 1970s. Gay men were socially feminized and overtly stigmatized by mainstream society (Nardi 1999). It is the historical and cultural specificity of this time—specifically the exceptional levels of homophobia in most Western cultures—that made HMT particularly suited to understanding the social organization of stratified masculinities (Grindstaff and West 2006).

Western homophobia of the 1980s is attributable to the rise of moralistic right-wing politics, the politicization of evangelical religion, and the AIDS crisis (Loftus 2001; McCormack and Anderson 2014). Crucially, because the social perception of homosexuality is determined by behavioral actions and social identifications, rather than ascribed characteristics (like skin color socially identifies "race"), heterosexuality had to be continually proved and reproved. This meant that young men of this generation went to great lengths to demonstrate that they were not gay (Mac an Ghaill 1994). They deployed homophobia against those who violated requisite gender norms, and esteemed masculinities remained within narrow gender boundaries that precluded emotional intimacy and physical tactility (Floyd 2000; Derlega et al. 1989; Pascoe 2007). This zeitgeist *required* homophobic attitudes and aggressive behaviors (Kreager 2007; Plummer 1999) if young men were to approximate the hegemonic form of masculinity and distance themselves from being thought gay.

HMT was therefore largely successful in describing intramasculine stratifications because it powerfully and pragmatically captured the masculine zeitgeist of the era in which it was conceived (Anderson 2009). Supported by a growing body of empirical research, HMT soon became the primary way of analyzing all masculinity issues to the point that the theory itself seems to have become hegemonic in the new sociology of masculinities scholarship by the turn of the century. Even scholars who did not explicate the theory nonetheless drew upon it (e.g., Plummer 1999).

CONNELL'S REVISION OF HMT

In 2005, Connell and Messerschmidt (2005) argued that HMT should be reformulated in several ways. They conceded that subordinated groups have agency and argued that gay men are not necessarily at the bottom of the hierarchy anymore, but that at best they can be both oppressed and tolerated at the same time.

The revised HMT therefore denies heterosexuals the ability to treat homosexuals equally. The conceptual logic of saying that hegemonic masculinity will always exist, and that it requires the oppression of gay men, structurally traps gay men into perpetual oppression. But this is not merely a structural/theoretical misjudgement; it is also prejudice. It is prejudice to suggest that straight men are incapable of inclusion and acceptance of gay men.

To use HMT, one relies on homophobia. In examining men, empirically then, one must therefore find homophobia, even if one has to shake it from trees, using a finer- and finer-grain lens to define it, hoping that one morsel of evidence drops for which they can then claim the entire forest is homophobic. At worse, scholars many times suggest that men are homophobic even when they find no evidence of it. Less contentiously, scholars define contemporary use of the term "that's gay," which has long lost homosexual contextualization the way "oh bugger" has, as homophobic (see McCormack 2012 for an excellent discussion of this). Yet, this term no longer has anything to do with homosexuality unless it's qualified —something we've known for over a decade (Thurlow 2001). Just as 'I was gypped" no longer connotes Roma, "uppity" no longer connotes American slaves, and "hooligan" no longer serves as a derogatory term for the Irish, "that's gay" no longer connotes homosexuality.

Several other problems with hegemonic masculinity theory also persist: (1) it still argues that HMT understands how masculine stratifications contribute to patriarchy, yet there remains neither the empirical evidence nor the conceptual logic to support this position; (2) it remains steadfast in using complicit, subordinated, and marginalized categories of masculinities, yet never concisely defines them (McCormack 2012); (3) there remains lack of clarity pertaining to HMT as a social process, rather than an archetype of masculinity; (4) it continues to employ a restricted notion of Gramscian hegemony (Beasley 2008); (5) its paradigmatic dominance has watered it down and damaged its utility as a theory (Moller 2007); and finally, (6) HMT's reformulation loses theoretical specificity, leaving little to distinguish it from the paradigm of social construction more broadly.

THE CENTRALITY OF HOMOPHOBIA

Despite Connell and Messerschmidt's revision, a substantial and growing body of newer work eschews HMT as a way of theorizing the social dynamics of the setting (e.g., Adams 2011; Duncanson 2009; Flood 2008). McCormack (2012), Bartholomaeus (2012), Lyng (2009), Swain (2006), Dean (2013), and dozens more argue that hegemonic masculinity does not capture the social dynamics of teenage or preteenage boys, instead choosing other theories. These studies reflect the effects of a masculinity shift evidenced among male youth today.

I offer the United States as an exemplar of this shift. Throughout the decades of the 20th century, awareness of homosexuality grew slowly; but the cultural belief that anyone could be gay skyrocketed (along with homophobia) in the 1980s. This was for three reasons: (1) HIV/AIDS, and the large percentage of even gender-typical men who acquired it through same-sex sex, proved to Americans that homosexuals existed in normal American families. The 1980s homophobia was also heightened by an increasingly noisy fundamentalist Christianity opposed to and which consequently demonized homosexuality (Anderson 2011a); and this effort/these religious leaders intermingled with the Republican Party. Thus the 1980s, the decade of religion, Rambo and Reagan, is when men began rapidly and safely distancing themselves from anything remotely associated with femininity.

In this homohysteric culture boys and young men (particularly those who were unmarried) needed to establish and re-establish themselves as heterosexual by aligning their gendered behaviors with idealized notions of masculinity. This is something that Kimmel (1994) aptly described as "masculinity as homophobia." It is within this era that I argue that hegemonic masculinity theory was an apt description of gendered identities and practices.

However, homohysteria is predicated upon homophobic attitudes, and there is an overwhelming body of quantitative evidence that cultural homophobia began to decrease in 1993 and has rapidly decreased since (e.g., Baunach 2012). Keleher and Smith (2012: 1324) show that *all* demographic groups have become more tolerant and, importantly, that they became more tolerant at the same rate; arguing that "we are witnessing a sweeping change in attitudes toward lesbians and gay men."

This means that youth grow up in a culture with radically different views than they used to. Thus, qualitative research has shown that the gendered behaviors of young boys, adolescents, and young men are radically different when they no longer fear being culturally homosexualized (Anderson 2009; McCormack 2012). This is something that I describe as a culture of inclusivity (Anderson 2014), the basis for my theory—inclusive masculinity.

APPLYING INCLUSIVE MASCULINITY THEORY

The American high school that I taught at in 1990 was near-perfectly theorized by Connell's theory. This was a social world in which a group of men (mostly football jocks) ruled *over* all others. Those who did not fit this model did their best to approximate it, looking up the hierarchy. Although those at the top could use some of their masculine capital (Anderson 2005) or "jock insurance" (Pascoe 2003) to engage in some homoerotic banter as a form of expressing their heterosexuality, all other forms of same-sex intimacy (physical or emotional) were taboo; their enactment brought physical punishment and social retribution (Pollack 1999). During this time, nothing could be worse to an adolescent male than to be thought a fag (Anderson 2000).

But Connell's theory does not seem to apply to this team today. Dozens of ethnographic studies, authored by myself and many other researchers, show that young men adopt inclusive attitudes toward homosexuality and that they associate much more freely with symbols that were once coded as homosexualizing of men (Adams 2011; Anderson 2008, 2009, 2011a,b; 2014; Anderson and McCormack 2014; Anderson et al. 2012; Anderson and McGuire 2010; Bullingham et al. 2014; Cavalier 2011; Cashmore and Cleland 2012; Channon 2012; Cleland 2014; Dean 2013; Dashper 2012; Drummond et al. 2014; Kian and Anderson 2009; Magrath et al. 2013;McCormack 2011a, 2011b, 2012; McCormack et al. 2014; Miller et al. 2014; Peterson 2011; Roberts 2012). As they do, those symbols lose their homosexualizing power. This means that even homophobic men can adopt softer gender codes. Take, for example, the color pink. In the 1980s, pink was for girls, and boys who wore it were labeled fags. Today, pink, purple, and lavender are popular men's dress shirt colors without homosexualizing the wearer. In England, I even see boys riding pink bicycles. Pink no longer homosexualizes a male in any of these contexts, unless a guy's bedroom looks as if it were hit with a Barbie bomb.

There is no definitive checklist of cultural attributes that define a culture as valuing what I call "orthodox" masculinity compared to one of inclusivity, but in attempt to give some specific behavioral traits (unlike HMT), I provide below some trends that will emerge when homophobia is socially unacceptable. These traits include same-sex emotional intimacy (bromances); same-sex physical intimacy (touch, kissing, cuddling); an expansion of desirable male bodies (i.e. today thin and muscular boys are sexualized); an expansion of acceptable gendered behaviors (men today can sit with their legs crossed); an expansion of gender-acceptable fashion, music, sport, gaming, and mass entertainment; avoidance of fights; homophobic intent removed from homophobic/gay/homosexualized discourse; less sexism; and a reduction in the "one-time rule of homosexuality" permitting gay sexual experiences without being culturally homosexualized.

Inclusive masculinity theory then argues that there will be a relationship between these above-mentioned behaviors and the social organization of masculinity types. In a culture of extreme homohysteria, boys will align, vertically, in a homophobic-hegemonic stratification similar, or perhaps identical, to the one Connell alludes to, while restricting the above-mentioned categories to what is perceived to be heterosexual. But in a culture of inclusivity—when a "so what" attitude exists around male homosexuality, as it does on the team I coach during the summers—a vertical, hegemonic stratification of masculinity types will not exist. Instead, multiple masculinity types will proliferate without inequality. I cannot prescribe the exact social arrangement of them, but they will not be vertical.

Thus, embedded into inclusive masculinity theory is the simple understating that homophobia hurts more than homosexuals; it profoundly (and negatively) impacts the lives of heterosexuals, too.

There is work yet to do with my theorizing. The preponderance of work using this theoretical paradigm is on young athletes. I selected these men intentionally because they exist at the center of masculine production in Western cultures. However, future work must examine what occurs among older men as the culture around them becomes more gay tolerant/friendly. Also, about 80 percent of the men I study are white. Although it is prejudice to suppose that non-whites, or non–university students, or non-middle-class men retain elevated rates of homophobia compared

to the groups I study without evidence (Pompper 2010), and given that recent quantitative data suggest changes are not restricted to white, middle-class youth (see Pryor et al. 2011), more research needs to be done on nonwhite demographics.

My theory also, intentionally, does not engage with patriarchy. I argue that hegemonic masculinity theory structures itself into a circular argument. In asserting causation between the hegemonic masculine stratifications of men and patriarchy and insisting that a form of masculine hegemony will always exist, Connell fails to recognize that she prescribes perpetual patriarchy for society. It is for this reason that I avoid an analysis of patriarchy with inclusive masculinity theory. Other theorists (i.e., Bridges 2014) examine the impact, or not, of inclusive masculinities on the gender order. For those who do examine the relationship between inclusive masculinities and patriarchy, I recommend a serious engagement with the breadth of scholarship (including beyond the discipline of sociology) on the topic.

Finally, I do not wish for users of my theory to portray *all* men as inclusive or to confuse hegemony (which requires willing compliance of the oppressed) with social capital or other measures of popularity. Dominance and privilege might still occur. Mark McCormack (2012) has added to my theory by showing how popularity could be established in a culture absent of a hegemonic form of masculinity, but more work must be done in this arena.

CONCLUSION

With this chapter, I hope to have provoked a critical reflection of the theory that has dominated our field for more than a quarter century. I hope to have shown a healthy respect for the theory/concept of hegemonic masculinity, as it transformed our understanding of the multiplicity of masculinities and their consequences nearly three decades ago, while simultaneously arguing that its usefulness is now germane only to cultures, or organizational cultures, that retain high degrees of homohysteria—the way America did in the 1980s.

Those married to hegemonic masculinity theory will undoubtedly cherry-pick isolated incidents of homophobia to verify their sustained belief in the utility of the theory. Masculinity scholars of the younger generation, however, are seeing matters quite differently. They see theoretical matters differently *because* they are generating different results in their empirical work.

This leads me to ask the reader: *how do you theorize the opening evidence?*

As a sociologist responsible for accurately portraying the participants I study, I cannot conceptually or ethically use hegemonic masculinity theory to explain my findings. To do this would be to ascribe undue prejudice to the men I study.

I cannot determine that the men of the team described at the beginning of this chapter at best "tolerate" gay men the way Connell and Messerschmidt (2005) claim they do; nor can I determine just what race it is that is to be marginalized on this team. I cannot determine which religion is associated with hegemonic masculinity, thus thrusting its nonbelievers into the category of complicit masculinities. More so, I find no evidence of any group of males—any archetype—dominating through hegemony at this school. And (again) without hegemony, there is no hegemonic masculinity theory. It is, after all, a hegemony-based theory.

I do not assume that my theory will cover all men in all situations, however. That is why, for example, McCormack (2014) has combined IMT with a neo-Bourdieuan understanding of class to analyze the intersection of class, masculinities, and decreasing homophobia. Indeed, I argue against intellectual fundamentalism or paradigmatic dominance. Instead, we need a plurality of social theorizing about masculinities. I welcome this.

REFERENCES

Adams, Adi. 2011. "'Josh Wears Pink Cleats': Inclusive Masculinity on the Soccer Field." *Journal of Homosexuality* 58 (5): 579–96.

Anderson, Eric. 2000. *Trailblazing: The True Story of America's First Openly Gay High School Coach.* Los Angeles: Alyson.

Anderson, Eric. 2002. "Openly Gay Athletes Contesting Hegemonic Masculinity in a Homophobic Environment." *Gender & Society* 16 (6): 860–77.

Anderson, Eric. 2005. *In the Game: Gay Athletes and the Cult of Masculinity.* New York: SUNY Press.

Anderson, Eric. 2008. "'Being masculine is not about who you sleep with . . .' Heterosexual Athletes Contesting Masculinity and the One-Time Rule of Homosexuality." *Sex Roles* 58 (1–2): 104–15.

Anderson, Eric. 2009. *Inclusive Masculinity: The Changing Nature of Masculinities.* New York: Routledge.

Anderson, Eric. 2011a. "The Rise and Fall of Western Homohysteria." *Journal of Feminist Scholarship* 1 (1): 80–94.

Anderson, Eric. 2011b. "Updating the Outcome Gay Athletes, Straight Teams, and Coming Out in Educationally Based Sport Teams." *Gender & Society* 25 (2): 250–68.

Anderson, Eric. 2014. *21st Century Jocks; Sporting Men and Contemporary Heterosexuality.* Basingstoke, UK: Palgrave–MacMillan.

Anderson, Eric, and Mark McCormack. 2014. "Cuddling and Spooning: Heteromasculinity and Homosocial Tactility among Student-Athletes." *Men and Masculinities.* Published online before print March 12, 2014, doi:10.1177/1097184X14523433.

Anderson, Eric, Mark McCormack, and Harry Lee. 2012. "Male Team Sport Hazing Initiations in a Culture of Decreasing Homohysteria." *Journal of Adolescent Research* 27 (4): 427–48.

Anderson, Eric, and Rhidian McGuire. 2010. "Inclusive Masculinity Theory and the Gendered Politics of Men's Rugby." *Journal of Gender Studies* 19 (3): 249–61.

Bartholomaeus, Clare. 2012. "'I'm Not Allowed Wrestling Stuff': Hegemonic Masculinity and Primary School Boys." *Journal of Sociology* 48 (3): 227–47.

Baunach, Dawn Michelle. 2012. "Changing Same-Sex Marriage Attitudes in America from 1988 through 2010." *Public Opinion Quarterly* 76 (2): 364–78.

Beasley, Christine. 2008. "Rethinking Hegemonic Masculinity in a Globalizing World." *Men and Masculinities* 11 (1): 86–103.

Bourdieu, Pierre. 2001. *Masculine Domination.* Stanford, CA: Stanford University Press.

Brannon, Robert, and Deborah David. 1976. "The Male Sex Role: Our Culture's Blueprint of Manhood, and What It's Done for Us Lately." In *The Forty-Nine Percent Majority: The Male Sex Role*, edited by Deborah S. David and Robert Brannon, 1–48. Reading, MA: Addison–Wesley.

Bridges, Tristan. 2014. "A Very "Gay" Straight? Hybrid Masculinities, Sexual Aesthetics, and the Changing Relationship between Masculinity and Homophobia." *Gender & Society* 28 (1): 58–82.

Bullingham, Rachael, Rory Magrath, and Eric Anderson. 2014. "Sport and a Cultural Shift away from Homohysteria." In *Routledge Handbook of Sport, Gender and Sexuality*, edited by Jennifer Hargreaves and Eric Anderson, 275. New York: Routledge.

Cashmore, Ellis, and Jamie Cleland. 2012. "Fans, Homophobia and Masculinities in Association Football: Evidence of a More Inclusive Environment." *The British Journal of Sociology* 63 (2): 370–87.

Cavalier, Elizabeth S. 2011. "Men at Sport: Gay Men's Experiences in the Sport Workplace." *Journal of Homosexuality* 58 (5): 626–46.

Channon, Alex. 2012. "Western Men and Eastern Arts: The Significance of Eastern Martial Arts Disciplines in British Men's Narratives of Masculinity." *Asia Pacific Journal of Sport and Social Science* 1 (2–3): 111–27.

Cleland, Jamie. 2014. "Association Football and the Representation of Homosexuality by the Print Media: A Case Study of Anton Hysén." *Journal of Homosexuality* 61 (9): 1269–87.

Connell, Raewyn. 1987. *Gender and Power: Society, the Person and Sexual Politics*. Stanford, CA: Stanford University Press.

Connell, Raewyn. 1995. *Masculinities*. Berkeley: University of California Press.

Connell, Raewyn, and James W. Messerschmidt. 2005. "Hegemonic Masculinity: Rethinking the Concept." *Gender & Society* 19 (6): 829–59.

Dashper, Katherine. 2012. "'Dressage Is Full of Queens!'Masculinity, Sexuality and Equestrian Sport." *Sociology* 46 (6): 1109–124.

Dean, James J. 2013. "Heterosexual Masculinities, Anti-homophobias, and Shifts in Hegemonic Masculinity: The Identity Practices of Black and White Heterosexual Men." *The Sociological Quarterly* 54: 534–60.

Demetriou, D. Z. 2001. "Connell's Concept of Hegemonic Masculinity: A Critique." *Theory and Society* 30: 337–61.

Derlega, Valerian, Robin J. Lewis, Scott Harrison, Barbara A. Winstead, and Robert Costanza. 1989. "Gender Differences in the Initiation and Attribution of Tactile Intimacy." *Journal of Nonverbal Behavior* 13 (2): 83–96.

Drummond, Murray J. N., Shaun M. Filiault, Eric Anderson, and David Jeffries. 2014. "Homosocial Intimacy among Australian Undergraduate Men." *Journal of Sociology*. Published online before print February 25, 2014. doi:10.1177/1440783313518251.

Duncanson, Claire. 2009. "Forces for Good? Narratives of Military Masculinity in Peacekeeping Operations." *International Feminist Journal of Politics* 11 (1): 63–80.

Ferree, Myra Marx, and Beth B. Hess. 1995. "Controversy and Coalition: The Feminist Movement across Three Decades of Change." In *Controversy and Coalition: The Feminist Movement across Three Decades of Change*. New York: Routledge.

Flood, Michael. 2008. "Men, Sex, and Homosociality: How Bonds Between Men Shape their Sexual Relations with Women." *Men and Masculinities* 10 (3): 339–359.

Floyd, Kevin. 2000. "Affectionate Same-Sex Touch: The Influence of Homophobia on Observers' Perceptions." *Journal of Social Psychology* 140 (6): 774–788.

Francis, Leslie J. 1999. "Personality and Attitude Toward Christianity Among Undergraduates" *Journal of Research on Christian Education* 8 (2): 179–195.

Gramsci, A. 1971. *Selections from Prison Notebooks*. London: New Left Books.

Grindstaff, Laura, and Emily West. 2006. "Cheerleading and the Gendered Politics of Sport." *Social Problems* 53 (4): 500–18.

Keleher, A., and Smith, E. 2012. Growing Support for Gay and Lesbian Equality since 1990. *Journal of Homosexuality* 59: 1307–26.

Kian, Edward (Ted) M., and Eric Anderson. 2009. "John Amaechi: Changing the Way Sport Reporters Examine Gay Athletes." *Journal of Homosexuality* 56 (7): 799–818.

Kimmel, Michael S. 1994. "Masculinity as Homophobia: Fear, Shame, and Silence in the Construction of Gender Identity." In *Theorizing Masculinities*, edited by Harry Brod and Michael Kaufman, 119-42. Research on Men and Masculinities Series. Thousand Oaks, CA: SAGE Publications, Inc.

Kreager, Derek A. 2007. "Unnecessary Roughness? School Sports, Peer Networks, and Male Adolescent

Violence." *American Sociological Review* 72 (5): 705–724.

Loftus, Jeni. 2001. "America's Liberalization in Attitudes Toward Homosexuality, 1973-1998." *American Sociological Review* 66 (5): 762–782.

Lyng, Selma Therese. 2009. "Is There More to 'Anti-schoolishness' Than Masculinity? On Multiple Student Styles, Gender, and Educational Self-Exclusion in Secondary School." *Men and Masculinities* 11 (4): 462–87.

Mac an Ghaill, Mairtin. 1994. *The Making of Men: Masculinities, Sexualities and Schooling.* Berkshire, United Kingdom: Open University Press.

McCormack, Mark. 2011a. "The Declining Significance of Homohysteria for Male Students in Three Sixth Forms in the South of England." *British Educational Research Journal* 37 (2): 337–53.

McCormack, Mark. 2011b. "Mapping the Terrain of Homosexually-Themed Language." *Journal of Homosexuality* 58 (5): 664–79.

McCormack, Mark. 2012. *The Declining Significance of Homophobia: How Teenage Boys Are Redefining Masculinity and Heterosexuality.* New York: Oxford University Press.

McCormack, Mark. 2014. "The Intersection of Youth Masculinities, Decreasing Homophobia and Class: An Ethnography." *The British Journal of Sociology* 65 (1): 130–49.

McCormack, Mark and Eric Anderson. 2014. "The Influence of Declining Homophobia on Men's Gender in the United States: An Argument for the Study of Homohysteria." *Sex Roles* 71 (3-4): 109–120.

McCormack, Mark, Eric Anderson, and Adrian Adams. 2014. "Cohort Effect on the Coming Out Experiences of Bisexual Men." *Sociology.* Published online before print February 17, 2014. doi:10.1177/0038038513518851.

Magrath, Rory, Eric Anderson, and Steven Roberts. 2013. "On the Door-step of Equality: Attitudes toward Gay Athletes among Academy-Level Footballers." *International Review for the Sociology of Sport.* Published online before print July 30, 2013. doi:10.1177/1012690213495747.

Miller, Peter, Samantha Wells, Rhianna Hobbs, Lucy Zinkiewicz, Ashlee Curtis, and Kathryn Graham.

2014. "Alcohol, Masculinity, Honour and Male Barroom Aggression in an Australian Sample." *Drug and Alcohol Review* 33 (2): 136–43.

Moller, Michael. 2007. "Exploiting Patterns: A Critique of Hegemonic Masculinity." *Journal of Gender Studies* 16 (3): 263–76.

Nardi, Peter. 1999. *Gay Men's Friendships: Invincible Communities.* Chicago, IL: University of Chicago Press.

New, Caroline. 2001. "Oppressed and Oppressors? The Systematic Mistreatment of Men." *Sociology* 35 (3): 729–48.

Pascoe, C. J. 2003. "Multiple Masculinities? Teenage Boys Talk about Jocks and Gender." *American Behavioral Scientist* 46 (10): 1423–38.

Pascoe, C. J. 2007. *Dude, You're a Fag: Masculinity and Sexuality in Adolescence.* Berkeley: University of California Press.

Peterson, Grant Tyler. 1999. "Clubbing Masculinities: Gender Shifts in Gay Men's Dance Floor Choreographies." *Journal of Homosexuality* 58 (5): 608–25.

Plummer, David. 1999. *One of the Boys: Masculinity, Homophobia, and Modern Manhood.* New York: Harrington Park Press.

Pollack, William. 1999. *Real Boys: Rescuing Our Sons from the Myth of Boyhood.* New York: Henry Holt and Company.

Pompper, Donnalyn. 2010. "Masculinities, the Metrosexual, and Media Images: Across Dimensions of Age and Ethnicity." *Sex Roles* 63 (9–10): 682–96.

Pryor, J, DeAngelo, L., Blake, L. P., Hurtado, S., and Tran, S. 2011. *The American Freshman: National Norms Fall 2011.* Los Angeles: Higher Education Research Institute, UCLA.

Roberts, S. 2012. "Boys Will Be Boys . . . Won't They? Change and Continuities in Contemporary Young Working-Class Masculinities." *Sociology* 47: 671–86.

Swain, Jon. 2006. "Reflections on Patterns of Masculinity in School Settings." *Men and Masculinities* 8 (3): 331–49.

Thurlow, Crispin. 2001. "Naming the 'Outsider Within': Homophobic Pejoratives and the Verbal Abuse of Lesbian, Gay and Bisexual High-School Pupils." *Journal of Adoles cence* 24 (1): 25–38.

MATTHEW B. EZZELL

13. HEALTHY FOR WHOM?—MALES, MEN, AND MASCULINITY: A REFLECTION ON THE DOING (AND STUDY) OF DOMINANCE

"Games," the men's group-accountability sessions at Substance Abuse Treatment Headquarters (SATH), were loud, aggressive, and confrontational.[1] Raised voices, angry pointing, and bulging veins in participants' necks were the norm. In key aspects of their lives, the male residents at SATH—disproportionately poor and black, with histories of addiction and criminal convictions—had lost control, a central tenet of patriarchal notions of manhood (Johnson 2005). This was compounded by their participation in SATH, a total institution (Goffman 1961) that orchestrated every aspect of their daily lives over a two-year period. In the games, the male residents had a chance to perform scripted manhood acts—acts that signify "a capacity to exert control over one's self, the environment, and others" (Schrock and Schwalbe 2009: 286; see also Schwalbe 2014)—based on aggressive competition, the subordination of a feminized Other, and emotion work consisting of both displays of anger and emotional restraint (see Ezzell 2012). Through interaction in the games the male residents signified (salvaged) masculine selves; but their performances reproduced inequality by reinforcing dominant ideologies of misogyny and homophobia along the way. The male residents' identity displays, analyzed as situated manhood acts, speak to the limitations of a "multiple masculinities" discourse and cast doubts on the efficacy of "healthy masculinity" campaigns to promote equality. In the rest of this chapter, I'll discuss gender as a category of inequality, review the shift from analysis of what males do to signify masculine selves to an analytic focus on masculinity(ies), highlight situated examples of manhood in action, and review campaigns to reconstruct versus deconstruct the gender system.

GENDER AS A CATEGORY OF INEQUALITY

Human beings are sexually dimorphic, a phrase that refers to the degree to which males and females within a species differ. Processes of evolution have resulted in the physical and reproductive differences that we refer to as "male" and "female," but as sociologist Lisa Wade (2013) has pointed out, the degree of difference between human males and females is so small compared to the degree of difference in other species that it makes more sense to focus on the ways human males and females are overwhelmingly the same:

> Yes, we're different. We reproduce sexually, so we do come in (with some exceptions) two types: one that potentially gestates, births and feeds new life and one that can mix up the genes of our species. Most men don't have a uterus and most women will never inseminate anyone. That's a fact of life.
>
> But we're not *that* different. We're just not that kind of species. (Wade 2013: paras. 12–13)

Males and females, in many respects, are not "opposite sexes." Variation within a sex category is greater than variation between categories. Biologist Anne Fausto-Sterling (2000: 31) has pointed out, in fact, that despite popular understandings of two-and-only-two discrete biological sexes, human bodies exist across

The author thanks Michael Schwalbe for his example, his analytic clarity, and his generosity in sharing early drafts of his book. The author further thanks Sherryl Kleinman, Beth Eck, and Brigid Bronik, without whom this reading could not have been envisioned or written, as well as the editors of this anthology for thoughtful feedback and their commitment to critical engagement of issues that matter.

a continuum of difference. "Neither sex nor gender," sociologist Judith Lorber argues, "are pure categories" (1993: 569). Biologically, males and females have more in common than they have in contrast. And yet "men" and "women," as gender categories, are cultural constructs created in opposition to one another. The constructed categories of sex and gender are sociologically distinct, yet they are regularly conflated in popular discourse. Even Wade's comments, above, seem to fuse biological sexual dimorphism and gender identity, treating men and women synonymously with male and female. Male and female bodies may well fall along a continuum of difference, but this is not gender.

Gender, in fact, is not a category of *difference*, it is a category of *inequality* (Lorber 1994, 2005; Schwalbe 2014). "Man" is A to "woman's" not-A (see Lorber 1994; also Jay 1981). Men and women do not occur naturally, nor are they the equivalent of maleness and femaleness. They are social creatures constructed through the attachment of different meanings to male and female bodies, coupled with the idea that these meanings reflect essential and natural internal differences. This continues as bodily differences are pointed to as the *source* of status differences, inequality, and exploitation. Legal scholar Catharine MacKinnon has pointed out that "differences are inequality's post hoc excuse" (1989: 218), meaning, in this instance, that gender does not follow from bodily difference but from the *use of difference* in the construction and maintenance of oppressive systems. Women and men, from a *critical gender theory* perspective (Schwalbe 2014), are "categories that are defined into existence as unequal from the start, with the category 'men' reserved for males who signify masculine selves and strive for dominance over others" (Schwalbe 2014: 13).

Women and men are necessary categories for the construction and reproduction of patriarchal social systems—that is, systems that are male-dominated, male-identified, and male-centered (Johnson 2005). Men in such systems are the social beings who construct themselves as members of the dominant gender category through situated action and institutional arrangements. Gender is not what we are, after all, but what we do (West and Zimmerman 1987). And doing manhood is doing dominance (Pascoe 2007).

Gender is accomplished by "doing" through situated action. But it is not simply a matter of stylized self-presentation. The situated doing of gender, instead, is linked to the larger social structures—political and economic systems—within which it takes place. Males (and some females) interacting and operating within larger social structures of white supremacy, capitalism, and patriarchy are compelled to become men, to compete for status as men by signifying masculine selves through manhood acts aimed at asserting control, eliciting deference, and resisting being controlled (Schrock and Schwable 2009; Schwalbe 2014). In this sense, gender is not a matter of play, but a matter of power, a matter of life and death.

MASCULINITIES VERSUS MEN

What is masculinity? In one respect, it's a folk notion revolving around ideas of an essential character and disposition associated with male social beings. In other words, it is popularly viewed as a trait that inheres naturally in men. As a constructed folk notion, the qualities and acts associated with popular understandings of masculinity shift across time and place. Drawing largely on the work of scholars in the 1980s and 1990s, modern sociological understandings of masculinity have tended to focus on it as a "configuration of practice" (see, e.g., Carrigan et al. 1985; Connell 1995; Connell and Messerschmidt 2005), a set of situated doings-together organized in relation to the gender structure. Taking this approach can be helpful in the sense of divesting masculinity from biological determinism and providing a framework from which to focus on the things that men do—both the things men do to mark themselves *as men* and the things men do collectively to uphold male supremacy. Scholarly work on men and masculinity has loosely been grouped into feminist/profeminist critical approaches, generally split between "men's studies" and "critical studies of men" (see Hearn et al. 2002), and non/antifeminist approaches, currently known as "male studies," which tend to be explicitly essentialist and portray males as victims (of feminism) (see Epstein 2010). Although men's studies and critical studies of men have tended to take more or less explicitly (pro)feminist approaches to the study of men and masculinity and although early work in these traditions had a critical edge, much of the work coming out of this field has been "de-radicalized" (Schwalbe 2014: 26–50), disconnected from considerations of oppression and inequality and, thus, failing to "adequately address power relations" (McCarry 2007: 406). In part, this trend has been enabled through the multiple masculinities discourse.

The focus on masculinity as a configuration of practice, as a form of doing, suggests that there are multiple ways to do it. And, indeed, there is ample evidence of the many ways social actors across time and place have signified masculine selves (see, e.g., Kimmel 1996). Tim Carrigan and colleagues (1985) pushed this idea further, arguing that within a given culture there will exist one form of masculinity—*hegemonic masculinity*—that is revered above others. This represents

> a particular variety of masculinity to which others— among them young and effeminate as well as homosexual men—are subordinated. It is particular groups of men, not men in general, who are oppressed within patriarchal sexual relations, and whose situations are related in different ways to the overall logic of the subordination of women to men. (Carrigan et al. 1985: 586)

Carrigan and colleagues' use of "hegemonic," drawing from the work of Italian Marxist Antonio Gramsci (1971), refers not only to a dominant understanding of masculinity but also to widespread acceptance and taken-for-grantedness of the superiority of a particular form of the doing of masculinity, to cultural and political processes that coerce such acceptance, and to cooperation with women who support men in the doing of it (see Hearn 2004). Raewyn Connell further refined the concept in the book *Masculinities*, describing it as the "configuration of gender practice that embodies the currently accepted answer to the problem of the legitimacy of patriarchy, which guarantees (or is taken to guarantee) the dominant position of men and the subordination of women" (1995: 77). In this sense, again, masculinity is something more than a style of self-presentation. It includes collective acts and practices that channel and concentrate males in positions of power and authority, acts that valorize and privilege males, male bodies, and men, and acts that shine the cultural focus of attention on males

and the things that males do—acts, as Connell notes, that secure "the dominant position of men." Further, hegemonic masculinity need not be enacted directly to have consequences; that it is collectively accepted as possible to be enacted is enough to address the "problem of the legitimacy of patriarchy." This is the mechanism through which every male enacting an identity as a man, *whether he strives to enact hegemonic masculinity or not*, is granted male privilege—cultural benefits and unearned advantages conferred by virtue of membership in the social category men.

Despite the critical origins and potential of the concept of hegemonic masculinity for clarifying the doing(s) of domination, scholars have pointed out that the definition of the concept is, overall, unclear and potentially contradictory (see, e.g., Donaldson 1993; Whitehead 1999)—a charge conceded by Connell and James Messerschmidt (2005) in a follow-up attempt to fine-tune the concept—and that, perhaps as a reflection of that, it has been inconsistently applied (see, e.g., Hearn 2004; Schwalbe 2014). Part of the confusion comes back to the question of what, exactly, masculinity is. If there is one revered form of masculinity as a configuration of practice, there are, as Carrigan and colleagues made explicit, other (subordinated) forms. Focusing on multiple masculinities can sensitize us to the realities of differences and inequalities among groups of men, and in that sense it is analytically exciting. But it can also muddy the waters, making it difficult to see what each configuration of gender practice has in common to make each a masculinity:

> The multiple masculinities concept reflects a laudable desire to value diversity. It is ironic, then, that this concept has fostered a kind of categorical essentialism in studies of men. To invoke, for example, the existence of black masculinity, Latino masculinity, gay masculinity, Jewish masculinity, working-class masculinity, and so on is to imply that there is an overriding similarity in the gender enactments of males who are black, Latino, gay, Jewish, or working class. The implicit claim is that all members of the category practice an identifiably unique form of masculinity. This strategy of using conventional categories of race, ethnicity, sexuality, religion, or class to define masculinities into existence is dubious. It can cause us to lose sight of what these allegedly diverse gender-signifying practices have in common

(again, other than enactment by male bodies) that makes them masculinity. It can also obscure important within-group variations. (Schrock and Schwalbe 2009: 280–81)

Again, what is masculinity? Looking across multiple masculinities scholarship, it is hard to say.

Reviewing studies of men and masculinity, it appears that masculinity isn't simply anything done by social agents with male bodies because scholars have pointed out that social actors with female bodies can signify masculine selves, even identifying "female masculinity" (see, e.g., Halberstam 1998; Pascoe 2007) as a type. Further, Connell and Messerschmidt (2005) argue in response to criticisms over their conceptualization of the concept that masculinity, in contradiction to Connell's (1995) earlier claim that hegemonic masculinity "guarantees . . the dominant position of men and the subordination of women," is not *necessarily* about domination and inequality: "the conceptualization of hegemonic masculinity should implicitly acknowledge the possibility of democratizing gender relations, of . . . [establishing] a version of masculinity open to equality with women" (1995: 853). Discussing the contradictory definitions of the concept, sociologist Michael Schwalbe points out that

> taking seriously what Connell and Messerschmidt say at different points in their essay, it seems that a configuration of practice can be a masculinity whether the practitioners are male or female, whether they are men or women, or whether they are striving for domination or equality. Thus whatever it is that makes a configuration of practice a masculinity, it is not necessarily body type, gender identity, or oppressive consequences. Neither actor, intention, goal, nor consequence seems to define a practice as a masculinity . . . But if a masculinity can be all of these things, then it has no clear referent. By pointing to everything, the concept points to nothing in particular. (2014: 40–41)

In the vacuum left by the lack of analytic clarity, scholarship in the field of men and masculinities has tended to provide a seemingly endless catalogue of various "types" of masculinity (Messner 2004). And although this can be done with the aim of analyzing different ways that men—social beings who signify masculine selves—interact with other men, with children, and with women to enact dominance and reproduce inequality across different social locations, the analysis of gender as a category of inequality—and the important foundational links between critical studies of men and feminist theory—has too often been lost or misrepresented (see, e.g., Hammer 1990; McCarry 2007; McMahon 1993; Pascoe 2007; Robinson 2003). There has further been a tendency to reify masculinity, to treat it as "an autonomous 'thing-in-itself'" (McCarry 2007: 409) and point to it as the *cause* of men's behavior. But to claim that masculinity is both the cause of what men do and constituted by what men do is tautological (see, e.g., McMahon 1993; MacInnes 1998). This "disembodies men from masculinity" (McCarry 2007: 409–10) and shifts our attention away from *what males actually do* to signify identities as men. Turning our analytic focus away from the material realities of men's behavior(s), this pattern leads to questions about how masculinity might be "redefined" or "reconstructed" instead of questions about men changing their behaviors and patterns of interaction (McMahon 1993).

Masculinity as a concept is not necessary to analyze the "how" of domination and subordination. We could, of course, analyze conceptions of masculinity *as accounts and ideological underpinnings* of men's interpersonal and collective doings-together, but the concept itself is a folk notion, not an analytic category (Schwalbe 2014). Sociologist Jeff Hearn calls for a shift away from analyses of hegemonic masculinity and toward analysis of "the hegemony of men":

> It is time to go back from *masculinity* to *men*, to examine the hegemony of men and about men. The hegemony of men seeks to address the double complexity that men are both a *social category formed by the gender system* and *dominant collective and individual agents of social practices.* . . . This involves addressing the formation of the social category of men, and its taken-for-grantedness, as well as men's taken-for-granted domination and control through consent. (2004: 59, emphasis in original)

In a similar vein, rather than focus our analytic lens on the categorization of *masculinities*, Doug Schrock and Michael Schwalbe (2009; see also Schwalbe 2014) call for an analysis of "manhood acts," acts aimed at "claiming privilege, eliciting deference, and resisting exploitation . . . [which] are inherently about upholding patriarchy and reproducing gender inequality" (2009: 281, 287). This approach discourages "the reification of masculinity and [redirects] analytic attention to what males actually do to achieve dominance" (Schrock and Schwalbe 2009: 281). Assuming it is our goal, a shift to focus on manhood acts is a necessary step in moving us toward a more just and egalitarian society. Taking men's violence against women as one example, policy studies scholar Melanie McCarry argues that

> it is necessary to understand the violence of men in order to challenge it and eradicate it from our lives. Therefore, it is important to have a critical examination of the *practices of men* and there is a need for the studies of men and masculinity precisely in order to analyse and deconstruct male power and the conditions resultant from gender inequalities. . . . However, unless masculinity studies authors critically analyse men and their material realities (in addition to theorising about 'masculinity') then rather than contribute to the critique of current gendered power relations they could actually be implicated in the maintenance of this system. (2007: 412, emphasis added)

What is needed to move us forward with an eye toward justice is analyses of manhood (dominance) in action. In the sections that follow, I'll offer some brief examples of manhood acts from my own study of men in a residential substance abuse treatment center and address the stunted progressive potential of reactive (Schwalbe 1996, 2002) and progressive (Macomber 2012) men's movements in their emphasis on masculinity(ies) instead of manhood acts.

MANHOOD IN ACTION

As I argued above, the analytic focus on masculinity(ies) has tended to shift our gaze away from what males actually do to achieve dominance. Multiple masculinities discourse has also obscured analytic clarity on men's identity work. For males (and some females) engaged in the doing of manhood, it's not about doing *different forms of manhood*, but about using different situationally available resources to enact hegemonic ideals of manhood with the goal of

signifying a masculine self—doing identity work, in other words, aimed at eliciting the imputation of a set of imagined characteristics ("masculinity") through expressive behavior. In every case, because it is what it means to signify a masculine self in a patriarchal gender order, this involves signifying dominance (control of self and others, resisting being controlled, resisting exploitation). Social beings known as men in different structural locations and across different situated contexts have access to different resources toward this end, and other aspects of identity can function as liabilities (e.g., having a female body, being gay, being a member of a racial minority group, having a physical disability, etc.) or assets (having a male body, being white, being wealthy, being conventionally able bodied, etc.) in the act of signification.

At SATH (see Ezzell 2012), this dynamic played out as males who were subordinated by virtue of their racial identities, class positions, identities as "addicts,"[2] and status as residents in a total institution interactionally struggled to signify a masculine self, to claim status as men. The men's access to semiotic resources for self-making were constrained: they had to forfeit all personal belongings outside of a small religious text and five or fewer photographs on entering the program; they were all given crew cuts, supplied with clothing, and forbidden from growing facial hair until they graduated to higher stages of the program; they were forbidden from acknowledging female residents for their first six months in the program; they worked for 16 hours a day for at least their first 30 days in the program; and, they were forbidden from challenging staff or other residents outside of the structured group accountability sessions, called "games," which were held three times a week. All of these facets of their daily structural realities, coupled with their subordinated identities within the larger economy of power, functioned as liabilities in their efforts to signify a masculine self. In this context, the importance of the games as a platform for identity work was heightened. Although they were structured by organizational rules and norms of interaction, and although they were officially policed by a "game strength," a resident game-leader with experience in the program and in the games, the games provided the male residents a chance to engage in (scripted) manhood acts tied to aggression, (verbal) violence, homophobia, and heterosexual display.

For example, during a game one evening early in my research, an older resident calmly singled out a younger resident for wearing a red-shirt—residents being disciplined were required to wear red as a visible form of social control: "So, John, what are you doing in that red shirt?" John's response was immediate and angry. He turned toward the older resident and screamed, "Man, fuck you! I'm not sayin' anything about that!" The room erupted into shouts and laughter because these bouts of verbal sparring functioned, among other things, as a form of manly competition and entertainment. The yelling went back and forth, with other residents joining in and also yelling at John. The first resident who challenged John claimed the floor and, starting calmly but with increasing anger, said, "Man, I don't know what you did; tell me what you fucking did so that I know not to do it myself!" John erupted with anger, jabbing his finger in the other resident's direction, "Fuck you, man. There are some motherfuckers that just get on my last goddamn nerve, and you're fucking one of 'em, man! Fuck you! Shut the fuck up!" Interactions like this, revolving around aggressive manhood acts, were the norm. Through them, males competed for status as "good game players" ("You're the only person I've seen who can out-shout him! Get him again!"), explicitly pushed one another to "be men" ("You need to grow some nuts and be a man!"), claimed status above women and nonconventional men ("It's just about pussy, man! That's all this is about! [The women here are] all bitches, and they're all interchangeable!"), and promoted a sense of self—in contrast to popular and organizational narratives that cast them as out of control—as explicitly in control ("I made that decision, motherfucker! I knew what I was doing!"). In other words, the games provided space in which the male residents could engage in situated manhood acts.

The male residents at SATH drew on the resources at their disposal to signify masculine selves and claim status as men, but it's not as if their collective identity work represented some discrete and unique form of "addict masculinity" that would be enacted by males with substance abuse problems across different contexts or situations. Indeed, the men's aggressive

verbal sparring in other contexts would likely cross a line and lead to a physical altercation—another manhood act, in and of itself, but one in which the residents in SATH may not have wanted to engage because it would have precipitated their expulsion from the program. In an interview, one resident commented on the disparity between interactive norms in the games and interactive norms in other settings:

> People were yelling and screaming and, I mean, I'm still in the prison mentality. . . . And there are just certain things you don't say to people without looking for a fight. And these people are freely cussing each other out back and forth, and I'm like . . . [stares with wide eyes, as if in disbelief].

Instead of representing "addict masculinity," the residents' identity work reflected the resources available within their specific situated performance of manhood. This was not a masculinity, in that sense, but the situated doings-together of males in the signification of dominance.

Although there are different intersections of identity, although the situated contexts are different, and although the particulars of the performances therein are different, there are shades of similarity in the identity performances of the residents at SATH and high school boys (Pascoe 2003, 2007), men with physical disabilities (Gerschick and Miller 1995), men in batterer intervention programs (Schrock and Padavic 2007), female-to-male transgender men (Dozier 2005), gay and "ex-gay" Christian men (Wolkomir 2006), male Mexican-immigrant gardeners (Ramirez 2011), and social actors in numerous other settings who are engaged in manhood acts. Across these settings and contexts, social agents are finding ways of approximating the hegemonic ideal through the use of available semiotic resources as they signify masculine selves. In that sense, what connects these disparate performances is the fact that, despite Connell and Messerschmidt's (2005) claim to the contrary, each instance is a signification of manhood—the doing of dominance—regardless of the situated resources used in the act of signification. Research into these social arenas can highlight the various ways that social agents known as men "do dominance" and, thus, reinforce inequality. This is important because inequality is not only structured through institutional arrangements but also reproduced (and/or resisted) through the situated interactions that make up daily life.

RECONSTRUCTION VERSUS DECONSTRUCTION

The tensions between an analytic focus on *masculinity* and a focus on *manhood acts* is on display more broadly in reactive and progressive men's movements that often aim to "refashion" or "reconstruct" masculinity while falling short of critiquing structural bases of male dominance and sexism. For example, both men in the mythopoetic men's movement (Schwalbe 1996) and men doing "engaging men" (EM) work in the antiviolence movement (Macomber 2012) were engaged in collective efforts to refashion conceptualizations of manhood that still provided access to male privilege by virtue of a credited signification of a masculine self. The mythopoetic men were driven by an individualist effort to change themselves, not to reform society. However, the men "rejected the more destructive aspects of hegemonic masculinity and resisted the soul-deadening effects of capitalist society" (Schwalbe 2002: 63) and thus "constituted a progressive challenge to traditional masculinity" (Schwalbe 1996: 243). And yet, the progressive potential of the men's collective work was stunted because the work "encouraged the men to think in psychological or, at best, cultural terms about gender and gender inequality" (Schwalbe 1996: 243). The men wanted to cultivate a fuller emotional life, in contradiction to the suppression of empathy and emotion endemic to current hegemonic ideals of manhood. Rather than use their personal frustrations as a springboard to challenge gender as a category of inequality that restricts males' abilities to access the full range of their own humanity, however, the men drew on Jungian psychology to redefine their more "feminine" characteristics as "deep" or "mature" masculinity. By distancing themselves from notions of the feminine, the men "implicitly reaffirmed the greater value of things masculine and male" (Schwalbe 1996: 179), thus reinforcing inequality.

In the antiviolence movement, male activists doing EM work—organizing efforts aimed at bringing more men into the movement—ostensibly have a more

explicitly political aim: ending men's violence against women. However, as sociologist Kristine Macomber (2012) found, many male activists' patterns of interaction and framing of the problems they faced was similar to the efforts of the mythopoetic men. EM activists explicitly separated men from masculinity, blaming patterns of male violence—in addition to their own frustrations with masculine restrictions on emotional display—on "traditional masculinity" (Macomber 2012: 41). By focusing on traditional masculinity as the *cause* of men's patterns of violence and as the *source* of their own personal frustrations, EM activists were able to "protect *men* [including themselves] from guilt-inducing critique" (Macomber 2012: 42). Explicitly drawing on multiple masculinities rhetoric and framing, EM activists then moved on to "redefine" (Macomber 2012: 43) masculinity, offering male activists and the male audience members they reached a "better," more open configuration of practice for being men. Like the mythopoetic men who constructed a notion of deep masculinity to cast themselves as honorable and manly, EM activists constructed males in the movement as virtuous, as "not only *different* kinds of men, but *better* men" (Macomber 2012: 45, emphasis in original). In keeping their commitment to manhood intact, however, the EM activists "drew from many of the same notions of the dominant male culture that they critiqued" (Macomber 2012: 48). Thus, they

> defined old aspects of masculinity in new ways, allowing them to be both strong *and* compassionate, courageous *and* empathic, assertive *and* thoughtful. Redefining masculinity in this way allowed activists to feel good about their involvement, but to also feel like *men* doing so. (Macomber 2012: 37, emphasis in original)

The EM activists, like the mythopoetic men, actively distanced themselves from the feminine by framing traditionally feminine characteristics (e.g., compassion, empathy, thoughtfulness) as explicitly masculine, thus (re)valorizing those things male and masculine and arresting the progressive potential of their organizing efforts.

Although their stated goals were different, the mythopoetic men and the male EM activists were both trying to broaden the resources available to males in the signification of manhood (dominance) without trying to dismantle structures of dominance, privilege, and inequality along the way. Reflecting the shift from analyzing *what males do* to a focus on *masculinities* in the academic literature, the focus on masculinity within these men's movements too often left men's patterns of interaction unexamined. For example, despite the EM activists' direct involvement in explicitly feminist and woman-centered movements and organizations, Macomber found resistance among the men to changing their own behavior. In interviews, male EM activists admitted to addictions to pornography, sexual objectification of women, conscious attempts to cash in on the patriarchal dividend, and resistance they often faced from women in the movement. Macomber interviewed some of the female activists with whom the male EM activists did organizing work and documented their frustrations with male activists talking over them, taking up too much space, objectifying women, sexually exploiting women, and receiving "undue praise and attention . . . in the movement, simply because they were men" (2012: 68). As Macomber notes, healthy masculinity (2012: 55) campaigns may well create more space for male activists to express a fuller range of emotions and feel better about themselves, *as men*, but they don't encourage males to resist structural inequality or change their own patterns of oppressive behavior. We have to ask: For whom is healthy masculinity healthy and at what costs?

Can masculinity be healthy? As a folk notion, currently dominant notions of what it means to be masculine can certainly be harmful to individual males who put their bodies and emotional lives on the line in the signification of masculine selves (see Sabo and Gordon 1995), not to mention the physical and symbolic acts of violence, enacted as manhood acts, that many males inflict upon females and other males. To be sure, a "healthier" approach to manhood is conceivable and could work to curb patterns of men's violence to self and others. And as Men Can Stop Rape's "Healthy Masculinity Action Project"[3] demonstrates, framing a campaign around healthy masculinity is an understandable political strategy in that it reaches out to men *as men* and seeks to offer/promote a different configuration of practice through which males can signify masculine selves. "To get men to 'stay at the table,' and not be threatened by anti-sexist messaging," Macomber notes, "activists [construct] pro-male and 'male-friendly' frames that [allow] men to feel good about themselves, as men" (2012: 141). At the very least, it seems clear that a healthy(ier) masculinity would be better than the hegemonic ideal as currently constructed.

And yet, because gender is a category of inequality and doing manhood is, by definition, doing dominance, you can't construct a masculinity or a definition of manhood that isn't predicated on inequality. The healthy masculinity frame protects "men *and the gender system in which men are the dominant group* from critique" (Macomber 2012: 142, emphasis added). In that sense, although it is conceivable to construct and promote a healthier masculinity *for individual men*, in the process we are still reinforcing larger structures of inequality by reinforcing the gender system. A kinder, gentler patriarchy is *still* patriarchy. Discussing healthy masculinity, then, is like discussing "healthy exploitation," "healthy dominance," or, as scholar and activist John Stoltenberg (2013) puts it, "healthy cancer." Schwalbe reminds us that "more inclusive manhood acts do nothing to change oppressive hierarchies" (2014: 159). They can work, however, to make such hierarchies "more emotionally bearable" (Schwalbe 2014: 159) and, thus, preserve them. Gendered campaigns that actively promote refashioned notions of manhood are, intentionally or not, thus implicated in the maintenance of the very systems they purport to critique.

If our goal is to dismantle systems of inequality, that goal is incompatible with academic and activist approaches that disembody men from masculinity, with the endless categorization of types of masculinity divorced from an analysis of power and inequality, and with efforts to refashion or reconstruct (rather than eradicate or deconstruct) categories of inequality (see Jensen 2007; Lorber 2005; Schwalbe 2014; and Stoltenberg 2000). If we accept the radical perspective that gender is, necessarily, about inequality, then we must see that "there is no preserving gender without preserving domination" (Schwalbe 2014: 170). The problem with healthy masculinity campaigns and, more broadly, with multiple masculinities discourses is that they do not "liberate conscience from gender. [They keep] conscience gendered" (Stoltenberg 2013, para. 25). They are, in short, gendering practices. We have the tools at our disposal to make sense of inequality and resist it (see Schwalbe 2000). All we need is the analytic clarity and will to use them.

REFERENCES

Carrigan, Tim, R. W. Connell, and John Lee. 1985. "Toward a New Sociology of Masculinity." *Theory and Society* 14: 551–604.

Connell, Raewyn. 1995. *Masculinities.* Cambridge, UK: Polity Press.

Connell, Raewyn, and James W. Messerschmidt. 2005. "Hegemonic Masculinity: Rethinking the Concept." *Gender & Society* 19: 829–59.

Donaldson, Mike. 1993. "What Is Hegemonic Masculinity?" *Theory and Society, Special Issue: Masculinities* 5: 643–57.

Dozier, Raine. 2005. "Beards, Breasts, and Bodies: Doing Sex in a Gendered World." *Gender & Society* 19: 297–316.

Epstein, Jennifer. 2010, April 8. "Male Studies vs. Men's Studies." *Inside Higher Ed*, retrieved September 24, 2013, from http://www.insidehighered.com/news/2010/04/08/males/.

Ezzell, Matthew B. 2012. "'I'm in Control': Compensatory Manhood in a Therapeutic Community." *Gender & Society* 26 (2): 190–215.

Fausto-Sterling, Anne. 2000. *Sexing the Body: Gender Politics and the Construction of Sexuality.* New York: Basic Books.

Gerschick, Thomas J., and Adam S. Miller. 1995. "Coming to Terms: Masculinity and Physical Disability." In *Men's Health and Illness: Gender, Power, and the Body, Research on Men and Masculinities Series,* edited by D. Sabo and D. F. Gordon, Vol. 8, 183–204. Thousand Oaks, CA: Sage.

Goffman, Erving. 1961. *Asylums: Essays on the Social Situation of Mental Patients and Other Inmates.* New York: Anchor Books.

Gramsci, Antonio. 1971. *Selections from the Prison Notebooks.* New York: International Publishers.

Halberstam, Judith. 1998. *Female Masculinity.* Durham, NC: Duke University Press.

Hammer, Jalna. 1990. "Men, Power and the Exploitation of Women." *Women's Studies International Forum* 13: 443–56.

Hearn, Jeff. 2004. "From Hegemonic Masculinity to the Hegemony of Men." *Feminist Theory* 5: 49–72.

Hearn, Jeff, Keith Pringle, U. Muller, E. Oleksy, E. Lattu, J. Chernova, H. Ferguson, O. G. Holter, V. Kolga, I. Novikova, C. Ventimiglia, E. Olsvik, and T. Tallberg. 2002. "Critical Studies on Men in Ten European Countries: The State of Academic Research." *Men and Masculinities* 4: 64–92.

Jay, Nancy. 1981. "Gender and Dichotomy." *Feminist Studies* 7: 38–56.

Jensen, Robert. 2007. *Getting Off: Pornography and the End of Masculinity.* Cambridge, MA: South End Press.

Johnson, Alan G. 2005. *The Gender Knot: Unraveling our Patriarchal Legacy.* Philadelphia: Temple University Press.

Kimmel, Michael S. 1996. *Manhood in America: A Cultural History.* New York: Free Press.

Lorber, Judith. 1993. "Believing Is Seeing: Biology as Ideology." *Gender & Society* 7: 568–81.

Lorber, Judith. 1994. *Paradoxes of Gender.* New Haven, CT: Yale University Press.

Lorber, Judith. 2005. *Breaking the Bowls: Degendering and Feminist Change.* New York: Norton.

Macinnes, John. 1998. *The End of Masculinity: The Confusion of Sexual Genesis and Sexual Difference in Modern Society.* Philadelphia: Open University Press.

MacKinnon, Catherine A. 1989. *Toward a Feminist Theory of the State.* Cambridge, MA: Harvard University Press.

Macomber, Kristine C. 2012. "Men as Allies: Mobilizing Men to End Violence against Women." Ph.D. diss., North Carolina State University.

McCarry, Melanie. 2007. "Masculinity Studies and Male Violence: Critique or Collusion?" *Women's Studies International Forum* 30: 404–15.

McMahon, Anthony. 1993. "Male Readings of Feminist Theory: The Psychologization of Sexual Politics in the Masculinity Literature." *Theory and Society* 22: 675–95.

Messner, Michael A. 2004. "On Patriarchs and Losers: Rethinking Men's Interests." *Berkeley Journal of Sociology* 48: 126–143.

Pascoe, C. J. 2003. "Multiple Masculinities?: Teenage Boys Talk about Jocks and Gender." *American Behavioral Scientist* 46: 1423–38.

Pascoe, C. J. 2007. *Dude, You're a Fag: Masculinity and Sexuality in High School.* Berkeley: University of California Press.

Ramirez, Hernan. 2011. "Masculinity in the Workplace: The Case of Mexican Immigrant Gardeners." *Men and Masculinities* 14 (1): 97–116.

Robinson, Victoria. 2003. "Radical Revisionings?: The Theorizing of Masculinity and (Radical) Feminist Theory." *Women's Studies International Forum* 26: 129–37.

Sabo, Don, and David F. Gordon. 1995. *Men's Health and Illness: Gender, Power, and the Body.* Thousand Oaks, CA: Sage.

Schrock, Doug, and Irene Padavic. 2007. "Negotiating Hegemonic Masculinity in a Batterer Intervention Program." *Gender & Society* 21: 625–49.

Schrock, Doug, and Michael Schwalbe. 2009. "Men, Masculinity, and Manhood Acts." *Annual Review of Sociology* 35: 277–95.

Schwalbe, Michael. 1996. *Unlocking the Iron Cage: The Men's Movement, Gender, Politics, and American Culture.* New York: Oxford University Press.

Schwalbe, Michael. 2000. "The Elements of Inequality." *Contemporary Sociology* 29: 775–81.

Schwalbe, Michael. 2002. "Everything Is Data: A Response to Brooke Harrington." *Qualitative Sociology* 25 (1): 63–65.

Schwalbe, Michael. 2014. *Manhood Acts: Gender and the Practices of Domination.* Boulder, CO: Paradigm.

Stoltenberg, John. 2000. *Refusing to Be a Man: Essays on Sex and Justice,* revised ed. London: UCL Press.

Stoltenberg, John. 2013, August 9. "Why Talking about 'Healthy Masculinity' Is Like Talking about 'Healthy Cancer.'" *feminist current,* retrieved September 24, 2013, from http://feministcurrent.com/7868/why-talking-about-healthy-masculinity-is-like-talking-about-healthy-cancer/.

Wade, Lisa. 2013, September 18. "Sex Shocker! Men and Women Aren't That Different." *Salon.com,* retrieved September 24, 2013, from http://www.salon.com/2013/09/18/sex_shocker_men_and_women_arent_that_different/.

West, Candace, and Don Zimmerman. 1987. "Doing Gender." *Gender & Society* 1: 125–51.

Whitehead, Steven. 1999. "Hegemonic Masculinity Revisited." *Gender, Work, & Organization* 6: 58–62.

Wolkomir, Michelle. 2006. *Be Not Deceived: The Sacred and Sexual Struggles of Gay and Ex-gay Christian Men.* New Brunswick, NJ: Rutgers University Press.

NOTES

1. All names of places, groups, and participants tied to my research are pseudonyms.
2. Reflecting popular and organizational discourses of addiction as a problem of personal responsibility, this identity translated as "out of control."
3. See http://www.mencanstoprape.org/Healthy-Masculinity-Action-Project/, retrieved September 24, 2013.

MICHAEL A. MESSNER

14. ON PATRIARCHS AND LOSERS: RETHINKING MEN'S INTERESTS

More than two decades ago, William Goode (1982) observed that when members of a superordinate group are even partly nudged from their positions of social centrality, they often experience this as a major displacement, and respond defensively. This, Goode concluded, is why men have so often resisted the movement for women's equality. Goode's analysis rested on an assumption fundamental to a feminist sociology: collectively, men have shared interests, opposed to those of women. In recent decades, social scientists have observed, measured, and described these opposing gendered interests with hundreds of studies of occupational segregation, glass ceilings, wage gaps, domestic labor, sex work, emotional labor, interpersonal violence, and media imagery.

The upshot of much of this research has been this: it is in men's collective interests to maintain the current relations in the gender order; it is in women's collective interests to change them. Casual observation will bear out the truth of this: overwhelmingly, it has been women who have put gender issues on the social agenda. While a few men throughout history have actively supported feminism (Kimmel & Mosmiller 1992), pro-feminist organizing by men never got much beyond the level of a loosely connected national and international network of men, most of them academics and therapists (Messner 1997).

Twenty years ago, as I drove one of those therapists back to Berkeley from my "men and masculinity" class at Cal State Hayward, to which he had delivered a guest lecture, he pointed at a young white guy speeding by in a pick-up truck with a gun rack. "I want that guy in the men's movement," he told me emphatically, "and to get him involved, we have to be able to convince him that the masculinity he has learned is self-destructive and toxic, and that feminist change is in his interests." I'm pretty sure that the guy in the pick-up never joined up. And I still wonder: is that because he didn't really see his "true" interests—he suffered from some kind of false consciousness? Or, is it perhaps because he did understand that his interests lie not in changing, but rather, in sustaining a gender status quo? Or, did perhaps his conception of his interests as a man—but also as a white man as a worker as an American, as a veteran, and, (as I imagined him) as heterosexual just get more and more complicated and contradictory as the years went by, leaving him with no clear sense of having interests that go beyond his individual self? Maybe he just needed, he found, a different car, a satellite dish, an iPod, better clothes, some purchased sex, and a men's cologne that made a statement about his rebellious individuality?

In this essay, I will share some reflections on the concept of "men's interests." First, using broad brush strokes, I will discuss the development of the scholarly focus on "men and masculinities." Then, I will draw examples from two of my recent projects as windows into the ways that "men's interests" in the U.S. are currently being articulated, respectively in commercial culture and in political discourse.

MULTIPLE MASCULINITIES AND MEN'S INTERESTS

By the late 1980s, the first scholarly collections of work on men—edited by Harry Brod (1987), Michael Kaufman (1987) and Michael Kimmel (1987)—grappled with a puzzle: how to take seriously and centrally the feminist critique of men's global power

This reading was originally published in the *Berkeley Journal of Sociology* 48 (2004): 74–88.

over women, while recognizing both the "costs of masculinity" that many men pay, as well as the existence of vast inequalities among men—inequalities grounded in social class, race/ethnicity, sexual orientation, and international relations. The answer that most scholars settled on was to think of masculinities as multiple. Hegemonic masculinity—the form of masculinity that, for the moment, codifies the collective project of men's domination of women—is defined in relation to emphasized femininity, but also in relation to marginalized and subordinated masculinities (Carrigan, Connell & Lee 1985; Connell 1987).

In practice, the idea of multiple masculinities was sometimes severed from its broad historical and structural moorings, and taken up by researchers investigating specific social contexts, resulting ultimately in a dizzying array of "types" of masculinities. Like 19th century biologists intent on building a taxonomy of the living world, scholars of the 80s and 90s seemed to find new forms of masculinity under every empirical stone, and seemed also intent on labeling them: The discovery of gay, black, Chicano, working class and middle class masculinity was followed by the detection of Asian masculinity, gay black masculinity, gay Chicano masculinity, white working class masculinity, militarized masculinity, transnational business masculinity, New Man masculinity, negotiated masculinity, versatile masculinity, healthy masculinity, toxic masculinity, counter masculinity, cool masculinity, and the one that I confess having deployed on occasion, complicit masculinity. Like all such deconstructive projects, the danger inherent in the multiple masculinities discourse is that, ultimately, we risk deconstructing down to each and every man having his own distinct form of masculinity: My masculinity; your masculinity. But why stop with men? As Judith Halberstam (1998) has argued, some women embody and display the cultural markers of masculinity. With "masculinities" multiplying seemingly by the hour, and with the concept now severed from its connection with "men," we now face the possibility of each and every individual on the planet expressing his or her own unique masculinity: Let six billion masculinities bloom!

What has kept the best social scientific studies of masculinities from devolving into a meaningless

radical individualism is a mooring in the concept of social structure. In particular, the structured inequalities of race, class, sexual orientation and gender are—and should remain—at the center of our intersectional theories of power and inequality (Baca Zinn & Dill 1996; Connell 2004). Keeping these categories of analysis central reminds us that theories of "multiple masculinities" aim not simply to describe different masculine "styles," but rather, to describe and understand complex group-based relations of power, and different—sometimes contradictory—relations to material interests (HondagneuSotelo & Messner 1994). Hence, my focus on interests here is partly a result of my sense that we have reached the limits of the "multiple masculinities" language; it represents an attempt to re-focus on how gender plays out in group-based relations of power.

THINKING ABOUT INTERESTS

The two examples from my recent research that I am going to share with you relate to sport. Sport is not patriarchal in a simple, seamlessly binary fashion (all men on top; all women on the bottom). Sport is "male dominated," but it is also constructed through what Don Sabo (1994) has called an "intermale dominance hierarchy," that is characterized by a very unequal distribution of resources and privilege among boys and men: star athletes over bench-warmers; athletic directors and head coaches over assistant coaches and players; athletes and coaches in central sports (especially football) over those in marginal "minor" sports (like cross country, swimming, gymnastics, wrestling, and golf). But some male athletes' experiences of marginality does not automatically translate into their seeing their interests as aligned with those of girls and women against the gluttony of football programs. Structural location does not always predict a group's perceptions of their interests. In a thoughtful essay, Bob Pease (2002: 170) argues that an analysis of "men's interests" cannot simply be reduced to a rational analysis of men's material interests in maintaining their patriarchal privilege. He argues that "people do not have objective interests as a result of their location; rather, they formulate . . . their interests, and they do so within the context of the available discourses in situations in which they are located and that they coproduce."

I offer two empirical windows into this situational formulation of men's interests. These two sites are not necessarily the best places to look at the issue of men's interests, but I draw from them because they are two research projects that I have been exploring over the past two or three years; they are the two windows that I have been looking through. The first is a study that I have been conducting with Jeffrey Montez de Oca, of beer and liquor advertisements in two mega sports media events aimed at male audiences. The second is a project I have been conducting with Nancy Solomon of the California Women's Law Center. Nancy and I spoke at one of the U.S. Secretary of Education's 2002 public hearings on Title IX, and together we have conducted an analysis of talk by the critics of Title IX. Though each of these two projects is broad, for my purposes here, I want to focus narrowly on how beer and liquor ads, and public arguments against Title IX offer us two windows into the situational articulation of "men's interests." I will suggest, across both of these empirical sites, that "men's interests" are not usually articulated overtly as men's interests; rather, stories about particular groups of men who are viewed as vulnerable, as actual or potential victims, serve as proxy for a larger articulation of men 's apparently threatened interests. I will suggest that the male "losers" that we see in beer advertising texts, and the male "victims" who are the centerpiece in the discourse of Title IX critics, are symbolic articulations of the supposedly threatened interests of white males.

BEER AND LIQUOR ADS: THE WHITE GUY AS LOSER

The televised Super Bowl ads that we examined construct a white male "loser" whose life is apparently separate from paid labor. He hangs out with his male buddies, is self-mocking and ironic about his loser status, is always at the ready to engage in voyeurism with sexy fantasy women, but holds committed relationships and emotional honesty with real women in disdain. I will offer [. . .] three brief examples here from Super Bowl commercials.

Two young somewhat nerdy-looking white guys are at a yoga class, sitting behind a class full of sexy young women. The two men have attached prosthetic legs to their bodies, so that they can fake the yoga moves. With two bottles of Bud Lite, these voyeurs watch in delight as the female yoga teacher uses her hands to push down on a woman's upright spread-eagled legs, and says "focus, focus, focus." The camera cuts back-and-forth from close-ups of the women's breasts and bottoms, while the two guys' gleefully enjoy their beer and their sexual voyeurism. In the final scene, the two guys are standing outside the front door of the yoga class, beer bottles in hand, and someone throws their fake legs out the door at them. As they duck to avoid being hit by the legs, one of them comments, "She's not very relaxed."

This ad contains, in various degrees, the dominant gender tropes that we found in the mega sports media events ads: First, men are often portrayed as chumps, losers. Masculinity—especially for the lone man—is precarious. Individual men are always on the cusp of being publicly humiliated, either by their own stupidity, by other men, or worse: by a beautiful woman. The precariousness of individual men's masculine status is offset by the safety of the male group. The solidity, primacy—and emotional safety—of male friendships are the emotional center of many of these ads. When women appear in these ads, it is usually as highly sexualized fantasy objects. These beautiful women serve as potential prizes for men's victories and proper consumption choices. They sometimes serve to validate men's masculinity, but their masculinity validating power also holds the potential to humiliate male losers. Wives, girlfriends or other women to whom men are emotionally committed are mostly absent from these ads. However, when they do appear, it is primarily as emotional or sexual blackmailers who threaten to undermine individual men's freedom to enjoy the erotic pleasure at the center of the male group.

To a great extent, these gender themes are intertwined in the Super Bowl "yoga voyeurs" ad. First, the two guys are clearly not goodlooking, high status, muscular icons of masculinity. More likely, they are intended to represent the "everyman," with whom many boys and men can identify. Their masquerade as sensitive men allowed them to transgress the female space of the yoga class, but they couldn't pull it off, and were eventually "outed" as losers, and rejected by the sexy women. But even if they realize that they are losers, they don't have to care, because they are so happy and secure in their bond with each other. Their friendship is cemented in frat-boy-style hijinks that allow them to share close-up voyeurism with sexy women who, we can safely assume, are way out of these men's league. In the end, the women reject the guys as pathetic losers. But the guys don't seem too upset by it. They have each other, and of course, they have their beers.

Consistently in these ads, white guy losers risk punishment or humiliation from beautiful women, but the level of punishment faced by the very occasional black men who appear in these ads is more severe. In "Pick-up Lines," a Bud Lite ad that ran during the 2002 Super Bowl, two black males are sitting at a bar next to an attractive black female. Paul, the man in the middle, is obviously a loser. He sounds a bit whiny as he confides in his male friend, "I'm just not good with the ladies like you, Cedric." Cedric starts to whisper opening pick-up lines to him. The loser turns to the woman and passes on the lines. But just then, the bartender brings another bottle of beer to Cedric, who asks the bartender, "So, how much?" Paul, thinking that this is his next pick-up line, says to the woman, "So, how much?" Her smile turns to an angry frown and she delivers a vicious kick to Paul's face, knocking him to the floor. After we see the Budweiser logo and hear the voice-over telling us that Bud Lite's great taste "will never let you down," we see a stunned Paul rising to his knees, beginning to pull himself up to his bar stool, but the woman knocks him down again with a powerful backhand fist to the face.

"Cedric" returns in another Bud Lite ad that ran during the 2004 Super Bowl. In this ad, the strutting, know-it-all pick-up artist falls victim to his own hypermasculine posturing. Thinking he's going to get a massage from a beautiful African-American woman, he has mistakenly stumbled in to the bikini waxing room. From behind a closed door, we hear him scream in agony, and then see him in the final scene with a towel wrapped around him like a skirt—feminized, punished and humiliated.

These Bud Lite ads—two of the very few ads that depicted relations between black males and black females—were the only ads in which we saw a man being physically beaten or physically humiliated by a woman. In both cases, the African American female-as-object turns to subject, inflicting direct physical

punishment on the African-American male. The existence of these very few "black" ads brings into relief something that might otherwise remain hidden: Most of these ads are about constructing a youthful white masculinity that is playfully selfmocking, always a bit tenuous, but ultimately lovable. The screw-ups that white guy losers make are forgivable, and we nearly always see them, in the end, with at least a cold beer in hand. By contrast, as Ann Ferguson (2000) has pointed out, the intersection of race, gender and class creates contexts of suspicion and punishment for African-American boys and men. In the beer ads, this translates into the message that a black man's transgressions are apparently deserving of a kick to the face.

These themes may find resonance with young men of today because they speak to basic insecurities that are grounded in historic shifts: deindustrialization, the declining real value of wages, cultural shifts brought about by over three decades of struggle by feminists and sexual minorities, and challenges to white male supremacy by people of color and by immigrants. This cluster of social changes defines the context of gender relations in which today's young men have grown toward adulthood. Examining beer and liquor ads gives us a window into the ways that commercial forces have seized on these destabilizing tendencies, constructing pedagogical fantasy narratives that aim to appeal to a very large group—18–34 year old men.

The sexual and gender themes of beer and liquor ads do not stand alone; rather they reflect, and in turn contribute to broader trends in popular culture and marketing to young white males. Television shows like "The Man Show," new soft-core porn magazines like "Maxim" and "FHM," and radio talk shows like the syndicated "Tom Leykus Show" share similar themes, and are targeted to similar audiences of young males. These magazines, television and radio shows construct young male lifestyles saturated with sexy images of nearly naked, surgically enhanced women; unabashed and unapologetic sexual voyeurism shared by groups of laughing men; and explicit talk of sexual exploit with "hotties" or "juggies." The erotic bonding among men is stitched together by a range of consumer products that include—often centrally, as in "The Man Show"—consumption of beer as part of the young male lifestyle. Meanwhile, real women are either absent from these media or they are disparaged as gold diggers (yes, this term has been resuscitated) who use sex to get men to spend money on them, and trick them into marriage. The domesticated man is viewed as a wimpy victim, who has subordinated his own pleasures (and surrendered his paychecks) to a woman. Within this framework, a young man should have sex with as many women as he can while avoiding (or at least delaying) emotional commitments to any one woman.

At first glance, these new media seem to resuscitate a 1950s "Playboy philosophy" of men's consumption, sexuality and gender relations (Ehrenreich 1983). Indeed, these new media strongly reiterate the dichotomous bitch-whore view of women that was such a lynchpin of Hugh Hefner's "philosophy." But today's tropes of masculinity do not simply reiterate the past; rather, they give a post-feminist twist to the Playboy philosophy. A half-century ago, Hefner's pitch to men to recapture the indoors by creating (purchasing) one's own erotic "bachelor pad" in which to have sex with women (and then send them home) read as a straightforwardly masculine project. By contrast, today's sexual and gender pitch to young men is delivered with an ironic, self-mocking wink that operates on two levels. First, it appears to acknowledge that most young men are neither the heroes of the indoors (as Hefner would have it), nor of the outdoors (as the 1970s and 1980s beer ads suggested). Instead, the ads seem to recognize that young white men's unstable status leaves them always on the verge of being revealed as losers. The irony works on a second level as well: the throwback sexual and gender imagery—especially the bitch-whore dichotomization of women—is clearly a defensive backlash against feminism and women's increasing autonomy and social power. The wink and self-mocking irony allow men to have it both ways: they can engage in humorous misogynist banter, and claim simultaneously that it's all in play. The humorous irony works, then, to deflect charges of sexism away from white males, allowing them to define themselves as victims, as an endangered species. We suspect too that this is a key part of the process that constructs the whiteness in these ads. Humorous "boys-will-be-boys" misogyny is unlikely to be taken ironically and lightly when delivered by men of color. Instead, the few "black" ads tend to project culturally delegitimized aspects of "traditional masculinity" on to black men, and then punish them for expressing it.

ANTI-TITLE IX POLITICAL DISCOURSE: THE WHITE GUY AS VICTIM

The 2002 public hearings about Title IX offer an opportunity to examine the ways that the spokespeople for men's sports articulate their interests in a highly politicized forum. Nancy Solomon and I analyzed talk at the 2002 San Diego hearings that we attended, and at which we both spoke. We focus on the various linguistic strategies employed by the critics of Title IX, most of whom spoke for groups and organizations that represented men in "marginal" sports that claimed to have been hurt or threatened by the enforcement of Title IX. I will begin to introduce these themes with an excerpt from the statement by Jon Vegosen, a Chicago attorney representing the U.S. Tennis Association:

> We support the tremendous strides that women have made through Title IX, and we want to preserve those gains. We are also concerned about its unintended consequences for both men and women . . . [including its] adverse impact on walk-ons. I was a walk-on at Northwestern and became captain my junior and senior year, and I was the first player to be selected at Northwestern to the All Big Ten Team. I experienced valuable life lessons, including goal-setting, time management, teamwork and travel. Today that wouldn't happen . . . I would be told, "Thanks for your interest, but there's no room for you," and that's what thousands of male athletes in tennis and other sports are told every year. They are turned away, while women's tennis teams struggle to fill their rosters . . . It is critical to appreciate the long-term impact of the unintended consequences of Title IX for tennis. If these trends continue, men's collegiate tennis will be jeopardized.

Vegosen's statement contained the major themes that we heard repeated in various forms by the Title IX critics. For my purposes here, I want to focus on the "walk-on" theme.

THE "WALK ON" AS VICTIM

A number of the critics invoked the image of the male student "walk-on" as a victim of Title IX's illogical and bureaucratic "quota system." (A "walk-on" is a college student who is neither recruited to play sports, nor given an athletic scholarship, but "who shows up and tries out for the team.") Sam Bell, President of the

National Track and Field Coaches Association told several stories of past "walk-on" athletes who had become successful in various ways. He then delivered a passionate defense of the walk-on, as threatened by Title-IX roster management and concluded, "We will lose a lot of this type of student athlete if we stay with quotas, with a quota mentality . . ."

The walk-on is a powerful image, we suggest, because it invokes the romantic ideal of the student-athlete as an untarnished amateur who loves the purity of sports. The invocation of this romantic ideal obscures the increasingly negative public image of the scholarship athlete in big-time college sports: He is viewed as spoiled by his privilege, he is often in legal or academic trouble, he is not fully deserving *as a student*, and—crucially—in the public image, he is African American. The walk-on, by contrast is first and foremost a *student*, who just happens to love sport. He does not seek fame and fortune; he just wants to be on the team. He is also, in the public imagination—like the character in the popular film *Rudy*—an admirably hard-working (albeit athletically limited) *white guy*. The critics' foregrounding the image of the walk-on is an accomplishment of political rhetoric: without mentioning race, white males are positioned as "regular kids," victimized by liberal policies gone amuck. The critics' image of the walk-on reveals the unintended victimization of white males as irrational, unfair, and un-American. The invocation of the walk-on, then, taps in to and reiterates familiar and highly charged sexist *and* racist anti-affirmative action narratives.

The image of the broken-hearted male wrestler or gymnast whose program has been eliminated is a powerful one, especially given the fact that some men's teams *have* been eliminated in recent years. Over the past twenty years, men's gymnastics and wrestling teams have declined in number. However, the critics of Title IX consistently fail to note that during this same period of time, the number of women's gymnastics and field hockey teams has also declined. And while many college women's sports have grown in number, men's participation in college sports has increased in football, baseball, crew, lacrosse, squash, track and volleyball.

Despite these facts, the periodic high-profile cuts of men's programs tend to fuel perceptions that gender equity works against the overall interests of men. In fact, it is only possible to hold this view if one accepts the logic of the football lobby, and argues against including football in calculations of sex equity. Football's enormous financial drain on resources—a lion's share of scholarships, skyrocketing salaries for coaches, huge equipment, travel and recruiting budgets—are often safely hidden behind the nickle-and-diming debates over which "non-revenue" men's sports should be eliminated to ensure compliance with Title IX proportionality measures (Zimbalist 1999). The football lobby shields its own interests by backing the claims that marginal men's sports and male "walk-ons" are being victimized by Title IX. And many advocates for marginal men's sports participate in this debate by aligning themselves with the football and basketball lobby, despite the fact that such allegiance may seem to run counter to their interests. Given their control of resources and their massive budgets, football programs can hardly claim hardship with a straight face. Rather, they have sought support for the anti-equity cause from the more vulnerable "minor" men's sports. But evidence suggests that the vulnerability of men's marginal sports is not due so much to the "unintended consequences" of Title IX. Rather, the vulnerability of marginal men's sports is a routine institutional consequence of the invisible and mostly unquestioned policy of affording football and men's basketball program is a privileged and untouchable status.

An entire social problems course could be taught using football as the empirical point of departure. Football is often at the center of problems related to sexual assault, campus bullying, and other forms of off-field violence by athletes (Messner 2002). The recent controversies about sexual assaults by football players, and the use of alcohol and women strippers to recruit high school football players at the University of Colorado are only the latest glimpses of what so often lies below the tip of the iceberg of college football (Sperber 2000). High school and college football programs gulp down huge resources, while occupying a mythic status that protects them as almost untouchable. So why do so many marginal boys and men—and their mostly male coaches—seem to identify with the interests of the football lobby? Why don't more of the men in marginalized "non-revenue sports"—the wrestlers, tennis players, swimmers, gymnasts, cross country athletes—identify their interests as consistent with those of women? Nina Eliasoph (1998: 251) argues that people "discover their interests" in everyday life, but the process through which they make this discovery " . . . is never a pure rational calculation." This echoes Pease's argument, introduced earlier, that men's understanding of their interests cannot be explained simply by describing their social location. Instead, we need to consider how men formulate their interests through interaction, in institutional contexts. In the case of the Title IX hearings, the spokesmen for men's marginal sports most likely formulated their interests within athletic department contexts, and these contexts are characterized by professional hierarchies headed by men from the central sports of football and basketball.

Football has played a key symbolic role in the U.S. gender order over the past half-century. In this feminist era, football stands in as a symbolic reference point for a general articulation of "men's interests." And here, I think, is a place where the concept of hegemonic masculinity is applicable and useful, precisely because it is directly tethered to an analysis of the interests of men. Connell (1987) argues that very few men fully conform to what we think of as hegemonic masculinity. The fact that it is nearly impossible for an individual man consistently to achieve and display the dominant conception of masculinity is an important part of the psychological instability at the center of individual men's sense of their own masculinity. Instead, a few men (real or imagined) are positioned as symbolic exemplars for a hegemonic masculinity that serves as a collective practice that continues the global subordination of women, and ensures men's access to a patriarchal dividend. What makes this masculinity "hegemonic" is not simply powerful men's displays of power, but also, crucially, less powerful men's consent and complicity with the institutions, social practices, and symbols that privilege men. To adapt a term that is now popular in market-driven bureaucracies, hegemonic masculinity requires a "buy-in" by subordinated and marginalized men, if it is to succeed as a strategy of domination.

So, though a rational assessment of the situation of, say, boys and men who run cross country, who wrestle, swim, play tennis or gymnastics might suggest that their interests run counter to those of big time football programs, more often than not, these men in marginal sports tend to identify with, and act in complicity with, the dominant discourse of the football lobby. This discourse tends to invoke a language of male victimization by the state, which is seen as unfairly representing women's interests. The language of bureaucratic victimization of individual men—especially as symbolized by the threatened "walk-on"—may find especially fertile ground among today's young white males, who face a world that has been destabilized by feminism, gay and lesbian liberation, the civil rights movement, and major shifts in the economy.

VICTIMS, LOSERS, AND MEN'S INTERESTS

Beer and liquor ads, and public narratives of Title IX critics are obviously two different things, both in form and content. But they are also similar, in that they involve a strategic address to an audience: the former, in a commercial electronic media context; the latter, in a public political context. In neither case are the interests of dominant men articulated overtly as "backlash." In fact, the interests of dominant men are not foregrounded against those of women. Instead, unfair or unintended victimization of heterosexual white males, and/or ironic humor serve as a facade, or as proxy for "men's" supposedly threatened interests. Arlene Stein (2001), in her study of a gay rights struggle in a small Oregon town, illustrates how dominant groups' appropriation of victim status allows them to sidestep their own shame, while stripping actual victims of moral authority. So too, I think, the cultural and political invocation of the white guy as victim/loser may offer white men a symbolic avenue of escape from the "hidden injuries" of a destabilized or insecure masculinity, while simultaneously delegitimizing the collective claims of women, sexual and racial-ethnic minorities.

Though they differ, the image of the walk-on in anti-Title IX narratives articulates neatly with the image of the "regular guy" in liquor commercials. We are encouraged to admire the walk-on, and to laugh at the loser. But embedded in both stories is an invitation to identify and sympathize with each, because both are potential victims: of the liberal state, of women's collectively-articulated interests; of individual women's put-downs. And both, we are led to believe, can rise above their victimization: the walk-on through heroic individual effort; the loser through consumption of beer with buddies.

So, in some objective sense that we can point to, are there "men's interests"? Perhaps this is not the best framing of the question. When we look at specific empirical sites, "men's interests" seem both to be united and divided, albeit differently, by context. So perhaps it's better to ask: What factors tend to unite white men in gender projects that re-assert patriarchal power, and men's social centrality? What cultural or institutional contexts tend to make salient an articulation of a seemingly unified "mens' interests"? What unites men (as men), across class, race, and age? Military threat and anti-terrorist imagery tends to unite privileged groups of men with many white working class men, as evidenced by the huge amount of support that President George W. Bush holds with white men (Hochschild 2003). Automobiles, in various ways, tend to unite men across these various groups (Connell 1987: 110). Commercial sports tend to unite many men, across generations, and across class and race lines. So, apparently, does the combination of beer with sexist sexual voyeurism.

This raises a corollary question: What factors tend to divide men, perhaps in ways that encourage some men to identify with and actively support feminist (and other) movements for equality and justice? Clearly, not simply having differential access to material resources. Unequal outcomes may, to many men, seem a "fair" outcome of individual competition with a meritocratic system. In fact, lower status boys and men tend often to look "up" to privileged men with admiration and identification (we see this with the slavish toeing of the football lobby's line by men from marginal sports).

But there are also other signs that warn us of the need to be careful with categorical thinking about men's unified interests. For instance, many of us are aware of stories of individual men who become overnight sex equity activists, when they find suddenly that their daughters have been denied access to sport, or have been offered substandard playing fields or unqualified coaches. In these cases, individual men clearly see their own interests as intertwined with the interests of their family members. But can this shift in the articulation of men's interests occur at the group level? At the San Diego Title IX conference, attendees were moved by the presentation of Joe Kelly, the executive director of a national advocacy organization called Dads and Daughters. Kelly spoke strongly of the need for fathers to support their daughters to play sports, and to take an active role in public issues that effect girls' access to athletic opportunities. Kelly told the Commission that gender equity in sports is not only good for girls—it is good for boys and men, too:

> Title TX opens doors for boys, and one of the most important ways it does is when our sons grow up to be fathers . . . Don't force fathers into the limited world where sons and daughters are valued differently just because of their gender. Fathers need a strongly enforced Title IX.

Kelly's speech—and the existence of his organization—suggest that it is possible for men to understand and articulate their own interests as consistent with those of girls and women, and opposed to the narrowly defined material interests of dominant men. How does this happen? Men's experiences in families—especially as fully involved fathers—encourage some men to identify their own interests as consistent with those of their daughters, and to fight for their daughters' rights within patriarchal contexts like sport. This example suggests that men do not always automatically see their interests as men, based on some rational calculation of men's global relations of power with women. As we have seen interests are formulated and articulated situationally, and this means that the construction of gender is potentially fluid and changeable. But this is not to say that contexts do not matter. People create gender within institutional contexts that are characterized by structured divisions of labor and power, and that are saturated with the play of cultural symbols (Messner 2002). And to further complicate this picture, men (and women) move daily in and out of various institutional contexts (e.g., families, workplaces, schools, sport, and the street)—contexts that are characterized by very different, sometimes contradictory gender regimes. For instance, the relationship between the university (which has been dramatically contested by feminism and other social movements), and university-based sport (which still often operates as a semi-autonomous men's fiefdom), offers an empirical example of the tensions and contradictions at the intersection of very different gender regimes. Men's movement across these different gender regimes pushes them to experience their own interests in more complicated ways. The confusion or instability that results from moving across these different gender regimes undoubtedly makes some men more open to the appeal of the kind of white-male-as-victim discourse that I have discussed, or to the ironic cultural sensibility of the white guy as loser. And this victim/loser sensibility, I have suggested, smuggles in a covert backlash against feminism, and against other movements for social justice.

But confusion among young men about gender does not automatically result in a backlash against women's equality; it also creates opportunities for less privileged groups of boys and men to rearticulate their interests. Today's shifting gender regimes of social institutions—especially those that encourage boys and men to interact with girls and women in ways that foster respect and empathy—can provide an emotional foundation for a dis-identification with the narrow interests of dominant men, and a commitment to take action with girls, women, and other men who are interested in building a more equitable and just world.

REFERENCES

Baca Zinn, Maxine, and Bonnie Thornton Dill. 1996. "Theorizing Difference from Multiracial Feminism." *Feminist Studies* 22: 321–331.

Brod, Harry, ed. 1987. *The Making of Masculinities: The New Men's Studies*. Boston: Allen & Unwin.

Carrigan, Tim, R. W. Connell, and John Lee. 1987. "Toward a New Sociology of Masculinity." *Theory & Society* 14: 551–604.

Connell, Raewyn. 1987. *Gender and Power*. Stanford, CA: Stanford University Press.

Connell, Raewyn. 2004. "Encounters with Structure." *International Journal of Qualitative Studies in Education* 17: 11–27.

Ehrenreich, Barbara. 1983. *The Hearts of Men: American Dreams and the Flight from Commitment*. New York: Anchor Doubleday.

Eliasoph, Nina. 1998. *Avoiding Politics: How Americans Produce Apathy in Everyday Life*. Cambridge, UK: Cambridge University Press.

Ferguson, Ann Arnett. 2000. *Bad Boys: Public Schools in the Making of Black Masculinity*. Ann Arbor: University of Michigan Press.

Goode, William J. 1982. "Why Men Resist." In *Rethinking the Family: Some Feminist Questions*, edited by B. Thorne and M. Yalom, 131–50. New York and London: Longman.

Halberstam, Judith. 1998. *Female Masculinity*. Durham, NC: Duke University Press.

Hochschild, Arlie. 2003. "Let Them Eat War." AlterNet.org, October 2, 2003.

Hondagneu-Sotelo, Pierrette, and M. A. Messner. 1994. "Gender Displays and Men's Power: The 'New Man' and the Mexican Immigrant Man." In *Theorizing Masculinities*, edited by Harry Brod and Michael Kaufman. Thousand Oaks, CA: Sage.

Kaufman, Michael, ed. 1987. *Beyond Patriarchy: Essays by Men on Pleasure, Power, and Change*. Toronto: Oxford University Press.

Kimmel, Michael S., ed. 1987. *Changing Men: New Directions in Research on Men and Masculinity*. Newbury Park, CA: Sage.

Kimmel, Michael S. and Thomas E. Mosmiller. 1992. *Against the Tide: Pro-feminist Men in the United States, a Documentary History*. Boston: Beacon Press.

Messner, Michael A. 1997. *Politics of Masculinities: Men in Movements*. Thousand Oaks, CA: Sage.

Messner, Michael A. 2002. *Taking the Field: Women, Men, and Sports*. Minneapolis: University of Minnesota Press.

Pease, Bob. 2002. "(Re)Constructing Men's Interests." *Men and Masculinities* 5: 165–77.

Sabo, Donald F. 1994. "Different Stakes: Men's Pursuit of Gender Equity in Sports." In *Sex, Violence and Power in Sports: Rethinking Masculinity*, edited by M. A. Messner and D. I. Sabo, 202–13. Freedom, CA: Crossing Press.

Sperber, Murray. 2000. *Beer and Circus: How Big-Time Sports Is Crippling Undergraduate Education*. New York: Holt.

Stein, Arlene. 2001. *The Stranger Next Door*. Boston: Beacon Press.

Zimbalist, Andrew. 1999. *Unpaid Professionals: Commercialism and Conflict in Big-Time College Sports*. Princeton, NJ: Princeton University Press.

JAMES W. MESSERSCHMIDT

15. MASCULINITIES AS STRUCTURED ACTION

To grasp the notion of "masculinity as structured action," we must turn to the intersectional theory of structured action that has been employed previously (Messerschmidt 1993, 1997, 2000, 2004, 2010, 2012, 2014) in understanding the relationship among sex, gender, race, class, age, sexuality, and nation. I begin by explaining how the theory of structured action conceptualizes "doing" sex, gender, and sexuality.

DOING SEX, GENDER, AND SEXUALITY

Reflecting various theoretical origins (Archer 2003, 2007, 2012; Connell 1987, 1995; Giddens 1976, 1984; Goffman 1963, 1972, 1979; Kessler and McKenna 1978; Mouzelis 2008; Sartre 1956; West and Fenstermaker 1995; West and Zimmerman 1987), structured action theory emphasizes the construction of sex, gender, and sexuality as situated social, interactional, and embodied accomplishments. In other words, sex, gender, and sexuality grow out of embodied social practices in specific social structural settings and serve to inform such practices in reciprocal relation.

Regarding "sex," historical and social conditions shape the character and definition of sex (social identification as "male" or "female"). Sex and its meanings are given concrete expression by the specific social relations and historical context in which they are embedded. In an important early work, Suzanne Kessler and Wendy McKenna (1978) argued that social action is constructed through taken-for-granted discourses, or what they call "incorrigible propositions." Our belief in two objectively real, biologically created constant yet opposite sexes is a telling discourse. We assume there are only two sexes; each person is simply an example of one or the other. In other words, we construct a sex dichotomy in which no dichotomy holds biologically, historically, cross-culturally, and contemporaneously (Messerschmidt 2004).

The key process in the social construction of the sex dichotomy is the active way we decide what sex a person is (Kessler and McKenna 1978: 1–20). A significant discourse of this sex attribution process is that men have penises and women do not. Thus we consider genitals the ultimate criterion in making sex assignments; yet, in our daily interactions we continually make sex attributions with a complete lack of information about others' genitals. Our recognition of another's sex is dependent on the exhibition of such bodily characteristics as speech, hair, clothing, physical appearance, and other aspects of personal front—through this embodied presentation we "do" sex and it is this doing that becomes a substitute for the concealed genitalia.

Nevertheless, "doing gender" (West and Zimmerman 1987) entails considerably more than the "social emblems" representing membership in one of two sex categories. Rather, the social construction of gender involves a situated social, interactional, and embodied accomplishment. Gender grows out of social practices in specific settings and serves to inform such practices in reciprocal relation. Although "sex" defines social identification as "male" or "female," "doing gender" systematically corroborates that sex identification and category through embodied social interaction. In effect, there are a plurality of forms in which gender is constructed: we coordinate our activities to do gender in situational ways (West and Zimmerman 1987).

Accordingly, early gender development in childhood occurs through an interactive process between child and parents, other children, and other adults. By reason of this interaction with others, children (for the most part) undertake to practice what is being preached and represented. Raewyn Connell defines the proactive adoption of specific embodied

---

From *Masculinities in the Making* (Rowman & Littlefield, forthcoming). Reproduced by permission of the publisher.

gender practices as the "moment of engagement" (1995: 122), the moment when an individual initiates a project of masculinity or femininity as his or her own. The young child has in effect learned to locate him- or herself in relation to others within a sexed and gendered social field (Jackson 2007). Children negotiate the embodied sexed and gendered practices that are prevalent and attributed as such in their particular milieu(s) and, in so doing, commit themselves to a *fundamental project* of sex and gender self-attribution—for example, "I'm a boy" or "I'm a girl." This fundamental self-attribution as a boy or as a girl is the primary mode by which agents choose to relate to the world and to express oneself in it, and thus—as I outline later in this chapter—serves as an important constraint and enabler in the social construction of sex, gender, and sexuality. Indeed, what makes us human is the fact that we construct ourselves by making reflexive choices that transcend given circumstances and propel us into a future that is defined by the consequences of those choices. Doing sex and gender—normally concurrently—is a continuing process in which agents construct patterns of embodied presentations and practices that suggest a particular sex and gender in specific settings and, consequently, project themselves into a future where new situations are encountered and subsequently new reflexive choices are made (Connell 1995). There exists unity and coherence to one's fundamental sex and gender project in the sense that we tend to embody this particular sexed and gendered self—for example, "I'm a boy" or "I'm a girl"—over time and space.

Nevertheless, and although agents construct a fundamental project as either male or female, the actual accomplishment of gender may vary situationally—that is, gender is renegotiated continuously through social interaction and, therefore, one's gendered self may be fraught with contradictions and diversity in gender strategies and practices. For example, agents may situationally construct a specific fundamental gender project (e.g., masculine) that contradicts their bodily sex category (e.g., female).

"Doing sexuality"[1] encompasses the same interactional processes just discussed for "doing gender" and therefore likewise involves children initially acquiring knowledge primarily about heterosexuality

through interaction with mothers, fathers, other children, and other adults. This initial process involves the acquisition of mostly non-erotic forms of heterosexual knowledge, such as male–female marital relationships that suggest this is "where babies come from." However, to adopt such rudimentary heterosexual knowledge, "doing sex" must take primacy. As Stevi Jackson and Sue Scott point out, "We recognize someone as male or female before we make assumptions about heterosexuality or homosexuality; we cannot logically do otherwise" (2010: 91–92). The homosexual/heterosexual dichotomy hinges on socially meaningful sexed categories, "on being able to 'see' two men or two women as 'the same' and a man and a woman as 'different'" (Jackson and Scott 2010: 92).

Once children begin to develop a sense of the erotic aspects of sexuality—which usually occurs through interaction with peers in secondary school—their sense-making is governed by their embodied sexed and gendered self (Jackson 2007). "Doing" sex, gender, and sexuality intersect here, so that our conceptualization of sex and gender impacts our understanding and practice of sexuality (both the erotic and the non-erotic aspects) and it is through sexual practices (once again both the erotic and the non-erotic) that we validate sex and gender. Agents adopt embodied sexual practices as a "moment of engagement," a moment when the individual begins to affix a specific sexual project to their fundamental sex and gender project, constructing, for example, heteromasculine and heterofeminine identities. Sex, gender, and sexuality are produced and reproduced by embodied individuals, and interaction with others is essential to one's ability to negotiate and fit in to ongoing and situationally constructed patterns of sex, gender, and sexuality.

Crucial to this negotiation and "fitting in" is the notion of "accountability" (West and Zimmerman 1987; Hollander 2013). Accountability refers to individuals anticipating assessment of their behavior and therefore they configure and orchestrate their embodied actions in relation to how such actions may be interpreted by others in the particular social context in which they occur. In other words, in their daily activities, agents attempt to be identified bodily as "female" or "male" through sex, gender, and sexual practices. Within social interaction, then, we encourage and expect others to attribute to us a particular sex category—to avoid negative assessments—and we facilitate the ongoing task of accountability through demonstrating that we are male or female by means of concocted practices that may be interpreted accordingly. The specific meanings of sex, gender, and sexuality are defined in social interaction and therefore through personal practice. Doing gender and sexuality renders social action accountable in terms of available gender and sexual practices appropriate to one's sex category in the specific social situation in which one acts. Thus, it is the particular gender and sexual relations in specific settings that give behavior its sexed, gendered, and sexual meanings.

In this view, then, although we decide quite early in life that we're a boy or a girl and later we adopt an identity as straight, gay, lesbian, bisexual, etc., the actual everyday doing of sex, gender, and sexuality is accomplished systematically and is never a static or a finished product. Rather, people construct sex, gender, and sexuality in specific social situations. In other words, people participate in self-regulating conduct whereby they monitor their own and others' embodied social actions. This perspective allows for innovation and flexibility in sex, gender, and sexuality construction—and the ongoing potentiality of normative transgression—but also underscores the ever-present possibility of any sexed, gendered, and sexual activity being assessed by copresent interactants. Sex category serves as a resource for the interpretation of situated social conduct, as copresent interactants in each setting attempt to hold accountable behavior as female or male; that is, socially defined membership in one sex category is used as a means of discrediting or accepting gender and sexual practices. Thus, although we construct ourselves as male or female, we situationally embody gender and sexuality according to our own unique experiences, and accountability attempts to maintain congruence among sex, gender, and sexuality; that is, male = masculinity = sexually desires females and female = femininity = sexually desires males.

Moreover, sex, gender, and sexuality construction results from individuals often—but not always—considering the content of their social action and

then acting only after internal deliberation about the purpose and consequence of their behavior. *Reflexivity* refers to the capacity to engage in internal conversations with oneself about particular social experiences and then decide how to respond appropriately. In reflexivity we internally mull over specific social events and interactions, we consider how such circumstances make us feel, we prioritize what matters most, and then we plan and decide how to respond (Archer 2007). Although we internally deliberate and eventually make such reflexive choices to act in particular ways, those choices are based on the situationally available sex, gender, and sexual practices. Notwithstanding that sex, gender, and sexuality simply may at specific times be a habitual and routine social practice (Martin 2003), accountability encourages people to do sex, gender, and sexuality appropriate to particular situations. And accountability and thus reflexivity especially come into play when agents are confronted with a unique social situation—such as a challenge to their sex, gender, or sexuality. Nevertheless, the resulting reflexive social action may not actually have been consciously intended to be a sex, gender, or sexuality practice.

STRUCTURED ACTION

As the forgoing indicates, although sex, gender, and sexuality are "made," so to speak, through the variable unification of internal deliberations and thus reflexive self-regulated practices, these embodied practices do not occur in a vacuum. Instead, they are influenced by the social structural constraints and enablements we experience. *Social structures*, defined as recurring patterns of social phenomena (practices and discourses) that tend to transcend time and space and thus constrain and enable behavior in specific ways, "only exist as the reproduced conduct of situated actors" (Giddens 1976: 127). In other words, agents draw on social structures to engage in social action and thus social structures (usually) are reproduced through that same embodied and accountable social action. In such duality, structure and action are inseparable (Giddens 1976). "Knowledgeable" human agents of sex, gender, and sexual practices enact social structures by reflexively putting into practice their structured knowledge. Social structures are the "medium" and "outcome" of social action: *medium* because it is through the use of social structures that social action occurs and *outcome* because it is through social action that social structures are reproduced—and sometimes transformed—in time and space (Giddens, 1976; Mouzelis, 2008). Because agents reflexively "do" sex, gender, and sexuality in specific social situations, they reproduce social structures. And given that agents often reproduce sex, gender, and sexual ideals in socially structured specific practices, there are a variety of ways to do them. Within specific socially structured settings, particular forms of sex, gender, and sexual practices are available, encouraged, and permitted. Accordingly, sexed, gendered, and sexual *agency* must be viewed as reflexive embodied structured action—what people, and therefore bodies, do under specific social structural constraints and enablements (Messerschmidt 1993, 1997, 2000, 2004, 2010, 2012, 2014).

Although there exists a variety of social structures, two are especially salient for conceptualizing sex, gender, and sexuality: relational and discursive. *Relational* social structures establish through social action the interconnections and interdependence among individuals in particular social settings and thus define social relationships among people in terms of sex, gender, and sexuality. Relational social structures constrain and enable social action. Examples of relational social structures are the informal yet unequal network of sexed, gendered, and sexual "cliques" in elementary and secondary schools and the sex and gender divisions of labor within workplaces. *Discursive* social structures are representations, ideas, and sign systems (language) that produce culturally significant meanings. Discursive social structures establish through social practice orders of "truth" and what is accepted as "reality" in particular situations. Like relational social structures, discursive social structures constrain and enable the possibilities of social action. Examples of discursive social structures are the notion of "two and only two sexes" mentioned above and social conventions defining styles of dress in terms of sex, gender, and sexuality.

Relational and discursive social structures intersect and work in combination and jointly, but also at times contradictorily. Both relational and discursive social structures are actualized only through particular forms of social action—they have a material base—yet such structured action produces simultaneously particular social relations *and* social meanings that are culturally significant because they shape a sense of what is "acceptable" and "unacceptable" behavior for co-present others in specific situations. Through embodied social action individuals produce relational social structures that concurrently proffer meaningful representations (through embodied appearance and practices) for others as a consequence of their social action. And in turn, through embodied social action individuals also produce discursive social structures that concurrently constitute social relations (through representations, ideas, and sign systems) for others as a consequence of their social action. In other words, discursive social structures often are a part of relational social structures and the latter often are a component of the former. The intersection of relational and discursive social structures then construct the knowledge we use to engage in particular practices—they recursively constrain and enable social action—and they actualize specific forms of understandings that define what is normal, acceptable, and deviant in particular social situations.

Nevertheless, relational and discursive social structures are not all-encompassing and are not always accepted by agents without question or objection (Mouzelis 2008). Through reflexivity agents actually may distance and separate themselves from particular social structures, clearing the path for improvisation and innovation in social action. For example, when confronting social structures, agents at times engage in reflexive internal deliberations and decide to break from and analyze, investigate, and possibly resist situational structural constraints and enablements (Mouzelis 2008). As Abby Peterson (2011) shows, it is in reflexivity where we find the mediatory processes whereby structure and action are connected or disconnected. And when such disconnect of agent from structure transpires—and thus dualism rather than duality occurs—the result often is unique forms of social action. Furthermore, social action may also be influenced by *supplemental* constraints and enablements, which are nonrecurring and thus nonstructural.

Examples of supplemental constraints and enablements are specific types of social interaction, such as a one-time intimate conversation with a trusted and influential individual, as well as our bodies because the body changes over time and situationally constrains and enables social action. In short, sex, gender, and sexual social action emerges from, and is constrained and enabled by, what is always possible within any particular social situation.

POWER

Power is an important structural feature of sex, gender, and sexual relations. Socially structured power relations among men and women are constructed historically on the bases of sex, gender, and sexual preference. In other words, in specific contexts some men and some women have greater power than other men or other women; some genders have greater power than other genders; some sexualities have greater power than other sexualities; and the capacity to exercise power and do sex, gender, and sexuality is, for the most part, a reflection of one's place in sex, gender, and sexual relations of power. Consequently, in general heterosexual men and women exercise greater power than do gay men, lesbians, and other sexual minorities; upper-class men and women exercise greater power than do working-class men and women; white men and women exercise greater power than do racial minority men and women; and cisgender people exercise greater power than do transgender people.[2] Power, then, is a relationship that structures social interaction not only between men and women but also among men and among women as well as in terms of gender and sexuality. Nevertheless, power is not absolute and at times may actually shift in relation to different axes of power and powerlessness.

Raewyn Connell's (1987, 1995) concept of *hegemonic masculinity* is relevant here. Initially, Connell conceptualized hegemonic masculinity as the form of masculinity in a given historical and society-wide setting that structures and legitimates hierarchical gender relations between men and women, between masculinity and femininity, and among men. The relational character was central to her argument, embodying a particular form of masculinity in hierarchical relation to a certain form of femininity and to nonhegemonic masculinities. Connell emphasized that hegemonic masculinity has no meaning outside its *relationship* to "emphasized femininity" (and to nonhegemonic masculinities) or to those femininities practiced in a complementary, compliant, and accommodating subordinate relationship with hegemonic masculinity. And in the *legitimation* of this relationship of superordination and subordination, the meaning and essence of both hegemonic masculinity and emphasized femininity are revealed. This emphasis on hegemony in gender relations underscored the achievement of hegemonic masculinity largely through cultural ascendancy—discursive persuasion—encouraging all to consent to, coalesce around, and embody such unequal gender relations.

Notwithstanding considerable favorable reception of the concept of hegemonic masculinity, it nevertheless attracted such criticisms as (1) concerns over the underlying concept of masculinity itself, (2) lack of specificity about who actually represents hegemonic masculinity, (3) whether hegemonic masculinity simply reduces in practice to a reification of power or toxicity, and (4) the concept's unsatisfactory theory of the masculine subject. Having successfully responded to each of these criticisms, Connell and Messerschmidt (2005) reformulated the concept in appropriately significant ways.

First, they discussed what must be retained from the original formulation, clearly noting that the relational idea among hegemonic masculinity, emphasized femininity, and nonhegemonic masculinities, as well as the conception that this relationship is a pattern of hegemony—not a pattern of simple domination—have well withstood the test of time. Also well supported historically are the seminal ideas that hegemonic masculinity need not be the most common and/or the most powerful pattern of masculinity in a particular setting and that any formulation of the concept as simply constituting an assemblage of "masculine" character traits should be thoroughly transcended.

Second, Connell and Messerschmidt nevertheless suggested that a reformulated understanding of hegemonic masculinity must incorporate a more holistic grasp of gender hierarchy that recognizes the agency of subordinated groups as much as the power of hegemonic groups and that appreciates the mutual conditioning (intersectionality) of gender with such other social dynamics as class, race, age, sexuality, and nation. Moreover, Connell and Messerschmidt asserted that a more sophisticated treatment of embodiment in hegemonic masculinity was necessary, as well as conceptualizations of how hegemonic masculinity may be challenged, contested, and thus changed.

Finally, Connell and Messerschmidt argued that instead of recognizing simply hegemonic masculinity at only the society-wide level, scholars should analyze empirically existing hegemonic masculinities at three levels: *local* (constructed in arenas of face-to-face interaction of families, organizations, and immediate communities), *regional* (constructed at the society-wide level of culture or the nation-state), and *global* (constructed in such transnational arenas as world politics, business, and media). Obviously, links among these levels exist: global hegemonic masculinities pressure regional and local hegemonic masculinities, and regional hegemonic masculinities provide cultural materials adopted or reworked in global arenas and utilized in local gender dynamics.

Hegemonic masculinities then construct both relational and discursive social structures because they establish relations of sex and gender inequality and at once signify acceptable discursive understandings of gender behavior and relations. In this regard, I find that Mimi Schippers' (2007) work is significant because it opens an extremely useful approach of conceptualizing how such *legitimacy* in hegemonic masculinity transpires. Schippers argues that embedded within the meanings of structured gendered relationships are the "qualities members of each gender category should and are assumed to posses" (2007: 90); therefore, it is in "the idealized *quality content* of the categories 'man' and 'woman' that we find the hegemonic significance of masculinity and femininity." For Schippers, certain gendered characteristics *legitimate* men's power over women "only when they are symbolically paired with a complementary and inferior quality attached to femininity" (2007:91). The significance of hegemonic forms of masculinity then is found in discursive meanings that legitimate a rationale for structured social relations and that ensure the ascendancy and power of

men as well as specific masculinities. What Schippers highlights, therefore, is first the *relationship* between masculinity and femininity and second how a certain masculinity is hegemonic only when it articulates discursively particular *gender qualities* that are *complementary* and *hierarchical* in relation to specific feminine qualities. For example, such a complementary and hierarchical relationship might establish masculinity as constituting physical strength, the ability to use interpersonal violence in the face of conflict, and authority, whereas femininity would embrace physical vulnerability, an inability to use violence effectively, and compliance (2007: 91). When both masculine and feminine qualities legitimate a complementary and hierarchical relationship between them, we have *gender hegemony*, involving the superordinate position of men and subordinate position of women (2007: 94).

Hegemonic masculinities form relational and discursive social structures that have cultural influence but do not determine social action. Hegemonic masculinities often—but not always—underpin the conventions applied in the enactment and reproduction of masculinities (and femininities)—the lived embodied patterns of meanings, which as they are experienced as practice, appear as reciprocally confirming. Hegemonic masculinities relationally and discursively shape a sense of "reality" for men and women in specific situations and are continually renewed, recreated, defended, and modified through social action. And yet they are at times resisted, limited, altered, and challenged. Hegemonic masculinities operate like other social structures as recurring "on-hand" meaningful practices that are culturally influential and thus available to be actualized into social action in a range of different circumstances. They provide a conceptual framework that is materialized in the design of daily practices and interactions. As individuals construct gender hegemony they simultaneously present those relations as culturally significant for others as a consequence of their embodied social action. Power then is constituted through acceptance of and consent to hegemonically masculine forms of knowledge and practice.

In addition to the above, the relationship between hegemonic masculinity and emphasized femininity underpins what has become known as *heteronormativity*, or the legal, cultural, organizational, and interpersonal practices that derive from and reinforce taken-for-granted assumptions that there are two and only two naturally opposite and complementary sexes (male and female), that gender is a natural manifestation of sex (masculinity and femininity), and that it is natural for the two opposite and complementary sexes to be sexually attracted to each other (heterosexuality). In other words, the social construction of sex differences intersects with the assumption of gender and sexual complementarity, or the notion that men's and women's bodies are naturally compatible and thus "made for each other"—*the* "natural" sex act allegedly involves vaginal penetration by a penis (Jackson and Scott 2010). Heterosexuality is understood culturally as the natural erotic attraction to sex/gender difference, as well as a natural practice of male active dominance and female passive receptivity, and thus this notion of natural attraction and practice reinforces hegemonic masculinity and emphasized femininity as natural and complementary opposites (Schippers 2007). Heteronormativity therefore refers to "the myriad ways in which heterosexuality is produced as a natural, unproblematic, taken-for-granted, ordinary phenomenon" (Kitzinger 2005: 478). Thus, gender hegemony and sexual hegemony intersect so that both masculinity and heterosexuality are deemed superior and femininity and homosexuality are judged to be inferior. The social construction of men and women as naturally different, complementary, and hierarchical sanctions heterosexuality as *the* normal and natural form of sexuality and masculine men and feminine women as *the* normal and natural gender presentation; any sexual or gender construction outside of these dichotomies is considered abnormal. Heteronormativity then reproduces a social structure based on an unequal sexual binary—heterosexuality and homosexuality—that is dependent on the alleged natural sexual attraction of two and only two opposite and complementary sexes that in turn constructs heteromasculine and heterofeminine difference. Nevertheless, some heterosexual practices are more powerful than other heterosexual practices; that is, normative heterosexuality determines its own internal boundaries as well as marginalizing and sanctioning sexualities outside those boundaries.

INTERSECTING WITH RACE AND CLASS

In addition to the significance of gender and sexuality, individuals construct race and class structured relations, and in their daily activities individuals attempt to be identified as, for example, "African American" or "white" and "working-class" or "middle-class." Nevertheless, the salience of gender, race, class, and sexual structured relations is important because although gender, race, class, and sexual constructions are ubiquitous, the significance of each shifts from context to context: for example, in one situation gender, race, and sexuality (but not class) may intersect and thus be important; in another, gender and class but not race and sexuality may intersect and be significant; and in still other situations sexuality may be more important than gender, race, and class. In other words, gender, race, class, and sexuality are not absolutes and are not always equally significant in every social setting in which individuals participate—they intersect in different ways depending upon the particular social situation.

Although gender, race, class, and sexuality vary in salience by social situation, socially structured relations of gender, race, class, and sexuality variously join us in a common relationship to others: we share gendered, race, class, and sexual structural space. Consequently, common or shared blocks of gendered, race, class, and sexual discursive knowledge about interpersonal practices evolve through interaction in which particular ideals and activities differ in significance. Through such interaction, gender, race, class, and sexuality become institutionalized, permitting, for example, men and women to draw on such existing but previously formed ways of doing or practicing gender, race, class, and sexuality to construct particular strategies for specific settings. The specific criteria of gender, race, class, and sexuality thus are embedded in the socially structured situations and recurrent practices by which gender, class, race, and sexual relations are structured. Nevertheless, accountability to gender, race, class, and sexuality is not always, in every social situation, critical to the particular interaction.

ADDITIONAL MASCULINITIES AND FEMININITIES

In addition to hegemonic masculinity and emphasized femininity, structured action theory identifies additional distinct masculinities and femininities: dominant, dominating, subordinate, and equality. "Dominant" masculinities and femininities differ from hegemonic masculinities and emphasized femininities in that they are not always associated with and linked to gender hegemony but refer fundamentally to the most celebrated, common, or current form of masculinity and femininity in a particular social setting (Beasley 2008). "Dominating" masculinities and femininities are similar to dominant masculinities but differ in the sense that they involve commanding and controlling specific interactions and exercising power and control over people and events—"calling the shots" and "running the show." Dominant and dominating masculinities and femininities do not necessarily legitimate a hierarchical relationship between men and women, masculinity and femininity. Although hegemonic masculinities and emphasized femininities at times may also be dominant or dominating, dominant and dominating masculinities and femininities are never hegemonic or emphasized if they fail culturally to *legitimate* unequal gender relations; in this latter scenario, dominant and dominating masculinities are thereby constructed *outside* relations of gender hegemony. However, dominant and dominating masculinities and femininities necessarily acquire meaning only in relation to other masculinities and femininities (see Beasley 2008; Messerschmidt 2008, 2010, 2012, 2014).

"Subordinate" masculinities and femininities refer to those masculinities and femininities situationally constructed as lesser than or aberrant and deviant to hegemonic masculinity or emphasized femininity as well as dominant/dominating masculinities and femininities. Depending on the particular context, such subordination can be conceptualized in terms of, for example, race, class, age, sexualities, or body display/behavior. Given the discussion above, it should be obvious that one of the most significant forms of subordination is that of gay boys/men and lesbian girls/women—the former are culturally feminized and the latter culturally masculinized. In a gender hegemonic culture, then, gayness is socially defined as the embodiment of whatever is expelled from hegemonic masculinity and lesbianism is the embodiment of whatever is expelled from emphasized femininity. Related to this, a second form of subordination usually occurs if there is incongruence within the sex–gender–heterosexuality structure. For example, girls and women perceived as female who construct bodily practices defined as masculine, such as expressing sexual desire for girls ("dyke"), acting sexually promiscuous ("slut"), and/or presenting as authoritarian, physically aggressive, or take charge ("bitch") are viewed as polluting "normal" and "natural" hegemonic gender and sexual relations and often are verbally, socially, and physically subordinated (Schippers 2007). Similarly, individuals perceived as male but who construct practices defined as feminine, such as sexually desiring boys or simply practicing celibacy ("fag"), being passive, compliant, or shy ("sissy"), and/or being physically weak or unadventurous ("wimp") likewise are seen as polluting "normal" and "natural" hegemonic gender and sexual relations and often are verbally, socially, and physically subordinated (Schippers 2007). Structured unequal gender and sexual relations then are sustained in part through the subordination of the above genders and sexualities. Finally, subordination can also occur among individuals that construct situationally accountable masculinities and femininities. For example, the masculinity of a son may be judged to be subordinate to the masculinity of his father, and the femininity of a daughter may be considered subordinate to the femininity of her mother. Both of these are subordinate primarily by reason of age, not because of any incongruence between sex and gender, and usually are established in relation to dominant/dominating masculinities and femininities and thus practiced independent of gender hegemony.

"Equality" masculinities and femininities are those that legitimate an egalitarian relationship between men and women, between masculinity and femininity, and among men and women and therefore are constructed exterior to gender hegemonic relations in any particular setting—these are additional forms of gender practiced external to relations of gender hegemony. Such masculinities and femininities do not assume a normal and natural relationship to sex and sexuality and usually they are not constructed as naturally complementary.

Sex, gender, and sexual structured practices operate as "on-hand" resources (developed from embodied social actions themselves) available to be actualized into practice in a range of different circumstances. They provide a conceptual framework that is materialized in the design of social structures and, therefore, materialized in daily practices and interactions. Structured action theory permits investigation of the different ways men and women experience their everyday worlds from their particular positions in society and how they relate to other men and women; the embodied sex, gender, and sexual practices are associated with the specific context of individual action and are for the most part self-regulated—through reflexivity—within that context; social actors self-regulate their behavior and make specific reflexive choices in specific contexts. In this way, then, men and women construct varieties of sex, gender, and sexuality through specific embodied practices. And by emphasizing diversity in sex, gender, and sexual construction, we achieve a more fluid and situated approach to our understanding of embodied sexes, genders, and sexualities.

EMBODIMENT

As I have emphasized, constructing sex, gender, and sexuality entails *embodied* social practices—reflexive structured action. Only through our bodies that we experience the social world, and the very possibility of a social world rests upon our embodiment (Crossley 2001). As Iris Marion Young long ago pointed out,

> It is the body in its orientation toward and action upon and within its surroundings that constitutes the initial meaning-given act. The body is the first locus of intentionality, as pure presence to the world and openness upon its possibilities. The most primordial intentional act is the motion of the body orienting itself with respect to and moving within its surroundings. (1990: 147–48)

We understand the world from our embodied place in it and our perceptual awareness of situational surrounding space. The body is a sensuous being—it perceives, it touches, and it feels; it is a lived body,

and given that consciousness consists of perceptual sensations, it is therefore part of the body and not a separate substance (Crossley 2001). The mind and the body are inseparably linked—a binary divide is a fiction—and live together as one in the social construction of sex, gender, and sexuality. In this conceptualization, then, the body forms the whole of our being and, therefore, one's reflexive sexed, gendered, and sexual self is located in the body, which in turn acts, and is acted upon, within a social environment. And in contemporary industrialized societies the body is central to the social construction of self (Giddens 1991). A proficient and able body is necessary for social action and, therefore, embodied discipline is fundamental to the competent social agent: "It is integral to the very nature both of agency and of being accepted (trusted) by others as competent" (Giddens 1991: 100).

Through embodied social action individuals do sex, gender, and sexuality while simultaneously reproducing structures and presenting such practices as resources for others as a consequence of their embodiment. The social situations in which embodied actions are oriented "are populated by others and it is these others, in part, toward whom the actions are oriented. Action is other oriented" (Crossley 1995: 141). Embodied social action is embedded within the specific social structural context of the agent, so that what we actually conceptualize are social situations that require specific "practical accommodation from our action" (Crossley 1995: 136)—we reflexively respect, acknowledge, reproduce, and sometimes resist structured embodied practices. And as Goffman acutely observes, such embodied actions are situational forms of "social portraiture" in which individuals discursively convey information that "the others in the gathering will need in order to manage their own courses of action—which knowledgeability he [sic] in turn must count on in carrying out his [sic] own designs" (1979: 6). Doing sex, gender, and sexuality therefore is necessarily both reflexive and physical; it is intelligent, meaningful, and embodied.

Bodies are active in the production and transmission of social structures as well as embodied social actions and are based on the reaction of others to our embodiment—whether or not it is judged accountable is important to our sense of self. Embodied account-ability is vital to an individual's situational recognition as a competent social agent. If an individual's embodied appearance and practice is categorized by others as "failed," that degradation may result in a spoiled self-concept (Goffman 1968). Consequently, adequate participation in social life depends on the successful presenting, monitoring, and interpreting of bodies.

Goffman helps us understand how doing sex, gender, and sexuality are socially structured in the sense that we accomplish all three bodily and in a manner that is accountable to situationally populated others. Individuals exhibit embodied sex, gender, and sexual competence through their appearance and by producing situationally appropriate "behavioral styles" that respond properly to the styles produced by others. In other words, "competent" individuals develop an embodied capacity to provide and to read structured depictions of sex, gender, and sexuality in particular settings, and appropriate body management is crucial to the smooth flow of interaction essential to satisfactory attribution and accountability by others. To be "read" by others as male, female, masculine, feminine, straight, gay, lesbian, etc., individuals must ensure that their proffered selves are maintained through situationally appropriate display and behavior—the body is social and social settings are created through intercorporeality.

But in addition, properly accountable bodies construct relational and discursive social structures; they signal and facilitate through their appearance and action the maintenance of sex, gender, and sexual power dynamics. To be sure, suitably adorned and comported bodies constitute the "shadow and the substance" of unequal sex, gender, and sexual social structures: "The expression of subordination and domination through the swarm of situational means is more than a mere tracing of symbol or ritualistic affirmation of social hierarchy. These expressions considerably constitute the hierarchy; they are the shadow and the substance" (Goffman 1979: 6). Individuals produce (and at times challenge) socially structured sex, gender, and sexual relations through their embodied appearance and actions.

The body is an essential part of sex, gender, and sexual construction in which we fashion appearance and actions to create properly and situationally adorned and performed bodies. The body is an inescapable and integral part of doing sex, gender, and sexuality, entailing social practice that constantly refers to bodies and what bodies do, it is not social practice reduced to the body (Connell 2000). Constructing sex, gender, and sexuality involves a dialectical relationship in which practice deals with the biological characteristics of bodies: "It gives them a social determination. The connection between social and natural structures is one of practical relevance, not causation" (Connell 1987: 78). In the social construction of sex, gender, and sexuality, then, bodily similarities between men and women are negated and suppressed, whereas bodily differences are exaggerated. Indeed, the body is essential to, for example, the discourse of "two and only two sexes" in the sense that "men have penises and women do not." The body is significant for our fundamental sex, gender, and sexual projects discussed above, our sense of sex, gender, and sexual self that we subjectively sustain through time and space. Bodies impact our recurring self-attributions and thus one's identity as male or female, masculine or feminine, and straight or gay. Because "sex" is associated with genitalia there is likely to be a degree of social standardization of individual lives—we recursively construct ourselves as, for example, a "boy/man" or as a "girl/woman" with a particular sexual orientation and thus such identities constrain and enable our social action. For most people sex is the primary claimed identity that is relatively solid and unchanging while gender and sexuality are qualifiers to sex (Paechter, 2006). Nevertheless, some turn this on its head—such as certain transgender people—whereby sex is the qualifier and gender is the primary mode in which one relates to the world (p. 2006: 259).

Bodies participate in social action by delineating courses of social conduct: bodies are agents of social practice and, given the context, will do certain things and not others; our bodies are *supplemental* constraints and enablers of social action and therefore they situationally mediate and influence social practices (Connell 1995). The body often is lived in terms of what it can "do" and the "consequence of bodily practice is historicity: the creation and transformation of situations. Bodies are drawn into history and history is constituted through bodies" (Connell 1998: 7). In short, the body is a participant in the shaping and generating of social practice. Consequently, it is impossible to consider human agency without taking sexed, gendered, and sexual embodiment into account.

CHALLENGES

Nevertheless, certain occasions present themselves as more effectively intimidating for demonstrating and affirming embodied sex, gender, and sexuality. In certain situations individuals may experience body betrayal and be identified by others as embodying sex, gender, race, class, or sexual "failure." The constitution of sex, gender, and sexuality through bodily appearance and performance means that sex, gender, and sexual accountability are vulnerable when the situationally appropriate appearance and performance are not (for whatever reason) sustained. Because the taken-for-granted sex, gender, and sexuality of individuals can be challenged in certain contexts, each may become particularly salient. They are, as David Morgan would put it, "more or less explicitly put on the line" (1992: 47), and the responding social action can generate an intensified reflexivity and a distinct type of sex, gender, or sexual construction. Such challenges are contextually embodied interactions that result in sex, gender, or sexual degradation—the individual is constructed as a sexed, gendered, or sexually "deviant" member of society. Such challenges arise from interactional threats and insults from peers, teachers, parents, or workmates and from situationally and bodily defined sex, gender, and sexual expectations that are not achievable. Such challenges, in various ways, proclaim a man or boy or a woman or girl subordinate in contextually defined embodied terms. Sex, gender, and sexual challenges may motivate social action toward specific situationally embodied practices that attempt to correct the subordinating social situation (Messerschmidt 1993, 1997, 2000, 2004, 2010, 2012, 2014). Given that such interactions question, undermine, and/or threaten one's sex, gender, or sexuality, only contextually "appropriate" sex, gender, and sexual embodied practices can help overcome the challenge. The existence of sex, gender, and sexual challenges alerts us to the transitory and fleeting nature of sex, gender, and sexual construction and to how particular forms of social action may arise as sexed, gendered, or sexual practices when they are regularly threatened and contested.

Social action is never simply an autonomous event but is amalgamated into larger assemblages—what is labeled here as socially structured embodied actions. The socially structured situational ideals of sex, gender, and sexuality encourage specific lines of social action, and relational and discursive social structures shape the capacities from which sex, gender, and sexuality actions are constructed over time. Men and boys and women and girls negotiate the situations that face them in everyday life and, in the process, pursue a sex, gender, and sexuality project. From this perspective, then, social action is often—but not always—designed with an eye to one's sex, gender, and sexual accountability individually, bodily, situationally, and structurally. Structured action theory, then, permits us to explore how and in what respects sex, gender, and sexual embodied practices are constituted in certain settings at certain times. In short, to understand masculinity, we must appreciate how structure and action are woven inextricably into the ongoing reflexive activities of "doing" embodied sex, gender, and sexual practices.[3]

REFERENCES

Archer, Margaret S. 2003. *Structure, Agency, and the Internal Conversation.* New York:Cambridge University Press.

Archer, Margaret S. 2007. *Making Our Way through the World: Human Reflexivity and Human Mobility.* New York: Cambridge University Press.

Archer, M.S. 2012. *The Reflexive Imperative in Late Modernity.* New York:Cambridge University Press.

Beasley, Christine. 2008. "Rethinking Hegemonic Masculinity in a Globalizing World." *Men and Masculinities* 11 (1): 86–103.

Connell, Raewyn. 1987. *Gender and Power.* Sydney, Australia: Allen & Unwin.

Connell, Raewyn. 1995. *Masculinities.* St. Leonards: Allen & Unwin

Connell, Raewyn. 1998. "Making Gendered People: Bodies, Identities, Sexualities." In *Revisioning*

Gender, edited by M. M. Ferree, J. Lorber, and B. B. Hess, 449–71. Thousand Oaks, CA: Sage.

Connell, Raewyn. 2000. *The Men and the Boys.* Sydney: Allen & Unwin.

Connell, Raewyn, and James W. Messerschmidt. 2005. "Hegemonic Masculinity: Rethinking the Concept." *Gender and Society* 19 (6): 829–59.

Crossley, Nick. 1995. "Body Techniques, Agency and Intercorporeality: On Goffman's *Relations in Public." Sociology* 29 (1): 133–49.

Crossley, Nick. 2001. *The Social Body: Habit, Identity and Desire.* Thousand Oaks, CA: Sage.

Giddens, Anthony. 1976. *New Rules of Sociological Method: A Positive Critique of Interpretive Sociologies.* New York: Basic Books.

Giddens, Anthony. 1984. *The Constitution of Society.* Berkeley: University of California Press.

Giddens, Anthony. 1991. *Modernity and Self-Identity: Self and Society in a Late Modern Age.* Stanford: Stanford University Press.

Goffman, Erving. 1968. *Asylums: Essays on the Social Situation of Mental Patients and Other Inmates.* New York: Doubleday & Company, Inc.

Goffman, Erving. 1979. *Gender Advertisements.* New York: Harper & Row.

Hollander, Jocelyn A. 2013. "'I Demand More of People': Accountability, Interaction, and Gender Change." *Gender & Society* 27 (1): 5–29.

Jackson, Stevi. 2007. "The Sexual Self in Late Modernity." In *The Sexual Self,* edited by M. Kimmel, 3–15. Nashville, TN.: Vanderbilt University Press.

Jackson, Stevi and Sue Scott. 2010. *Theorizing Sexuality.* New York: McGraw–Hill.

Kessler, Suzanne and Wendy McKenna. 1978. *Gender: An Ethnomethodological Approach.* New York: Wiley.

Kitzinger, Celia. 2005. "Heteronormativity in Action: Reproducing the Heterosexual Nuclear Family in After-Hours Medical Calls." *Social Problems* 52 (4): 477–98.

Martin, Patricia Yancey. 2003. "'Said and Done' Versus 'Saying and Doing': Gendering Practices, Practicing Gender at Work." *Gender and Society* 17 (3): 342–66.

Messerschmidt, James W. 1993. *Masculinities and Crime: Critique and Reconceptualization of Theory.* Lanham, MD: Rowman & Littlefield.

Messerschmidt, James W. 1997. *Crime as Structured Action: Gender, Race, Class, and Crime in the Making.* Thousand Oaks, CA: Sage.

Messerschmidt, James W. 2000. *Nine Lives: Adolescent Masculinities, the Body, and Violence.* Boulder, CO: Westview Press.

Messerschmidt, James W. 2004. *Flesh & Blood: Adolescent Gender Diversity and Violence.* Lanham, MD: Rowman & Littlefield.

Messerschmidt, James W. 2008. "And Now, the Rest of the Story . . ." *Men and Masculinities* 11 (1): 83–101.

Messerschmidt, James W. 2010. *Hegemonic Masculinities and Camouflaged Politics: Unmasking the Bush Dynasty and Its War against Iraq.* Boulder, CO: Paradigm.

Messerschmidt, James W. 2012. *Gender, Heterosexuality, and Youth Violence: The Struggle for Recognition.* Lanham, MD: Rowman & Littlefield.

Messerschmidt, James W. 2014. *Crime as Structured Action: Doing Masculinities, Race, Class, Sexuality, and Crime.* Lanham, MD: Rowman & Littlefield.

Mouzelis, Nicos P. 2008. *Modern and Postmodern Theorizing: Bridging the Divide.* New York: Cambridge University Press.

Morgan, David. 1992. *Discovering Men.* New York: Routledge.

Paechter, Carrie. 2006. "Masculine Femininities/Feminine Masculinities: Power, Identities, And Gender." *Gender and Education* 18 (3): 253-263.

Peterson, Abby. 2011. "The 'Long Winding Road' to Adulthood: A Risk-Filled Journey for Young People in Stockholm's Marginalized Periphery." *Young* 19 (3): 271–89.

Sartre, Jean Paul. 1956. *Being and Nothingness.* New York: Washington Square Press.

Schippers, Mimi. 2007. "Recovering the Feminine Other: Masculinity, Femininity, and Gender Hegemony." *Theory & Society* 36 (1): 85–102.

West, Candance and Sarah Fenstermaker. 1995. "Doing Difference." *Gender and Society* 9: 8–37.

West, Candace and Don Zimmerman. 1987. "Doing Gender." *Gender and Society* 1 (2): 125–51.

Young, Iris Marion. 1990. *Throwing Like a Girl and Other Essays in Feminist Philosophy and Social Theory.* Bloomington: Indiana University Press.

NOTES

1. *Sexuality* involves all erotic and non-erotic aspects of social life and social being that relate to bodily attraction or intimate bodily contact between individuals, such as desires, practices, discourses, interactions, relationships, and identities (see Jackson and Scott 2010).
2. *Cisgender* denotes a person whose gender matches the sex assigned at birth and *transgender* designates a person whose gender does not match the sex assigned at birth.
3. For a broader discussion and empirical assessment of structured action theory, see my forthcoming book, *Masculinities as Structured Action: From the Local to the Global* (Lanham, MD: Rowman & Littlefield, 2015).

PART

3

NAVIGATING MASCULINITIES

CHAPTER 3

NAVIGATING MASCULINITIES

An Introduction

In Marilyn Frye's (1983) classic essay—"Oppression"—she uses a birdcage as a metaphor for considering the meanings, causes, and consequences of systems of social and cultural dominance. Initially, she asks readers to consider just one wire of the cage, inviting the comparison with a consideration of a single form of inequality. "You could look at that one wire," she writes, "up and down the length of it, and be unable to see why a bird would not just fly around the wire any time it wanted to go somewhere" (Frye 1983: 4). Frye compares the individual wires of the birdcage to distinct forms of oppression. Considering any single one on its own, she suggests, inadequately defines the experience of oppression. It is only by altering one's perspective, stepping back and refocusing on the entire cage rather than a single wire, that we can more completely appreciate systems of power and inequality. This refocusing enables a different and powerful understanding of inequality: "It [will be] perfectly obvious that the bird is surrounded by a network of systematically related barriers, no one of which would be the least hindrance to its flight, but which, by their relations to each other, are as confining as the solid walls of a dungeon" (Frye 1983: 5).

The perspectives represented in the *Navigating Masculinities* section take this metaphor seriously. This line of scholarship primarily examines the ways that various axes of power and inequality (e.g., gender, race, class, sexuality, age, religion) intersect to constitute masculinities in different ways. This theory and research examine the ways that systems of power and inequality are best understood as working together, simultaneously. For instance, how can we best understand the inequality faced by a 65-year-old, working-class, Latino, gay man who recently converted to Islam and lives in rural Iowa? Should we focus on the inequality he might face as a result of his age, his class, his race, his sexuality, his religion, his gender, or something else? Scholars who utilize what we call a "navigating masculinities" approach would probably simply answer this question with a definitive "Yes!"

This type of inequality may be difficult to theorize given that the vast majority of research on men and masculinities has focused primarily on populations of male, cisgendered,[1] white, heterosexual, middle-class, Western men (likely reflecting the positionality of many of the researchers themselves). In writing about his own experience in gender studies classrooms watching white and nonwhite women discuss their experiences, for instance, Michael Kimmel writes,

> When I looked in the mirror, I thought I saw a "human being," a generic person, universally generalizable. What had been concealed—race, gender, and class—was suddenly visible. As a middle-class white man, I was able to not think about the ways in which class and race and gender had shaped my existence. Marginality is visible, and painfully visceral. Privilege is invisible, and painlessly pleasant. (Kimmel 1990: 94)

This type of privilege informed initial efforts to address other forms of inequality, even as efforts were made to make masculinity more visible. In fact, making masculinity visible as gender was a major project of initial theory and research in the field.

The sorts of advantages Kimmel describes are a part of what Raewyn Connell (1995) refers to as the "patriarchal dividend"—the surplus advantages men receive as a result of gender inequality. Although the wage gap and additional income is perhaps the easiest way of thinking about the systems of collective advantage from which men benefit, Connell considered wages one small piece of a system of gender relations whereby men are afforded more money, respect, authority, status, safety, and more. In societies structured by inequality, privilege is largely unrecognized, taken for granted.

As Kimmel's example illustrates, Connell argues that the patriarchal dividend refers to the systems of structured advantage men (as a group) are collectively afforded. Yet Connell stressed that not all men benefit in the same ways or to the same degree. For instance, working-class men may not profit economically from the patriarchal dividend. So, some groups may be systematically excluded from aspects (e.g., money) of the patriarchal dividend. Gay men, for instance, may lack access to the authority, respect, and safety afforded other groups of men that might more closely live up to culturally exalted forms of masculinity. Yet, many gay men might benefit economically from the patriarchal dividend in ways working-class men do not, even if they receive more cultural authority and respect in many contexts. So, Connell's patriarchal dividend begins an important conversation about intersections between gender and other categories of identity.

Some scholarship has dealt with discrepancies in the accrued advantages from the patriarchal dividend between different groups of men with the conceptualization of what Karen Pyke (1996) calls "compensatory masculinity." The idea here is that men who are unable to embody culturally idealized models of masculinity (or are marginalized by those models) may "compensate" for these "losses" by overemphasizing other "masculine" configurations of practice. Pyke's analysis concentrates on the different kinds of power men hold in heterosexual marriages, contingent on their economic class. As Pyke writes,

> The different conjugal power processes available across social class further feed into the cultural legitimations of higher-class men's superior position. In the absence of legitimated hierarchical advantages, lower-class husbands are more likely to produce hypermasculinity by relying on blatant, brutal, and relentless power strategies in their marriages, including spousal abuse. In so doing, they compensate for their demeaned status, pump up their

sense of self-worth and control, and simulate the uncontested privileges of higher-class men. The production of an exaggerated masculinity in some working-class subcultures also serves the interests of higher-class men by deflecting attention from their covert mechanisms of power and enabling them to appear egalitarian by contrast. (1996: 544–45)

Pyke suggests that compensatory masculinities are best understood in two ways. First, she understands compensatory masculinity as composed of strategies in which men with less cultural power and authority might engage to collect forms of privilege that flow more seamlessly to groups of men less marginalized by culturally dominant forms of masculinity. Second, however, Pyke argues that we must pay close attention to the ways that compensatory masculinities also play a key role in obscuring power-retaining strategies among groups of men who may not need to participate in compensatory masculine practices. In this way, marginalized men are often cast as the scapegoats of gender inequality (see also Hondagneu-Sotelo and Messner [1994] on this point).

Although Pyke discussed compensatory masculinity with respect to class inequality, the term has most often been used to address racial inequality. Although they do not explicitly use the term, Richard Majors and Janet Mancini Billson's analysis of black men in *Cool Pose: The Dilemmas of Black Manhood in America* (1992) is a classic example of this type of argument. Majors and Billson argue that the "cool pose" culturally recognized as stereotypically characteristic of black masculinity is a compensatory strategy in which black men may engage to recuperate masculinity lost because of institutionalized racism and inequalities that structurally prevent many from achieving masculinity via other routes (see also hooks [2003] and Collins [2004]). Whereas some scholars in the *Multiple Masculinities* section deploy this term as well, intersectional uses of the term do not necessarily frame compensatory masculinity within the multiple masculinities theoretical framework. Rather, they deploy the term to intersectionally interrogate masculinities.

The perspectives in the *Navigating Masculinities* section build on feminist intersectional approaches to inequality to understand the ways in which men are positioned differently vis-à-vis the patriarchal dividend. Navigating masculinities approaches are distinct from those in the *Multiplying Masculinities* section because they do not always consider gender the primary axis of analysis. Rather, they examine intersections with other categories of identity and systems of power and inequality that structure masculinities. Navigating masculinities scholars are open to the idea that class, race, sexuality, or something else might best help us understand distinct configurations of gender identities, practices, and inequalities. This approach suggests two things: (1) gender inequality is always only *one* form of inequality and (2) gender is not always the most important category helping us understand different configurations of masculinity and forms of inequality.

Navigating masculinities perspectives often do two things. They examine masculinities from what Kimmel (1990) calls "visible" and "visceral" positions in systems of power and inequality. But they also call attention to the challenges we face when trying to situate people as *either* suffering from existing systems of power and inequality *or* privileged by existing systems of power and inequality. Many individuals and groups are better understood as *both* suffering from *and* privileged by existing social structures and relations. And to more completely understand this complex reality, we must consider how different forms of power and inequality work together. By implicitly (and sometimes explicitly) questioning the centrality of gender in their analysis, scholars relying on navigating masculinities perspectives consider other identity categories and systems of power and privilege alongside gender.

THINKING INTERSECTIONALLY ABOUT MASCULINITIES

Navigating masculinities approaches reflect attention to multiple systems of power and inequality. These approaches examine the world from positions of marginality and subordination, focusing on perspectives of individuals and groups located at multiple axes of power and inequality. Beginning with the experiences, identities, and perspectives of those at the margins, these approaches reverse the way in which a great deal of scholarship looks at the world and, as a result, provides a more multidimensional understanding of enduring patterns in gender identities and inequality. As bell hooks (1984) famously put it, these perspectives look at the world "from margin to center." Such an approach privileges voices and experiences often left out of social theory that address inequality from the position of the more powerful, revealing how multiple vectors of power construct inequality.

Drawing on theories of intersectionality, navigating masculinities approaches not only examine different systems of power and inequality separately, but also seek to understand how various forms of power and inequality work together. Like Frye's bird cage, navigating masculinities scholars examine how different forms of power and inequality create webs of oppression that are best understood (from this perspective) by considering the complexity of the whole than by concentrating on a single strand of the web or wire of the cage.

This approach to understanding inequality—one that takes intersections between different identity categories (e.g., gender, race, class, sexuality) and systems of power and inequality as critically important—grew out of legal scholar Kimberlé Crenshaw's groundbreaking work (1989, 1991). Crenshaw suggests we look at a traffic intersection as a metaphor for different forms of inequality. When an accident happens at an intersection, it often happens for more than one reason. Isolating a *single* cause based on bystanders' and participants' observations may be next to impossible given their unique locations and perspectives, none necessarily more objectively "true" than the others.

Crenshaw applied this model of thinking to a consideration of black women's experiences of discrimination. How are we to know, she asked, whether it was racial or gender discrimination? And is it really even possible (or desirable) to separate these different forms of discrimination? As Crenshaw writes, "the intersection of racism and sexism factors into black women's lives in ways that cannot be captured wholly by looking at the race or gender dimensions of those experiences separately" (1991: 1244). Crenshaw argues that multiple vectors of power are not additive; they are "intersectional." By this, she means that we cannot simply add and subtract inequalities to get a sense of individual experiences. In fact, attempting to deploy mathematical metaphors to explore the dynamics of overlapping and intersecting inequalities is unproductive and often leads to a sort of "contest of oppressions."

Patricia Hill Collins (1990) refers to these sorts of webs of intersecting identities and oppressions as the "matrix of domination." This language assists in avoiding thinking of oppressions hierarchically (i.e., which one is more/most important?) and toward an understanding of them as collaborative (i.e., how do different kinds of oppression work together to produce something more difficult to name?). Much like Frye's metaphor using the birdcage, oppression based on a single facet of identity (e.g., race, gender, class, sexuality)—considered alone—does not make sense from this perspective. Rather, only by looking at the ways in which inequalities work together, as a "matrix," can we understand the complexities of systems of inequality. Collins writes about this distinct contribution in this way:

> Viewing relations of domination for black women for any given sociohistorical context as being structured via a system of interlocking race, class, and gender oppression expands the focus of analysis from merely describing the similarities and differences distinguishing these systems of oppression and focuses greater attention on how they interconnect. Assuming that each system needs the others in order to function creates a distinct theoretical stance that stimulates the rethinking of basic social science concepts. (1990: 222)

As Collins argues, intersectional approaches focus on the interconnections between systems of oppression, examining the ways in which they work together in ways that are not wholly appreciated by examining each alone.

Collins also introduced the concept of "controlling images" to facilitate intersectional analysis. Controlling images refer to the cultural stereotypes surrounding specific groups—images that situate them within social hierarchies and work to produce a "truth" about that group. Collins was particularly interested in interrogating the cultural power surrounding controlling images of black women.

> Ideologies represent the process by which certain assumed qualities are attached to black women and how those qualities are used to justify oppression. From the mammies, Jezebels, and breeder women of slavery to the smiling Aunt Jemimas on pancake mix boxes, ubiquitous black prostitutes, and ever-present welfare mother of contemporary popular culture, the nexus of negative stereotypical images applied to African-American women has been fundamental to black women's oppression. (Collins 1990: 7)

Certainly, there are many counter-images. But Collins theorizes that even counter-images are made sense of in light of institutionalized inequalities. Cultural stereotypes about and controlling images of the masculinities associated with different groups of men are powerful forces that structure men's lives, identities, opportunities, and more.

Some of the scholars who make up what we refer to as the navigating masculinities tradition might not be readily considered (or consider themselves) "masculinities scholars" per se. And this is significant. Precisely because they may be focusing on other dimensions of inequality (such as race and class) that shape gendered inequality, this approach may not be reflected in the canon of masculinities scholarship as it is currently recognized. Two influential ethnographic accounts of urban life and education, respectively, exemplify this categorization process: Elijah Anderson's *Code of the Street* and Paul Willis's *Learning to*

Labour. Both studies address men and masculinity, yet neither is typically taught in courses on men and masculinities.

The Code of the Street (Anderson 1999) is traditionally taught as an ethnography about race and class as Anderson follows young African American men navigating the challenges of urban poverty. However, Anderson's study is a great example of some of the tensions that navigating masculinities perspectives seek to address. He discusses the intricate ways that young black men living in the inner city learn how to alter their performances of self in public—a practice he refers to as "code switching"—in ways that enable them to collect respect, to maintain status, and perhaps, most importantly, to avoid violence. He writes, "There is a sense that violence is just below the surface in some pockets of the community. That fact necessitates a careful way of moving, of acting, of getting up and doing the streets" (Anderson 1999: 23). The interactional strategies on which these young men rely are gendered, but Anderson uses race and class as the primary lenses through which he seeks to explain their identities and experiences. In doing so, he articulates how young, mostly black men living in the inner city *navigate* masculine identities in ways that draw on intersections among their gender, race, class, age, location, and more.

Learning to Labour (Willis 1977) addresses similar intersecting forms of oppression in his study of education, class, and gender. In Willis's analysis of class reproduction in England, he sets out with the following premise: "The difficult thing to explain about why middle class kids get middle class jobs is why others let them. The difficult thing to explain about how working class kids get working class jobs is why they let themselves" (1977: 1).[2] Willis shows how the groups of boys he studied make meaning out of some of the harshest conditions English industrial society had to offer. Willis was fascinated by "shop floor culture" and the ways in which men working in industrial factories found ways of forging identities and making meaning out of the alienating and dehumanizing conditions industrial economies produce. And yet, "despite the dispossession, despite the bad conditions, despite the external directions, despite the subjective ravages, people do look for meaning, they do impose frameworks, they do seek enjoyment in activity, they do exercise their abilities" (Willis 1979: 188). For working-class boys and men enduring or preparing to endure industrial wage labor on the shop floor, Willis suggests that we simply cannot understand their experience, their performances of self, or their conceptualizations of masculinity without paying attention to their social class and the economic conditions under which their identities and practices were forged.

Although much of the research relying on this perspective considers race and class equally important to (if not more important than) gender, navigating masculinities perspectives do not all highlight racial or class dynamics. Rather, they are critically interested in interrogating intersections between distinct (although inseparable) systems of inequality and axes of identity. For some scholars, this means taking the role of religion seriously when seeking to understand masculinities (e.g., Archer 2001; Robinson and Spivey 2007; Wolkomir 2001, 2006) or the role of location or context (e.g., Coltrane 1994; Bridges 2009). For others, it means considering the ways that masculinity and sexuality are intimately interconnected (e.g., Lehne 1976; Connell 1992; Kimmel 1994; Pascoe 2007). Still others stress the significance of class (e.g., Fine et al. 1997; Lamont 2000; Pyke 1996) and race (e.g., Ferguson 2001; Gutmann 1996; hooks 2003; Marriott 2000; Staples 1982) as central in any meaningful understanding of masculinities. By stressing different axes of identity, this body of scholarship illustrates how different groups forge masculinities out of different sets of circumstances and resources.

Often, however, as Crenshaw (1991) and Collins (1990) suggest, navigating masculinities scholarship does negotiate multiple identities and inequalities simultaneously. This makes breaking these scholars up into those who simply consider gender *and* class or gender *and* race, for instance, less meaningful. Many of these scholars also do not cite the feminist theory initially conceptualizing intersectionality. Indeed, they may not even use the term. Yet, we suggest that intersectional theorizing about inequality was a necessary precondition for navigating masculiniti*es* theory and perspectives to emerge. Chong-suk Han's (2007) essay on gay men of color highlights this in a dynamic way. In Han's essay, he carefully unpacks the ways that stereotypes of gay men (from both within and outside the gay community itself) promote a very white image of "gay" (see also Muñoz 1999). Using Collins's (1990) language, we might suggest that the controlling image for gay masculinity is a white man. Han addresses the variety of explicit and implicit forms of racial bias that create different experiences of sexual identification for gay men of color. As Muñoz (1999) argues, sexual identification for men of color is often a dual process of, first, "disidentifying" with controlling images of "gay," and, next, forging gay identities that counter these images in significant ways. Beyond this, Steve Valocchi (1999) discusses gay identities as "class inflected" as well, charting the historical path along which gay identities started out as politically motivated and turned into what Valocchi refers to as "lifestyle categories"—lifestyles only a portion of those identifying as gay can economically achieve. From a navigating masculinities perspective, this means that theorizing about masculinity and sexuality requires attending to race and class dynamics as well. As this brief example illustrates, navigating masculinities approaches do not simply add an identity element to the mix. Rather, they attempt to illustrate the complexity of systems of power and inequality by examining how different forms of inequality deeply rely on and reinforce one another.

SECTION SUMMARY

Although multiple masculinities is established in the field, with Connell's (1995) theoretical framework serving as the dominant model, navigating masculinities perspectives lack a common reliance on a key set of texts. Thus, it would be more difficult, for instance, to argue that there is a central scholar—and potentially even a group of scholars—primarily associated with this theoretical perspective. Scholars exploring the tensions between masculinities and different sets of intersecting identities, issues, and ideologies continue to chart new territory in scholarship on masculinities. Thus far, however, we suggest that there have been two dominant conceptual breakthroughs within the navigating masculinities perspective. First, scholars have deployed intersectional feminist approaches to examining groups of socially and structurally marginalized men. Some scholars even turn this intersectional lens back on relatively privileged groups of men as well—"studying up" on inequality, as Messner (1996) refers to the practice. Second, scholars have applied Pierre Bourdieu's (1984) theory (initially intended to address class inequality) to considerations of masculinity. This latter approach offers fresh theoretical insights on intersecting in-equalities and may help avoid the trap of individualizing by categorizing masculinities as an ever-expanding array of "types" that Messner (Reading 14) warned against in the multiple masculinities section. The first four essays in this section illustrate some of the groundbreaking work utilizing insights from intersectional theory. Kristen Barber's essay (Reading 19)—explained in more detail below—is a powerful illustration of both of these trends. And the final four essays take a Bourdieuian approach to address issues with which navigating masculinities theories are primarily concerned.

We begin this section with Richard Mora's (Reading 16) theorization of the role of puberty in gender identification processes among Latino boys. Whereas puberty is often understood as a physiological process, Mora is interested in the social and cultural dynamics by which boys learn to view their own and their peers' bodies as masculine (or not). He investigates intersections among race, nationality, gender, sexuality, age, and embodiment, structuring the ways the boys he studied learned about the significance of their bodies from their peer groups, families, popular culture, and overlapping (yet dissimilar) gender orders in the United States and Puerto Rican and Dominican society. Although he does not directly frame his work with Collins's (1990) theory of intersectionality, the boys in Mora's research can be made sense of by considering the "images" with which they identify and by which they are identified by others. In Reading 17, Mark Anthony Neal builds on an intersectional theorization of black masculinity. Neal provides a cultural and textual analysis of hip-hop artist Shawn Carter (Jay-Z) to address the ways in which controlling images work to structure the ways black masculinities are produced and consumed in commercial hip-hop culture. Jay-Z's cosmopolitanism creates what Neal refers to as an "illegible" black masculinity. What makes distinct configurations of masculinity legible or illegible provides a powerful intersectional analysis of systems of power and inequality.

Amy Wilkins (Reading 18) and Kristen Barber (Reading 19) both turn an intersectional lens on young, straight, white men. But in looking at this group intersectionally, both scholars critically interrogate how whiteness and heterosexuality meaningfully intersect with and shape masculinities among populations of men not often considered intersectionally. Wilkins introduces the term "masculinity dilemmas" to theorize the ways that young, white, straight Christian men discursively masculinize abstinence in ways that are not so different from the discursive strategies among a subcultural group of goth men that similarly attempt to rework dominant meanings associated with masculinity. Wilkins's concept and research result in a powerful illustration of how dominant ideologies can be intersectionally upheld, even among groups that might seem fundamentally at odds with each other and with dominant meanings associated with masculinity. Barber's analysis of professional, white, straight men who participate in culturally feminized grooming practices by frequenting expensive hair salons builds on a similar line of analysis. Like Wilkins, Barber illustrates how masculinity is profitably understood as a discourse such that any behavior can be "masculinized" in ways that shore up existing systems of power and inequality. Barber also relies on the social theory of Pierre Bourdieu to theorize the ways that the white, heterosexual men she studied relied on the hair salon as a way of embodying class and drawing symbolic boundaries between themselves as "Other" men. We briefly explain Pierre Bourdieu's central theoretical project before explaining how other scholars in this section use this framework to build intersectional theories.

Pierre Bourdieu is not a scholar typically associated with intersectionality. He was a French social theorist primarily interested in the reproduction of class inequalities through tastes and aesthetic dispositions. His most famous text—*Distinction: A Social Critique of the Judgement of Taste* (1984)—critically addresses the ways that social inequalities are reproduced via individual tastes.[3] Tastes are, for Bourdieu, far from individual. They are part of the building blocks that allow different groups (for Bourdieu, social classes) to come to think of themselves as radically different from one another. Everything from tastes in food and drink, to music preferences, to clothing, and more are part of a social process that situates desires hierarchically and establishes what sociologists Michèle Lamont and Annette Lareau (1988) refer to as "symbolic boundaries" between groups of individuals (see also Lamont and Molnár 2002). Tastes, Bourdieu suggests, get inside of us and become some of the primary materials out of which systems of power and inequality reproduce themselves. His basic idea is that we all appropriate, through choice and desire, routines and practices that actually result from material constraints. Simply put, Bourdieu is interested in the ways that tastes stratify. Some navigating masculinities scholars apply Bourdieu's analysis of class reproduction to forge a more intersectional theoretical framework for considerations of masculinity and inequality.

Masculinities scholars have deployed Bourdieu's theory in a number of different ways. Kristen Barber (Reading 19) relies on Bourdieu to analyze intersections among gender, race, class, and embodiment in ways that allow her to illustrate how straight men's participation in typically feminized salon hair care practices produce a "styled masculinity" strategically deployed in ways that further entrench these men's race, class, gender, and sexual privilege.[4] In Reading 20, Matthew Desmond uses Bourdieu's theorization of class inequality to investigate how and why young men growing up in rural communities become wildland firefighters. Similar to Willis's consideration of working-class boys in England, Desmond theorizes the ways that gender and class socialization intersect in ways that produce what he refers to as a "country boy habitus"—a configuration of identity that produces the raw materials for the identities required of wildland firefighters. Next, Adam Reich (Reading 21) applies a Bourdieuian perspective to make sense of the experiences of groups of boys in a youth correctional facility. Reich builds on Messerschmidt's (Reading 15) theorization of masculinity as "structured action" by relying on Bourdieu's metaphor of social life as a game to make sense of the masculine identity projects he observed among primarily nonwhite, lower-class boys and young men. Reich suggests that the boys come to the correctional facility invested in one game—"outsider masculinity"—and the institution attempts to get them to invest in a new game—"insider masculinity." This metaphor enables Reich to interrogate intersections between systems of inequality and social institutions. Although he does not frame his analysis with the compensatory masculinity framework, Reich's analysis implicitly infuses a greater sense of agency to the performances of masculinity that have often been framed solely as *reactions* to existing structures of power (e.g., Majors and Billson 1992; hooks 2003; Collins 2004). Subsequently, Anthony Ocampo (Reading 22) theorizes how gay, second-generation Mexican American and Filipino

American men navigate gendered and racialized sexual identities in different contexts. Stereotypes of gay masculinity are often associated with white, middle-, and upper-class men. Yet, the men in Ocampo's study did not recognize their sexual identities or desires in these controlling images of gay masculinity. Ocampo relies on Bourdieu's notion of "fields" to theorize the ways Latino and Filipino gay men navigate gender, sexual, racial, and cultural identities in distinct social contexts, creatively adapting contextually contingent gendered scripts for identity and behavior.

The final reading in this section—Tony Coles's "Negotiating the Field of Masculinity"—(Reading 23) fuses Connell's theory of masculinities with Bourdieu's theory of social reproduction. Coles articulates a theoretical model capable of acknowledging a diversity of culturally dominant masculinities bound by an overarching field of masculinity. Coles's blending of theoretical insights from both Connell and Bourdieu to conceptualize what he refers to as the "field of masculinity" addresses many of the concerns central to the navigating masculinities perspective: intersections among gender, race, class, sexuality, embodiment, setting, and more. And, significantly, Coles does not understand his model as incompatible with Connell's multiple masculinities perspective. Bourdieu's conceptualization of "field," Coles suggests, offers a theoretical device for the consideration of overlapping systems of power and inequality. From intersectional analyses, to controlling images and the matrix of domination, to compensatory choreographies of masculinity among marginalized and subordinated groups, navigating masculinities scholars examine the unequal access different groups have to culturally exalted forms of masculinity, their attempts to symbolically gain access, and the production of multiple dominant masculinities. Throughout this theorizing, navigating masculinities scholars all make sure to highlight the ways that different forms of power and inequality (e.g., gender, class, race, sexuality) are best understood as working collaboratively to reproduce existing forms of power and inequality.

REFERENCES

Anderson, Elijah. 1999. *Code of the Street: Decency, Violence, and the Moral Life of the Inner City.* New York and London: Norton.

Archer, Louise. 2001. "'Muslim Brothers, Black Lads, Traditional Asians': British Muslim Young Men's Constructions of Race, Religion and Masculinity." *Feminism & Psychology* 11 (1): 79–105.

Bettie, Julie. 2003. *Women without Class: Girls, Race, and Identity.* Berkeley: University of California Press.

Bourdieu, Pierre. 1984. *Distinction: A Social Critique of the Judgement of Taste.* Cambridge, MA: Harvard University Press.

Bourdieu, Pierre, and Loïc Wacquant. 1992. *An Invitation to Reflexive Sociology.* Chicago: University of Chicago Press.

Bridges, Tristan. 2009. "Gender Capital and Male Bodybuilders." *Body & Society* 15 (1): 83–107.

Collins, Patricia Hill. 1990. *Black Feminist Thought: Knowledge, Consciousness and the Politics of Empowerment.* Boston: HarperCollins.

Collins, Patricia Hill. 2004. "Booty Call: Sex, Violence, and Images of Black Masculinity." In *Black Sexual Politics: African Americans, Gender, and the New Racism,* 149–80. London: Routledge.

Coltrane, Scott. 1994. "Theorizing Masculinities in Contemporary Social Science." In *Theorizing Masculinities*, edited by Harry Brod and Michael Kaufman, 39–60. London: Sage.

Connell, Raewyn. 1992. "A Very Straight Gay: Masculinity, Homosexual Experience, and the Dynamics of Gender." *American Sociological Review* 57 (6): 735–51.

Connell, Raewyn. 1995. *Masculinities*. Berkeley: University of California Press.

Crenshaw, Kimberlé. 1989. "Demarginalizing the Intersection of Race and Sex: A Black Feminist Critique of Antidiscrimination Doctrine, Feminist Theory and Antiracist Politics." *University of Chicago Legal Forum* 1989: 139–67.

Crenshaw, Kimberlé. 1991. "Mapping the Margins: Intersectionality, Identity Politics, and Violence against Women of Color." *Stanford Law Review* 43 (6): 1241–99.

Ferguson, Ann Arnet. 2001. *Bad Boys: Public Schools in the Making of Black Masculinity*. Ann Arbor: University of Michigan.

Fine, Michelle, Lois Weis, Judi Addelston, and Julia Marusza. 1997. "(In)Secure Times: Constructing White Working-Class Masculinities in the Late 20th Century." *Gender & Society* 11 (1): 52–68.

Frye, Marilyn. 1983. *Politics of Reality: Essays in Feminist Theory*. Trumansburg, NY: Crossing Press.

Gutmann, Matthew. 1996. *The Meanings of Macho: Being a Man in Mexico City*. Berkeley: University of California Press.

Han, Chong-suk. 2007. "They Don't Want to Cruise Your Type: Gay Men of Color and the Racial Politics of Exclusion." *Social Identities* 13 (1): 51–67.

Hondagneu-Sotelo, Pierette, and Michael Messner. 1994. "Gender Displays and Men's Power: The 'New Man' and the Mexican Immigrant Man." In *Theorizing Masculinities*, edited by Harry Brod and Michael Kaufman, 200–18. London: Sage.

hooks, bell. 1984. *Feminist Theory: From Margin to Center*. Cambridge, MA: South End Press.

hooks, bell. 2003. *We Real Cool: Black Men and Masculinity*. New York: Routledge.

Jenkins, Richard. 1992. *Pierre Bourdieu*. London: Routledge.

Kimmel, Michael. 1994. "Masculinity as Homophobia: Fear, Shame and Silence in the Construction of Gender Identity." In *Theorizing Masculinities*, edited by Harry Brod and Michael Kaufman, 119–41. London: Sage.

Kimmel, Michael S. 1990. "After Fifteen Years: The Impact of the Sociology of Masculinity on the Masculinity of Sociology." In *Men, Masculinities and Social Theory*, edited by Harry Brod and David Morgan, 93–109. London: Unwin Hyman.

Lamont, Michèle. 2000. *The Dignity of Working Men: Morality and the Boundaries of Race, Class, and Immigration*. Boston: Harvard University Press.

Lamont, Michèle, and Annette Lareau. 1988. "Cultural Capital: Allusions, Gaps and Glissandos in Recent Theoretical Developments." *Sociological Theory* 6(2): 153–68.

Lamont, Michèle, and Virág Molnár. 2002. "The Study of Boundaries in the Social Sciences." *Annual Review of Sociology* 28: 167–195.

Lehne, Gregory. 1976. "Homophobia among Men." In *The Forty-Nine Percent Majority*, edited by Deborah David and Robert Brannon, 66–88. Reading, MA: Addison-Wesley.

Majors, Richard, and Janet Mancini Billson. 1992. *Cool Pose: The Dilemmas of Black Manhood in America*. New York: Touchstone.

Marriott, David. 2000. *On Black Men*. New York: Columbia University Press.

Messner, Michael. 1996. "Studying Up On Sex." *Sociology of Sport Journal* 13 (3): 221–37.

Muñoz, José Esteban. 1999. *Disidentifications: Queers of Color and the Performance of Politics*. Minneapolis: University of Minnesota Press.

Pascoe, C. J. 2007. *Dude, You're a Fag: Masculinity and Sexuality in High School*. Berkeley: University of California Press.

Pyke, Karen D. 1996. "Class-Based Masculinities: The Interdependence of Gender, Class, and Interpersonal Power." *Gender & Society* 10 (5): 527–49.

Robinson, Christine M., and Sue E. Spivey. 2007. "The Politics of Masculinity and the Ex-Gay Movement." *Gender & Society* 21 (5): 650–75.

Staples, Robert. 1982. *Black Masculinity: The Black Male's Role in American Society*. San Francisco: Black Scholar Press.

Valocchi, Steve. 1999. "The Class-Inflected Nature of Gay Identity." *Social Problems* 46 (2): 207–24.

Willis, Paul. 1977. *Learning to Labor: How Working Class Kids Get Working Class Jobs*. New York: Columbia University Press.

Willis, Paul. 1979. "Shop Floor Culture, Masculinity and the Wage Form." In *Working-Class Culture: Studies in History and Theory*, edited by John Clarke, Chas Critcher, and Richard Johnson, 185–98. London: Hutchinson.

Wolkomir, Michelle. 2001. "Wrestling with the Angels of Meaning: The Revisionist Ideological Work of Gay and Ex-Gay Christian Men." *Symbolic Interaction* 24 (4): 407–25.

Wolkomir, Michelle. 2006. *Be Not Deceived: The Sacred and Sexual Struggles of Gay and Ex-Gay Christian Men*. New Brunswick, NJ: Rutgers University Press.

NOTES

1. "Cisgender" is a term that compliments transgender. It emerged to avoid terms like "non-transgender," "bio man," or "bio woman" (both of which reiterate the symbolic power of biological sex). Cisgender refers to individuals whose gender identities match the identities they were assigned at birth. For instance, a person who identifies as a man and who was born with a male body would qualify as a cisgender man.

2. Willis's subtitle—*How Working Class Kids Get Working Class Jobs*—reveals the extent to which he himself doesn't think of himself as a masculinities scholar. A key function of the way these kids get these jobs is through the way masculinity works. Thus, the title might more accurately read *How Working Class Boys Get Working Class Jobs*, an issue Julie Bettie (2003) thoughtfully addresses in her ethnography of race, class, and gender dynamics in an American high school.

3. For an introduction to the social theory of Pierre Bourdieu, see Richard Jenkins's (1992) introduction to Pierre Bourdieu's theory and Pierre Bourdieu and Loïc Wacquant's (1992) *An Invitation to Reflexive Sociology*.

4. See also Bridges (2009) for an analysis of Bourdieu's theory of class reproduction to make sense of symbolic boundaries between male bodybuilders and other men.

RICHARD MORA

16. LATINO BOYS, MASCULINITY, AND PUBERTY

Pubescence brings about the most noticeable changes to the male body, second only to neonatal development (Martin 1996). The social meanings ascribed to these physical changes, and puberty itself, are locally situated (Janssen 2006). Hence, understanding how boys make sense of puberty and how they interpret and socially construct their bodies during pubescence may illuminate how boys' bodies figure into their gender identities. Yet the literature lacks thorough and sustained *in situ* examinations of how diverse boys employ their bodies to construct masculine identities during pubescence across a range of sociocultural contexts.

The present chapter contributes to the literature on masculinity by examining how 10 sixth-grade, second-generation immigrant Dominican and Puerto Rican boys, who publicly acknowledge that they are experiencing puberty, construct their masculine identities and employ their bodies at school. The relationship between the boys' gender construction and physiological development emerged early in a two-and-a-half year ethnographic study. Not assuming *a priori* that puberty mattered to the boys allowed for emic understandings of how the peer group influenced boys' views of their bodies and pubescence. The data suggest that among the boys, puberty was a social accomplishment connected to masculine enactments informed by the dominant gendered expectations of peers at school and in their neighborhoods, the hegemonic masculine practices espoused by commercial hip-hop rappers, and the dominant gender orders in the United States and both Dominican and Puerto Rican societies.

LITERATURE

Currently, boys enter puberty approximately 2 1/2 years earlier than their counterparts did at the beginning of the twentieth century (Frankel 2003). The age range for the onset of puberty in boys today is 9 to 14 years (compared to 8 to 13 years in girls) (Katz and Misra 2011). The mean age of initial growth spurts for boys is approximately 11 years, roughly 2 years later than for girls (Abbassi 1998; Katz and Misra 2011). As a result, sixth-grade classrooms are spaces that may include boys yet to experience pubescence and girls who look like young women (Eccles 1999). Boys who experience puberty later than their peers tend to experience greater anxiety and be less popular (Martin 1996). Retrospective data based on interviews with a group of mostly white working- and middle-class high school students suggest that, compared to girls, boys tend to experience puberty alone and hardly discuss such matters with peers (Martin 1996).

The few empirical studies that consider the relationship between puberty and masculinity are retrospective medical and psychological works that include few, if any, nonwhite participants. These studies suggest that adolescent boys view masculinity as an accomplishment, with no clear connection to sexual maturation (Martin 1996; Stein and Reiser 1994). Since the body undergoes biological and social changes over the life course (Schilling 1993), however, it seems likely that there is a connection among boys' construction of masculinity, their social identities, and their physiological development. Consequently, an *in situ* study of boys' enactments of masculinity during puberty is warranted.

Aware that their bodies are interpreted and gendered by others, boys from distinct socioeconomic and racial backgrounds work on their bodies with the intent of achieving the ideal male physique ascribed with high masculine status (McCabe and Ricciardelli

This reading is an author adaptation of Richard Mora's article, "'Do It for All Your Pubic Hairs!': Latino Boys, Masculinity, and Puberty," *Gender & Society* 26 (2012): 433–60.

2004; Pope et al. 2000). Consequently, boys consider a "flabby body" less manly (Lilleaas 2007: 42). British research suggests that males of varying ages associate fat with lack of control and weakness (Grogan and Richards 2002). Although there is some evidence that Latino men may also disapprove of flabbiness (Pope et al. 2000: 206), little is known about Latino boys' views of their bodies.

In schools, boys of distinct ages, races, and social classes negotiate masculine identities and social standing by demonstrating their physical dexterity, strength, and athleticism (Davison 2000; Eder et al. 1995; Hasbrook and Harris 1999). On school campuses, sports often provide a venue for successful gender performances (Connell 2005). Boys who use their bodies successfully during sporting activities can amass "physical capital" and, thus, gain "masculine" status.

Although boys at school typically try on and test masculine identities in the presence of friends (Ferguson 2001; Pascoe 2007), they nonetheless often construct their masculinities by regulating gender boundaries (Ferguson 2001; Kehily 2001; Pascoe 2007; Renold 2001, 2005; Swain 2003; Witt 2000). Often it is high-status boys who dictate the hegemonic masculinities that regulate and maintain the gender order (Gardiner 2000; Lopez 2003; Mac an Ghaill 1994; Martino 1999, 2000; Martino and Pallotta-Chiarolli 2003; McGuffey and Rich 1999; Pascoe 2007; Swain 2000, 2003). Among boys, masculinity typically involves performing dominant heterosexual identities (Martino and Pallotta-Chiarolli 2003; Renold 2005), with peers regularly policing heterosexuality (Chambers et al. 2004; Epstein et al. 2000; Nayak and Kehily 2001; Pascoe 2007). The "panopticonic regimes of surveillance" present in peer groups normalize heterosexuality (Martino and Pallotta-Chiarolli 2003) and promote "compulsory heterosexuality" within peer groups (Korobov 2005; Pascoe 2007; Redman et al. 2002). Hence, many boys across racial and class groups define their gender identities against "the dual Others," namely girls and boys deemed feminine (Epstein 2001: 106; Gilbert and Gilbert 1998; Haywood and Mac an Ghaill 2001; Nilan 2000; Thorne 1993). Peers accuse those who do not live up to heteronormative expectations of being homosexuals (Dalley-Trim 2007; Eliasson et al. 2007;

Pascoe 2007; Renold 2003), interactionally reiterating the importance of heterosexuality.

Boys from varied racial and class backgrounds construct masculinity differently. For second-generation Caribbean youth, for example, proving masculinity is an experience that involves racial stigma (Lopez 2003). Furthermore, some young men of color in the United States, especially those who are working-class or poor, adopt coping mechanisms, such the "cool pose" used by African Americans males (Majors and Billson 1993) and the "masculine protest behaviors" of urban youth, including Puerto Ricans (De La Cancela 1993: 34), to deal with marginalized positions in society. Boys and young men from low-income neighborhoods may enact masculinities that include the use of stoic personas—"tough fronts" by black youth (Dance 2002) and "cara de palo" (wooden club-face) by U.S.-based Puerto Ricans (Thomas 1987)—and the use of their bodies as weapons to gain status and ward off potential assailants (Majors and Billson 1993). Such presentations of self by urban youth are oftentimes part of a situated "code of the street," a set of cultural ideas that dictate social expectations and conduct in urban localities, particularly those where neighborhood violence is common (Anderson 2000).

Studies of masculine practices among U.S. Latinos and Latin American men tend to focus on *machismo*, or the cult of manliness (Arciniega et al. 2008; De La Cancela 1993; Falicov 2010; Gutmann 1996; Mirandé 1997; Torres et al. 2002). Early research equated machismo with behaviors attributed to working-class men and peasants from Latin America (Ramírez 1999), including male dominance, assertiveness, aggressiveness, and the valuing of physical strength and courage (Mosher 1991). However, Latin American women and individuals from various non–Latin American cultures and countries also display characteristics associated with machismo (Doyle 1995). In addition, the term carries different meanings in different Latin American countries (De La Cancela 1993), and some variants are not rooted in the dominance of women (Doyle 1995). As a result, many scholars have moved away from simplified conceptualizations of the meanings of machismo (De La Cancela 1991; Gutmann 1996; Mirandé 1997; Torres et al. 2002). Rather than focusing on characteristics that may be classified as machismo (which simultaneously essentializes Latino cultures), the present study examines the influence of dominant gender norms from various gender orders on the boys' masculine performativity.

Let us turn, then, to studies examining the dominant masculine expectations in both the Dominican Republic and Puerto Rico. In the Dominican Republic, De Moya (2004) finds hegemonic masculinity to be associated with heteronormativity and displays of power and both physical and rhetorical dominance. In Puerto Rico, "masculine ideology" also includes the objectification of women, stresses sexuality and heteronormativity, demands that men be providers, and emphasizes male competition (Ramírez 1999: 43–44). Research suggests that, like their Puerto Rican counterparts, Puerto Rican youth in the United States who embrace hypermasculinity typically identify strongly with their ethnicity and nationality (Saez et al. 2009). These three studies and those discussed prior to them inform this chapter's theoretical framework.

RESEARCH AND METHODS

This chapter is based on data collected in the first four months of a two-and-a-half-year ethnography that followed a group of sixth graders at Romero Elementary and Middle School, a bilingual school in the greater metropolitan area of a northeastern city. (All names, including that of the school, have been changed.) At the time of the study, Romero had a total student enrollment of approximately 380, of which approximately 85 percent were Latina/o. The middle school had approximately 90 students, of which more than 95 percent were Latina/o. More than 75 percent of all students received free lunches. The focus of this chapter is primarily on 10 of the boys—7 second-generation Dominicans and 3 second-generation Puerto Rican boys who acknowledged, enacted, and maintained their heritages, as described below. Throughout the school day, I observed the boys and their peers in and out of the classroom.

At Romero, students of Latin American heritage referred to whites as Americanos (Americans) and regularly identified themselves and each other by their nations of origin. Students whose parents were born in the Dominican Republic, for example, referred to themselves as "Dominicans" and less often as "Latino," "Hispanic," or "Spanish." Many of the students publicly demonstrated their national pride by writing "DR#1" (i.e., Dominican Republic is no. 1) or "PR#1" (i.e., Puerto Rico is no. 1) on desks and in textbooks and by wearing accessories with their home country's national flag. These students had such strong attachment to their Caribbean countries of origin because they visited regularly and participated in transnationalism, sustaining "multi-stranded social relations that link[ed] their societies of origin and settlement" (Basch et al. 1994: 8). During their visits, the boys were exposed to gender norms that gave primacy to dominant, heteronormative masculinity.

Like many young men in their neighborhoods, the boys defined themselves as urban, working-class males with ties to their respective countries of origin. As such, they identified with Latino and black rappers who view the streets as "the school of hard knocks." The boys especially liked rappers who embodied a tough, heterosexual masculinity and displayed dominance, physical strength, and a willingness to use violence. Conversely, the boys rejected wholesome-seeming singers, like the white Justin Timberlake, whose masculine embodiment did not reflect the urban, ethnoracial masculinities they imagined themselves achieving someday.

In the boys' neighborhoods, fights among youths were regular occurrences. Those who did not defend themselves or seek retribution were ridiculed and called "pussies," "bitches," and/or "fags." Thus, in line with the local "code of the street," the boys adopted tough personas and expressed a willingness to fight. Many of their teachers worried that some of the boys would join local street gangs. The boys, however, expressed no interest.

The analysis of the data did not utilize the term machismo. The term was not emic because none of the students observed used the term machismo to describe masculine behavior. Furthermore, the negative connotations associated with machismo would racially bias the interpretation of the data. The fact that a wide range of characteristics are associated with *machismo* limits its explanatory power. As a result, machismo is an inadequate descriptor of these findings.

FINDINGS

Representative data in the following sections illustrate how Latino boys at Romero performed masculinity within their peer group during pubescence. The first section documents how the boys referenced their bodies and puberty during playful interactions. The second section considers the boys' longing for muscular male physiques like those in their multiple social worlds. The third section examines how the boys displayed physical strength and punished their bodies to prove their manliness. The last and final section briefly discusses how the boys enacted masculinity after the sixth grade.

"PUBERTY IS NOW": CHANGING BODIES

While in the sixth grade, the boys were experiencing sexual maturation—a fact they declared publicly. During a science class discussion on physical development, for example, one boy loudly interjected, "Puberty is now." In addition, the boys' exchanges regularly included references to puberty and the accompanying biological changes. When a boy appeared exceedingly "wild" (i.e., hyperactive), the other boys attributed it to hormonal changes brought on by puberty and, using language introduced by one of them, jokingly rebuked him with statements such as, "Control your hormones!" and "Let your hormones relax, c'mon. Your hormones are gonna get tired." Contrary to retrospective accounts of high school students (Martin 1996), the boys at Romero experienced puberty within their homosocial group, rather than alone.

The boys also referenced puberty in ways that defined the construction of and boundaries surrounding masculine status within their peer group. An exchange about male genitalia, for example, led Brandon to ask Steven whether he had experienced his first menstruation:

> [In class] Michael makes fun of Steven by referencing an episode of *South Park* in which a boy has a penis and scrotum growing on his chin. Michael says: "Steven got a little dicky and scrotum on his chin. And it is growing every day."
>
> Brandon joins in: "Steven, did you get your period yet?"

Brandon's depiction of Steven as a premenstrual girl called both Steven's gender and his pubescent development into question. Here menarche, as a signifier of femininity, is used to interactionally undermine Steven's masculinity. Participating in banter and verbal one-upmanship was a cultural, gendered expectation the boys willingly met. Like other working-class Dominican (De Moya 2004) and Puerto Rican (Ramírez 1999) youth, the boys constructed gender identities and relations of power within their verbal exchanges.

Like other boys (Dixon 1997; Martino and Pallotta-Chiarolli 2003), the boys at Romero viewed penises as appendages distinguishing boys from girls and as associated with males' manhood and dominance. They frequently brought up male genitalia to playfully disparage one another's masculine identities, highlighting the interplay between the body and the construction of gendered identities (Butler 1993; Connell 2005). One afternoon, banter about a banana resulted in the charge that Rudy, the shortest boy, had an undersized penis:

> During lunchtime, Michael holds out a peeled banana, wiggles it, and says, "Look, it's crooked." A two-inch long piece of banana breaks off and lands on the table. Michael says, "Look, Steven—he lost his manhood. It fell off."
>
> Steven smiles and says, "That's Rudy's." Cesar chimes in, "Yeah, it's like this"—Cesar holds out his pinkie finger and smiles.

Steven and Cesar used Rudy to demarcate the low masculine status attributed to smaller male bodies. As the only boy referred to as "shrimp," "small fry," or "enano" ["midget"], Rudy was not perceived as physically dominant, which led to the accusation that he had a small penis. In all, I documented 43 references to secondary sex characteristics during the sixth grade, of which nearly two dozen were public acts of verbal one-upmanship.

The boys mentioned penises much more during the sixth grade than during any other period thereafter and stopped publicly referencing puberty after the sixth grade. This stark difference in the boys' interactions reveals just how significant the initial phases of their physical development were to them.

BODIES IN TRANSITION

The boys compared the size of their flexed biceps and the firmness of their abdomens on almost a daily basis. They also openly shared their desire to possess the "sociocultural ideal male physique"—strong, lean, muscular, and fit (McCabe and Ricciardelli 2004). A telling example of how much they yearned for muscular bodies worthy of admiration is a portrait one of them drew of himself and his four closest classmates. The drawing, which according to the illustrator depicted his friends and him "in five or six years," was of five stoic young men, each wearing a tank top and baggy pants, with extremely muscular arms and chests, relatively small waists, and a weapon—a knife, gun, or crowbar—in his hand. The figures represented the physiological aesthetic the boys were interested in replicating—namely, that of the muscular rappers they favored and of young men in their social worlds who valued strong, dominant bodies.

Both broad and localized cultural expectations associated with masculinity and male bodies informed the boys' imaginings of their future bodies and selves. Consider Michael's reference to gladiators in a fantasy replete with his desire for a tough, sculpted body:

> As students worked independently on an assignment on ancient Rome, Michael says to me, "Richard, I'm going to build a time machine and go back [to ancient Rome]. I'm going to work out so when I go I'm strong. I'm going to get a scar." He moves a finger along his right cheek. "I'm going to fight like the gladiators."

For both cultural and practical reasons, Michael and the rest of the boys valued tough, strong bodies skilled at fighting. Their cultural expectation was that men defend themselves (De Moya 2004; Ramírez 1999). Practically, Michael and the boys were cognizant that in their neighborhoods strong male bodies became dangerous weapons during physical fights and, because of their association with the capacity to inflict harm, were also highly valued outside of fights.

Since the boys prized musculature, they were preoccupied with the amount of fat (or "flubber") on their bodies. Like other boys (James 2000), they held fatness in low regard, equating it with a lack of bodily control and strength. A telling incident transpired after the nurse summoned the entire class for an annual health examination. Pedro and Rodrigo came into the room smiling and in a celebratory tone simultaneously yelled, "I don't have no flubber!" Aware that others scrutinized their bodies, many of the boys "with flubber" masked their concerns with self-deprecating humor. Michael, who wanted to be a gladiator, occasionally lifted his shirt, exposing his stomach, and asked peers, "Do you think I'm fat?" The handful of boys who had flubber also sought to communicate that they were physically strong. For example, while discussing his physical appearance with a thinner, taller female classmate, a boy stated, "I don't care if I don't have a six-pack. I got muscles. That's why you couldn't take the ball away from me [during the basketball game]." Similarly, consider what James said to Michael during a tense dispute:

> Michael says James is fatter than he is. James frowns and says, "I work out with my [adult] brother. I bet you don't even work out. I am better than you in every sport, except baseball. I don't play baseball."

By highlighting his superior athleticism, James dismissed Michael's comment and communicated that although fatter, his was the more "successful body" (Drummond 2003). As the data show, the boys ascribed masculine status to musculature, which they considered proof of a boy's physical transition beyond boyhood and of his willingness to transform his physique.

PHYSICAL STRENGTH, TOUGHNESS, AND MASCULINE STATUS

At Romero, there were no school-sanctioned sports teams. Thus, unlike the boys in other studies (Eder et al. 1995; Swain 2000, 2003), the boys at Romero lacked the opportunity to gain masculine status on the field or court. This may partially explain why boys engaged in a wide array of other physical activities—arm wrestling matches, bloody knuckles, and slap hands—banned by the school to curtail confrontations. With these physical enactments, the boys sought to initiate themselves into manhood while exploring, defining, and patrolling the boundaries of their collective masculine practices.

The boys regularly tried to convince each other to engage in public physical challenges. For example, one afternoon, Raul held out his right clenched fist and invited another boy to play "bloody knuckles" with him: "C'mon, punch my knuckles. It's like a massage. It doesn't hurt me. It's like a massage. C'mon, give me a massage." When rebuffed, boys usually tried to goad prospective competitors with statements such as "Don't be a sissy" and "Don't be a girl." More often than not, boys who declined a challenge were met with ridicule. All this peer pressure and gender policing rarely failed.

Most notably, the boys publicly asserted masculine identities during arm wrestling matches, the outcomes of which the boys used to rank themselves. Each match was an opportunity for boys to display physical strength and acquire "physical capital" within their social world regardless of their physical size (Swain 2000, 2003). Note the following lunchtime arm wrestling session:

> Pedro, Ignacio, Bernardo, Adam, and Jason take turns arm wrestling one another.
> Jason beats Ignacio, looks over at me, and says nonchalantly, "Kids."
> Pedro points at Armando and says, "He's number one in arm wrestling."
> Jason nods and says, "Yeah, I don't know how he does it. I'm, like, number three." Pedro then says, "I'm, like, number four."

With his comment, Jason playfully associated his physically weaker peers with boyhood and, by contrast, himself with adolescence and manliness. Moreover, Armando, who despite being among the smallest boys in the group was the best arm wrestler, was praised for his feat. I observed roughly a dozen arm wrestling matches during each visit.

The boys arm wrestled older boys with bigger, more developed physiques. Most of the seventh- and eighth-grade boys accepted challenges only after the younger boys playfully took on tough personas and accused them of being "scared." The older boys won these matches decisively. However, interactions with older, male schoolmates were chances for the boys to test their physical strength and try on the stoic demeanor embodied by many rappers and many of the youth in their social worlds.

Over the course of the semester, the girls in their class peer group and those in the other sixth-grade class challenged the boys to arm wrestle approximately two dozen times. The boys rebuffed these challenges because many of their female peers were physically stronger, a fact the boys acknowledged only among themselves. For the boys, to arm wrestle girls *and lose* would have been humiliating since they publicly claimed that males are physically stronger than females.

The banter punctuating arm wrestling matches reified their notions of masculine dominance and heteronormativity. The boys belittled any boy who did not adequately display physical strength or other perceived masculine traits by calling him "a girl" or "a woman"—a finding echoed in previous research (e.g., Thorne 1993; Fine 1987). They levied such accusations, which reduced gender to a male–female binary, more than 50 times. Moreover, the boys' homosocial peer group also offered them "a performative space where heterosexuality and masculinity can be fused and displayed" (Kehily 2001: 179). Consistent with Pascoe's (2007) research, the boys also regularly lobbed joking accusations of homosexuality and unmanliness at one another. Here is a case in point:

> Ignacio asks Albert, "You're the son of a fag?"
> Albert smiles and screams, "Do it [arm wrestle] for all your pubic hairs!"

Using a homophobic slur that was common within the boys' peer group (see Mora 2013), Ignacio implied that Albert's poor performance was evidence of his father's homosexuality. Like his peers, Ignacio coupled heterosexual masculinity and physical strength—a perspective in line with the hegemonic masculinities in the boys' neighborhoods, in their respective countries of origin (De Moya 2004; Ramírez 1999), and in the United States (Connell 2005; Kimmel and Messner 1998). Albert, for his part, then associated boys' corporeal might with pubic hairs, a key signifier of puberty.

Whenever they used their bodies to best male peers, the boys made public declarations of manliness. On average, there were six brash comments, like "I'm a man" or "I'm the man," per day of observation. These loud proclamations drew the attention of teachers, one of whom assured me the boys "don't think of themselves as boys; they think of themselves as men." However, in time, I learned that when they referred to themselves as "men," the boys were simply voicing masculine aspirations. In one another's presence, the boys readily admitted being—as they put it—"pre-teenagers." Thus, with their declarations, the boys attempted to both make sense of their ongoing and impending physical development and shore up what they imagined to be their future masculine identities.

LITTLE BOYS, NO MORE

The boys were viewed as children by both their female classmates and their teachers. Similar to girls in previous research (Dixon 1997), the sixth-grade girls at Romero, who were generally taller and appeared older than their actual age, viewed their bodies as being closer to adulthood and maturity than the boys' bodies and, thus, associated the boys with childhood. Throughout my observations, there were 26 instances in which girls publicly referred to the boys as "little boys" because of what they deemed their "childish" behavior, such as punching lockers, arm wrestling, and play fighting. The boys' teachers also infantilized the boys with frequent, public chastisements for acting "like babies" when they "whined" about one another's behavior. Partly to avoid derision, the boys maintained their homosocial peer group during the sixth grade.

After the summer between the sixth and seventh grade, the boys returned to school physically transformed. All of them were taller, most of them taller than their female classmates, and most of them having shed much of the "flubber" that had occupied their minds months earlier. At the beginning of the seventh grade, their teachers and female peers complimented them on their physiological development, which may explain why many walked with swagger and confidence. Furthermore, from the seventh grade on, the boys rarely engaged in the physical games and challenges of "little boys." That is, they hardly made a public show of their physical strength or their ability to endure physical pain.

Instead, they ventured beyond their homosocial peer group and turned much of their attention to public displays of heteronormative masculinity. More to the point, they flirted with and tried to woo teenage girls, much like peers in the Dominican Republic, who, by the age of 12 or 13, were expected to "show a vivid and visible erotic interest in all females that come close" (De Moya 2004: 74). The most common form of flirting involved *piropos*, or "'amorous compliments,' often undesired by the females at whom they are directed" (Bailey 2000: 562). Among the 51 documented piropos were phrases used in Spanish songs and by older peers and relatives in their neighborhoods and countries of origin. For example, some of the boys regularly said something like, "¡Oh, mami! Tu sí 'tas buena. (Oh, baby! You are fine)." The boys delivered most of their piropos in the presence of male peers, who acknowledged particularly clever compliments and who were likely the *actual* audience for the boys' piropos.

Into the flirtatious exchanges, the boys and girls often incorporated sexual innuendos that called attention to their own developed bodies and to those of the individuals they desired. During these suggestive exchanges, boys displayed their compliance with compulsory heterosexuality and augmented their masculine status among male and female peers. Since charming teenage girls could enhance a boy's masculine status, many of the boys claimed to have done so during their visits to Puerto Rico and/or the Dominican Republic—a claim that was, conveniently, not possible to prove.

CONCLUSION

Contrary to retrospective research on high school students (Martin 1996), the boys at Romero did not experience puberty on their own but rather within their homosocial group. Overall, the findings highlight pubescence as a *social* process as much as a biological transformation—a social process that is interactional, collective, embodied, and situated in classed, gendered, and ethnoracialized contexts. The boys yearned for musculature bodies and participated in physical activities to signal that, although their sexual maturation was not readily apparent, they were in fact transitioning beyond childhood. They utilized their bodies in public displays of physical strength and toughness—attributes that they and those in their social worlds associated with manliness and relied on during physical confrontations—to gain masculine status. The physical challenges and accompanying verbal one-upmanship are characteristic of the dominant masculinities in the Dominican Republic (De Moya 2004), Puerto Rico (Ramírez 1999), and the United States (Kimmel 2008). Consequently, via references to and enactments of their bodies, puberty became a social accomplishment connected to masculine identities influenced by multiple cultural interpretations of gender.

The data inform research examining masculinity and the body (Butler 1993; Connell 2000, 2005; Swain 2000, 2003), heteronormativity at schools (Dalley-Trim 2007; Eliasson et al. 2007; Kehily 2001; Mac an Ghaill 1994; Martino 2000; Martino and Pallotta-Chiarolli 2003; McGuffey and Rich 1999; Pascoe 2007; Renold 2003, 2005; Swain 2000, 2003), and the intersection of racial identity and masculinity (Ferguson 2001; Lopez 2003; Majors and Billson 1993). This research also points to areas of further study. At present, the few studies on boys and puberty offer limited insight into how boys perceive and utilize their changing bodies or the dialectic between *localized* masculine enactments and more macrocultural interpretations of changing male bodies. The data presented herein, however, suggest the need for longitudinal ethnographic studies examining how boys from various social backgrounds experience the ongoing gendered process of "becoming" during their pubescent development. Last, scholarship on boys and masculinity would benefit from additional research on the intersection of masculine, ethnoracial, class, and sexual identities.

REFERENCES

Abbassi, Val. 1998. "Growth and Normal Puberty." *Pediatrics* 102: 507–11.

Arciniega, G. Miguel, Thomas C. Anderson, Zoila G. Tovar-Blank, and Terence J. G. Tracey. 2008. "Toward a Fuller Conception of Machismo: Development of a Traditional Machismo and Caballerismo Scale." *Journal of Counseling Psychology* 55: 19–33.

Anderson, Elijah. 2000. *Code of the Streets: Decency, Violence and the Moral Life of the Inner City.* New York: Norton.

Bailey, Benjamin. 2000. "Language and Negotiation of Ethnic/Racial Identity among Dominican Americans." *Language in Society* 29 (4): 555–82.

Basch, Linda, Nina Glick-Schiller, and Christina S. Blanc. 1994. *Nations Unbound: Transnational Projects, Postcolonial Predicaments, and Deterritorialized Nation-States.* Amsterdam: Gordon & Breach.

Butler, Judith. 1993. *Bodies That Matter: On the Discursive Limits of "Sex."* New York: Routledge.

Chambers, Deborah, Estella Tincknell, and Joost Van Loon. 2004. "Peer Regulation of Teenage Sexual Identities." *Gender and Education* 16: 297–315.

Connell, Raewyn. 2000. *The Men and the Boys.* Berkeley: University of California Press.

Connell, Raewyn. 2005. *Masculinities*, 2nd ed. Berkeley: University of California Press.

Dalley-Trim, Leanne. 2007. "'The Boys' Present . . . Hegemonic Masculinity: A Performance of Multiple Acts." *Gender and Education* 19: 199–217.

Dance, Lory J. 2002. *Tough Fronts: The Impact of Street Culture on Schooling.* New York: RoutledgeFalmer.

Davison, K. G. 2000. "Boys' Bodies in School: Physical Education." *Journal of Men's Studies* 8: 255–66.

De La Cancela, Victor. 1991. "Working Affirmatively with Puerto Rican Men: Professional and Personal Reflections." In *Feminist Approaches for Men in Family Therapy*, edited by M. Bograd. Binghamton, NY: Harrington Park Press.

De La Cancela, Victor. 1993. "'Coolin': The Psychosocial Communication of African and Latino Men." *Urban League Review* 16: 33–44.

De Moya, E. Antonio. 2004. "Power Games and Totalitarian Masculinity in the Dominican Republic." In *Interrogating Caribbean Masculinities: Theoretical and Empirical Analyses*, edited by R. E. Reddock. Kingston: University of West Indies Press.

Dixon, Carolyn. 1997. "Pete's Tool: Identity and Sex-Play in the Design and Technology Classroom." *Gender and Education* 9: 89–104.

Doyle, James A. 1995. *The Male Experience*, 3rd ed. Madison, WI: Brown & Benchmark.

Drummond, M. J. N. 2003. "The Meaning of Boys' Bodies in Physical Education." *Journal of Men's Studies* 11: 131–43.

Eccles, Jacquelynne S. 1999. "The Development of Children Ages 6 to 14." *Future of Children* 9: 30–44.

Eder, Donna, Catherine C. Evans, and Stephen Parker. 1995. *School Talk: Gender and Adolescent Culture.* New Brunswick, NJ: Rutgers University Press.

Eliasson, Miriam A., Kerstin Isaksson, and Lucie Laflamme. 2007. "Verbal Abuse in School: Constructions of Gender among 14- to 15-Year-Olds." *Gender and Education* 19: 587–605.

Epstein, Debbie. 2001. "Boyz' Own Stories: Masculinities and Sexualities in Schools." In *What about the Boys?: Issues of Masculinity in Schools*, edited by W. Martino and B. Meyenn. Philadelphia: Open University Press.

Epstein, Debbie, Sarah O'Flynn, and David Telford. 2000. "'Othering' Education: Sexualities, Silences, and Schooling." *Review of Research in Education* 25: 127–79.

Falicov, Celia J. 2010. "Changing Constructions of Machismo for Latino Men in Therapy: 'The Devil Never Sleeps.'" *Family Process* 49: 309–29.

Ferguson, Ann Arnet. 2001. *Bad Boys: Public Schools in the Making of Black Masculinity*. Ann Arbor: University of Michigan Press.

Fine, Gary Alan. 1987. *With the Boys: Little League Baseball and Preadolescent Culture*. Chicago: University of Chicago Press.

Frankel, Loren. 2003. "Puberty." In *Men and Masculinities: A Social, Cultural, and Historical Encyclopedia*, edited by M. Kimmel and A. Aronson, Vol. II. Santa Barbara, CA: ABC-CLIO.

Gardiner, Judith Kegan. 2000. "Masculinity, the Teening of America, and Empathic Targeting." *Signs* 25: 1257–61.

Gilbert, Rob and Pam Gilbert. 1998. *Masculinity Goes to School*. New York: Routledge.

Grogan, Sarah, and Helen Richards. 2002. "Body Image: Focus Groups with Boys and Men." *Men and Masculinities* 4: 219–32.

Gutmann, Matthew C. 1996. *The Meanings of Macho: Being a Man in Mexico City*. Berkeley: University of California Press.

Hasbrook, Cynthia A., and Othello Harris. 1999. "Wrestling with Gender: Physicality and Masculinities among Inner-City First and Second Graders." *Men and Masculinities* 1: 302–18.

Haywood, Chris, and Maírtín Mac An Ghaill. 2001. "The Significance of Teaching English Boys: Exploring Social Change, Modern Schooling and the Making of Masculinities." In *What about the Boys?: Issues of Masculinity in Schools*, edited by W. Martino and B. Meyenn. Philadelphia: Open University Press.

James, A. 2000. "Embodied Being(s): Understanding the Self and the Body in Childhood." In *The Body, Childhood, and Society*, edited by A. Prout. Houndmills: Macmillan.

Janssen, Diederik F. 2006. "'Become Big, and I'll Give You Something to Eat': Thoughts and Notes on Boyhood Sexual Health." *International Journal of Men's Health* 5: 19–35.

Katz, Michelle and Madhusmita Misra. 2011. "Delayed Puberty, Short Stature, and Tall Stature." In *The Mass General Hospital for Children Adolescent Medicine Handbook*, edited by Mark A. Goldstein. New York: Springer.

Kehily, Mary. 2001. "Bodies in School: Young Men, Embodiment, and Heterosexual Masculinities." *Men and Masculinities* 4: 173–85.

Kimmel, Michael S. 2008. *Guyland: The Perilous World Where Boys Become Men*. New York: Harper Collins.

Kimmel, Michael S. and Michael A. Messner, eds. 1998. *Men's Lives*, 4th ed. Boston: Allyn & Bacon.

Korobov, Neill. 2005. "Ironizing Masculinity: How Adolescent Boys Negotiate Heteronormative Dilemmas in Conversational Interaction." *Journal of Men's Studies* 13: 225–46.

Lilleaas, Ulla-Britt. 2007. "Masculinities, Sport, and Emotions." *Men and Masculinities* 10: 39–53.

Lopez, Nancy. 2003. *Hopeful Girls, Troubled Boys: Race and Gender Disparity in Urban Education*. New York: Routledge.

Mac An Ghaill, Maírtín. 1994. *The Making of Men: Masculinities, Sexualities and Schooling*. Buckingham, UK: Open University Press.

Majors, Richard and Janet M. Billson. 1993. *Cool Pose: The Dilemmas of Black Manhood in America*. New York: Touchstone.

Martin, Karin A. 1996. *Puberty, Sexuality, and the Self: Boys and Girls at Adolescence*. New York: Routledge.

Martino, Wayne. 1999. "'Cool Boys,' 'Party Animals,' 'Squids,' and 'Poofters': Interrogating the Dynamics and Politics of Adolescent Masculinities in School." *British Journal of the Sociology of Education* 20: 239–63.

Martino, Wayne. 2000. "Policing Masculinities: Investigating the Role of Homophobia and

Heteronormativity in the Lives of Adolescent Schoolboys." *Journal of Men's Studies* 8: 213–36.

Martino, Wayne and Maria Pallotta-Chiarolli. 2003. *So What's a Boy?: Addressing Issues of Masculinity and Schooling*. Berkshire, UK: Open University Press.

McCabe, M. P., and L. A. Ricciardelli. 2004. "A Longitudinal Study of Pubertal Timing and Extreme Body Change Behaviors among Adolescent Boys and Girls." *Adolescence* 39: 145–66.

McGuffey, C. Shawn, and B. Lindsay Rich. 1999. "Playing in the Gender Transgression Zone." *Gender & Society* 13: 608–27.

Mirandé, Alfredo. 1997. *Hombres y Machos: Masculinity and Latino Culture*. Boulder, CO: Westview Press.

Mora, Richard. 2013. "'Dicks Are for Chicks': Latino Boys, Homosexuality, and the Abjection of Homosexuality." *Gender and Education* 25 (3): 340–56.

Mosher, Donald L. 1991. "Macho Men, Machismo, and Sexuality." *Annual Review of Sex Research* 2: 199–247.

Nayak, Anoop and Mary Kehily. 2001. "'Learning to Laugh': A Study of Schoolboy Humour in the English Secondary School." In *What about the Boys?: Issues of Masculinity in Schools*, edited by W. Martino and B. Meyenn. Philadelphia: Open University Press.

Nilan, Pam. 2000. "'You're Hopeless, I Swear to God': Shifting Masculinities in Classroom Talk." *Gender and Education* 12: 53–68.

Pascoe, C. J. 2007. *Dude, You're a Fag: Masculinity and Sexuality in High School*. Berkeley: University of California Press.

Pope, Harrison G., Katharine A. Phillips, and Roberto Olivardia. 2000. *The Adonis Complex: The Secret Crisis of Male Body Obsession*. New York: Free Press.

Ramírez, Rafael L. 1999. *What It Means to Be a Man: Reflections on Puerto Rican Masculinity*, translated by Rosa E. Casper. New Brunswick, NJ: Rutgers University Press.

Redman, Peter, Debbie Epstein, Mary Kehily, and Maírtín Mac an Ghaill. 2002. "Boys Bonding: Same-Sex Friendship, the Unconscious and Heterosexual Discourse." *Discourse* 23: 179–91.

Renold, Emma. 2001. "Learning the 'Hard' Way: Boys, Hegemonic Masculinity and the Negotiation of Learner Identities in the Primary School." *British Journal of Sociology of Education* 22: 369–85.

Renold, Emma. 2003. "'If You Don't Kiss Me, You're Dumped': Boys, Boyfriends and Heterosexualised Masculinities in the Primary School." *Educational Review* 55: 179–94.

Renold, Emma. 2005. *Girls, Boys and Junior Sexualities: Exploring Children's Gender and Sexual Relations in the Primary School*. London: Routledge Falmer.

Saez, Pedro A., Adonaid Casado, and Jay C. Wade. 2009. "Factors Influencing Masculinity Ideology among Latino Men." *Journal of Men's Studies* 17: 116–28.

Schilling, Chris. 1993. *The Body and Social Theory*. London: Sage.

Stein, James H. and Lynn W. Reiser. 1994. "A Study of White Middle-Class Adolescent Boys' Responses to 'Semerache.'" *Journal of Youth and Adolescence* 23: 373–84.

Swain, Jon. 2000. "'The Money's Good, the Fame's Good, the Girls Are Good': The Role of Playground Football in the Construction of Young Boys' Masculinity in a Junior School." *British Journal of Sociology of Education* 21: 95–109.

Swain, Jon. 2003. "How Young Schoolboys Become Somebody: The Role of the Body in the Construction of Masculinity." *British Journal of Sociology of Education* 24: 299–314.

Thomas, Piri. 1987. *Down These Mean Streets*. New York: A..

Thorne, Barrie. 1993. *Gender Play: Girls and Boys in School*. New Brunswick, NJ: Rutgers University Press.

Torres, José B., V. Scott H. Solberg, and Aaron H. Carlstrom. 2002. "The Myth of Sameness among Latino Men and Their Machismo." *American Journal of Orthopsychiatry* 72: 163–81.

Witt, Susan D. 2000. "The Influence of Peers on Children's Socialization to Gender Roles." *Early Child Development and Care* 162: 1–7.

MARK ANTHONY NEAL

17. "MY PASSPORT SAYS SHAWN": TOWARD A HIP-HOP COSMOPOLITANISM

[. . .]

You got rappers afraid to be themselves.

—*Jay-Z, Fade to Black (2004)*

Can a nigga be cosmopolitan? Such a question might have been unthinkable two decades ago, even as hip-hop itself—the cultural phenomenon largely responsible for circulating the idea of the "nigga" as a trope of contemporary transnational blackness—was largely premised on the innovations and contributions of a wide range of diasporic bodies. Manthia Diawara made such an observation in his essay "Homeboy Cosmopolitan," in which he constructs a cosmopolitanism for hip-hop that is an "expression of poor people's desire for the good life," noting that the "search for the good life is not only in keeping with the nationalist struggle for citizenship and belonging, but also reveals the need to go beyond such struggles and celebrate the redemption of the black individual through tradition" (Diawara 1998: 238). As Ekow Eshun writes more than a decade after Diawara's observation, "Success in the music industry has allowed young black people to breach the furthest territories of white exclusivity. As with Jack Johnson, . . . who enraged white America with his diamond rings and expensive cars, their flaunting of wealth is intended as provocation against a society that has striven to confine the aspirations of black people" (Eshun 2005). And while I'd be remiss not to mention that the homeboy cosmopolitanism that Diawara constructs is rife with a nostalgia for the so-called glory days of hip-hop (and hip-hop scholarship, for that matter), I'd very much like to endorse his observations about contemporary hip-hop's unfettered pursuit of leisure, wealth, capital, and movement.

It is in this context that I'd like to posit my own notion of a hip-hop cosmopolitanism, marked in part by a symbolic homelessness from notions of mainstream American morality, political relevancy, and cultural gravitas. I am evoking a cosmopolitanism that finds resonance in the concept of the "Katrina generation," those black bodies deemed little more than "refugees" by corporate media, reinforcing the presumed inhumanity and *foreignness* of this population. In the early moments of the Hurricane Katrina disaster, the evoking of "refugees" also cast a pall of illegitimacy on those so-called refugees who viewed themselves as national subjects deserving of relief at a moment of national crisis *and* citizenship in whatever locale they chose—or were forced—to relocate to. In other words, media depictions of "refugees" cast aspersions on the desires of the "Katrina generation" to see themselves as cosmopolitan. Ifeoma Kiddoe Nwankwo (2005) suggests that such aspersions are historically related to the fear among whites of blacks who view themselves as cosmopolitan subjects. [. . .]

Nwankwo's notion that the collapsing of cosmopolitan possibilities is related to efforts to limit the breadth and diversity of black identity is particularly compelling in an era when hip-hop identities are intensely wedded to racial truisms that are often legitimized by some of the most visible (and highly compensated) hip-hop artists, but are often out of sync with those who might otherwise reference their hip-hop identities within a broad range of civic, political, cultural, spiritual, economic, and intellectual activities. [. . .] [A] hip-hop cosmopolitanism is undergirded by desires for physical, social, and economic mobility, including, for my own purposes, a

---

This reading is an excerpt from the chapter "'My Passport Says Shawn'—Toward a Hip-Hop Cosmopolitanism," in Mark Anthony Neal's *Looking for Leroy: Illegible Black Masculinities* (New York: New York University Press, 2013). © 2013 by New York University.

mobility from or even within the essential tropes—playa, pimp, hustler, thug, and nigga—that define contemporary mainstream hip-hop masculinities.

The possibilities that cosmopolitanism affords hip-hop at this moment can be summarized by Dereka Rushbrook, who argues that "As identity is constituted through consumption, these practices allow for the creation of multiple, shifting identities, of lifestyles that can be tried on, discarded and reformulated" (2002: 188–89). However problematic the idea that one can construct identities via consumption, especially for those preoccupied with more "authentic" experiences, in the world of mainstream hip-hop that desire for the "authentic" is even more palpable. Indeed, those who embrace the kinds of "multiple, shifting identities" that Rushbrook cites are easily marginalized and even queered in the discourses of hip-hop, as "authenticity" is often gendered and sexualized. Thus it is perhaps the defining irony of contemporary commercial hip-hop that as the culture itself becomes more cosmopolitan—a legitimate global culture—hip-hop artists remain wedded to concepts of realness or authenticity that are decidedly local.

[. . .] John L. Jackson Jr. notes that "Hip-hop's preoccupation with realness is predicated upon deep-seated doubts about what usually passes for *real*, skepticism toward social performances/presentations offered up as indexical links to realness" (2005: 177). Jackson's analysis partly explains the anxieties produced in response to the increasingly cosmopolitan nature of commercial hip-hop in the United States. [. . .] [H]ip-hop cosmopolitanism represents a fertile location to challenge the larger society's desire to impose constraints on how hip-hop constituencies choose to embody themselves, as well as a site to challenge stridently parochial notions of masculine identity (and gender) in hip-hop, particularly those solely rooted in the local. Indeed, I'd like to argue that the constraints placed on hip-hop-infused identities are analogous to the historical difficulties experienced by those blacks desiring to be read as cosmopolitan—legitimate citizens of the world.

The title of the chapter refers to a highly publicized Hewlett Packard ad campaign that featured the hip-hop icon Jay-Z (Shawn Carter). With individual wealth rumored to exceed $300 million, ownership stake in a professional basketball team, a resume that includes presidencies of a major recording label and clothing line, a groundbreaking recording and concert deal worth $150 million, and a reputation as one of the handful of legitimate arbiters of highbrow urban style, Jay-Z is the very embodiment of "homeboy cosmopolitanism." As Jay-Z once told the activist and writer Bakari Kitwana (2004), "People don't say anything about all of these White people that own Fortune 500 companies [who] take private jets . . . It seems like black people ain't deserving of some of the same things." Jay-Z's cognizance of the value of cosmopolitanism to his own masculine identity can be heard in the lyrics of "30 Something," where he disparages his younger peers with the quip, "You ain't got enough stamps in your passport to fuck with young H-0, international, show you young boys how to do this thing" (Jay-Z 2006). In his artistic memoir, *Decoded*, Jay-Z recalls his first trip abroad: "Up until that point my life could be mapped with a triangle: Brooklyn, Washington Heights, Trenton. So everything about the trip to London—going to Rockefeller Center to get my passport, packing for a month-long trip, preparing for a trans-Atlantic flight—was new to me. It was a surreal, disorienting experience" (Jay-Z 2010: 76). Jay-Z's regular referencing of his working-class Brooklyn roots, though, is reflective of his ongoing concerns for the local. [. . .]

As such, I'd like to argue that Jay-Z/Shawn Carter serves as an entry point to examine more concretely how black bodies (as constructed via the discourses of mainstream American hip-hop) travel through the world, but also how the world travels through those bodies. I am particularly concerned with the productive value of having the theoretical worlds of black feminist and queer theory—rendered as discursive interventions—travel through the body of a highly visible and influential masculine icon of hip-hop, as an alternative iteration of diaspora. [. . .]

TRAFFICKING IN MONIKERS

Around 1977, the poet Audre Lorde began to introduce herself at poetry readings as a "black, lesbian, feminist, mother poet warrior." According to Alexis De Veaux [. . .], her fellow poet June Jordan was disturbed, in particular, by Lorde's need to articulate her lesbian identity, because "she felt distanced from Lorde's complex definitions as more than black" (De Veaux 2004: 179). [. . .] Lorde's conceptualization of a complex black identity was fully articulated in her book *Zami: A New Spelling of My Name.* According to DeVeaux, *Zami* "originated a new discursive space for more complex renderings of black women's lives [. . .]" (De Veaux 2004: 311). [. . .]

Nearly twenty years after the publication of *Zami* (Lorde 1982), Jay-Z taped a performance eventually broadcast as part of MTV's *Unplugged* series. Sitting on a stool, wearing a Che Guevara t-shirt and jokingly referring to the session as "Jay-Z's poetry reading," Jay-Z begins his performance stating that "I go by a couple of names. . . . Sometimes they call me Jay-Z, sometimes they call me Jigga, sometimes they call me young hov' [Iceberg], tonight I'm 'H to the Izzo, V to the Izza' [sung by vocalist Jaguar Wright]." Here Jay-Z articulates what has been a time-tested practice in hip-hop: the multiple personas. But whereas most hip-hop artists simply adopt alternative personas, often referencing underground drug lords or fictional Mafia figures, Jay-Z created a complex "hip-hop" identity that speaks to concepts such as fluidity, mobility, and social capital. Christopher Holmes Smith suggests that among so-called hip-hop moguls, including Jay-Z, a "major aspect of the mogul's utopian sense of freedom is one of identity shifting, or at the least, identity layering." Smith adds that "while hip-hop moguls can never be said to deny their racial and ethnic heritage, they are encouraged to use the material aspects of gangster social formations . . . to expand the options for social performativity normally afforded blacks or Latinos" (Smith 2003: 82). [. . .] This collapsing of stage(d) personas and "real" identities by some hip-hop figures plays into the desires of audiences concerned with notions of authenticity: "Are these cats for real?"

[. . .] In a telling and at times bizarre profile of Jay-Z on an episode of *60 Minutes II* broadcast in November 2002, the interviewer, Bob Simon, says to the rapper, "Now people have told me that in the business, you've got the best flow. My problem is, I don't know what that means." Jay-Z responds, "Here's the melody [hums]. Me I'll rhyme like [making rhyming sounds].

So I'm in sync with the beat, like when the music's going [hums] I'm going [making rhyming sounds], with words though. See?" What Jay-Z has articulated to his somewhat befuddled interviewer is the concept of flow as a metaphor for adaptability. [. . .] In addition to the identities that Jay-Z articulates at the opening of his *Unplugged* performance, he has also been known by his birth name, Shawn Carter, and S. Carter. Each moniker that Jay-Z references serves distinct purposes related to his ability to exhibit social capital and remain fluid in the various publics in which he has influence, be it the upper echelons of the recording industry, the mainstream pop charts, Madison Avenue taste makers, or of course the "hood." For example, Jigga relates to his identity as the "ghetto everyman." "Hova"—as in Jehovah, the "savior" of hip-hop— represents a moniker that has value to hard-core hip-hop fans who desire the most "authentic" product, the hard-core ghetto thug. "S. Carter" initially represented Jay-Z's song publishing identity, the name that shows up in the songwriting credits of his recordings and those for whom he ghost writes. Given the history of black musicians—early blues musicians and hip-hop artists in particular—who sold off their potential publishing royalties for paltry advances, "S. Carter" is evidence of Jay-Z's savvy in the recording industry. "S. Carter" also adorned his signature athletic shoe line (in partnership with Reebok), which was one of the best-selling signature shoe lines not named for a professional athlete. [. . .] Of course, the moniker Jay-Z is the quintessential hip-hop commodity that is at the root of the rapper's social fluidity. In addition, there are Roc-A-Fella and Rocawear, the urban entertainment and clothing companies that Jay-Z founded with Kareem "Biggs" Burke and Damon Dash. The names of the companies are an obvious play on the Rockefeller family wealth and New York State's Rockefeller drug laws. What these examples make clear is the extent to which Jay-Z's various monikers represent distinct *brands*.

Much of Jay-Z's music is rooted in his own "biomythography": the world of "Shawn Carter the hustler," the drug dealer from Brooklyn's Marcy Projects. It is "Shawn Carter" who embodies the rapper's hustling instincts ("More than a hustler, I'm the definition of it. . . . I'm a hustler's hope, I'm not his pipedreams"), instincts that have helped translate his street wit into a rap career of some distinction. [. . .] In the guise of the hustler, Shawn Carter embodies the improvisational aspects of both his persona and his vocation. In this regard it should not be surprising that Jay-Z urged journalists and others to refer to him only as "Shawn Carter" when he made the transition from best-selling artist to the new "hustle" as president of the Island Def Jam recording label. According to his "biomythography," Jay-Z's initial investment in Roc-A-Fella came from his profits from the crack cocaine trade. [. . .] This is a history that Jay-Z shares with many rappers; what has made Jay-Z significant is that he has, as successfully as any of his contemporaries, mainstreamed his "thug-nigga" persona over an extended period of time without losing social capital in the "ghetto-hoods" that helped produce him and continue to inform his musical narratives.

Jay-Z's social capital among ghetto denizens (including those who are socially constructed as such) is best articulated by the fact that he is one of the most bootlegged artists in rap music but has also consistently topped the pop charts for his opening-week sales. Whereas bootlegging represents the outright theft of his music, given its location in the hood it is also evidence of his viability as an authentic "thug-nigga." His first-week sales figures—the more traditional and legal consumption of his music—are emblematic of his popularity as a mainstream pop artist. The best example of such popularity was the first-week sales of his recording *The Blueprint*, which sold nearly 500,000 copies and was released on September 11, 2001. In the midst of one of the largest domestic crises in US history, 493,000 people bought copies of Jay-Z's CD during the week of the attack.

I'd like to suggest that Jay-Z embraces a "post-nigga" identity that coyly destabilizes constructions of the essential "nigga" that remains at the root of hip-hop's circulation across the globe. I hesitate, though, to read Jay-Z's efforts in the "queer" context in which Lorde articulated the notion of Zami, however enticing the possibility of such a read. Instead, I find Fred Moten's conceptualizations of queerness and discontinuity useful. As Moten writes, "Perhaps political upheaval is in the nonlocatability of discontinuity. Art tries to fictionalize and/or redeploy such location

among other things. . . . What one begins to consider, as a function of the nonlocalizable nature or status of discontinuity, is a special universalization of discontinuity, where discontinuity could be figured as ubiquitous minority, omnipresent queerness" (Moten 2003: 69). Thus in the context of hip-hop, flow still retains its utility in the service of adaptability, but this notion of adaptability is less about fluidity and more about managing discontinuity, or in this particular case, managing Jay-Z's queerness (per Moten's use of the term).

And it is the marketplace that is the all-too-willing compatriot in Jay-Z's attempt to manage his monikers. For example, in May 2006 Hewlett Packard unveiled the first in a series of commercials featured in its ad campaign "The Computer Is Personal Again." The initial commercial in the campaign featured the Olympic snowboarding champion Shaun White. The second commercial, featuring Jay-Z, was initially broadcast during the National Basketball Association championships in June 2006. In the latter commercial a disembodied Jay-Z—only his torso, attired in a business suit, appears in the commercial—states, "My whole life is on this thing," referring to his Hewlett Packard laptop computer. [. . .] The ad exemplifies a particular brand of commercial cosmopolitanism— "I'm not a 'businessman', I'm a *business*, man"—which Jay-Z has come to embody. [. . .] Well taken is Halberstam's point that "promoting flexibility at the level of identity and personal may sound like . . . a queer program for social change. But it easily describes the advertising strategies like the Gap, who sell their products by casting their consumers as simultaneously all the same and all different" (Halberstam 2005). And yet I remain committed to fully exploring the very gestures that Jay-Z makes toward a more progressive and even radical conceptualization of black masculine identity in hip-hop, even as his skill at manipulating and exploiting those very gestures in the name of branding is quite apparent.

"TAKE THIS BEAT, I DON'T MIND / GOT PLENTY OTHERS . . ."

In the song "Moment of Clarity" from *The Black Album* (2003), Jay-Z asserts that "hustlers and boosters embrace me and the music I be makin' / I dumbed down for my audience to double my dollars. . . . if skills sold, truth be told, I'd probably be Talib Kweli / Truthfully I wanna rhyme like Common Sense / But I did Five Mil—I ain't been rhymin' like Common since." At the time of its release, the lyric was Jay-Z's most public acknowledgment that many of his core hip-hop identities were little more than constructions aimed at keeping his music relevant in an industry that by definition reduces black identity to the most simplistic terms. As Imani Perry observes, [. . .] thug narrators are "especially vulnerable to being understood in terms of prescribed racial narratives, regardless of the more nuanced levels on which they communicate or aspire to communicate" (Perry 2004). As the quality of music video production improved for hip-hop artists (a measure of how important the genre had become for the recording industry), music videos became valuable forums for artists to further complicate their commercial and personal identities. With regard to Jay-Z's career, I am particularly interested in the music videos for the songs "Girls, Girls, Girls" (2001) and "'03 Bonnie and Clyde" with Beyoncé Knowles (2002). The two music videos give the earliest indication of a budding hip-hop cosmopolitanism in Jay-Z's work, highlighting his flow (in the broadest sense), while undermining the essential character of the "nigga" that he naturally embodies in the context of the marketplace.

The original version of Jay-Z's "Girls, Girls, Girls," like the remix, is largely a celebration of Jay-Z's heterosexual masculine flow within what could only be described as a transnational femininity. The first verse of "Girls, Girls, Girls" begins with Jay-Z listing the kinds of women he dates: a Spanish chick, a black chick, a French chick, and a woman who, while referred to as an "Indian Squaw," is clearly East Indian. By linking these women to various ethnic food products like fried chicken, curry chicken, arroz con pollo (chicken and rice), and crepes, Jay-Z articulates a well circulated belief in hip-hop that women are little more than consumables. In the song's second verse a second group of women is identified—a young chick, a project chick, a model chick, and a stewardess chick, but instead of these women embodying Jay-Z's appetite, if you will, they are emblematic of the various publics in which his "product" resonates—the neophyte hip-hop fan, the hard-core ghetto, the fashion industry, and international hip-hop audiences. The rather problematic

gender politics aside, the video serves as an indicator of Jay-Z's emerging cosmopolitan taste.

In the third verse Jay-Z highlights his relationships with a wider range of women, including a narcoleptic and a "weed-head chick." His reference to an "African chick with Eddie Murphy on her skull" reads as most problematic, however, as Jay-Z alludes to a particularly misogynist and homophobic rant from Eddie Murphy's concert film *Raw*. Though the video for "Girls, Girls, Girls" seems to reinforce common perceptions of hip-hop's proclivity for sexist and misogynistic sensibilities, the video's narrative ultimately unravels as little more than a literal video set—a stage. Thus Jay-Z performs the song's last chorus while walking off the set, in the process giving handshakes and nods to many of the women who appeared in the video. Tellingly, Jay-Z removes his shirt—his uniform, if you will—and walks off the set by himself. While I hesitate to give Jay-Z any credit for anything close to feminist vision in this context, I will suggest that the video creates a significant distance between the essential "nigga" who embodies his music (including the notion that he is promiscuous) and "Shawn Carter." The video's closing frame, which focuses on a sign that says "Girls, Girls, Girls—Closed Set," leaves open the possibility that Jay-Z is nothing more than a constructed persona; this gesture is a radical move in a commercial subculture largely premised on highly contrived essentialist notions of black masculinity.

"'03 Bonnie and Clyde" was released in the fall of 2002, amid rumors that romantically linked Jay-Z and Destiny Child's lead singer Beyoncé Knowles. Knowles's performance on the song and appearance in the video were the first public acknowledgment that the pair had a relationship, professional or otherwise. "'03 Bonnie and Clyde" is essentially a remake of Tupac Shakur's "Me and My Girlfriend," which was an ode, not to a woman, but to Tupac's gun. The title of the Jay-Z and Knowles remake highlights their status as "outlaws," though in the context of the lyric that asserted that they were the "new Bobby and Whitney"—a reference to the scandal-filled marriage between Bobby Brown and the late Whitney Houston—their presumed outlaw status may simply be the product of what might be perceived as an unusual union, between a former drug dealer and a mainstream pop princess. [. . .]

The narrative for the "'03 Bonnie and Clyde" music video is premised on the couple trying to escape law enforcement led by an officer portrayed by the actor Lance Reddick, most widely known in his role as Lieutenant Cedric Daniels in the critically acclaimed HBO series *The Wire*. The series, set in West Baltimore, often presented "queered" visions of urban blackness that consistently challenged essentialized notions of black sexuality and black masculinity. I use the term "queer" here deliberately, referencing not just sexuality but also modes of blackness that are often seen as out of sync and at odds with acceptable notions of who black people are and what black culture is supposed to be. [. . .]

"'03 Bonnie and Clyde" was produced by Kanye West, who along with Just Blaze (Justin Smith) was the primary producer of Jay-Z's recording *The Blueprint* and its follow-up *The Blueprint 2*. The two producers are well known for mining obscure soul recordings from the 1960s and 1970s and changing the pitch of the voices they sample from those records. This technique has given Jay-Z's music a distinct soulfulness, particularly on tracks like the West-produced "Izzo (H.O.V.A.)," which samples the Jackson Five's "I Want You Back," or "Never Change," which samples David Ruffin's "Common Man." According to one critic, West's production style creates a context where "men sound like women and women sound like chipmunks" (Edlund 2004: 18). This style of production presents yet another vantage point from which to interpret the queering of Jay-Z's music. West suggests as much when he recalls his first production efforts with Jay-Z on the track "This Can't Be Life" (2000): "Man, I really wanted more like of the simple type Jay-Z, I ain't want like the, the more introspective, complicated rhyme." The point here is that Jay-Z was working in a narrative framework that could be perceived as queer in the context of traditional hip-hop narratives and his earlier body of work.

The "queerness" of Jay-Z and Knowles's relationship is also conveyed musically, notably in the bridge to "'03 Bonnie and Clyde," where Knowles sings a hook appropriated from Prince's 1987 recording "If I Was Your Girlfriend." The song was originally recorded by Prince as a side project for an artist named Camille (Prince's vocals sped up to sound like a "female" voice). Though the Camille project was scrapped, "If I Was Your Girlfriend" with the cross-gendered vocals intact, was included on Prince's career-defining recording *Sign O' the Times*. The literary critic C. Leigh McInnis Jr. writes that the song "builds on this notion of finding happiness and inner peace by breaking the walls of prescribed normality that regulate our romantic relationships, which are the building blocks for society" (2000: 214). Prince deliberately heightens the sexual ambiguity of "Camille" with lyrics like "if I was your girlfriend? / Would you remember to tell me all of the things you forgot when I was your man?" Thus when Prince (credited as Camille in the liner notes) sang "If I Was Your Girlfriend," the song could alternately be read as a woman addressing a woman, a woman addressing a man, or even the possibility, since Prince is in fact a man, of a man addressing another man.[1] [. . .]

Of particular interest to me here is the importing of Prince into the texts of a mainstream hip-hop artist. For example, there is a subtle reference to Prince on the track "My 1st Song," where Jay-Z suggests that his so-called retirement was his "second major break-up / my first was with a pay truck and a hooptie, a cook pot and the game / This one's with the stu', with the stage, the fortune," only to quickly assert "naw, maybe not the fortune." [. . .]. Jay-Z's cadence, delivery, and intent here directly mirror a line from Prince's ballad "Adore," where he claims to his lover that he would do anything for her, including burn up his clothes and "smash up my ride," only to quickly recant, "well, maybe not the ride." [. . .] Prince's construction of his own masculine persona was often at odds with the masculinities that have historically circulated in hip-hop. In the mid-1980s, for example, the images of Run-DMC, LL Cool J, and Chuck D of Public Enemy seemed direct responses to the performances of popular black male R&B artists during that era, such as Prince, Michael Jackson, Rick James, and Luther Vandross, who often trafficked in androgyny or, in the case of Vandross, a decidedly "sentimental" performance of masculinity (King 2000). The tensions between these versions of black masculinity are perfectly captured by the rapper

KRS-One's homophobic quip "Are there any straight singers in R&B?" [. . .] Given the intensification of hypermasculine performance in hip-hop since the mid-1980s, Jay-Z's identification with the music of Prince, however clever and nuanced, strikes me as potentially undermining his "authenticity" among the genre's core constituencies.

Jay-Z's [. . .] *Black Album* accentuates a moment in Jay-Z's career when an openness toward—dare I say, a willingness to be penetrated by—influences not in sync with mainstream hip-hop became more pronounced. His subsequent use of Indian Bhangra music on the track "Beware the Boys," his signing of the British-born rapper Lady Sovereign to the Island Def Jam label, and his comical cameo on the remix of the late British musician Amy Winehouse's "Rehab" are all examples of Jay-Z's interests in not simply traveling the world, but also allowing the world to travel through him. [. . .]

CHANGE CLOTHES AND GO

However interesting the issues of fluidity and hybridity in the context of the core masculinities of commercial hip-hop culture it is important to remember that "niggas" largely circulate in transnational commercial culture as flattened images, images that are a projection of historic fears of black masculinity in the United States, the desires of young white men (and others) to consume the supposed visceral pleasures and dangers associated with black masculinity, and the willingness of young black men (and others) to make those images available for consumption. Not surprisingly, it would be in the arena of fashion that "niggas" would arguably be most accessible. In this regard the desire of young hip-hop fans to consume the uniform of the "nigga"—as produced by companies like FUBU, Phat Farm, Sean John, or Rocawear—has helped hip-hop transition from subculture to mega-brand. [. . .] In other words, the wearing of the uniform of the "nigga" conveys an authenticity to the act of consuming said "nigga" that simply listening to *his* music would never convey.

Though there are examples of hip-hop fashion that are seemingly accoutrements to young black criminality—real and imagined—hip-hop has for some time laid claim to the world of haute couture.

In the mid-1980s, the images of shell-top Adidas, velour running suits, gold chains, and Kangol caps, as displayed by the group Run-DMC, were synonymous with hip-hop culture, but as hip-hop moved into different commercial and discursive markets, hip-hop fashion has become more diverse. The examples of Tommy Hilfiger (purportedly the first major designer to take notice of hip-hop's potential to sell fashion) and the black designer Karl Kani are regularly cited as critical to a shift in hip-hop fashion where "trends were specifically created for hip-hop markets" (Fleetwood 2005: 330). [. . .] Fleetwood notes that "Central to the evolution of hip-hop fashion and its transformation into an industry is the fixity of the black male icon of hip-hop. Examining the significance of urban male fashion and the iconic, racialized, adorned male body of hip-hop's material and visual culture offers insight into the relationship among materiality, representation and consumption within black popular culture" (2011: 151–52).

Fleetwood also cautions, though, that contemporary hip-hop fashion is often fraught with ambivalence and anxiety. "Embedded in representation of the fashioned black male body of hip-hop is the interplay between a highly stylized and reproducible racial alterity, nationalism, and hypermasculinity," Fleetwood writes, adding that the "black male body signifies within and outside of black communities a form of coolness through racialized and masculine difference and diaphanous 'outlawness'" (2011: 152). The result of these tensions is an ambivalence that, according to Fleetwood, is "central to the success of hip-hop fashion marketing campaigns" (2011: 165).

The ambivalences that Fleetwood references are easily correlated with some of the anxieties associated with contemporary hip-hop culture in general. Fleetwood suggests that these anxieties are in part related to the fears of artists and other representational figures in hip-hop of being marginalized as "ethnic" or some other identity construction that marks them as non-American at a moment when hip-hop's stake in Americana is so pronounced. [. . .] This partly explains the move by hip-hop's elite fashion producers from so-called urban fashion to what could be described as upscale or even metrosexual in the case of male fashion. For elite hip-hop icons like

Russell Simmons, Sean Combs, and Jay-Z, the shift from urban to upscale mirrors their own ascendance to the higher echelons of American celebrity culture.[2] This shift is initially evident in the work of Jay-Z in the music video for "Excuse Me Miss" (2002). The video's primary labor is to articulate the branding power of Jay-Z, but it also provides a transitory landscape on which to read the emotional and existential complexities that mainstream rap music largely and, I would suggest, deliberately obscures.

Tweaking the accepted uniform of the "nigga," Jay-Z and other artists signed to the Roc-A-Fella label appear in the video for "Excuse Me Miss" donning business suits. With Jay-Z uttering phrases like "this is for the grown and sexy" and "Can I get my grown man on?" throughout, the video anticipates the emergence of the hip-hop metrosexual as exemplified by artists like Kanye West, Andre 3000, Pharrell Williams, and later Drake and Kid Cudi. In the context of hip-hop, these men's [. . .] consumption habits—particularly in the realm of fashion—are akin to those that mainstream American society generally assigns to women (Simpson 1994). The attention to highbrow style throughout the video, directed by Little X, is an attempt to identify Jay-Z and the other members of the Roc-A-Fella clique as exceptional men, among the clichéd archetypes of black masculinity that have historically circulated in hip-hop culture. [. . .]

The song and video for "Excuse Me Miss" are rife with product placements, with references to "S. Dots" (the S. Carter sneaker collection), Armadale (a Scottish-produced vodka that was briefly distributed in the United States by Roc-A-Fella), and Zino Platinum Crowns, upscale cigars targeted to hip-hop-generation consumers. What links these products was Jay-Z's relationship with Peter Arnell, the chief creative officer of the Arnell Group, which specializes in "product creation" and "brand invention" and Steve Stoute, a longtime music industry executive, who with Arnell formed PASS, an agency dedicated to linking high-end producers with hip-hop consumers. [. . .] In her book *Modern Blackness*, the cultural anthropologist Deborah Thomas cautions that "if we approached a more complex understanding of the politics of popular culture we would, for example, reveal the emphasis on consumerism as something more than consciousness and a capitulation to Americanized commodification of desire" (Thomas 2004: 260). Indeed, Jay-Z makes clear that what he traffics in is not simply about products; he tells Bakari Kitwana (2004), "Hip-hop is culture. This is somebody's life and a way of thinking. This isn't like a place to go. . . . There's no culture attached to a raincoat. There's culture attached to hip-hop and it runs deeper that just [vacationing in] St. Barts."

[. . .] What is being bought and sold in Jay-Z as "proprietary intellectual property"? The branding of Jay-Z as an elite "product"? Yes, of course, but less pronounced is Jay-Z's attempt—a simple gesture, really—to broaden the contours of a commercially viable black masculinity. Notable about Jay-Z's gesture is that he has chosen to do so in the context of branding, thus making claims on a progressive notion of hip-hop masculinity at the level of consumption. [. . .]

The image of hard-core hip-hop acts wearing Armani suits would not normally elicit much comment if the images were not buttressed by the musical narrative of "Excuse Me Miss," created by Jay-Z and his collaborator Pharrell Williams. "Excuse Me Miss" borrows from the chorus of Luther Vandross's song "Take You Out." With Vandross as a referent here, I'd like to suggest that Pharrell Williams's deliberate use of elements of "Take You Out" creates a narrative that destabilizes the accepted heteromasculine narrative of the song and video. Vandross never responded to queries about his sexuality, but it was widely believed among audiences and industry peers that he was gay. Vandross often appeared opposite women in his music videos, but his record company, perhaps sensing how palpable questions about his sexuality were becoming, blatantly attempted to "heterosexualize" Vandross's image for "Take You Out," the lead single from his 2001 recording *Luther Vandross*. Thus Vandross appeared in the video for "Take You Out" wearing Sean John clothing (a normative, youthful masculinity tailored just for Vandross), while pursuing the actress Garcelle Beauvais. [. . .] Pharrell Williams's use of "Take You Out" [is] evidence of the levels of complexity that almost always reside in the crevices of mainstream popular culture, that is, if one is willing to submit to the illegibility of it all. [. . .]

Rather than read "Excuse Me Miss" as simply a celebration of the "bling" that Jay-Z's celebrity and branding power affords, I'd like to suggest that there is a performative labor associated with bling, beyond its ability to provide access to the radio, video, and clothing outlets that mainstream rappers find absolutely necessary for crossover success. In other words, I'd like to argue that in line with bling's singular attribute, it literally blinds audiences (and critical readers) to the complexities that "lay in the cut" and in fact, this blindness is more than a residual effect of artists trying to provide nuanced and progressive performances in the full glare of mainstream popular culture, in that it is concretely related to attempts by artists and critics to make a progressive politics "illegible" in an era when anxieties about the legibility of such politics are heightened.

Set in a club, "Excuse Me Miss" opens with Jay-Z and his entourage being greeted by the gaze of virtually every woman—all conveniently scantily clad—in the club. The club setting establishes one of the defining clichés of rap music at the time as expressed in the track "Do It Again (Put Your Hands Up)" from Jay-Z's 1999 recording *Volume Three . . . The Life and Times of S. Carter.* On the track Jay-Z and his label mate Beanie Sigel, who also appears in the video for "Excuse Me Miss," make explicit references to the kinds of sexual favors they receive from women at clubs, all ostensibly related to the celebrity and social capital that even second-rate rappers are thought to possess. Additionally, an earlier collaboration between Jay-Z and Pharrell (The Neptunes), "I Just Want to Love," explicitly celebrated Jay-Z's inability to commit to a single woman. In comparison to those narratives, the video for "Excuse Me Miss" features Jay-Z and others simply engaging in casual conversation with some of the women in the club.

The critical action, though, in the "Excuse Me Miss" video occurs in an elevator, where Jay-Z is rendered speechless (he literally bites his lip) by an attractive woman—the embodiment of bling—who enters the elevator. As such I would also like to argue that there is some significance to the fact that Jay-Z's fantasy occurs in the proverbial closeted space—an elevator. Rather than use Jay-Z's heterosexual gaze to construct another cliché of male objectification of

black female sexuality, the director, Little X, employs Jay-Z's gaze to fuel a romantic fantasy in which the rapper imagines that this woman is "the one," the love of his life. The scenes of Jay-Z romancing the woman are not particularly extraordinary, except when juxtaposed with some of the rapper's previous musings about women—"The only time you love them is when your dick's hard." [. . .] Here the director has established a broader context—beyond the bling—to catch a "glimpse of Shawn." Jay-Z's fantasy—in part simply a longing to just be "Shawn"—ends when the rapper utters the line, "I'm about to give you all the keys and the security codes, . . . but before I jump out the window, what's your name?" In the narrative of the video, Jay-Z wakes from his fantasy, still speechless, as he and the woman exit the elevator. Referencing Moten (2003) again, I'd like to argue that Jay-Z's query "What's your name?" is the invocation of the lack of language available to represent the politics and poetics of a cosmopolitan masculinity in contemporary rap music. [. . .]

In the case of "Excuse Me Miss" [. . .], the closeted cosmopolitan space renders Jay-Z's embodied queerness palpable in the context of mainstream hypermasculine hip-hop, where he can be queered only in the most idiosyncratic ways. Such was the case when Jay-Z encountered his longtime business partner Damon Dash in an elevator, shortly after the two had dissolved their professional relationship and Jay-Z became the president of Island Def Jam. According to Dash, "[Jay] was coming from whatever he was doin' at Def Jam . . . and he had on a suit with shoes and a trench coat. And I had on my State Property [clothing line] and my hat to the side. It was ill. Our conversation was brief, wasn't no malice, but he was not the same person I had met. *I would never expect him to wear a trench coat and shoes*" (Toure 2005, my emphasis). In the context of Dash's description, simple apparel like a pair of shoes and a trench coat were enough evidence that somehow Jay-Z had changed. The implication here was that Jay-Z was no longer "real" in the sense that mainstream hip-hop traffics in the "real" as emblematic of the overwrought caricatures of black masculinity that have become one of hip-hop's most treasured commodities. [. . .]

[. . .]

"WATCH THE THRONE?": A POSTSCRIPT

Kingdom Come (2006), Jay-Z's first full-length post-retirement recording, represents the possibilities that critically resonate in his discursive rebirth. In a revealing profile of Jay-Z in the December 2006 edition of *GQ*, Mark Healy observes that with previous recordings, the artist often sequestered himself from the world, but as if he was cognizant of the myriad meanings that could be attached to his discursive body, Jay-Z chose a different strategy. According to Healy, "For *Kingdom Come*, [Jay-Z] hasn't kept the world at bay but rather exposed himself to it-burning through Europe, Africa and the Middle East" (Healy 2006: 286). Jay-Z's travels included a much-celebrated trip to the African continent on behalf of the United Nations and its efforts to address the fresh water crisis across the continent. [. . .] Though not the focus of Healy's profile—Jay-Z was named one of GQ's "Men of the Year"—it illuminates that as Jay-Z travels the world, embodying the notion of a hip-hop cosmopolitanism, the "world" inevitably travels through him. One of the by-products of Jay-Z's evolved persona is what Samuel Delany calls a "discursive collision," where the "Jay-Z" that first emerged in the mid-1990s is always going to be at odds with the "Jay-Z" that is discursively reproduced in the context of a hip-hop cosmopolitanism. [. . .] [T]hese discursive collisions are often exploited by those unwilling or unable to grant hip-hop culture at large the gravitas it demands, particularly in the political realm.

In her acclaimed profile of Jay-Z, the journalist Elizabeth Mendez Berry describes him as a "confidence artist"—a con man—and it's a fair criticism, given the efficiency with which Jay-Z has trafficked in such disparate markets and publics. [. . .] Thus it's not surprising that a figure like the noted hip-hop critic and activist Jeff Chang would take such a cynical view of *Kingdom Come*, as he did in the pages of the *Nation*. Commenting on the aforementioned GQ profile, Chang (2007) writes, "Jay-Z threw up a black power fist while dressed in a Club Monaco cardigan, a Purple Label button-down and his own Rocawear sweats," adding that Jay-Z had "repackaged hip-hop's rebellion into a symbol of the postmulticulturalist good life." [. . .] And again, this is a valid critique of Jay-Z, but when such imagery is interpreted in a broader discursive context, the image of Jay-Z in *GQ* can be read as a critical revision of the often problematic masculinities that undergirded some of the radical and black nationalist politics of the 1960s. Chang's commentary on Jay-Z anticipates one of the most enduring critiques of him, namely, that Jay-Z's fixation with the accumulation of wealth sits uncomfortably with many, including those who have some amount of faith in his discursive possibilities.

The wealth that Jay-Z and figures like Russell Simmons and Sean Combs have amassed is in many ways unprecedented, particularly given their ages; all were under forty when they achieved their wealth. Their financial success has created anxieties among traditional black political leadership and various activist communities, particularly among those located on the political left. Given the ways that poverty and frugality have been romanticized, even fetishized, on the political left—particularly in relation to one's commitment to "struggle"—it's understandable that it is difficult to think of Jay-Z and his reported $400 million net worth in progressive political terms. Indeed, a Black Power fist or Che Guevara t-shirt is not a substitute for concrete political activity, but the wealth of individuals like Jay-Z and Simmons can be leveraged on behalf of their particular social and political passions in ways that conservative figures like the Koch brothers have done rather effectively. Even some so-called conscious rappers have admitted that the accumulation of wealth and the subsequent pursuit of the "good life" are not antithetical to the pursuit of social justice. For example, on his track "It's Your World (part 1 and 2)," the Chicago-based rapper Common asserts that "My generation never understood workin' for the man / And, of bein' broke I ain't a fan." [. . .] His fellow "political" rapper Talib Kweli takes the critique a step further, holding black political organizations accountable for their failure to consider the importance of finances: "You join an organization that know black history / But ask them how they plan to make money and it's a mystery." [. . .]

Many of these issues came to the forefront when Jay-Z and Kanye West collaborated on the project *Watch the Throne* (2011). Few artists in the prime of their careers have ever decided to come together in the ways that Jay-Z and West do on *Watch the Throne*, which begs the question, what was in it for each? [. . .] Indeed, when word of *Watch the Throne* began to surface—the project took over a year to complete—some fans and critics reacted with cynicism, despite that fact that Jay-Z and West often expressed real affection and respect for each other. [. . .] Such cynicism was likely the product of collective fears that Jay-Z and West's pairing would not only *not* produce great art, but would confirm their unwillingness—or, more troubling, their inability—to say anything of consequence at a moment when many desire mainstream pop artists to index their secular and spiritual concerns. Yet part of what possibly made *Watch the Throne* attractive for Carter and West is the fact that they were all too aware of their disconnect from the working-class worlds that produced them, and the unique and isolated positions that each holds at the pinnacle of his craft and celebrity, as well as the relative power, or lack of power, associated with those positions. [. . .]

As such, *Watch the Throne* serves as a meditation on Black Power, not in the sense of the social movement that challenged America in the 1960s and beyond to live up to its radical democratic tenets, but rather in the will of so many generations of black folk to imagine the highest quality of life for themselves. In line with Diawara's earlier point about the desire to live "the good life," what has often made hip-hop matter to the working-class communities that produced it, even in the days of "party and bullshit," is its ability to be aspirational. This is a point that the branding expert Steve Stoute (2011) argues. [. . .] [H]e writes that the "force of aspiration" is the "power that turns nothing into something [. . .]" (Stoute 2011: 7).

In a country marked by the richness of immigrant cultures, black Americans may represent some of the most aspirational of peoples—willing themselves off of plantations and into some semblance of a still unrealized full citizenship—long before Shawn Carter and Kanye West ever walked into a recording studio. Black aspiration is Black Power, dating to the time, per the late poet Sekou Sundiata, when some "slave" dreamed of a freedom that she would never fully experience.[3] [. . .]

Hip-hop's genius move from the outset was to make the trinkets of everyday life the stuff of hyperconsumption—a story at least as old as Pig Feet Mary selling chitlins', hog maws, and of course pig feet out of a baby carriage in Harlem in the early twentieth century and later becoming a real estate tycoon, or the Fisk Jubilee Singers traveling around the globe providing European audiences with a taste of those good old Negro spirituals in the late nineteenth century, or Henry Box Brown re-creating his escape act for European audiences years before the Emancipation Proclamation (Lewis 1989: 109–10; Brooks 2006: 66–130). Perhaps no commodity was as valuable to hip-hop as the conceit of the lyrical boast, itself intimately related to the traditions of black expressive culture, whether expressed by school kids playing the dozens, the dandy on Chicago's Stroll in the 1920s, or Nikki Giovanni's 1969 poem "Ego Tripping," a direct precursor to rap music.

When the late Notorious B.I.G. opined, "Fuck a dollar and a dream"—putting into context the way that hood-controlled numbers running had been appropriated by the state—he did so knowing that he was of a generation of young blacks who were part of a commercial culture that no longer simply had to dream. [. . .] There's no denying that rap music has changed over the years; the conceits that were once simply metaphors—yes, the dreams of Black Power—are now quantifiable assets. [. . .]

In one of the more popular lyrics from *Watch the Throne*, West describes the project as "luxury rap"—cited often by detractors as evidence of how out of touch West and Jay-Z were—yet the lyric is followed by a lyric that describes West as the "Hermes of verses." Hermes is, of course, one of the important messengers in Greek mythology and often described as a guide to the underworld. West's juxtaposing of the lyrics was likely just a means of recognizing his ability to speak to both highbrow and lowbrow audiences, a notion seemingly confirmed with the following lyric, "sophisticated ignorance." Later, though, Jay-Z picks up on the theme of the underworld or underground, referencing Fidel Castro's Cuba (saluting the Cuban dictator while standing in front of a customized American flag in the song's video) and economic success among Spanish-speaking immigrant communities, before adding, "not bad, huh, for immigrants? / Build your fences, we diggin' tunnels / Can't you see we gettin' money up under you?" Here Jay-Z uses the metaphors of American immigration policy and the underground economies to construct political and economic affinity with immigrant communities. Even Jay-Z's gesture to Castro suggests more an acknowledgment of his ability to stay in political power while facing down American efforts to destabilize the Cuban government in the region for more than fifty years. [. . .]

Many of those who dismiss Jay-Z's potential—discursive or otherwise—do so because they disregard the so-called subaltern consciousness that is palpable throughout his music and informs some of his choices as a corporate taste maker. Jay-Z and West's seemingly throwaway lines about their Mercedes Benzes and paparazzi ("They ain't seen me cause I pulled up in my other Benz / Last week I was in my other other Benz. . . . Photoshoot fresh, lookin' like wealth / I'm 'bout to call the paparazzi on myself") are as much about the modes of surveillance that are often associated with celebrity, a space that both men share with many other black men in American society. In another example, when Jay-Z was asked about his interest in purchasing a London-based soccer club—the presumed coming together of hip-hop and "soccer hooligans"—Jay-Z quipped, "There's a ghetto everywhere," highlighting again Nwankwo's notion of a cosmopolitanism that is both local and global (Youngmisuk 2005). That Jay-Z's music doesn't concretely address the poverty and misery that exist among the black poor (and what music has?) and his wealth does not allow him (and hip-hop, for that matter) to speak back to the state in the ways that might more directly address subaltern concerns, does not detract from the fact that his wealth does allow him to speak back to corporate power. Jay-Z's lyric "Just sent a million dollars through a hands-free / that's big money talk can you answer me" from *Kingdom Come*'s "Prelude" is not just a simple boast when read alongside his widely reported admonishment of Frederic Rouzaud, president of Champaign Louis Roederer (producer of the hip-hop elite's champagne of choice, Cristal), for comments that Jay-Z deemed racist (Century 2006). More importantly, with the conflation of the state and the corporate sphere—of which the privatization of the state is but one example—Jay-Z's wealth, and that of the hip-hop generation, is not a minor conceit.

Perhaps a more compelling example of Jay-Z's subaltern sensibilities can be found on the track "Minority Report," which also appeared on *Kingdom Come*. Written in the aftermath of Hurricane Katrina's destruction of the Gulf Coast, "Minority Report" represents Jay-Z at his most politically lucid, as he holds the state accountable for failing to deliver goods and services to its citizens. Jay-Z's critique then goes a step further as he also admonishes his peers with the observation "Silly rappers, 'cause we got a couple Porsches / MTV stopped by to film our fortresses / We forget the unfortunate." But rather than revel in his own propensity for giving—Jay-Z and Sean Combs donated $1 million of their own money to relief efforts—Jay-Z holds a mirror up to himself: "Sure I ponied up a mil' but I didn't give my time / So in reality I didn't give a dime or a damn / I just put my monies in the hands of the same people that left my people stranded. . . . Damn, money we gave was just a band-aid." [. . .] The lyrics are revealing because Jay-Z is willing to be self-critical as he grapples with the limits of his capacity to directly address the conditions of the Gulf Coast and the recognition that, at the time, there was not an infrastructure in place that could better serve the needs of those in the region. [. . .]

The larger point that I'm making here is that the popularity and influence of hip-hop demand that we develop the language to better address the seeming contradictions between the pursuit of the good life and all of its material accoutrements. "Modern blackness," a concept employed by the cultural anthropologist Deborah A. Thomas to discuss contemporary cultural practices in Jamaica, provides some critical perspective here. According to Thomas, modern blackness "requires that we abandon the binaries of hegemony and resistance, global and local, and instead try to understand the range of cultural formations among . . . African descended people throughout the diaspora" (Thomas 2004: 15). For Thomas, modern blackness is "unapologetically presentist and decidedly mobile. It challenges the past-tenseness of 'folk' blackness and African heritage as well as the notion of an evolving future based on creole nationalists' modernist visions" (2004: 13).

REFERENCES

Brooks, Daphne. 2006. *Bodies in Dissent: Spectacular Performances of Race and Freedom, 1850–1910*. Durham, NC: Duke University Press.

Century, Doublas. 2006. "Jay-Z Puts a Cap on Cristal." *New York Times*, July 2, sec. 9, p. 1.

Chang, Jeff. 2007. "Moving On Up." *The Nation*, January 22.

De Veaux, Alexis. 2004. *Warrior Poet: A Biography of Audrey Lorde.* New York: Norton.

Diawara, Manthia. 1998. "Homeboy Cosmopolitan." In *In Search of Africa*. Cambridge, MA: Harvard University Press.

Edlund, Martin. 2004. "Turning the Tables." *New York Sun*, February 17, p. 18.

Eshun, Ekow. 2005. "Battle of the Brands." *New Statesman*, January 15, p. 40–41.

Fleetwood, Nicole. 2005. "Hip-Hop Fashion, Masculine Anxiety, and the Discourse of Americana." In *Black Cultural Traffic: Crossroads in Global Performance of Popular Culture*, edited by Harry J. Elam and Kennell Jackson. Ann Arbor: University of Michigan Press.

Fleetwood, Nicole. 2011. *Troubling Vision: Performance, Visuality, and Blackness*. Chicago: University of Chicago Press.

Halberstam, Judith. 2005. *In a Queer Time and Place: Transgender Bodies, Subcultural Lives*. New York: New York University Press.

Healy, Mark. 2006. "Renaissance Mogul," *GQ*, December.

Jackson, John L. Jr. 2005. *Real Black: Adventures in Racial Sincerity*. Chicago: University of Chicago Press.

Jay-Z. 2006. "30 Something." *Kingdom Come*. Island Def Jam/Roc-A-Fella.

Jay-Z. 2010. *Decoded*. New York: Spiegel Grau.

King, Jason. 2000. "Any Love: Silence, Theft and Rumor in the Work of Luther Vandross." *Callaloo* 23 (1): 422–47.

Kitwana, Bakari. 2004. "Jay Z: Hip-Hop and High Society." *Black Book Magazine*, Spring.

Lewis, David Levering. 1989. *When Harlem Was in Vogue*. New York: Oxford University Press.

Lorde, Audrey. 1982. *Zami: A New Spelling of My Name*. Freedom, CA: Crossing.

McInnis, C. Leigh Jr. 2000. *The Lyrics of Prince Rogers Nelson: A Literature Look at a Creative, Musical Poet, Philosopher, and Storyteller*. Jackson, MS: Psychedelic Literature.

Moten, Fred. 2003. *In the Break: The Black Radical Tradition*. Minneapolis: University of Minnesota Press.

Nwankwo, Ifeoma Kiddoe. 2005. *Black Cosmopolitanism: Racial Consciousness and Transnational Identity in the Nineteenth-Century Americas*. Philadelphia: University of Pennsylvania Press.

Perry, Imani. 2004. *Prophets of the Hood: Politics and Poetics in Hip-Hop*. Durham, NC: Duke University Press.

Rushbrook, Dereka. 2002. "Cities, Queer Space, and the Cosmopolitan Tourist." *GLQ* 8 (1–2): 183–206.

Simpson, Mark. 1994. "Here Come the Mirror Men." *Independent* (UK), November 15.

Smith, Christopher Holmes. 2003. "'I Don't Like to Dream about Getting Paid': Representations of Social Mobility and the Emergence of the Hip-Hop Mogul." *Social Text* 77 (21): 69–97.

Stoute, Steve. 2011. *The Tanning of America: How Hip-Hop Created a Culture That Rewrote the Rules of the New Economy*. New York: Gotham Books.

Thomas, Deborah A. 2004. *Modern Blackness: Nationalism, Globalization, and the Politics of Culture in Jamaica*. Durham, NC: Duke University Press.

Toure. 2005. "The Book of Jay." *Rolling Stone*, December 15, pp. 80–89.

Youngmisuk, Ohm. 2005. "No Sleep till Brooklyn: Jay-Z Won't Rest Until Nets Take Over Town." *New York Daily News*, November 15.

NOTES

1. "If I Was Your Girlfriend" was also covered by TLC on their album *CrazySexyCool* (1994). The lead singer T-Boz's voice also has the effect of challenging notion of gender address.

2. In this regard Jay-Z's anxieties about is newfound celebrity are palpable on a track like "Hollywood" from *Kingdom Come* (2006), where he laments both the multiple gazes he now faces as well as his deference to his wife, Beyoncé, who is clearly the more visible celebrity.

3. Sekou Sundiata, "Urban Music," *Longstoryshort* (Righteous Babe Records, 2000).

AMY C. WILKINS

18. MASCULINITY DILEMMAS: SEXUALITY AND INTIMACY TALK AMONG CHRISTIANS AND GOTHS

In this article, I compare seemingly antithetical groups of white middle-class young adult men. The first, members of a university-based evangelical organization I call University Unity, engage in a conservative cultural agenda, abstain from partying and sex, and commit themselves to self-discipline and moral cleanliness. The second, goths, self-consciously use dark clothes and dark emotions to transform themselves into self-proclaimed freaks. Apparent boundary transgressors, they adopt elements of gender blending and queer play. Christianity and goth provide distinct ways of navigating the space between adolescence and adulthood, yet their masculinity projects achieve similar things. Both evangelical Christian and goth men attempt to ameliorate some of the more restrictive expectations of masculinity by crafting masculinity projects out of available cultural resources.

[. . .] [T]he elusive ideal of hegemonic masculinity creates particular gender dilemmas for different boys and men as they struggle to create socially recognized masculinities. The ensuing negotiations over masculinity are embedded in power relations both between men and women and among men. Heterosexuality and emotional stoicism are central (and often linked) components of hegemonic masculinity. The persistent expectation that boys will be boys mandates and excuses the performance of aggressive heterosexuality among young men. Not only are boys and men assumed to be heterosexual, but they are assumed to be heterosexual in particular ways. For young men especially, heterosexuality is imagined as a relentless drive, endlessly preoccupying and always potentially out of control. Accordingly, men are assumed to be heterosexually predatory and dominant, and more interested in sex than in emotions. Nonetheless, men's heterosexual

dominance and emotional stoicism have both come under attack, complicating the cultural terrain of men's dominance (Messner 1993). In this article, I examine the ways in which young men use unconventional sexualities and intimacy talk, an emotional vocabulary associated with a "feminine" style of love, to resolve their masculinity dilemmas.

These young men do not enact gender projects in isolation. Subcultures make alternative gender identities more possible because they provide community and support for practices that might otherwise be isolating. Both the Unity Christian and the goth subcultures create conditions for the staging of alternative heterosexual performances and collectively manipulate dominant meanings of masculinity. In both cases, new collective meanings of heterosexuality and manhood, not the practices themselves, allow participants to manage their masculinities. [. . .] By examining the similarities and differences between seemingly antithetical masculinities, we can begin to see not just a plurality of ways of being masculine but also patterns among them. Despite striking differences in the gender projects of Unity Christian and goth men, they similarly navigate dilemmas posed by masculine expectations. Each group of men differently renounces components of dominant notions of masculinity, achieving more flexibility in the performance of masculinity. Yet, in the end, both the Christians' conservative project and the goths' gender-blending project fail to challenge gendered power hierarchies.

THINKING ABOUT MASCULINITIES

Feminists and other social commentators are concerned about the implications of a masculine culture of aggression and sexual dominance for both boys and girls (Eder 1995), as well as the suppression of "soft" emotionality among boys. [. . .] As a result of these concerns, feminists and progressive youth often applaud boys' and men's adoption of unorthodox behaviors. These challenges to definitions of "real" masculinity have opened up some cultural space for the acceptable performance of a wider range of masculine styles (see Schippers 2002; Anderson 2005).

Cultural change is never univocal, however. While some social commentators lament the loss of feelings among boys, others complain that contemporary boys are becoming too soft. Sut Jhally documents an increasing emphasis on masculine toughness in the media (*Tough Guise* 1999). In his research on the families of boys who have been sexually abused, C. Shawn McGuffey (2008) also found that fathers, in part, attribute their sons' abuse to a vulnerability stemming from "softer" parenting strategies. These fathers attempt to cure their sons by deliberately instilling qualities of emotional toughness and heterosexual dominance in them. These examples seem to suggest a cultural struggle in which, on one hand, restrictive notions of masculinity are questioned by progressives while, on the other hand, a conservative backlash reasserts masculine toughness.

But masculinities are more complex than they initially appear. First, masculinities are not static but are contingent and negotiated. Boys and men draw on available resources to actively manage their masculinities (Chen 1999). For example, young men are able to use high-status masculine traits as bargaining chips that allow them to also exhibit lower status traits (McGuffey and Rich 1999). In a study of a California high school, C. J. Pascoe (2003) found that boys who were athletically successful could exhibit "soft" feelings without consequence but nonathletic boys could not. These examples suggest that high-status boys and men have more flexibility in their gender performances. Because their masculinities are already anchored by investments in high-status dimensions of masculinity (e.g., sports), they are able to play with less manly forms of gender expressions [. . .]. But even lower-status boys and men can position themselves as masculine by claiming high-status elements of masculinity. Rather than challenge

dominant understandings of masculinity, this maneuvering allows a spectrum of men to "claim this masculinity for themselves" (Pascoe 2003, 1425; see also Chen 1999).

Second, because masculinities are historically and spatially contingent, the gendered meanings that attach to particular behaviors vary by organizational culture (Dellinger 2004). Moreover, as Melanie Heath (2003) argues, "contradictory gender . . . ideologies can fuel collective identities and social movements" (426). Thus, conservative spaces can offer challenges to restrictive definitions of masculinity, and progressive spaces can simultaneously reproduce masculine dominance. The Promise Keepers, for example, promote community and caring among men while also reaffirming a man's role as family patriarch (Heath 2003). Gay men's spaces also loosen the tight link between masculinity and heterosexuality, yet may not challenge the bases for men's dominance over women. Peter Hennen (2004) documents the ways in which the Radical Faeries, a subculture of "gentle gender warriors," "active[ly] embrace" (2004: 500) the stereotype of gay men's effeminacy yet invoke essentialist gender distinctions (see also Yeung, Stombler, and Wharton 2006).

These examples caution us to temper both our celebrations and condemnations; it is more difficult than it initially seems to classify masculinities as either resistant or complicit. Challenges to undesirable or restrictive dimensions of masculinity not only are compatible with continued male dominance but may even further it. In addition, the historical and contextual specificity of hegemonic masculinity gives men more latitude in their masculine negotiations than is commonly recognized. [. . .] [And some] men are able to use these cultural challenges as resources in their gender projects.

THE DATA

This [chapter] is based on ethnographic studies of local Christian and goth subcultures. The claims I make in the [chapter] are not intended to be generalized to all Christians or goths but instead to document similarities and differences in local projects. I conducted twelve months of participant observation at University Unity meetings as well as at the home church of most of my participants and carried out formal, open-ended interviews with fifteen (six men and nine women) self-identified evangelical Christians. [. . .] Although I frequently use interview data with the men to illustrate my claims, my understanding of the dynamics of masculinity in both scenes emerges from the broader ethnographic projects and from the interviews with the women as well as the men. Participant observation allowed me to see masculinities in action, but interviews with women also gave me insight into how the women in the subcultures perceive the men's projects. [. . .]

The Christians in my study participate in a nondenominational organization that I call University Unity. With roots outside the Northeast, University Unity is interdenominational, although conservative Protestant in focus and flavor. For these Christians, participation in University Unity organizes their identities. University Unity claims about forty active members, has a weekly Thursday night meeting, sponsors six different student-led Bible study groups, and coordinates regular trips and events, including fall retreats and evangelizing spring break trips to popular spring break locales. [. . .]

The goths in this study are part of a local self-identified goth community, with ties to an international goth scene, which emerged in the early 1980s, and from which they take many of their meanings. In part a music scene, goth nonetheless implies much more than just shared musical taste. These goths come together weekly at a local dance club and maintain daily connections through their prolific community listserv. Although participants interact with nongoths in their daily lives, they think of themselves as part of a distinct community. Goth is defined by its "dark" aesthetic, woven into "freaky" goth fashion and expressed through participants' shared fascination with the macabre.

Both Christianity and goth seem to be open to anyone, regardless of race or class. But while there are no formal boundaries to participation in either group, both are overwhelmingly white and middle class, reflecting the general pattern of segregated associations common among white young people. Like most white people (see Bonilla-Silva 2003), the participants do not think of their projects in terms of race or class,

even while participants are culled from class-stratified institutions (colleges and universities) and participation requires substantial economic expenditures (for clothes, going out, spring break trips, etc.). [. . .]

[. . .] I argue that participants in each subculture use sexual strategies to recuperate their masculinities. Because their sexual strategies are distinct, I examine them separately. In the final section, I show that, despite these differences, University Unity Christians and goths make similar links between sexuality, intimacy talk, and masculinity.

MASCULINITY DILEMMAS AND SUBCULTURAL SOLUTIONS

Like other men, the men in this study face the central problem of achieving masculinity in the face of a cultural system that denigrates some of their practices as unmasculine. For these men, this problem seems especially pronounced. The particular problem these men face is shaped by their age, race, and class. They are white middle-class men on the cusp of adulthood. Among older boys and young men, toughness, athletic prowess, social visibility, power over others, and heterosexual success are typically key signs of real masculinity (Eder 1995; McGuffey and Rich 1999). Boys and young men who do not meet these criteria often suffer from isolation and/or harassment (Eder 1995).

Accordingly, both groups of men report being marginalized by their peers before becoming evangelical Christians or goths. While some were simply invisible, others were more actively ostracized or picked on. Crow describes himself and other goths as "outcasts," explaining that the "head of the football team" had a "personal vendetta" against him. University Unity men do not tell stories as dramatic as the goths, but they also tell stories about not fitting in, not being able to get a girlfriend, not being good at sports, being too smart or too studious, or having "uncool" interests or concerns [. . .].

As geeks, these young men occupied the lower rungs of youth status hierarchies that are sorted, in part, by gender performance. "If you're a man," Sean, a goth, explains, "it doesn't make your life good to sit down at recess and read rather than play. . . . Doing well in school does not endear you to your peers." However, the development of technological and other academic skills associated with geekiness (even described by goths as "geeking") provides valuable masculine resources in the long run, allowing men to develop the requisite skills for adult careers and thus setting them up for the eventual acquisition of one kind of successful adult masculinity (see Cooper 2000).

This process is tied to race and class. As white middle-class boys enter adulthood, they learn to transfer their skill investments from athletics to academics, whereas black and poor boys, faced with few other opportunities for the performance of validated masculinities, do not (Messner 1989). Similarly, while boys of color may accrue status through the performance of hypermasculine traits associated with being cool, men of color are marginalized for those same performances (see also Kelley 1997; Wilkins 2004a). Thus, as white middle-class boys enter adulthood, they have new and enhanced opportunities for the performance of esteemed masculinities and more to gain from distancing themselves from elements of the masculinities associated with racially and socioeconomically subordinated men. Race and class privilege allow more flexibility in gender performances by anchoring University Unity and goth men to other high status markers. [. . .] Thus, both Christian and goth men occupy the paradoxical position of having low status among youth while benefiting from whiteness, middle-class status, and masculinity more generally, all of which are, however, invisible resources.

Both the University Unity and the goth subcultures provide solutions to young men's dilemmas. Evangelical Christianity and goth culture provide them with community, social support, and tools for thinking about themselves differently. [. . .] In both subcultures, participants also learn to think about themselves differently, transforming some of the attributes associated with their marginality into subcultural virtues (Schwalbe and Mason-Schrock 1996). [. . .] Unity Christians remake themselves as good men. Goths remake themselves as "freaks." In both cases, their new identities are chosen, valorized, and used to make claims about themselves as men.

Sexuality is a principal arena in which both Unity Christians and goths remake their masculinities.

In this [chapter], I am concerned not with what Unity and goth men actually do sexually but with how they use sexual practices and rhetoric to reconstitute their masculinities. The sexual performances of Unity and goth men are distinct, even antithetical, yet each violates dominant notions of young men's sexuality as voracious, resolutely heterosexual, sexually dominant, and emotionally shallow. Unity members are sexually abstinent, whereas goths are sexually exploratory and endorse some forms of queer play. Moreover, both sets of men portray sexuality as emotionally intimate and evince concern for women's emotions. [. . .] In both cases, however, their sexual performances manage, rather than jeopardize, their masculinities. [. . .]

UNIVERSITY UNITY SEXUAL STRATEGIES

University Unity Christians are sexually abstinent. They are universally committed to postponing sex until marriage. In addition, most do not date at all. Abstinence is particularly striking among young men since relentless sexual desire is central to cultural understandings of adolescent and young adult masculinity. [. . .] However, in contrast to goth practices such as polyamory (explicit and consensual nonmonogamy), Unity men's commitment to abstinence is endorsed by an adult-run international organization and aligns with a popular, conservative-led political agenda that condemns premarital sexual activity. The institutionally structured expectation of abstinence provides resources to protect the masculinity of Unity men. First, the Christian identity provides a reasonable explanation for nonparticipation in heterosexual conquest, hiding other, potentially more gender-discrediting reasons for nonparticipation. Second, ritual attention to "the problem of [hetero]sexual temptation," as a Unity pamphlet put it, allows Unity men to prove themselves sufficiently heterosexual in the absence of actual heterosexual practices.

Before becoming Christians, Unity men were generally not heterosexually successful. Their heterosexual problems took a variety of forms, including the inability to get a girlfriend, a lack of interest in sexuality or dating, and the desire to avoid crushing heartbreak. In an abashed tone, Unity Christian Jon reveals, "I wasn't that popular with girls in high school. It's kind of embarrassing." Kevin expresses disinterest in both dating and sexuality. Aaron regrets that he had sex before becoming a Christian, emphasizing his heartbreak, rather than sin or shame: "Sometimes I think God tells us not to do something because it's just hurtful if we do." For young men, each of these problems is potentially stigmatizing. [. . .] For Unity men, the expectation of abstinence provides a way to transform the meaning of their heterosexual experiences. [. . .]

Lucas's story is illustrative of the broader pattern in the data. Lucas was harassed in high school. He was raised in a Christian family, but he initially viewed church as a place to seek girls, not God. He explains: "In high school, I was, like, not very popular and I was trying to get a girlfriend. I wasn't very popular and they were all mean to me so I decided to go where there would be nice and good-looking girls: church." Lucas hoped that getting a girlfriend, especially a good-looking one, would ease his humiliation, both because a girlfriend would provide him with intimacy and because she would salvage his masculinity by proving his heterosexual prowess. At church, though, Lucas found something different: "I found my identity in God. It gave me so much joy," he explains. Committing himself to the Christian identity, he abandoned his quest for a girlfriend: "I still haven't had a girlfriend. I made a conscious decision. I just saw people who had girlfriends—they always broke up, and as soon as they broke up, they wanted another girlfriend. Like obsessive. I didn't want that. I wanted to focus on schoolwork and on my relationship with God." Christianity did not make Lucas heterosexually successful. Instead, it transformed the meaning of his heterosexual nonparticipation. Lucas had wanted a girlfriend, but after becoming a Christian, he explains, he chose not to date girls. Once rejected by girls, Lucas is now the rejecter (at least in the abstract): he is choosing not to become romantically or sexually involved. [. . .] Drawing on University Unity discourse, Lucas neutralizes his heterosexual nonparticipation and turns it into a mark of masculine self-discipline. The Unity group provides Christian men with a label—"abstinence"—and an explanation for heterosexual nonparticipation that allows them to think of themselves not only as sufficiently heterosexual but as better men.

This rationale is not convincing to all audiences, to be sure. [. . .] But it is convincing, at least to him and to other Christians like him. Moreover, for outsiders like me, it provides a cogent explanation, one that deflects attention from his possible heterosexual failure. In sum, then, University Unity men use the expectation and rhetoric of Christian abstinence to transform embarrassing heterosexual records into purposefully chosen sexual identities. [. . .] Rather than abandon the centrality of heterosexuality, they temporarily privilege other aspects of masculinity such as self-control; indeed, they claim self-control on the basis of resisting heterosexuality.

In addition, University Unity men perform their heterosexuality collectively, aligning themselves with conventional assumptions about masculinity through the ritual invocation of temptation. [. . .] Temptation is a necessary part of the performance of abstinence: without temptation, heterosexual nonparticipation is not abstinence. While Unity men do not identify temptation as a problem in their pre-abstinence stories, in becoming members of University Unity, Christian men acquire the language of temptation. Christian temptation talk helps transform heterosexual nonparticipation into abstinence—a moral identity achieved through self-discipline and commitment. But, at the same time, it also maintains the assumptions that heterosexual desire is a central component of masculinity and that Christian men are, in fact, real men.

Temptation talk peppers University Unity materials. The question of why everyone struggles with sexual immorality is a theme addressed in reading materials and by the group leaders. Although the word "everyone" suggests that this is a problem faced by both women and men, Susan told me a story about a University Unity–sponsored summer retreat, for example, that underscored the ways in which temptation talk is gendered. At the retreat, Susan explains, she learned in a conversation with the young men about their struggles with temptation: "I really had no idea, like, for guys, struggling to be sexually pure. They were brutally honest: 'it's a minute by minute thing for us [men] . . . even a spaghetti strap can be hard.' I think girls struggle with different things."[1]

This conversation collectively reaffirmed the masculinity of young University Unity men, allowing them to prove their heterosexuality by talking about it. Instead of bragging about "scoring," they talked about how hard they struggled to be sexually pure. [. . .] The ritual profession of sexual temptation thus does part of the work of stabilizing the heterosexuality of sexually abstinent men.

Tied as it is to a collective identity, abstinence takes the heat off Christian men, allowing them to deflect not only their own inability to attract women but also imputations of inadequate heterosexual drive that would compromise their masculine identities. Instead, the collective performances allow them to claim masculine heterosexual desire in the absence of heterosexual practice. This strategy minimizes the costs of their unorthodox performances of masculinity, shores up qualities associated with long-term masculine success (such as self-discipline and autonomous decision making), and allows them to think of themselves as real men. [. . .] Although the Unity Christian strategy challenges the assumption that real men are sexually predatory, it does not challenge the assumption that men are naturally more sexual than women.

GOTH SEXUAL STRATEGIES [. . .]

In contrast to University Unity abstinence, the goth scene facilitates heterosexual success. Goths pride themselves on being sexually adventuresome. By fostering a space in which sexuality is encouraged, is public, and is built into community practices, goth men are able to use goth sexual culture to perform a kind of successful masculinity and heterosexuality. The goth scene provides these opportunities by transforming conventionally unattractive men into sexually desirable men (at least within the subculture) and by creating occasions for sexual contact with multiple partners. [. . .] Despite these conventional forms of success, goth men violate two central assumptions of normative heterosexuality: First, in a reversal of dominant heterosexual courtship norms, goths expect women to be sexually aggressive. Second, goth men engage in elements of queer play.

Like the Christians, goths use talk to establish sexual identities. Instead of talking about sexual temptation, however, they showcase their sexual experiences, sexual knowledge, and comfort with

unconventional forms of sex. Goth men participate in forms of sexual boasting associated with men in other contexts. Hunter, for example, told me, "since [his last girlfriend], I've had eighteen partners. I'm a guy. We keep count." Goths also convey their varied sexual repertoire by bragging about their comfort with bondage, group sex, and, as I discuss below, bisexuality. [. . .]

The organization and expectations of the goth scene also enable successful heterosexual practice. Many goth men would not be viewed as attractive in other young adult arenas. Some of the men are overweight, others are short or very thin, and many appear effeminate. These men, however, are desirable to goth women. As Jeff explains, "Before the Sanctuary, I didn't feel unattractive, I didn't feel noticed. I think that's the case for a lot of people. Over time, I'm more and more noticed because I get better at it [making himself attractive to other goths]. No one wants to be ugly. It's sort of like a bubble from the outside world." Goth aesthetic expectations redefine desirability in ways that incorporate goth men, and the goth emphasis on creativity means that men can reinvent themselves as desirable. [. . .]

Because of its climate of sexual openness and experimentation, and because the community is organized around weekly dance nights and regular parties, the goth scene provides men with opportunities to add to their sexual coffers. Goth norms discourage monogamy and "vanilla" sex, instead encouraging polyamory, group sex, and "freaky" sexual experimentation. These norms mean that, even when they are in relationships, goth men are able to access sex with a variety of women and are able to frequently fulfill stereotypical male fantasies of sexual encounters with several women at the same time. [. . .]

Goth further facilitates heterosexual liaisons through its culture of sexual openness and adventurousness. Before becoming a goth, Graham states, he was sexually inexperienced and uninterested. He explains that the sexual experimentation at goth parties "sped along his breaking," encouraging him to experiment sexually in a way he had previously avoided. For example, he describes a party at which "five girls were giving me hickies because I look like [some other guy]." In this story, Graham reports his participation in a stock masculine sexual fantasy in which he is given sexual attention by multiple women—but he did not have to initiate the interaction. Thus, with its centrality of sexual adventure, the goth scene provides a conventional means of fortifying the masculinities of goth men. And yet, the dynamics of gender and sexuality in the goth scene are unconventional in many ways: goth men gain, rather than lose, heterosexual cachet through their willingness to violate dominant heterosexual scripts.

Goth norms reverse mainstream courtship scripts. Goth women are expected to be sexually aggressive, and goth men are discouraged from being sexually predatory. This reversal is chiefly achieved through goth etiquette about spatial boundaries. These rules elaborate a set of collective assumptions about appropriate "pick-up" behavior. For example, men are not supposed to approach unknown women. Instead, as I was told, they should arrange an introduction through a mutual friend. These rules help create a space in which women feel freed from the more distasteful aspects of mainstream clubs: overly aggressive men and unsolicited touching. [. . .]

Goth women experience this reversal as empowering.[2] Goth men, however, are not disempowered by it. Instead, men who had little prior experience picking up women can be sexually successful without engaging in behavior that they may also find distasteful, that they are unskilled at, or that runs the risk of rejection and painful humiliation. They are able to see themselves as respectful of women without sacrificing sexual opportunities. For example, as Sean earnestly explains, "I don't really flirt with people first. I don't really try to pick someone up. Mostly from having conversations with women about people flirting with them, it makes them feel bad. I don't want to make anyone's day bad. I know I am not the most nonthreatening person ever. I am not small, not feminine. I am often leathery and spiky." By expecting women to be the sexual aggressors, goth men do not lose out on heterosexual opportunities, but rather, they likely gain them. [. . .]

In addition to assuming the role of sexual catch, goths violate gender boundaries by incorporating some elements of queer play. Regardless of a goth's own sexual predilections, one is expected to demonstrate gothness through tolerance for and familiarity with different kinds of sexual play. Accordingly, many, but not all, goth men "gender blend." Greg comments, "It's hard enough finding clothes for men that are interesting. I am not going to limit myself to men's clothes. It's fun." [. . .] In contrast to other contexts, these men's use of feminine accouterments does not signal a rejection of heterosexuality. Rather, it can increase their heterosexual success with goth women, who confess their attraction to androgynous men and to men in women's clothing. As one goth woman posts, "Men in skirts are yummy!"

In addition, some goth men perform a kind of symbolic bisexuality. Women's bisexuality is increasingly more hip in some circles, but men's bisexuality is less so (e.g., see Schippers 2002; Wilkins 2004b). The community in which this study takes places has a large and visible lesbigay population; in addition, both sexual tolerance and sexual experimentation are central to the goth identity. Within this context, goth men situate themselves on the border of bisexuality. Hunter says, "I've kissed men, kissed women. I'm completely straight though; nothing bothers me." [. . .] Goth men are proud of their willingness to experiment physically with other men. Indeed, when they kiss other men, it is public, not private. By flirting with bisexuality, they reinforce their identities as tolerant, enlightened, experimental, and secure in their manhood. At the same time, these men claim to be straight. In the same breath, Crow laments, "Sadly, I'm straight," professes his attraction to men, and explains why he is unwilling to have sex with the men to whom he is attracted. [. . .] By refusing to relinquish their identities as straight, despite bisexual behavior, goth men are able to maintain the privileges of heterosexuality and to maintain some distance from a potentially discrediting association with gay men. [. . .] In short, this strategy makes them hip without making them gay.

Siobhan indicates that these men are at least partially successful: "In my group, there are a few men who are out as bisexual. I really admire them. . . . It's sexy for women to be bisexual but not for men—not as many gay men . . . are considered manly." It's not clear from Siobhan's comment whether being bisexual requires owning the label (as the men I interviewed do not) or just kissing other men in public, as many of these men do. What she does make clear is that the putative added stigma attached to bisexuality for men means that men who dare to explore feelings for other men, or who even suggest that they are open to the possibility, are able to accrue status in a scene that prides itself on its ability to transgress conventional sexual norms, even while they avoid taking on the label "bisexual." [. . .] Critical of the way goth men are able to capitalize on bisexual symbolism, Rory says, "Most men in the goth scene—theoretically bisexuality [sic], practice heterosexuality. It's cooler. Chicks dig bisexual guys; it makes them sound open minded."

For goth men, departures from dominant gendered sexual scripts are likely sincere attempts to break down gender and sexual barriers. The quest to be gender alternative, however, does not dismantle the gender status quo. This happens because the goth scene is a space in which men accrue status from being alternative, women are grateful for their freedom from lecherous men, and participants presume that it is harder for men than for women to engage in queer play. Thus, within the goth scene, alternative gendered behavior is a resource that men can use both to increase their heterosexual desirability and to bolster their status in a way that is less available to women (see Wilkins 2004b, 2008).

The sexual strategies of the goth men are very different from those of the Christians. Goths remake themselves as heterosexually successful by participating in a subculture in which they have opportunities to have sex. But as with University Unity men, goth subcultural meanings allow goth men to use their unconventional heterosexual strategies as resources to shore up their heterosexuality. These transformations are furthered, I show next, through the common use of intimacy talk.

INTIMACY TALK AND MASCULINITIES

Although University Unity Christians are abstinent and goths are sexually adventuresome, both sets of men use what I call intimacy talk to manage their sexual practices and to claim a certain kind of manhood. By intimacy talk, I refer to an emotional vocabulary that includes talk about emotional vulnerability; the desire for communication, trust,

and intimacy; and respect for, or appreciation of, women. Francesca Cancian (1987) argues that these qualities are feminized and associated with love, whereas sex and instrumental support are masculinized and less likely to be seen as love. Intimacy talk therefore responds to feminist and popular concerns about men's participation in relational emotion work.

To be sure, Christian and goth men do not erect identical masculinity projects: Christian men draw more, but not exclusively, on images associated with old-fashioned chivalry, whereas goth men draw more on rhetoric associated with feminism (e.g., notions of women's empowerment). Christian men are more likely to reference a hypothetical future relationship, but goth men often reference lived experiences (although goth men too may use intimacy talk as a hypothetical). Nonetheless, both sets of men use intimacy talk in strikingly similar ways. First, both University Unity and goth men use intimacy talk to justify their sexual practices. Their sexual practices are desirable, they both say, because they lead to greater relational intimacy. Second, both sets of men use intimacy talk to claim masculinities that are presumably more moral and more desirable than the masculinities of other sorts of men. Unity men describe themselves as "better men." Goths portray themselves as "evolved."[3]

Both University Unity and goth men talk about sex and relationships in a way that suggests their ability to engage in a feminine style of love. By talking about intimacy in this way, they seem to violate notions of men as nonemotive. But, as with their unconventional sexualities, intimacy talk is recuperative: their violation is a way for Christians and goths to think about themselves as different kinds of men. [. . .] Both Christian and goth men describe sex as less important than relational intimacy. Aaron, who is the only University Unity man to claim he has had sex (which occurred before he was a Christian), explains, "The point of sex is not ultimately because it feels good; the best part of sex is the moment right after." Hunter, a goth, sounds much like Aaron: alternating his sexual boasting with an admission of his own emotional vulnerability, he tells me, "One of the reasons I like sleeping next to people at night [is that] the shells go away." In emphasizing their desire for closeness and their vulnerability, these men suggest that they are different from other (young adult) men because they privilege emotional intimacies associated with sharing, self-disclosure, and mutual vulnerability over the physical pleasures of sex. [. . .]

In these comments, neither University Unity nor goth men are necessarily that different from other men. Indeed, their comments sound much like the comments I hear from my students, women and men, when I ask them what makes a good relationship. Cancian (1987) too finds that most men associate love with the kinds of intimacies these men discuss. Regardless, these men think about themselves as different, and they connect this difference to their particular sexual practices. Both sets of men claim that their sexual strategies are a way to achieve greater intimacy in their relationships with women, although they use opposing logic. For Christian men, exclusivity creates greater intimacy. For goth men, participation in a broader range of relationships requires more attention to relational emotion work and thus leads to improved intimacy.

Christian men argue that because sex is so intimate, it should occur only in the context of a committed relationship. [. . .] Intimacy talk lays out a path to a particular kind of manhood—one in which they can become men who care about the needs and concerns of their future wives and who are best able to meet the expectation of exclusive emotional closeness because they have not shared themselves with anyone else. For goths, polyamory, not abstinence, is the path to greater relational intimacy. Polyamory, goth men tell me, pushes them to work on their emotions in their heterosexual relationships. [. . .] Thus, like University Unity men, goths posit their sexual strategies as a means of developing heterosexual relationships that work better because men are more attuned to and respectful of the emotional needs of the relationships and their partners. [. . .]

Intimacy talk is thus supple enough to be linked to a range of sexual practices. For University Unity men, intimacy talk is another heterosexual performance in that it suggests their long-term interest in women while also proposing that their abstinence will make them better partners than men who do not wait. For goth men, it is a way to navigate a middle ground: they are able to be heterosexually exploratory while also distinguishing themselves from the assumed shallow licentiousness of the average man. [. . .]

The intimacy talk of both University Unity and goth men occurs in tandem with a continued investment in essential gender difference. Lucas, a Christian, told me, "Women and men are different. Women are more emotional than men. Women focus more on love and loving. Men focus more on significance, acceptance, and making themselves known." Jeff, a goth, said, "[My girlfriend's] more threatened by my emotional connections to someone else. I'm more threatened by her sexual connections." [. . .] Essentialism also helps men garner a greater payoff for their intimacy talk than that received by women. In the economy of gratitude (Hochschild 1989), men's intimacy talk takes on greater significance because it is assumed to be a greater gift than that of women, for whom it is presumed to be natural. If women are better at relational work, then men deserve more credit for their efforts and skills. [. . .] Intimacy talk, then, does not necessarily undo privilege in heterosexual relationships and can even maintain it.

Like other resources, intimacy talk is more valuable if it is rare. Intimacy talk works because it circulates in a cultural space in which some men are assumed to be uncaring, untrustworthy, and disrespectful partners—and in which many women expect more from the men with whom they are involved. This strategy, then, is predicated on distinctions among men. These distinctions are achieved, in part, through the formulation of new identities as "better" (Christian) or "more enlightened" (goth) men. [. . .]

For both sets of men, popular critiques of masculine relational skills make intimacy talk available as a resource men can use to prove their relational worthiness. In this context, intimacy talk can be used to enhance sexual strategies and to bolster masculinity. Jack Sattel (1976) argues that men use situational disclosure strategically in their relationships with women. [. . .] The irony here is that both University Unity and goth men engage in intimacy talk. This commonality suggests that intimacy talk may be more widespread among men than the Unity group or the goths, both men and women, think. The widespread use and flexibility of intimacy talk further suggest that acceptable performances of masculinity have expanded even while most men are still presumed to behave in old ways. This paradox allows the structural bases of gender inequality to remain unchecked. [. . .] Jennifer Dunn (1999) demonstrates that women are less likely to interpret stalking behavior as predatory when men incorporate symbols of romance (e.g., when they show up with flowers). Symbols of intimacy, then, can be used by men not just to maintain privilege but also to reduce the perception that they are engaging in acts of domination.

[. . .]

REFERENCES

Anderson, Eric. 2005. "Orthodox and Inclusive Masculinity: Competing Masculinities among Heterosexual Men in a Feminized Terrain." *Sociological Perspectives* 48 (3): 337–55.

Bonilla-Silva, Eduardo. 2003. *Racism without Racists: Color-Blind Racism and the Persistence of Racial Inequality in the United States*. Lanham, MD: Rowman & Littlefield.

Cancian, Francesca M. 1987. *Love in America: Gender and Self-Development*. Cambridge, UK: Cambridge University Press.

Chen, Anthony S. 1999. "Lives at the Center of the Periphery, Lives at the Periphery of the Center: Chinese American Masculinities and Bargaining with Hegemony." *Gender & Society* 13 (5): 584–607.

Cooper, Marianne. 2000. "Being the 'Go-to Guy': Fatherhood, Masculinity, and the Organization of Work in Silicon Valley." *Qualitative Sociology* 23 (4): 379–405.

Dellinger, Kirsten. 2004. "Masculinities in 'Safe' and 'Embattled' Organizations: Accounting for Pornographic and Feminist Magazines." *Gender & Society* 18 (5): 545–66.

Dunn, Jennifer L. 1999. "What Love Has to Do with It: The Cultural Construction of Emotion and Sorority Women's Responses to Forcible Interaction." *Social Problems* 46 (3): 440–59.

Eder, Donna. 1995. *School Talk: Gender and Adolescent Culture*. New Brunswick, NJ: Rutgers University Press.

Heath, Melanie. 2003. "Soft-Boiled Masculinity: Renegotiating Gender and Racial Ideologies in the Promise Keepers Movement." *Gender & Society* 17 (3): 423–44.

Hennen, Peter. 2004. "Fae Spirits and Gender Trouble: Resistance and Compliance among the Radical Faeries." *Journal of Contemporary Ethnography* 33 (5): 499–533.

Hochschild, Arlie Russell. 1989. *The Second Shift: Working Parents and the Revolution at Home*. New York: Viking.

Hondagneu-Sotelo, Pierette, and Michael A. Messner. 1994. "Gender Displays and Men's Power: The 'New Man' and the Mexican Immigrant Man." In *Theorizing Masculinities*, edited by Harry Brod and Michael Kaufman, 200–18. Thousand Oaks, CA: Sage.

Kelley, Robin D. G. 1997. *Yo' Mama's Disfunktional! Fighting the Culture Wars in Urban America*. Boston: Beacon.

McGuffey, C. Shawn. 2008. "'Saving Masculinity': Gender Reaffirmation, Sexuality, Race, and Parental Responses to Male Child Sexual Abuse." *Social Problems* 55 (2): 216–37.

McGuffey, C. Shawn, and B. Lindsay Rich. 1999. "Playing in the Gender Transgression Zone: Race, Class, and Hegemonic Masculinity in Middle Childhood." *Gender & Society* 13 (5): 608–27.

Messner, Michael. 1989. "Masculinities and Athletic Careers." *Gender & Society* 3 (1): 71–88.

Messner, Michael. 1993. "'Changing Men' and Feminist Politics in the United States." *Theory and Society* 22 (5): 723–37.

Pascoe, C. J. 2003. "Multiple Masculinities? Teenage Boys Talk about Jocks and Gender." *American Behavioral Scientist* 46 (10): 1423–38.

Pyke, Karen D. 1996. "Class-Based Masculinities: The Interdependence of Gender, Class, and Interpersonal Power." *Gender & Society* 10 (5): 527–49.

Sattel, Jack W. 1976. "The Inexpressive Male: Tragedy or Sexual Politics?" *Social Problems* 23 (4): 469–77.

Schippers, Mimi. 2002. *Rockin' Out of the Box: Gender Maneuvering in Alternative Hard Rock*. New Brunswick, NJ: Rutgers University Press.

Schwalbe, Michael, and Douglas Mason-Schrock. 1996. "Identity Work as Group Process." In *Advances in*

Group Processes, edited by Barry Markovsky, Michael J. Lovaglia, and Robin Simon, 113–47. Greenwich, CT: JAI.

Tough Guise: Violence, Media, and the Crisis in Masculinity. 1999. Directed by Sut Jhally. Northampton, MA: Media Education Foundation.

Wilkins, Amy C. 2004a. "Puerto Rican Wannabes: Sexual Spectacle and the Marking of Race, Class, and Gender Boundaries." *Gender & Society* 18 (1): 103–21.

Wilkins, Amy C. 2004b. "'So Full of Myself as a Chick': Goth Women, Sexual Independence, and Gender Egalitarianism." *Gender & Society* 18 (3): 328–49.

Wilkins, Amy C. 2008. *Wannabes, Goths, and Christians: The Boundaries of Sex, Style, and Status.* Chicago: University of Chicago Press.

Yeung, King-To, Mindy Stombler, and Renee Wharton. 2006. "Making Men in Gay Fraternities: Resisting and Reproducing Multiple Dimensions of Hegemonic Masculinity." *Gender & Society* 20 (1): 5–31.

NOTES

1. As I discuss elsewhere (Wilkins 2008), for University Unity women the temptation problem is romantic involvement with non-Christian men.
2. See Wilkins (2004b) for an analysis of the limitations of this empowerment.
3. These forms of masculinity are also classed. Not only do they draw on class resources, but they also reproduce class distinctions. As Pierette Hondagneu-Sotelo and Michael A. Messner (1994) argue, the "new man," with which the Unity and goth masculinity projects resonate, is a formulation of manhood that is counterposed to the stereotype of the disrespectful, untrustworthy, lower-class man/man of color (see also Pyke 1996; Wilkins 2004a).

KRISTEN BARBER

19. STYLED MASCULINITY: MEN'S CONSUMPTION OF SALON HAIR CARE AND THE CONSTRUCTION OF DIFFERENCE

Brad Pitt's hair gets a lot of media coverage. Whether he wears it shaggy, in a ponytail, bleaches it blond, or buzzes it off on the sides to reveal a contemporary "high and tight" mohawk, people want to know what's going on with Brad Pitt's hair. Online, you can find a "Brad Pitt Movie-Hair Quiz" and slideshows that take you through his "hair evolution" (Fox 2013; *UsWeekly* 2011). He is an international movie star, but also represents carefully styled masculinity. In a 2012 *Chanel No. 5* glossy advertisement, Pitt wears a tailored tuxedo and leans confidently against a reflective sliding glass door. He holds a glass of scotch in one hand, and his long wavy hair and goatee, although relaxed, are perfectly manicured. Even when he's caught by the paparazzi walking through the LAX airport, media outlets report on his casual designer duds.

Men's appearances are increasingly scrutinized in the media, and magazine columns provide advice to help men sort through their "sartorial conundrums" (O'Brien 2013). For example, *GQ*'s "Style Guy," Glenn O'Brien, answers men's questions about hair loss, recommends them seasonal accessories, and assuages their anxieties about the emasculating potential of using a hair dryer or receiving a manicure. So, we should not be surprised that some men are spending more money on beauty products and services, especially as they become increasingly available and marketed specifically to men (Barber forthcoming; Euromonitor International 2010; IBISWorld 2010). Some scholarship, however, has mistaken men's participation in beauty regimes and emphasis on styled masculinity as destabilizing unequal gender arrangements (e.g., Bordo 1999; Salzman et al. 2005). This is

because the body beautiful is linked to current definitions of femininity and thus associated with women and gay men (see Bridges 2014 for a discussion of men's appropriation of "gay aesthetics"). Indeed, Susan Bordo claimed, "I never dreamed that 'equality' would move in the direction of men worrying *more* about their looks rather than women worrying *less*" (1999: 217).

Yet, to claim that styled masculinity—and the time and energy spent cultivating it—signals the dissolution of gender differences ignores how race, class, and sexuality intersect to differently shape the meaning of men's bodily aesthetic practices. Brad Pitt's masculinity is rarely questioned despite his careful attention to his appearance. Instead, he embodies styled masculinity in a way that signals a privileged class and celebrity status. Men actually have a long relationship with stylized embodiments, fretting over their looks and decorating their bodies to signal social locations. For example, Augustus Caesar, concerned with his standing as Rome's first emperor and "Principal Citizen," wore his legendary ceremonial wreath to hide the fact that he was balding (Luciano 2001). Even Hannibal, a Carthaginian commander who defeated the Romans, waged war while wearing a wig and "kept a second one on hand for social occasions" (Luciano 2001: 14). The aesthetic cultivation of bodies, then, becomes important in understanding men's negotiations of, associations with, and stakes in larger social relations of power and status.

Few scholars have examined the meaning of men's participation in the contemporary beauty culture. Women, we know, express *difference* (West and Fenstermaker 1995) as they groom their bodies. They

---

Portions of this reading are mentioned in an earlier publication in *Gender & Society* (Barber 2008) and appear in the book *Styling Masculinity: Gender, Class, and Inequality in the Men's Grooming Industry* (Barber, 2016).

forge racialized, classed, and sexualized gender identities by cutting their hair, doing their nails, and otherwise styling their bodies in particular ways (Battle-Walters 2004; Candelario 2000; Cogan 1999; Craig 2006; Gimlin 1996; Jacobs-Huey 2006; Kang 2003; Taub 1999). To understand how men today make sense of their participation in what might otherwise be seen as "feminine" practices of beauty or aesthetic enhancement, I studied male clients of a small hair salon in Southern California—*Shear Style*. *Shear Style* is dedicated to and occupied largely by women and so allowed me to analyze how men engage with gendered cultural meanings of beauty. I wanted to know: How might the cultivation of a styled masculinity be wrapped up with men's multiple social locations? How do men at *Shear Style* make sense of their consumption and experience of salon hair care? How do they navigate the feminized association of salon hair care while evoking racialized, classed, and sexual gendered locations? And how does the everyday practice of hair care support the persistence of difference or distinction among men?

THE STUDY

I spent four and a half months studying *Shear Style*, clocking in 40 hours of ethnographic observations, as well as conducting formal in-depth interviews with 15 of the salon's male clients and a group interview with 3 of the 4 women stylists. The salon was small, with four workstations, so it was easy for me to observe interactions from the waiting bench. When I approached men for interviews, they were often surprised because they had assumed I was waiting for a hair appointment. In addition to being well positioned to observe all four work stations, spending time on the waiting bench provided me many informal conversations with men as they waited for or exited the salon after their appointments. I asked men about how they discovered *Shear Style* and what kept them coming back. These quick conversations helped me to structure my questions for the more formal interviews with clients.

Observations allowed me to evaluate *how* men were using and moving about the salon and interacting with stylists; but it was during the in-depth interviews that I explored *why* men come to the salon—their

attempts to make sense of their interest in purchasing salon hair care. I asked their opinions on why they and other men chose salon hair care, what they looked for in a haircut and a stylist, how they discovered the salon, and what they liked and would change about their experiences at *Shear Style*. They also discussed their previous experiences at and impressions of popular places for men to get a haircut, such as the barbershop or chain stores like *Supercuts*. I analyzed the major themes and patterns that emerged from men's narratives about what *Shear Style* and a salon haircut meant to them.

Most of the men I interviewed and observed at the salon were white. Although I recorded 1 Asian man and 2 Latino men making appointments at *Shear Style*, only 1 of the 15 men I interviewed identified as Mexican, whereas the other 14 identified as white. This is significant since the men's whiteness was often assumed in their descriptions of themselves and of other men. Thirteen of the men also identified as straight. Two did not disclose their sexual orientation. The men ranged in age from 30 to 63, with the average being 49. And although 1 participant was a stay-at-home dad, all of the other men occupied professional, white-collar jobs such as engineer, orthodontist, lawyer, art director, and college professor. Of the 11 men who reported their incomes, the average salary was approximately $194,000. These men spent $45 for a haircut, or about three times more than they would have spent at the barbershop or *Supercuts* located across the street from *Shear Style*. Although I saw 1 man have his hair colored, all other men who came through the salon were there for haircuts and sometimes to stock up on their favorite styling products.

REPUDIATING THE FEMINIZED SALON

Masculinity and femininity are dichotomized categories that make sense only in relation, and in opposition, to each other. Masculinity is defined as the absence or rejection of femininity; and because characteristics associated with masculinity are often highly valued, the process of creating dichotomies relies on the repudiation of femininity and is integral to the perpetuation of male dominance (Connell 1995; Kimmel 1994). Insulting or making jokes about women and expressing disgust in practices or symbols associated with femininity, for example, allow men to claim masculinity at women's expense. These kinds of practices were typical of men's narratives at *Shear Style*. They rejected the salon as "feminine" while simultaneously seeking the services offered therein. If we understand gender as a situational "state of play" (e.g., Connell 1987; Messner 1990), then such contradictions and complexities involved in accomplishing gender (West and Zimmerman 1987) make more sense. Gender relations are constantly and imperfectly negotiated via physical and discursive interactions with others. Men at *Shear Style*, for instance, discursively squelched the notion that purchasing a particular stylized embodiment at the salon brought them closer to women. Instead, they maintained differences in preferences between men and women, which situated them as anomalies while also allowing them to participate in the feminine aesthetic enhancing practice of stylizing.

Shear Style is a small, feminized salon that caters mostly to women. It is marked by fresh-cut flower arrangements, dusty-pink walls, and daily cookie platters served alongside a variety of hot teas. The men crossed gender boundaries to have their hair cut at *Shear Style*, risking potential feminization (Kimmel 1994) via association with a "women's" space. Most of the men I interviewed followed their stylists from other salons they described as more gender neutral. So, they recognized *Shear Style* as a feminine place.

The salon sat on the bottom floor of an old house with large Greek revival columns flanking the entrance of the wraparound front porch. Inside, long, thin track lighting snaked down from the ceiling. The floors were a dark glossy wood, and old kitchen cabinets spanned the back wall to display mousse and hairspray available for purchase, as well as locally crafted jewelry, purses, and self-help books. Styling tools including curling irons and blow dryers were stowed on the bottom shelves. On the weekends, the salon was packed with women having their hair cut, waiting for their color to set under hot upright dryers, and waiting for appointments. On busy days the salon rang out with the chatter and laughter of women as they talked with stylists and each other about their family lives and celebrity gossip.

The men I interviewed were keenly aware that they were outnumbered by women in the salon and reported seeing few other men during their appointments. They were both literal and ideological anomalies—men who clearly pursued stylized embodiments in a feminized space designed for women. Hamilton, a white 57-year-old investment manager, pointed to the women around him and explained, "It's jammed full of housewives . . . and there are bimbos walking around chatting." Disparaging women who were at the salon in the middle of the day as "housewives" highlighted the fact that he was also there midweek. But by trivializing women's interactions at the salon as "catty," Hamilton situated himself in opposition to *Shear Style*'s typically gendered client. As a privileged white, upper-middle-class professional, Hamilton's social status likely allowed him to feel entitled to insult and reject the women around him.

Some clients recognized *Shear Style* as a feminized space not set up for men, recommending steps the salon could take to better serve them. For example, two men asked me to envision flat-screen televisions affixed to the walls and tuned to sports or news channels to help men feel like they belonged. Wanting more than "gossip" magazines to read while he waited for his appointments, Evan, a white 37-year-old stay-at-home father, said men's magazines would be "kind of nice to see . . . Maybe I'll suggest that next time I see [my stylist]." He laughed, "Where's my *GQ*? Where's my *Esquire*?" His laughter implied that he understood *Shear Style* as a "women's" salon. Men positioned themselves in contrast to the women in the salon by suggesting they were inherently and obviously interested in different types of amenities. Recommending magazines that target middle- and upper-middle-class white men—instead of, say, *Ebony* or *JET*—Evan also suggested that he and the other men who frequent the salon were invested in appropriating a white, professional-class masculinity.

Shear Style is a "fairly feminine atmosphere," Neil, a white 43-year-old engineer, told me. I asked him to describe the salon and what exactly made it feminine. You have to "perch" on a cushioned waiting bench, he told me, "and men don't perch." He gestured to the purple, maroon, and gold tasseled throw pillows surrounding him, looking at me as if the pillows spoke for themselves. "[T]he pillows, food, [and] décor," he said, made him feel as if he were in a "woman's space." Expressing distaste for the decoration of the salon, Neil communicated to me that although he had his haircut at *Shear Style* every few weeks, as a man he did not actually *belong* in or *like* the salon. Further, he highlighted gendered behavior, whereby women are prone to carefully and passively perch and men are more active and present in their embodiment and possession of space. This helped Neil to separate himself, and other men, from the feminine and potentially feminizing character of *Shear Style*—repudiating the feminine as something undesirable and unrelatable to men.

PROFESSIONALLY STYLED HAIR FOR PROFESSIONAL MEN

"Difference," according to West and Fenstermaker (1995), is "done." That is, people routinely participate in practices and discourses that both locate them at particular axes of race, class, gender, and sexuality (among other things) and separate them from others. Classed cultural symbols such as expensive sports cars and finely tailored clothing display a privileged status and a fat pocketbook. And it is in *interactions* that this status is accomplished. Similarly, the body is an available social symbol—tangible, plastic, and frequently manipulated to communicate deep-seated identities and locations to others (e.g., Cregan 2006; Crossley 2001; Featherstone et al. 1992). For example, women might take for granted that wearing a skirt signals to others a sex category (female) as well as an appropriately gendered persona (feminine) (e.g., West and Zimmerman 1987), styling their bodies in ways that distinguish them from men. Everyday aesthetic-oriented rituals—and the meanings we give these rituals—cultivate raced, classed, gendered, and sexual divisions between people.

Yet, most take these rituals for granted because we are socialized to accept various treatments of our bodies as appropriate; and because we practice these rituals daily, they become routinized and normalized. We often reduce our relationships to clothes, makeup, and grooming to expressions of individual tastes. But, according to Bourdieu (1984), taste itself is social. Our lifestyles, values, preferences, and dispositions—or *habitus*—are tied to our social locations. So class privilege, for example, provides some with access to and experiences with luxury goods and practices that are then folded into constructions of inherent taste. Bourdieu uses the term *bodily hexis* to describe the corporeal expression of habitus, whereby the body becomes a "site of incorporated history" (1984: 437) or an expression of entrenched social relations. Men at *Shear Style* expressed a classed habitus as they linked their interest in "stylish" hair to both their professional occupations and their supposedly inherent "priorities," preferences, and progressiveness. Individualizing these priorities both shored up and naturalized distinctions between the men and their white, working-class counterparts.

Men who frequented *Shear Style* distinguished themselves by framing their ritual salon-going practices as expressions of "stylish" professional-class white masculinity. The salon, they said, is an important resource for the purchase of "personalized" style and contemporary haircuts. "[If I] want something a little more stylish, I'll come to the salon because the salon develops more current styles [and] different techniques [that are] more relevant," said Mack, a white 39-year-old art director. Unlike at chain stores, men said, stylists at salons keep up with current trends in hair. And unlike barbershops, salons are stocked with women stylists, whom the men argued have a "high taste level" and are inherently skilled at delivering style. The men trusted their female stylists, whom they essentialized as superior beauty providers. "I know that I'm going to have a consistently good haircut every time I go," one man told me. Men likened the barbershop or chain store, on the other hand, to "rolling the dice" with their haircuts, as well as a place for less refined, blue-collar men.

Popular associations of beauty with women and femininity mean that men's desires for and practices to promote aesthetic enhancement are potentially emasculating. After all, men's self-worth is not supposed to be tied up with how they look. Many of the men I spoke with embedded their commercial aesthetic pursuits in attempts to succeed in their professional jobs. Looking "stylish", they said, helped them to compete in the workplace. They might work with clients, whom they have to persuade to hire them and their firms, for example; they told me that looking "good" helps to convince clients that they can and will do the job well (see Luciano 2001 for a historical discussion of men's appearances being tied to capitalist notions of white-collar success). Tom, a white 58-year-old educational consultant, explained:

> I mean, you know, I have clients. That means before they become clients, I have to win them over. Now, who are they going to go with? The person who has . . . this great appearance package [points to himself], including grooming, style, professionalism, mannerism. Who are they going to go with, that person, or are they going to go with somebody who looks like they came in and dressed by accident or [are] indifferent about their hair?

Hamilton similarly expressed feeling pressured to cultivate a particular stylized masculine embodiment because he works with "wealthy clients." "When you walk in a room and there are billionaires sitting there, you need to uphold the same appearance," he explained. Although gender scholars have found that there are often unwritten appearance rules in the workplace that control women's bodies and are associated with different rewards and disadvantages (Dellinger and Williams 1997), the men I interviewed suggested this is not unique to women.

Although connecting their purchase of salon hair care to professional requirements for particular embodiments, men at *Shear Style* did not directly acknowledge that their workplace embodiments were accessible *because* of their privileged classed locations. Kerry, a white 50-year-old marketer, was the exception. He described the typical male client of *Shear Style* as "somebody who has more money than somebody who can only afford 10 dollars." But he quickly reassessed his answer, telling me that "It doesn't matter how rich or how poor you are, you have budgets and you have allocations. And some people who make less money will spend more on entertainment than people who make a lot of money. What's your priority?" Although he recognized that not all men could afford a $45 haircut every six to eight weeks, he also framed it as a *decision*, an issue of "priorities." If a man saw "stylish" hair as important, he suggested, he

would splurge despite his income. Kerry's explanation marked him, and all male clients at *Shear Style*, as distinct from other men in terms of "priority" rather than privilege. Making invisible class privilege (Kimmel and Ferber 2009; Pease 2012), he ultimately evoked a classed habitus and bodily hexis, claiming an inherent preference for "stylish" hair that distinguishes him from (and above) men who will not (or *cannot*) spend money on pricey haircuts.

Highlighting taste differences between themselves and others, men at *Shear Style* rejected the barbershop as a place for crass, working-class white men. They discussed the "old-school" barbershop as stuck in time, in terms of both hairstyle and masculinity. One client told me, "I think there is a difference; I think [my stylist] cuts hair a little bit better [than a barber]." The men generally defined a "good," "stylish" haircut as one that is up to date and is in contrast to the haircut they believed they would get from "old" barbers. "The male barber is just bad," Hamilton said. "80-year-old barbers who can't see just chop your hair." These men wanted the "superior" and "customized" haircuts they believed the barbershop could not deliver. They saw the barbershop as synonymous with white, working-class men satisfied with "inferior" haircuts. For example, Evan evoked derogatory, classist rhetoric when explaining just who would choose a barbershop or chain store over *Shear Style*. "I can't see a mechanic working at, or a grease-monkey working at Jiffy-Lube, or something like that, going to a shop that charges $65 for a haircut." Evan essentialized working-class masculinity, as well as his difference from such men. If "grease monkeys" choose the barbershop, and he was *inherently*—not just occupationally—different from these men, then it made sense he would have his hair cut at a salon.

Eking out classed associations between men's professional status and their choice of hair care, clients made sense of their consumption of salon hair care by setting themselves apart from men whom they saw as inferior in taste and priority—and ultimately in masculinity. They referred to the barbershop as "old" and outdated, framing themselves as contemporary men who rightfully seek out the beauty services offered at *Shear Style* and delivered by women beauty service workers. For example, Mack justified his presence at the salon by connecting the barbershop with passé, aggressive, and misogynist masculinity—men who are closer to their "primitive" heterosexual roots, or what McCaughey (2008) refers to as "the caveman mystique."

> [The barbershop's] got the owner's old boxing gloves up on the wall, black and white photos from being in the war, the Naugahyde seats, [and] the pile of *Playboys* in the corner . . . I guess it just depends on how machismo I was feeling at the time, if I wanted to go "Grrr" [pretending to be "machismo" as he furrows his brow, grunts, and shakes his head from side to side] and go old school [to the barbershop], or, you know, if I wanted to come here [to the salon].

Mack painted the barbershop as a place for working-class men and the cultivation of working-class masculinity. Neil also classed the barbershop by describing it as having "no music, vinyl flooring, and *Auto Week* magazines." Situated alongside the "old-school" masculinity and "machismo" they framed the barbershop as embodying, clients at *Shear Style* represented "new men" (see Hondagneu-Sotelo and Messner 1994): progressive, contemporary, stylish, and professional.

CLASSED LEISURE, HETEROSEXUALIZED CONSUMPTION

Although aesthetic treatments are popular within feminized beauty regimes, they are also wrapped up with classed experiences of leisure. This is especially true for middle- and upper-middle-class whites, who expect carefully executed physical care when they have their nails done (Kang 2003), for example. In their study of women beauty "therapists," Sharma and Black found that "'pampering' was seen as a service that the stressed and hardworking (female) client deserved and needed" (2001: 918). Black (2004), whose work has focused on the meanings and experiences of women workers and women clients in the beauty industry, suggests that men "groom" and women "beautify," situating men's aesthetic routines as solely utilitarian. Yet, men at *Shear Style* rooted their consumption of salon hair care partly in their desires for a particularly classed leisure experience and a break from their hectic professional schedules.

Pampering could be considered a feminine form of leisure that brings men's proximity to hegemonic (or culturally idealized) notions of masculinity (Connell 1995) into question. The men maintained, however, that the pampering haircuts they purchased at *Shear Style* were *less* feminine than other services (e.g., manicures). Some of them heterosexualized their interactions with stylists in a way that symbolically worked to prove the point. Consuming the gendered work and bodily labor of women who touch and pamper their clients, these men link their experiences of salon hair care with conventional projections of heterosexual masculinity. In so doing, they masculinized pampering as a heterosocial and heterosexual interaction.

Many of the men I spoke with at *Shear Style* described the salon as a place of leisure. They were professionals living fast-paced lives in the metropolis of Southern California, where work and family life collide and compete. The salon, they suggested, acted as a much-appreciated retreat from hectic routines. "I don't have a lot of time for myself," Colby, a Mexican 30-year-old realtor, said. "I'm really busy during the week. I have a son; I have a five-year old. So, I don't have a lot of time to do things for myself. So, this is cool. I like to just come out and get some coffee or something . . . it's kind of relaxing; it's something I do for myself." Colby told me that he is always happy with his haircut, but he emphasized the pleasure in sipping coffee while *waiting* for his haircut—despite the girly pillows decorating the waiting bench. *Shear Style* served an important function in these men's lives, as they look for spaces where they can pay for and experience an escape from their busy lives.

There are numerous places the men could go to relax and find time, so why choose a "women's" salon? For one, the services at *Shear Style* came with pampered touch, a form of leisure associated with privileged class locations. Cutting hair requires workers and clients to be in close contact, violating otherwise conventional and taken-for-granted social rules that regulate interactions between strangers, especially between women and men. And whereas stylists at *Supercuts* avoid washing clients' hair in an effort to turn them over in mere minutes, *Shear Style* is focused on providing a "full-service" experience. And touch is built into full-service beauty work in a way that is not part of other service occupations. For example, I observed a typical interaction between a stylist and her client:

> When Rosa was done cutting Evan's thick brown hair, she took him to the other room to wash and rinse off the fine bits that had fallen around his neck and were nestled in his hair. She dug her fingers deep into his hair and scratched his scalp as she lathered in the shampoo. This is when most clients close their eyes, relax into their chair, and let their heads hang loose in the shampoo bowl. After rinsing the soap from his hair, Rosa escorted Evan back to her station, where she vigorously toweled off his head and neck. She proceeded to blow-dry his hair, ruffling her fingers through it. (fieldnote)

Men described the scalp massage that accompanied the shampoo as one of their favorite aspects of salon service. As Don, a white 50-year-old animator, told me, "[T]hey put you in a chair, flip you back, wash your hair . . . It's just a lovely experience." Mack echoed this sentiment, "You know, there's nothing like putting your head back and getting a little head massage while you're getting your hair washed . . . Sal's [a hypothetical barber] not going to do that." Both Don and Mack emphasized the physical pleasure that accompanied hair care at *Shear Style*. Barbers, Mack suggested, do not offer this sort of experience. Reflecting on his gendered, sexualized, and racialized experiences at the black barbershop, Alexander (2003) discusses the secret pleasures of being touched by a male barber. Although he enjoyed having the barber touch his scalp, Alexander argues that the potential homoerotic interpretation of pleasurable touch between men pushes the discussion of this touch underground. Comparatively, the heterosocial interactions men had with women stylists at *Shear Style* allowed them to access pampering touch without their presumed heterosexuality (and thus, masculinity) coming under suspicion.

The fact that the pampering experience at *Shear Style* was marked by the intimate labor of women helped men to resist potential feminization or association with gay masculinity. "It's like when you go to get a massage [and] they want to know if you want a man or a woman; I'm like, 'a woman sounds nice,'" Don

told me. He and others suggested that they come to *Shear Style* not only for a stylishly professional haircut or a leisurely experience, but also because they are invested in the purchase of intimacy with women (see Zelizer 2005). Noting the pleasure of being touched by a woman, the men implicitly (and sometimes explicitly) claimed to be uncomfortable being touched by a man. "I would say I prefer women," said Sam, a white 53-year-old architect. "It's kind of like a massage, too. They ask, 'do you want a man or a woman?' I always prefer a woman." Getting stuck with male stylists was not possible at *Shear Style*, where all of the stylists were women. Whether they actually identified as straight, the ability to heterosexualize intimate interactions with their hairstylists allowed men to fold the consumption of beauty work into a class-privileged, heterosexual masculinity. As Alexander (2003) mentioned above, men might very well enjoy being touched by a male barber, but a heteronormative masculine culture rewards men for keeping this to themselves.

CARING RELATIONSHIPS WITH WOMEN

Service work is gendered. Women are typically hired because of their supposed innate docility, friendliness, and deferential attitudes (e.g., Erickson 2009; Hochschild 1983; Leidner 1991). This reveals how the cultivation and expression of care and concern for the customer is wrapped up with commerce—formally or informally required by an organization, and expected and rewarded by customers (e.g., Wharton 1996). Hairstyling, although different from most other service occupations because workers require schooling and licensure, generally includes providing an emotional product in addition to the more tangible haircut. Some beauty workers even maintain job satisfaction by emphasizing the emotional content of their service (Sharma and Black 2001). At the same time, the gendering of *emotional labor* (Hochschild 1983) in service work reinforces men's dominance as women serve up deference alongside the primary product.

Yet, the emotive experience available when consuming salon hair care is often overlooked in studies of beauty work. Although we know workers report that customers demand different forms and degrees of emotional labor during the service exchange (e.g., Black 2004; Gimlin 1996; Kang 2003), we do not know much about how customers interpret the care work they receive. And we know less about how men make sense of this, especially since masculine presentations are often linked to appearing emotionally detached (Bird 1996). This is particularly the case in homosocial interactions, where pressure from other men to squelch personal feelings impacts men's interpretations and expressions of emotions. Messner (1990) suggests that emotional detachment, and the negative effect it has on building relationships, is a "cost" of attempting to embody culturally idealized forms of masculinity. *Shear Style*, and presumably other salons like them, however, might mitigate these costs for men.

In addition to paying for and enjoying the touch wrapped up with purchasing a haircut at *Shear Style*, men also reported enjoying the personal, intimate, and friendly relationships they had with stylists. They generally booked appointments with the same stylist every six to eight weeks, and so they had commercially moderated, yet ongoing, interactions with the women. As a result, the men described becoming attached and loyal to their stylists. As Don explained,

> It's like totally a relationship . . . It's a person you talk to on a regular basis and they're really good listeners . . . Rosa [his stylist] always says, "So, where are you going this weekend?" . . . It's like this is Rosa, this is my friend; I tell her what I'm doing this weekend. It's like another kind of relationship that's really important.

Describing his stylist as a "good listener," Don boasted that he told Rosa intimate details about his life. Although I often observed light bantering between clients and stylist, I also overheard men sharing intimate details about what was going on in their lives, including details about relationships with spouses and children. Many of them prided themselves on these familiar relationships with stylists.

Asking and talking about a client's family, however, is built into the occupational repertoires of many hairstylists. Beauty workers often draw clients into conversation by asking them questions about their families and recent events in their lives (Sharma and Black 2001); and the men generally perceived the women's interest in their families as sincere and mutual. Patrick, a white 61-year-old corporate official, reported that he and his stylist had "become kind of

friends . . . she tells me about [her daughter] and stuff, and I tell her about my sons and daughter." This personalized relationship motivated men like Patrick to come back to the salon and to follow their stylists if they moved salons. One man told me that he came to Rosa for haircuts because "She's very friendly and she knows my kid's, my son's name. We keep kind of going on what happened last time. If something happened in my personal life, we talk about it." In my later research (Barber forthcoming), I found that even when men acknowledged that their female stylists "have to" care about them, they expressed appreciation for these relationships.

I witnessed the pleasure men received when talking with stylists about their personal lives and when their stylists demonstrated interest in their families. Many clients upheld the notion that care work is gendered, claiming men who work in barbershops "don't care about you." The homosocial character of barbershop interactions between such white men may be shaped by the avoidance of emotional exchange. The salon and the female stylist consequently become the natural choice for hair *care*; and men emphasized the sincerity of women who presumably wanted to "talk about life."

As I wrapped up my research, I treated the stylists at *Shear Style* to dinner to thank them for their cooperation, and I interviewed them as a group about their experiences working with male clients. Unlike the men, these three stylists described their relationships with clients to be largely "part of the job." Although they indeed formed friendships with clients whom they socialized with outside of the salon, more often they were not interested in the intimate details of their clients' lives. Instead, they recognized the *work* involved in caring, claiming that men come to see them because "it's cheaper than a psychiatrist." The men, however, did not recognize stylists as paid informal therapists. Emotional labor, especially that performed by women, is often interpreted by others as natural expressions of a "feminine" disposition (Hochschild 1983; Tancred 1995). Overlooking the paid aspect of the care they received from stylists, men both enjoyed personal and intimate exchanges at the salon and reinforced the invisibility of women's care work.

In addition to consuming the gendered work of women stylists, men's descriptions of their relationships with the women established them as members of a particular class. They positioned themselves as "classy" by distinguishing "salon talk" from the "garage talk" they said takes place at barbershops. Barbershops, they suggested, are places where men talk about "beer and pussy," as well as sports and cars; and therefore they are places for the expression of working-class masculinity and misogyny. In addition to classing the barbershop and hair salon, the men also implicitly racialized these environments. Although they did not plainly discuss race (which is typical for whites who often experience themselves as un-raced—see Kimmel and Ferber 2009), by situating the barbershop as a place for the expression of masculinity that differed from their own, they defined it as a space for *white* working-class masculinity. One man described the barbershop and hair salon as "night and day" and explained that "You have garage talk and you have salon talk." Similar to Mack, he drew associations between the barbershop and auto shop, both places for blue-collar men. Many of the men explained that the gendered difference between the barbershop and hair salon lay in conversation. "[T]he masculine view is that you're supposed to go to the barbershop and get a standard haircut from a man, talk about football, locker rooms, [and] sex," Mack told me. He and others expressed a desire for the more intimate conversations at *Shear Style*.

As a place that does not provide them with caring and close relationships, men at *Shear Style* described the barbershop as less progressive than the hair salon. Differentiating themselves from men who presumably go to the barbershop to talk about "beer and pussy," men at *Shear Style* situated themselves as progressive, professional-class men. They described the salon as a place where they could avoid some of the costs of masculinity, like emotional detachment. And at the same time they took the gendered work of women occupationally required to care for them for granted.

CONCLUSION

The body "is a site where something social happens" (Connell 2002: 48). Scholars who study the body show that it is a malleable tool for the expression of difference; and although current research focuses largely on the consequences of women's beauty

practices, men, too, invest in meaningful stylized embodiments. Looking at men's constructions of salon hair care at *Shear Style*, I show that class, sexuality, and race mitigate the potentially emasculating experience of commercial aesthetic enhancement. These men are invested in a classed bodily hexis, whereby they pursue a "stylish" aesthetic that works to frame their "priorities" as what differentiates them from other men. And it is in the naturalization of distinction between themselves and other working-class white men that they reveal a deeply ingrained habitus. They overlook how their power and status over white men with less financial privilege and social clout both facilitated their desire for and ability to access pricey hair care and worked in ways that naturalized difference and inequality. Like the class and status wrapped up in Brad Pitt's carefully styled aesthetic and in *GQ*'s Style Guy's recommendations for men's accessories, men's participation in commercial efforts to enhance their appearances says something about the stake these men have in reproducing larger relations of power and distinction.

REFERENCES

Alexander, Bryant Keith. 2003. "Fading, Twisting, and Weaving: An Interpretive Ethnography of the Black Barbershop as Cultural Space." *Qualitative Inquiry* 9 (1): 105–28.

Barber, Kristen. 2008. "The Well-Coiffed Man: Class, Race, and Heterosexual Masculinity in the Hair Salon." *Gender & Society* 22 (4): 455–76.

Barber, Kristen. 2016 (forthcoming). Styling Masculinity: Gender, Class, and Inequality in the Men's Grooming Industry. New Brunswick, NJ: Rutgers University Press.

Battle-Walters, Kimberly. 2004. *Sheila's Shop: Working-Class African American Women Talk about Life, Love, Race, and Hair.* New York: Rowman & Littlefield.

Bird, R. Sharon. 1996. "Welcome to the Men's Club: Homosociality and the Maintenance of Hegemonic Masculinity." *Gender & Society* 10 (2): 120–32.

Black, Paula. 2004. *The Beauty Industry: Gender, Culture, Pleasure.* New York: Routledge.

Bordo, Susan. 1999. *The Male Body: A New Look at Men in Public and in Private.* New York: Farrar, Straus and Giroux.

Bourdieu, Pierre. 1984. *Distinction: A Social Critique of the Judgement of Taste.* Cambridge, MA: Harvard University Press.

Bridges, Tristan. 2014. "A Very "Gay" Straight?: Hybrid Masculinities, Sexual Aesthetics, and the Changing Relationship between Masculinity and Homophobia." *Gender & Society* 28 (1): 58–82.

Candelario, Ginetta. 2000. "Hair Race-ing: Dominican Beauty Culture and Identity Production." *Meridians: Feminism, Race, and Transnationalism* 1 (1): 128–56.

Cogan, Jeanine C. 1999. "Lesbians Walk the Tightrope of Beauty: Thin Is In but Femme Is Out." *Journal of Lesbian Studies* 3 (4): 77–89.

Connell, Raewyn. 1987. *Gender and Power: Society, the Person, and Sexual Politics.* Stanford, CA: Stanford University Press.

Connell, Raewyn. 1995. *Masculinities.* Berkeley: University of California Press.

Connell, Raewyn. 2002. *Gender.* Cambridge, MA: Polity.

Craig, Maxine Leeds. 2006. "Race, Beauty, and the Tangled Knot of Guilty Pleasure." *Feminist Theory* 7 (2): 159–77.

Cregan, Kate. 2006. *The Sociology of the Body: Mapping the Abstraction of Embodiment.* Thousand Oaks, CA: Sage.

Crossley, Nick. 2001. *The Social Body: Habit, Identity, and Desire.* London: Sage.

Dellinger, Kirsten, and Christine L. Williams. 1997. "Makeup at Work: Negotiating Appearance Rules in the Workplace." *Gender & Society* 11 (2): 151–77.

Erickson, Karla A. 2009. *The Hungry Cowboy: Service and Community in a Neighborhood Restaurant.* Jackson: University Press of Mississippi.

Euromonitor International. May 2010. *Men's Grooming Products in the U.S.: Country Sector Briefing.*

Featherstone, Mike, Mike Hepworth, and Bryan S. Turner. 1992. *The Body: Social Process and Cultural Theory.* Thousand Oaks, CA: Sage.

Fox, Jesse David. October 25, 2013. *Take the Brad Pitt Movie-Hair Quiz.* Accessed: March 1, 2014, at http://www.vulture.com/2013/10/take-the-brad-pitt-movie-hair-quiz.html/.

Gimlin, Debra. 1996. "Pamela's Place: Power and Negotiation in the Hair Salon." *Gender & Society* 10 (5): 505–26.

Hochschild, Arlie Russell. 1983. *The Managed Heart: Commercialization of Human Feeling.* Berkeley: University of California Press.

Hondagneu-Sotelo, Pierrette, and Michael A. Messner. 1994. "Gender Displays and Men's Power: The "New Man" and the Mexican Immigrant Man." In *Theorizing Masculinities*, edited by H. Brod and M. Kaufman, 200–18. Thousand Oaks, CA: Sage.

IBISWorld. 2010. "Hair and Nail Salons in the U.S.: 81211." *IBISWorld Industry Report.*

Jacobs-Huey, Lanita. 2006. *From the Kitchen to the Parlor: Language and Becoming in African American Women's Hair Care.* New York: Oxford University Press.

Kang, Miliann. 2003. "The Managed Hand: The Commercialization of Bodies and Emotions in Korean Immigrant-Owned Nail Salons." *Gender & Society* 17 (6): 820–39.

Kimmel, Michael. S. 1994. "Masculinity as Homophobia: Fear, Shame and Silence in the Construction of Gender Identity." In *Theorizing Masculinities*, edited by Harry Brod and Michael Kaufman, 119–42. Thousand Oaks, CA: Sage.

Kimmel, Michael S., and Abby L. Ferber. 2009. *Privilege: A Reader.* Boulder, CO: Westview Press.

Leidner, Robin. 1991. "Serving Hamburgers, Selling Insurance: Gender, Work, and Identity in Interactive Service Jobs." *Gender & Society* 5 (2): 154–77.

Luciano, Lynne. 2001. *Looking Good: Male Body Image in Modern America.* New York: Hill and Wang.

McCaughey, Martha. 2008. *The Caveman Mystique: Pop-Darwinism, and the Debates over sEx, Violence, and Science.* New York: Routledge.

Messner, Michael A. 1990. "When Bodies Are Weapons: Masculinity and Violence in Sport." *International Review for the Sociology of Sport* 25 (3): 203–20.

O'Brien, Glenn. October 2013. *The Style Guy Solves Your Sartorial Conundrums: From Black Shirts to Dad Jeans, GQ's Glenn O'Brien Has the Answers.* Accessed February 15, 2014, at http://www.gq.com/style/style-guy/201310/gq-style-guy-october-2013#slide=1/.

Pease, Bob. 2012. *Undoing Privilege: Unearned Advantage in a Divided World.* London: Zed Books.

Salzman, Marian, Ira Matathia, and Ann O'Reilly. 2005. *The Future of Men.* New York: Palgrave MacMillan.

Sharma, Ursula, and Paula Black. 2001. "Look Good, Feel Better: Beauty Therapy as Emotional Labor." *Sociology* 35 (4): 913–31.

Tancred, Peta. 1995. "Women's Work: A Challenge to the Sociology of Work." *Gender, Work & Organization* 29 (1): 11–20.

Taub, Jennifer. 1999. "Bisexual Women and Beauty Norms: A Qualitative Examination." *Journal of Lesbian Studies* 3 (4): 27–36.

UsWeekly. December, 18, 2011. *Brad Pitt's Hair Evolution.* Accessed: March 1, 2014, at http://www.usmagazine.com/celebrity-beauty/pictures/brad-pitt-hair-gallery-20111612/19411/.

West, Candace, and Sarah Fenstermaker. 1995. "Doing Difference." *Gender & Society* 9 (1): 8–37.

West, Candace, and Don H. Zimmerman. 1987. "Doing Gender." *Gender & Society* 1 (2): 125–51.

Wharton, Amy S. 1996. "Service with a Smile: Understanding the Consequences of Emotional Labor." In *Working in the Service Society*, edited by Cameron Lynn MacDonald and Carmen Sirianni, 91–112. Philadelphia: Temple University Press.

Zelizer, Vivian. 2005. *The Purchase of Intimacy.* Princeton, NJ: Princeton University Press.

MATTHEW DESMOND

20. BECOMING A FIREFIGHTER

The profession of wildland firefighting requires seasonal workers to abandon whatever job they held in the colder months for one that pays roughly 10 dollars an hour (give or take) and that obliges most of them to live in a forest encampment, largely isolated from family and friends, in surroundings that can at best be described as less than glamorous. It [. . .] demands that firefighters make themselves radically available. Sometimes, crewmembers do not come in contact with people besides other members of the firecrew and occasional campers for weeks at a time. Summer days are monopolized by the priority of fire, and when a blaze busts, firefighters rush off to the scene armed only with hand tools, flame-resistant clothing, hard hats, and fire shelters (nick-named "shake and bakes") to "dig line" in front of a lethal and combustive force that [. . .] has no purpose other than to destroy. Those who choose to square off with "the Black Ghost" must regularly work 14 (or more) hours on end, crawling through ash and dirt, hiking through steep terrain carrying 20 pounds of gear, swinging axes and shovels, sometimes miles away from the nearest paved road, let alone the nearest hospital. And they don't always win. Between 1990 and 1998, 133 firefighters died while involved in wildland fire activities. Wildfire claims, on average, between 12 and 22 firefighters' lives per year, while injuring hundreds more. [. . .]

Why do individuals choose to take part in such a demanding and dangerous enterprise? What compels them to accept the burdens of firefighting, and how do they become acclimated to this universe? In response to these questions, we might surmise that firefighters long for the *rush*, that they are overtaken by a need to test themselves, and, accordingly, that they carefully weigh the exhilaration gained on the fireline against the painful consequences of smoke inhalation, broken bones, and a fiery death. [A problem with this account is the] assumption that individuals who partake in behavior defined as risky do so through rational calculation and share the same understanding of "risk" as the analyst who studies that behavior. It is this assumption that I wish to confront here.

Firefighting—that is, marching, digging, chopping, crawling, and running amongst torching trees and smoldering ash—is a carnal activity, and in the swelter of infernos firefighters' bodies react to the dangers they face. *How far should I go down the canyon wall? How much heat can I take? Is this dangerous or am I scared? Is that oak burnt straight through? Is that smoke or steam? Should I keep digging or should I fall back?* On the fireline, thousands of questions such as these must be asked and answered with such celerity that they exist in cognitive form only for fleeting moments, if at all. Decisions of risk are made at the bodily level and cannot be fully translated into articulate verbal accounts. [. . .]

[. . .] To comprehend how firefighters, soldiers, or police officers come to develop a specific disposition toward the dangers of wildfire, warfare, or wrongdoing, we must examine the degree to which the dispositions they bring to the firehouse, military base, or police station correspond to the culture and practices of these supporting organizations. In other words, we must trace the development of individuals' *habitus* over time and space, exploring how one's *primary* or *general habitus* transforms into a *specific habitus*. As Bourdieu pointed out in *Pascalian Meditations* (2000 [1997]), a

This reading is an excerpt from Matthew Desmond's article in *Ethnography* 7 (2006): 387–421.

general habitus is a system of dispositions and ways of thinking about and acting in the world that is constituted early on in life, while a *specific habitus* is acquired later through education, training, and discipline within particular organizations. If some individuals take to certain professions better than others—if some seem to be "naturals" at soldiering or are "born to be police officers"—it is because they bring to the organization a general *habitus* that transforms into a specific *habitus* with little friction, while others possess a general *habitus* that is at odds with the fundamental structures and practices of the organization. [. . .]

Accordingly, this [chapter] inquires into how the general *habitus* of self-described "country boys" (the social embodied) gracefully transforms into the specific *habitus* of firefighters (the organization embodied). More precisely, it attempts to understand how individuals gravitate and acclimate to the universe of wildland firefighting by focusing on how firefighters' dispositions and skills acquired from their rural, masculine, and working-class upbringings connect with the organizational common sense of the US Forest Service. As we will see, country boys come to the Forest Service already ready to fight fire and take to the rigors of firefighting *secundum naturam*, with nearly instinctual proficiency. For this reason, the Forest Service does not need to exert much effort when sculpting the deployable firefighter. [. . .] Rather, his dispositions and skills need only to be tweaked and adjusted slightly, since the country boy is "adjusted in advance" to the requirements of wildland firefighting. [. . .]

[. . .] [T]his article is based upon ethnographic data I collected while serving as a member of the Elk River Wildland Firefighting Crew, one of a dozen crews stationed in northern Arizona. Most of the material upon which the following arguments are built was collected during the summer of 2003, though I had served as a wildland firefighter at Elk River in previous seasons—from 1999 to 2000, and again in 2002. By taking the "participant" in "participant observation" seriously, by offering up my mind and body, day and night, to the practices, rituals, and thoughts of the crew, I gained insights into the universe of firefighting, insights I gleaned when I bent my back to thrust a pulaski[1] into the dirt during a direct assault on a fire or when I moved my fingers through new warm ash to dig for hot spots (cf. Wacquant 2004). [. . .] My body became a field note, for in order to comprehend the contours of the firefighting *habitus* as deeply as possible, I had to feel it growing inside of me.

SEEING LIKE A COUNTRY BOY

Five of the crewmembers at Elk River are following a path well-worn by their fathers. As Kris, a 21-year-old in his second season whose father has fought fire for over 30 years, put it, "We've been around fire for years . . . My father told me stories about having to lead crews on ridge tops at night where you would have to crawl. He told me stories about having to lead crews, you know, to get to a safety zone, having to walk through a little bit that was on fire." As children, these men became familiar with the smell of smoke wafting from their fathers' garments. As teenagers, they knew the terminology, commands, and regulations of firefighting, and as 18-year-olds, these "Forest Service brats" all joined wildland firefighting crews through a virtually natural reflex. As for the first-generation firefighters at Elk River, most came from working-class families with personal ties to the Forest Service [. . .] recruited through small-town social connections. [. . .] Their fathers and friends had dug line before them, and because of their embeddedness in networks of firefighters, they did not find the profession an alien one. [. . .]

Of the 14 male crewmembers at Elk River, most are young, in their late teens and early 20s, though one recently turned 40 and another is 55. These two older men have over 20 years of experience under their belts. For the rest of the crew, however, the modal number of seasons is three. All the men are single except for two, both of whom are married with children. Four men are Native American, four are Hispanic, two are biracial (African American and white), and four are white. Crewmembers vary in racial composition, age, religion, and what they do after the season ends. However, all share [. . .] a rural upbringing. In fact, every wildland firefighter that I have ever met comes from rural America. [. . .]

Raised in small towns with populations under 10,000, most crewmembers have known each other from kindergarten, were on the football team together, and are familiar with each other's families. Three Native Americans on the crew were raised on reservations. Most are not proud of their hometown per se; rather, they take pride in being from a small town in general, as opposed to a big city. Crewmembers are, in their own words, "country boys," and the culture of the country—that "small town way of life" thought to be distinctly different from urban modes of existence—greatly influences how they perceive themselves and how they understand the meaning of manhood (Bell 1995; Connell 2006).

Most crewmembers are deeply familiar with the woods they protect. They know where the best fishing spots are and where to find wild turkey at the right time of the season. They know the different vegetation, where to gather the best firewood for the winter, and the hundreds of miles of dirt roads, mapped and uncharted, careening like tributaries through millions of acres of forestland. "I've always liked being in the woods," reflects Diego, a 20-year-old in his third season. "I would come here since I was little: camping, hunting, fishing. I've been here forever." Most of the men at Elk River feel the same way. [. . .] To these firefighters, the fact that they can earn a paycheck while "playing in the woods" seems like a too-beautiful con. This is why most of them pick up odd jobs in the offseason that allow them to work outside, like construction work or furring, and why most fantasize about securing a full-time position with the Forest Service.[2] Crewmembers come from working-class rural America, and they bring with them specific masculine dispositions structured by their working-class and country backgrounds. In other words, they come to the Elk River Fire Station with a *country-masculine habitus*. [. . .]

The country-masculine *habitus* divides the world into two types of people: indoors people and outdoors people, city people and country people. As "outdoors people," crewmembers fervently reject any type of indoor work, regularly symbolized by the dull, predictable, sanitary desk. "I guess I've always been an outdoors person," remarks the 40-year-old Nicholas, who has fought fire each consecutive summer since he was 18 years old. "You know, I've never been like an indoor type of guy, a desk or

something." The rejection of "indoor work" is both a *class demarcation* and a *regional separation*. By rejecting the desk, crewmembers reject middle-class occupations. Although they would enjoy a larger salary, they view the cubical, computer, and necktie that accompany white-collar professions as too large a sacrifice. The desk represents the world of paper work, sycophancy, and middle-class managerial masculinity; whereas the forest represents freedom, wilderness, and working-class masculinity (Collinson 1992; Willis 1977). [. . .]

Thus, for the men at Elk River, the division between "the city" and "the country" functions as the "fundamental principle of opposition," as Lévi-Strauss (1966 [1962]) would call it, since, more than any other antipodal cultural pairing (e.g. man/woman, white/black, rich/poor), it reinforces a foundational boundary separating known from unknown, familiar from foreign, and pure from polluted. This principle of differentiation orders Elk River by classifying who does and does not belong, and it can be seen at work in the words of Clarence Kraus, the 60-year-old lookout, who believes that "the Buick crowd" most certainly does not belong in the forest, while the "pickup crowd" is always welcome. [. . .]

"You know," Clarence remarks to a gathered crowd of firefighters, who had climbed some hundred aluminum steps up to visit him in his lookout tower, an eight-by-eight foot perch looming 160 feet above the ground. "I was talkin' to someone here the other day about that new development down there, where that millionaire, Hutchinson or whatever his name is, is buildin' dem fuckin' luxury vacation cabins, and supposedly he is gonna buy more land across the road and build there too. They say he's gonna dig two lakes on his property and gonna stock 'em with fish . . ." [. . .]

Clarence reddens, and his voice grows sharper. "You know, that's a damn shame. You know what's gonna happen don't-ja? Pretty soon, we're gonna be pavin' these damn roads and all sorts of fuckin' people are gonna be comin' in from Phoenix and from Tucson and wherever. They're gonna be driving their little Buicks up here. Shit, the Buick crowd is gonna replace the pickup crowd if Hutchinson has dem roads paved."

"What's the difference between the Buick crowd and the pickup crowd?" I ask.

"The pickup crowd is guys like us, people that aren't afraid to eat beans out of a can," Clarence replies.

I wait for more, but Clarence only gives me a "you-know-what-I-mean" look before turning to glance at the trees below. A few seconds pass before Clarence turns back to the crew and asks, "Do you know that the public has no idea about this? This is a whole 'nother world out here. You're good people, you know, people that keep America runnin', who the military draws from. You are middle America right here!"

[. . .] Although "the city" functions as the general space of the Other in the minds of crewmembers, the city is not a homogeneous entity. Many types of men live in metropolitan areas, and certainly not all of them fit the mold of "city boy" as defined by the crewmembers. Who is the city boy? Is he the president of a major corporation, a university professor, a bank teller, or a homeless man? I believe Clarence's loathed Buick can be found parked in the driveway of a nice *suburban* home. The suburbanite drives his shiny new car into the forest, leaving his three-car garage and well-trimmed lawn behind for a weekend in "the great outdoors." He looks forward to a comfortable stay in Hutchinson's cabins. But the "wimpy suburbanite" is not the only city boy who is referenced by the crewmembers at Elk River. The hard and violent *inner-city* dweller also lurks in their representations of the city. If the suburbs are weak, wealthy, and vain, then the inner city is impure, dangerous, and poor.

"In a small town you get to know your neighbors," explains Donald, a 22-year-old firefighter in his fourth season. "You don't have ambulances and police cars driving by every night. You don't have those problems . . . But in a big city, you don't know who [your kids are] hanging out with at school. You never meet their families because there is so many kids there . . .

"You have to be scared all the time when you're driving in the city because there's always an idiot. There's always an idiot you have to watch out for. There's just so many people. You go to the mall and you'll be walking around. There's gangsters walking by you, and they're just looking for someone to mug

or whatever they're going to do. They might even get in a gang fight and you get caught in the middle of it. So, you gotta watch your back really bad there."[3]

Thus, the symbolic construction of the country gravitates between two equally rejected conceptions of the city. The inner city is associated with crime, danger, and vice; the suburbs with money, fashion, and manners. The inner city is too dangerous; the suburbs, too safe. The country resembles the inner city in that it is gritty and the weak-willed cannot survive, but it is unlike the inner city in that it is a place of security and wholesomeness. In its security it resembles the suburbs, but the country is unlike the suburbs in that it is rough—this safety cannot be bought; it must be earned.

Crewmembers come to Elk River from similar positions in the social landscape and with a similar vision and division of the world constituted by that social landscape. They come knowing, implicitly or explicitly, that the kind of men who fight wildfire are the kind of men their fathers are, the kind they are, or at least the kind of men they want to be. [. . .] "Out here," a phrase often invoked by crewmembers, no one considers hunting to be a barbaric practice. It is simply what men do in the winter. Out here, one would not think to criticize the owner of an oversized truck for its poor fuel-economy. One needs such a truck to get around these parts. Because crewmembers know such things in advance, because they come to Elk River with a preformed country-masculine *habitus*, they gravitate to the world of wildland firefighting not only for the money or the adventure, but also—and more importantly—for the *espirit de corps* that comes with a collectively shared lifestyle. [. . .] [T]hese country-masculine principles of vision and division align with the principles of vision and division of the US Forest Service, as I shall demonstrate below.

COUNTRY COMPETENCE

A city boy, or "valley rat" in the words of one crewmember ("valley" refers to the Greater Valley Area, which constitutes Phoenix and all its suburbs), could not distinguish poison oak from wild sumac. He is ignorant of all things wild. The men at Elk River, by contrast, see themselves as possessing a specific body of knowledge—a country competence [. . .]—which makes them country boys and the lack of which makes other men city boys. Country masculinity is practiced and displayed primarily through country competence. Crewmembers' practical knowledge of the woods, their embodied outdoorsmanship acquired through a rural upbringing—the way a hand grips an axe, the way a foot mounts a trail—is directly bound up with their core sense of self, their masculinity and identity. [. . .] This means that an attack on one's outdoorsmanship translates into a direct attack on one's masculinity. This is why Bryan, a 22-year-old fourth-season firefighter, did not take it lightly when he heard that George, a 21-year-old third-season firefighter, thought he could run a chainsaw better than him.

[. . .] Bryan stomped into the shop, marched straight up to George, stopping inches from his face, and in a loud and confrontational voice barked, "You think you can run a saw better than me?"

Everyone in the shop turned to observe the event. Bryan's voice signaled the commencement of an altercation both in tone and in subject. He was referencing a chainsaw, a crucial tool used in wildland firefighting. Because of its mass, violence, and ability to harm, a saw is wielded only by the strongest, most skilled, and most experienced firefighters. Thus, sawyering skills signal much more than the ability to drop a full grown oak; they represent a skilled firefighter—more, a competent and mature country man. Bryan had advanced a serious challenge in response to a serious challenge supposedly advanced by George.

[. . .] George was at once confused, startled awake, and a bit scared. He slowly peeled his body away from the wall and stuttered, "Wha-what?"

Immediately Bryan snapped back, "Someone told me that you were saying that you could run a saw better than me. Is that true, *George*?" [. . .]

"Uh, uh, no. No. I never said anything like that," George denied. [. . .]

"Are you *sure* George? 'Cause somebody told me that you said that."
Bryan wanted to hear George deny it again.

"Yeah. I mean, I don't know who told you that, but I didn't say nothin' about that."

"Well, do *you* think you can run a saw better than me, George?"

George thought about the question before answering. "No. Not *better*."

"Are you sure?"

"Yeah."

After a few seconds, Bryan turned away from George and marched stone-faced out of the shop and said, "That's what I thought, *George*."

A week later, the crew responded to a one-acre fire called the Alligator Juniper Fire. I was assigned the task of spotting the sawyer. Bryan made sure to grab the chainsaw first. I hoisted an army-green bag full of chainsaw equipment, such as hatchets and wedges, on my back, and we went to work. We policed the fire in search of trees with the potential to topple and came upon a medium-sized pine seared most of the way up, which, we thought, needed to be dropped.

Bryan stood in the ashes and began to cut into the trunk while I looked on to make sure the tree was stable and would fall in the direction we wanted. He maneuvered the saw in and out of the trunk by making two front slices forming a pie-cut a quarter of the way into the wood followed by a perfectly straight back cut [. . .] He shut off the saw with a flick of his thumb and, turning to me, bragged, "And George thought he could run a saw better than me. I said, 'George, I've been running a saw since I was 13!'"

Just as working-class men tend to judge the measure of a man through a value system that prioritizes attainable attributes (breadwinning, a hard work ethic, integrity) over ones perceived as unattainable (wealth, education, a powerful career; see Halle 1984; Lamont 2000), country boys define masculinity through standards of country competence. The men at Elk River value their "human capital," country competence, over economic capital and city competence. This is why, although Hutchinson might *own* some land, Clarence and other crewmembers *know* the land, and as such, they feel that they have more rights to the forest than some millionaire developer. They, country boys, belong at Elk River, and they feel it belongs to them.

Knowledge of the country is a practical and specific type of knowledge. If one can gut an elk, string a catfish line, reload .45 bullets, fall a Juniper with a

20-pound chainsaw, or throw a rig into four-low and climb up a rocky hill, then one exhibits country competence. This knowledge not only binds crewmembers together [. . .]; it also allows those who possess it to adapt to the rigors of wildland firefighting, as well as to the organizational common sense of the US Forest Service, with quickness and aptness.

SEEING LIKE THE US FOREST SERVICE

[. . .] The skills new recruits bring to their host organization allow them to adapt to the demands of firefighting almost effortlessly. [. . .] [W]ildland firefighting competence must be understood as a specified extension of country competence.

When an organization commands its members to stand inches away from a gigantic and violent wall of flame burning with such blistering torridity that it destroys the very soil beneath its monstrous flames, leaving the land barren for generations, it goes without saying that the organization must obtain from its membership a high degree of trust. How do firefighters come to trust the Forest Service? [. . .] [One] way firefighters come to trust the Forest Service is by participating in the symbolic struggles of their host organization. Through these struggles, new recruits quickly learn of the organization's enemies and allies, and, soon enough, they find themselves joining in the fight. They begin to see how the world looks through the eyes of the organization and start to accept the needs of the organization as their own. [. . .]

Here, I focus on one symbolic struggle—the battle against environmental groups—through which crewmembers come to gain a deep understanding of the essence of wildland firefighting and begin to think like the Forest Service. By joining in this symbolic struggle, crewmembers begin to accept the culture of the Forest Service. [. . .] And if they accept the classificatory schemes of the Forest Service with little question, it is, in part, because the symbolic binaries pitting environmental groups against the Forest Service align with the symbolic binaries, cultivated within them from childhood, separating city boys from country boys.

A few hours into my first day on the job of the 2003 season, Peter, a 27-year-old engine operator in his seventh season, pulled me aside after the morning briefing and asked, "Have you seen that billboard outside of Jameson?" [. . .] "Dude, you have *got* to see this!" he replied excitedly—and immediately began logging onto the computer in the main office.

"Oh man," Donald added, approaching us, "it's a *cool* billboard." Peter pulled up a website displaying a picture of the sign. A full-sized billboard sponsored by a group called "AZ F.I.R.E." (which I later learned stands for Fighting Irresponsible Radical Environmentalism) displayed the caption, "Thank You EnvironMENTALists for Making the 2002 Fire Season All It Could Be!" against the backdrop of a hillside engulfed by flames. [. . .]

[. . .] During the summer of 2002, Arizona glowed red and orange. Nearly half-a-million acres were scorched and over 400 homes were destroyed. Many individuals around the state, including those who formed AZ F.I.R.E., blamed "those damn environmentalists," as they were regularly referred to by crewmembers, for the severity of the fire season.

Arguments over where the fault of a devastating fire season lies, how best to manage forests, the politics of logging and thinning, the treatment of endangered species, and hunting and camping rights are all manifestations of a power struggle between independent environmentalist groups (such as the Sierra Club or the Forest Guardians) and governmental organizations such as the US Forest Service. In recent years, the Forest Service has come under hard-hitting criticism advanced by several organizations that identify with the Green movement. [. . .] Through legislative victories, they have subjected the Forest Service to intense legal pressure and supervision (most powerfully manifest in laws such as the Endangered Species Act), decreasing its ability to thin, burn, and log at will. Some so-called environmentalists argue that the Forest Service destroys wildlife habitats, including those of endangered species, by over-logging and over-burning, while supporters and members of the Forest Service retort that a hands-off approach to forestry will only bring bigger and deadlier forest fires.

When crewmembers commit themselves to the Forest Service each summer, they also commit themselves to this power struggle. To them, "environmentalist" comes to mean "opponent of the US Forest Service," and once they recognize the Forest Service as the rightful overseer of the land, they join in the struggle and caricature environmentalists as misinformed, blindly zealous, and, indeed, "mental." For instance, Diego believes that the only thing the environmentalists do is tie the Forest Service's hands behind its back. [. . .]

"[W]hat we want to do in the fire department area of the Forest Service, they won't let us do because we've got environmentalists, we've got the freakin' timber people, mostly environmentalists," Diego replied, raising his right hand and his voice. "But they won't let us do, like, Thurman wants to do a burnout [to light a prescribed fire] and some things, they won't let us do it because then we are screwing up the National Forest look or we're destroying the *owl habitat*."

Diego rolled his eyes and painted the words "owl habitat" with a thick coat of sarcasm. He was referencing the Spotted Owl, an endangered species now protected by law, which was often contemptuously evoked as the mascot of environmentalist policy. Rex Thurman, the 47-year-old head supervisor of the Elk River Firecrew, regularly referred to the Spotted Owl as "that goddamn bird." [. . .]

Recognizing that environmental policy has real consequences for them on the fireline, crewmembers passionately participate in these struggles. For instance, Peter, like Thurman, believes that less thinning and burning will result in deadlier fires. One day he vented to me: "What they [the environmentalists] do affects me, affects *everybody*. [. . .] [T]hey can't log this, so the first-year firefighters are going to be going into a fire in a dog hair thicket that they can't thin, or can't log or whatever, and that kid's *life is in danger* because they can't thin it. You know? [. . .] You've got your people that bitch about 'Oh, you're cutting all the trees.' But then they're bitching about these big wildfires. So, you can't thin it. So, then you're like, 'Well, we can control burn it.' But *then* they bitch about the smoke. [. . .] You know, it's like *fuck*! What the fuck!" [. . .]

I asked him: "So, people have bitched about thinnin' and burnin' to you before?"

Peter grinningly replied, "Ohhhh, yeah. I was talking to a guy in Scottsdale [a suburb of Phoenix known for its wealth]. This guy named Bob [. . .] He's got money [. . .] and I said, 'I think we need to log it,

thin it, burn it. We need to do something or it's just going to keep on getting worse.'

"'Oh, you can't log it! You can't log it! When they log it, they only want to cut the big trees.'" Peter erupted, mimicking Bob's nasally voice and frantic gesticulations.

Then he turned into a calm discussant. "Well that's not true. They don't want the big ones. . . . It's like a *garden*. If you don't pull the weeds, you're not going to have good tomatoes or peas or green beans or whatever you're growing because there's only so much water and so much nutrition. Now, if you pull all the weeds, the plants that you do want are going to flourish. They are going to do great."

Peter nodded and smiled at me, confident in his simile, before imitating Bob again. "And he's like, 'No, no, no. They only want the big trees!'" [. . .] Peter sighed heavily. "I argued with him for an hour, and I said, 'You just need to come up there. You need to come *up there* and spend a day with me.'"

To Peter, Bob was sorely mistaken. What was needed was a more interventionist, not a hands-off, approach. And the source of Bob's wrongheaded outlook was precisely his lack of country competence and first-hand experience. [. . .]

Most crewmembers [. . .] do not know any environmentalists personally, and if they do meet advocates of anti-interventionist forestry, it is usually in passing moments such as barstool conversations. Nevertheless, all (the word is not an exaggeration) the firefighters at Elk River decry meddlesome "environmentalists," their amorphous enemies, because their fight is not with people but with a specific position within the field of environmental politics, a field where the symbolic struggle over the best way to do forestry takes place. The fire sector of the Forest Service occupies a certain position in this field while environmental groups, including groups within the Forest Service such as wildlife biologists, occupy an opposing position, and when crewmembers commit themselves to fighting fires for the Forest Service, they enter into this field and join in its struggles. [. . .]

By adopting the enemies of the Forest Service as their own enemies and the problems of the Forest Service as their own problems, crewmembers come to identify with and trust the Forest Service. They begin to understand their world through its categories and classifications and aim their critical energies and doubtful queries not at their host organization but at outside organizations and individuals classified by the Forest Service as deserving of criticism.

Becoming a wildland firefighter involves much more than simply learning how to dig line, back burn, fall dead trees (snags), recognize fire behavior, and interpret weather patterns; it also involves learning how to communicate and think like other wildland firefighters and to like and dislike certain things and individuals which wildland firefighters "should" like and dislike. [. . .] [T]hough they are not aware of it, crewmembers have been preparing to trust and to accept the common sense of the US Forest Service since childhood; they began developing a disposition that "fits" within this organization long before they even knew of the organization.

FIREFIGHTING COMPETENCE

[. . .] How do country boys acclimate themselves to the act of firefighting? How do they acquire the deep-seated, bodily competence that they employ on the fireline? If firefighting is not easy, and if the principal source of firefighting competence is not to be found in training, being but a brief and mnemonic education transmitted through video tapes, experience, since most crewmembers lack extensive exposure to wildfire, [. . .] then how are firefighters able to synchronize their actions on the fireline, to work together seamlessly, safely, and efficiently? A significant [. . .] part of the answer lies in the fact that country boys come to the Forest Service already acclimated to the tasks of wildland firefighting. Country competence serves as the foundation for wildland firefighting competence. [. . .]

I once battled an especially volatile and enormous fire with George and J. J., a 22-year-old in his third season of firefighting, under the guidance of Rex Thurman. We were stationed in a small mountain community that was threatened by the blaze. J. J., George, and I worked side-by-side, quickly coordinating our actions and acclimating to different scenarios. In order to foam down houses using the hose, the three of us separately worked towards the accomplishment of a shared goal: J. J. primed the engine pump, I procured the hose, and George secured the nozzle. These independent (yet corresponding) actions allowed us to get water on the houses as soon as possible. We did not intentionally coordinate each action; we did not formulate a game plan; rather, our actions seemed to coordinate themselves. Part of this process involved offering and accepting each others' suggestions ("let's use a foam nozzle instead of a forester," "don't use too much water"), which were always delivered in a hasty and forceful manner. If we were able to understand and act upon these minimal suggestions, changing direction and making adjustments in response to utterances that barely formed sentences, it was because we shared a linguistic *habitus*, one formed in past pressure situations. Growing up, all three of us took orders from a football coach who barked terse commands, as Thurman did, and we orchestrated plays on the gridiron on the basis of pithy phrases ("45 is the Mike," "shift left," "watch the draw," "wing-right, 38 sweep"). We knew the language of firefighting, so to speak, because we shared a linguistic disposition formed (and informed) by a shared country-masculine history. [. . .]

J. J., George, and I adjusted our bodily movements to one another. [. . .] [T]his was possible because we shared a country-masculine history that predisposed us to such actions. When my country-masculine *habitus* encountered itself in the postures, movements, rhythms, gestures, and orientations of my crewmembers, it recognized something familiar, something known deep down, and, accordingly, it synchronized with other manifestations of itself, creating a chemistry of sorts that coordinated action.

Crewmembers easily found the isolated mountain community, even though they had never been there before, because the roads they navigated to find smoke in the summer were the same ones they drove to find deer in the winter. [. . .] Since many crewmembers took their driver's license test in the seat of a four-by-four pickup, it was not difficult for them to adjust to driving the engine or the pickup that trails it, called the chase truck. J. J., George, and I knew how to swing a pulaski to destroy a half-burnt porch because we had been chopping our parents' and grandparents' wood since we were children. As young men who were raised in the woods [. . .] we knew how to observe the forest because our eyes had been search-ing the tips of pines and the trunks of oaks for years. Our ears knew what to listen for; our noses knew what the forest was supposed to smell like. Our footing and balance, posture and hiking style, sense of touch and movement were attuned to the forest, and this height-ened sense of awareness, this woodsy know-how in-scribed in our histories and in our very bodies, allowed us quickly to adapt to the challenges of the fire.

When J. J., George, and I returned to fire camp after doing battle on the line, our faces, necks, arms, and legs were caked with a thin crust of dried sweat, ash, dirt, and hardened foam. Our filthy fire shirts and pants bore the evidence of the dirty work of firefight-ing; globs of mud stuck to our boots; and we smelled of body odor and smoke. But we were used to getting dirty. As children, all three of us were encouraged to muck around in the outdoors, and as teenagers, we fur-ther were encouraged to muddy ourselves on the foot-ball field. This is not a trivial point, for if one chooses to fight wildfire, one must not mind being coated in dirt, ash, and sweat for days on end. One crewmember returned to Elk River from a 14-day fire stint, where showers were unavailable, with large pus-filled swell-ings under his armpits that later had to be lanced and drained. The doctor informed him that the swellings were brought on by the thick layer of dirt and ash that had accumulated on his skin and clogged up his pores, drastically hindering his ability to perspire.

Stories like this are not uncommon, for wildland firefighters must function under extremely primitive conditions stripped of many modern amenities such as running water and warm food. [. . .] Far from shying away from such discomforts that affront cleanliness and the ways of civilization, crewmem-bers embrace them. They take pride in the soot that covers their faces, arms, legs, and even teeth after a full day's work on the fireline, and, more to the point, they have known the taste and feel of dirt ever since they were children.

Most wildland firefighters acquire many of the dispositions and skills necessary to perform their job long before they become employees of the US Forest Service. In the same way, new firefighters who do not come from rural backgrounds and who do not possess a core set of country competences have a very difficult

time acclimating to the demands of firefighting. This was the case for Vince. Although he was raised in a small town, Vince, 23, was not brought up the same way many of his crewmembers were. Vince did not grow up with family camping trips or with weekend woodland outings. While most other crewmembers at Elk River were raised by their biological fathers, who introduced them to the Great Outdoors at very young ages, Vince was raised by a stepfather who taught him much about the receiving end of a leather strap and little about the delicate movement of a home-tied fly-lure atop a still lake or the rash action of deer in the rut. Thus, he did not acquire much country compe-tence growing up. Moreover, Vince was not socialized into a masculine sporting culture. Whereas most crewmembers had spent a considerable amount of time in homosocial male environments, Vince's first significant experience in such an environment came when he joined the Forest Service. Accordingly, Vince was not accustomed to masculine styles of communi-cation and joking; he did not possess years of experi-ence working beside other men in a collective setting, nor was he used to taking curt orders from a mascu-line boss. Vince *grew up* in the country, but he was not *brought up* with a country-masculine upbringing. [. . .] As a result, he had a much more difficult time accli-mating to the demands of firefighting than did his fellow crewmembers.

Although the summer of 2003 marked Vince's seventh season as a wildland firefighter, he did not hold a position of authority as did other crewmem-bers with comparable years of experience; in fact, many crewmembers with less experience outranked him. [. . .] [H]e did not assert himself as a confident leader or demonstrate a significant degree of firefight-ing competence. This became clear through dozens of everyday practices which took place on and off the fireline, practices which, when taken together, served to separate Vince from other crewmembers, stripping him of firefighting (and masculine) capital. For ex-ample, during fires, Vince never grabbed (nor was he ever handed) a pulaski, the lead tool; thus, when dig-ging line, he never directed his crewmembers but always followed behind someone else. Although the most experienced firefighters carry radios during a fire, I never saw Vince carrying one. When we were assigned to sharpen tools, Vince usually sanded the handles, a task understood by crewmembers as easier and less important than taking a file to metal and grinding on the edge of a combi or the blade of a pulaski. Although he was certified to do so, Vince rarely drove the chase truck, and on the rare occasion that he did, he was overly grateful for a turn behind the wheel. In short, Vince did not take to the formal and informal requirements of the job with the same degree of confidence and competence that other crewmembers did.

Whereas most crewmembers came to Elk River with a refined and well-developed set of country-masculine skills, Vince came to the Forest Service with fewer resources to draw upon. Most crewmembers adapted to the everyday practices of wildland firefighting—from digging line to repairing vehicles—easier than did Vince. Thus, although it seems strange that Vince was not well-adjusted to the world of wildland firefighting after seven years of experience, we might now say that he *only* had seven years of experience, whereas other crewmembers, regardless of the number of summers they had been employed by the Forest Service, had lifetimes' worth.

When we attempt to identify the source of firefighters' practical knowledge, when we pursue a genealogical trail leading back through young adulthood, adolescence, and childhood in an effort to put into words the unspoken intuitive competence that allows firefighters, simply, to do what they do, we discover that neither organizational socialization nor direct experience within the organization can lay full claim to the source of this knowledge. While the Forest Service accounts for firefighters' competence through training courses and regulations and firefighters themselves tend to attribute their know-how to their time spent on the fireline, there is a deeper source. There is something in the background, something alive, though invisible, and present in nearly every action of wildland firefighting; this "something" is the country-masculine *habitus*. Crewmembers' shared history manifests itself in firefighters' very bodies. It is brought to life through their skillful actions, but it usually resides under the surface, acting as the unnoticed bind that holds everything in place. Firefighters are practical actors, who have

adapted, *modus operandi*, to the demands of firefighting not through a drastic transformation (after all, training can be described accurately as meager at best), nor by following ordinances, or even through direct experience fighting fire, but rather, through subtle modifications of already established dispositions and skills. The skills involved in battling a wildfire come to firefighters almost naturally, because firefighters' rural working-class masculine upbringings, *opus operatum*, have already laid the groundwork. [. . .] [T]he wildland firefighter comes to the setting pre-formed, pre-conditioned, and thus, in the root sense, *prepared*—from the Latin *praeparare*, literally meaning "previously procured"—for the demands and dangers of firefighting.

AFTERWORD: ETHNOGRAPHY OF THE HABITUS

By tracing the conversion of a general *habitus* to a specific one, I was able to show that the process of becoming a wildland firefighter starts long before one joins a firefighting crew. In fact, the process begins with thousands of experiences specific to working-class rural backgrounds. Through these experiences, crewmembers acquire embodied competences and naturalized ways of apprehending the world that serve them well on the fireline. Moreover, I was able to uncover how the country-masculine *habitus* "helps to determine what transforms it" (Bourdieu 2000 [1997]: 149). In other words, I was able to break with current accounts of risktaking, which would venture to guess that new recruits are seduced into the world of firefighting by promises of *adventure* [. . .]. By contrast, I was able to demonstrate that crewmembers gravitate "naturally" to the ranks of firefighting because the country-masculine *habitus* seeks out a universe in which it can recognize itself, an environment in which it can thrive. For the men at Elk River, the decision to fight fire was not a bold leap into a brave new world, but rather, a mild step into familiar territory. Therefore, this article has demonstrated that we must study not only the organization, but the individual (and his history) within the organization, not only the US Forest Service, but the country boy as a member of the Forest Service.

In the same way, if researchers wish to reconstruct the practical logic of executives, Marines, street hustlers, or nurses [. . .] then they must explore the interface between individuals' general *habitus* and the culture and practices of the office building, the military, the street, or the hospital. Examining the emergence of a specific *habitus* from the configuration of skills and dispositions that constitute the general *habitus* requires much more than simply researching individuals' personal histories. [. . .] If this were the case, investigations into the transformation of a *habitus* would be no different than the pursuits of bread-and-butter anthropology, a discipline built upon the examination of kinship patterns and genealogies. What makes a *habitus*-driven approach distinct is its insistence on ferreting out *specific linkages* connecting personal histories with present-day social contexts (such as the linkage between country competence and firefighting competence). It requires rigorously examining the origins of acquired dispositions and skills as well as the precise ways in which they handicap or advantage individuals in various organizational, educational, cultural, social, or political settings. [. . .]

REFERENCES

Bell, Michael. 1995. *Childerley: Nature and Morality in a Country Village*. Chicago: University of Chicago Press.

Bourdieu, Pierre. 2000 [1997]. *Pascalian Meditations*. Stanford, CA: Stanford University Press.

Collinson, David. 1992. *Managing the Shopfloor: Subjectivity, Masculinity, and Workplace Culture*. New York: de Gruyter.

Connell, Raewyn. 2006. "Country/City Men." In *Country Boys: Masculinity and Rural Life*, edited by Hugh Campbell, Michael Bell, and Margaret Finney, 255–66. University Park: Pennsylvania State University Press.

Halle, David. 1984. *America's Working Man: Work, Home, and Politics among Blue-Collar Property Owners*. Chicago: University of Chicago Press.

Lamont, Michèle. 2000. *The Dignity of Working Men: Morality and the Boundaries of Race, Class, and Immigration*. Cambridge, MA: Russell Sage Foundation/Harvard University Press.

Lévi-Strauss, Claude. 1966[1962]. *The Savage Mind*. Chicago: University of Chicago Press.

Wacquant, Loïc. 2004. *Body & Soul: Notebooks of an Apprentice Boxer*. New York: Oxford University Press.

Willis, Paul. 1977. *Learning to Labour: How Working Class Kids Get Working Class Jobs*. Farnborough, UK: Saxon House.

NOTES

1. A pulaski is a furrowing tool with the head of an axe melded with an adze trenching blade; it usually serves as the lead tool during line construction.
2. Since wildfires primarily dance across the landscape only during the summer months, most wildland firefighters are temporary workers who hold odd jobs or attend college during the off-season.
3. Though it is clear that a fear of crime abounds in their construction of the city, no crewmember used racial stereotypes when describing their fears. Further, white and minority crewmembers alike viewed the inner city as a site of violence and vice.

ADAM REICH

21. CAN BOURDIEU HELP US UNDERSTAND MASCULINITY, AND CAN MASCULINITY HELP US UNDERSTAND BOURDIEU?

... [M]y mayhem is bringing
me closer to death
But I enjoy it cuz if I die
It'll be over respect.

—G-Bo, Hidden TREWTH, *Rhode Island Training School*
(2005)

The maximum-security unit of the Rhode Island Training School (RITS)—the state's only juvenile detention facility—was called the Youth Correctional Center, or YCC for short. The YCC was a prison within a prison. Security was relatively casual when one arrived at the main entrance of the Training School. In the YCC, on the other hand, all visitors had to empty their pockets of keys, cell phones, pens, and anything else that might conceivably be a threat. While many residents of the Training School were allowed relatively unrestrained movement around the fenced campus of the facility, YCC residents lived behind a second fence and three heavy locked doors. Unlike in the main building, all the classrooms in the YCC have large windows out to the hallway, so that the juvenile program workers (JPWs) could keep a close watch to ensure teachers' safety. In several years of directing the facility's newspaper, *Hidden TREWTH*, the only time I ever worried about my safety was in the YCC, when one young man flashed a blade he had made out of a piece of filing cabinet.

When I sat down with Doug, a white resident in the YCC, he told me that it was "hard to be white" in maximum security. Out of twenty-eight residents in the unit, he said, only four were white. "Usually you'd think I'd get picked on," he told me. But he was able to handle it. While "dudes that are soft try to be hard," he said, "dudes that are hard sit back and be quiet." That's what he had done. And now he was "the only white guy in the RITS that has respect." Doug's approach to life was etched onto his arm, the initials "M.P.R." tattooed in large block letters. When I asked him what it stood for, he answered, "money, power, respect." Allen, an African American resident of the YCC, used the same acronym as he began to describe himself: "M.P.R.—money, power, respect. I get respect anyway. Say you're not selling drugs. Average nigga. Say you're making money. People start respecting you. Others see that they're respecting you. So you got influence on others. If you could tell them to do something they do it. That's power."

In one way, these two young men seemed only to make explicit the classical typologies by which people distinguish themselves from others. Sociologists have long observed that people tend to use their economic standing, their power over others, and their social esteem as markers of their positions in social hierarchies. But in another way these young men's accounts are strikingly paradoxical. Young men's participation in crime certainly does not deliver money, power, or respect according to standard conceptions of the terms. The economic rewards of participation in the drug trade are less, on average, than those of working a minimum-wage job (Levitt and Venkatesh 2000). It is hard to imagine a more powerless position than that of incarceration—a direct result of many young men's criminality. And, if anything, criminal activity undermines young men's respectability in the eyes of the broader social world. These young men were striving for social distinction but seemed to define and distribute this distinction

This reading is adapted from Adam Reich's *Hidden Truth: Young Men Navigating Lives In and Out of Juvenile Prison* (Berkeley: University of California Press, 2010). © 2010 by the Regents of the University of California. Published by the University of California Press.

in opposition to the ways that it was understood in the wider world.

In this chapter I argue that young men's participation in street crime represents a self-defeating assertion of an ideal of masculinity that has been, in critical ways, decoupled from the institutional processes by which men as a group have perpetuated the domination of women (Connell 1987: 183). In turn, administrators and staff-members of the Rhode Island Training School work to inculcate among these same young men new ways of understanding themselves and their lives—understandings consistent with an alternative ideal of masculinity that will keep them out of trouble and yet forces them to accept their own powerlessness more directly. Out of the intersection of these ideal-types, I suggest, there exists the possibility of critical practice—a less gendered, reflexive understanding of both oneself and of the broader structural conditions within which one lives.

But what is *masculinity*? Sociologists have long considered gender to be a flexible but persistent social boundary, based on perceived sex differences, through which men establish power over and expropriate resources from women. From this perspective, "masculinity"—like "femininity"—might be understood as a set of meanings and identities that uphold and legitimate the boundary. Note that from this perspective the contents of the categories are entirely variable, meaningful only in relationship to one another.

Raewyn Connell (1987, 1995), importantly, complicated the notion of a gender dichotomy and analyzed the multiple ways that masculinity is enacted within any given society. For her, masculinities can usefully be understood as being arranged in a hierarchy, in that some ways of being masculine are "hegemonic," more "socially central, or more associated with social power, than others" (Connell and Messerschmidt 2005: 846). While most men have some access to the "patriarchal dividend" of men's general domination of women, she suggested, the profits are unequally distributed.

Despite the intuitive appeal of this approach, the young men at the Training School are difficult to place within Connell's framework. This is because the term *hegemonic masculinity* seems at once to refer to that conception of masculinity practiced and perpetuated by those men with institutional power, and to that conception of masculinity most *culturally* dominant (e.g., Connell 1995: 77–78). But these are not necessarily the same. Young men involved in crime (and governed by the criminal justice system) are some of the most institutionally powerless young men in U.S. society, yet they simultaneously serve as potent cultural symbols of masculinity. The music, fashion, video-game, entertainment, sports, and automobile industries, to name a few, splash these young men across their glossy advertisements, and the halls of high schools across the country mirror the trends that these young men start. Scholars would be hard-pressed to show *either* that these men enacted hegemonic masculinity as Connell defines it, *or* that this kind of masculinity was subordinate to others, given its cultural prominence and power (Sewell 1997). This is certainly not to say that these young men are in control of the cultural representations of them. But images of poor young men involved in crime remain potent symbols of masculinity in U.S. culture.

James Messerschmidt advances Connell's framework in relationship to men's involvement in crime. Messerschmidt takes seriously the relative autonomy of masculinity's cultural significance from men's institutional power. The way Messerschmidt understands "hegemonic masculinity," then, is in terms of specific practices of social interaction that are commonly accepted as masculine across different settings. In contemporary society, he suggests, these involve "practices toward authority, control, competitive individualism, independence, aggressiveness, and the capacity for violence" (Messerschmidt 1993: 82). No longer is hegemonic masculinity that conception "more associated with social power," as Connell would have it. Rather, it is a set of understandings and practices common to men in many different contexts.

In turn, Messerschmidt argues that masculinity is a "situated accomplishment" (1993: 79), meaning that in order to enact hegemonic masculinity, in order to *feel* masculine—feel competitive and independent—men in different structural positions must make use of the different resources over which they have some control (1993: 117). Based on this theoretical reconceptualization, Messerschmidt understands young men's involvement in crime as an attempt by those men without institutional power to assert masculinity outside of institutional channels, "when other resources are unavailable" (1993: 85). Messerschmidt thus retains the idea of hegemonic masculinity but abstracts it to make it consistent with *both* the businessman and the young man at the Training School. This is a valuable analytic move.

But if Connell conflates masculinity and other forms of institutional power with her concept of hegemonic masculinity, Messerschmidt risks too clean a break between masculinity and other forms of power. What distinguishes the businessman's aggressive pursuit of profit and the young man's criminality, for Messerschmidt, are merely their different situations, the different resources that they have to "do gender" (West and Zimmerman 1987). What is missing are the particular ways in which *crime* allows marginalized young men to "do gender." What does crime provide that other pursuits cannot? More generally, what does it mean to use something as a "resource" to do gender? Despite the usefulness of Messerschmidt's analysis, and his attention to what unifies different conceptions of masculinity across different social settings, his account is ultimately unsatisfying when it comes to explaining variation in the understandings and practices associated with masculinity across different groups.

Pierre Bourdieu's conception of game-playing helps to enrich Messerschmidt's notion of masculinity as a "situated accomplishment." According to Bourdieu, humans in general tend to establish hierarchies among themselves through competition within socially agreed upon arenas, or "fields." People use different kinds of resources to compete for power in different fields and can strategically use high status in one field (e.g. money when it comes to the economic field, or a doctorate when it comes to the cultural field) to gain status in another. The metaphor Bourdieu uses most commonly to describe this process is that of the game. Players' focus, when immersed in a game, is less on the presuppositions of the game than on one's strategic activity relative to other players. When one is playing chess, for example, one is not consistently questioning *why* one cares about winning, how chess came to be a game in the first place, or what the rewards of winning are

(of which there are likely none). One's attention is on the next move, or the series of moves necessary to win.

Bourdieu suggests that people's very conceptions of what kinds of power *matter*, and therefore which games they play and find meaningful, are structured by their objective positions in social space. While all people may be striving to accumulate social power, the particular kind of social power for which they strive is structured by the opportunities and constraints they face.

According to Bourdieu, such processes of game-playing are inescapable. Competition within agreed-upon fields is essential to what it means to be human. Bourdieu's most explicit explanation for the emergence of games, however, is a functionalist one. He writes that through

> investment in a game and the recognition that can come from cooperative competition with others, the social world offers humans that which they most totally lack: a justification for existing. (Bourdieu 2000: 239).

For Bourdieu, game-playing provides a solution to the opposite (and seemingly *instinctual*) poles of the boredom of routine and the radical uncertainty of existential meaninglessness. The combination of collaboration and competition inherent in games provide players with a manageable level of uncertainty that draws them into playing. A game provides players with enough uncertainty to feel engaged, but with enough control to feel as if their actions are related to the outcomes at stake (Burawoy 1979: 87). People are able to find a "justification for existing" through social interaction that lets them identify their position vis-à-vis others, and lets them feel that their own behavior has something to do with this position.

But a need for a justification for existing does not in itself produce that justification. And the particular justification for existing the game seems to provide—a kind of individual, positional identity within a group—seems to be only one of several conceivable justifications. What about the bond one feels for another human? What about a freedom to posit one's own goals outside of these games? Bourdieu seems to turn everything into a game, when the metaphor might explain some patterns of social interaction better than others.

But feminist scholarship implicitly calls into question the ubiquity of such game-playing. For example, in her book *The Bonds of Love* (1988), Jessica Benjamin observes that the modern world relegates emotional connection and intersubjective recognition to a "feminine" private sphere, which then becomes the object of a separate, calculating, public masculinity. A public, masculine ethic of "means" then comes to dominate a private, feminine ethic of "ends." Reasoning is disconnected from values—with the former understood as masculine and the latter as feminine (Benjamin 1988: 186).

Other scholars working within the psychoanalytic tradition make similar arguments. For them, the fact that mothers tend to be primary caregivers to infants has real and different effects on the way that men and women come to understand themselves and to relate to the world. Gender is not only a social boundary, but is also an unconscious pattern of interaction and identity forged in the family. For example, according to Chodorow in her classic *The Reproduction of Mothering* (1979), an infant boy is forced to distinguish himself from his mother earlier than a girl, because the mother begins to treat him as a sexual object rather than, in the case of the girl, as an extension of herself. The boy is then forced to compete with his father over his (now cognitively separate) mother's love. The processes of distinction and competition are likely taught to the infant boy earlier and more fully than to the infant girl (Chodorow 1979). Supporting this psychoanalytic perspective, several scholars have suggested that masculinity can be characterized by a strict adherence to and high regard for impersonal rules; a competitive and strategic orientation to other people; and a tendency to organize people in hierarchies (e.g., Lever 1976; Thorne 1993).

In other words, game-playing might better explain *men's* understandings of their place in the social world than it explains behavior, interactions, and motivations in social world more generally. In light of this, we might consider masculinity as an orientation towards action that places a premium on the individualized pursuit of power for its own sake. These insights of Messerschmidt, as well as those of Benjamin, help us reconceptualize game-playing—and perhaps the very drive for individualized distinction—less as

universal human behavior than as gendered action. In turn, what Bourdieu contributes to Messerschmidt's approach is the idea that game-playing (i.e., masculinity) is centrally about the pursuit of social power and distinction. Moreover, Bourdieu draws attention to the ways that game-playing (i.e., masculinity) opens up possibilities for certain kinds of insights while precluding others. I now turn to these two ways in which Bourdieu can enrich the study of masculinities.

MASCULINITY AND POWER

Importantly, Bourdieu suggests that people's very conceptions of what kinds of power *matter*, and therefore the games that they play, are influenced by their objective positions in social structure. Seen through a gendered lens, while all men may be game-playing for social power, the ways in which *power* is understood is structured by the opportunities and constraints they face.

Young men involved in crime typically have little access to institutional sources of social power, have little claim on the patriarchal dividend through these channels. They are excluded from or, at best, offered the lowest positions in the labor market; they have little or no political power; and they are regarded as social pariahs at school and by many in society at large. They cannot play those games that would distinguish themselves as men through the arenas of work, politics, or status.

As an adaption to this institutional exclusion, they conceive of power as something *physical*, external. "Money, power, and respect" are displayed on men's bodies and at stake in daily interaction. Money is displayed garishly through the "bling bling" of clothes, cars, and jewelry. Power is equated with physical strength and not backing down from a fight. And respect is something threatened through the smallest violations of what Anderson (1999) calls the "code of the street." I call this "*outsider* masculinity," then, for two reasons. First, and most obviously, it takes place outside the boundaries of the law. But it also takes place on the outside of men's bodies.

The metaphor of the "game" is actually used quite explicitly by many young men caught up in crime. For example, one of the young men I interviewed described his life as follows: "I'm eighteen years old, that's eighteen years gone to the game." And some young men *are* able to achieve a kind of mythical stature through their participation in crime, at least among other young men in their communities—memorialized in death or in incarceration as the embodiment of an ideal toward which others strive.

Men who have access to institutional sources of social power, on the other hand, tend to stake their masculinity less on daily interactions. Instead, the games they play are games related to their trajectories through the workplace, political power, and social standing. This is not to say that these games do not also involve outward "displays" of masculinity, or jockeying for position within social interactions. But these games are more firmly rooted within existing arrangements of economic, political, and social power. I call this "*insider* masculinity," again as a play on the word "inside." Masculinity understood in this way is, most obviously, inside the boundaries of the law. Yet men invested in *insider masculinity* also relate to power as something that inheres in the person rather than being expressed or worn externally. Masculinity is demonstrated less through one's daily presentation-of-self and physical force, and more through institutional position and the ongoing accumulation of resources by legal means.

Michael Messner's (1992) study of sports and masculinity is useful in its demonstration of the relationship between what I refer to as outsider and insider masculinity. He highlights variations by social class in the ways that young men relate to sports as they grow from the relative powerlessness of adolescence to positions of varied social standing. Sports serve as a kind of analogy to the conception of outsider masculinity elaborated above. While still within the boundaries of the law, sports offer an arena within which men's physical prowess is rewarded through strategic action within a set of rules. As an interviewee of Messner observed, in some low-income communities of color young men feel "you were either one of two things: you were in sports or you were out on the streets being a drug-addict, or breaking into places" (Messner 1992: 38). For these young men, sport quite literally becomes a substitute for crime.

Yet where men of lower social class continued to depend on sports as a marker of masculinity as they

grow up, Messner found, middle-class men tended to come "to view a sport career as 'pissing in the wind' or as 'small potatoes'" compared to their "other educational or professional goals" (Messner 1992: 135). As the possibility of hinging one's masculinity on one's more general power in society opened up, the need to prove it within the sports arena faded. This was clearest in the contrast Messner draws between Ray, a Vietnam veteran and bus driver, and Jim, a dentist. For Ray, his continued attachment to sports—despite severe injuries—helped him feel that he is "still somebody" (1992: 135). Despite his previous athletic accomplishments, on the other hand, Jim thought, "I'm thirty-two years old, and so what if I'm out of shape?" (1992: 136).

According to this framework, masculinity might be seen as bipolar. Outsider masculinity—defined by physical toughness, material display, dominance in interaction, opposition to the law—is at one pole, where insider masculinity—defined by one's position in institutional hierarchies, one's capacity to create the law—is at the other. This is too neat a distinction, of course. But the important point is that young men involved in crime likely face a "masculinity cost" to the marginal gains in institutional power and respectability they could acquire through "reform" (as defined by correctional programming). In order to become law-abiding, these young men would have to give up elements of outsider masculinity, but my research builds on others to illustrate that insider masculinity remains out of reach. For example, if they can find jobs at all, these young men have to accept positions at the bottom of hierarchies they heretofore had rejected altogether—having to assume dispositions consistent with such subordinated positions. Thus, masculinity is likely an under-appreciated mechanism that reproduces young men's criminality and undermines the success of rehabilitative programming.

Staff at the Rhode Island Training School worked to reconceptualize "reform" as consistent with masculinity (albeit a subordinated one), setting up a micro-game within which incarcerated young men could win small and symbolic gains in status. Young men won behavioral "points" for behavior in keeping with the managerial needs of the facility. These points were aggregated over the course of weeks and

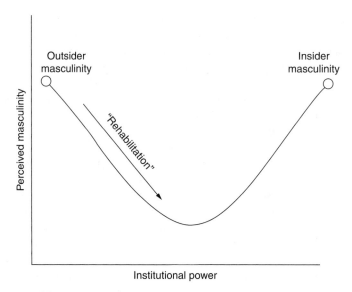

FIGURE 1   is an illustration of the argument above. For young men involved in crime, who have staked their masculinity on their opposition to those forms of power considered legitimate by larger publics, small gains in institutional power (i.e., a low-wage job or enrollment in community college) likely demand a degree of subordination inconsistent with their (and others') sense of their masculinity. Desistance from crime thus means the loss of one of the only forms of power to which they have been able to lay claim.

months into "levels." Residents who follow the rules of this "game" are able to win privileges such as later bed-times and more contact with the outside world. But, points could be lost with any indiscretion.

The regime served two purposes simultaneously. First, it served as a lubricant for the daily operations of the facility. To the extent that points became a currency important to young men in the facility, Training School staff were able to maintain a degree of control over their charges. In this way, this game resembled the shop floor games articulated by scholars of the labor process (e.g., Willis 1977; Haraszti 1978; Burawoy 1979). The Training School (like the firm) set the terms of the game in such a way so as to fulfill banal organizational mandates, all the while letting players feel a sense of agency or control in their daily lives.

Yet this regime served a second broader, if less fully articulated or acknowledged, purpose. Staff quite often viewed a resident's "level" as an indication of some internal process of rehabilitation, assuming that those young men who walked with their hands behind their backs on command would be able to handle the responsibilities of work and family

life. In other words, this regime was seen as a mechanism through which young men's marginal position within broader systems of social power could become meaningful to these young men. In other words, the Training School sought to turn *submission* into sport. When successful, it made possible a process by which young men became invested enough in conforming to the law that they consented to remaining relatively powerless within society as a whole.

MASCULINITY AND MEANING

For Bourdieu, the process by which people make sense of their lives tends not to challenge the existing order of things, since the games they enter (and the way they think about competing) merely reproduce the world as they know it. Indeed, throughout the sociological literature, the metaphor of the game chiefly has been employed to explain social reproduction (e.g., Willis 1977; Burawoy 1979). Participation in a game systematically shuts down the possibility of questioning how the game emerged or reflecting on the goals around which the game is organized. This makes the transformation of games difficult, especially from a position of uncritical investment. At best, then, the understandings generated through participation take the form of what Paul Willis calls "partial penetrations," or half-articulated criticisms of those games that *are not* played.

Participation in crime deprives young men of a view of this game's place within broader social structures (i.e., how this "game" works to systematically perpetuate existing positions of power and inequality). Yet this same participation offers young men a whole constellation of meanings and motivations within which to make sense of their lives. Young men's understandings of the world emerge alongside the constraints they face and practices they take part in among others. This sentiment is elaborated by Michael Burawoy who writes, "[I]t is lived experience that produces ideology, not the other way around. Ideology is rooted in and expresses the activities out of which it emerges" (Burawoy 1979: 18). Masculinity is not—by and large—imposed from the top down. Rather, it emerges in practice through the contests and contestations that make up young men's lives.

Yet given these young men's *lack* of investment in the insider masculinity associated with institutional power, they have several important—if partial—insights into the social world from which they are excluded. For example, Joel was part of the first group of writers I ever worked with at the Training School. In the premier issue of the newspaper, he wrote our cover story on the state's Department of Children, Youth, and Families (DCYF)—the department that also administers the Training School:

> In critical slang it is known as the Department that Controls Your Families. Reasons vary. . . . DCYF take children away from their families when there is a conflict within the family that may make that family live dysfunctionally. Of course there really aren't any set rules or limits that states what makes a dysfunctional family. Supposedly if your family isn't, happy and . . . getting along like "Full House" episodes then there is a problem. . . . More specifically, if a parent is a crackhead, apparently she cannot take care of her child. DCYF can. If a parent is a weed smoker she too cannot provide for the family, but DCYF can. . . . A child is neglected, call DCYF. A child getting spanked, has marks and bruises, call

> DCYF. . . . Sounds real good. Why is it thought of negatively? . . . Maybe DCYF sticks their nose in families who don't need the assistance of the state. Maybe when children and youths enter the system they leave more corrupt than they ever were. Maybe DCYF corrodes the benefits of a struggling family. . . . The government benefits off of us and our families in more ways than one. We are taught to live the lives we lead, without DCYF, the state or the government we'd be free to learn, teach, discover and grow in the ways of nature naturally.

For those most invested in outsider masculinity, it seemed to make possible a particular kind of insight into the social world from which it represents a partial rebellion. More generally, it is the groups *not* invested in particular games that are most easily able to critique them. The games created by the marginalized, then, can have paradoxical effects: on the one hand, they reproduce powerlessness; on the other hand, they offer some of the most radical insight into the systems of power from which they are excluded. This paradoxical quality of game-playing by the marginalized—that it opens up possibilities for insight at the same time it reproduces the social world out of which it emerges—has been well captured by other scholars (e.g., Willis 1977; Burawoy 1979), if rarely linked explicitly to masculinity.[1]

Of course, Bourdieu's theory provides a much clearer conception of social reproduction than it does of social change. For him, the games people play are framed by their positions in social structure, and their playing tends to reproduce these structures. Yet by considering game-playing as a way men "prove" masculinity, rather than as a ubiquitous pattern of interaction, we are able to imagine a transcendence of game-playing altogether, which might involve at the same time a *degendering* of young men's activity.

Many young men in the Training School seemed caught between the outsider masculinity in which they had been invested on the outside and the disciplinary game that organized life in the Training School. Some spoke from juvenile prison about being at war with themselves, like in this piece by Richard that he entitled "My Enemy":

> I get the feeling that someone is out to get me, destroy what I have become. . . . I have found this man

to be a savage and I must destroy him, he is what brought me here, he is what keeps me from successfully changing my life, he tells me to do what I never wanted to do, he is what I have become, he is me.

Many young men understand these conflicting identities as internal, psychological. Encouraged by the Training School to conceive of himself as responsible, disciplined, Richard's investment in another conception of himself felt like something dangerous, outside of his full control.

Young men often spoke from juvenile prison about these internal struggles for self-definition and understanding, or the difficulty of extracting themselves from the "roles" they had been occupying. A game perspective helps us "sociologize" young men's internal struggles. We are able to see them less as internal battles between good and evil, and more as the dissonant effects of the collision of two different (and often competing) conceptions of masculinity. Some young men were able to subsume one within the other, either using their time in the Training School to increase their status on the street, or "seeing the light" and working to a disciplined, subordinated masculinity within themselves. Yet some, feeling the irreconcilability of these two games from a position of investment in either one, seem able to develop a second-order understanding of these games and their limitations. Through the synthesis of these opposing conceptions of masculinity, some young men began to envision a world in which they could consciously create and pursue their own ends. Interestingly, this possibility seems to emerge not with a divestment from games entirely, but rather from a position of deep investment in two *contradictory* games. Where a position of non-investment could open up a certain amount of insight into those games that are *not* played, a position of contradictory investments seems to create the possibility of the *transcendence* of games altogether.

Yet among others, this contradiction between outsider masculinity and the demands of life "inside" seemed to create the possibility for critical practice, a kind of synthesis of two different games. I call this set of understandings "critical practice." Young men involved in critical practice reframe money as important only in terms of meeting their natural needs,

and are no longer concerned with displaying or saving their money to distinguish themselves. They reimagine power as the capacity to address their problems collectively, through political praxis. And respect, formerly something "won" through competition with other young men, becomes something akin to mutual recognition, or love.

Critical practice was also associated with a kind of *degendering* for these young men, as they become less invested in proving their masculinity through narrow game-playing. This is not to say that gender categories lose their salience entirely. One might argue that critical practice constitutes merely a new form of masculinity—masculinity as "redone" rather than "undone" (e.g., West and Zimmerman 2009). But at the very least, masculinity loses its rigidity, and becomes one of many different identities and boundaries with which these young men experiment and play. Indeed, it seems, a full critique of the social world is possible for these young men only once they begin to divest from the games on which they have staked their masculinity. This argument offers a twist to an emerging literature on "undoing gender," which has argued for an understanding of the variability of the salience of gender in different times and places (Deutsch 2007).

For these young men, both *outsider masculinity* and the subordinated *insider masculinity* put forward by the Training School came to be understood as narrow and unreflective orientations towards the social world. The ends of young men's activity, previously unquestioned, themselves became the object of consciousness and reflection. They began to understand their own involvement in crime as a *part* of the social structure from which they wished to rebel, part of the same structure that offered them only marginal positions in the social world. Crime became "falling into the trap" of the society they see as confining while low-wage work is seen as its own kind of trap.

For example, Tony described his own previous participation in crime as "just another illegal life." Like many other young men deeply invested in crime, he seemed to view crime as indistinguishable from legal work. Yet Tony was critical of *each*:

Kay, from like, just watching everything I seen grow up, people hustling, everyone in a rush to get something accomplished but no one really sure what. Drug dealer's a perfect example. Like, they hustle all day just to get money. At the end of the day is all they do with their money is buy more drugs, or buy clothes and shit that doesn't really matter. But they go out and just look, so they can look better in front of the next person on the block who they really don't care about. And it's the same thing in any form of life. Like a doctor works seventy hours a week to buy a brand new Mercedes to impress people he doesn't even know. Probably doesn't want the car, but because he's a doctor, and because he makes a certain amount of money a year he has to have that status symbol, to appear successful, regardless of how happy he is.

Tony saw similarities between the drug dealer and the doctor—how they each worked to make money, but made money only in order to prove they are of some status in relationship to others. He saw both lives as being driven by forces outside of their control, both the drug-dealer and the doctor as trying to achieve a kind of status without regard for "how happy" they are. Tony seemed to recognize the unreflectiveness of both insider masculinity *and* outside masculinity, and to work towards a transcendence of both.

This transcendence seemed possible because of the contradictory identities young men were asked to assume in juvenile prison. The juvenile prison intensified the pressures of outsider masculinity, as young men from different neighborhoods and gangs were forced into close proximity with each other and labeled juvenile delinquents. Yet it also intensified the pressure to reform, to assume a subordinated version of insider masculinity, as staff enforced a rigid disciplinary regime on young men. Implicitly asked to simultaneously play two different and opposing games in juvenile prison, to assume two contradictory ideals of masculinity, some young men were able to synthesize the two through a kind of second-order reflection on each game as a game. This seemed a first step towards being able to step out of the games entirely.

MASCULINITY AS A FUNDAMENTAL CAUSE OF CRIME?

According to the Bureau of Justice Statistics, as of December 31, 2011, there were 1,487,393 men under the jurisdiction of state and federal prisons, compared with 111,387 women. The gender disparity in crime and incarceration is so longstanding and so taken-for-granted that it has rarely been subject to serious analysis.[2] Moreover, most criminologists are interested in uncovering causes of crime that are more proximate to criminal activity than gendered understandings and practices. After all, *most* men (even within marginalized neighborhoods) are not regularly involved in street crime. Once one controls for more proximate causes of crime—antisocial cognitions, antisocial personality, antisocial associates— gender is an even weaker predictor (Andrews and Bonta 2010: 329–32).

Of course, it seems likely that masculinity *is* a fundamental cause of crime, in that it puts people at risk of the risks more proximately related to criminal behavior, particularly when in interaction with marginality (measured by class, race, something else) (Link and Phelan 2001). As epidemiologists remind us, the causes of a distribution are rarely the same as the causes of an individual's place within a distribution (Rose 1985; Lieberson 1997). Stanley Lieberson argues that, before one tries to understand individual outcomes, "[o]ne has to first consider any basic driving force that generates a certain outcome independent of the characteristics of the units in the population." He continues,

> Our current practices tend to infer the driving forces by examining the empirical association of the dependent variable with a variety of independent variables. Alas, these independent variables are secondary in the sense that they operate only within the context of affecting which units fall where in the distribution . . . but they do not create the distribution. (Lieberson 1997: 19)

In just such a way, masculinity seems likely to skew the distribution of social behavior in such a way that crime is more prevalent—in a neighborhood, community, or society.

This chapter has used Bourdieu to explore *why* masculinity might serve as such a fundamental cause of crime. In turn, it relies on gender scholarship and theory to question the universalism inherent in Bourdieu's account of game-playing. If game-playing for power is not a universal human tendency, but is rather a gendered practice, then there is at least the possibility of its transcendence, as I try to capture in my (admittedly utopian) conception of critical practice.

REFERENCES

Anderson, Elijah. 1999. *Code of the Street: Decency, Violence, and the Moral Life of the Inner City*. New York: Norton.

Andrews, D. A., and James Bonta. 2010. *The Psychology of Criminal Conduct*. New Providence, NJ: Elsevier.

Benjamin, Jessica. 1988. *The Bonds of Love: Psychoanalysis, Feminism, & the Problem of Domination*. New York: Random House.

Bourdieu, Pierre. 2000. *Pascalian Meditations*. Stanford, CA: Stanford University Press.

Burawoy, Michael. 1979. *Manufacturing Consent: Changes in the Labor Process under Monopoly Capitalism*. Chicago: University of Chicago Press.

Carlsson, Christoffer. 2013. "Masculinities, Persistence, and Desistance." *Criminology* 51 (3): 661–93.

Chodorow, Nancy J. 1979. *The Reproduction of Mothering: Psychoanalysis and the Sociology of Gender*. Berkeley: University of California Press.

Connell, Raewyn. 1987. *Gender and Power: Society, the Person and Sexual Politics*. Stanford, CA: Stanford University Press.

Connell, Raewyn. 1995. *Masculinities*. Stanford, CA: Stanford University Press.

Connell, Raewyn, and James W. Messerschmidt. 2005. "Hegemonic Masculinity Rethinking the Concept." *Gender & Society* 19 (6): 829–59.

Deutsch, Francine M. 2007. "Undoing Gender." *Gender & Society* 21 (1): 106–27.

Haraszti, Miklós. 1978. *A Worker in a Worker's State*. New York: Universe Books.

Klubock, Thomas Miller. 1996. "Working-Class Masculinity, Middle-Class Morality, and Labor Politics in the Chilean Copper Mines." *Journal of Social History* 30 (2): 435–63.

Lever, Janet. 1976. "Sex Differences in the Games Children Play." *Social Problems* 23 (4): 478–87.

Levitt, Steven D., and Sudhir Alladi Venkatesh. 2000. "An Economic Analysis of a Drug-Selling Gang's Finances." *The Quarterly Journal of Economics* 115 (3): 755–89.

Lieberson, Stanley. 1997. "Modeling Social Processes: Some Lessons from Sports." *Sociological Forum* 12 (1): 11–35.

Link, Bruce G., and Jo C. Phelan. 2001. "Conceptualizing Stigma." *Annual Review of Sociology* 27: 363–85.

Messerschmidt, James W. 1993. *Masculinities and Crime: Critique and Reconceptualization of Theory*. Lanham, MD: Rowman & Littlefield.

Messner, Michael A. 1992. *Power at Play: Sports and the Problem of Masculinity*. Boston: Beacon Press.

Rose, Geoffrey. 1985. "Sick Individuals and Sick Populations." *International Journal of Epidemiology* 14: 32–38.

Sewell, Tony. 1997. *Black Masculinities and Schooling: How Black Boys Survive Modern Schooling*. London: Trentham Books.

Thorne, Barrie. 1993. *Gender Play: Girls and Boys in School*. New Brunswick, NJ: Rutgers University Press.

West, Candace, and Don H. Zimmerman. 1987. "Doing Gender." *Gender & Society* 1 (2): 125–51.

West, Candace, and Don H. Zimmerman. 2009. "Accounting for Doing Gender." *Gender & Society* 23 (1): 112–22.

Willis, Paul E. 1977. *Learning to Labor: How Working Class Kids Get Working Class Jobs*. New York: Columbia University Press.

NOTES

1. For an exception see Klubock (1996).
2. For a recent exception, however, see Carlsson (2013).

ANTHONY C. OCAMPO

22. "MANNING UP TO BEING GAY": MINORITY MASCULINITIES IN THE COMMUNITY AND AT THE CLUB

Jimmy Avila could not pinpoint the exact moment he "discovered" that his uncle Cristián was gay, but for as long as he could remember, his *tío* was "clearly a homosexual." Like many other Mexican Americans, Jimmy grew up in a household not only with his parents and siblings, but also with a number of other relatives—aunts, uncles, cousins, grandparents, family friends—most of whom were from the same area in Guadalajara, Mexico, where he and his parents were born. At the age of three, Jimmy had settled with his family in Orange County where his father found work as a security guard at a local airport. Once the Avilas were able to purchase a home, there seemed to be a revolving door of relatives who would stay with them for weeks or even months upon migrating from Mexico. When he was younger, Jimmy's parents had offered to house his mother's cousin Rosa, and *Tío* Cristián was Rosa's overtly effeminate younger brother.

"My dad would always talk shit about *Tío* Cristián. Always calling him a *maricón* or a *puto*," Jimmy recalled. At first, Jimmy had no real conception of what these terms meant, but it was evident from his father's disdainful tone that these were bad things to be called. "I was a kid and didn't really understand," he continued, "So I asked my older brother what those words meant, and he goes, 'Oh, it's bad. It's when a boy likes another boy.' From that point on, I figured out quick that I'm not supposed to like my Superman action figures too much, even though I found their buff bodies attractive."

Like Jimmy, Kevin Orozco came to this country as a young child. Although he and his parents were from the Philippines, he shares vivid memories similar to Jimmy's recollections of his *Tío* Cristián. Kevin remembers spending many afternoons after school watching *The Filipino Channel*, or "TFC" for short, with his mother, father, and siblings. It seemed that every *novela* that his parents watched had a hyperfeminine male character who was the best friend of the female protagonist. "Look at that *bakla*!" Mr. Orozco would say, in the same disparaging demeanor as Mr. Avila's treatment of Jimmy's *Tío* Cristián. In the Philippines, *bakla* literally translates as half female (*babae*) and half male (*lalake*) and is the equivalent of the English pejorative term "fag." Mr. Orozco would always warn Kevin about the *baklas* every time he went to get his haircut at the local Filipino-owned salon, referring to the male stylists who worked there. "Be careful, son," he would tell Kevin, "Make sure they don't touch you."

Jimmy and Kevin were 2 of the 50 young men I interviewed who grew up in Southern California with immigrant parents. They are both part of the "new second generation"—the rapidly growing population of Latinos and Asian Americans who come of age in households and communities where they actively straddle the cultural value systems of their parents' home country and the United States (Portes and Zhou 1993). They also happen to identify as gay men (although as this chapter will show, this was not always the case). What is fascinating is that Jimmy, Kevin, and many of the other men I studied shared story after story of parents and relatives casually stigmatizing gay people throughout their childhood (and even adulthood), and they recounted these moments with the most vivid of detail—as if these incidents occurred just yesterday. During interviews, some men seemed to relive the emotions of these moments, some on the verge of tears, but many others with a stoicism characteristic of attempts to block out traumatic memories. These were the moments when they learned that gay was wrong. These were also the moments when they realized there was something "off" about them that needed to be fixed or—at the very least—hidden at all costs.

The experiences of the gay second generation remain invisible in the existing literatures in research on immigration and sexualities. As such, this chapter "queers" assimilation frameworks (Manalansan 2006) by highlighting the critical role that cultural conceptions of masculinity play in the lives of second-generation Latino and Filipino gay men. Specifically, my analysis utilizes a "cultural capital" framework to consider the consequential effects that different types of *masculinities* have in how second-generation gay men navigate their relationships with family, the co-ethnic community, and the larger gay community (e.g., Ocampo 2012). Although there is overlap in how masculinities are constructed within these social environments, there are also differences that can be put into stark relief by focusing on the intersectional identities of second-generation gay men. As I will show, the centrality (and marginality) of race, ethnicity, and class differs in how masculinities are defined in the immigrant family versus white gay communities. These men's experiences allow us to understand gender and sexual identities and inequalities in new ways.

Eventually, the men I interviewed found themselves "manning up to being gay," as one respondent astutely characterized that moment when he owned his sexual identity and began to identify himself as "gay." In privileging this young man's catchphrase in the chapter title, I am aware of the problematic nature of reinforcing the association between masculinity and courage and its implications for the devaluing of femininity (which can be embodied by any person—man, woman, or other). At the same time, this phrasing signals the accomplishment of an interesting shift in the gender and sexual identity development of second-generation gay men. How is it that these men go from understanding gay and masculine as dialectically opposed concepts to eventually seeing them as congruent? By delving into the way Latino and Filipino gay men negotiate sexuality and masculinity in conjunction with other competing identities, I investigate this process.

GAY CHILDREN OF IMMIGRANTS: WHERE THEORIES OF IMMIGRATION, CULTURE, AND MASCULINITY COLLIDE

ASSIMILATION THEORY

There was a period in American sociology when immigration experts believed that all immigrants would eventually become part of the American middle class (e.g., Park 1950; Gordon 1964). And, if we look at the assimilation patterns of the groups that early American sociologists studied—turn-of-the-century European immigrants—this prediction turns out to be largely true. Capitalizing on their white racial status and the economic opportunities afforded to them through a booming industrial economy, even European groups with minimal education and occupational skills were able to climb the socioeconomic ranks of American society within three or four generations (Alba 1990; Waters 1990).

However, after Congress passed the 1965 Hart–Cellar Act,[1] the face of immigration changed dramatically and reopened U.S. borders to immigrants from Latin America and Asia, who for decades had been subject to federal exclusion laws barring their entry (Baldoz 2011; Takaki 1998). Since the passage of the law, more than 80 percent of immigrants have come from countries like Mexico, the Philippines, China, and El Salvador. Unlike their European predecessors, Latino and Asian immigrants lacked the white racial privilege that would allow their children to fully blend in with the larger American middle class. Beyond this, however, they were also entering a postindustrial labor market where employment opportunities were bifurcated—available jobs were either professional or low-wage with few in the middle (Portes and Rumbaut 2001). The increased racial and socioeconomic situation of contemporary immigrant waves prompted scholars of immigration to retheorize assimilation. Rather than viewing assimilation as unidirectional— as a "one size fits all" process—scholars began to recognize how the assimilation patterns of immigrants today were better characterized as "segmented" (Portes and Zhou 1993).

The rapid influx of Latino and Asian migration to the United States has been accompanied by an emerging interest in the fate of immigrants' U.S.-born children: the "second generation." Contemporary immigration scholars have theorized extensively about how the dialectical relationship between structure and agency influences the experiences and opportunities afforded the second generation. With respect to structure, Alejandro Portes and Ruben Rumbaut (2001) highlight the importance of the "context of reception" that children of immigrants face—what educational, socioeconomic, social, and cultural opportunities are available to them. In terms of agency, scholars have pointed to the constellation of factors—class status, language proficiency, co-ethnic support networks—that affect their ability to secure different kinds of futures for themselves (Feliciano 2001; Waters 1999; Zhou and Bankston 1998).

Notably absent within assimilation frameworks, however, are the unique social conditions faced by children of immigrants who are gay. Only recently have LGBT Americans gained the right to legally marry, serve openly in the military, and receive protections from employment discrimination and hate crimes (Hunter 2013; Huffman and Huffman 2012). There are incidents of school bullying throughout the country at every level of education and reports of teachers failing to protect LGBT students from such harassment (Pascoe 2007). All of these factors suggest that there are countless ways in which the adaptation experiences of gay children of immigrants differ significantly from that of their heterosexual peers.

BOURDIEU'S RELEVANCE FOR THE STUDY OF IMMIGRATION AND SEXUALITY

Contemporary theories of immigration emphasize the role of family and community in the assimilation patterns of the second generation (Portes and Rumbaut 2001; Zhou and Bankston 1998; Zhou 2009). The family and community both provide sources of economic, social, and emotional support that buffer the negative effects of racism and socioeconomic disadvantage. For gay children of immigrants, their sexual identities often compromise their ability to access familial and community resources because of the stigma associated with being gay within both contexts (Cantú et al. 2009; Espin 1999; Decena 2008; Hom 2007; Ng 2004; Manalansan 2003). As Jimmy and Kevin's stories both demonstrate, second-generation gay men are

cognizant of and feel responsible for having to navigate these contexts.

Pierre Bourdieu's theory of cultural capital provides a useful framework to better understand the process by which second-generation gay men navigate both their families and their communities. At the heart of cultural capital theory is the idea that groups in power utilize cultural tastes, mannerisms, behaviors, and knowledge as gatekeeping mechanisms precluding subordinate classes from accessing their social circles and institutions. Traditionally, scholars employing Bourdieu's framework have concerned themselves mainly with the relationship between culture and the reproduction of the dominant class (e.g., Beisel 1990; Bourdieu 1984; Bryson 1996; DiMaggio 1982; DiMaggio and Mohr 1985). In doing so, studies have overlooked the role of culture in acquiring noneconomic forms of capital (e.g., street credibility, racial authenticity, symbolic status), which can heavily influence the everyday lives of groups that are socially or culturally marginalized within the larger society (e.g., Carter 2005; Bridges 2009; Reich 2010; Rios 2011).

As a result of their intersectional identities, second-generation gay men occupy multiple social environments—the immigrant family, the ethnic community, and the gay community. Within each of these contexts, there is a system of power relations that determines the allocation of resources—both economic and noneconomic—that these men must navigate. Bourdieu (1996) refers to theses spaces as "fields." What is common between these fields is the symbolic value of masculinity. Masculinity functions as a symbolic form of currency that second-generation gay men use to "purchase" love, support, and acceptance from the different social actors in each of these fields (Ocampo 2012; Rodríguez 2006). At the same time, however, there are qualitative differences in how masculinity is defined in each space. As Raewyn Connell (2005) has demonstrated, there is not one form of masculinity, but rather multiple *masculinities*.

As such, the processes by which these men socially construct and navigate masculinities will vary both by context and by their stage in the coming-out process. In the following sections, I draw from the narratives of Latino and Filipino gay men to show

how they develop their own consciousness of what masculinity means in their family, ethnic community, and the gay community and show how these conceptions in turn shape their interactions in those different worlds.

NEGOTIATING MASCULINITY AND SEXUALITY WITHIN THE FAMILY AND ETHNIC COMMUNITY

Research on children of immigrants highlights the context of reception as a space in which groups have differential access to resources facilitating (or hindering) their assimilation into American life (Portes and Rumbaut 2001). Typically, studies focus on socioeconomic outcomes. I argue that the family and ethnic community are important contexts of *moral* reception because heterosexual and homosexual children of immigrants have differential access to emotional and social support from their parents and co-ethnics (Ocampo 2014). In these contexts, Latino and Filipino gay men grow up learning that gender normativity (i.e., masculinity—and a particular "type" of masculinity) is rewarded, whereas gender transgressions are severely sanctioned. Enrique, a 30-year-old Mexican American banking employee, recalled how his now late father instilled this lesson in him as a child:

> One of my earliest memories of my dad was of him watching *Telemundo* (the Spanish channel) and seeing a very feminine gay guy on one of the shows. I remember him looking disgusted and saying that all the faggots should be lined up and be shot. When I heard that, I was like, "Holy shit. My dad would literally kill me if he ever found out about [my sexuality]."

Although previous studies suggest that Latin American and Filipino societies are not distinctly antigay relative to Western societies (Carrillo 2004), Enrique's remark demonstrated how Latino and Filipino gay men felt that their ethnic culture was "more conservative," with "more *machismo*" than American culture. In this respect, these men understood masculinity as an important performance that helped them establish status and respect among their family and other relatives.

Although not all of the men described their families as overtly homophobic as Enrique's father, most recalled hearing antigay comments on a regular basis and particularly noticed that such remarks were never sanctioned by their loved ones. Whenever their immigrant relatives watched television shows from their home country, they openly mocked gay characters or openly voiced disgust. Paolo, a 19-year-old Mexican American student, said his grandmother told him that gay characters on the *Telemundo* or *Univisión* soap operas "had demons inside of them." He also noted that whenever he would talk or laugh like one of these gay characters, his grandmother would yell at him: "Don't sound like that, you're gonna sound like a gay!" Filipinos noted similar experiences. Several Filipino men pointed out their tremendous fear of seeing gay people on *The Filipino Channel*. Nick, a 26-year-old military employee, said, "My dad would always comment on all the gay guys on the game shows, calling them *bakla*. And I was always afraid of that [word] being used on me." Although Nick never saw any shame in acting effeminate, he felt that if he were to act in a way that might get him labeled "*bakla*" in front of his parents, it would compromise his ability to receive validation or love from them. Here, masculinity constituted a symbolic form of capital that translated into not only status and recognition, but also love and emotional support from family members.

Latino and Filipino men also expressed their frustration at how religion was often used by their families and community members to justify antigay views. Several respondents noted how their local Catholic parishes voiced disapproval of same-sex marriage, particularly during the 2008 election season. During church sermons, many men noted how priests overtly stated, "marriage should only be between man and woman, not man and man." Dario, a 31-year-old Mexican American social worker, told me that after coming out, both of his parents were extremely upset and used religion to dissuade him from "accepting" his sexuality. "My parents said that [being gay] wasn't the way God intended me to be. I found this ironic considering neither of my parents were even religious!" Coming to terms with being gay was particularly hard for those whose parents raised them to attend church on a weekly basis. For both Latinos and Filipinos, ethnicity and religion were closely intertwined. Many of the ethnic cultural practices were deeply infused with Catholic traditions, and the Catholic Church and other religious activities were important spaces within which their ethnic communities could maintain intimate social relations (Rodriguez 2012).

Jason, a 19-year-old Filipino college student, said that this close association made it very hard to develop a sense of camaraderie with other Filipino Americans growing up:

> It was really hard coming from a predominantly Catholic family. I was really struggling with my religion, and that put a big strain on my relationship with my dad. When I went to church, it just seemed that they would always tell us all the reasons we would go to hell. I really hated it. I hated going. I hated being Catholic. But at the time, my dad and mom really relied on religion as a crutch for them. "Let's just pray and everything will be fine," they'd say. In my mind, I thought, God hates me. I'm going to hell because I'm gay. And it's because of this, I never really had any relationships with the Filipinos in my church community.

Jason felt that the Catholic Church was not particularly welcoming of gays. Yet, because of the link between Filipino culture and religion, he extended this sense of isolation to his ethnic community as well.

Because of the negative connotations associated with being gay within their family and ethnic communities, like Jason, many of my respondents chose to distance themselves personally and emotionally from their parents and relatives. For those who made attempts to sustain close familial and community ties, they painstakingly managed their masculine presentation of self. One primary concern many addressed was to be highly selective about the friends and partners they brought home to meet the family. Josh, a 27-year-old business owner, said he would only introduce friends who "weren't too gay or too feminine and still appear like boys" to his parents, despite his acknowledgment that he had friends of diverse gender presentations. He feared that his more overtly effeminate friends would cause his parents to question his sexuality and that he would ultimately be "outed" were he to introduce them. Even those

who came out within their families were selective about the people who entered their family networks so that they could be perceived as the "right" kind of gay. Although this helps them to maintain rapport with their families, it also symbolically remarginalizes segments of the gay community who present themselves as gender conforming.

Some men applied an even higher threshold of masculinity when it came to the men that they dated. Tommy and Matt, two Mexican Americans from Inglewood and South Los Angeles, said that they were attracted to the "homeboy aesthetic" (Rodriguez 2006), or Latinos who embodied urban masculine styles prevalent within their families and predominantly minority neighborhood contexts. Francisco, a 30-year-old Mexican American from the San Fernando Valley, explained that having a "masculine" partner was important part of keeping one's own masculinity intact in the eyes of family and the community. He noted that although it was generally "accepted" for him to be openly gay, to transgress gender boundaries and perform gender in a way that resembled women would "rock the boat too much" among his family members and his community, who might in turn shame his parents for raising him poorly. Ultimately, having a masculine partner allowed both Latino and Filipino gay men the opportunity to bring their partners into their most intimate social circles without having sexuality become too much of an issue. It allowed for their relationships to be more tacitly accepted among parents, relatives, and the larger community (Decena 2008).

RACIALIZED MASCULINITIES WITHIN THE GAY SCENE

When the men first started exploring their sexuality, their conceptions of gay identity were nearly as stereotypical as those of their parents. Given how family and community members quickly sanctioned deviance from "masculine" behavior, most expressed fear about openly learning more about gay culture and lifestyles. As such, they were often left with the default media images of gay community that Alan Bérubé defines as "upscale, mostly male, and mostly white" (2010: 179). Even when these men first dabbled into exploring their sexual desires and identities in high school or college through a gay club or organization, they generally found that white men and lesbians dominated these spaces. The majority of my respondents grew up in predominantly minority neighborhoods, and many expressed discomfort with social spaces that were mostly white. Armando, a 28-year-old city planner from the heavily Mexican neighborhood in Los Angeles' San Gabriel Valley, recalls his reaction to the white people he met in his first days of college:

> What was crazy was that I was never around white people before. Now they weren't just everywhere on TV. They were everywhere in real life! TV was really my only real exposure to white people before. As for the LGBT organizations, I wasn't part of those because those were all the white kids. . . . I felt more Latino than gay.

Armando's remarks exemplified the close association that most respondents made between gay identity and whiteness. Although he shared the same sexual orientation as the members of the LGBT organizations, his experiences as working-class and Latino prevented him from feeling comfortable around the "white gay guys who wore designer jeans and got all prettied up to go to the 'bougie' white clubs."

Armando's comment also demonstrated how respondents conflated the gender identities and performances of white gay men with being effeminate, which further deterred them from developing relationships with whites in their early days of coming out. EJ, a 27-year-old Filipino American banker from San Diego, talked about his impressions of the gay white men he met while working at a retail store.

> I never entertained the idea of dating a boy. I was working retail, and there were lots of gay people, but they were mostly white. I wouldn't relate to the gays there. They were so queeny and bitchy. One of them, Allen, he would be the most flamboyant and he would come to work in colorful outfits. I mean, I was always cool with people. I respected who they are, but if they tried to flirt, I'd freak out.

EJ's characterization of Allen fit most respondents' early ideas of what "gay" meant. As his story illustrates, meeting gays who fit the racial and gendered stereotypes associated with gay culture prompted

resistance from Latino and Filipino men. Because of the racial and gendered connotations of the word "gay," many recalled utilizing euphemisms to describe their sexual identities. Arturo, a 24-year-old Mexican American from East Los Angeles, noted, "I don't really say I'm gay." Instead, he preferred to say, "I sleep with guys," or "I date *men*." In certain respects, although Arturo's *behavior* is admittedly same-sex oriented, his discourse and tone are reminiscent of the "locker room" speak of heterosexual men (Pascoe 2007; Ward 2008). For him, being white and being gay were both associated with a devalued sense of manhood in the neighborhood where he was raised. This alternative method of signaling his sexuality also resembled the "compulsive heterosexuality" that Pascoe (2007) documented among high school youth where straight men brag about their sexual prowess to play up their masculinity.

EJ's entry into the gay scene demonstrated the key role that ethnicity played in finding a community of gay friends. Latinos' and Filipinos' first encounters with the gay community occurred at ethnic-specific social events, such as neighborhood house parties and ethnic-themed club nights. EJ's entrée into the gay lifestyle came only when he discovered that Randall, a "thugged out" Filipino student from his high school, was gay. He was different from the gay co-workers at EJ's store who "dressed gay." For instance, in contrast to the tight jeans that Allen wore, EJ felt that Randall was more similar to him in terms of his choice of attire, his interests, and performance of self. Randall wore baggier jeans, jerseys, and sported sneakers typical of any hip hop artist at the time. Randall acted "hard and masculine . . . just like the other minorities" in his high school, which was located near the working-class neighborhood where EJ grew up.

Through hanging out with Randall, EJ warmed up to the idea of attending a gay party—something he could never have imagined himself doing at the time—and this further opened his eyes to the diversity within the gay community. EJ learned from Randall of an annual bonfire thrown by gay Filipino men and women during pride week in San Diego:

EJ: Since San Diego pride didn't have that many minorities, a bunch of the Filipinos decided to have their own thing and it just became this big event.

AO: What was it like?

EJ: I was amazed. It was perfect. That's where I found my friends. They were different. They weren't as flamey. It was very urban and it was something that I could relate to and be comfortable around. So I was like, "Oh shit, *these* are the people that I want to be surrounded by." And these were the guys that took me to my first gay club.

AO: Which club was that?

EJ: Bar 81 in West Hollywood. We would drive up all the way from San Diego to LA like every Friday to go to their Asian night. And we'd drive back home the same night!

EJ's comments illustrate the sentiments that many gay men of color felt about the gay community—that it was predominantly white and effeminate. This further prompted their ambivalence about gay identity. Upon encountering spaces where gay embodied an urban masculinity reminiscent of the other young men of color in their neighborhood, however, EJ started to see the possibility that he could embrace *both* his ethnicity *and* his sexuality simultaneously. Moreover, his willingness to travel more than 100 miles weekly to attend an Asian American party in West Hollywood demonstrated the importance of ethnic-specific spaces in these gay men's lives. These spaces enabled them to mitigate some of the challenges associated with their competing identity projects—allowing them to frame their gender, sexuality, and ethnicity as congruent, rather than contradictory. As EJ recounted about his first time at Bar 81, "That's when I thought, 'Oh my God. The gay scene is bigger than I ever imagined.'"

Interestingly, beyond ethnic-themed events, many of the Latino and Filipino men expressed ambivalence about West Hollywood and other predominantly white gay spaces, especially when they were first coming out. EJ said that for years, he never ventured into the gay clubs and bars in West Hollywood adjacent to Bar 81 *because* they were mostly white. Armando noted his own discomfort about the racial demographics of West Hollywood and the classed connotations of that space:

> I get this sense that it's stuck up, bourgeois, and it's all about designer fashion and how flat your stomach is. . . . I prefer my gay *cholo* bars like Club Caliente.

They have Latino hipsters too, and even Latinos who only speak Spanish. They're not so uppity there and people are nice. There's another club called Metro that's a hole in the wall, and it's where all the immigrant gay Latinos are, and I like it. I think the Latinos who go to West Hollywood are the upper class gay Latinos who prefer those rich white guys.

Similar to Armando, gay men of color felt that the type of masculinity that other young men from their neighborhoods and immigrant communities had no place in majority white gay social environments, such as West Hollywood.

Rafa, a 29-year-old Salvadoran American, not only felt excluded for looking "too urban," but also felt that his appearance would elicit harassment from club owners and police. He noted that a Wednesday night event catering to Latino and African American patrons had suddenly been canceled without notice. The club owners simply told him that they wanted to "change the vibe." However, Rafa felt this move was a covert act of racism, especially because this weekly party was among the most well-attended events on Wednesday nights: "You see, [canceling the events] had nothing to do with business. West Hollywood is just trying to get rid of all the minorities. That's why they stopped playing hip hop. It's so we'll stop coming. They [the venue owners and police] think that we'll just cause trouble." Echoing Rafa's remarks, I often overheard patrons in West Hollywood describe ethnic-specific gay venues in disparaging or even voyeuristic ways. Often times, white gay men (as well as gay men of color who assimilated into the West Hollywood scene) dismissed places like Bar 81, Club Caliente, and Metro as "ghetto" and said they would "never be caught dead going there" or only go there on nights they were "slumming it." Beyond the different music choices or racial makeup of the patrons, these clubs were not different from predominantly white clubs in West Hollywood. They charged similar entrance fees and drink prices were comparable. In this respect, such comments revealed how the different configurations of masculinity popular within communities of color were negatively sanctioned, which in turn made many Latino and Filipino gay men feel unwelcome in gay social environments that were mostly white.

Whereas *sexuality* deterred Latino and Filipino gay men's ability to secure emotional support within their families and communities, *race* and *class* became barriers to finding such support within predominantly gay social spaces. Within the immigrant context, these men "lost points" for their sexuality, but salvaged status, emotional ties, dignity, and respect by maintaining a masculine presentation of self—both in their appearance and in their choice of social networks (Ocampo 2012). In turn, respondents could not necessarily find refuge in the most visible of gay spaces or media representations (which were mostly white) because many did not relate to either because of their nonwhite status or working-class background. As such, ethnic-specific spaces became extremely important for Latino and Filipino gay men because these contexts provided them unique opportunities to not be penalized for embracing the cultural aspects of either their ethnic or their sexual identities.

MERGING MASCULINITIES: THE BRIDGING OF ETHNIC AND SEXUAL IDENTITIES

Do the multiple—and often competing—identities of ethnicity and sexuality permanently relegate second-generation gay men to the margins of their families, ethnic communities, and (white) gay culture? Although these narratives might seem to suggest this, the overall pattern I observed is that these men, over time, make tremendous efforts to merge their social worlds. Within the family and community context, Latino and Filipino gay men may at first be strategic in only revealing images of gay life that coincide with their parents' and co-ethnics' conceptions of masculinity. However, these actions serve as catalyst opportunities to dialogue more openly about LGBT people and communities, rather than sweep the issue under the rug, which is more customary among immigrant circles (Decena 2008; Ocampo 2012, 2014). After expanding their gay social networks within ethnic-specific gay spaces, many of the men met "cultural brokers," other men of color with similar backgrounds who helped them feel more comfortable in predominantly white gay environments.

Other men have used artistic outlets to tackle the sense of cultural dissonance they once felt for being

FIGURE 1   (Credit: SEDiego)

both a man of color *and* gay. Local playwright Miguel Garcia created and produced a series of community-based plays in East Los Angeles—"Brown & Out"—exploring the diverse experiences of LGBT Latinos who attempt to navigate their ethnic culture and gender and sexual identities. Similarly, filmmaker Jonathan Menendez Benavides's documentary film "Gay LAtino" profiled Latino gay men of different neighborhoods, legal statuses, and national origins to demonstrate how masculinity shapes their lives in distinct ways. Filipino visual artist Elmer Manlongat, more popularly known by the name SEDiego, merges homoeroticism with images of urban masculinity that he grew up with in his working class Latino and Filipino neighborhood in San Diego (see Figures 1 and 2).

These three artists' early lives very much resemble the experiences of Jimmy, Kevin, Armando, and other men interviewed for this study. After growing

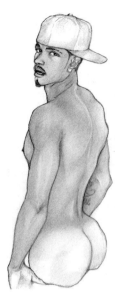

up their entire lives feeling that their race and sexuality were incompatible, these men have utilized art to demonstrate how Latino and Filipino gay men indeed forge new identities by creatively adapting elements of cultural capital associated with different contexts and groups that has the ability to raise the social consciousness of their families, ethnic communities, and the white gay community.

REFERENCES

Alba, Richard. 1990. *Twilight Ethnicity*. New Haven, CT: Yale University Press.

Baldoz, Richard. 2011. *The Third Asiatic Wave*. New York: New York University Press.

Beisel, Nicole. 1990. "Class, Culture, and Campaigns against Vice in Three American Cities, 1872–1892." *American Sociological Review* 55: 44–62.

Bérubé, Allan. 2010. "How Gay Stays White and What Kind of White It Stays." In *Privilege*, edited by M. Kimmel and A. Ferber, 179–212. Boulder, CO: Westview Press.

Bourdieu, Pierre. 1984. *Distinction: A Social Critique of the Judgment of Taste*. Cambridge, MA: Harvard University Press.

Bourdieu, Pierre. 1996. *State Nobility: Elite Schools in the Field of Power*. Stanford, CA: Stanford University Press.

Bridges, Tristan. 2009. "Gender Capital and Male Bodybuilders." *Body & Society* 15 (1): 83–107.

Bryson, Bethany. 1996. "Anything but Heavy Metal: Symbolic Exclusion and Musical Dislikes." *American Sociological Review* 61 (5): 884–99.

Cantu, Lionel. Nancy Napes, and Salvador Vidal-Ortiz. 2009. *The Sexuality of Migration: Border Crossings and Mexican Immigrant Men*. New York: NYU Press.

Carrillo, Hector. 2004. "Sexual Migration, Cross-Cultural Sexual Encounters, and Sexual Health." *Sexuality Research and Social Policy: Journal of NSRC* 1 (3): 58–70.

Carter, Prudence. 2005. *Keepin' It Real: School Success beyond Black and White*. New York: Oxford University Press.

Connell, Raewyn. 2005. *Masculinities*. Berkeley: University of California Press.

Decena, Carlos. 2008. "Tacit Subjects," *GLQ: A Journal of Lesbian and Gay Studies*, 14 (2–3): 339–59.

DiMaggio, Paul. 1982. "Cultural Entrepreneurship in Nineteenth-Century Boston: The Creation of an Organizational Base for High Culture in America." *Media, Culture, and Society* 4: 33–50.

DiMaggio, Paul, and John Mohr. 1985. "Cultural Capital, Educational Attainment, and Marital Selection." *American Journal of Sociology* 90 (6): 1231–59.

Espin, Oliva. 1999. *Women Crossing Boundaries*. New York: Routledge Press.

Feliciano, Cynthia. 2001. "The Benefits of Biculturalism: Exposure to Immigrant Culture and Dropping out of School among Asian and Latino Youths." *Social Science Quarterly* 82 (4): 865–79.

Gordon, Milton. 1964. *Assimilation in American Life*. New York: Oxford University Press.

Hom, Alice. 2007. "Stories from the Homefront: Perspectives of Asian American Parents with Lesbian Daughters and Gay Sons." In *Contemporary Asian America*, edited by M. Zhou and J. Gatewood. New York: New York University Press.

Huffman, J. Ford, and Huffman, Tammy, eds. 2012. *The End of Don't Ask Don't Tell*. Washington, DC: Marine Corps University Press.

Hunter, Marcus. 2013. "Race and the Same Sex Marriage Divide." *Contexts* 12 (3): 74–76.

Manalansan, Martin. 2003. *Global Divas: Filipino Gay Men in the Diaspora.* New York: New York University Press.

Manalansan, Martin. 2006. "Queering Intersections," *International Migration Review* 40 (1): 224–49.

Ng, Mark. 2004. "Searching for Home: Voices of Gay Asian American Youth in West Hollywood." In *Asian American Youth: Culture, Identity, and Ethnicity,* edited by J. Lee and M. Zhou. New York: Routledge Press.

Ocampo, Anthony C. 2012. "Making Masculinity: Negotiations of Gender Presentation among Latino Gay Men." *Latino Studies* 10 (4): 448–72.

Ocampo, Anthony C. 2014. "The Gay Second Generation: Sexual Identity and the Family Relations of Latino and Filipino Gay Men." *Journal of Ethnic and Migration Studies* 40 (1): 155–73.

Park, Robert E. 1950. *Race and Culture.* Glencoe, IL: Free Press.

Pascoe, C. J. 2007. *Dude, You're a Fag.* Berkeley: University of California Press.

Portes, Alejandro, and Rumbaut, Ruben. 2001. *Legacies.* Berkeley and New York: University of California Press and Russell Sage.

Portes, Alejandro, and Zhou, Min. (1993) "The New Second Generation." *Annals of the American Academy of Political and Social Science* 530: 74–95.

Reich, Adam. 2010. *Hidden Truth: Young Men Navigating Lives in and out of Juvenile Prison.* Berkeley: University of California Press.

Rios, Victor. 2011. *Punished: Policing the Lives of Black and Latino Boys.* New York: New York University Press.

Rodriguez, Evelyn. 2012. *Celebrating Debuts and Quinceañeras.* Philadelphia: Temple University Press.

Rodríguez, Richard. T. 2006. "Queering the Homeboy Aesthetic." *Aztlán* 31 (2): 127–37.

Takaki, Ronald. 1998. *Strangers from a Different Shore.* Boston: Little, Brown.

Ward, Jane. 2008. "Dude-Sex: White Masculinities and 'Authentic' Heterosexuality among Dudes Who Have Sex with Dudes." *Sexualities* 11 (4): 414–34.

Waters, Mary. 1990. *Ethnic Options.* Berkeley: University of California Press.

Waters, Mary. 1999. *Black Identities: West Indian Dreams and American Realities.* Cambridge, MA: Harvard University Press.

Zhou, Min. 2009. *Contemporary Chinese America.* Philadelphia: Temple University Press.

Zhou, Min, and Bankston, Carl. 1998. *Growing up American.* New York: Russell Sage Foundation.

NOTE

1. Nearly four decades before the Hart–Cellar Act, the U.S. government passed the 1924 Immigration Act, which created quotas that essentially halted immigration from most of Asia and Southern and Central Europe. The only exception to the restrictive immigration laws were Filipinos, who as U.S. nationals were eligible to migrate. However, one decade after the 1924 Immigration Act, Congress passed the Tydings–McDuffie Act, which granted the Philippines independence, but also put a stop to the mass migration of Filipinos to the United States. It would not be until the passage of the 1965 Hart–Cellar Act that nonwhite immigrants from Asia, as well as Latin America, would be allowed to legally migrate to the United States (Baldoz 2011).

TONY COLES

23. NEGOTIATING THE FIELD OF MASCULINITY: THE PRODUCTION AND REPRODUCTION OF MULTIPLE DOMINANT MASCULINITIES

This [chapter] presents a theoretical model of masculinities based on a combination of Connell's theories on hegemonic masculinity and Bourdieu's concepts of habitus, capital, and fields. The work of Connell has been both profound and pervasive in its influence on the study of men and masculinities. However, there are limitations, particularly in relation to the disparity between the theoretical concept of hegemonic masculinity as the culturally dominant ideal and men's lived experiences of a variety of dominant masculinities. The model presented herein introduces the possibility of multiple dominant masculinities that operate within subfields bound by a field of masculinity. The model also outlines the ways in which masculinities are both produced and reproduced as a consequence of struggles between dominant and subordinate groups of men. These struggles also provide a rationale for resistance and complicity determined by what is deemed to be valued capital within the field of masculinity.

Men's masculinities are constantly in flux. As men age and move through the course of their lives, so too do their identities as men shift to accommodate the changes in their lives. Moreover, what masculinity means at the societal level changes across epochs, and individual conceptualizations of what masculinity means necessarily shift to accommodate these changes as well. Yet the fluidity of masculinity is rarely given critical consideration in the context of men's lives. While masculinity is understood to be a fluid, socially constructed concept that changes over time and space (i.e., historically and culturally), it is often only discussed at the structural level with little consideration given to the strategies men use to negotiate masculinities in their everyday lives.

Furthermore, the concept of hegemonic masculinity as the descriptor of the culturally dominant ideal only takes into consideration dominant and subordinate/marginalized masculinities at the structural level without taking into account men's lived realities of their own masculinities as dominant in relation to other men, despite being subordinate in relation to the cultural ideal. Indeed, hegemonic masculinity may have a marginal impact upon the lives of men who choose to disassociate themselves from the mainstream and operate in social milieux where their masculinity is dominant in relation to other men.

It is therefore necessary to consider looking at the more subtle interplay of masculinities that exists in men's lives. To do this, the work of Bourdieu has been incorporated with Connell's concept of hegemonic masculinity to present a theoretical model of a field of masculinity in which various subfields exist to account for the variety of dominant masculinities that may be present at any given time. Capital, habitus, and fields are brought to the fore in an effort to describe how masculinities operate in and over men's lives. Before proceeding, however, to the concept of a field of masculinity, it is first necessary to give a brief description of hegemonic masculinity and how it has been used in the study of men and masculinities and unpack the Bourdieuian concepts of fields, habitus, and capital.

HEGEMONIC MASCULINITY

Much of the theoretical work currently circulating in the study of men and masculinities revolves around the concept of hegemonic masculinity. Hegemonic

This reading is an excerpt from Tony Coles's article in *Men and Masculinities* 12, no. 1 (2009): 30–44.

masculinity, according to Carrigan, Connell, and Lee (1987), is "a question of how particular groups of men inhabit positions of power and wealth, and how they legitimate and reproduce the social relationships that generate their dominance" (92). Connell (1987, 1995) elaborates on this idea, stressing the importance of the fluidity of hegemonic masculinity and the mechanics that mobilize it at a structural level:

> At any given time, one form of masculinity rather than others is culturally exalted. Hegemonic masculinity can be defined as the configuration of gender practice which embodies the currently accepted answer to the problem of the legitimacy of patriarchy, which guarantees (or is taken to guarantee) the dominant position of men and the subordination of women. This is not to say that the most visible bearers of hegemonic masculinity are always the most powerful people. They may be exemplars, such as film actors, or even fantasy figures, such as film characters. Individual holders of institutional power or great wealth may be far from the hegemonic pattern in their personal lives. . . . Nevertheless, hegemony is likely to be established only if there is some correspondence between cultural ideal and institutional power, collective if not individual. (Connell 1995: 77)

Even though hegemonic masculinity may not be the most common form of masculinity practiced, it is supported by the majority of men as they benefit from the overall subordination of women, what Connell (1995) terms the "patriarchal dividend" (p. 82). According to Connell, the patriarchal dividend benefits men in terms of "honour, prestige and the right to command," as well as in relation to material wealth and state power. Structurally, men as an interest group are inclined to support hegemonic masculinity as a means to defend patriarchy and their dominant position over women.

The strength of hegemonic masculinity as a theoretical tool lies in its ability to describe the layers of multiple masculinities at the structural level and the intricacies of their relations to one another, and to recognize the fluidity of gender identities and power (Hearn 2007). Indeed, it is the flux of gender relations and the challenges that hegemonic masculinity endures that validate it. [. . .] Thus, the concept of hegemonic masculinity and its position in relation to femininities

and other masculinities has been useful in outlining the various nuances of power (resistance and subordination) set within a hierarchical framework. [. . .]

In recognizing multiple masculinities, however, one must be wary to avoid oversimplification (Clatterbaugh 1990; Connell 1995; Hearn 1996; Beynon 2002; Pease 2002). Just as the term masculinity cannot be applied to all men equally, so too are there problems associated with reducing groups of men into stereotypes based on their behavior (e.g., gay men as overly sensitive, black men as sexually aggressive, working-class men as physically violent). To avoid reducing various masculinities into simplified categories or stereotypes, Connell suggests,

> We have to examine the relations between them. Further, we have to unpack the milieux of class and race and scrutinize the gender relations operating within them. There are, after all, gay black men and effeminate factory hands, not to mention middle-class rapists and cross-dressing bourgeois. A focus on the gender relations among men is necessary to keep the analysis dynamic, to prevent the acknowledgement of multiple masculinities collapsing into a character typology. (Connell 1995, 76)

The relationships through which these masculinities operate involve levels of dominance and subordination. Furthermore, as Connell (1995) notes, men's masculinities may be marginalized by factors such as age or ethnicity. Although these hierarchical relations appear rigidly structured, they are continuously open to challenge and change (by both men and women) such that the dominance of hegemonic masculinity is susceptible to the challenges of subordinated and marginalized masculinities (e.g., gay men excelling in sports epitomizing hegemonic masculinity, such as football and rugby) and femininities (Gardiner 2002).

However, while the concept of hegemonic masculinity has proved to be pervasively popular in the study of men and masculinities, there are limitations.[1] Firstly, hegemonic masculinity does little to account for the variety of dominant masculinities that exist under this umbrella term and how they are interconnected (Hearn 2007).[2] If hegemonic masculinity is one form of masculinity that is culturally exalted over others (Connell 1995: 77), then this disregards the complexities of various dominant masculinities that exist. For example, within the offices of a multinational corporation, dominant masculinity may be epitomized by the slender, fit, young, aggressive businessman dressed in his designer-label suit. However, within a working-class pub, dominant masculinity may be epitomized by the unkempt, middle-aged man with a large beer belly who can consume vast quantities of alcohol. Hegemonic masculinity may be that which is culturally exalted at any given time, but dominant masculinities need to be drawn from this and contextualized within a given field (or subfield), as well as located culturally and historically. It is possible to be subordinated by hegemonic masculinity yet still draw on dominant masculinities and assume a dominant position in relation to other men.

Secondly, while power is certainly important in terms of understanding relations between groups of men as well as between men and women (i.e., patriarchy), hegemony is limiting as it assumes that groups act (at a structural level) to either achieve or maintain a dominant position over others that is to their own advantage, perpetuated through social institutions. Although Connell and Messerschmidt (2005) argue that "the concept of hegemonic masculinity embeds a historically dynamic view of gender in which it is impossible to erase the subject" (2005, 843) and that there are numerous examples of empirical studies investigating how hegemonic masculinity is lived by men, hegemonic masculinity as a theoretical concept still tends to be used to describe male power at a structural level with no real understanding of how power is organized in terms of complicity and resistance at the individual level (Whitehead 2002). There is also an over-tendency to focus on hegemonic masculinity in relation to patriarchy and male power over women. While male power in the form of patriarchy needs to be critically examined in the study of men and masculinities, it makes little sense to use patriarchy to describe the power differentials in and between various subpopulations of men where much of the tensions and struggles over masculinities occur.

Furthermore, there is a distinct need to take masculinity away from the structural and consider masculinities as collective human projects that are individually

lived out (Watson 2000; White 2002). Masculinity does not mean the same thing to all men. It is varied in how it is understood, experienced, and lived out in daily practice. For example, whereas some health professionals may perceive drinking as an unhealthy masculine pastime, for those men who live in relative social isolation, having a drink at the pub provides an opportunity to congregate, bond, and build relationships with other men that they would otherwise have little chance of achieving (Pease 2001).

To overcome these theoretical limitations, the work of Pierre Bourdieu and his notions of habitus, capital, and fields will be used to complement the concept of hegemonic masculinity and provide a legitimate way of understanding how men do gender effectively. Unlike many poststructuralist theories that attempt to move beyond the concept of hegemonic masculinity (e.g., Whitehead 2002), Bourdieu's concepts of habitus, capital, and fields work with hegemonic masculinity to produce a theoretical model that ably describes how men negotiate masculinities over the life course within a range of broad social fields, as well as describing the relations of power that center on capital and the tensions that exist between dominant and subordinate groups of men.

BOURDIEU: HABITUS, CAPITAL, AND FIELDS

[. . .] Bourdieu's popularity stems from his ability to cross the structure/agency divide by theoretically integrating both subjective experience and objective structures. [. . .] Bourdieu rejects the more orthodox visions of each in preference of a theoretical synthesis that considers how individual practice is shaped and the various strategies that are employed by agents in everyday life. In doing so, Bourdieu introduces the notion of constructivist structuralism that considers how individuals support and challenge dominant social structures through their individual practices. The inference of Bourdieu's theory of practice is that individuals are neither completely free to choose their destinies nor forced to behave according to objective norms or rules imposed upon them (Swartz 1997; Lane 2000).

Habitus is central to Bourdieu's theory of practice, forming the crux in the nexus between structure and agency (Strathern 1996; Swartz 1997; Margolis 1999; Fowler 2000; Smith 2001). Habitus refers to the ways in which individuals live out their daily lives through practices that are synchronized with the actions of others around them, functioning to produce a social collective that is not ordered by rules per se but influenced by objective structures (Robbins 1991; Bohman 1999). In the words of Bourdieu, habitus is described as

> systems of durable, transposable dispositions, structured structures predisposed to function as structuring structures, that is, as principles of the generation and structuring of practices and representations which can be objectively "regulated" and "regular" without in any way being the product of obedience to rules, objectively adapted to their goals without presupposing a conscious aiming at ends or an express mastery of the operations necessary to attain them and, being all this, collectively orchestrated without being the product of the orchestrating action of a conductor. (Bourdieu 1977: 72)

In essence, habitus allows individuals to navigate their way through everyday situations that require a degree of flexibility and improvisation (Smith 2001). That individuals are able to do this "owe[s] their specific efficacy to the fact that [habitus] function[s] below the level of consciousness and language, beyond the reach of introspective scrutiny or control by the will" (Bourdieu 1984, 466). Habitus is not based on conscious reasoning but rather is impulsive and nonreflexive; it is a strategy without having a strategic intention (Calhoun 1993). Successful practice requires the individual to adjust his or her dispositions according to the situation in play and "to act creatively beyond the specific injunctions of its rule" (Fowler 1997, 18). [. . .]

Yet objective structures may dictate the situation to which the individual may have to adjust, thus impinging upon habitus. However, the objective structures do not necessarily constrain people in the ways that rules and norms do. They are more like guidelines or boundaries in which the individual is able to operate with a degree of flexibility. Individuals are still in the position of choosing the disposition that best suits their requirements and may even actively choose what they appear constrained to choose in

order to distance themselves from the imposition of objective structures. [. . .] For example, men born into working-class families who are denied access to middle-class occupations by their limited social, economic, and cultural capital and who must opt for working-class jobs may not necessarily see their situation as forced upon them. They may refuse white-collar work as an effeminate, soft alternative and "will the inevitable" by taking on blue-collar work that they view as skilled and makes them "real" men by allowing them to use their bodies to perform masculinity (e.g., strength, competency, risk taking).

Importantly, the dispositions and practices that form one's habitus are "acquired in social positions within a *field* and imply a subjective adjustment to that position" (Mahar, Harker, and Wilkes 1990, 10, emphasis added). Fields are central to the operation of habitus and subsequently to practice and the configuring of complex societies (Mahar, Harker, and Wilkes 1990; Swartz 1997; Butler 1999; Fowler 2000; Smith 2001). As Butler (1999, 114) suggests, dispositions and practices do not spontaneously appear but rather emerge as a result of conjuncture between habitus and fields. [. . .]

The concept of field is a metaphor for domains of social life (Swartz 1997; Smith 2001). Although the spatial metaphor of field implies boundaries and limits, Bourdieu argues against such limitations and instead focuses on fields as relational and elastic, to be defined using the broadest possible range of factors, including those overlapping with other fields, that influence and shape behavior (Swartz 1997). Fields shape the structure of the social setting in which habitus operates and include social institutions such as law and education. However, they are not to be conflated with institutions: "fields may be inter- or intra-institutional in scope; they can span institutions, which may represent positions within fields" (Swartz 1997, 120). For example, the field of gender overlaps with many other fields (e.g., class, education, government) and also accommodates a variety of subfields (such as the field of masculinity and the field of femininity) and social institutions (such as the family and courts of law). Thus, individuals are not necessarily beholden to objective structures but instead are able to negotiate and traverse fields and subfields (though they may not always be able to step outside of the influence of the field or the social institutions therein).

Bourdieu's concept of capital is also important to consider in relation to fields and habitus as the accumulation and value of capital has the potential to influence the position of individuals within any given field. Capital is a resource that is the object of struggle within fields and which functions as a social relation of power (Bourdieu 1993: 73). Broadly, Bourdieu observes three types of capital that tend to exist perennially within most fields: economic capital, which refers to financial resources; social capital, which refers to one's social networks and the status of individuals therein; and cultural capital, which broadly considers one's cultural skills, tastes, preferences, qualifications, and so forth that operate as class distinctions. The possession of valued capital within a field determines the rank of individuals, groups, and organizations [. . .] (Swartz 1997). The value of capital is contested within fields to become the site of struggle. Those in dominant positions are able to define what constitutes legitimate or valued capital and thus reproduce their status by preserving the worth of their capital (Webb, Schirato, and Danaher 2002). However, examples of the changing value of capital and shifts in power resulting from subversive strategies of agents are possible, such as pop art's gaining legitimate value as cultural capital in the field of highbrow art.

Through habitus (in conjunction with one's capital) and fields, practices are formed and individuals are able to use strategies to navigate their way through daily life (McNay 2000). One does not operate in isolation to the other, and both are forming and formative, reproducing and generative. Thus, habitus, capital, and fields allow for the consideration of how individuals and groups function to support or subvert structures within the social order and the strategies that are used at the subconscious level to negotiate positions.

THE FIELD OF MASCULINITY

Using the work of Bourdieu to build on the concept of hegemonic masculinity, the theoretical model proposed herein considers a *field of masculinity* (see Figure 1) and the struggles and contestations for positions [. . .] between men. Within the field of masculinity, there are sites of domination and subordination, orthodoxy (maintaining the status quo) and heterodoxy (seeking change), submission and usurpation. Individuals, groups, and organizations struggle to lay claim to the legitimacy of specific capital within the field of masculinity. Those in dominant

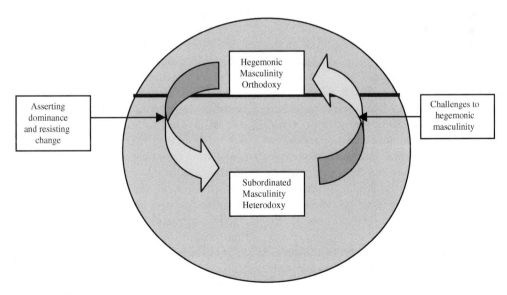

FIGURE 1 The Field of Masculinity.

positions strive to conserve the status quo by monopolizing definitions of masculinity and the value and distribution of capital, while subordinate challengers look to subversive strategies [. . .] generating flux and mechanisms for change.

[. . .] [E]conomic capital, social capital, and cultural capital are all contested by individuals, groups, and organizations within the field of masculinity. However, to these must be added another resource that is heavily contested within the field of masculinity and must be recognized as a form of capital—the male body. Although social, economic, and cultural capital all carry weight in the field of masculinity, the centrality of the male body to men's masculinities means that physical capital requires critical attention. The male body as physical capital and its primary importance in the field of masculinity as a valued resource in relation to men's masculinities requires it to be a central theme in discussing the field of masculinity.

The concept of the body as a form of physical capital is not new. Bourdieu (1984) himself suggests that the internalization of objective structures is often manifested in bodily form (such as posture, gait, speech) to become a materialization of class taste. Drawing on this idea, Shilling (1991, 1993) develops the argument that the body is capable of being developed into forms of physical capital that become the site of tensions contributing to the reproduction of social inequalities and shows how physical capital is able to be converted into other forms of capital. For Shilling, the body as a marker of physical capital is impinged [upon] by other factors: most notably class. [. . .] Shilling predominantly focuses on the ways in which social classes tend to produce distinct bodily forms that are assigned symbolic value and where physical capital is valued in parallel with class dispositions. While class is certainly important to how bodies are valued as physical capital in the field of masculinity, there are many other factors that influence the value of physical capital including age, ethnicity, health, and sexuality.

In relation to the field of masculinity, the ways in which the male body is represented to personify dominant images of masculinity make it the object of struggles and valued as capital. It is a resource that men use to project an image of masculinity. [. . .] [T]he size and shape of the body are as important as how it is used (e.g., gait, speech, dexterity, deportment, demeanor, sexual practices). Muscles have come to be equated with hegemonic masculine ideals of strength and power; low body fat is equated with being active and disciplined; youth is associated with health and virility. Thus, men with bodies that epitomize hegemonic masculinity and match the cultural ideal (i.e., lean, muscular, youthful) have the physical capital most valued in the field of masculinity.

Also important to the formation of men's masculinities in the field of masculinity are external sources of influence such as class, age, and ethnicity. These external forces intersect with the field of masculinity to form complex matrices that allow for a variety of masculinities to exist. [. . .] However, these external sources do not impinge directly on men's masculinities; rather, they are "mediated through the structure and dynamics of fields" (Swartz 1997: 128). For example, class may bear heavily in terms of defining what masculinity means to individuals; however, class must be considered in relation to the effects of internal struggles within the field of masculinity and the relations of power premised on the value of various forms of capital. The significance of external forces is dependent on power struggles and hierarchies within the field of masculinity.

The concept of habitus also works to describe how men negotiate masculinity. Being both durable and transposable, men use masculinity as a resourceful strategy to function in their everyday lives. Without [. . .] being consciously aware of it, men's actions reflect this strategy (e.g., posture, gait, gestures, speech, etc.) of performing masculinity. At the individual level, it is used to negotiate everyday situations. In conjunction with the field of masculinity, the performance becomes a practice in conservation or subversion. In so doing, the practices are regular without being forced. These practices are based on opportunities or constraints that are presented through the continuum of time and space (Swartz 1997).

As mentioned above, one of the strengths of habitus is its ability to function without introspective scrutiny, below the level of conscious reasoning and deliberate will to action. This "feel for the game" gives the impression that one's actions and dispositions are in effect instinctual (McNay 2000). [. . .] The struggle for legitimacy that exists in the field of masculinity between dominant and subordinated masculinities is validated by habitus and the belief that one's own masculinity is "natural" and "true." Thus, even those men in subordinated positions in the field of masculinity may not see their masculinity as subordinated or marginalized, particularly if they operate in social fields and domains in which the actions and dispositions of other men are similar to their own. Masculinity as an unconscious strategy forms part of the habitus of men that is both transposable and malleable to given situations to form practical dispositions and actions to everyday situations.

Finally, the notion of fields and subfields that exist within, and overlap with, the field of masculinity also need to be considered to understand how men subordinated or marginalized by hegemonic masculinity are able to deny or refute their position as subordinated or marginalized (see Figure 2). Subfields have their own sets of struggles over capital, which in turn create distinctions between dominant and subordinated groups of men. Therefore, subfields allow for dominant masculinities to exist within subordinated positions within the field of masculinity.

For example, the field of gay masculinity has its own contested boundaries of dominant gay masculinities and subordinate gay masculinities. Although located in the field of masculinity in a subordinated position by hegemonic definitions of masculinity, gay men may feel that their masculinity is not one that is subordinated if they fit dominant gay masculinities within the field of *gay* masculinity. Dominant gay masculinities may draw upon and share values associated with hegemonic masculinity (e.g., sexually

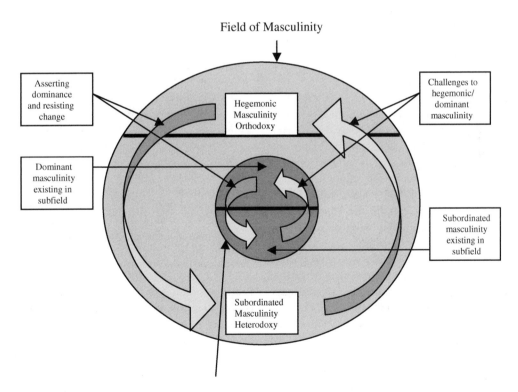

FIGURE 2   Subfields in the Field of Masculinity.

aggressive, independent) that may lend to further legitimizing the value of their gay masculinity. In doing so, gay men may feel that the masculinity they perform is dominant in relation to other masculinities. In effect, this may mean that men's lived experiences of masculinity may be far from perceived as having a relegated status in comparison to other men's masculinities.

Furthermore, fields operate across a continuum in which [. . .] struggles in one field have implications in others. For example, the field of gender contains the struggles of men as the dominant group over women as the subordinated group, resulting in a patriarchal power differential.

> In the field of gender, men have persistently and tirelessly worked to establish a case for the superiority of men's essential nature in all of those domains which are said to determine the "real" worth of a person—from superiority in the moral sense through to superiority in regard to the possession of those highly regarded capacities of logic and rational argument. This case has been central to the maintenance and extension of the inequitable arrangements between the genders—to the justification of the oppression of women, and for the support of male power, privilege and violence. (White 1996: 167)

Men use their dominant position in the field of gender to maintain male hegemony (orthodoxy) that privileges men, while feminists look to subversion and change (heterodoxy). Influenced by a variety of other fields (most notably the field of economic production), feminism has been able to make ground in its struggle against male hegemony and legitimize the rights of women and push for a move towards equality in certain social spheres, both public and private.

In turn, men have tried to defend their position of dominance by falling on essentialist arguments that necessarily separate men from women. This struggle in the field of gender has influenced struggles in the field of masculinity. The essentialist argument creates instability in the field of masculinity as subordinated men use the argument of essentialism (i.e., that men are genetically predisposed to masculine behavior such as aggression, promiscuity, and risk taking) generated in the field of gender to subvert hegemonic masculinity. For example, using the essentialist

argument, sexual orientation becomes redundant in relation to masculinity as men are masculine by virtue of their biology, not their sexuality. Thus, social change is capable of being produced as change in one field has the potential to lay down foundations for subversion and change in other fields.

CONCLUSION

Bourdieu's concepts of fields, habitus, and capital, and the identification of the struggles that exist between positions of orthodoxy and heterodoxy that generate fields can be considered to be complementary to the theoretical concept of hegemonic masculinity.[3] Indeed, hegemony as a theoretical concept fits quite neatly into Bourdieu's concept of fields and the dominant position of orthodoxy taken within fields. For, as Williams (1977) demonstrates in defining hegemony,

> A lived hegemony is always a process. It is not, except analytically, a system or a structure. It is a realized complex of experiences, relationships, and activities, with specific and changing pressures and limits. [. . .] [Hegemony] does not just passively exist as a form of dominance. It has continually to be renewed, recreated, defended, and modified. It is also continually resisted, limited, altered, challenged by pressures not at all its own. We have then to add to the concept of hegemony the concepts of counter-hegemony and alternative hegemony, which are real and persistent elements of practice. . . . The reality of any hegemony, in the extended political and cultural sense, is that, while by definition it is always dominant, it is never either total or exclusive . . . [. . .] The reality of cultural process must then always include the efforts and contributions of those who are in one way or another outside or at the edge of the terms of the specific hegemony. (Williams 1977: 112–13)

Williams's definition of hegemony (and by default, counter-hegemony) is remarkably similar to the struggles between orthodoxy and heterodoxy that are played out in fields described by Bourdieu.

If one is to use the above definition of hegemony in relation to the concept of hegemonic masculinity, then hegemonic masculinity can be used to appropriately describe that form of masculinity that is considered culturally to be most dominant at any given time (remembering that it is fluid and subject to change) within the field of masculinity. Where the concept of hegemonic masculinity is currently lacking is in its ability to account for other dominant masculinities that exist in fields overlapping with the field of masculinity and subfields within the field of masculinity. There, too, struggles exist between orthodoxy and heterodoxy (or to use Williams's framework, hegemony and counter-hegemony), meaning that other dominant masculinities necessarily exist that may not conform to hegemonic masculinity in the field of masculinity.

Within any given field, there are those in positions of dominance and those who are subordinated. While hegemonic masculinity can be used to describe the dominant version of masculinity within the field of masculinity, there are subfields within the field of masculinity that have their own dynamics of dominant and subordinate masculinities. [. . .]

Bourdieu's concept of fields allows for a variety of dominant masculinities to exist. As there are a multitude of fields in which masculinities operate, so too are there necessarily different versions of dominant (and subordinate) masculinities. For example, in the field of business and finance where economic capital is highly valued, dominant masculinity is exemplified in the aggressive market exploits of men. In the field of militia, toughness and brute physical strength represent dominant versions of masculinity, and the body is valued as physical capital. Furthermore, these dominant masculinities are crosscut by external fields such as ethnicity and age to form a complex matrix of masculinities. While the concept of hegemonic masculinity is centrally important to the study of men and masculinities, it needs to be contextualized within Bourdieu's concept of fields to allow for consideration of multiple dominant masculinities.

Furthermore, habitus allows masculinity to be both transposable and adaptable, a strategy by which men are able to adapt to given situations. Importantly, habitus also allows for individuality and difference in how men perform masculinity. It helps to explain why some men choose to reject hegemonic masculinity, why some men support it, or why men may reject some components of hegemonic masculinity while simultaneously supporting others. Their position depends on

their relationship to others in the field of masculinity and the resources they have available at their disposal. [. . .] It may also depend on the subfield in which they operate in the field of masculinity as to whether they believe their masculinity to be a dominant or legitimate form of masculinity. [. . .] Using both Bourdieu and Connell provides [. . .] insight into how masculinities are produced and reproduced [. . .] at the structural level and the individual level; the hierarchies involved; and how men come to negotiate masculinities over the life course [and across contexts].

REFERENCES

Beynon, John. 2002. *Masculinities and Culture*. Buckingham, UK: Open University Press.

Bohman, James. 1999. "Practical Reason and Cultural Constraint: Agency in Bourdieu's Theory of Practice." In *Bourdieu: A Critical Reader*, edited by R. Shusterman. Oxford, UK: Blackwell.

Bourdieu, Pierre. 1977. *Outline of a Theory of Practice*. Cambridge, UK: Cambridge University Press.

Bourdieu, Pierre. 1984. *Distinction: A Social Critique of the Judgement of Taste*. London: Routledge & Kegan Paul.

Bourdieu, Pierre. 1993. *Sociology in Question*. London: Sage.

Butler, Judith. 1999. "Performativity's Social Magic." In *Bourdieu: A Critical Reader*, edited by R. Shusterman. Oxford, UK: Blackwell.

Calhoun, Craig C. 1993. "Habitus, Field, and Capital: The Question of Historical Specificity." In *Bourdieu: Critical Perspectives*, edited by C. Calhoun, E. LiPuma, and M. Postone. Chicago: University of Chicago Press.

Carrigan, Tim, R. W. Connell, and John Lee. 1987. "Toward a New Sociology of Masculinity." In *The Making of Masculinities: The New Men's Studies*, edited by H. Brod. Boston: Allen & Unwin.

Clatterbaugh, Kenneth. 1990. *Contemporary Perspectives on Masculinity: Men, Women, and Politics in Modern Society*. Boulder, CO: Westview.

Coles, Tony. 2009. "Negotiating the Field of Masculinity: The Production and Reproduction of Multiple Dominant Masculinities." *Men and Masculinities* 12 (1): 30–44.

Collier, Richard. 1998. *Masculinities, Crime and Criminology: Men, Heterosexuality and the Criminal(ised) Other.* London: Sage.

Connell, Richard. 1987. *Gender and Power: Society, the Person and Sexual Politics.* Stanford, CA: Stanford University Press.

Connell, Raewyn. 1995. *Masculinities.* Sydney: Allen & Unwin.

Connell, Raewyn and James W. Messerschmidt. 2005. "Hegemonic Masculinity: Rethinking the Concept." *Gender & Society* 19: 829–59.

Fowler, Bridget. 1997. *Pierre Bourdieu and Cultural Theory: Critical Investigations.* London: Sage.

Fowler, Bridget, ed. 2000. *Reading Bourdieu on Society and Culture.* Oxford, UK: Blackwell.

Gardiner, Judith Kegan, ed. 2002. *Masculinity Studies and Feminist Theory.* New York: Columbia University Press.

Hearn, Jeff. 1996. "Is Masculinity Dead? A Critique of the Concept of Masculinity/Masculinities." In *Understanding Masculinities: Social Relations and Cultural Arenas*, edited by M. Mac an Ghaill. Buckingham, UK: Open University Press.

Hearn, Jeff. 2004. "From Hegemonic Masculinity to the Hegemony of Men." *Feminist Theory* 5 (1): 49–72.

Hearn, Jeff. 2007. "Masculinity/Masculinities." In *Encyclopedia of Men and Masculinities*, edited by M. Flood, J. Gardiner, B. Pease, and K. Pringle. London: Routledge.

Lane, Jeremy F. 2000. *Pierre Bourdieu: A Critical Introduction.* London: Pluto.

Mahar, Cheleen, Richard Harker, and Chris Wilkes. 1990. "The Basic Theoretical Position." In *An Introduction to the Work of Pierre Bourdieu: The Practice of Theory*, edited by R. Harker, C. Mahar, and C. Wilkes. London: Macmillan.

Margolis, Joseph. 1999. "Pierre Bourdieu: Habitus and the Logic of Practice." In *Bourdieu: A Critical Reader*, edited by R. Shusterman. Oxford, UK: Blackwell.

McNay, Lois. 2000. *Gender and Agency: Reconfiguring the Subject in Feminist and Social Theory.* Cambridge, UK: Polity.

Pease, Bob. 2001. "Moving beyond Mateship: Reconstructing Australian Men's Practices." In *A Man's World? Men's Practices in a Globalized World*, edited by B. Pease and K. Pringle. London: Zed.

Pease, Bob. 2002. *Men and Gender Relations.* Melbourne: Tertiary Press.

Petersen, Alan. 1998. *Unmasking the Masculine: "Men" and "Identity" in a Sceptical Age.* London: Sage.

Robbins, Derek. 1991. *The Work of Pierre Bourdieu: Recognizing Society.* Buckingham, UK: Open University Press.

Shilling, Chris. 1991. "Educating the Body: Physical Capital and the Production of Social Inequalities." *Sociology* 25: 653–72.

Shilling, Chris. 1993. *The Body and Social Theory.* London: Sage.

Smith, Philip. 2001. *Cultural Theory: An Introduction.* Malden, UK: Blackwell.

Strathern, Aandrew. 1996. *Body Thoughts.* Ann Arbor: University of Michigan Press.

Swartz, David. 1997. *Culture & Power: The Sociology of Pierre Bourdieu.* Chicago: University of Chicago Press.

Watson, Jonathan. 2000. *Male Bodies: Health, Culture and Identity.* Buckingham, UK: Open University Press.

Webb, Jen, Tony Schirato, and Geoff Danaher. 2002. *Understanding Bourdieu.* Crows Nest, Australia: Allen & Unwin.

White, M. 1996. "Men's Culture, the Men's Movement, and the Constitution of Men's Lives." In *Men's Ways of Being: New Directions in Theory and Psychology*, edited by C. McLean, M. Carey, and C. White. Boulder, CO: Westview.

White, Rob. 2002. "Social and Political Aspects of Men's Health." *Health: An Interdisciplinary Journal for the Social Study of Health, Illness and Medicine* 6 (3): 267–85.

Whitehead, Stephen M. 2002. *Men and Masculinities: Key Themes and New Directions.* Cambridge, UK: Polity.

Williams, Raymond. 1977. *Marxism and Literature.* Oxford, UK: Oxford University Press.

NOTES

1. This is not an exhaustive list of the limitations by any means. In particular, there have been a number of poststructuralist and (pro)feminist

theoretical critiques in recent years that have emerged challenging the concept of hegemonic masculinity on the grounds that it adds to the problem of the subordination of women and marginalized groups of men by legitimizing the hierarchical ordering of masculinities (Collier 1998; Petersen 1998; Whitehead 2002; Hearn 2004). However, the purpose of this [chapter] is not to analyze or critique the various arguments challenging the concept of hegemonic masculinity (for a good synopsis of the various challenges to hegemonic masculinity, see Hearn 2007). Instead, the focus is on how best to use hegemonic masculinity and build on it to develop a more sound rationale for how men negotiate masculinities. [. . .]

2. Connell and Messerschmidt (2005) have attempted to rectify this by suggesting that there are multiple hegemonic masculinities that exist at the global, regional, and local levels. I would argue, however, that to consider multiple hegemonic masculinities runs counter to definitions of hegemony and runs the risk of being contradictory. For example, can one be exemplary of the hegemonic masculine ideal locally and subordinated regionally? That is, can one be both a holder of hegemonic masculinity and simultaneously subordinated by it? [. . .]

3. Connell and Bourdieu also share commonalities in their theoretical positions in more subtle ways: both believe class and economic materialism to be a prominent social issue that exists perennially, cutting through other issues such as gender; both recognize masculine domination as a problematic social principle; and both acknowledge the necessity to consider individuals and how they perform gender while simultaneously considering the effects of social structures such as education and law that pervade individual choices. There are also parallels between Connell's (1987) concept of cathexis and Bourdieu's notion of habitus in that they both cross the structure/agency divide (although cathexis is more tightly bound by structures and interrelated with power and the division of labor whilst habitus operates more freely, allowing individuals to more readily negotiate their position within fields).

4

DISLOCATING MASCULINITIES

CHAPTER 4

DISLOCATING MASCULINITIES

An Introduction

If scholars are to effectively challenge the power relations of gender, race, and sexuality, it is important that they critically examine the discursive frameworks that shape the fabrication of concepts, the definition of problems, and the formulation of research questions.

—ALAN PETERSEN, 2003

A popular parenting blog recently featured a picture of a child's room with the following words written decoratively on the wall: "boy, *n.* 1. noise with dirt on it." Fans of the site responded with humorous comments about the truth of that statement in their own lives—affirming that yes, boys are messy, loud, and generally a handful. Surely, many of us have heard this sort of "boys will be boys" explanation for all manner of behavior. The idea behind it is that boys are, somehow, unavoidably . . . well, unavoidably *something*. The point is less about what that particular "something" is and more about the fact that whatever it is, it is inevitable and hardwired into boys and men. So inevitable is this "something," in fact, that "boys will be boys" and similar comments are deployed to make sense of all manner of bad or destructive behaviors enacted by boys and men. Interestingly, "boys will be boys" is something we say about others; it is not something a boy generally says about himself. Rather, it is a discourse others use to excuse boys for all manner of bad behavior. As they get older, we have discourses that allow them to excuse themselves (e.g., "A man's gotta' do what a man's gotta' do"). In this light, "boys will be boys" might be best understood as a socializing discourse—one that is so embedded in our culture that we can often invoke it without directly saying it. Sometimes, a wall decal says it for us.

Interestingly, another, contradictory discourse often appears alongside this essentialist one. Rather than claiming that male-bodied persons are inherently one way or another, a set of competing claims situate masculinity as much more tenuous, implying that it may be shaped by social forces. Take, for instance, the outcry about a 2011 J. Crew advertisement depicting a young boy and his mother painting their toenails pink (see advertisement on next page). Fox News suggested that the child would need therapy because "J. Crew plants the seeds for gender identity." These responses are emblematic of more general parental fears about their sons wearing pink, playing with dolls, or participating in a range of "feminized" activities (e.g., Kane 2006). Rather than suggesting that masculinity is some inherent trait, these concerns reflect understandings of masculinity as something that is not fully predetermined. That is, if a boy engages in feminized activities, the fear is that they may shape his gender identity such that he is less masculine than other men. Such a line of thought suggests that what we think of "masculinity" is not inherent, but something that is easily changeable.[1]

These contradictions raise the following questions: Is masculinity stable or is it not? Is it inevitably produced, solid and unwavering? Or is it tenuous, delicate, and in need of constant support and supervision to ensure its continued existence? Can it be both of these things at the same time? Or is it something else altogether? *Dislocating masculinities* scholarship takes the incongruities raised by these questions seriously, engaging with two bodies of theory to address these contradictions—poststructuralist and, more specifically, queer theories.

Poststructuralism emerged in the humanities to address the ways that language (such as the discourses about masculinity highlighted above) shapes meaning, experience, and reality itself. The ways in which we are capable of speaking and writing about something influence our understanding of that thing—*language shapes experience* (e.g., McGowan 1991). Inherent in this approach is the understanding that things, categories, identities, and phenomena as well as reality itself are a lot less stable than how we are accustomed to treating them. These various "things" that we study, poststructralists suggest, are not actually "out there" in any stable or enduring way, but are actively created through the way we talk and write about them. This is not to deny the reality or *realness* of the things we study—it simply questions the origins, longevity, and durability of this reality (e.g., Petersen 1998).

In many ways, the readings that structure the *Dislocating Masculinities* section are not a part of "masculinities studies" proper. Indeed, some of the authors in this section (even as they were writing about masculinity) expressed hesitation about being included in a book focusing on "theorizing masculinities." These readings are less likely to engage with the multiple masculinities scholarship than are other essays in this volume. Masculinities scholarship

J. Crew Advertisement

was—and still is—largely recognized by theoretically framing one's argument with respect to founding scholars largely associated with the multiple masculinities perspective. As a result, a great deal of research and theorizing about masculinity goes unrecognized as such precisely because it is situated with respect to alternate literatures. This has—inadvertently—produced a segregated field in which theoretically rich research outside of "masculinities studies" proper might have a great deal to say to those of us studying masculinities.

For instance, until this point, essays in this book have anchored gender and sexuality in particular bodies or bodies with specific anatomical configurations. Although masculinities scholars have long attempted to detach the study of masculinity from biological maleness, the majority of work in this field considers populations of people with penises. Scholars who form the dislocating masculinities perspective challenge this relationship (e.g., Petersen 1998). That is, women of all sexualities, gay men, and straight men enact different gender projects, although all are subject to the expectations of hegemonic masculinity. Queer theory suggests a different relationship among sexualities, bodies, and gender, one that deeply informs much of the writing in this section. Queer theory emphatically does *not* treat sexuality as a discrete identity category (homosexual, heterosexual, or bisexual, for instance) located in a particular sexed (male or female) body. Queer theory moves beyond a focus on categories by looking at how sexuality shapes and is shaped by social life, is embedded in multiple institutions, and is implicated in social theorizing that neglects to mention sexuality (but is nonetheless based on assumptions about sexuality) (Warner 1993).

Dislocating masculinities scholarship and theory serves as a corrective to that tendency in widening the scope of masculinities studies and bringing into the dialogue scholars who (due to intellectual commitments, theoretical framings, or disciplinary boundaries) may not be typically understood as "masculinities scholars." In doing so, we hope to respond to Peterson's call in this section's opening essay (Reading 24) for attention to the "discursive frameworks that shape the fabrication of concepts, the definitions of problems and the formulation of research questions." Indeed, this discursive focus may be the hallmark of the writing in this section. These essays move beyond the endless taxonomies of men and shift our attention to the dynamics between and among gendered beings in discursive and symbolic realms.[2] They take seriously the way in which masculinity is actively created by the way we write, talk, and study it. How is it that we even identify masculinity as an object of study? What are we talking about? Where do we find it? How can we study it? Does it always have to do with men? Answers to these questions are not incidental. Indeed, the ways we answer these questions define the very field of study itself. In essence, theory and research within the dislocating masculinities tradition critically calls into question the stability of masculinity.

QUEER THEORY

Queer theory originated out of a need to think about, understand, and study sexualities using the tools of poststructuralism. Scholars have since expanded the application of queer theoretical perspectives beyond sexuality. For example, as a theoretical perspective, queer theory deconstructs things we tend to think of as "going together." It looks at possibilities, dissonances, lapses, and excesses of meaning (Warner 1993). It attends, for instance, to the instability of discourses around difference and meaning—much like those found in the opening examples about how we understand masculinity both as essential and as constructed (Petersen 1998; Warner 1993). As Stein and Plummer (1996) argue, queer theory analyzes power, contradiction, and knowledge production in three primary ways. First, queer theory sees sexual power as embodied in different levels of social life—primarily through *discourses* constituted of binary oppositions (e.g., gay/straight, black/white, masculine/feminine, man/woman). Second, it problematizes sexual and gender categories and *identities* in general, claiming that identities are always uncertain and unstable. Third, it interrogates areas normally not seen as the terrain of sexuality, challenging traditional framings of society in *social theory* (Stein and Plummer 1996).

DISCOURSE

Attention to *discourse* may be the key feature of this particular section. Rather than seeing masculinity as something that belongs to or is solely enacted by a biologically male body, the scholarship in this section turns our attention to how gender (and sexuality) is discursively produced and, in turn, *becomes* embodied. Rather than seeing the body as the beginning of gendered enactment (West and Zimmerman 1987), these essays understand gender (and, often, race and sexuality too) *performatively*—as implicated in and produced by discourse. This section encourages us to consider masculinity discursively, not just in terms of male bodies or categories of men. To be sure, however, discursive does not mean *not embodied*; it just calls into question assumptions about embodiment, like the assumption that masculinity proceeds from bodies that are sexed as male.

The concept of "binary oppositions" is central to understanding how discourse works. Binary oppositions, queer theory points out (Sedgwick 1990), refer the ways in which inequality is linguistically constructed, framed, and reflected. Binary oppositions are categorical pairs that define each other—man/woman, masculinity/femininity, black/white, homosexual/heterosexual, masculine/feminine, public/private, health/illness, active/passive, natural/artificial, knowledge/ignorance (Sedgwick 1990). Each word in the pair depends on another unequal category to define itself. This inequitable interdependence highlights the instability of the categories themselves.

For scholarship on masculinity, attention to binary oppositions means that we might not think of masculinity and femininity in opposition. What would it mean to be *both* masculine and feminine? Or *neither* masculine nor feminine? Or a little masculine and a lot feminine? What would it mean if we did not dichotomize sexual identities like homosexual or heterosexual? Or link such identities with sexed bodies? What would it mean to think, as David Halperin (2012) suggests, of something like "gay culture" as analytically separable from "collections of gay individuals"? By allowing us to ask (and sometimes answer) questions like these, queer theory enables an investigation of the very knowledge production processes that undergird masculinities studies itself and exposes the normative assumptions on which it may rely.

IDENTITIES

Queer theory does not address identity in the singular. Rather, it demands we think of identi*ties*, in the plural. Queer theory posits that identities are always *multiple, fractured*, and a *composite* with infinite potential combinations and intersections (e.g., sexuality, race, class, gender, able-bodiedness, nationality, age). These identities are not stable. They are arbitrary and exclusionary. Thus, by "taking these categories as givens or as reified, we do not fully consider the ways that inequalities are constructed by the categories in the first place. These categories exert power over individuals, especially for those who do not fit neatly within their normative alignments" (Valocchi 2005: 752).

In a semantic history of the term, the historian Philip Gleason (1983) argues that "identity" began to be used to support a discourse about the individual that entailed a stability of self that queer theory fundamentally questions. This includes the questioning of a stable heterosexual or homosexual identity taken for granted by many academic in-quiries. Such inquiries ask, for example, whether Shakespeare or Michelangelo was gay. According to queer theory, they were not. They could not have been gay, because *being gay* did not yet exist (e.g., Foucault 1978; D'Emilio and Freedman 1988; Chauncey 1994). And neither did heterosexuality (e.g., Katz 1995; Blank 2012). Homosexuality (and hetero-sexuality) only became an available identity category in the late 1800s and took much longer to actually take hold. In other words, people's sexual practices were not translat-able into some immutable identity (e.g., Weeks 1986). People did not always think of their sexual desires or behavior as implying something about who they "really are" on a fundamental level.

Given its recent appearance as a way of understanding human behavior, dislocating masculinities approaches are suspicious of the concept of "identity." As Alan Petersen writes, "The critique of identity does not necessarily mean that one should disavow iden-tity, but rather that one needs to be constantly aware of the fictitious character of identity and of the dangers of imposing an identity" (pp. 342 in this volume). For queer theorists, identity is not just *liberatory*; it is *disciplinary*. Beginning with Foucault (1978), most queer theorists see identity not as something that sets one free (e.g., "If only I could figure out what my true identity is, I'd be fine"), but as a way in which power operates. Identities are templates for defining selves and behaviors. But, as templates, they are exclusionary, pre-cluding the full range of possible ways to understand and experience selves, bodies, desires, actions, emotions, and more. Yet, we are all controlled by a discourse about identities that disciplines us to inhabit, craft, and embrace recognizable identities. We do so by constantly monitoring ourselves, our behaviors, and all manner of identity practices. The more closely we are able to approximate "normal" identities, the more social rewards we receive.

Part of understanding identities as disciplinary has to do with what Judith Butler calls "performativity." Performativity is the compelled and repeated citation of a social norm (Butler 1990, 1993a). To be culturally recognizable, we must all engage in performativity. That is, to be a man, one must cite the norms of masculinity (and vice versa to be a woman). For Butler, these citationary practices actively create the very identity category itself—the category from which these practices are then said to emerge. The risk of not citing them means that one risks not being culturally intelligible, being what Butler calls an "abject identity"—one that cannot fit into society or be recognized by others.

Performativity, for Butler, is different from "performance," as we may casually understand the term. Consider Butler's explanation:

> Gender is not a performance that a prior subject elects to do, but gender is *performative* in the sense that it constitutes as an effect the very subject it appears to express. . . . To claim that there is no performer prior to the performed, that the performance is performative, that the performance constitutes the appearance of a "subject" as its effect is difficult to accept. This difficulty is the result of a predisposition to think of sexuality and gender as "expressing" in some indirect or direct way a psychic reality that precedes it. (Butler 1993b: 314–15)

Butler's theory of *performativity* suggests that a kind of biological reductionism remains in the ways gender is treated in a great deal of social theorizing and in the masculinities literature itself. In considering masculinity, for instance, Butler suggests not only that masculinity is a performance—it is a performance that, if done well, produces the belief in a stable subject position behind that performance. The idea that a stable subject lies behind the performance, for Butler, is one of the many accomplishments of the performance. Postmodern approaches to masculinities studies challenge us not to treat masculinities as "expressed" (in Butler's sense), but as constituted by a performance that solidifies what we think of as the "it" we discussed above.

Although masculinities scholars have long held that masculinity is socially constructed, a body of theory and scholarship challenges theory and research on masculinities to push these boundaries further. To actually understand masculinity as separate from male bodies necessitates acknowledging that *women can do masculinity too*. This, among other insights, structures the challenges put forth in this section. It is a dramatic break with a great deal of masculinities scholarship and pushes the boundaries of what it means to understand and write about masculinities as social constructs.

DECENTERING SOCIAL THEORY

Finally, queer theory issues a call for "decentering" social theory (Warner 1993; Butler 1990). In this model, sexuality cannot simply be *added* to a theory; rather, sexuality must be understood as being at the center of social theory. The sexual order blends with a wide range of institutions and social ideologies, informing them in a variety of ways that are not immediately visible without a queer analysis (Warner 1993). Traditional social theories have been based on heteronormative understandings of society (Warner 1993). In other words, queer theory is positing a "growing, assertive insistence that the sociological study of sexuality is not necessary simply to understand those realms of life already designated as 'sexual'" (Gamson and Moon 2004: 59). Rather, queer theory proposes to uncover the *sexual* dynamics also structuring and at play in those realms of life we tend not to think of as "sexual" in the first place.

There are two particularly good examples of this. In the first, Michael Warner (1993) analyzes an area of life not usually thought of as sexual—the U.S. space program. On NASA's *Pioneer 10* (1972)—the first spacecraft to leave our solar system—Carl Sagan designed an image of the solar system with two naked human beings standing next to each other, one anatomically appearing male and one female (see image below). Warner points out that this image frames the heterosexual couple as the foundation of humanity, each imbued with normative gender traits reflective of middle-class Western ideals:

> They are not just sexually different; they are sexual difference itself. They are nude but have no body hair; the woman has no genitals; their heads are neatly coiffed according to the gender norms of middle-class young adults. The man stands square, while the woman leans one hip slightly forward. To a native of the culture that produced it, this bizarre fantasy-image is immediately recognizable not just as two gendered individuals, but as a heterosexual couple. . . . It testifies to the depth of the cultures assurance (read: insistence) that humanity and heterosexuality are synonymous. (Warner 1993: xxiii)

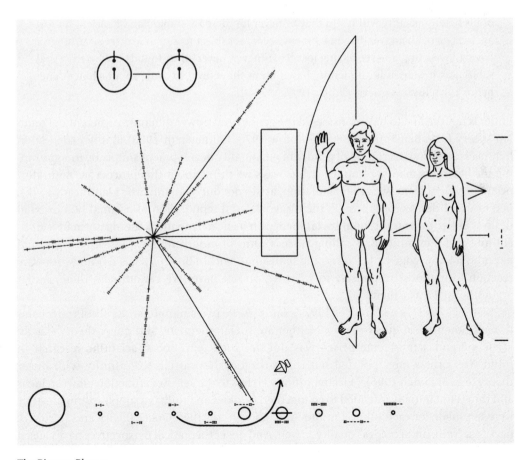

The Pioneer Plaque

Warner doesn't comment on the apparent race of the pair. But these are features we might mention as well. Warner uses this image as a way of talking about how heteronormativity structures gender, our experience of the world, and, indeed, even our attempts to represent "humanity." But there are other structuring discourses apparent in this image as well—race, class, bodily ability.

Judith Butler turns a similar deconstructive lens on Freud's theories of human psychological development, specifically the Oedipus complex. In her essay entitled "Melancholy Gender/Refused Identification," Butler asks, what if our original love objects were not assumed to be *heterosexual*, as Freud suggests? That is, what if it weren't his mother the young boy gave up under threat of castration from his father, but his father himself? What if original love were a same-sex love? By reframing Freud's Oedipal drama and questioning the heteronormativity on which Freudian theory ultimately rests, Butler develops a theory of gender that situates the enactment of gender itself as pathological. As Butler writes,

> If we accept the notion that heterosexuality naturalizes itself by insisting on the radical otherness of homosexuality, then heterosexual identity is purchased through a melancholic incorporation of the love that it disavows: the man who insists upon the coherence of his heterosexuality will claim that he never loved another man, and hence never lost another man. That love, that attachment becomes subject to a double disavowal, a never having loved, and a never having lost. This "never–never" thus founds the heterosexual subject, as it were; it is an identity based upon the refusal to avow an attachment and, hence, the refusal to grieve. (Butler 1997: 139–40)

Butler is not the first to have considered the gender and power dynamics inherent in Freudian theory (e.g., Benjamin 1988; Chodorow 1978; Dinnerstein 1976). But her suggestion here *queers* our understanding of gender in personality development simply by foregrounding the heteronormativity implicit in the ways we think about this process as "naturally" occurring. Gender, in Butler's formulation, arises not out of an intrinsic identification with heterosexual desires, but through the disavowal and repudiation of original homosexual desires. Butler turns traditional social theory on its head by pathologizing normative masculinity and femininity and calling them a form of mourning for a lost love that could never be acknowledged. Masculine and feminine—within Butler's revised framework—are reaction formations[3] responsive to what we cannot have. We cannot *have* them, Butler argues, so we *become* them.

Warner's (1993) and Butler's (1997) examples are two small illustrations of the revolutionary potential of queer theory. Neither are social scientists, and queer theory—as an academic and activist enterprise—was not designed with social scientific research in mind. Yet, others have pointed out that sociology has an elective affinity with queer theory (e.g., Seidman 1996). "Elective affinity" refers to the sense of attraction between ideas and things not initially intended to go together. Cookies and milk is a simple example—they were not made for each other, but they sure go well together. Queer theory and sociology have that "milk-and-cookies" quality as well. And queer theoretical perspectives have caused some scholars of masculinity to investigate just how far we can push a social constructionist argument and what we learn by getting to the limits of such an argument.

QUEERING MASCULINITIES STUDIES

Dislocating masculinities perspectives deploy insights from queer theory that allow us to look at masculinity in a different way. Like the multiple masculinities approach, it allows us to understand masculinity as multiple roles rather than as a singular role. Like the navigating masculinities approach, it allows us to see masculinity as intersecting with other forms of inequality (Gamson and Moon 2004). What it adds to these approaches is a more refined sense of how gender and sexuality (in addition to other categories of identity) simultaneous constitute each other as social categories. In other words, contained within constructions of sexuality are assumptions about masculinity (and femininity) and contained within constructions of masculinity are assumptions about sexuality. Scholarship highlighted in this section interrogates assumptions about embodiment in the masculinities literature, analyzes meanings of sexuality implicit in conceptualizing masculinity, and frames sexuality not only as identity, but also as discursive culture.

Much literature tying masculinity to the male body (e.g., masculinity is what men do) is at least implicitly biologically reductionistic in that it fails to grapple with what it means when something we recognize as masculinity does not proceed from a biologically male body. In this section, both Jack Halberstam (Reading 25) and Eve Kosofsky Sedgwick (Reading 26) theorize ways of strategically "dislocating" masculinity from the male body. Halberstam, for instance, argues that the social sciences, especially, have unreflexively posited a male body as central to masculinity. As such, he examines the varied ways we might begin to question the relationship between embodiment and gender. Similarly, Sedgwick posits three ways we might begin to think differently about masculinity in terms of challenging binary relationships between concepts of masculinity and femininity (Reading 26). Emily Kazyak investigates female masculinity from a social scientific perspective in "Midwest or Lesbian?" (Reading 27). Kazyak suggests that gendered identities, such as female masculinity and male femininity, are deeply informed by both sexuality and place. She also highlights the significance of context in determining whether these sorts of gender transgressions are understood as "deviant." Building on Kazyak's finding that place is important in terms of gender and embodiment, Miriam Abelson's (Reading 30) reading not only complicates the relationship between sexed bodies and gendered identities, but also highlights the role of place in shaping violence or potential violence in constructing contemporary masculinity.

Dislocating masculinities approaches also tease out the complicated relationship between sexuality and gender (and age) by highlighting instabilities and the co-constituting nature of the categories themselves. Karl Bryant's reading (Reading 28) highlights the way in which childhood gender nonconformity produces panic about sexual identity. Instead of examining sexuality as a discrete, stable identity separate from gender identity, Bryant investigates the way in which childhood gender nonconformity calls into question adult sexual identities. In "William's Doll and Me," Bryant unpacks the messages in the classic early feminist song, "William Wants a Doll" from the *Free to Be . . . You and Me* (1972) album to illustrate the power of childhood gender nonconformity for little boys and the way in which such nonconformity is rendered palatable through the promise of adult heterosexuality. This linkage of gender transgression for boys to deviant sexuality later in life undergirds parents' different reactions to female masculinity and male femininity (e.g., Kane 2006). This sort of childhood gender panic deeply informs gendered violence in adult life as demonstrated by Laurel Westbrook and Kristen Schilt's analysis of interactions between cisgender[4] and transgender individuals in Reading 29, "Penis Panics." These pieces lay bare the way in which power, inequality, and violence manifest through processes of gendered and sexualized identities and that the instability in one term necessarily panics the other. All three demonstrate the diverse ways in which gender and sexual identities work not only as liberatory social forms, but also as disciplinary ones.

The final two readings suggest ways in which we might begin to think of sexualized *cultures* and *interactions* rather than *identities* or *desires*. In Reading 31, Jane Ward's research documenting same-sex sexual encounters between men who do not self-identify as "gay" teases out complex relationships among gender, racial identity, sexual practice, and sexual cultures. She suggests that heterosexuality is not so much a constellation of sexual practices and desires as it is a "cultural identity" that can coexist alongside particular sexual practices that might seem to contradict it—at least to outsiders. Similarly, Bridges and Pascoe (Reading 32) allow us to think about what happens when masculinity and sexuality are not necessarily about particular embodied identities or sexual desires and practices. In analyzing relationships between homophobia and masculinity, they suggest that homophobia is best understood as a disciplinary practice rather than an actual fear of same-sex relationships. In other words, both of these readings take into account what it means when sexual identities are not inhered in particular bodies, but understood as capable of existing as *cultures* and *discourses* identified with and deployed in a variety of ways that reflect and inform the contemporary ordering of gendered, racialized, and sexualized inequalities.

REFERENCES

Benjamin, Jessica. 1988. *The Bonds of Love: Psychoanalysis, Feminism, and the Problem of Domination*. New York: Pantheon.

Blank, Hanne. 2012. *Straight: The Surprisingly Short History of Heterosexuality*. Boston: Beacon Press.

Butler, Judith. 1990. *Gender Trouble: Feminism and the Subversion of Identity*. New York: Routledge.

Butler, Judith. 1993a. *Bodies That Matter: On the Discursive Limits of Sex*. New York: Routledge.

Butler, Judith. 1993b. "Imitation and Gender Insubordination." In *The Lesbian and Gay Studies Reader*, edited by Henry Abelove, Michele Aina Barale, and David M. Halperin, 307–20. New York: Routledge.

Butler, Judith. 1997. *The Psychic Life of Power: Theories in Subjection*. Stanford, CA: Stanford University Press.

Chauncey, George. 1994. *Gay New York: Gender, Urban Culture, and the Making of the Gay Male World, 1890–1940*. New York: Basic Books.

Chodorow, Nancy J. 1978. *The Reproduction of Mothering: Psychoanalysis and the Sociology of Gender*, updated ed. Berkeley: University of California Press.

Connell, Raewyn. 1987. *Gender and Power: Society, the Person and Sexual Politics*. Stanford, CA: Stanford University Press.

Connell, Raewyn. 1995. *Masculinities*. Berkeley: University of California Press.

Connell, Raewyn. 2002. *Gender: Short Introductions*. London: Polity Press.

D'Emilio, John, and Estelle B. Freedman. 1988. *Intimate Matters: A History of Sexuality in America*. Chicago: University of Chicago Press.

Dinnerstein, Dorothy. 1976. *The Mermaid and the Minotaur: Sexual Arrangements and Human Malaise*. New York: Open Press.

Epstein, Steven. 1993/1994. "Gay Politics, Ethnic Identity: The Limits of Social Constructionism." *Socialist Review* 17 (3/4): 9–54.

Foucault, Michel. 1978. *The History of Sexuality, Volume I: An Introduction*. New York: Pantheon Books.

Gamson, Joshua, and Dawne Moon. 2004. "The Sociology of Sexualities: Queer and Beyond." *Annual Review of Sociology* 30 (1): 47–64.

Gleason, Philip. 1983. "Identifying Identity: A Semantic History." *The Journal of American History* 69 (4): 910–31.

Halperin, David M. 2012. *How to Be Gay*. Cambridge, MA: Harvard University Press.

Kane, Emily W. 2006. "'No Way My Boys Are Going to Be Like That!': Parents' Responses to Children's Gender Nonconformity." *Gender & Society* 20 (2): 149–76.

Katz, Jonathan. 1995. *The Invention of Heterosexuality*. New York: University of Chicago Press.

Kimmel, Michael S. 1993. "Sexual Balkanization: Gender and Sexuality as the New Ethnicities." *Social Research* 60 (3): 571–87.

McGowan, John. 1991. *Postmodernism and Its Critics*. Ithaca, NY: Cornell University Press.

Petersen, Alan. 1998. *Unmasking the Masculine: 'Men' and 'Identity' in a Sceptical Age*. Thousand Oaks, CA: Sage.

Petersen, Alan. 2003. "Research on Men and Masculinities: Some Implications of Recent Theory for Future Work." *Men and Masculinities* 6 (1): 54–69.

Sedgwick, Eve Kosofsky. 1990. *Epistemology of the Closet*. Berkeley: University of California Press.

Seidman, Steven, ed. 1996. "Introduction." In *Queer Theory Sociology*, 1–29. Cambridge, MA: Blackwell.

Stein, Arlene, and Ken Plummer. 1994. "'I Can't Even Think Straight': 'Queer' Theory and the Missing Sexual Revolution in Sociology." *Sociological Theory* 12 (2): 178–87.

Thomas, Marlo, and Friends. 1972. *Free to Be . . . You and Me*. New York: Bell Records.

Valocchi, Stephen. 2005. "Not Yet Queer Enough: The Lessons of Queer Theory for the Sociology of Gender and Sexuality." *Gender & Society* 19 (6): 750–70.

Warner, Michael. 1993. *Fear of a Queer Planet: Queer Politics and Social Theory*. Minneapolis: University of Minnesota Press.

Weeks, Jeffrey. 1986. *Sexuality*. New York and London: Routledge.

West, Candace, and Don H. Zimmerman. 1987. "Doing Gender." *Gender & Society* 1 (2): 125–51.

NOTES

1. Sexuality suffers from similarly contradictory popular understandings. So, for instance, Epstein (1993/1994) addresses the ways in which people often simultaneously consider homosexuality something people are "born with," combined with concerns over whether people can be "seduced" into it. These are logically contradictory views, but this does not mean people do not hold onto both simultaneously without recognizing any contradiction (see also Kimmel 1993).

2. Connell's (1987, 1995) initial theory of gender relations only considered three separate dimensions: power relations, production relations, and emotional relations (or relations of

cathexis). (See the Introduction for more details.) In subsequent iterations, however, Connell (2002) added what she refers to as "symbolic relations." We bring this up here because it is a dynamic illustration of the fact that Connell has always considered her theory "open" in the sense that it might be amended, added to, etc., as we gain new knowledge and focus on different elements of social life. Symbolic relations refer to some of the discursive terrain on which scholars within the dislocating masculinities tradition seek to build: systems of meaning, language, truth claims, symbols, and more. This dimension of Connell's theory, however, is less theorized than the initial three. Dislocating masculinities scholarship and theory step in here.

3. Psychoanalytic theory uses the concept *reaction formation* to refer to a psychologically defensive process whereby people manage "unacceptable" impulses or emotions with an exaggerated or mastered display of an opposing impulse or emotion.

4. "Cisgender" is a term referring to individuals whose gender identity matches the identity they were assigned at birth. See Note 1 in the *Navigating Masculinities* section introduction for a more complete explanation.

ALAN PETERSEN

24. RESEARCH ON MEN AND MASCULINITIES: SOME IMPLICATIONS OF RECENT THEORY FOR FUTURE WORK

This article offers some reflections on the challenges posed by recent trends in social theory to the field of masculinity studies. The emergence of postmodernism and poststructuralism in the social sciences and humanities during the 1980s and 1990s has been a significant theoretical development that has offered new tools of analysis and opened up new lines for exploration and critique. The poststructural ideas of Michel Foucault in particular have influenced many areas of critical enquiry, including feminism, queer theory, and antiracist and postcolonial studies, prompting scholars to reappraise core concepts and research foci. Feminists have interrogated such fundamental concepts as woman, gender, patriarchy, femininity, and women's experience and have begun to place greater emphasis on diversity and plurality (Barrett and Phillips 1992; Grant 1993). Along with other scholars, they have drawn attention to the dangers of essentializing identity and universalizing experience and to the exclusions involved in deploying particular categories. The sex/gender division, which has been foundational to second-wave feminism and which posits a separation between a natural or biological sex and a socially constructed gender, has also been challenged on the grounds of its biological determinism, essentialism, and implicit heterosexism.

In this article, I describe a number of aspects of these developments and draw some implications for future work in the field of masculinity studies. The critique of the concepts of gender and identity and of the sex/gender binary raises important questions about the directions of research and the politics of knowledge. It points to the need for a more reflexive use of categories and concepts and some reorientation of research focus, with more attention to issues of epistemology and history. If scholars are to effectively challenge the power relations of gender, race, and sexuality, it is important that they critically examine the discursive frameworks that shape the fabrication of concepts, the definition of problems, and the formulation of research questions. The article concludes by proposing a revised and broadened agenda for research on men and masculinities, which pays greater attention to the politics of knowledge and makes greater use of historical methods to analyze power relations and the constructions of masculine identity and the male body.

THE POSTSTRUCTURAL CHALLENGE

The recent poststructural turn in social theory challenges conventional ways of thinking about the relationship between knowledge, power, truth, and subjectivity. Eschewing structuralists' search for the underlying rules, codes, and systems that govern social phenomena, and the urge to develop grand synthesizing theories, poststructuralists have focused on the inextricable links between power and knowledge and on how individuals are constituted as subjects and given unified identities. Poststructuralists have drawn attention to micropolitics and emphasize subjectivity, difference, and everyday life (Best and Kellner 1991: 19, 24). Universalist and scientistic claims to be able to know, objectively, all there is to know (i.e., "the truth") have been rejected in favor of the view that knowledge is socially and historically specific and always grounded in a particular experience. In recent years, poststructural ideas have found wide application in research in the social

This reading is an excerpt from Alan Petersen's article in *Men and Masculinities* 6, no. 1 (2003) 54–69.

sciences and humanities, including a number of areas of critical scholarship such as feminism, queer theory, and antiracist and postcolonial studies. This has led to the reinvigoration of many fields of academic enquiry, involving the critique of basic concepts and strategies and the development of novel topics of investigation.

In particular, the dualistic distinctions that underlie our descriptions of the world (e.g., subject/object, self/other, nature/culture, mind/body, private/public, sex/gender, and heterosexual/homosexual) have been vigorously interrogated, showing how they may serve to exclude and limit understanding. There have been many innovative studies focusing on taken-for-granted categories, for example, the cultural representation of whiteness rather than blackness or color, which has been the usual focus in studies of race (e.g., see Dyer 1997). New kinds of historical study have been undertaken, drawing particularly on Foucault's genealogical method, elaborated in his writings such as *The History of Sexuality* (1980). Foucault's concept of discourse, which links power and knowledge, has found applications in the study of diverse topics, offering new insights and new ways of understanding familiar topics (e.g., sexuality and deviance). Historical studies of sexuality and sex have helped recast thinking about these phenomena, which are no longer seen as intrinsic and fixed aspects of the person, but rather understood as discursive constructions or inventions (e.g., Katz 1995; Laqueur 1990; Weeks 1985, 1990).

The questioning of identity has occurred across the social sciences and humanities, leading scholars and activists in the fields of feminism, gay and lesbian studies, and antiracist and postcolonial studies to rethink the strategic role of identity politics in contemporary radical practice. Queer theorists, for instance, have explored the implications and consequences of the identity politics of the gay and lesbian movements, that is, the strategy of "coming out of the closet" (e.g., Sedgwick 1994). In the above areas, fundamental issues of epistemology have been highlighted, leading scholars to reflect on the politics of their adherence to particular ways of seeing. Within feminism, there has been increasing acknowledgement of the politics of location (Rich 1986),

which implies attention to where one is speaking from and a consciousness of the exclusions that one's politics perpetuate. It is recognized that the politics of white feminists—who produce most of the published feminist theory—have often excluded the interests of black and Third World women (Jordan and Weedon 1995, 215).

The insights generated by scholars working in the above areas have direct implications for the field of masculinity studies. In particular, they should prompt scholars to consider the extent to which essentialism and dualistic distinctions are embedded in the categories and concepts that they employ. Evidence of essentialism, that is, "a belief in true essence . . . that which is most irreducible, unchanging, and therefore constitutive of a given person or thing" (Fuss 1989, 2), is widespread in writings on gender, perhaps most evidently in popular (e.g., mythopoetic) literature on men. The tendency to essentialize gender differences is not limited to the political or religious right, or even to popular men's movements. It is also a feature of some feminist writings where gender differences are characterized as fundamental and timeless (Coltrane 1994: 45). As Grosz (1995: 47–48) argued, essentialism is seen to entail the belief that those characteristics defined as women's/men's essences are shared in common by all women/men at all times and underlie all apparent variations differentiating women/men from each other. It implies a limit on the variations and possibilities for change and thus of social reorganization, and for this reason has been of central concern to contemporary feminists and other critical theorists. Most contemporary theorists reject essentialism, although some recognize the necessity of occasionally employing essentialist descriptions for strategic purposes, that is, "strategic essentialism" (Sayer 1997: 454–55). Essentialism is likely to be sustained by the governing frameworks of knowledge that influence the choice of research topics and the selection of categories, concepts, and methodologies. The recent emergence of antiessentialism in the social sciences represents a significant challenge to all studies of gender since it involves a fundamental questioning of established categories and concepts, especially those that assume the existence of fixed, homogenous, and mutually exclusive identities, including man and woman. The antiessentialist critique should cause scholars to reflect on the use of categories and, where necessary, rethink their strategic value.

It is important that writers be aware of the implications of adhering to the dualistic distinctions (i.e., in/out, either/or) that underlie discussions about differences. Second-wave feminists have critiqued the notion that observed differences between the situation and experiences of men and women are fundamentally a product of nature—the biology-as-destiny argument—on the grounds that this has been frequently used to explain and legitimize inequalities. When masculinity scholars and feminists rally against essentialism, in most cases they are targeting the assumption that there is an underlying essential, usually biologically based, dichotomy between men and women. Thus, much cross-cultural comparative work has been undertaken with the aim of debunking this claim by showing that there is considerable cross-cultural variation in the organization and expression of gender (e.g., see Coltrane 1994: 45–48; Cornwall and Lindisfarne 1994). In difference feminism, essentialism has less to do with biological facts than with the ways in which "culture marks bodies and creates specific conditions in which they live and recreate" (Gatens 1992: 133). As Gatens (1992: 135) explained, difference feminism is "concerned with the mechanisms by which bodies are recognized as different only insofar as they are constructed as possessing or lacking some socially privileged quality or qualities," which are then taken as fundamental ontological differences.

Much recent research on men and masculinities has focused on socially constructed differences between men and on how some masculinities come to be constructed as hegemonic (e.g., Connell 1995; Kaufman 1994; Kimmel 1994). The replacement of the unitary concept of masculinity with the pluralized concept of masculinities occurred because it was recognized that there are hierarchies among men, as well as between women and men, and that the power relations of gender are complex and multifaceted (Kimmel 1994: 124–26). However, as it became popularized, masculinities has sometimes lost its dimension of power and simply come to signify diversity or

plurality (Brod 1994: 86; Hearn and Collinson 1994: 112–14). Definitions of masculinity often entail little more than the compilation of lists of what are seen to be characteristic masculine qualities or attributes such as aggressivity, competitiveness, and emotional detachment, which, it is implied, distinguish it from its counterpart, femininity (passivity, cooperativeness, emotionality, etc.). That is, despite scholars' rejection of essentialism, masculinity is often referred to as though it had a definable, distinctive essence. Scholars often seem not to recognize that masculinity escapes precise empirical definition and that such identified traits at best represent "tendencies and possibilities that individuals have more or less access to at different points in time, and coexist in an uneasy and messy alliance" (MacInnes 1998, 15). The notion of masculinity may contain many images and behaviors that may be competing, contradictory, and mutually undermining, and that "completely variant notions of masculinity can refer simultaneously or sequentially to the same individual" (Cornwall and Lindisfarne 1994: 12). As Cornwall and Lindisfarne [. . .] noted,

> Meaning depends on who is speaking and who is being described in what setting. Masculinity has multiple and ambiguous meanings which alter according to context and over time. Meanings of masculinity also vary across cultures and admit to cultural borrowing; masculinities imported from elsewhere are conflated with local ideas to produce new configurations. (1994: 12)

The notion of masculinity as a composite of distinct qualities or attributes or a single definable essence is a myth that is perpetuated by scholars through their research and writing, particularly in their failure to acknowledge the history of, and particular significations attached to, the term masculinity. The specific historical and social constructions of masculinity cannot be dissociated from constructions of femininity and, like other terms such as male, men, female, and women, it is difficult to speak of masculinity without implying a binary notion of gender (Cornwall and Lindisfarne 1994: 11, cited in Threadgold 1990).

An enduring problem in research on gender, from any perspective, has been the tendency to focus on differences between women and men and to over-look extensive similarities between the sexes and even the extensive variation within each sex (Howard and Hollander 1997, 12). The reasons for this focus on difference are manifold, and include the enduring historical influence of post-Enlightenment theories of sexual complementarity, which postulate that the minds and bodies of men and women are quite different in ways that make them complementary; the pervasiveness of psychological theories of identity formation that tie the quest for self-identity to distinctions of gender (knowing who we are implies knowing who we are not); and the inclination of academic journals and mainstream publishers to focus on research findings of difference, which is seen as more newsworthy than research on similarities (Lloyd 1984; Howard and Hollander 1997: 12–13). Both research and writing reinforces "the essentialist belief that there are large, stable, innate differences between the sexes and encourages biological explanations for those few differences that are resilient" (Howard and Hollander 1997: 12).

Feminist historians and philosophers of science have drawn attention to the implicit dualistic thinking and biological determinism underlying the concept of gender. As Haraway (1991: 134) argued, the concept of gender was formulated within the so-called gender identity paradigm in the decades after World War II as part of broad liberal reformulation of the life and social sciences. However, this reformulation "failed to interrogate the political–social history of binary categories like nature/culture, and so sex/gender, in colonialist western discourse." While early second-wave feminists criticized the nature/culture dualism, argued Haraway, they hesitated to extend their criticism fully to the derivative sex/gender distinction. Biological determinism and dualistic thinking was carried over into feminist theorizing in the correspondence of sex with nature and gender with culture. The development of a second-wave feminist politics based on biological determinism versus social constructionism and the sex/gender distinction was prestructured by a discourse that was functionalist and essentialist in its orientation and took the field of biology as a given rather than as a discourse open to intervention. Within this discourse,

the world is posited as an object of knowledge in which the resources of nature are to be appropriated by culture. In their arguments against biological determinism and in favor of social constructionism, Haraway (1991: 134) maintained, feminists have failed to enquire into how bodies, including sexualized and racialized bodies, appear as objects of knowledge and sites of intervention in biology.

As queer theorists and many feminist scholars have argued, theories of gender rely on an implicit heterosexual dualism whereby males and females learn to become men and women through attaining opposite and distinct traits based on sex (e.g., see Ingraham 1996). It is taken as an unproblematic given that opposite sexes are naturally attracted to each other, much like other aspects of the physical world, for example, magnetic fields. A heterosexual bias can be seen most clearly in theories of socialization, whereby males and females are seen to become men and women attaining opposite and distinct traits based on sex. Many sociological discussions rely on an unstated heterosexual dualism which implies a static and normative understanding of gender. Moreover, few theorists explain the necessity of gender. The theory of gender as an achieved status never addresses the question of "to what ends gender is acquired" (Ingraham 1996: 185–86). As Ingraham [. . .] commented,

> Contemporary sex–gender ideology provides limited options for how we organise sexuality, but expanding these options is not simply a matter of attending to marginalized sexualities. Instead, it seems to me that we need to question our assumptions about sex and gender as to how they organize difference, regulate investigation, and preserve particular power relations, especially those linked to institutionalized heterosexuality. (1996: 184)

The assumed sex/gender binary of second-wave feminist theory has been undermined by recent historical and theoretical enquiries into the changing constructions or materializations of sexed bodies (e.g., Butler 1993; Laqueur 1990; Schiebinger 1986, 1993; Hood-Williams 1996, 1997). Thomas Laqueur's *Making Sex* (1990) was an especially influential source in debates in the 1990s. In this book, Laqueur describes a shift, around the time of the Enlightenment, from a one-sex model in which women were seen to have the same sex organs as men but on the inside of their bodies rather than the outside, to a two-sex model, in which there are seen to be fundamental differences between the male and female sexes, and thus between man and woman, in discoverable biological distinctions. Laqueur's fundamental point is that claims about sex always involve claims about gender and power (1990: 11). While in both the one-sex model and the two-sex model there is a hierarchy obtaining between men and women, in the one-sex model the differences between the sexes are of degree rather than of nature. Man is the yardstick of perfection, against which the female sex is measured. Before the emergence of the two-sex model, to be a man or a woman was above all a rank or cultural role, and not one form of being biologically different from the other (Badinter 1995: 6). However, during the Enlightenment, the body began to appear as real and cultural significations as epiphenomena, that is, "biology became the epistemological foundation for social prescriptions" (Badinter 1995: 7).

This interrogation of gender and sex/gender has far-reaching implications for how masculinity scholars think about the subject of their investigations. In many studies, sex has been taken as a pregiven, natural domain, unmediated by culture and history, while gender is seen as the concomitant cultural construction, practice, or enactment. Thus, the primary concern has been with such questions as—What is definitive of manhood (as a gendered state of being or practice)? How one becomes a man (as an acquisition of gender role and/or gender identity)? What are the personal implications of the crisis in male identity (loss of gender role and/or gender identity)? An assumed sex/gender or nature/culture dualism underpins much work in this area. It is taken as given that sex is the stable bedrock for the social constructions of gender and that there is a necessary correspondence between biological sex and social gender. An analysis of how differences in sex become seen as natural, and how these differences then become the foundation for definitions of gender, would seem to be critical to the task of denaturalizing the sex/gender dualism and its supportive relations of power.

Denaturalizing sex/gender undermines the heterosexist idea that there are two and only two complementary sexes/genders. It allows us to imagine other ways of having sex, organizing domestic life, and so forth, which construct gender differently, and potentially to put them into practice (VanEvery 1996: 52). Such critical deconstructive work is especially important with the recent rise of genetic reductionist explanations of difference in science and popular culture. Appeals to explanations of natural sex difference can be used to explain and legitimize social inequalities in work, domestic arrangements, health status, and so forth. For example, inequalities between men and women in types of occupational representation are sometimes explained in terms of natural sex differences in biological makeup or cognitive functioning (e.g., see Moir and Jessel 1991).

THE REASSESSMENT OF IDENTITY

The antiessentialist movement in the social sciences has also led to a reassessment of identity as an analytic category, which has profound implications for identity-based politics. As Epstein (1993/1994) noted, social science conceptions of identity—originally developed in the 1950s—lean toward either one of two oppositional views, one a psychological reductionism, the other a sociological reductionism. The first view treats identity as a relatively fixed and stable characteristic of the person. It reflects the notion that we can know who someone really is. The second conception treats identity as acquired, involving "the internalisation or conscious adoption of socially imposed or socially constructed labels or roles." According to the acquired definition, identity is not so deeply inscribed in the psyche of the individual, and so there is scope for transforming identity. It reflects the belief that the individual can voluntarily choose to identify as such-and-such (Epstein 1993/1994, 28–29).

Of course, these are ideal-type conceptions, and in the social sciences attempts have been made to mediate between these contending positions. For example, psychoanalytic explanations of identity posit a complex interaction between intrapsychic processes and social expectations. However, the above two basic conceptions have dominated thinking about identity up to the present and have influenced the development of so-called identity politics, whereby one bases one's politics on a sense of personal identity—as gay, Jewish, black, a male, a female, and so forth (Fuss 1989, 97). As Fuss argued, the tendency has been to assume that there is a causal relationship between identity and politics, with the former determining the latter. Thus, there is the expectation that individuals will claim or discover their true identity before they elaborate a personal politics. This is especially evident in the gay and lesbian literature, where there is a familiar tension between a view that identity is something that is always present (but has been repressed) and that which has never been socially permitted (but remains to be created or achieved). This has often led to the reduction of the political to the personal, and the limitation of political activity to self-discovery and personal transformation (Fuss 1989, 99–101). In feminist psychology, in particular, the dictum "the personal is political" has usually meant that the political is personalized, as can be seen in the use of the notions of empowerment, revolution from within, and the focus on validating women's reality (Kitzinger 1996).

Increasingly, identity is seen in the social sciences and humanities as a discursive construction—one that is arbitrary and exclusionary and acts as a normative ideal for regulating subjects. This is not to deny human agency and the possibility for the self to fashion itself. However, to view identity as fabricated disturbs the widely held assumption that identity is relatively stable and is made up of various fixed components, particularly gender, sexuality, race, and ethnicity, conceived as relatively independent aspects of one's being. As Edwards (1990) pointed out, there has been a tendency to treat sex and gender, and sexuality and gendered identity, as separate entities or aspects of identity. Moreover, race has been either totally neglected or viewed, like sex, as a natural category. The separation of these categories in research and writings reflects the dualism between nature and culture, referred to above, that has been part of Western thinking since the nineteenth century (Edwards 1990, 111). One of the legacies of this dualistic thinking is that, in writings about men and masculinities, masculine identity is often conceived as being simply a composite of various natural and socially constructed attributes. Thus, one is a

homosexual man, a black man, a white heterosexual man, an able-bodied young man, and so forth. The problem with the use of this additive model of identity is that no matter how exhaustive the description, there will always be exclusions and disjunctions between imposed identity labels and personal experiences. There is literally an infinite number of ways in which the components of identity can intersect or combine to make up masculine identity. There is an arbitrariness about any identity construction, which will inevitably entail the silencing or exclusion of some experiences. The critique of identity does not necessarily mean that one should disavow identity, but rather that one needs to be constantly aware of the fictitious character of identity and of the dangers of imposing an identity. On some occasions, there may be some strategic benefit in mobilizing around an identity, conceived as a fixed and unitary category, as when appeals to women are used to redress gender inequalities in health care (e.g., Broom 1991) and advance affirmative action goals (e.g., see Bacchi 1996: 163). However, recent theoretical work questions the notion that identities must always be secure so that one can do political work (Fuss 1989: 105).

Queer scholars, in particular, have raised questions about the dangers of essentializing sexual identity and the deployment of simple additive (and, by implication, exclusionary) models of identity. Writers such as Eve Sedgwick (1994), Diana Fuss (1989), and Judith Butler (1990) have drawn attention to the profound impact of the heterosexual/homosexual distinction on our thinking about categories and distinctions such as masculine/feminine, secrecy/disclosure, majority/minority, natural/artificial, domestic/foreign, health/illness, same/different, active passive, and in/out. As Sedgwick (1994: 41) explained, "There currently exists no framework in which to ask about the origins or development of individual gay identity that is not already structured by an implicit, trans-individual Western project or fantasy of eradicating that identity." The recent queer critique of sexual epistemology and of identity politics involves a reexamination of assumptions about the relationship between sexuality and identity, particularly the idea that people have a natural sexual orientation that is normally heterosexual. This work draws attention to the political and practical implications of the loosening of the connection between sexuality and identity. It leads one to question the meanings of gay-affirmative work as promoted by many scholars and activists. Discussions about masculine identity are generally prefigured by a discourse that takes as given the heterosexual/homosexual division and all that that implies; for example, the assumption that subjects have relatively fixed and mutually exclusive identities, the denial of the construction and fluidity of desire, and the marginalization of those who identify as neither gay nor heterosexual. As queer theorists have pointed out, political projects designed to liberate subjects, whether they be small-scale confessional or therapeutic practices or large-scale social movements, often amount to ways of fixing identities and shaping subjectivities through the knowledges that they generate. Recent work underlines the arbitrariness of the sexual classificatory system and the ways in which an appeal to nature may be used to regulate sexual identities by allowing corporeal distinctions to be drawn between the pure and the impure, the hygienic and the unhygienic, the healthy and the unhealthy, and so forth. As a consequence of this work, the notion of a natural sexual orientation is increasingly difficult to sustain.

SHIFTING THE RESEARCH FOCUS

Recent theoretical work emphasizes the importance of scrutinizing basic categories, concepts, and assumptions that guide research on men and masculinity. As Frank (1993) noted, insofar as masculinity studies fails to critically examine man-made explanations of the world, it offers no profound oppositional discourse. Although gender has become an object of enquiry, this tends to be conceived as yet another variable to be added to "the already long list of variables to be measured" while business continues as usual (Frank 1993: 336).

> Even with the awareness of the social construction of gender within patriarchal relations, there is still either the lack of recognition—or the purposeful avoidance—of any analysis of the historicity and the social construction of the actual theories and the methods themselves that produce knowledge.

> The power of these historical and social products (the theoretical stance and methodological procedures) produced within the patriarchal gaze used to gain an understanding of people's lives and the resulting consequences, are taken for granted, and thus temporalized and depoliticized. In-so-far as these disciplinary practices produce women, and some men, as subordinate, their methods of observation and inquiry and the resulting production of theory do little to reorganize the objectified "ways of knowing." (Frank 1993: 336–37)

One of the important contributions of recent theoretical and historical work has been to highlight the role of the social and natural sciences in the construction of knowledge of human subjects and in shaping people's awareness of themselves as subjects. Although in the broader culture there is a tendency to view natural and social knowledge as mutually exclusive, increasingly it has become clear that all knowledge, including biological knowledge, is socially produced and reflects prevailing assumptions about normal embodiment and subjectivity. Historical deconstruction has proved invaluable in demonstrating the historical variability of our ways of knowing and thus underlining the fact that things could be otherwise. It has been successfully employed by sexuality scholars and feminists in the past (e.g., Laqueur 1990; Lloyd 1984; Ehrenreich and English 1973, 1979; Oudshoorn 1994; Schiebinger 1989; Weeks 1985, 1990) and could be useful employed by masculinity scholars to investigate questions pertaining to the epistemology of masculinity. Some interesting work on the history of the constructions of masculinity and the male body has already been undertaken—for example, George Mosse's *The Image of Man* (1996), Joanna Bourke's *Dismembering the Male* (1996), Anthony Rotundo's *American Manhood* (1993), and Graham Dawson's *Soldier Heroes* (1994). Through such investigations, writers have demonstrated that what are taken to be the norms of masculinity and male embodiment are historically contingent, constantly in flux, and open to contestation. By disrupting our taken-for-granted assumptions about men and masculinity, historical deconstruction serves an important strategic function in allowing us to imagine alternative futures. For example, much of the above work emphasizes that aggressive or militaristic behavior need not be an integral and inevitable aspect of masculine identity. Further research is required to elaborate on the complex linkages between the power relations of gender, sexuality, race, and various constructions of masculine identity and the male body, and show how these constructions serve to exclude and oppress.

Recent work in the social sciences has drawn attention to the importance of the body as a site for investigations into gender, sexuality, and power. Under the influence of the ideas of Michel Foucault in particular, many writers have challenged the naturalistic view of the body, which has a fixed structure and immutable desires and behaviors. For example, the idea of a normal masculine heterosexual desire is questioned by recent Foucauldian-inspired social constructionism (see Katz 1995). Rather than seeing bodies as biologically given, or prediscursive, bodies have come to be seen as fabricated through discourse as an effect of power/knowledge (e.g., see Butler 1993). Masculinity scholars could take their cue from this work to reveal the ways in which the male body has been posited as both object and site for the exercise of power and to explore the implications of this for the subjectivities of men. It needs to be asked why some male bodies are invested with more visibility and power than others and how natural knowledge is deployed in the construction of differences between the sexes. As yet, there has been relatively little analysis of how different male bodies have been constructed in discourse and how differences between men and women, and between men, have come to be seen as natural differences. Feminist historians and philosophers of science and supportive male scholars have shown how the production of natural knowledge, for example, in the discipline of anatomy, has been shaped by social assumptions about male/ female difference (e.g., Giacomini, Rozée-Koker, and Pepitone-Arreola-Rockwell 1986; Lawrence and Bendixen 1992; Moore and Clarke 1995; Petersen 1998; Schiebinger 1986, 1989, 1993). This work underscores the necessity to challenge the representations of science and its constructions of masculinity and femininity. This analysis needs to be extended to the social sciences as well, including psychology and sociology, which are often underpinned by theories of natural difference (e.g., see Domenici and Lesser 1995; Petersen and Davies 1997; Seidman 1996). Scholars can usefully contribute to the task of exposing the diverse ways in which the sciences normalize differences by making those differences appear as inevitable by-products of nature, for example, by undertaking discourse analyses of scientific texts that focus on sex differences.

The recent resurgence of interest in biological, particularly genetic, explanations of human differences in science and the broader culture (e.g., see Nelkin and Lindee 1995; Petersen 1999) should prompt scholars to reflect on the context within which knowledge is produced and disseminated. Such theories have appeared with renewed vigor during a period in which there has been a conservative backlash against virtually all minority groups and against the gains made by feminists, gay and lesbian people, and peoples of non-European descent. They have been strategically employed by dominant groups to draw boundaries between Self and Other, justify rights, and deny rights. As Nelkin and Lindee argued (1995, 399), the findings of genetic research can be used by those who believe that education will make no difference in the social status of indigenous peoples, by those who would seek to change homosexual behavior through medical intervention, and by those who are opposed to equality in general. It needs to be asked why there has been a renewed interest in genetic explanations of human differences in popular culture and science, and how such work is used to argue for discriminatory policies and practices. Work such as that of Simon LeVay (1994) and Dean Hamer (Hamer & Copeland 1994) in the United States, which focus on the biological bases of male homosexuality, and of Moir and Jessel (1991) in the United Kingdom, which focuses on biological differences between men and women, has struck a resonant chord among a broad section of the population. There have been numerous efforts in the past to intervene into the bodies and lives of women on the assumption that their bodies are naturally inferior, and various forms of treatment have been meted out to homosexuals on the assumption that their condition is a result of a failure of some biological function (e.g., see Birke 1982;

Ehrenreich & English 1979; Minton 1996; Terry 1995). It is likely that studies of biological difference will continue to be used in these ways so long as science, and biological science in particular, remains unchallenged as the privileged arbiter of the truth on questions of difference. There needs to be greater sensitivity to the history of the deployments of natural knowledge for the control and/or annihilation of that which is deemed to be different and to the potential for such knowledge to be used to delineate boundaries between the normal (i.e., included) and the abnormal (i.e., excluded). If scholars are to usefully contribute to our understanding of the social structuring of gender-based power and inequality and of the mechanisms for social change, it is important that they remain reflexive in their social theorizing and aware of the implications of their adherence to particular ways of knowing.

REFERENCES

Bacchi, Carol L. 1996. *The Politics of Affirmative Action: "Women," Equality, and Category Politics*. London: Sage.

Badinter, Elizabeth. 1995. *XY: On Masculine Identity*. New York: Columbia University Press.

Barrett, Michèle and Anne Phillips, eds. 1992. *Destabilizing Theory: Contemporary Feminist Debates*. Cambridge, UK: Polity Press.

Best, Steven and Douglas Kellner. 1991. *Postmodern Theory: Critical Interrogations*. New York: Guilford.

Birke, Linda I. A. 1982. "From Sin to Sickness: Hormonal Theories of Lesbianism." In *Biological Woman—The Convenient Myth: A Collection of Feminist Essays and a Comprehensive Bibliography*, edited by R. Hubbard, M. S. Henifin, and B. Fried. Cambridge, MA: Schenkman.

Bourke, Joanna. 1996. *Dismembering the Male: Men's Bodies, Britain and the Great War*. London: Reaktion Books.

Brod, Harry. 1994. "Some Thoughts on Some Histories of Some Masculinities." In *Theorizing Masculinities*, edited by H. Brod and M. Kaufman. Thousand Oaks, CA: Sage.

Broom, Dorothy H. 1991. *Damned If We Do: Contradictions in Women's Health Care*. Sydney: Allen & Unwin.

Butler, Judith. 1990. *Gender Trouble: Feminism and the Subversion of Identity*. New York: Routledge.

Butler, Judith. 1993. *Bodies That Matter: On the Discursive Limits of "Sex."* New York: Routledge.

Coltrane, Scott. 1994. "Theorizing Masculinities in Contemporary Social Science." In *Theorizing Masculinities*, edited by H. Brod and M. Kaufman. Thousand Oaks, CA: Sage.

Connell, Raewyn. 1995. *Masculinities*. Berkeley: University of California Press.

Cornwall, Andrea and Nancy Lindisfarne, eds. 1994. *Dislocating Masculinity: Comparative Ethnographies*. London: Routledge.

Dawson, Graham. 1994. *Soldier Heroes: British Adventure, Empire and the Imagining of Masculinities*. London: Routledge.

Domenici, Thomas and Ronnie C. Lesser, eds. 1995. *Disorienting Sexuality: Psychoanalytic Reappraisals of Sexual Identities*. New York: Routledge.

Dyer, Richard. 1997. *White*. London: Routledge.

Edwards, Tim. 1990. "Beyond Sex and Gender: Masculinity, Homosexuality and Social Theory." In *Men, Masculinities and Social Theory*, edited by J. Hearn and D. Morgan. London: Unwin Hyman.

Ehrenreich, B., and D. English. 1973. *Witches, Midwives and Nurses: A History of Women Healers*. New York: Feminist Press.

Ehrenreich, Barbara and Deirdre English. 1979. *For Her Own Good: 150 Years of the Experts' Advice to Women*. New York: Anchor Books.

Epstein, Steven. 1993/1994. "Gay Politics, Ethnic Identity: The Limits of Social Constructionism." *Socialist Review* 17 (3/4): 9–54.

Foucault, Michel. 1980. *The History of Sexuality, Volume One: An Introduction*. New York: Vintage Books.

Frank, B. W. 1993. "The 'New Men's Studies' and Feminism: Promise or Danger?" In *Men and Masculinities: A Critical Anthology*, edited by T. Haddad. Toronto: Canadian Scholars Press.

Fuss, Diana. 1989. *Essentially Speaking: Feminism, Nature and Difference*. New York: Routledge.

Gatens, Moira. 1992. "Powers, Bodies and Difference." In *Destabilizing Theory: Contemporary Feminist Debates*, edited by M. Barrett and A. Phillips. Cambridge, UK: Polity Press.

Giacomini, M., P. Rozée-Koker, and F. Pepitone-Arreola-Rockwell. 1986. "Gender Bias in Human Anatomy Textbook Illustrations." *Psychology of Women Quarterly* 10: 413–20.

Grant, Judith. 1993. *Fundamental Feminism: Contesting the Core Concepts of Feminist Theory.* New York: Routledge.

Grosz, Elizabeth. 1995. *Space, Time and Perversion.* New York: Routledge.

Hamer, Dean and Peter Copeland. 1994. *The Science of Desire: The Search for the Gay Gene and the Biology of Behaviour.* New York: Simon & Schuster.

Haraway, Donna. 1991. *Simians, Cyborgs, and Women: The Reinvention of Nature.* New York: Routledge.

Hearn, Jeff and David L. Collinson. 1994. "Theorizing Unities and Differences between Men and between Masculinities." In *Theorizing Masculinities*, edited by H. Brod and M. Kaufman. Thousand Oaks, CA: Sage.

Hood-Williams, John. 1996. "Goodbye to Sex and Gender." *Sociological Review* 44 (1): 1–16.

Hood-Williams, John. 1997. "Real Sex/Fake Gender." *Sociological Review* 45 (1): 42–58.

Howard, Judith, and Jocelyn Hollander. 1997. *Gendered Situations, Gendered Selves: A Gender Lens on Social Psychology.* Thousand Oaks, CA: Sage.

Ingraham, Chrys. 1996. "The Heterosexual Imaginary: Feminist Sociology and Theories of Gender." In *Queer Theory/Sociology*, edited by S. Seidman. Cambridge, MA: Blackwell.

Jordan, Glenn and Chris Weedon. 1995. *Cultural Politics: Class, Gender, Race and the Postmodern World.* Oxford, UK: Blackwell.

Katz, Jonathan Ned. 1995. *The Invention of Heterosexuality.* New York: Penguin.

Kaufman, Michael. 1994. "Men, Feminism, and Men's Contradictory Experiences of Power." In *Theorizing Masculinities*, edited by H. Brod and M. Kaufman. Thousand Oaks, CA: Sage.

Kimmel, Michael S. 1994. "Masculinity as Homophobia: Fear, Shame, and Silence in the Construction of Gender Identity." In *Theorizing Masculinities*, edited by H. Brod and M. Kaufman. Thousand Oaks, CA: Sage.

Kitzinger, Celia. 1996. "Therapy and How It Undermines the Practice of Radical Feminism." In *Radically Speaking: Feminism Reclaimed*, edited by D. Bell and R. Klein. North Melbourne, Australia: Spinifex.

Laqueur, Thomas. 1990. *Making Sex: Body and Gender from the Greeks to Freud.* Cambridge, MA: Harvard University Press.

Lawrence, Susan C. and Kae Bendixen. 1992. "His and Hers: Male and Female Anatomy in Anatomy Texts for U.S. Medical Students, 1890–1989." *Social Science and Medicine* 35 (7): 925–34.

LeVay, Simon. 1994. *The Sexual Brain.* Cambridge, MA: The MIT Press.

Lloyd, Genevieve. 1984. *The Man of Reason: "Male" and "Female" in Western Philosophy.* London: Methuen.

MacInnes, John. 1998. *The End of Masculinity: The Confusion of Sexual Genesis and Sexual Difference in Modern Society.* Buckingham, UK: Open University Press.

Minton, Henry L. 1996. "Community Empowerment and the Medicalization of Homosexuality: Constructing Sexual Identities in the 1930s." *Journal of the History of Sexuality* 6 (3): 435–58.

Moir, Anne and David Jessel. 1991. *Brainsex: The Real Difference between Men and Women.* London: Mandarin.

Moore, Lisa Jean and Adele E. Clarke. 1995. "Clitoral Conventions and Transgressions: Graphic Representations in Anatomy Textbooks, c1900–1991." *Feminist Studies* 21 (2): 255–301.

Mosse, George L. 1996. *The Image of Man: The Creation of Modern Masculinity.* New York: Oxford University Press.

Nelkin, Dorothy and M. Susan Lindee. 1995. *The DNA Mystique: The Gene as Cultural Icon.* New York: Freeman.

Oudshoorn, Nelly. 1994. *Beyond the Natural Body: An Archeology of Sex Hormones.* London: Routledge.

Petersen, A. 1998. "Sexing the Body: Representations of Sex Differences in *Gray's Anatomy*, 1858 to the Present." *Body & Society* 4 (1): 1–15.

Petersen, Alan. 1999. "The Portrayal of Research into Genetic-Based Differences of Sex and Sexual Orientation: A Study of "Popular" Science Journals, 1980 to 1997." *Journal of Communication Inquiry* 23 (2): 163–82.

Petersen, Alan and Deirdre Davies. 1997. "Psychology and the Social Construction of Sex Differences in Theories of Aggression." *Journal of Gender Studies* 6 (3): 309–20.

Rich, Adrienne. 1986. *Blood, Bread and Poetry: Selected Prose, 1979–1985*. New York: Norton.

Rotundo, E. Anthony. 1993. *American Manhood: Transformations in Masculinity from the Revolution to the Modern Era*. New York: Basic Books.

Sayer, Andrew. 1997. "Essentialism, Social Constructionism, and Beyond." *Sociological Review* 45 (3): 453–87.

Schiebinger, Londa. 1986. "Skeletons in the Closet: The First Illustrations of the Female Skeleton in Eighteenth-Century Anatomy." *Representations* 14 (Spring): 42–83.

Schiebinger, Londa. 1989. *The Mind Has No Sex? Women in the Origins of Modern Science*. Cambridge, MA: Harvard University Press.

Schiebinger, Londa. 1993. *Nature's Body: Gender in the Making of Modern Science*. Boston: Beacon Press.

Sedgwick, Eve Kosofsky. 1994. *Epistemology of the Closet*. London: Penguin.

Seidman, Steven. 1996. "Introduction." In *Queer Theory/Sociology*, edited by S. Seidman. Cambridge, MA: Blackwell.

Terry, Jennifer. 1995. "Anxious Slippages between "Us" and "Them": A Brief History of the Sexual Search for Homosexual Bodies." In *Deviant Bodies: Critical Perspectives on Difference in Science and Popular Culture*, edited by J. Terry and J. Urla. Bloomington: Indiana University Press.

Threadgold, Terry. 1990. "Introduction." In *Feminine, Masculine and Representation*, edited by T. Threadgold and A. Cranny-Francis. London: Allen & Unwin.

VanEvery, Jo. 1996. "Heterosexuality and Domestic Life." In *Theorising Heterosexuality*, edited by D. Richardson. Buckingham, UK: Oxford University Press.

Weeks, Jeffrey. 1985. *Sexuality and Its Discontents*. London: Routledge.

Weeks, Jeffrey. 1990. *Coming Out: Homosexual Politics in Britain from the Nineteenth Century*, rev. ed. London: Quartet Books.

J. JACK HALBERSTAM

25. AN INTRODUCTION TO FEMALE MASCULINITY: MASCULINITY WITHOUT MEN

THE REAL THING

What is "masculinity"? This has been probably the most common question that I have faced over the past five years while writing on the topic of female masculinity. If masculinity is not the social and cultural and indeed political expression of maleness, than what is it? I do not claim to have any definitive answer to this question, but I do have a few proposals about why masculinity must not and cannot and should not reduce down to the male body and its effects. I also venture to assert that although we seem to have a difficult time defining masculinity, as a society we have little trouble in recognizing it, and indeed we spend massive amounts of time and money ratifying and supporting the versions of masculinity that we enjoy and trust; many of these "heroic masculinities" depend absolutely on the subordination of alternative masculinities. [. . .] [F]ar from being an imitation of maleness, female masculinity actually affords us a glimpse of how masculinity is constructed as masculinity. In other words, female masculinities are framed as the rejected scraps of dominant masculinity in order that male masculinity may appear to be the real thing. But what we understand as heroic masculinity has been produced by and across both male and female bodies.

This chapter does not simply offer a conventional theoretical introduction to the enterprise of conceptualizing masculinity without men; rather, it attempts to compile the myths and fantasies about masculinity that have ensured that masculinity and maleness are profoundly difficult to pry apart. [. . .] I detail the many ways in which female masculinity has been blatantly ignored both in the culture at large and within academic studies of masculinity. This widespread indifference to female masculinity, I suggest, has clearly ideological motivations and has sustained the complex social structures that wed masculinity to maleness and to power and domination. I firmly believe that a sustained examination of female masculinity can make crucial interventions within gender studies, cultural studies, queer studies, and mainstream discussions of gender in general.

Masculinity in this society inevitably conjures up notions of power and legitimacy and privilege; it often symbolically refers to the power of the state and to uneven distributions of wealth. Masculinity seems to extend outward into patriarchy and inward into the family; masculinity represents the power of inheritance, the consequences of the traffic in women, and the promise of social privilege. But, obviously, many other lines of identification traverse the terrain of masculinity, dividing its power into complicated differentials of class, race, sexuality, and gender. If what we call "dominant masculinity" appears to be a naturalized relation between maleness and power, then it makes little sense to examine men for the contours of that masculinity's social construction. Masculinity [. . .] becomes legible as masculinity where and when it leaves the white male middle-class body. Arguments about excessive masculinity tend to focus on black bodies (male and female), Latino/a bodies, or working-class bodies, and insufficient masculinity is all too often figured by Asian bodies or upper-class bodies; these stereotypical constructions of variable masculinity mark the process by which masculinity becomes dominant in the sphere of white middle-class maleness. But all too many studies that currently attempt to account for the power of white masculinity recenter this white male body by concentrating all their analytical efforts on detailing the forms and expressions of white male dominance. Numerous studies of Elvis, white male youth, white male feminism, men and marriage, and domestications of maleness amass information about a subject whom we know intimately and ad nauseam. [. . .]

[. . .] To illustrate my point that modern masculinity is most easily recognized as female masculinity, consider the James Bond action film, in which male masculinity very often appears as only a shadow of a more powerful and convincing alternative masculinity. In *Goldeneye* (1995), for example, Bond battles the usual array of bad guys: Commies, Nazis, mercenaries, and a superaggressive violent femme type. He puts on his usual performance of debonair action adventure hero, and he has his usual supply of gadgetry to aid him—a retractable belt, a bomb disguised as a pen, a laser weapon watch, and so on. But there's something curiously lacking in *Goldeneye*, namely, credible masculine power. Bond's boss, M, is a noticeably butch older woman who calls Bond a dinosaur and chastises him for being a misogynist and a sexist. His secretary, Miss Moneypenny, accuses him of sexual harassment, his male buddy betrays him and calls him a dupe, and ultimately women seem not to go for his charms—bad suits and lots of sexual innuendo—which seem as old and as ineffective as his gadgets.

Masculinity, in this rather actionless film, is primarily prosthetic and, in this and countless other action films, has little if anything to do with biological maleness and signifies more often as a technical special effect. In *Goldeneye* it is M who most convincingly performs masculinity, and she does so partly by exposing the sham of Bond's own performance. It is M who convinces us that sexism and misogyny are not necessarily part and parcel of masculinity, even though historically it has become difficult, if not impossible, to untangle masculinity from the oppression of women. The action adventure hero should embody an extreme version of normative masculinity, but instead we find that excessive masculinity

turns into a parody or exposure of the norm. Because masculinity tends to manifest as natural gender itself, the action flick, with its emphases on prosthetic extension, actually undermines the heterosexuality of the hero even as it extends his masculinity. So, in *Goldeneye*, for example, Bond's masculinity is linked not only to a profoundly unnatural form of masculine embodiment but also to gay masculinities. In the scene in which Bond goes to pick up his newest set of gadgets, a campy and almost queeny science nerd gives Bond his brand-new accessories and demonstrates each one with great enthusiasm. It is no accident that the science nerd is called Agent Q. We might read Agent Q as a perfect model of the interpenetration of queer and dominant regimes—Q is precisely an agent, a queer subject who exposes the workings of dominant heterosexual masculinity. The gay masculinity of Agent Q and the female masculinity of M provide a remarkable representation of the absolute dependence of dominant masculinities on minority masculinities.

When you take his toys away, Bond has very little propping up his performance of masculinity. Without the slick suit, the half smile, the cigarette lighter that transforms into a laser gun, our James is a hero without the action or the adventure. The masculinity of the white male, what we might call "epic masculinity," depends absolutely, as any Bond flick demonstrates, on a vast subterranean network of secret government groups, well-funded scientists, the army, and an endless supply of both beautiful bad babes and beautiful good babes, and finally it relies heavily on an immediately recognizable "bad guy." The "bad guy" is a standard generic feature of epic masculinity narratives: think only of Paradise Lost and its eschatological separation between God and Devil; Satan, if you like, is the original bad guy. Which is not to say that the bad guy's masculinity bars him from the rewards of male privilege—on the contrary, bad guys may also look like winners, but they just tend to die more quickly. Indeed, there is currently a line of clothing called Bad Boy that revels in the particular power of the bad guy and reveals how quickly transgression adds up to nothing more than consumerism in the sphere of the white male. Another line of clothing that indulges in the consumer potential of male rebellion is No Fear gear. This label features advertisements with skydiving, surfing, car-racing men who show their manliness by wearing the No Fear logo and practicing death-defying stunts in their leisure time. To test how domesticated this label actually is, we have only to imagine what No Fear might mean for women. It might mean learning how to shoot a gun or working out or taking up a martial art, but it would hardly translate into skydiving. Obviously, then, No Fear is a luxury and can in no way be equated with any form of social rebellion.

There is also a long literary and cinematic history that celebrates the rebellion of the male. If James Stewart, Gregory Peck, and Fred Astaire represent a few faces of good-guy appeal, James Dean, Marlon Brando, and Robert De Niro represent the bad-guy appeal, and really it becomes quite hard to separate one group from the other. Obviously, bad-boy representations in the 1950s captured something of a white working-class rebellion against middle-class society and against particular forms of domestication, but today's rebel without a cause is tomorrow's investment banker, and male rebellion tends toward respectability as the rewards for conformity quickly come to outweigh the rewards for social rebellion. To paraphrase Gertrude Stein, what's the point of being a rebel boy if you are going to grow up to be a man? Obviously, where and when rebellion ceases to be white middle-class male rebellion (individualized and localized within the lone male or even generalized into the boy gang) and becomes class rebellion or race rebellion, a very different threat emerges.

TOMBOYS

What happens when boy rebellion is located not in the testosterone-induced pout of the hooligan but in the sneer of the tomboy? If we are to believe general accounts of childhood behavior, tomboyism is quite common for girls and does not generally give rise to parental fears. Because comparable cross-identification behaviors in boys do often give rise to quite hysterical responses, we tend to believe that female gender deviance is much more tolerated than male gender deviance.[1] I am not sure that tolerance in such matters can be measured or at any rate that responses to childhood gender behaviors necessarily

tell us anything concrete about the permitted parameters of adult male and female gender deviance. Tomboyism tends to be associated with a "natural" desire for the greater freedoms and mobilities enjoyed by boys. Very often it is read as a sign of independence and self-motivation, and tomboyism may even be encouraged to the extent that it remains comfortably linked to a stable sense of a girl identity. Tomboyism is punished, however, when it appears to be the sign of extreme male identification (taking a boy's name or refusing girl clothing of any type) and when it threatens to extend beyond childhood and into adolescence.[2] Teenage tomboyism presents a problem and tends to be subject to the most severe efforts to reorient. We could say that tomboyism is tolerated as long as the child remains prepubescent; as soon as puberty begins, however, the full force of gender conformity descends on the girl. Gender conformity is pressed onto all girls, not just tomboys, and this is where it becomes hard to uphold the notion that male femininity presents a greater threat to social and familial stability than female masculinity. Female adolescence represents the crisis of coming of age as a girl in a male-dominated society. If adolescence for boys represents a rite of passage (much celebrated in Western literature in the form of the bildungsroman), and an ascension to some version (however attenuated) of social power, for girls, adolescence is a lesson in restraint, punishment, and repression. It is in the context of female adolescence that the tomboy instincts of millions of girls are remodeled into compliant forms of femininity. [. . .]

CONSTRUCTING MASCULINITIES

Within cultural studies itself, masculinity has recently become a favorite topic. I want to try here to account for the growing popularity of a body of work on masculinity that evinces absolutely no interest in masculinity without men. I first noticed the unprecedented interest in masculinity in April 1994 when the DIA Center for the Performing Arts convened a group of important intellectuals to hold forth on the topic of masculinities. On the opening night of this event, one commentator wondered, "Why masculinity, why now?" Several others, male critics and scholars, gave eloquent papers about their memories of being young boys and about their relationships with their fathers. The one lesbian on the panel, a poet, read a moving poem about rape. At the end of the evening, only one panelist had commented on the limitations of a discussion of masculinity that interpreted "masculinity" as a synonym for men or maleness.[3] This lonely intervention highlighted the gap between mainstream discussions of masculinity and men and ongoing queer discussions about masculinity, which extend far beyond the male body. Indeed, in answer to the naive question that began the evening, "Why masculinities, why now?" one might state: Because masculinity in the 1990s has finally been recognized as, at least in part, a construction by female- as well as male-born people.[4]

The anthology that the conference produced provides more evidence of the thoroughgoing association that the editors have made between masculinity and maleness. The title page features a small photographic illustration of a store sign advertising clothing as "Fixings for Men." This illustration has been placed just below the title, *Constructing Masculinity*, and forces the reader to understand the construction of masculinity as the outfitting of males within culture. The introduction to the volume attempts to diversify this definition of masculinity by using Judith Butler's and Eve Sedgwick's contributions to suggest that the anthology recognizes the challenges made by gays, lesbians, and queers to the terms of gender normativity. The editors insist that masculinity is multiple and that "far from just being about men, the idea of masculinity engages, inflects, and shapes everyone" [Berger, Wallis, and Watson 1996: 7]. The commitment to the representation of masculinity as multiple is certainly borne out in the first essay in the volume, by Eve Sedgwick, in which she proposes that masculinity may have little to do with men, and is somewhat extended by Butler's essay "Melancholy Gender." But Sedgwick also critiques the editors for having proposed a book and a conference on masculinity that remain committed to linking masculinity to maleness. Although the introduction suggests that the editors have heeded Sedgwick's call for gender diversity, the rest of the volume suggests otherwise. There are many fascinating essays in this anthology, but there are no essays specifically on female

masculinity. Although gender-queer images by Loren Cameron and Cathy Opie (1996) adorn the pages of the book, the text contains no discussions of these images. The book circles around discussions of male icons such as Clint Eastwood and Steven Seagal; it addresses the complex relations between fathers and sons; it examines topics such as how science defines men and masculinity and the law. The volume concludes with an essay by Stanley Aronowitz titled "My Masculinity," an autobiographically inflected consideration of various forms of male power.

None of my analysis here is to say that this is an uninteresting anthology or that the essays are somehow wrong or misguided, but I am trying to point out that the editorial statement at the beginning of the volume is less a prologue to what follows and more of an epilogue that describes what a volume on masculinity should do as opposed to what the anthology does do. Even when the need for an analysis of female masculinity has been acknowledged, in other words, it seems remarkably difficult to follow through on. What is it then that, to paraphrase Eve Sedgwick's essay, makes it so difficult not to presume an essential relation between masculinity and men?

By beginning with this examination of the Constructing Masculinity conference and anthology, I do not want to give the impression that the topic of female masculinities must always be related to some larger topic, some more general set of masculinities that has been, and continues to be, about men. Nor do I want to suggest that gender theory is the true origin of gender knowledge. Rather, this conference and book merely emphasize the lag between community knowledges and practices and academic discourses [Berger, et al. 1996]. I believe it is both helpful and important to contextualize a discussion of female and lesbian masculinities in direct opposition to a more generalized discussion of masculinity within cultural studies that seems intent on insisting that masculinity remain the property of male bodies. The continued refusal in Western society to admit ambiguously gendered bodies into functional social relations (evidenced, for example, by our continued use of either/or bathrooms, either women or men) is, I will claim, sustained by a conservative and protectionist attitude by men in general toward masculinity. Such an attitude has been bolstered by a more general disbelief in female masculinity. I can only describe such disbelief in terms of a failure in a collective imagination: in other words, female-born people have been making convincing and powerful assaults on the coherence of male masculinity for well over a hundred years; what prevents these assaults from taking hold and accomplishing the diminution of the bonds between masculinity and men? Somehow, despite multiple images of strong women (such as body-builder Bev Francis or tennis player Martina Navratilova), of cross-identifying women (Radclyffe Hall or Ethel Smyth), of masculine-coded public figures (Janet Reno), of butch superstars (k. d. lang), of muscular and athletic women (Jackie JoynerKersee), of female-born transgendered people (Leslie Feinberg), there is still no general acceptance or even recognition of masculine women and boyish girls. This book addresses itself to this collective failure to imagine and ratify the masculinity produced by, for, and within women.

In case my concerns about the current discussions of masculinity in cultural studies sound too dismissive, I want to look in an extended way at what happens when academic discussions of male masculinity take place to the exclusion of discussions of more wide-ranging masculinities. While it may seem that I am giving an inordinate amount of attention to what is after all just one intervention into current discussions, I am using one book as representative of a whole slew of other studies of masculinity that replicate the intentions and the mistakes of this one. In an anthology called *Boys: Masculinities in Contemporary Culture*, [. . .] [Paul] Smith suggests that masculinity must always be thought of "in the plural" as masculinities "defined and cut through by differences and contradictions of all sorts" [1996: 3]. The plurality of masculinities for Smith encompasses a dominant white masculinity that is crisscrossed by its others, gay, bisexual, black, Asian, and Latino masculinities. Although the recognition of a host of masculinities makes sense, Smith chooses to focus on dominant white masculinity to the exclusion of the other masculinities he has listed. Smith, predictably, warns the reader not to fall into the trap of simply critiquing

dominant masculinity or simply celebrating minority masculinities, and then he makes the following foundational statement:

> And it may well be the case, as some influential voices often tell us, that masculinity or masculinities are in some real sense not the exclusive "property" of biologically male subjects—it's true that many female subjects lay claim to masculinity as their property. Yet in terms of cultural and political power, it still makes a difference when masculinity coincides with biological maleness. (1996: 4)

What is immediately noticeable to me here is the odd attribution of immense power to those "influential voices" who keep telling us that masculinity is not the property of men. There is no naming of these influential voices, and we are left supposing that "influence" has rendered the "female masculinity theorists" so powerful that names are irrelevant: these voices, one might suppose, are hegemonic. Smith goes on to plead with the reader, asking us to admit that the intersection of maleness and masculinity does "still" make a difference. His appeal here to common sense allows him to sound as if he is trying to reassert some kind of rationality to a debate that is spinning off into totally inconsequential discussions. Smith is really arguing that we must turn to dominant masculinity to begin deconstructing masculinity because it is the equation of maleness plus masculinity that adds up to social legitimacy. As I argued earlier in this chapter, however, precisely because white male masculinity has obscured all other masculinities, we have to turn away from its construction to bring other more mobile forms of masculinity to light. Smith's purpose in his reassertion of the difference that male masculinity makes is to uncover the "cultural and political *power*" of this union in order to direct our attention to the power of patriarchy. The second part of the paragraph makes this all too clear:

> Biological men—male-sexed beings—are after all, in varying degrees, the bearers of privilege and power within the systems against which women still struggle. The privilege and power are, of course, different for different men, endlessly diversified through the markers of class, nation, race, sexual preference and so on. But I'd deny that there are any

men who are entirely outside of the ambit, let's say, of power and privilege in relation to women. In that sense it has to be useful to our thinking to recall that masculinities are not only a function of dominant notions of masculinity and not constituted solely in resistant notions of "other" masculinities. In fact, masculinities exist inevitably in relation to what feminisms have construed as the system of patriarchy and patriarchal relations. [Smith 1996: 4–5]

The most noticeable feature of this paragraph is the remarkable stability of the terms "women" and "men." Smith advances here a slightly old-fashioned feminism that understands women as endlessly victimized within systems of male power. Woman, within such a model, is the name for those subjects within patriarchy who have no access to male power and who are regulated and confined by patriarchal structures. [. . .] Smith, in other words, cannot take female masculinity into account because he sees it as inconsequential and secondary to much more important questions about male privilege. Again, this sounds more like a plaintive assertion that men *do* still access male power within patriarchy (don't they?), and it conveniently ignores the ways in which gender relations are scrambled where and when gender variance comes into play.

[. . .] Because I have criticized Smith for his apparent lack of investment in the project of producing alternative masculinities, let me take a moment to make my own investments clear. Although I make my own masculinity the topic of my last chapter, it seems important to state this book is an attempt to make my own female masculinity plausible, credible, and real. For a large part of my life, I have been stigmatized by a masculinity that marked me as ambiguous and illegible. Like many other tomboys, I was mistaken for a boy throughout my childhood, and like many other tomboy adolescents, I was forced into some semblance of femininity for my teenage years. When gender-ambiguous children are constantly challenged about their gender identity, the chain of misrecognitions can actually produce a new recognition: in other words, to be constantly mistaken for a boy, for many tomboys, can contribute to the production of a masculine identity. It was not until my midtwenties that I finally found a word for my particular gender configuration: butch. [. . .]

THE BATHROOM PROBLEM

If three decades of feminist theorizing about gender has thoroughly dislodged the notion that anatomy is destiny, that gender is natural, and that male and female are the only options, why do we still operate in a world that assumes that people who are not male are female, and people who are not female are male (and even that people who are not male are not people!)? If gender has been so thoroughly defamiliarized, in other words, why do we not have multiple gender options, multiple gender categories, and real-life nonmale and nonfemale options for embodiment and identification? In a way, gender's very flexibility and seeming fluidity is precisely what allows dimorphic gender to hold sway. Because so few people actually match any given community standards for male or female, in other words, gender can be imprecise and therefore multiply relayed through a solidly binary system. At the same time, because the definitional boundaries of male and female are so elastic, there are very few people in any given public space who are completely unreadable in terms of their gender.

Ambiguous gender, when and where it does appear, is inevitably transformed to deviance, thirdness, or a blurred version of either male or female. As an example, in public bathrooms for women, various bathroom users tend to fail to measure up to expectations of femininity, and those of us who present in some ambiguous way are routinely questioned and challenged about our presence in the "wrong" bathroom. For example, recently, on my way to give a talk in Minneapolis, I was making a connection at Chicago's O'Hare airport. I strode purposefully into the women's bathroom. No sooner had I entered the stall than someone was knocking at the door: "Open up, security here!" I understood immediately what had happened. I had, once again, been mistaken for a man or a boy, and some woman had called security. As soon as I spoke, the two guards at the bathroom stall realized their error, mumbled apologies, and took off. On the way home from the same trip, in the Denver airport, the same sequence of events was repeated. Needless to say, the policing of gender within the bathroom is intensified in the space of the airport, where people are literally moving through space and time in ways that cause them to want to stabilize some boundaries (gender) even as they traverse others (national). However, having one's gender challenged in the women's rest room is a frequent occurrence in the lives of many androgynous or masculine women; indeed, is so frequent that one wonders whether the category "woman," when used to designate public functions, is completed outmoded.[5]

It is no accident, then, that travel hubs become zones of intense scrutiny and observation. But gender policing within airport bathrooms is merely an intensified version of a larger "bathroom problem." For some gender-ambiguous women, it is relatively easy to "prove" their right to use the women's bathroom—they can reveal some decisive gender trait (a high voice, breasts), and the challenger will generally back off. For others (possibly low-voiced or hairy or breastless people), it is quite difficult to justify their presence in the women's bathroom, and these people may tend to use the men's bathroom, where scrutiny is far less intense. Obviously, in these bathroom confrontations, the gender-ambiguous person first appears as not-woman ("You are in the wrong bathroom!"), but then the person appears as something actually even more scary, not-man ("No, I am not," spoken in a voice recognized as not-male). Not-man and not-woman, the gender-ambiguous bathroom user is also not androgynous or in-between; this person is gender deviant.

For many gender deviants, the notion of passing is singularly unhelpful. Passing as a narrative assumes that there is a self that masquerades as another kind of self and does so successfully; at various moments, the successful pass may cohere into something akin to identity. At such a moment, the passer has *become*. What of a biological female who presents as butch, passes as male in some circumstances and reads as butch in others, and considers herself not to be a woman but maintains distance from the category "man"? For such a subject, identity might best be described as process with multiple sites for becoming and being. To understand such a process, we would need to do more than map psychic and physical journeys between male and female and within queer and straight space; we would need, in fact, to think in fractal terms and about gender geometries. Furthermore,

when and where we discuss the sexualities at stake in certain gender definitions, very different identifications between sexuality, gender, and the body emerge. The stone butch, for example, in her self-definition as a nonfeminine, sexually untouchable female, complicates the idea that lesbians share female sexual practices or women share female sexual desires or even that masculine women share a sense of what animates their particular masculinities.

I want to focus on what I am calling "the bathroom problem" because I believe it illustrates in remarkably clear ways the flourishing existence of gender binarism despite rumors of its demise. Furthermore, many normatively gendered women have no idea that a bathroom problem even exists and claim to be completely ignorant about the trials and tribulations that face the butch woman who needs to use a public bathroom. But queer literature is littered with references to the bathroom problem, and it would not be an exaggeration to call it a standard feature of the butch narrative. [. . .]

If we use the paradigm of the bathroom as a limit of gender identification, we can measure the distance between binary gender schema and lived multiple gendered experiences. The accusation "you're in the wrong bathroom" really says two different things. First, it announces that your gender seems at odds with your sex (your apparent masculinity or androgyny is at odds with your supposed femaleness); second, it suggests that single-gender bathrooms are only for those who fit clearly into one category (male) or the other (female). Either we need open-access bathrooms or multigendered bathrooms, or we need wider parameters for gender identification. The bathroom, as we know it, actually represents the crumbling edifice of gender in the twentieth century. The frequency with which gender-deviant "women" are mistaken for men in public bathrooms suggests that a large number of feminine women spend a large amount of time and energy policing masculine women. Something very different happens, of course, in the men's public toilet, where the space is more likely to become a sexual cruising zone than a site for gender repression. Lee Edelman [. . .] argues that "the institutional men's room constitutes a site at which the zones of public and private cross with a distinctive psychic charge."

[Edelman 1994: 158] The men's room, in other words, constitutes both an architecture of surveillance and an incitement to desire, a space of homosocial interaction and of homoerotic interaction.

So, whereas men's rest rooms tend to operate as a highly charged sexual space in which sexual interactions are both encouraged and punished, women's rest rooms tend to operate as an arena for the enforcement of gender conformity. Sex-segregated bathrooms continue to be necessary to protect women from male predations but also produce and extend a rather outdated notion of a public–private split between male and female society. The bathroom is a domestic space beyond the home that comes to represent domestic order, or a parody of it, out in the world. The women's bathroom accordingly becomes a sanctuary of enhanced femininity, a "little girl's room" to which one retreats to powder one's nose or fix one's hair. The men's bathroom signifies as the extension of the public nature of masculinity—it is precisely not domestic even though the names given to the sexual function of the bathroom—such as cottage or tearoom—suggest it is a parody of the domestic. The codes that dominate within the women's bathroom are primarily gender codes; in the men's room, they are sexual codes. Public sex versus private gender, openly sexual versus discreetly repressive, bathrooms beyond the home take on the proportions of a gender factory.

Marjorie Garber (1992) comments on the liminality of the bathroom in *Vested Interests* in a chapter on the perils and privileges of cross-dressing. She discusses the very different modes of passing and cross-dressing for cross-identified genetic males and females, and she observes that the restroom is a "potential waterloo" [1992: 47] for both female-to-male (FTM) and male-to-female (MTF) cross-dressers and transsexuals.[6] For the FTM, the men's room represents the most severe test of his ability to pass, and advice frequently circulates within FTM communities about how to go unnoticed in male-only spaces. Garber notes: "The cultural paranoia of being caught in the ultimately wrong place, which may be inseparable from the pleasure of 'passing' in that same place, depends in part on the same cultural binarism, the idea that gender categories are sufficiently uncomplicated to permit

self-assortment into one of the two 'rooms' without deconstructive reading" (1992: 47). It is worth pointing out here (if only because Garber does not) that the perils for passing FTMs in the men's room are very different from the perils of passing MTFs in the women's room. On the one hand, the FTM in the men's room is likely to be less scrutinized because men are not quite as vigilant about intruders as women for obvious reasons. On the other hand, if caught, the FTM may face some version of gender panic from the man who discovers him, and it is quite reasonable to expect and fear violence in the wake of such a discovery. The MTF, by comparison, will be more scrutinized in the women's room but possibly less open to punishment if caught. Because the FTM ventures into male territory with the potential threat of violence hanging over his head, it is crucial to recognize that the bathroom problem is much more than a glitch in the machinery of gender segregation and is better described in terms of the violent enforcement of our current gender system.

Garber's reading of the perilous use of rest rooms by both FTMs and MTFs develops out of her introductory discussion of what Lacan calls "urinary segregation." Lacan used the term to describe the relations between identities and signifiers, and he ultimately used the simple diagram of the rest room signs "Ladies" and "Gentlemen" to show that within the production of sexual difference, primacy is granted to the signifier over that which it signifies; in more simple terms, naming confers, rather than reflects, meaning. In the same way, the system of urinary segregation creates the very functionality of the categories "men" and "women." Although restroom signs seem to serve and ratify distinctions that already exist, in actual fact these markers produce identifications within these constructed categories. Garber latches on to the notion of "urinary segregation" because it helps her to describe the processes of cultural binarism within the production of gender; for Garber, transvestites and transsexuals challenge this system by resisting the literal translation of the signs "Ladies" and "Gentlemen." Garber uses the figures of the transvestite and the transsexual to show the obvious flaws and gaps in a binary gender system; the transvestite, as interloper, creates a third space of possibility within which all binaries become unstable. Unfortunately, as in all attempts to break a binary by producing a third term, Garber's third space tends to stabilize the other two. [. . .]

[. . .] [F]ocusing exclusively on the drama of the men's room avoids the much more complicated theater of the women's room. Garber writes of urinary segregation: "For transvestites and transsexuals, the 'men's room' problem is really a challenge to the way in which such cultural binarism is read" (1992: 14). She goes on to list some cinematic examples of the perils of urinary segregation and discusses scenes from *Tootsie* (1982), *Cabaret* (1972), and the *Female Impersonator Pageant* (1975). Garber's examples are odd illustrations of what she calls "the men's room problem" if only because at least one of her examples (*Tootsie*) demonstrates gender policing in the women's room. Also, Garber makes it sound as if vigorous gender policing happens in the men's room while the women's room is more of a benign zone for gender enforcement. She notes: "In fact, the urinal has appeared in a number of fairly recent films as a marker of the ultimate 'difference'—or studied indifference" (1992: 14). Obviously, Garber is drawing a parallel here between the conventions of gender attribution within which the penis marks the "ultimate difference"; however, by not moving beyond this remarkably predictable description of gender differentiation, Garber overlooks the main distinction between gender policing in the men's room and in the women's room. Namely, in the women's room, it is not only the MTF but all gender-ambiguous females who are scrutinized, whereas in the men's room, biological men are rarely deemed out of place. Garber's insistence that there is "a third space of possibility" occupied by the transvestite has closed down the possibility that there may be a fourth, fifth, sixth, or one hundredth space beyond the binary. The "women's room problem" (as opposed to the "men's room problem") indicates a multiplicity of gender displays even within the supposedly stable category of "woman."

So what gender are the hundreds of female-born people who are consistently not read as female in the women's room? And because so many women clearly fail the women's room test, why have we not begun to count and name the genders that are clearly emerging at this time? One could answer this question in two ways: On the one hand, we do not name and notice new genders because as a society we are committed to maintaining a binary gender system. On the other hand, we could also say that the failure of "male" and "female" to exhaust the field of gender variation actually ensures the continued dominance of these terms. Precisely because virtually nobody fits the definitions of male and female, the categories gain power and currency from their impossibility. In other words, the very flexibility and elasticity of the terms "man" and "woman" ensures their longevity. To test this proposition, look around any public space and notice how few people present formulaic versions of gender and yet how few are unreadable or totally ambiguous. The "It's Pat" character on a *Saturday Night Live* skit dramatized the ways in which people insist on attributing gender in terms of male or female on even the most undecidable characters. The "It's Pat" character produced laughs by consistently sidestepping gender fixity—Pat's partner had a neutral name, and everything Pat did or said was designed to be read either way. Of course, the enigma that Pat represented could have been solved very easily; Pat's coworkers could simply have asked Pat what gender s/he was or preferred. This project on female masculinity is designed to produce more than two answers to that question and even argue for a concept of "gender preference" as opposed to compulsory gender binarism. The human potential for incredibly precise classifications has been demonstrated in multiple arenas; why then do we settle for a paucity of classifications when it comes to gender? A system of gender preferences would allow for gender neutrality until such a time when the child or young adult announces his or her or its gender. Even if we could not let go of a binary gender system, there are still ways to make gender optional—people could come out as a gender in the way they come out as a sexuality. The point here is that there are many ways to depathologize gender variance and to account for the multiple genders that we already produce and sustain. Finally, as I suggested in relation to Garber's arguments about transvestism, "thirdness" merely balances the binary system and, furthermore, tends to homogenize many different gender variations under the banner of "other."

It is remarkably easy in this society not to look like a woman. It is relatively difficult, by comparison, not to look like a man: the threats faced by men who do not gender conform are somewhat different than for women. Unless men are consciously trying to look like women, men are less likely than women to fail to pass in the rest room. So one question posed by the bathroom problem asks, what makes femininity so approximate and masculinity so precise? Or to pose the question with a different spin, why is femininity easily impersonated or performed while masculinity seems resilient to imitation? Of course, this formulation does not easily hold and indeed quickly collapses into the exact opposite: why is it, in the case of the masculine woman in the bathroom, for example, that one finds the limits of femininity so quickly, whereas the limits of masculinity in the men's room seem fairly expansive?

We might tackle these questions by thinking about the effects, social and cultural, of reversed gender typing. In other words, what are the implications of male femininity and female masculinity? One might imagine that even a hint of femininity sullies or lowers the social value of maleness while all masculine forms of femaleness should result in an elevation of status.[7] My bathroom example alone proves that this is far from true. Furthermore, if we think of popular examples of approved female masculinity like a buffed Linda Hamilton in *Terminator 2* (1991) or a lean and mean Sigourney Weaver in *Aliens*, it is not hard to see that what renders these performances of female masculinity quite tame is their resolute heterosexuality. Indeed, in *Alien Resurrection* (1997), Sigourney Weaver combines her hard body with some light flirtation with co-star Winona Ryder and her masculinity immediately becomes far more threatening and indeed "alien." In other words, when and where female masculinity conjoins with possibly queer identities, it is far less likely to meet with approval. Because female masculinity seems to be at its most threatening when coupled with lesbian desire, in this book I concentrate on queer female masculinity almost to the exclusion of heterosexual female masculinity. I have no doubt that heterosexual female masculinity menaces gender conformity in its own way, but all too often it represents an acceptable degree of female masculinity as compared to the excessive masculinity of the dyke. It is important when thinking about gender variations such as male femininity and female masculinity not simply to create another binary in which masculinity always signifies power; in alternative models of gender variation, female masculinity is not simply the opposite of female femininity, nor is it a female version of male masculinity. Rather, as we shall see in some of the artwork and gender performances to follow, very often the unholy union of femaleness and masculinity can produce wildly unpredictable results.

[. . .] Gender policing in public bathrooms [. . .] and gender performances within public spaces produce radically reconfigured notions of proper gender and map new genders onto a utopian vision of radically different bodies and sexualities. By arguing for gender transitivity, for self-conscious forms of female masculinity, for indifference to dominant male masculinities, and for "nonce taxonomies," I do not wish to suggest that we can magically wish into being a new set of properly descriptive genders that would bear down on the outmoded categories "male" and "female." Nor do I mean to suggest that change is simple and that, for example, by simply creating the desegregation of public toilets we will change the function of dominant genders within heteropatriarchal cultures. However, it seems to me that there are some very obvious spaces in which gender difference simply does not work right now, and the breakdown of gender as a signifying system in these arenas can be exploited to hasten the proliferation of alternate gender regimes in other locations. From drag kings to spies with gadgets, from butch bodies to FTM bodies, gender and sexuality and their technologies are already excessively strange. It is simply a matter of keeping them that way.

REFERENCES

Berger, Maurice, Brian Wallis, and Simon Watson, eds. 1996. *Constructing Masculinity*. New York and London: Routledge.

Bordo, Susan. 1993. "Reading the Male Body." *Michigan Quarterly Review* 32 (4): 696.

Burke, Phyllis. 1996. *Gender Shock: Exploding the Myths of Male and Female*. New York: Anchor Books.

Edelman, Lee. 1994. "Tearooms and Sympathy, or the Epistemology of the Water Closet." In *Homographesis: Essays in Gay Literary and Cultural Theory.* New York: Routledge.

Garber, Marjorie. 1992. *Vested Interests: Cross-Dressing and Cultural Anxiety.* New York: Routledge.

Opie, Catherine. "Catherine Opie with Russell Ferguson," interview by Russell Ferguson, *Index* (April 1996): 29.

Smith, Paul, ed. 1996. *Boys: Masculinities in Contemporary Culture.* Boulder, CO: Westview Press.

NOTES

1. For an extension of this discussion of tomboys see my article "Oh Bondage up Yours: Female Masculinity and the Tomboy," in *Sissies and Tomboys: A CLAGS Reader* (New York: New York University Press, [1996]).

2. For more on the punishment of tomboys see Phyllis Burke, *Gender Shock: Exploding the Myths of Male and Female* (New York: Anchor Books, 1996). [. . .]

3. The conference papers were collected in a volume called *Constructing Masculinity*, ed. Maurice Berger, Brian Wallis, and Simon Watson (New York: Routledge, 1996), and the one intervention on behalf of nonmale masculinities was made by Eve Kosofsky Sedgwick [Reading 26 in this edited volume].

4. I am using the terms "female born" and "male born" to indicate a social practice of assigning one of two genders to babies at birth. My terminology suggests that these assignations may not hold for the lifetime of the individual, and it suggests from the outset that binary gender continues to dominate our cultural and scientific notions of gender but that individuals inevitably fail to find themselves in only one of two options.

5. The continued viability of the category "woman" has been challenged in a variety of academic locations already: Monique Wittig, most notably, argued that "lesbians are not women" in her essay "The Straight Mind," 121. Wittig claims that because lesbians are refusing primary relations to men, they cannot occupy the position "woman." In another philosophical challenge to the category "woman," transgender philosopher Jacob Hale uses Monique Wittig's radical claim to theorize the possibility of gendered embodiments that exceed male and female (see Jacob Hale, "Are Lesbians Women?" *Hypatia* II, no. 2 [Spring 1996]). Elsewhere, Cheshire Calhoun suggests that the category "woman" may actually "operate as a lesbian closet" (see Cheshire Calhoun, "The Gender Closet: Lesbian Disappearance under the sign 'Women,'" *Feminist Studies* 21, no. I [Spring 1995]: 7–34).

6. Obviously Garber's use of the term "waterloo" makes a pun out of the drama of bathroom surveillance. Although the pun is clever and even amusing, it is also troubling to see how often Garber turns to punning in her analysis. The constant use of puns throughout the book has the overall effect of making gender crossing sound like a game or at least trivializes the often life-or-death processes involved in cross-identification. This is not to say gender can never be a "laughing matter" and must always be treated seriously but only to question the use of the pun here as a theoretical method.

7. Susan Bordo argues this in "Reading the Male Body," *Michigan Quarterly Review* 32, no. 4 (Fall 1993). She writes: "When masculinity gets 'undone' in this culture, the deconstruction nearly always lands us in the territory of the degraded; when femininity gets symbolically undone, the result is an immense elevation of status" (721).

EVE KOSOFSKY SEDGWICK

26. GOSH, BOY GEORGE, YOU MUST BE AWFULLY SECURE IN YOUR MASCULINITY!

The title I have chosen for this text is borrowed from a hapless Long Island disc jockey who was overcome with admiration while interviewing a celebrity, only to finally hear himself blurting it out—"Gosh, Boy George . . . !" My intent is to propose some axioms that may be helpful for stimulating, and even possibly disrupting, the conversation on the topic of masculinity.

The first axiom I would like to propose is what I have always imagined as Boy George's response to the Long Island disc jockey:

1. SOMETIMES MASCULINITY HAS GOT NOTHING TO DO WITH IT

Nothing to do, that is, with men. And when something is about masculinity, it is not always "about men." I think it is important to drive a wedge in, early and often and if possible conclusively, between the two topics, masculinity and men, whose relation to one another it is so difficult not to presume. Even in the prospectus prose for a serious book [. . .] whose aim seems to be to problematize every conceivable aspect of masculinity, it is still notable that the distinctive linkage between masculinity and the male subject, or the subject of men, goes unquestioned. In asking "What Is Masculinity?" for instance, [Berger, Wallis, and Watson (1996)] begin: "Men of all ages and cultural backgrounds—straight, gay, and bisexual—are beginning to ask and explore key issues about the nature of masculinity. . . ."

Maybe we could update that to "Men of all ages and cultural backgrounds straight, gay, bisexual, and female"?

Later in the same document, I am invited to consider how "traditional representations of masculinity have played a crucial role in shaping the economic, cultural, and political status of men"; how science views "traits that are typical to men"; whether it is "possible to imagine a critical men's movement"; and finally, climactically, "How *men* [can] rethink their power in an effort to reconstruct themselves personally and politically."[1]

Of course, the last thing I want to do is to minimize the importance of questions like these. But it does seem necessary to emphasize how crucially the force of such questions is vitiated when they are presented as the questions about masculinity per se—when, that is, an inquiry begins with the presupposition that everything pertaining to men can be classified as masculinity, and everything that can be said about masculinity pertains in the first place to men.

Gosh, Boy George must really be secure in *something* when he has the courage to perform in drag—and he is a boy, at least his name says he is, so what he is secure *in* must be "masculinity," "his" masculinity. It is less obviously absurd, but all the more insidious, when, for example, nominally gay-affirmative psychologists such as Richard Friedman assume that the only form self-respect can take in boys, in boys gay or straight, is and has to be something called "masculine self-regard."[2] The boys I know who were so profoundly nourished, and with such heroic difficulty, by their hard-won feminine and effeminate self-regard—and for that matter, the girls who extracted the same precious survival skills from a sturdily masculine one—ought to present much more of a challenge than they have so far to the self-evidence of such formulations.

I would ask that we strongly resist, then, the presupposition that what women have to do with masculinity

---

This reading was originally published in Maurice Berger, Brian Wallis, and Simon Watson's (eds.) *Constructing Masculinity* (New York: Routledge, 1995).

is mainly to be treated less or more oppressively by the men to whom masculinity more directly pertains. My purpose is not to file an *amicus curiae* brief with the "men of all ages and cultural backgrounds" who are "beginning to explore key issues about the nature of masculinity." I am exploring them myself. Nor do I mean to issue a *Consumer Reports* test-kitchen rating on the new masculinities. As a woman, I am a consumer of masculinities, but I am not more so than men are; and, like men, I as a woman am also a producer of masculinities and a performer of them.

It seems to me that the women who might better speak to these issues are some of those who are beginning to write so directly and eloquently about masculinity and/or about butch identity in women, largely but not exclusively in lesbian contexts: Leslie Feinberg, for example, or Judith Halberstam, or the contributors to Joan Nestle's "femme-butch anthology," or Judith Frank, who originated the ineradicably compelling notion of "butch abjection."[3] I myself, embarrassingly, can only speak from the subject position newly classified by Minnie Bruce Pratt as "adult children of mothers who couldn't figure out whether to be butches or femmes."[4] (Actually, my mother finally did figure it out; but it took her until the age of seventy, so I am trying to be patient with my own confusions on this topic.)

In another sense, though, it may be that there is an even *stronger* case to be made in this regard by a writer who self-identifies, roughly speaking, as a confused femme (or do you consider the epithet redundant?). At any rate, that is the experience out of which I am trying to figure out how to articulate this. More specifically, in very briefly framing three further propositions on masculinity, I want to draw on what I occasionally have the composure to describe as the most interesting experiment I have undergone (or, euphemistically, "conducted") in the semiotics of gender, something I have written a little bit about before—namely, the half-year or so I spent in 1991 doing intensive chemotherapy following a diagnosis of node-positive breast cancer. The treatment involved, among other things, a by-no-means-uncommon disruption in the somatic signifiers (and for that matter the signifieds) of gender—and more profoundly and simply, of bodily health. I do not want to dwell now on the encounter with mortality entailed in this experience; rather on, for instance, the many, many encounters in the mirror with my bald and handsome father and my bald and ugly grandfather; or the phantom conversations, more haunting than a phantom breast, in which sometimes I still hear myself challenging some imaginary sexual assailant by—what? It is hard to piece this together but I think what I am doing in these fantasies is defiantly exposing my mastectomy scar, and cementing my triumph over this attacker by making clear to him that underneath the clothing and the prosthesis, I am really a man whom he has had the poor judgment to mistake for a vulnerable woman.

When I first got the breast cancer diagnosis, one of the good friends who called to check in and cheer me up was a gay man I had known and loved for a long time, a psychoanalytic theorist, who reminded me that he, too, had had a pretty bad breast cancer scare several years before. But his lump had turned out to be benign—"And it was a good thing too," he said on the phone, "because you know what the treatment of choice is for male breast cancer? Castration!" I congratulated him on his narrow escape from a fate evidently seen as worse than death. And I did not make any connection between that and the moment, months later, when I was finishing chemotherapy and the question of hormone therapy came up, when I suddenly noticed that both my cheerful oncologist and the matter-of-fact medical textbooks I could not seem to stop reading apparently had the same question on their mind; to castrate—me!—or not to castrate. I did not even know what the word could really mean, in this context, but that did not keep me from bursting into the tears that mark the heaping of injury on insult; here I thought I already was! All these years my Lacanian friends had me convinced I had nothing to lose.

Maybe the weirdest part of this story is that even now, at the end of it, I actually do not know whether I got castrated or not. It turns out that for women, as indeed for men, there exist the alternatives of surgical ablation or chemical ablation (also I thought "ablation" was something done by Latin nouns) of the gonads, which for women means the ovaries—and since the chemo had already knocked my reproductive system into a cocked hat, the question of further abla-tion turned out to be, as they say, moot. I believe, but I am not sure, that that is a way of saying that the cas-tration had, indeed, already happened. *Maybe* of saying that *any* postmenopausal woman is by defini-tion, as Germaine Greer would put it, a female eunuch.

But the point of this shaggy-dog medical thriller, right now, is to mark how different, and how rather unpredictably different, the notion of castration is in a female context from a male context. For a man, it seems clear enough what is signified by castration; that is, a threat to masculinity. But it is still fully am-biguous to me whether the tears I was bawling out at the mention of castration were wept in response to a threat against my masculinity, or my femininity.[5] A rather too fancy way of broaching the commonplace—but it is an important commonplace, and one that people always forget—that . . .

2. MASCULINITY AND FEMININITY ARE IN MANY RESPECTS ORTHOGONAL TO EACH OTHER

Orthogonal: that is, instead of being at opposite poles of the same axis, they are actually in different, perpendicular dimensions, and therefore are inde-pendently variable. The classic research on this was, of course, Sandra Bem's work on psychological an-drogyny; she had people rated on two scales, one measuring stereotypically female-ascribed traits and one measuring stereotypically male-ascribed ones; and found that many lucky people score high on both, many other people score low on both, and most importantly that a high score on either of them does not predict a low score on the other.[6]

If we may be forgiven a leap from two-dimensional into *n*-dimensional space, I think it would be inter-esting, by the way, to hypothesize that not only mas-culinity and femininity, but in addition effeminacy, butchness, femmeness, and probably some other superficially related terms, might equally turn out in-stead to represent independent variables—or at least, unpredictably dependent ones. I would just ask you to call to mind all the men you know who may be both highly masculine and highly effeminate—but at the same time, not a bit feminine. Or women

whom you might consider very butch and at the same time feminine, but not femme. Why not throw in some other terms, too, such as top and bottom? And an even more potent extension into *n*-dimensional space could, ideally, make representable a factor such as race, as well. I am thinking, for instance, of a fasci-nating recent paper by Riche Richardson in which she analyzes the differential meanings, in African-American men's (effeminate) drag performance, of imitations of "white" femininity compared to imita-tions of "black" femininity.[7]

One implication of work like Sandra Bem's is that not only are some people more masculine or more fem-inine than others, but some people are just plain more *gender-y* than others—whether the gender they mani-fest be masculine, feminine, both, or "and then some."

Which brings us to . . .

3. MASCULINITY AND FEMININITY ARE THRESHOLD EFFECTS

This includes masculinity and femininity and, we might add, some of the other gender-salient dimen-sions that we have also been discussing. By "threshold effects," I mean places where quantitative increments along one dimension can suddenly appear as qualita-tive differences somewhere else on the map entirely. I will offer only one example of this—which must also serve to introduce Proposition 4, as a matter of fact—and unfortunately it involves only my hunches about an issue on which I am probably the least expert wit-ness available: that is to say, the reception history of my own gendered self-presentation around the time of the chemotherapy "experiment." But, for what it's worth, here is my observation. It so happened that the end of the half-year of chemo, during which time I was totally bald, and at the end of which I suddenly developed this fabulous babylike fuzz (which I almost wore away with the sheer joy of having it to fondle), it so happened that this moment, the first moment when I felt able—indeed, irrepressibly eager—to ven-ture out into the world without one of those little penitential ethnic beanies on my head, coincided with the fifth annual Lesbian and Gay Studies Confer-ence, that year being held at Rutgers. So, of course, I went and displayed my wares, and my hairs.

Now, I had been fortunate enough to attend all four of the previous conferences in this series (three at Yale, one at Harvard). And, much as I had treasured the almost overwhelming stimulus and camaraderie that was on tap at each one of them and the sense that as scenes they were among the most fun I had ever happened on, I had nonetheless the sense, at each one, of being, as a body, erotically invisible to most of the other participants, both male and female. This did not get me down too much, but I did notice it, and at some level felt a bit forlorn. Strikingly different was the feeling of being in this particular body at that particular conference, the Rutgers conference, at that particular moment. Suddenly, it seemed to me—outlandish, near-bald, and extremely happy—that I had had the great pleasure of *clicking*, with an almost audible click, into visibility in the grid of a certain lesbian optic. I felt, really for the first time, that I looked exactly as I ought and wished to look, and was visible as so doing.

Now, here is the part of it that was really instructive—and by instructive I mean that it took me forever to catch on to. It was clear to me that this vibrant sense of having a body, having a visible body, was tied to the butchness of, as a woman, swaggering around in the world, or at least in New Brunswick, with almost no hair. So far so good, I thought; I had always been attracted to very butch women, and now, it seemed to me, by some miracle, I was going to get to turn into one. And wasn't this what I had wanted?

What emerged over time, however, as I learned to read myself and to read other women's (and indeed men's) responses to my bodily habitus in a somewhat more subtle and differentiated way, was not the story of this particular miracle. It was something else: that what I had become visible as was, in fact (no big surprises here), quite femme. The surprise was in seeing that it required the crossing over a threshold of, precisely, butchness, to become visible as, precisely, if it is precisely, femme. That is to say, I had to stumble my way onto a map of sexy gender-y-ness in the first place; and the portal to that place, for women, or for lesbians, or for queers, or just for me, I do not know yet, is marked "butch." The rheostat that you might think would adjust the seamless gradations from feminine to femme seemingly has to get interrupted by the on/off switch of butch.

4. IN MASCULINITY/FEMININITY, A DYNAMIC OF SELF-RECOGNITION MEDIATED BETWEEN ESSENTIALISM AND FREE PLAY

Proposition 4 is about transformations like the one I have just sketched: about trying to find, not a middle ground, but a ground for describing and respecting the inertia, the slowness, the process that mediates between, on the one hand, the biological absolutes of what we always are (more or less) and, on the other hand, the notional free play that we constructivists are always imagined to be attributing to our own and other people's sex-and-gender self-presentation. I want to mark here a space in which there might be broached some description at a psychological level of how such changes may actually occur: namely through a slow and rather complicated feedback mechanism that I would summarize in the phrase: "Will I be able to recognize myself if I . . . ?"

This proposition interests me especially because I would want to argue that, while to some degree it is probably true of everybody, it seems likeliest to be truest of people who experience their bodies in the first place as not just problematic, but precisely stigmatic. I am sure that not every visibly handicapped person, or transgendered person, or person of color, or fat person, or visibly sick person, or person with gender-"inappropriate" voice or demeanor in fact experiences his or her body as stigmatic most or necessarily even any of the time. But it is a very plain fact that many of us do. And I would like with this proposition to open something like a door into the mix of paralysis or transfixion, with extraordinary daring and often outrageousness, with strange sites of stylistic conservatism, with an almost uncanny discursive productiveness, that many of us experience as we struggle to continue the adventure of recognizing ourselves and being recognized in these problematic femininities and masculinities that constitute us and that we, in turn, constitute.

REFERENCES

Berger, Maurice, Brian Wallis, and Simon Watson, eds. 1996. *Constructing Masculinity*. New York and London: Routledge.

NOTES

1. Maurice Berger, Brian Wallis, and Simon Watson prospectus for *Constructing Masculinity*, n.p.
2. The phrase occurs in Richard C. Friedman, *Male Homosexuality: A Psychoanalytic Perspective* (New Haven, CT: Yale University Press, 1988), p. 245.
3. Leslie Feinberg, *Stone Butch Blues* (Ithaca, NY: Firebrand Books, 1993); Judith Halberstam, "F2M: The Making of Female Masculinity," in Laura Doan, ed., *The Lesbian Postmodern* (New York: Columbia University Press, 1994); Joan Nestle, ed., *The Persistent Desire: A Femme-Butch Reader* (Boston: Alyson, 1992); and Judith Frank, personal communication.
4. Pratt described herself in approximately these terms during an informal talk at Duke University, Feb. 21, 1994.
5. It is interesting to me that when I try to tell people this story, often concluding with "—but now I realize I *was* castrated?" they incorrectly assume that I am describing the supposedly traumatic psychological impact of the loss of a breast. It is easy for people to arrive at the crisp homology "breast:femininity::phallus:masculinity," and that neatly metaphorical substitution offers a kind of presumptive pseudosense that altogether effaces the literal fact that women are indeed castratable; effacing, as well, the challenge that this fact offers to conventional gender schematics.
6. Sandra Bem, "The Measurement of Psychological Androgyny," *Journal of Consulting and Clinical Psychology* 42 (April 1974): 155–62; Bem, "The Theory and Measurement of Androgyny: A Reply to the Pedhazur–Tetenbaum and Locksley–Colten Critiques," *Journal of Personality and Social Psychology* 37 (June 1979); and Bem, *The Lenses of Gender: Transforming the Debate on Sexual Inequality* (New Haven, CT: Yale University Press, 1993).
7. Riché Richardson, "Sistuh Girl Terry McMillan: Crossing the Threshold to the Trenches," paper delivered at the College Language Association, Durham, NC, Apr. 15, 1994.

EMILY KAZYAK

27. MIDWEST OR LESBIAN?: GENDER, RURALITY, AND SEXUALITY

Growing up in a small town, I worked on a farm. A lot of women worked on farms or in road construction or nontraditional jobs for women. I told somebody that if you were to drive by [my town], you'd think the place is full of lesbians! They're all wearing flannel shirts and cowboy boots.

This quote from one of my participants, Nancy, a lesbian woman living in a small Midwestern town, illustrates the way space, gender, and sexuality are intertwined and underscores two important issues.[1] It indicates that gender presentations are central to understandings of sexuality, insofar as lesbian sexuality is conflated with masculinity. Masculine gender practices, from wearing flannel shirts to working in traditionally male dominated jobs, are part of how the category "lesbian" is constructed. Nancy's quote also indicates that such practices of masculinity for women in rural communities are "not uncommon," illustrating that the meanings of gender presentations vary by geographic context. Although female masculinity is the most visible gender presentation of lesbian identity in urban contexts, it does not have the same meaning in rural contexts, since both straight and lesbian women might enact it. People therefore might erroneously think her town is "full of lesbians" since all women might enact more masculine gender presentations.

Research does indicate a gendered dimension to the geography of sexual minorities. Gay couples are more likely to live in urban areas than are lesbian couples (Gates and Ost 2004: 28), suggesting that gender might matter for how sexual minorities experience rural areas. Drawing on data from 60 interviews with rural gays and lesbians, I analyze the mutually constitutive relationships among place, gender, and sexuality to assess how acceptance of gays and lesbians in small towns is gendered. I find that constructions of male femininity align with gay sexuality but not rurality, which may mean that for some gay men, the ability to stay put in rural areas might be constrained. However, masculinity underpins both the categories rural and lesbian, which may afford some lesbians the ability to stay in rural places. How these categories are co-constructed sheds light on the gendered nature of acceptance for sexual minorities in rural areas: Both lesbian women and gay men gain acceptance by doing masculinity.

[. . .] [Focusing] on how rural lesbians do masculinity, the current study provides an instance of female masculinity (Halberstam 1998). As such, it underscores the importance of recognizing that masculinity extends beyond male bodies (Pascoe 2007). Some research argues that women doing masculinity is culturally disruptive and personally transgressive (Halberstam 1998; Schippers 2007; Shapiro 2007). In contrast, my research shows that some practices of female masculinity are normative. [It] shows that the meanings of gender presentations differ not only by generation and race (Moore 2006) but also by geography. Female masculinity is the most visible gender presentation of lesbian identity in urban contexts (Kennedy and Davis 1993; Moore 2006: 117). However, it does not hold the same meaning in rural contexts, because masculine gender presentations are acceptable for all rural women, regardless of sexuality. [. . .]

INTERSECTIONALITY AND MASCULINITY

Intersectional approaches consider how the categories and identities of race, class, gender, and sexuality (Bettie 2003; Hill Collins 1990; Nagel 2003; Wilkins 2004) are constructed simultaneously. For example, in her work on the gendered–classed–raced category

This reading is an excerpt from Emily Kazyak's article in *Gender & Society* 26, no. 6 (2012): 825–48.

"Puerto Rican wannabe," Wilkins (2004) demonstrates how sexuality works in constructing this category, insofar as it refers to white young women who, among other things, date black and Puerto Rican men and thus eschew white middle-class gender and sexual norms. The current study employs a similar type of analysis in its focus on how the construction of sexual and spatial categories rests on meanings shaped by gender. [. . .] Specifically, asserting sameness is crucial to being seen as belonging in rural communities. The racial homogeneity in rural areas (U.S. Bureau of the Census 2000) no doubt means that whites, unlike people of color, have a greater ability to assert such belonging and have it legitimated.

[. . .] Scholars define masculinity as encompassing both practices (what people do—gender displays) and discourses (assumptions and expectations about what men and women should be like) (Connell 1995; Pascoe 2007; Schippers 2007). Importantly, the practices and discourses that establish what it means to be an ideal man position femininity and other kinds of masculinities as subordinate and thus justify and perpetuate gender inequality and male dominance (Connell 1995). Recently, scholars have asserted the need to extend beyond a definition that ties masculinity to what men do, arguing that women (and girls) also engage with masculinized practices and discourses (Halberstam 1998; Pascoe 2007). Building on such work, this [research] extends analyses of gender by focusing on a neglected group within masculinity studies: women. It provides more empirical evidence of the importance of not reducing masculinity to the male body and femininity to the female body.

Halberstam (1998) calls women's engagements with practices and discourses associated with masculinity, including embodying and performing masculinity, "female masculinity." Such engagements can shape people's own transgressive sense of gender identity. Shapiro (2007), for instance, finds that through participating in drag king troupes, many participants adopt new gender identities, including "genderqueer" and "butch," and see themselves as "gender outlaws." Moreover, female masculinity is culturally disruptive (Halberstam 1998). Since U.S. culture so tightly links masculinity with maleness, Halberstam (1998) notes the paradox that masculinity enacted by women has been both ignored and met with much anxiety. For instance, butch lesbians, one exemplar of women's embodiments of masculinity, have been pathologized (Halberstam 1998, 9). In fact, some argue that when women enact features of dominant masculinity, it should not be considered masculinity, but rather "pariah femininity," given that it is seen as contaminating the appropriate relationship between masculinity and femininity (Schippers 2007). Schippers (2007) also argues that such enactments are met with stigma and disapproval.

Yet other work shows that some forms of female masculinity are accepted (Pascoe 2007). In other words, when girls or women enact masculinity, it is not always met with hostility. In her ethnography, Pascoe (2007) highlights two groups of high school girls who were considered masculine by themselves and others. The masculine practices of one group—the "basketball girls"—including dressing like boys and being aggressive, were accepted by their peers. And not only were they accepted but those practices increased the girls' popularity and social status (Pascoe 2007: 120). Likewise, Pascoe (2007) argues that not all enactments of female masculinity challenge the gender order. Only those enactments that are coupled with an explicit, critical assessment of the accepted gender and sexual norms are challenging.

Scholars have also addressed contexts in which women (and men) can produce alternative genders and redefine the relationship between masculinity and femininity—what Schippers (2002) calls "gender maneuvering." In alternative hard rock subcultures, for example, girl bands challenge the homophobia common in rock as well as transform stigmatized femininities (like "slut" or "bitch") into markers of power. In her ethnography of the sport of roller derby, Finley (2010) also finds that women in this context are able to cultivate alternative femininities. Similarly, drag performances can challenge dominant understandings of gender and sexuality (Rupp, Taylor, and Shapiro 2010). However, not all forms of gender resistance result in a disruption of the gender order. Synthesizing across previous work, Finley asserts that in contexts where men dominate and control resources, it is less likely that women's enactment of unconventional femininity will transform the gender order (2010: 366).

In sum, scholars point not only to women's gender identity (exemplified by women who are seen by themselves and others as more masculine) but also to women's engagement with practices and discourses associated with masculinity to provide examples of female masculinity. In this article, I too draw on participants' gender identity and their engagement with practices and discourses associated with masculinity in rural areas, including doing farmwork or being "country" or "redneck." Debate exists regarding whether female masculinity, and other enactments of alternative genders, challenges or reproduces the dominant gender order. Similar to Pascoe's work, this article provides an example of a context wherein female masculinity is not necessarily stigmatized, presenting an account of which women's engagements with practices and discourses associated with masculinity are seen as normative and which are seen as disruptive. As such, this work illustrates the importance of addressing how context matters for how female masculinity is viewed.

RURAL GENDER AND SEXUALITY

Research reveals the patriarchal nature of rural life, but simultaneously recognizes the multiple masculinities that exist in rural communities and that rural masculinities change (Campbell, Bell, and Finney 2006). Working and laboring are crucial to constructions of masculinity. In contrast, constructions of rural femininity are tied to domesticity (Hughes 1997; Little and Austin 1996). These constructions of masculinity and femininity work to sustain gender inequality insofar as they justify men as rightfully positioned in paid labor, public spheres and women in unpaid, private spheres. For instance, Bird (2006) illustrates how male owners of rural small businesses are seen as providing for their families and for the community itself by employing men who in turn take care of their families. When women work in these small businesses, they are viewed as helpers. The same is true in farming, where farmwork is seen as the sole domain of men and women are seen as helpers in the domestic sphere (Sachs 1983). Even with the increasing absence of traditionally defined male jobs in rural areas due to economic restructuring (Falk and Lobao 2003), physical toughness continues to constitute local constructions of

masculinity (Morris 2008). Hard work and laboring are also part of what it means to be a "local," which contributes to the alienation and possibly even departure of groups positioned outside of working and laboring, including women (Campbell, Bell, and Finney 2006; Laore and Fielding 2006).

This is not to suggest that no women stay in rural areas or work in small towns. Indeed, many women want to stay, even if opportunities exist elsewhere (Tickamyer et al. 2000). Also, Tickamyer and Henderson (2003) find that rural economic restructuring has necessitated the presence of women in the paid labor market. Nonetheless, research suggests that domesticity remains central to constructions of rural femininity. Taking care of the home and family are important routes to achieve femininity and are often seen as incompatible with paid employment (Little 1997). Rural women's caretaking expectations even inform rural activism (Bell and Braun 2010). The emphasis on domesticity underscores how heterosexuality underpins rural femininity. Some suggest that heterosexuality and domesticity are so central to constructions of rural femininity, in part, to combat the fact that some practices commonly performed by rural women, such as being outdoorsy or doing farmwork, are masculinizing (Smyth 2007). In this way, whereas "rural men equal real men" (Sachs 2006: 2), the opposite is true for rural women. Indeed, some rural women struggle with being perceived as masculine and work to assert femininity (Brandth 2006; Smyth 2007). Yet others view rural areas as offering the space to reject traditional notions of femininity, namely, women part of lesbian land movements (Bell and Valentine 1995).

Constructions of rural masculinity and femininity matter for the experiences of rural gay men, as those who are perceived as feminine face greater hostility than those who are perceived as masculine (Boulden 2001; Gray 2009; Howard 1999). Analyzing a bashing that occurred after a drag performance at a local Wal-Mart, Gray (2009) links the bashing to the fact that the young men were transgressing gender norms. She argues that for rural men, "publicly disrupting normative gender expectations arguably remains as, if not more, contentious than homoerotic desires" (Gray 2009, 110). Yet other research suggests that some gender nonnormative black men in small towns in the South find acceptance (Johnson 2008), indicating a complex interplay among identities of rurality, region, masculinity, race, and sexuality. Furthermore, there have been movements, such as the radical faeries, to create rural spaces where men can reject traditional notions of masculinity (Hennen 2008; Herring 2007). These accounts provide rich detail of how gender expectations matter for gay men in rural places, but we know less about the experiences of lesbian women. This article fills this gap.

Informed by these theoretical and empirical literatures, this study asks how acceptance for rural sexual minorities is gendered. Utilizing a definition of masculinity that encompasses identity, practices, and discourse reflects the fact that some rural gay men and lesbian women described their own gender identities or gender displays (practices), while others talked more explicitly about the expectations that circulate in rural areas about what men and women are supposed to be or do (discourses). As in previous work, I find constructions of masculinity to entail laboring, working hard, and being tough. I also find heterosexuality and domesticity to be important parts of constructions of rural femininity. Unlike the radical faeries, the gay men in this study did not reject masculinity. The rural lesbian women were not part of lesbian land movements, although they did reject traditional femininity. Unlike rural women in previous studies, many defined their gender as more masculine, engaged with masculinized practices and discourses, and did not express discomfort about others perceiving them as masculine. Both rural gay men and lesbian women engage with practices and discourses associated with masculinity, which bolsters their acceptance in small towns. Importantly, not all female masculinities are wholly accepted in rural areas, including practices and discourses that are seen as antithetical to what it means to be "country."

COCONSTRUCTIONS OF RURALITY, GENDER, AND SEXUALITY

Using an intersectional approach highlights how understandings about gay and lesbian sexuality, masculinity and femininity, and urban and rural are constructed simultaneously. I first describe how both

men and women thought that being gay or lesbian meant enacting nonnormative gender. I then describe how interviewees articulated an understanding that gay femininity is not compatible with rurality, whereas lesbian masculinity is. Whereas both gay and lesbian sexualities are intertwined with gender nonnormativity, the category "gay" shares a different relationship to rurality than does the category "lesbian."

GAY FEMININITY AND LESBIAN MASCULINITY

Interviewees repeatedly talked about the equation of gay male sexuality with effeminacy. Adam described the stereotypes he once had about gay men in this way: "Theater, drama, music, you have to dress nice . . . you have to be kinda effeminate, you have to be very effusive and talk in a high voice." Justin's description echoes Adam's. When discussing the stereotype of a gay man, he said:

> That feminine guy, that cross-dressing [guy], the guy that acts like a woman, that doesn't play sports, [is] into fashion and makeup and hair and shopping, and [who] does nothing that a typical straight guy would do [like] run outside with a chainsaw cutting a tree down, working in the yard, building stuff, and playing sports.

Jesse agreed, saying, "I guess I just thought that if you're gay, you have to act really flamboyant and queeny."

Women also described the model of same-sex sexuality that collapses lesbianism with masculinity. Elise said, "I would never have thought that you could be a lesbian and look feminine." Chelsea and Andrea, a lesbian couple who both participated in the project, described a magnet on their refrigerator that said: "I once was a tomboy but now I'm a lesbian." Similarly, Jenny referenced how she had the "stereotypical" markers for being lesbian growing up: "[I] played softball, I was a tomboy, [had] short hair, hated to dress up. I'd rather be outside doing something than bored and playing a musical instrument." Stephanie said, "I don't dress the most feminine and that usually leads people to stereotype me as a lesbian." Here participants both reference their own sense of gender and circulating discourses about what it means to be a lesbian.

THE COMPATIBILITY OF GAY (EFFEMINATE) AND LESBIAN (BUTCH) WITH RURALITY

The construction of gay as effeminate also contains geographical meanings, namely, as being incompatible with rurality. In contrast, lesbian as butch coincides with rurality. The incompatibility of rurality and effeminacy is evident in how interviewees described gender expectations for boys and men in small towns. Phil said, "I think in a rural area, if you're not into the sports, if you are interested in theater, then that causes a lot of problems, because [with] all these farm boys, you're supposed to be into the football and wrestling." Todd explained how his dad forced him to participate in sports: "You've got to, this is what little boys do in [this town]." Experiences Alice had going to gay bars in a nearby city when she first came out further underscore this point: "It was mostly made up of flamboyant, soft-spoken, and sensitive [gay men]. Growing up in [my town], I wasn't exposed to that." These quotes indicate the degree to which feminine characteristics conflated with gay sexuality, such as being flamboyant, soft-spoken, sensitive, or interested in theater, do not fit with the gender expectations for rural men.

That most of the men living in rural areas created a distinction between their sexuality and discourses about effeminate gay sexuality illustrates another way that rurality and effeminacy are constructed as incompatible. Except for Kevin, all men distanced themselves from the gay as effeminate model. Gene adamantly expressed this distancing: "I don't wanna be lumped together with a bunch of homos running around dressed in women's clothes, funky make-up, [and] dancing to Cher." Justin also made a distinction between his identity and what he sees as a stereotypical feminine gay identity, saying: "I'm not that guy." He elaborated:

> I don't mind shopping, but I'm not into fashion. If you look at [how] I'm dressed today, I'm dressed like any normal person would be: I have a T-shirt and blue jeans on. I have three chainsaws at home. I love being outside. I love playing sports. I love to do home projects. I've got my power tools and I know how to use them.

Interestingly, Justin links his sense of not being what he sees as a stereotype to living in a small town:

> Being here really changed my mindset because . . . I was getting flirted with what I thought were straight men . . . [but] they weren't straight men, they were gay men, but they looked very straight, they acted very masculine . . . that changed everything. It was, like, this wasn't what I thought of as a gay man. So being in this town really changed how I thought of myself and the gay community. I was really happy that I could be a normal masculine type guy and be gay and not be . . . the stereotype.

As Justin's words underscore, what it means to be a "normal, masculine" rural guy conflicts with femininity, including gay male effeminacy associated with urban spaces. Distancing their identities from femininity strengthens the ability of rural gay men to pursue local masculinity.

By contrast, rurality and more butch-like gender presentations are constructed as compatible. One way this compatibility is demonstrated is in how interviewees explained that rural areas allowed for, as Teresa put it, "a range of female gender." By this, interviewees meant that it is acceptable for women to do masculinity.[2] Although some practices of masculinity are accepted, interviewees also articulated the expectation that women be heterosexually married and have children. As Natalie said, "It's just that mentality there that a woman can't live without a man, that you have to be married and you have to have 13 kids." Even though women can do things associated with masculinity, rural femininity still rests on heterosexuality and domesticity.

Explaining the "wider" range of female gender in rural areas, Teresa said, "There were farm girls [who] might dress up for the prom, but they also could slaughter a hog." Many had childhood stories relating to the fact that, as Lisa put it, "Tomboyishness was somewhat more acceptable than it might be somewhere else." Echoing this observation, Ester talked about her enjoyment of being raised on a farm: "I helped my dad a lot on the farm, raising . . . livestock. . . . I really enjoyed driving the farm machinery! It just empowered me, driving a tractor or truck." Ester's quote shows how some practices associated with masculinity are not seen as inappropriate for girls or women in rural contexts. In Rita's story, playing sports entailed being around a lesbian community while growing up in a small town. She said, "I played softball, so I was around really strong women and a really strong lesbian community from almost day one. I didn't get negative feedback from that." Her story, along with the others', underscores that gender expectations for rural women complement the discursive construction of lesbian sexuality that conflates it with masculinity.

Furthermore, most of the women living in rural areas did not create a distinction between their own gender and sexual identity and butch lesbian sexuality. There were nuances in how women talked about "butchness" ("butch," "soft butch," and "butchy"). However, there was not the same distancing from the gender nonnormative model of lesbian sexuality as there was for the gay men I interviewed. Take, for instance, Jenny, who described herself as butch, a stereotypical lesbian, and as a "redneck": "I'm so excited to go to the old gas tractor show. We fix our own things, we build our own stuff." When I asked if being a redneck fit with being a lesbian, she said, "Oh, it fits perfectly! It fits perfectly with being butch, but wouldn't fit at all [with] being femme." A similar narrative emerged in Tara's interview: "I ride a Harley. . . . I have two dogs, [the] stereotype, you know, I play softball. Yeah, it all fits!" Here she references one stereotype of being a lesbian, including riding a motorcycle, having dogs, and playing softball. She said that her last girlfriend told her she looked "butchy" or "softbutch," adding, "I always have boots on. . . . I'll never wear a dress . . . and all the Harley stuff." The stereotype of being a lesbian equates with being "butchy," and in her case, driving a motorcycle exemplifies both.

Later in the interview, Tara also pointed to riding a Harley as one of the components that makes her think of herself as "country" or a "good old redneck girl." She explains: "I mow for farmers or do fieldwork. [I] haul grain . . . I'm a redneck because I drive a Harley, [because] I drive a 4×4, [because of] the way I dress and I clod around." This example illustrates that it is not uncommon for rural women to engage in practices associated with masculinity, such as

those she describes. Moreover, her comments illustrate that lesbian–butch and rural are seen as compatible. Some of the components that make her fit the stereotype of a lesbian are the same ones that make her "country."

For most of the gay men, living in a small town entailed not enacting gender presentations stereotypically associated with their sexual identity. The opposite was true for the lesbian women. They enact masculinity by claiming more butchlike identities and engaging with practices and discourses associated with masculinity in rural contexts. Their identification as "country" or "redneck" further signals the degree to which rural women can embrace traditionally masculinized redneck discourses (Hubbs 2011). Importantly, these lesbian–butch–rural identities are white insofar as the components of these identities are different, for instance, from what constitutes more masculine gender practices in urban black lesbian communities (Moore 2006).

In highlighting these narratives, I do not intend to argue that only butch lesbians live in rural areas. Rather, the only lesbian women I was able to recruit from small towns saw their gender as more masculine. This might reflect the fact that even though rural women commonly engage in practices like farmwork or being outdoorsy, these practices are still associated with masculinity, which impacts rural women's gender identities (Smyth 2007). It could also be that those who do not adhere to rural masculinity leave for more urban areas, as Laore and Fielding (2006) suggest. Relatedly, participating in urban lesbian communities might entail exposure to a diversity of lesbian gender identities, including femme lesbian. These questions warrant attention in future research. Here, I argue that the way in which spatial, gender, and sexual categories are mutually constitutive has implications for the gendered nature of acceptance for rural sexual minorities, as I now turn to.

GENDERED EXPERIENCES IN RURAL AREAS

Census data indicate that more lesbian women than gay men live outside urban areas (Gates and Ost 2004), which raises a question about the gendered experiences of sexual minorities in rural areas. I focus on acceptance and visibility in addressing this question.

ACCEPTANCE

Rural gays and lesbians describe that being seen as belonging in their communities bolsters others' acceptance of their sexuality (Gray 2009; Kazyak 2011a). What it means to belong is informed by class and racial meanings, insofar as being a "hick" is one way to signal an embrace of rural ways of life (Kazyak 2011b). The term hick creates a distinction between privileged (hick) and polluted (white trash) whiteness and illustrates how rural is constituted as white (Wray 2006). I argue that understandings about what it means to belong are not only classed and raced but also gendered. For gay men and lesbian women, being accepted as a good person who belongs entails embracing masculinizing practices and discourses.

Consider the two narratives presented earlier from Tara and Jenny. They both understood that being country, being a lesbian, and being more masculine entails similar interests and activities. That Tara is a "country girl" who has lived in the same area where her family has been for generations is part of her understanding about why she is accepted as an out lesbian woman in her town. Importantly, the country and "butchy" aspects of her gender are one and the same. However, not all female masculine gender presentations are seen as so intertwined with being country. Some presentations, as Rita's story illustrates, might be seen as urban and thus as incompatible with a rural way of life. Rita talked about how she has a "more urban look," noting that her "hair's cut off." When I asked her to elaborate on what she meant by an "urban look," she said, "My hair's bleached and sometimes I dye the tips. . . . I tend to wear sweaters and neat ties and things that you wouldn't see a lot of in rural areas." She also told a story about visiting her hometown after cutting off her hair: "People were staring at me and I was, like, 'Why are people staring at me?' I couldn't for the life of me really wrap my mind around it until I realized, 'Oh my god, I look totally different than everybody else here.'" This quote suggests that female masculinity is read

differently across geographic contexts. Rita links short hair, dyed tips, and wearing ties to urban settings and tells a story of being stared at in a small town because of such gender presentations. This is in contrast to what others said: that they did not necessarily feel out of place for looking more masculine. These narratives suggest that only practices of female masculinity that underpin what it means to be country are accepted.

Unlike female masculinity, no practices of male femininity cultivate claims to belonging. Many interviewees spoke of how effeminate men face disapproval and harassment in their towns. Consider, for instance, Tom, who spoke of his concern growing up about being "too femmy." He said, "I started smoking [because] I was afraid my voice wouldn't get deep enough and I didn't want anybody to think I had a lisp and that I was too femmy." Likewise, Kevin explained how his manager at work told him he needed to "learn how to drop my voice." Bethany reflected on how high school officials "were very harsh on boys," noting that "the guys who were thought to be a little more effeminate were pulled in once in a while and told by the superintendent how [they're] expected to behave." Xander, who lives in an urban area, talked about feeling uncomfortable when going back home: "I'm not the biggest flaming person, but I feel like I'm well enough on that way, that I feel like people [think] it's a little off." To further explain his point, he brought up the example of getting his car fixed: "When I go home and I'm going to get my oil changed . . . and they're, like, 'What about this gauge?' and I'm, like, 'I have no idea what you're talking about!' I see the way that people look at me."

Indeed, doing masculinity strengthens claims to belonging and thus acceptance for gay men living in small towns. Jake was typical of those who were currently living in a small town: He saw his identity as distinct from effeminate gay sexuality. He said that his friend refers to him and his partner as her "flannel gays." Elaborating on that description, he said, "We're always doing projects outside in the yard, building things. So yeah, sometimes I guess I feel like a little bit of a hick . . . maybe that's why I fit in so well up here!" In Jake's assessment, the fact that he is a "little bit of a hick" is tied to his engagement with practices of rural masculinity. Importantly, he also points to these facts as reasons why he "fit[s] in so well up here." Like practices of female masculinity, practices of male masculinity can signal belonging in small towns.

Xander also expressed a sense that masculinity could lead to acceptance in small towns: "I think it has to do with what you do [or] how you make your living. . . . If you're a flaming gay queen, they're like, 'Oh, you're a freak, I'm scared of you.' But if you're a really butch woman and you're working at a factory, I think it's a little easier." He thinks acceptance is easier "if you're doing something that the town thinks is really useful to the community, [or if you're] doing the things that they're doing." Acceptance is predicated on masculinized discourses of work and "use" in the community—and a "flaming gay queen" is seen as having little ability to contribute to the community, in contrast to a "butch woman."

Like gay men who distanced themselves from effeminacy, lesbian women embraced practices and discourses associated with masculinity. In fact, female masculinity, so long as it was entangled with the country rather than the city, further strengthened women's ability to assert belonging in small towns. Since being able to signal belonging is integral to having one's sexual identity accepted, these data highlight how the nature of acceptance for rural gays and lesbians is gendered.

VISIBILITY

Another way that the experience of sexual minorities in rural towns is gendered is that, unlike effeminacy, which is assumed to be linked to gay sexuality for men, more masculine gender presentations are not understood as linked only to lesbian sexuality for women. Therefore, visibility of lesbian identity is achieved differently in rural areas than in urban areas. Unlike in urban areas, more butch gender presentations are not enough make lesbian identity visible in rural areas. Rather, being seen around town with a same-sex partner is a way lesbian sexual identity is visible in rural areas given the close-knit nature of rural life. Thus, one route to visibility in rural contexts is relational (via connection with a same-sex partner) rather than individual (via butch gender presentations).

Speculating on how effeminate men are visible in rural areas, Xander said: "I think it'd be hard anywhere

rural if you were, like, a really flamboyant gay guy. There's really no way to read that [other than] feminine. It's always off from what they're expecting." Whereas effeminate men have no other way of being understood than as gay in rural towns, the opposite is true for butch women. Like Nancy, in her comments presented at the beginning of this article, many women maintained that it is difficult to distinguish between rural heterosexual and lesbian women by using butch gender presentation. Rita said that, in the rural Midwest, "you can't tell whether women are or aren't because they all have potential!" Chelsea echoes this sentiment:

> It's kinda funny around here, because you're, like, "Hey, honey, is she 'family'?" We'll be talking and it'll be, like, "I don't know, she might just be a farmer hick." You know, here's a woman with short hair, hiking boots, with a wallet in her back pocket . . . no, she's just a farmer!

Chelsea's example of a woman who is "just a farmer," but who also could be a lesbian because of her more butch gender practices, highlights how female masculinity is not categorically linked with lesbian sexuality in small towns.

Thus, the meanings of gender presentations are geographically specific. Although gender presentations, particularly more butch self-presentations, are a route to visibility for lesbians in urban areas, they do not always translate the same way in rural towns. For instance, when I asked Jenny if she thought she was visible as a lesbian in her small town, she replied, "We're pretty stereotypical. I mean, look at me, I'm in jeans, a T-shirt, and a hat . . . but that's like the general attire of so many women here!" That non-feminine attire aligns with the "general attire" of heterosexual women in the area makes it less salient in achieving lesbian visibility. Xander agrees, noting that "if you're a flannel-wearing lesbian, they may not see the lesbian part of it," which he thinks makes life "easier" for rural lesbian women than for gay men.

I argue that these data reveal how individual butch gender presentations are not *enough* to make women's nonnormative sexuality visible in rural areas. Rather, being seen around town with a same-sex partner is a rural specific way of achieving visibility. This is particularly important for couples who describe themselves as more masculine, as most of the coupled rural women did. For instance, when I asked Jenny if other people knew she was in a same-sex couple, she said, "I just assume people know we are, because we go in together all the time." Evelyn's reflections echo Jenny's. Evelyn, who described "some parts of herself as butch," was living in a city, but wanted to move to the country. Interestingly, she imagines that being away from the city would lead to a decrease in the visibility of her sexual identity. Elaborating, she said, "In the city you're more visible to more people. In the country they aren't going to necessarily think anything of it unless they see you with somebody else." Particularly telling are her words "unless they see you with somebody else." Although Evelyn sees her sexual identity as visible in the city, she speculates that it would not be so in the country unless she was with a same-sex partner.

Understandings of female same-sex sexuality have historically been linked to displaying masculine gender presentations and having a same-sex sexual partner (Chauncey 1982), and both continue to circulate. Although more butch-like individual gender presentations make lesbian identity visible in urban contexts (Kennedy and Davis 1993; Moore 2006), this is not the case in rural areas, where having a same-sex partner is more paramount in signaling lesbian sexuality. Interestingly, this is also the case for femme lesbian women across geographic contexts (Walker 2001). Although the sexual identity of rural butch lesbian women is not invisible in urban lesbian cultures, their more butch gender presentations do not do the same work in rural areas because those gender presentations are also tied to normative (hetero)sexuality.

CONCLUSION

Presuming that more lesbian than gay couples live outside urban areas in the United States, I analyze the mutually constitutive relationships among place, gender, and sexuality to assess why this might be the case. Constructions of female masculinity align with those of rurality and lesbian sexuality, which may leave room for some lesbians to be able to stay in rural places. Likewise, that constructions of male femininity align with gay sexuality but not rurality may mean that the ability for some gay men to stay put in rural areas might be constrained. How these categories are coconstructed sheds light on the gendered nature of acceptance for rural sexual minorities: Both lesbian women and gay men gain acceptance by engaging with masculinized practices and discourses. Finally, visibility of lesbian sexuality is achieved relationally (via a same-sex partner) rather than individually (via more butch gender presentations) given the degree to which all rural women, regardless of sexuality, enact more masculine presentations.

Rural lesbians' engagement with masculinity both reproduces and challenges the gender order in small towns. Rural lesbians challenge the rural gender order insofar as they assert sexuality not tied to men and disrupt the expectations that rural women be heterosexual. Yet their engagement with masculinizing practices and discourses reproduce the conflation of masculinity and rurality, which works to marginalize femininity as well as people who display nonnormative gender presentations. Thus, that more bodies may be privy to masculinity does not necessarily entail a revaluation of what practices constitute dominant and subordinate masculinities or femininities in rural areas.

These findings extend knowledge about rural sexual minorities by showing how gender matters for lesbian women in rural areas. Although both heterosexual and lesbian women might embrace female masculinities, this is not to say that sexuality is irrelevant. Rural sexual minorities face unique constraints not faced by rural heterosexuals or their urban counterparts, including, for instance, isolation and a lack of a visible, sustained gay community (Coby and Welch 1997; McCarthy 2000). [. . .]

This work also provides insights useful to understanding sexuality more broadly. First, it underscores the degree to which nonnormative sexuality is becoming delinked from nonnormative gender (Valentine 2007). Valentine (2007) argues that the emergence of the category "transgender" reflects how mainstream gay movements worked to distance gay and lesbian identity from gender variance. He suggests that the delinking might be more true for gay men than for lesbian women. Given the degree to which rural gay men, but not lesbian women, created a clear distinction between their sexual identity and gender nonnormativity, this article provides one empirical example that supports his assessment. Second, these findings also suggest that analyses of sexual minorities would benefit from a more explicit focus on femininity and masculinity. Work focused on gays and lesbians in other contexts should assess how the experiences of gay men or lesbian women might differ by gendered presentations.

In addition, this work extends understandings of masculinity. It indicates that the meanings of gender presentations differ across geographic contexts. Although female masculinity is the most visible gender presentation of lesbian identity in urban contexts, it does not hold the same meaning in rural contexts because masculine gender presentation is acceptable for all rural women, regardless of sexuality. Extending this finding more broadly, this work underscores that the meanings and values attributed to masculinity and femininity vary across context. [. . .] Furthermore, in contrast to previous researching suggesting that women doing masculinity is culturally disruptive and personally transgressive, this work shows one instance of female masculinity that is normative. Importantly, the practices of masculinity in which rural lesbian women engage must be understood as specific to rurality.

These findings draw attention to how an intersectional approach can enrich theorizing of masculinity. Overall, this work provides more empirical weight to the call in gender studies to disentangle masculinity from men and male bodies.

REFERENCES

Bell, D., and G. Valentine. 1995. "Queer Country: Rural Lesbian and Gay Lives." *Journal of Rural Studies* 11: 113–22.

Bell, S. E., and Y. A. Braun. 2010. "Coal, Identity, and the Gendering of Environmental Justice Activism in Central Appalachia." *Gender & Society* 24: 794–813.

Bettie, Julie. 2003. *Women without Class*. Berkeley: University of California Press.

Bird, S. 2006. "Masculinities in Rural Small Business Ownership: Between Community and Capitalism." In *Country Boys: Masculinity and Rural Life*, edited by Hugh Campbell, Michael Bell, and Margaret Finney. University Park: Pennsylvania State University Press.

Boulden, Walter T. 2001. "Gay Men Living in a Rural Environment." *Journal of Gay and Lesbian Social Services* 12: 63–75.

Brandth, Berit. 2006. "Agricultural Bodybuilding: Incorporations of Gender, Body and Work." *Journal of Rural Studies* 22: 12–27.

Campbell, H., M. M. Bell, and M. Finney, eds. 2006. *Country Boys: Masculinity and Rural Life*. University Park: Pennsylvania State University Press.

Chauncey, George Jr. 1982. "From Sexual Inversion to Homosexuality: Medicine and the Changing Conceptualization of Female Deviance." *Salmagundi* 58/59: 144–46.

Coby, P., and P. Welch. 1997. "Rural Gay Men in Northern New England: Life Experiences and Coping Styles." *Journal of Homosexuality* 33: 51–67.

Connell, Raewyn. 1995. *Masculinities*. Berkeley: University of California Press.

Falk, W., and L. M. Lobao. 2003. "Who Benefits from Economic Restructuring? Lessons from the Past and Challenges for the Future." In *Challenges for Rural America in the Twenty-First Century*, edited by D. L. Brown and L. E. Swanson. University Park: Pennsylvania State University Press.

Finley, N. J. 2010. "Skating Femininity: Gender Maneuvering in Women's Roller Derby." *Journal of Contemporary Ethnography* 39: 359–87.

Gates, G. J., and J. Ost. 2004. *The Gay and Lesbian Atlas*. Washington, DC: Urban Institute.

Gray, Mary L. 2009. *Out in the Country: Youth, Media, and Queer Visibility in Rural America*. New York: New York University Press.

Halberstam, Judith. 1998. *Female Masculinity*. Durham, NC: Duke University Press.

Hennen, Peter. 2008. *Faeries, Bears, and Leathermen: Men in Community Queering the Masculine*. Chicago: University of Chicago Press.

Herring, Scott. 2007. "Out of the Closets, into the Woods: RFD, Country Women, and the

Post-Stonewall Emergence of Queer Anti-urbanism." *American Quarterly* 59: 341–72.

Hill Collins, Patricia. 1990. *Black Feminist Theory: Knowledge, Consciousness, and the Politics of Empowerment*. New York: Routledge.

Howard, John. 1999. *Men Like That: A Southern Queer History*. Chicago: University of Chicago Press.

Hubbs, Nadine. 2011. "'Redneck woman' and the Gendered Poetics of Class Rebellion." *Southern Cultures* 17: 44–70.

Hughes, Annie. 1997. "Rurality and 'Cultures of Womanhood.'" In *Contested Countryside Cultures*, edited by P. Cloke and J. Little. New York: Routledge.

Johnson, Patrick E. 2008. *Sweet Tea: Black Gay Men of the South*. Chapel Hill: University of North Carolina Press.

Kazyak, Emily. 2011a. "Disrupting Cultural Selves: Constructing Gay and Lesbian Identities in Rural Locales." *Qualitative Sociology* 34: 561–81.

Kazyak, Emily. 2011b. "'If We Were Rednecks': The Classed and Raced Meanings of Space." Unpublished manuscript.

Kazyak, Emily. 2012. "Midwest or Lesbian? Gender, Rurality, and Sexuality." *Gender & Society* 26 (6): 825–48.

Kennedy, E., and M. Davis. 1993. *Boots of Leather, Slippers of Gold: The History of a Lesbian Community*. New York: Penguin Books.

Laore, C., and S. Fielding. 2006. "Rooted and Routed Masculinities among the Rural Youth of North Cork and Upper Swaledale." In *Country Boys: Masculinity and Rural Life*, edited by H. Campbell, M. Bell, and M. Finney. University Park: Pennsylvania State University Press.

Little, J., and P. Austin. 1996. "Women and the Rural Idyll." *Journal of Rural Studies* 12: 101–11.

Little, Jo. 1997. "Employment Marginality and Women's Self-identity." In *Contested Countryside Cultures*, edited by Paul Cloke and Jo Little. New York: Routledge.

McCarthy, Linda. 2000. "Poppies in a Wheat Field." *Journal of Homosexuality* 39: 75–94.

Moore, Mignon. 2006. "Lipstick or Timberlands? Meanings of Gender Presentation in Black Lesbian Communities." *Signs: Journal of Women in Culture and Society* 32: 113–29.

Morris, Edward W. 2008. "'Rednecks,' 'ruters,' and ''rithmetic': Social Class, Masculinity, and Schooling in a Rural Context." *Gender & Society* 22: 728–51.

Nagel, Joane. 2003. *Race, Ethnicity, and Sexuality: Intimate Intersections, Forbidden Frontiers*. Oxford: Oxford University Press.

Pascoe, C. J. 2007. *Dude You're a Fag: Masculinity and Sexuality in High School*. Berkeley: University of California Press.

Rupp, L. J., V. Taylor, and E. I. Shapiro. 2010. "Drag Queens and Drag Kings: The Difference Gender Makes." *Sexualities* 13: 275–94.

Sachs, Carolyn E. 1983. *The Invisible Farmers*. Totowa, NJ: Rowman & Allanheld.

Sachs, Carolyn E. 2006. "Foreword." In *Country Boys: Masculinity and Rural Life*, edited by H. Campbell, M. Bell, and M. Finney. University Park: Pennsylvania State University Press.

Schippers, Mimi. 2002. *Rockin' out of the Box: Gender Maneuvering in Alternative Hard Rock*. New Brunswick, NJ: Rutgers University Press.

Schippers, Mimi. 2007. "Recovering the Feminine Other: Masculinity, Femininity, and Gender Hegemony." *Sociological Theory* 36: 85–102.

Shapiro, Eve. 2007. "Drag Kinging and the Transformation of Gender Identities." *Gender & Society* 21: 250–71.

Smyth, Jolene D. 2007. "Doing Gender When Home and Work Are Blurred: Women and Sex-Atypical Tasks in Family Farming." Ph.D. diss., Washington State University, Pullman, WA.

Tickamyer, A. R., D. A. Henderson, J. A. White, and B. L. Tadlock. 2000. "Voices of Welfare Reform: Bureaucratic Rationality versus the Perceptions of Welfare Participants." *Affilia* 15: 173–92.

Tickamyer, A. R., and D. A. Henderson. 2003. "Rural Women: New Roles for a New Century." In *Challenges for Rural America in the Twenty-First Century*, edited by D. L. Brown and L. E. Swanson. University Park: Pennsylvania State University Press.

U.S. Bureau of the Census. 2000. *2000 Summary File 1. Table GCT-P6: Race and Hispanic or Latino–State–Urban/Rural and Inside/Outside Metropolitan Area*. Washington, DC: U.S. Census Bureau.

Valentine, David. 2007. *Imagining Transgender*. Durham, NC: Duke University Press.

Walker, Lisa. 2001. *Looking Like What You Are: Sexual Style, Race, and Lesbian Identity*. New York: New York University Press.

Wilkins, Amy C. 2004. "Puerto Rican Wannabes: Sexual Spectacle and the Marking of Race, Class, and Gender Boundaries." *Gender & Society* 18: 103–21.

Wray, Matt. 2006. *Not Quite White*. Durham, NC: Duke University Press.

NOTES

1. [The data for this reading come from 60 interviews with gay men and lesbians living in the Midwest. More information on the study and research methods can be found in the full version of the article (*Gender & Society* 26: 825–48)].

2. Thanks especially to Nadine Hubbs for this point.

KARL BRYANT

28. WILLIAM'S DOLL AND ME

For people unfamiliar with *Free to Be . . . You and Me*, it's hard to imagine the impact it had when it first appeared in the early 1970s. An album, a children's book, and an Emmy-winning television "special," *Free to Be . . . You and Me* was a children's media blockbuster. The project was the brain child of actress Marlo Thomas, who went looking for non-sexist children's books for her young niece Dionne but was shocked to find only stories based on extremely traditional gender stereotypes (in reflecting on those experiences, Thomas noted one particularly egregious example, a book telling kids that "boys invent things, girls use what boys invent"[1]). Finding nothing in the way of alternatives, Thomas set out to create one herself. With input from friends like Gloria Steinem and a partnership with the newly minted Ms. Foundation for Women, Thomas and her colleagues amassed a team of writers, actors, artists, and singers to produce fresh material that would "help children to be unencumbered by stereotypes—to capitalize on their unique strengths and understand that whatever their gender, race, or ethnic identity, or their economic origins, they were free to pursue their talents and their dreams."[2] Instead of recycling post-war "Leave It to Beaver" fantasies of white, middle class, normatively gendered propriety and conformity, Marlo Thomas and friends told children to be who they wanted to be, and that they were free to be just about whatever they could dream up for themselves.[3]

A child of that era, lots of people of my generation hold on to extremely fond memories of *Free to Be*. When I mention *Free to Be* to friends and colleagues, their first response is often to begin singing their favorite song from the album, and more than one friend has told me about how much they've looked forward

to passing on those songs and stories to their own children. Yet, unlike many kids of my generation, I didn't wear out a *Free to Be* album on my kiddie record player, nor do I have a treasured copy of the book on a shelf or in a box somewhere. Granted, at ten years old when the record debuted I was a little outside the target demographic (my eight year old brother was closer to the age range the stories spoke to). However, age aside, there were other reasons why the book and record might have been kept from my childhood home.

No, I didn't grow up in a conservative, overtly anti-feminist household. My family held some at least vaguely left-leaning values, especially concerning "social issues." There were both Democrats and Republicans among us, but no Phyllis Schlaflys. Instead, most of us thought that "women's lib"—at least the egalitarian-focused liberal feminism with which we were most familiar—was reasonable, fair, and good. Along with this mild commitment to (or at least tolerance for) some forms of feminism, my extended family was not exactly a study in egregious gender stereotypes: my dad and uncles were soft spoken, sometimes referred to as "gentle" men by my aunts, whereas the women on both sides of my family struck me as leaders rather than followers. What's more, my parents were well-versed in post-war parenting approaches that touted a new answer to the question of what kids should be when they grow up ("anything as long as you're happy"), where children's self-actualization became the hallmark of successful parenting. We seemed like the kind of family where *Free to Be* would be welcomed in with open arms. Except that for many years my parents had received expert advice directing them away from many of the messages found in *Free to Be*.

This reading is an excerpt from Lori Rotskoff and Laura L. Lovett's (eds.) *When We Were Free to Be: Looking Back at a Children's Classic and the Difference It Made* (Chapel Hill: University of North Carolina Press, 2012). Copyright © 2012 by the University of North Carolina Press. Used by permission of the publisher. http://www.uncpress.unc.edu/.

Some of my earliest memories are of wanting to be a girl. I expressed this in many ways—through the toys I asked for, the clothes I dressed up in, the games I played, and my fantasies for the present and the future. My parents started out tolerating this as "just a phase," but when my desires, behaviors and identifications hadn't diminished by the time I started kindergarten, any tolerance was overshadowed by deep concern. It turned out that by being born in Southern California in the early 1960s, I was within striking (and driving) distance of what was then a hotbed of research on "childhood gender variance." At the time, a small coterie of researchers and clinicians at UCLA were developing a new area of expertise by studying and treating children who did not conform to standard notions of what it meant to be boys and girls. Through a family friend, my parents learned about psychiatrist Richard Green, then a young rising star and already a leading figure in this new area.[4] We started seeing Dr. Green every other Saturday morning, where through play and talk therapy I would learn subtle and not-so-subtle lessons about how boys were really supposed to act. At the time I didn't know it, but I was part of a long-term study designed to track the adult outcomes of profound forms of childhood gender variance. Dr. Green (and others) wanted to know how boys like me turn out when we grow up, especially concerning adult sexual orientation and gender identity. Would I be homosexual, heterosexual, transsexual? A cross-dresser, bisexual, or something else altogether?

Whether or not my parents discussed *Free to Be*, it's a fair guess that they would have had some hesitations about introducing it into our household. One goal of the time spent at UCLA was that I more clearly, and normatively, experience and express myself *as a boy*. The kind of expert advice my parents were getting, and the journey they'd begun when they started somewhat ambivalently down a path that included therapy for their gender nonconforming son, meant that the messages in *Free to Be* might not have been exactly what they were looking for.

Nonetheless, I did come into contact with *Free to Be*. It was too much a part of the social landscape of childhood in the United States during the 1970s for me to remain unaware of it for long. I don't remember

exactly where or how I first came across *Free to Be*. Maybe we played the record and learned the songs while visiting my cousins. Maybe I saw the book when I was over at a friend's house. We might have even watched the television special at home when it first aired in 1974. But, one way or another, I did encounter it.

Free to Be is repeatedly described (in the original introduction, in retrospectives, and in news reports) as a collection of stories that replaces messages about what kids *should* be with messages about what they *could* be. It did this primarily by challenging the gender stereotypes that were (and mostly still are) prevalent in the cultural products that saturate children's lives. As a result, *Free to Be* included many portrayals of gender nonconforming girls and boys, men and women—that is, people doing things that aren't typically or traditionally associated with their presumed gender. In other words, people kind of like me! From mommies and daddies with unconventional occupations to athletic princesses who chose adventure over marriage, *Free to Be* often challenged gender stereotypes through individual expressions of ostensibly non-traditional genders.

William's Doll is one such story. Adapted in *Free to Be* from Charlotte Zolotow's 1972 children's book,[5] it introduces us to William, a young boy who wants a doll of his own to "hug and hold." For this, he is taunted by his older brother and other boys who call him a "sissy" and a "jerk." William's father, also initially anti-doll, has a solution: he gets William a slew of sports gear. It turns out that William excels at and enjoys all these "things a boy would love." Yet, he still wants a doll. Finally, along comes William's grandmother, who buys him the doll, explaining to William's father that a doll is just fine for William, "cause some day he may want to be a father, too."

Not surprisingly, this was the one story in the collection that most caught my attention. As a gender nonconforming child, I was able to identify in some ways with a character like William. It's true, I wasn't all that interested in having a *baby* doll that I could "wash and clean and dress and feed." What I really wanted was a doll I could dress *up*, say, maybe a Barbie (something that was never going to show up in *Free to Be*). Even so, here was a boy who wanted a doll, said it out loud, was reprimanded for those desires, yet in the end prevailed and got what he was after all along. In some ways, it seemed like *William's Doll* was written specifically for kids like me.

William's Doll and *Free to Be* were just two examples of a larger phenomenon. When Marlo Thomas went looking for stories to read to her young niece Dionne yet found none that met her expectations, she discovered firsthand something that feminist scholars were learning through more systematic inquiry: existing children's books forcefully reinforced traditional, stereotypic notions of gender. The same year that *Free to Be* was first released, a now classic study[6] found that portrayals in prize-winning children's picture books reinforced traditional gender stereotypes. Boys and men were active, leaders, independent, self-confident, and found camaraderie in their male friendships. Girls and women, on the other hand, were passive, immobile, pleasing, helping, and relied on men. Men and boys were praised for achievement and cleverness; women and girls, for their attractiveness. Occupations and social roles also reflected traditional gender stereotypes. Grown women, for example, were universally portrayed as wives and mothers.

This overabundance of traditional representations inspired Marlo Thomas to conceive *Free to Be*; it inspired others as well to create representations for children that worked to undo gender stereotypes. Beginning in the early 1970s, feminist-inspired writers, illustrators, editors, and even entire presses created a mini-boom of new "non-sexist" children's books.

Motivated in part by my own experiences reading *William's Doll*, a few years ago I carried out a systematic study of children's stories about gender nonconformity that were part of this boom of "non-sexist" literature produced in the wake of second-wave feminism. There was plenty for me to look at—books about athletic girls, dancing men, sports-writer moms, and of course boys who had (or wanted) dolls.[7] I found these books through indexes of non-sexist children's literature, the kinds of resources that feminist educators, librarians, or even parents might have turned to.

Yet as I examined these books comprehensively, I also found that they tacitly reinforced traditional ideas about gender even as they tried to promote alternatives. This was especially the case in stories about boys, but also in stories about girls as well. For example, girls' gender nonconformity was most often tolerated or valorized when it served others' interests. Girls' gender nonconformity was permitted or even welcomed when it served immediate and basic interests (for example, in wilderness stories where girls' skill at "men's work" like hunting could help keep people alive),[8] or in situations where there weren't enough boys on hand (for example, where a ball-playing girl could fill out a school baseball team).[9] Other times, a girl's competence at gender nonconforming behaviors was used to shame or encourage boys to be more manly ("if a *girl* can do X, shouldn't you be able to, too?").[10]

By contrast, boys' gender nonconformity was tolerated or valorized when either the boy or the gender nonconformity itself was masculinized. For instance, in one story, a boy dancer's father can tolerate ballet because it "is certainly good exercise for athletes,"[11] and in the well known *Oliver Button Is a Sissy*, Oliver's father (who strongly disapproved of his son's gender nonconformity) allows that Oliver can take dance lessons "especially for the exercise."[12] Other times, a boy's skill and success in masculine-coded endeavors, such as baseball, worked to offset his gender nonconformity, as in dancing.[13] And in some stories, the struggles themselves that are associated with being a gender nonconformist (being teased, getting in fights) served to prove one's masculinity, as illustrated when Doug, who is teased and physically bullied mercilessly for being a ballet dancer, fights back even when outnumbered and overpowered. When the ordeal ends, the bully ringleader tells Doug, "'[y]ou're no sissy. You put up a good fight.'"[14]

The child characters in these stories had their own ways of explaining their gender nonconformity, too. Whereas girls overwhelmingly explained it as an active refusal to adhere to traditional gender norms, boys sometimes explained their gender nonconformity as a "second choice" that they were forced to make because of their lack of skill, capacity, or competence to succeed at more "properly" gendered behaviors. Girls critiqued a gender system that they found to be fundamentally unfair (and where they saw traditional "women's roles" as limiting, silly, drudgery, or boring); boys used an individualist mode for understanding and explaining their gender nonconformity. The upshot was that none of the stories about boys I looked at included a critique of traditional notions of masculinity, whereas stories about girls overtly critiqued traditional notions of femininity.

While this meant that gender expectations themselves were being critiqued and expanded for girls and women, that critique and expansion came at a price: things that had been stereotypically associated with women (such as housework or motherhood) were sometimes denigrated in the process of expanding other options for women; this denigration often happened in the process of attaching positive value to girls' and women's gender nonconformity. There was little room for girls to enjoy "girly" things, or to have aspirations associated with traditional notions of femininity. This aspect of *Free to Be* and other "non-sexist" children's literature has sometimes been critiqued in a liberal humanist vein for the way that it limits girls' *choices*; however, such an approach also risks undervaluing what have traditionally been considered forms of "women's work" and "ways of being." And for boys and men, there was little in the way of critique at all; instead, gender nonconforming behaviors were redefined as actually adhering to traditional gender expectations.

William's Doll shared some of the features of the broader body of children's literature I've been describing. In the story, we are repeatedly reassured of William's masculinity via the skill he exhibits and the pleasure he takes in sports as a boy; we're also assured, at least implicitly, of his heterosexuality via the future that is mapped out for him as a father. It's made clear that William is a "real" boy and will become a man. This same reassurance is also expressed in *Free to Be*'s "Parents are People," where we are told that Mommies can be just about anything *except* "grandfathers . . . Or daddies" and Daddies can be anything *except* "grandmas . . . Or mommies." Maybe not so surprisingly, then, my own initial reactions to the story left me feeling uneasy. Why should William first have to take part in and enjoy "boy's stuff" like baseball and basketball, I asked myself, in order to get his doll? Later, I wondered why William's desire for a doll had to be justified by linking him with a future as a father, where William was at least tacitly heterosexualized.

My desire for a doll represented for me something completely different. It was but one example of a profound, pleasurable, and sometimes painful *identification* with girls, women, and femininity. There was very little, it seemed to me, suggesting any feminine identification in William. Instead, William fit into the trend in the broader non-sexist children's literature from the time where masculinity was shored up and traditional forms of femininity were implicitly devalued. As a decidedly and self-consciously *feminine* child who was both deeply ashamed of this fact and yet also struggled to somehow be proud of it, I sensed that despite the promise conveyed in its title, *William's Doll* wasn't really about kids like me. In some respects, the story even felt like a betrayal.

So, in retrospect, do I believe that *William's Doll*, *Free to Be*, and the broader set of related children's literature, should be seen as failures? No, I don't think so. During the 1970s, *William's Doll* and the *Free to Be* project as a whole were breaking new ground: they are examples of early, notable attempts to attach positive value to gender nonconformity through mass-produced cultural products. Up until that time, there had been virtually no conscious attempts in this realm to represent gender nonconformity except in pathologizing, stigmatizing or otherwise denigrating terms. Today there are listservs and peer support groups for parents of gender nonconforming children; advocacy organizations and annual conferences for trans* and gender variant kids and their families; children's books with gender-queer characters, TV shows and news reports (sometimes sensationalist, sometimes sensitive) about kids with a range of gender identities, and so on: in other words, a host of representations and an emerging social support network for gender nonconforming children. When *Free to Be* was first conceived, *none* of this existed. And in important ways, work like *Free to Be* helped pave the way for the kind of thinking, organizing, and advocating that exists today. Yet, early "affirmative" representations of marginalized groups that have previously been negatively portrayed—or not portrayed at all—are up against a daunting and almost impossible task. There's an incredible burden on such representations. They animate the expectations, or simply the secret hopes, of people who may have never seen more than a hint of their true experiences represented. So maybe it's not surprising when such attempts sometimes fall short of such high expectations.

What's more, *William's Doll*, *Free to Be*, and similar books from this era are limited by the vision of social change that was at the heart of these stories. While the stories are very obviously about gender, the world they imagined was really about a "gender-blind" society, where equality and justice would be achieved largely through getting *beyond* gender. What this often meant was that the notion of gender nonconformity (or even gender writ large) was effectively erased. For example, in a story about a group of girls who are creating a "tomboy" club, one of the girl's mothers objects that a tomboy club is "old-fashioned" because girls can do anything that boys can do.[15] This kind of narrative not only presumed a level of gender equity that did not yet exist in reality, but it also erased any notion of gender nonconformity, or worse, made it seem retrograde. The impetus behind such visions of social change—which many progressive minded people still hold to—was ultimately to make gender irrelevant so that it ceased to be a primary vector through which inequality was produced. Given this model for achieving equality, it's not surprising that *William's Doll* and other children's stories produced in a similar vein did not fully validate the lived experiences of being a gender nonconforming child.

In writing this essay, I went back to the various versions of *William's Doll* and *Free to Be* and became familiar with them all over again for the first time in several years. In doing so, I've found myself reconciling with William, if not completely with *William's Doll*. Yes, it's true that William is presented as a masculine boy who wants a doll. And yes, it's true that the final justification for getting the doll is linked to later fatherhood and presumptive heterosexuality. But it's the *grandmother* and the voice of the *author* presenting these perspectives, not William. When real life kids digress from others' expectations about their presumed gender, this also often gets "narrated" as trivial, a phase, as somehow *not* about a profound

sense of one's own gender identity or embodiment. But the fact that adults spin children's gender nonconformity in such ways doesn't tell us much at all about kids' own interior lives, or about the meanings and pleasures that they attach to their actions and desires. And maybe that's true of *William's Doll*, too. While others both torment William and provide explanations of who William is, there's very little that we hear directly from William. The one thing we do know is that William wants a doll and doesn't ever give up on that desire. That's a part of William's story well worth remembering and honoring today.

If we heard William speak today, maybe a different story would emerge. Instead of a world where gender no longer mattered, maybe gender and its relevance to our lives would be imagined in multiple forms *and* in ways that resist reproducing inequalities. Instead of reassurances of William's masculinity, maybe we'd hear about feminine identifications, including the pleasures and pains that are at the heart of so many people's complex gendered experiences. Certainly William still dreams of being "free to be," but perhaps in a slightly different cast and hue than the story written over forty years ago.

Acknowledgments: Thanks to Suzanne Kelly, Laura L. Lovett, Lori Rotskoff, and Jane Ward for their insightful comments on the original version of this essay. Thanks to Tristan Bridges and CJ Pascoe for including a revised version here.

NOTES

1. From Whitney Darrow, I'm Glad I'm a Boy! I'm Glad I'm a Girl! (Windmill Books, 1970), quoted in Marlo Thomas, "Prologue." Pp. 13–20 in When We Were Free to Be: Looking Back at a Children's Classic and the Difference It Made. Chapel Hill: University of North Carolina Press.

2. Letty Cottin Pogrebin, consulting editor for *Free to Be . . . You and Me*. Quoted at http://www.freetobefoundation.org/history.htm/.

3. For more on the genesis of *Free to Be . . . You and Me*, including the broader social context in which it was conceived, see Lori Rotskoff and Laura L. Lovett (Eds), *When We Were Free to Be: Looking Back at a Children's Classic and the Difference It Made*. Chapel Hill: University of North Carolina

Press; Marlo Thomas and Letty Cottin Pogrebin, "The History of Free to Be You and Me," http://www.freetobefoundation.org/history.htm/.

4. Richard Green had begun his work with gender nonconforming children while still a medical student at Johns Hopkins University in the 1950s under the mentorship of John Money. Money was well known at the time and remains (in)famous for his work on intersex infants and children. It was through Money that Green found his first gender nonconforming child to study as part of a yearlong student research project. Green and Money went on to publish work together across the 1960s, thus helping to lay the foundation for the development of a niche subspecialty on childhood gender variance within psychology and psychiatry. At the time, this work was largely motivated by an interest in understanding psychosexual development, and by the possibility of preventing a set of non-normative adult sexual orientation and gender identity outcomes, especially transsexuality.

5. Charlotte Zolotow, *William's Doll* (New York: Harper & Row, 1972).

6. Lenore J. Weitzman, Deborah Eifler, Elizabeth Hokada, and Catherine Ross, "Sex-Role Socialization in Picture Books for Preschool Children," *American Journal of Sociology* 77 (1972): 1125–50.

7. Examples of the books I looked at include John Beatty and Patricia Beatty, *Master Rosalind* (New York: William Morrow, 1974); Carol H. Behrman, *Catch a Dancing Star* (Minneapolis, MN: Dillon Press, 1975); Tomie De Paola, *Oliver Button Is a Sissy* (New York: Harcourt Brace Jovanovich, 1979); Louise Fitzhugh, *Nobody's Family Is Going to Change* (New York: Farrar, Straus and Giroux, 1974); Norma Klein, *Tomboy* (New York: Four Winds Press, 1978); Elizabeth Levy, *The Tryouts* (New York: Four Winds Press, 1979); Ben Shecter, *Hester the Jester* (New York: Harper & Row, 1977); Mary W. Sullivan, *What's This about Pete?* (Nashville, TN: Thomas Nelson, 1976); and Miriam Young, *No Place for Mitty* (New York: Four Winds Press, 1976). In total, I examined 29 children's books.

8. See, e.g., Patricia Beatty, *By Crumbs, It's Mine!* (New York: William Morrow, 1976); Moses L. Howard, *The Ostrich Chase* (New York: Holt, Rinehart and Winston, 1974).

9. See, e.g., Beatty and Beatty, *Master Rosalind*; Julia First, *Flat on My Face* (Englewood Cliffs, NJ: Prentice Hall, 1974); Mildred Lawrence, *Touchmark* (New York: Harcourt Brace Jovanovich, 1975).

10. See, e.g., Howard, *The Ostrich Chase*; Lawrence, *Touchmark*.

11. Marcia L. Simon, *A Special Gift* (New York: Harcourt Brace Jovanovich, 1978), p. 24.

12. De Paola, *Oliver Button Is a Sissy*, p. 20.

13. See, e.g., Elizabeth Winthrop, *Tough Eddie* (New York: Dutton, 1985); Zolotow, *William's Doll*.

14. William H. Hooks, *Doug Meets the Nutcracker* (New York: Frederick Warne, 1977), p. 72.

15. Klein, *Tomboy*.

LAUREL WESTBROOK AND KRISTEN SCHILT

29: PENIS PANICS: BIOLOGICAL MALENESS, SOCIAL MASCULINITY, AND THE MATRIX OF PERCEIVED SEXUAL THREAT

In January 2014, California law AB1266—the School Success and Opportunity Act—went into effect. This state law allows transgender youth "to participate in sex-segregated programs, activities and facilities," such as bathrooms and sports teams, that align with their gender identity (California State Legislature 2013). Although many applaud the law as a cutting-edge step in transgender equality, others have expressed outrage. Those opposed to the law claim that it puts children at risk. Part of what "risk" entails in this context is simply the knowledge that transgender people exist and are increasingly being validated institutionally and socially—an idea that some argue promotes a "dangerous" transgender "lifestyle" and is too "radical" to present to children (Bohon 2013). Karen England, executive director of the Capital Resources Institute, for example, argues that "AB 1266 forces San Francisco values on all California schools" (Starnes 2013). The other meaning of risk referenced by opponents is the idea that transgender people, particularly trans women and girls, become potential sexual threats when they are allowed to enter certain social spaces, such as gender-segregated bathrooms, locker rooms, and sports teams. As opponent Matt Staver, founder and director of the Liberty Counsel, warns, "Now, girls in elementary and high school will be forced to shower and change in locker rooms with boys masquerading as a girl. When an incident happens—and no question, it will—Governor Brown will have the innocence of that abused girl on his hands" (Bohon 2013).

AB1266 is just one of a number of recent transgender rights bills in the United States. The increasing (although sporadic and relatively limited) institutional legitimization of transgender rights in the United States suggests that the social determinants of who counts as a man and who counts as a woman are slowly changing. As the sex/gender/sexuality system (Seidman 1995) has encountered liberal values of self-determinism (Meyerowitz 2002) and transgender rights activism, the criteria for "determining gender" (Westbrook and Schilt 2014) have shifted from pure biological essentialism to some degree of self-determination.[1] However, as public debates about transgender inclusion demonstrate, the validation of such self-determination faces space-specific limitations. We argue that in two particular contexts—gender-segregated spaces and (hetero)sexual[2] interactions—transgender people, and in particular transgender women, face demands to provide proof that they hold the "biological credentials" (West and Zimmerman 1987) considered appropriate and necessary for participation in such settings.

Heteronormativity and gender inequality—the hallmarks of the current sex/gender/sexuality system—structure these context-specific oppositions to transgender people. The vocal fears of some cisgender[3] people about the "wrong body" in gender-segregated spaces or (hetero)sexual interactions generate "gender panics" (Westbrook and Schilt 2014), situations in which people frantically attempt to reassert the naturalness and rightness of a male/female binary (and, by proxy, heterosexuality). Situations and spaces that gain their logic and legitimacy from gender difference, such as (hetero)sexual interactions and gender-segregated public spaces, often are the sites of such panics. We explore such gender panics through an analysis of five case studies: (1) public debates over the expansion of transgender rights in employment, housing, and public accommodations, (2) policies determining eligibility of transgender people for competitive sports, (3) a proposal to remove the genital surgery requirement for a change of sex marker on birth certificates, (4) an ethnographic study of transgender men's workplace experiences, and (5) a textual analysis of media narratives about the killings of transgender people in the United States, almost all of whom are trans women.

We suggest that these contexts are best analyzed through what we term a "matrix of perceived sexual threat" (see Figure 1). This matrix delineates ways in which cisgender people interpret particular combinations of contexts, bodies, and gender identities as representing different degrees of potential sexual threat.[4] Although many scholars conflate masculinity and maleness as forms of embodiment that are socially constructed as potential sexual threats (e.g., Day 2001; Lane et al. 2009; Wilcox et al. 2006), our multi-context analysis indicates that presumed *biological maleness* (the state of having a penis) emerges as a stronger potential threat than *social masculinity* (self-identifying and presenting as a man). This distinction means that transgender women, who are widely assumed by cisgender people to still have penises, are seen as sexually threatening in a way that transgender men, who are often imagined to not have a "real" penis, are not—creating a *spectrum of perceived sexual threat*.[5] Because trans men do not have a "naturally occurring" penis, their gendered appearance becomes, for many cisgender people, social masculinity without biological maleness—a state that, although potentially stigmatized, is not imagined as particularly sexually threatening. Trans women, people who have or had "naturally occurring penises," in contrast, are seen as biologically male and thus sexually threatening. This spectrum of perceived sexual threat accounts for why cisgender opposition to transgender inclusion organizes predominantly around the presence of transgender women (not transgender men) in sexual interactions and gender-segregated spaces. This spectrum further suggests that gender panics around transgender people might more accurately be termed "penis panics" because they are fueled by terror of penises where they "should not" be or a lack of penis where one "should" be present. In the following sections, we illustrate how such panics both rely on and reproduce heteronormativity, homophobia, and gender inequality.

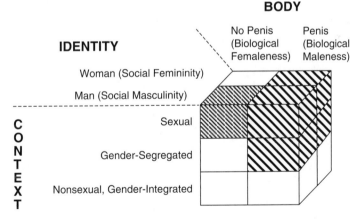

Different combinations of bodies, identities, and social contexts produce different social perceptions of potential sexual threat.

= Higher levels of perceived sexual threat. Can threaten both those with invincible and vulnerable subjecthoods.

= Lower levels of perceived sexual threat. Only a threat to those with vulnerable subjecthoods.

FIGURE 1 The Matrix of Perceived Sexual Threat

CONCEPTUAL FRAMEWORK

Our current sex/gender/sexuality system rests on a series of cultural assumptions: there are only two sexes, sex and gender are assumed to "match," heterosexuality is the norm, gender and sexuality are mutually dependent and reinforcing, and men and women are thought to have innately opposite personality traits and physical bodies. In this dimorphic imaginary, men have what we term an *invincible subjecthood* in which they actively accomplish masculinity through visible (hetero)sexual desire, ridicule of homosexuality and femininity, and demonstrated imperviousness to physical threats from other men (Pascoe 2007). In this masculinity duality, men are both protector and predator—the superhero who looks after women, but also the caveman with a biological propensity for heterosexual rape (Marcus 1992). Women's "vulnerable subjecthood" (Westbrook 2008), in contrast, positions them as passive tableaus on which the achievement of masculinity, and, as a result, heterosexuality, is enacted. In the cultural narrative of innate vulnerability, women are always at risk from "dangerous" men (Hollander 2001), typically imagined as strangers lurking in dark alleys—a risk that is warded off only through "protection" from other men.

Ideas about innate gender differences reinforce *heteronormativity*, a worldview that positions heterosexual coupling as the only natural and legitimate form of sexuality and assumes all bodies to be heterosexual. Heteronormativity deeply influences ideas about what sorts of bodies should interact in various social contexts, as well as the criteria used to "determine" someone's gender by placing them in a gender category (Westbrook and Schilt 2014). This process is evident in the different outcomes of interactions between cis and trans people in various social contexts. In most social interactions, cis people accept trans people's gender self-identity (Schilt 2010; Schilt and Westbrook 2009). However, in sexual contexts, opposite bodies are the norm because of cultural schemas about men and women's natural differences—an assumption commonly understood as the notion of "opposites attract" (Connell 1995; Schilt and Westbrook 2009), making normative sexual contexts homophobic. Because heterosexual interactions demand bodily oppositeness, people typically use genitals, not self-identity, as the criteria for determining a potential partner's gender in these contexts. In (hetero)sexual interactions, trans people who may have bodily configurations that do not align in normatively expected ways with their gender expression can face negative and, at times, violent reactions from heterosexual cisgender people who feel "tricked" into what they perceive as a "homosexual" interaction—"homosexual" because the heteronormative expectation of bodily oppositeness has been challenged (Schilt and Westbrook 2009).

Gender-segregated spaces present another potential context for gender panics about trans people. Although men and women freely interact in many public settings, such as the workplace, they sometimes are segregated into "men's spaces" and "women's spaces" on the basis of assumed differences in their bodies, as well widely shared beliefs about what activities are normal and appropriate for men or women (Goffman 1977; Lorber 1993; West and Zimmerman 1987). If sexual situations are where "opposites attract," these gender-segregated spaces are where "like meets like," and oppositeness is forbidden. As "sexuality-free zones," gender difference is a source of discomfort and a great deal of cultural fear can be generated when the "wrong bodies" gain access (Westbrook and Schilt 2014). Women's assumed vulnerability translates bodily difference in women's spaces into a potential sexual threat, making gender-segregated spaces *heterophobic* (Westbrook and Schilt 2014). Because the context of gender-segregated spaces relies on (and reproduces) an idea of gender oppositeness, in these contexts, like (hetero)sexual interactions, genitals, not self-identity, are used to determine gender (Westbrook and Schilt 2014).

Past scholarship on perceptions of men's dangerousness and women's vulnerability have highlighted that people perceive certain men (young, straight, poor, and/or of color) as more dangerous than their older/gay/wealthy/white counterparts (Hollander 2001). Here, we build on such scholarship, highlighting spectrums of perceived threat. We examine how cisgender people's reactions to transgender women and men in various social contexts indicate that discussions of "men" being seen as dangerous must be even more nuanced. As we show, it is biological maleness that presents a sexual threat to heterosexual cis men and women. In contrast, social masculinity coupled with biological femaleness is only seen as a sexual threat insofar as it can be a source of homosexual contamination to heterosexual cis women. In the matrix of perceived sexual threat, biological maleness and social masculinity sit on a spectrum such that not all "men" are seen as equally sexually threatening.[6]

CASE STUDIES

We analyze five case studies in this chapter, all of which draw on cisgender people's responses to transgender people, in an effort to explore the inner workings of the sex/gender/sexuality system. The first three come from collections of mainstream news articles about moments of conflict over transgender inclusion and rights: (1) federal and state proposals made between 2009 and 2011 to prohibit discrimination based on gender identity and expression in the arenas of employment, housing, and public accommodations (often called "transgender rights bills"); (2) a 2006 proposed policy in New York City to remove the genital surgery requirement for a change of sex marker on birth certificates; and (3) controversies over trans women and men participating in competitive sports. Our fourth data source is a systematic collection of mainstream news media coverage in the United States between 1990 and 2005 of the murders of transgender people (7,183 individual news stories about 232 murder victims, 228 of whom were trans women and transfeminine people). Our fifth and final case study is interviews with trans men and their coworkers about their "before and after" workplace experiences. For more details on the collection of the data used for these case studies, please see Westbrook and Schilt (2014) for the first three and Schilt and Westbrook (2009) for the last two.[7]

FINDINGS

Much of the literature on transgender discrimination attributes it to cis people responding negatively to what they perceive as "breaking gender norms" or exhibiting "gender non-conformity" (e.g., Lombardi et al. 2002; Namaste 2000; Stotzer 2009). Our data reveal an additional explanation. In all of our data sources, cis

people's fear of trans people as an actual or potential sexual threat is a central, organizing theme. However, cisgender people did not attribute threat to transgender people equally. Instead, we identify a matrix of perceived sexual threat, in which cis people's fears vary by the *context, gender identity,* and actual or imagined *bodies* of trans people. In gender-segregated spaces and sexual interactions, transgender people—and, in particular, trans women assumed to have penises—were positioned as dangerous in a way not seen in interactions in gender-integrated spaces, such as the workplace.

By far the most common threat imagined by cisgender people in our case studies is a transgender woman who has not undergone genital surgery. Because the penis is the hallmark of maleness (Connell 1995), transgender women with such real or imagined biological credentials are classified as male in narratives about their homicides and by opponents to transgender rights, regardless of their gender identity and appearance. Further, due to the cultural equation of male = potential rapist (Marcus 1992), the specter of trans woman as both a homo- and heterosexual threat to cis men, women, and children haunts these discussions. In news stories about transgender rights bills, participation on sports teams, and birth certificate policies, opponents portray trans women as heterosexually threatening to cisgender women and children in women's-only spaces, such as public bathrooms and locker rooms—spaces that, due to their heterophobia, have no adult men present as protection.[8] Cisgender opponents imagine scenarios in which trans women use their feminine appearance to gain access to women-only spaces and then use their innate male strength (and penis) to overpower and rape the cisgender women and children who have a "right" to be there on the basis of biological femaleness. In narratives around the murder of transgender people, in contrast, trans women are imagined by the news media to use their feminine appearance to trick straight, cisgender men into sexual encounters that, due to the presence of two "penises," are interpreted to be homosexual.

Showing how gender identity and bodies shape cis people's perceptions of sexual threat in the two contexts we identify as salient, trans men are rarely portrayed as sexually threatening to anyone. They can be integrated into many workplaces, allowed to play on men's sports teams without genital or hormonal modifications, and their presence in other men-only spaces such as bathrooms and locker rooms creates little imagined panic for opponents to transgender inclusion. We posit that this different perception of trans men is not a result of greater cultural acceptance. Rather, this difference illustrates our distinction between biological maleness and social masculinity. Trans men's social masculinity, which emerges from their male gender identity and masculine appearance, is accepted by many cisgender people in gender-integrated spaces. And, their assumed lack of a naturally occurring penis, the hallmark of biological maleness, renders them nonthreatening in gender-segregated spaces. Making this point, the only instances we documented where cis women expressed a sexual concern about trans men happened when they imagined a trans man to be in a sexual interaction with a straight cis woman who did not know that he was "really a woman" (meaning he did not have a naturally occurring penis). Trans men in these cases were not framed as rapists, or even as frightening, but rather as dishonest for "pretending to be" biologically male. The threat, then, is about deception, not rape. This distinction illustrates our point that biological maleness and social masculinity exist on a spectrum of perceived sexual threat, where bodies with invincible subjecthood (cis men) are only seen as sexually threatened by those with biological maleness, whereas those with vulnerable subjecthood (cis women and sometimes children) can be both heterosexually threatened by those with biological maleness and homosexually threatened by those with (penis-less) social masculinity.

In the following sections, we explore the roles of social masculinity and biological maleness in the matrix of perceived sexual threat by examining "penis panics" in gender-segregated spaces and sexual interactions.

CONTEXT: GENDER-SEGREGATED SPACES

In newspaper articles about the pro-transgender rights policies we analyzed, critics expressed their opposition as stemming from fears about people with "male anatomies" (Cave 2006) or "male genitalia" (Kwok 2006) being allowed in women's spaces such as restrooms, locker rooms, and prison cells. A common imagined interaction that generated gender panic was trans women with "male anatomies" being housed with female prisoners (Cave 2006; Staff 2006; Weiss 2006; Yoshino 2006) or trans women "who still have male genitalia" using women's bathrooms (Kwok 2006; Yoshino 2006). The common allusion to "male" genitalia when discussing the use of women-only spaces demonstrates that some cis people, at least those speaking out against transgender rights, conceive of woman-identified and feminine-presenting people who also have penises as really men on the basis of biological maleness.

When opponents to these policies worried about "male genitalia" in sex-segregated spaces, they were hinting at the possibility that those with "male anatomies" would sexually assault the women with whom they shared space. While most articles merely suggested this possibility, some were more explicit. An opinion piece about the New York City proposal argued that one of the dangers of the proposed law was "personal safety: Many communal spaces, like prison cells and public bathrooms, are segregated by sex to protect women, who are generally physically weaker than men, from assault or rape" (Yoshino 2006). Explaining his opposition to a New Hampshire transgender rights bill, Representative Robert Fesh similarly noted, "Parents are worried about their kids and sexual abuse" (Macarchuk 2009). Thus, in the minds of these opponents, trans women are males and all males are potential rapists. Moreover, there is an assumption of heteronormativity here, where all bodies with male anatomies, regardless of gender identity, desire female bodies, and many of them (enough to elicit concern from the public) are willing to use force to get access to those bodies.

In debates around transgender participation in sports, the specter of trans woman as (hetero)sexual threat also (oddly) features centrally in the discussion. For example, the United Kingdom's 2004 Gender Recognition Act, a law intended to grant more rights to transgender people, includes a provision that prohibits trans athletes' competition in cases that endanger the "safety of competitors" (Cavanagh and Sykes 2006). Discussion of safety in this case generally revolved around regulating access to contact sports. Yet, during debate around this act, another meaning of safety surfaced. Lord Moynihan is reported as saying that "many people will be greatly concerned at the idea of themselves or their children being forced to share a changing room with a trans-sexual person" (Mcardle 2008: 46). The allusion is that transgender people present a sexual danger to vulnerable others. Opponents conflate being transgender with sexual deviance and cast the penis as a dangerous sexual weapon.

That these imagined sexual assaults occur only in women-only spaces is worth further analysis because women share space with men daily without similar concerns. We suggest that women-only spaces generate intense *androphobia* because, by definition, these spaces should not contain bodies with penises. If women are inherently unable to protect themselves, and men (or, more specifically, penises) are inherently dangerous (Hollander 2001), the presence of a penis in women's space becomes terrifying because there are no other men there to protect the women. The "safe" (read: gender-segregated) space is transformed into a dangerous, (hetero)sexual situation by the entrance of an "improper body," a proverbial fox in a henhouse. These fears rely on and reproduce gender binarism, specifically the assumption of strong/weak difference in male/female bodies, as opponents assume that people who could be "unnaturally" gaining access to women's space (people with penises) are inherently stronger than cis women and easily able to overpower them. Because those "improper" bodies (those with invincible subjecthood) entering the space look like women, the danger is compounded. In our current cultural moment, "rapist" is a deeply gendered category and people are supposed to be able to quickly tell who is safe and who is potentially a rapist by appearance alone (here, a proxy for biological credentials). For opponents to transgender rights, trans women are wolves in sheep's clothing—potential rapists masquerading as women—a deception they position as legitimized by the passage of transgender-inclusive bills and policies.

By contrast to trans women, trans men in gender-segregated spaces were referenced only once by opponents in our analysis. In this case, they were not positioned as sexual threats to cis men and, instead, were viewed as biological females who should use the women's restroom no matter their masculine gender expression (Ball 2009). We suggest that trans men and trans women are policed differently because of the spectrum of perceived sexual threat created by different cultural beliefs about the dangerousness of biological maleness versus social masculinity. Trans men's perceived lack of a natural penis renders them biologically female and, under the logic of vulnerable subjecthood, unable to be highly sexually threatening (and, therefore, unlikely to generate public outcry). Cisgender men, the group who would share a bathroom or locker room with trans men, also are not seen in the public imagination as potential victims of sexual threat from bodies without penises because such an image is contradictory to cultural constructions of maleness and masculinity (Lucal 1995) as forms of invincible subjecthood. Trans men enter a liminal state, in some ways, because they cannot hurt men (making them women), but are not seen as warranting protection from men (making them part of a "pariah femininity" [Schippers 2007]). This gender difference in the matrix of perceived sexual threat derives from the interplay between heteronormativity and gender inequality. Feminine bodies imagined to have penises retain biological maleness and thus are sexually threatening in women's spaces in a way that masculine bodies without biological maleness are not in men's spaces, producing a spectrum of perceived sexual threat.

CONTEXT: SEXUAL INTERACTIONS

Trans women, who comprise more than 98 percent of the murder victims in the analyzed news stories, also are positioned as a sexual threat in narratives about the murder of transgender people. Showing the importance of context in our matrix of perceived sexual threat, these news stories portrayed trans women as biologically male and, therefore, homosexually threatening to straight cisgender men. Many articles describe the perpetrators (almost always straight, cisgender men[9]) and victims (almost always transfeminine people) as strangers or very recent acquaintances. In these narratives, cisgender men approach or are approached by an attractive woman for what they assume, on the basis of her appearance, is heterosexual sex. In this sexual interaction, the cisgender man "discovers" that the trans woman has a penis and reacts with physical violence. Articles often explain the resulting violence as caused by the perpetrators feeling deceived by the trans women about their "true gender" and, thereby, being "tricked" into a homosexual encounter.

The accusation of deception stems from the dominant cultural belief that anyone who has a penis is a man (biological maleness), even if that person identifies as and/or presents as a woman (social femininity). It is notable that none of the news articles about the murder of trans people who had had genital surgery employed the deception narrative. By contrast, the stories about murdered trans women who had not had genital surgery are peppered with phrases such as "secret," "lied," "tricked," "misled," "posed as a woman," "true gender," "really a woman," "true identity," "double life," "fooled," "deceit," "pretended," "masquerade," and "gender secret." In the minds of the journalists and perpetrators, biological maleness overrides social femininity. The deception narrative is so culturally resonant that even in cases where there is extensive evidence that the perpetrator knew the victim was transgender prior to the sexual act, such as the murder of Chanelle Pickett by William Palmer in 1995, many people involved in the case, including journalists, police officers, and jurors, still offer a deception frame in explaining the resulting murder.

The news stories portray the perpetrator's violent response to what they viewed as gender deception as reasonable because engaging in a sexual interaction with someone else with biological maleness (even unwittingly) rendered the interaction homosexual. Although trans women may self-identify as heterosexual women who desire men (their opposite), reporters and perpetrators categorize them as gay men on the basis of their genital configuration. These sexual interactions carry a heavy social weight through what we term the "one-act rule of homosexuality" (Schilt and Westbrook 2009). Similar to the idea that anyone with one drop of black blood is black (Davis 1991), both straight and gay people

often believe that engaging in sexual encounters with people of the same gender demonstrates an innate, previously hidden, homosexuality, no matter what sexual identity one may personally avow. In interviews and court testimony, the accused killers of Gwen Araujo articulate a belief that for a man to have sex with a person who has male-shaped genitals makes them homosexual, even if they were unaware of those genitals at the time. Mainstream news stories describe one of the convicted killers as starting to cry and repeating "I can't be gay" over and over again when the group of men "discovered" that Gwen Araujo had testicles (Airoldi 2003). It should be noted that the one-act rule applies mostly to men. Unlike straight cisgender women, who can publically be sexual with other women with little chance of having their claim to heterosexual privilege questioned (Hamilton 2007; Rupp and Taylor 2010), straight men's claim to straightness is more tenuous because the maintenance of invincible subjecthood (as well as, of course, gender inequality) requires active distancing from femininity and homosexuality, two ways of being associated with vulnerable subjecthood.

Taking the idea of sexual threat further, some news articles about these homicide cases cast trans women victims as rapists, a frame that attempts to justify the murder as done in "self-defense" (for example, see Connelly 2001, Cook 2002, and Lazenby 2002). This story is perceived as plausible, unlike stories about cis women as rapists, since the trans women are seen as biological males with invincible subjecthood who both desire and are capable of raping others. Interestingly, the accused murderers also sometimes frame the "deception" as a form of rape. To return to the murder of Gwen Araujo, one of her killers, Jaron Nabors, argued during the 2004 trial that Araujo raped his friends. When asked to explain, Nabors said, "He (Araujo) did not come clean with being what he really was. I feel like he forced them into homosexual sex, and my definition of rape was being forced into sex." When the attorney followed up with, "She forced them?," Nabors answered, "Through deception" (St. John 2004; see Wolf 1998 for a different case using the same framing). In this narrative, their masculinity is challenged because they feel "raped" and feminized through their connection to homosexuality. In the construction of invincible subjecthood, a sense of being a "real man" must be reclaimed through violence and force—the cultural logic that underlies these cases and accounts for why trials often end in hung juries or justified homicide verdicts (Schilt and Westbrook 2009; Westbrook 2009).

Unlike trans women, trans men are not seen as hetero- or homosexually threatening to cis men. Some cis men coworkers of trans men were, in contrast, happy to be in (hetero)sexualized spaces with them. Although some trans men personally identify as gay or queer, heteronormativity ensures that their co-workers imagine they are transitioning to become heterosexual men. When an open workplace transition has employer support, heterosexual cis men are willing in many cases to relate to trans men on the basis of a presumed shared sexual desire for women. Illustrating this, one co-worker describes taking his trans man colleague to Hooters because they both enjoy looking at "scantily clad women." It is notable that trans men are not seen as threatening to cis men in sexual situations. Although they may be seen as gender deviant, because of heteronormativity, they are assumed to share a sexual interest (women), and so are not a rape threat to cis men. Moreover, they are not perceived as having a penis and so are likely also not perceived as sexual competition.

As we note, in interviews with trans men we found a few instances of straight cis women positioning trans men as potentially threatening to other straight cis women. Showing how, when their sexuality becomes a topic of interest, trans men's self-identities can be trumped in the minds of others by people's ideas of their biological femaleness, Preston remembers telling a woman co-worker that he had a new girlfriend. He was shocked when she yelled across the room, "How do you have sex if you don't have a dick?" Her comment shows that, in his co-worker's mind, Preston does not have the essential signifier of manhood and therefore cannot really have penis/vagina intercourse—the hallmark of heterosexuality. In other instances, straight cis women take this rejection of self-identity a step farther, framing trans men as homosexual women who might "trick" unsuspecting heterosexual women into homosexual interactions. But, biological maleness and social masculinity are on a spectrum, the

perceived sexual threat is not that trans men will rape cis women—which they are imagined to be unable to do without a naturally occurring penis—but rather that they will taint unsuspecting straight cis women with the stigma of homosexuality. These cis women co-workers perceive a mismatch between their colleague's biological credentials and his gender identity, which comes to the forefront when they see trans men engaging in heterosexual flirtations with cisgender women.

These same women may accept the social masculinity of trans men when they do masculine roles at work, such as heavy lifting or killing spiders. But in these imagined sexualized situations, trans men become anchored to biological femaleness and, as a result, are labeled as homosexual women. Chris encountered such views in his first job as a man. Hired as a man, he planned not to come out as transgender at work. However, his transition became public knowledge when a high school colleague recognized him. Although she originally agreed not to tell anyone, she changed her mind. He says, "So basically for the first time in my life—I was nineteen—I had girls like like me, you know. And I think what happened was [this former classmate] was thinking, 'Oh that's sick, I better warn them.'" Although his co-workers continued to treat him as a man in nonsexual interactions, a woman he had set up a date with canceled. He had no further romantic interest shown to him by women at that job. His experience shows how women's acceptance of trans men's gender identity can be negated in sexualized interactions. Perhaps drawing on their own surprise at learning that someone who looks like a man might not have a penis, they want to alert other women who could be "tricked" into homosexuality.

As we have illustrated, the positioning of transgender people, particularly transgender women, as sexual threats to cisgender women and, at times, cisgender men highlights the distinction between biological maleness (sexually threatening to both those with invincible and those with vulnerable subjecthoods) and social masculinity (only threatening to those with vulnerable subjecthoods). In sexual interactions, like gender-segregated spaces, transgender people's gender identities are negated by their actual or imagined bodily configuration. Yet, highlighting the importance of gender in the matrix of perceived sexual threat, transgender women—those who are socially feminine but perceived of as biologically male—carry a greater threat than transgender men and social masculinity.

CONCLUSION: THE CONSEQUENCES OF PERCEIVED SEXUAL THREAT FOR TRANSGENDER RIGHTS

Scholars have long focused on cisgender people's policing of perceived transgressions of gender norms as the cause for most discrimination against transgender people. Our data suggest, in contrast, that such discrimination is not only about gender, but also about sexuality. The liberal moment of gender (Meyerowitz 2002) has enabled much more institutional legitimization of transgender people and transgender lives. Yet, because the sex/gender/sexuality system still relies on and reproduces heteronormativity, gender inequality, and homophobia, we see the expansion of transgender inclusion resulting in the current matrix of perceived sexual threat we outline in this chapter. In this matrix, trans people are accepted in some social contexts, but seen as sexual threats in others, and an imagined penis, even one attached to a body that expresses social femininity, is seen as much more of a threat than a body that expresses social masculinity but is not imagined to have a "real" penis.

As we show, such panics are not just about the terror that the sex/gender/sexuality system will break down if not carefully enforced. The panic caused by "gender deviance" is also about a fear of sexual threat. The way a person does gender in social interactions is assumed to reflect their genitals. People take these public performances of gender to be confirmatory evidence about who is acceptable to desire sexually, who should be sexually avoided, and who should be sexually feared. Our culture currently understands rapist to be synonymous with maleness. Doing gender in non-normative ways (where gender and genitals "don't match") disrupts beliefs about sexual safety because the rapist/man is not identifiable on the basis of appearance. Cisgender fears of transgender women, then, are about a concern that social femininity can render biological maleness undetectable, heightening sexual risk. As we have demonstrated, because these

fears center around a sexually threatening penis, we suggest that gender panics are often also "penis panics." This terror relies on beliefs that our current sex/gender/sexuality system must stay in place because women are vulnerable, men are invincible and dangerous, and everyone is heterosexual. Although some participants in penis panics express sympathy for individual trans people, they argue (successfully in some cases) that transgender rights must be sacrificed for the rights of normative cisgender women and children. This use of the assumed innate vulnerability of women to deny rights to transgender people maintains and reifies gender inequality more broadly.

Two types of sexual threat predominated throughout the texts and interviews we examined: heterosexual rape and homosexual "conversion" through the "one-act rule of homosexuality." To link transgender people with these forms of sexual threat requires a particular form of androphobia in the equation of maleness with being a potential (or even probable) rapist. These narratives rely on, and reproduce, a belief that men (or, really, penises) are sexually driven and strong and will use that strength to satisfy sexual desires at any cost. The texts and interviews we examined also reveal the inner workings of homophobia because the belief that "same-sex" sexual encounters are something to be avoided provide a cultural justification to out, assault, and even kill someone who expresses desire for a person of the "same sex." In addition, women's spaces are heterophobic in that, due to the lack of available protection from adult males, there is a significant level of fear of assault by males. Finally, for many of these narratives to work, one must believe in women's inherent weakness. Trans women can only be seen as threatening if one believes that cis women are weaker than biological males. Because cis women are seen as incapable of protecting themselves from these threats, "defenders" of women turn to policies to protect them. Thus, because of the beliefs that men are sexual predators, homosexuality is wrong, and women are weak, trans people (particularly trans women) are denied rights. These processes result in a reproduction of gender inequality, gender conformity, and heteronormativity.

But what cultural work do these threats accomplish? There is a long history that reveals how perceived sexual threats, particularly sexual threats to socially vulnerable and valuable groups such as white, middle- and upper-class cisgender women and children, have been particularly effective in maintaining social inequality (Foucault 1990; Nagel 2003). There is an extensive literature on the role of perceived sexual threat to white women by men of color in maintaining colonialism (Nagel 2003) as well as slavery, Jim Crow laws after the abolition of slavery in the United States, and more modern forms of racial inequality in the United States (Collins 2005). Similarly, gender inequality has been reinforced at various historical moments under the guise of protecting (mainly white) women from sexual threats from men (Campbell 2005). As Foucault argued, sexuality is "an especially dense transfer point for relations of power" (1990: 103). Claims that a policy will protect people from a perceived sexual threat can be used to control a variety of populations. In the cases we examined, this threat is utilized to deny transgender people the rights of safety from violence, protections from discrimination in employment and housing, access to public spaces, and documents conferring personhood.

REFERENCES

Airoldi, Robert. 2003. "Teen Changes Plea to Guilty: Nabors Says Friends Had 'Plan to Kill' Araujo a Week before Party." *The Argus (Fremont–Newark, CA)*, 25 February.

Ball, Molly. 2009. "Robocall Distorts Record." *Las Vegas Review–Journal*. April 6: B2.

Berns, Nancy. 2004. *Framing the Victim: Domestic Violence, Media, and Social Problems*. New Jersey: Transaction.

Bohon, Dave. 2013. "California Becomes First State to Pass Dangerous 'Transgender' Law." The New American. 15 August. http://www.thenewamerican.com/culture/faith-and-morals/item/16318-california-becomes-first-state-to-pass-dangerous-transgender-law/. Accessed February 3, 2014.

California State Legislature. Assembly Bill No. 1266. Aug. 12, 2013. http://leginfo.legislature.ca.gov/faces/billNavClient.xhtml?bill_id=201320140AB1266/. Accessed October 15, 2013.

Campbell, Alex. 2005. "Keeping the 'Lady' Safe: The Regulation of Femininity through Crime Prevention Literature." *Critical Criminology* 13 (2): 119–40.

Cavanagh, Sheila L., and Heather Sykes. 2006. "Transsexual Bodies at the Olympics: The International Olympic Committee's Policy on Transsexual Athletes at the 2004 Athens Summer Games." *Body & Society* 12: 75–102.

Cave, Damien. 2006. "No Change in Definition of Gender." *The New York Times*, 6 December.

Collins, Patricia Hill. 2005. *Black Sexual Politics*. New York; London: Routledge.

Connell, Raewyn. 1995. *Masculinities*. Berkeley: University of California Press.

Connelly, Sherryl. 2001. "I, the Jury Foreman: An Inside View of the Pitfalls of Justice." *The Daily News* (New York), 7 October.

Cook, Dick. 2002. "Jury Finds Jackson Guilty in Childress Murder Case." *Chattanooga Times Free Press*, 19 October.

Davis, Floyd James. 1991. *Who Is Black?: One Nation's Definition*. University Park: Pennsylvania State University Press.

Day, Kristen. 2001. "Constructing Masculinity and Women's Fear in Public Space in Irvine, California." *Gender, Place & Culture* 8 (2): 109–27.

Foucault, Michel. 1990. *The History of Sexuality: An Introduction*. New York: Vintage Books.

Gamson, William A., David Croteau, William Hoynes, and Theodore Sasson. 1992. "Media Images and the Social Construction of Reality." *Annual Review of Sociology* 18: 373–93.

Goffman, Erving. 1977. "The Arrangement between the Sexes." *Theory and Society* 4(3): 301–31.

Hamilton, Laura. 2007. "Trading on Heterosexuality." *Gender & Society* 21 (2):145–72.

Hollander, Jocelyn A. 2001. "Vulnerability and Dangerousness: The Construction of Gender through Conversation about Violence." *Gender and Society* 15: 83–109.

Jansen, Sue Curry. 2002. "When the Center No Longer Holds: Rupture and Repair." In *Critical Communication Theory: Power, Media, Gender, and Technology*, edited by Nick Couldry and James Curran. Lanham, MD: Rowman & Littlefield.

Kessler, Suzanne, and Wendy McKenna. 1978. *Gender: An Ethnomethodological Approach*. Chicago: University of Chicago Press.

Kwok, Stephan. 2006. "N.Y. Gender Law Not Realistic." *Daily Trojan*, 10 November.

Lane, Jodi, Angela R. Gover, and Sara Dahod. 2009. "Fear of Violent Crime among Men and Women on Campus: The Impact of Perceived Risk and Fear of Sexual Assault." *Violence and Victims* 24 (2): 172–92.

Lazenby, Brian. 2002. "Local Man Sentenced to 24 Years in Prison for Stabbing Death." *Chattanooga Times Free Press*, 10 December.

Lombardi, Emilia, Riki Anne Wilchins, Dana Priesing, and Diana Malouf. 2002. "Gender Violence." *Journal of Homosexuality* 42 (1): 89–101.

Lorber, Judith. 1993. "Believing Is Seeing: Biology as Ideology." *Gender & Society* 7: 568–81.

Lucal, Betsy. 1995. "The Problem with 'Battered Husbands.'" *Deviant Behavior* 16: 95–112.

Macarchuk, Alexis. 2009. "N.H. Transgender Bill Aims to Extend Protections." *University Wire*, 10 April.

Macdonald, Myra. 2003. *Exploring Media Discourse*. London, UK: Arnold.

Marcus, Sharon. 1992. "Fighting Bodies, Fighting Words: A Theory and Politics of Rape Prevention." In *Feminists Theorize the Political*, edited by Judith Butler and Joan W. Scott, 385–403. New York: Routledge.

Mcardle, D. 2008. "Swallows and Amazons, or the Sporting Exception to the Gender Recognition Act." *Social & Legal Studies* 17: 39–57.

Meyerowitz, Joanne. 2002. *How Sex Changed: A History of Transsexuality in the United States*. Cambridge, MA: Harvard University Press.

Nagel, Joane. 2003. *Race, Ethnicity, and Sexuality: Intimate Intersections, Forbidden Frontiers*. New York: Oxford University Press.

Namaste, Viviane K. 2000. *Invisible Lives: The Erasure of Transsexual and Transgendered People*. Chicago: University of Chicago Press.

Pascoe, C. J. 2007. *Dude, You're a Fag: Masculinity and Sexuality in High School*. Berkeley: University of California Press.

Rupp, Leila J., and Verta Taylor. 2010. "Straight Girls Kissing." *Contexts* 9 (3): 28–32.

Schilt, Kristen. 2010. *Just One of the Guys? Transgender Men and the Persistence of Gender Inequality*. Chicago: University of Chicago Press.

Schilt, Kristen, and Laurel Westbrook. 2009. "Doing Gender, Doing Heteronormativity: 'Gender Normals,' Transgender People, and the Social Maintenance of Heterosexuality." *Gender & Society* 23: 440–64.

Schippers, Mimi. 2007. "Recovering the Feminine Other: Masculinity, Femininity, and Gender Hegemony." *Theory & Society* 36 (1): 85–102.

Seidman, Steven. 1995. "Deconstructing Queer Theory or the Under-theorization of the Social and the Ethical." In *Social Postmodernism: Beyond Identity Politics*, edited by Linda Nicholson and Steven Seidman. Cambridge, UK: Cambridge University Press.

St. John, Kelly. 2004. "Defense Grills Star Witness in Teen Murder Trial: 'You're Lying,' Lawyer Says to Man Who Pleaded Guilty." *The San Francisco Chronicle*, 28 April.

Staff. 2006. "Facing Facts Dec. 3–Dec. 9." *The New York Times*, 10 December.

Starnes, Todd. 2013. "Will California Let Boys Use Girls Locker Rooms?" Fox News Radio, 17 June. http://radio.foxnews.com/toddstarnes/top-stories/will-california-let-boys-use-girls-locker-rooms.html/. Accessed October 15, 2013.

Stotzer, R. L. 2009. "Violence against Transgender People: A Review of United States Data." *Aggression and Violent Behavior* 14 (3), 170–79.

Weiss, Jillian Todd. 2006. "NYC Rejects Birth Certificate Change Regs." Transgender Workplace Diversity (blog), December 5, 2006, http://transworkplace.blogspot.com/.

West, Candace, and Don Zimmerman. 1987. "Doing Gender." *Gender & Society* 1 (2): 125–51.

Westbrook, Laurel. 2008. "Vulnerable Subjecthood: The Risks and Benefits of the Struggle for Hate Crime Legislation." *Berkeley Journal of Sociology* 52: 3–24.

Westbrook, Laurel. 2009. *Violence Matters: Producing Gender, Violence, and Identity through Accounts of Murder*. Ph. D. diss., University of California, Berkeley.

Westbrook, Laurel, and Kristen Schilt. 2014. "Doing Gender, Determining Gender Transgender People, Gender Panics, and the Maintenance of the Sex/Gender/Sexuality System." *Gender & Society* 28 (1): 32–57.

Wilcox, Pamela, Carol E. Jordan, and Adam J. Pritchard. 2006. "Fear of Acquaintance versus Stranger Rape as a 'Master Status': Towards Refinement of the 'Shadow of Sexual Assault.'" *Violence and Victims* 21 (3): 355–70.

Wolf, Leslie. 1998. "Man to Stand Trial in Stabbing Death of Female Impersonator." *The San Diego Union–Tribune*, 21 October.

Yoshino, Kenji. 2006. "Sex and the City." *Slate Magazine*, 11 December.

NOTES

1. Following Kessler and McKenna (1978), we highlight the social construction of both "sex" and "gender" using the term "gender" throughout this article, even in moments where most people use the term "sex" (e.g., "gender-segregated" rather than "sex-segregated"). We reserve "sex" for references to intercourse, unless using a specific term such as "sex marker."

2. We use the term "(hetero)sexuality" to highlight that when many social actors speak of "sexuality" they are inferring heterosexuality.

3. Cis is the Latin prefix for "on the same side." It compliments trans, the prefix for "across" or "over." Cisgender replaces the terms "non-transgender" or "bio man/bio woman" to refer to individuals who have a match between the gender they were assigned at birth and their personal identity.

4. It should be noted that none of the examined narratives conceive of transgender people as potentially sexually endangered; they are always the threat, never the threatener. The ability to harm others attributed to trans people in these narratives and the lack of focus on the injury, including violence and discrimination, experienced by transgender people should be problematized; to cast murder victims as dangerous assailants requires a particular departure from logic. The trans people imagined by those opposed to transgender rights function as monstrous specters, so there is often little nuance in these portrayals of trans lives. By contrast, arguments made for transgender rights bills and for access to gender-segregated spaces often include descriptions of trans folks as victims of violence and harassment and there is extensive scholarship on the high levels of sexual assault experienced by transgender people (e.g. Lombardi et al. 2002).

5. When we refer in this article to transgender women as "having penises," we are referencing how cisgender opponents frame their negative reactions to transgender inclusion and how journalists and accused murders explain the motivation for homicides. It is important to note that transgender women, in contrast, may describe or conceptualize their bodies in very different ways.

6. The use of quotes here around the term "men" is intended to problematize the fact that some cisgender people see trans women as men.

7. Because four of the five data sources for this chapter are from the mainstream media, it should be noted that the mainstream media is an excellent site for exploring the sex/gender/sexuality system, because the media tend to both reflect and shape prevailing understandings (Berns 2004; Gamson et al. 1992; Jansen 2002; Macdonald 2003).

8. It is notable that the articles we examined often spoke of "women and children" as in danger in women-only spaces. This indicates that boys who are young enough that a female caregiver would be bringing them into "women's" restrooms are considered vulnerable in similar ways to women and girls.

9. Of the reported murders in which both the gender of the victim and that of the perpetrator were known, 94.9 percent (149 of 157 cases) were instances of cisgender men killing transgender women. The remaining cases included 3 in which a cis woman killed a trans woman (1.91 percent), 2 in which a trans woman killed another trans woman (1.27 percent), and 3 in which one or more cis men killed a trans man (1.91 percent).

MIRIAM J. ABELSON

30. NEGOTIATING VULNERABILITY AND FEAR: RETHINKING THE RELATIONSHIP BETWEEN VIOLENCE AND CONTEMPORARY MASCULINITY

Author Thomas McBee and his girlfriend experienced a particularly frightening mugging in 2010. On that night a man held them at gunpoint facedown on the ground for more than 10 minutes, demanding money they did not have. The incident was especially scary, as McBee relayed, because it lasted for so long and the man seemed particularly agitated. Stunned into silence for most of the encounter, McBee eventually joined in his girlfriend's protests that they had no money to give. Upon hearing his voice, the mugger let them go. They found out later that their assailant had held up other couples at gunpoint but in each of the other incidents he had killed the man. Although the mugger assumed McBee to be a man throughout most of the robbery, McBee's voice must have suggested something else. "That's why he let us go as soon as I spoke. Since I hadn't started testosterone at that point, my voice hadn't changed. We were released because I wasn't yet a man" (McBee 2014). This story illustrates both the terrifying capacity of men to perpetuate violence and a much less talked about relationship to violence in men's lives: that is, how men manage the violence that they encounter from other men.

From playground bullying to large-scale war, men perpetrate much of the violence we see in the modern world. Masculinities scholars and educators have worked to uncover the relationship among men, masculinity, and violence (e.g., Kimmel 1994; Katz 2006). Yet, what we often ignore when we look at the connection among men, masculinity, and violence in the contemporary United States is that men are far more likely to be the subject of all kinds of violent crime, except rape and sexual assault, than women (Schafer et al. 2006). Differing social locations mean that not all men will experience the same amount of actual or possible violence, nor do they respond to it

in the same way. Social and individual characteristics also shape men's risk of and responses to threatened and actual violence. Trans men,[1] people who are assigned as female at birth and transition to live as men, most often begin to learn these negotiations as adults, and their experiences reveal much about how these perceptions of potential violence shape men's lives, interactions, and identities.

This chapter is based on a qualitative analysis of interviews with 49 trans men from the U.S. Midwest and West Coast. Notably, this analysis relies on trans men's self-reports of feelings of fear and experiences of violence and my interpretation of those experiences across the total group of men in the two regions. Men experience shifting perceptions of safety as they move through their everyday lives. When they feel their safety is threatened, they are more likely to engage in conforming gender practices (Abelson 2014). This analysis focuses on the complex role that violence takes in constituting normative masculinity in the contemporary United States.

As Schilt (2010) has shown in the case of workplace inequality, the lives of trans men are a valuable site of inquiry for understanding the social construction of gender and, particularly, adding to the study of men and masculinities. Yet, with few exceptions, Schilt (2010) being the most notable, trans men are rarely included in research on men and masculinities. Trans men's view of masculinity may be particularly insightful, not because trans men experience gender more than other men, but because it may be more conscious. This awareness is a result of their female biography and the process of transition, which likely make trans men's practice of masculinity and experience of other men's masculinities more salient than that of other men. Consequently, the exclusion of trans men in the field of men and masculinities not only leaves out a group of men, but also leads to the loss of valuable insight relevant to other men.

Trans men's stories show that their perceptions of vulnerability to violence changed dramatically when they began living as men. Their fears and the ways in which they negotiate the threat of violence now depend on how they spatially map out the possibility of danger as men, as well as their understanding of the vulnerability of their bodies in comparison to other men. The experiences of this group of men suggest that this management of fear and perceived vulnerability are central elements of contemporary masculinity. The fear of transphobic violence was present, especially in connection to rural spaces, in trans men's stories, but this was not the most common fear they reported. In fact, none of the men in this study reported experiencing physical violence in public from strangers because they were transgender. Instead, their fears and actual experiences of violence stemmed from other men assuming the trans men were men and thinking they did not appear to be appropriately manly. This chapter expands existing knowledge of the production of gender inequality by focusing not on how men exhibit violent behavior but on how the *fear* of violence shapes men's masculine practices.

Perceived vulnerability to and actual experiences of violence shape individual lives in highly gendered ways. The difference between men and women in their levels of fear of crime and their actual rates of violent victimization is the most consistent finding in the literature on fear of crime (Stanko 1995). Men usually report low levels of fear, whereas women report high levels of fear, although men have the highest rates of victimization for all violent crimes except rape and sexual assault (Ferraro 1995; May et al. 2010; Schafer et al. 2006). The disjuncture between fear and victimization is often conceived in criminological literature as women's "irrational fear" (May et al. 2010) or the "gender-fear paradox" (Ferraro 1996), but feminist scholars have pointed out that men's lack of fear may be what is most irrational (Pain 1997; Stanko 1990).

This lack of fear does not mean that men are free from negotiating the potential for violence (Reid and Konrad 2004). One way men start to learn to negotiate this violence is through rough childhood play and fighting with other boys (Stanko 1990) and it is important to note that men often perform fearlessness as part of negotiating a masculine self and identity in the face of possible violence (Brownlow 2005; Hollander 2001). Race, sexuality, class, disability, and other aspects of social location also affect men's fears and experiences of violence (Meyer 2012; Schafer et al. 2006) and men manage routine harassment based on their perceived racial and sexual identities (Stanko and Hobdell 1993). Transgender men may feel particularly vulnerable since transgender people face high levels of harassment and discrimination (Grant et al. 2011; Valentine 2007). In addition, political organizing around transphobic violence may have had the unintended effect of discursively constructing transgender people as inherently vulnerable (Westbrook 2008). With this understanding of fear and violence as a background, we can better see how trans men negotiate vulnerability and the contemporary contours of masculinity.

PERCEPTIONS OF VULNERABILITY AND NORMATIVE MASCULINITY

Shifting perceptions of their vulnerability to violence was one of the most commonly reported changes that trans men experienced in their interactions with other men when they transitioned. Nearly all claimed that their fear of violence or harassment stemmed from the worry that other men would react violently if they judged the interviewees' masculine practices as effeminate or not appropriately masculine. They also expressed fears that if they acted aggressively or challenged other men, they would incite violence in interactions. These fears were especially heightened in spaces where they expected to encounter particularly violent men, especially in rural spaces. The possibility of violence was exceptionally threatening when they felt like their bodies were more vulnerable and they would not be able to physically handle or resist the aggression of other men. Although being transgender is one of the few things these men have in common, transphobic violence was not the reported source of most of their everyday fears because others routinely saw them as just men. Yet, even when they presented as normatively masculine men, as most did, they had to manage the threat of violence from other men and their perception of their own vulnerability. This negotiation shaped their lives as men.

"THE PRIVILEGE OF MALE VIOLENCE"

The men in this study reported that the most significant factor affecting their perception of vulnerability was the difference between living as women and living as men. As men, they said that they no longer were afraid of being sexually assaulted by a stranger in public walking alone at night. As their geography of fear shifted, this allowed them increased access to public space and a sense of freedom. However, they had a new set of fears brought on by what Leo called "the privilege of male violence." Leo used privilege in a sarcastic sense. Instead of the usual meaning of the term, he used it to highlight how the transition to a relative position of power, in this case being seen as a man as opposed to a woman, came with the unexpected consequence of being potentially targeted for a new kind of violence from other men. This new sense of vulnerability actually more accurately reflects large-scale patterns of crime and victimization since, as noted above, men are far more likely than women to experience nonsexual physical assault from strangers who are men.

The change to both the fears and the actual experience of violence that accompanied trans men's transitions from living as women to living as men was triggered by others seeing them as men, rather than their understanding of their own gender identity. For example, Ken reported that this recognition of his manhood created a difference between his experience and the experiences of trans masculine people who were still viewed by strangers as women. He explained,

> It's little things that you just can't know until you are experiencing it. . . . Having a little bit more of guys stepping to you. Like if you're in a bar or something, some guy wants to pick a fight with you. He's not going to start a fight with a girl, but he might start a fight with you.

These newfound experiences of violence and perceptions of vulnerability were likely especially jarring because trans men do not have the experiences of learning to manage violence from other men at a young age that many other men share (Stanko 1990). It was clear throughout these stories that learning to manage this potential violence from other men, rather than perpetuating violence themselves, was perhaps more important in becoming a man. Maintaining appropriate masculinity entailed avoiding victimization more so than perpetuating violence.

The most heightened fears of victimization and reports of violence as men across the trans men's stories came from not appearing appropriately masculine or heterosexual. Aaron, living in a large Midwestern city, described frequent harassment from strangers on the street for a more feminine gender presentation. This verbal harassment, and even physical violence on occasion, included homophobic slurs. To avoid this violence he said,

> I did stop wearing purple. I stopped wearing flowers. I stopped wearing any of that stuff. I stopped wearing anything that I really thought was going to trigger somebody saying, "Fag."

Aaron did not identify as gay, but the homophobic harassment and violence he experienced was not based on his actual sexual identity or really even his identity as a trans man. Rather, the treatment he experienced seemed to be directed at the femininity he presented as a man, which was conflated with his sexuality. Thus, other men used homophobia as a tool to police his behavior as a man. The threat of further harassment ultimately pushed him to dress in a more normatively masculine fashion. Aaron's experience suggests that normative masculinity is heterosexual at its core.

Gender, in terms of being viewed as either a man or a woman, or perceived sexuality alone did not shape these new experiences of violence or perceived vulnerability, but were also influenced by race, class, ability, and other aspects of social location. Black trans men reported that although they were seen as newly threatening by others in public interactions, they were also subject to new violence and potential vulnerability from other men in positions of institutional power, namely from police officers and other representatives of the criminal justice system. I often asked interviewees whether they could tell when other people recognized them as men, besides the use of masculine pronouns. Ethan said that he knew he was being seen as a man rather than a woman because of the frequency of being stopped and interrogated by police officers. He explained,

> I get harassed a lot more by the police . . . I've been spread-eagled plenty of times. And I'm not that type of person, so for you just to [siren sound] pull up on me, just up out of the blue . . . and be like, "Okay, assume the position," I'm like, "Again?" You know, "You fit the description." "Of what? A typical black man?"

These frequent interactions with the police were a reminder of his own vulnerability as a black man. As another black respondent, Seth, reported, these experiences and the kind of perceived vulnerability connected to them was what it meant to be a "black man in America." The actual interactions with the police were jarring, but were heightened by the possibility that they could result in physical harm, the threat of incarceration, or even death. This caused respondents to avoid public space, to avoid interactions with the police, and to work to present themselves as less threatening when encountering others. This suggests that whiteness, in addition to heterosexuality, plays a role in maintaining normative masculinity.

MAPPING FEARS

Interviewees mapped out geographies of fear as they described changing feelings of vulnerability across different locations. These changing feelings were often based on the men they expected to find in those places. There was some agreement among men across the two regions that cities, especially those on the East and West Coasts, were far safer for a wide range of masculine expressions and for men of color and transgender people in general. Interestingly, individuals tended to map out a more nuanced geography of fear in their local area. For example, men who lived in San Francisco marked some neighborhoods as safer than others or other local cities as more dangerous. At the same time, men living in the rural Midwest described some towns or areas as safer or even particular individuals in their small towns as more threatening than others. All said, there was little difference between the urban and rural interviewees or Midwestern and Western men in their reports

of experiencing violence from stranger men. This suggests that perhaps the spatially based fear of victimization, which very much seems to shape how the men behave in various settings, does not necessarily reflect a spatial distribution of violence. It could also mean that their efforts to alter their behavior around supposedly more dangerous men are often effective. Either way, rural spaces spark particular fears of homophobic and even transphobic violence.

Homophobic violence was the most commonly reported source of fear in rural places. This more heightened sense of fear of violence from other men in rural places stemmed from the assumption that the interviewees would find more homophobic and violent men there. Jason lived with his husband in a Midwestern city known for a large gay population and a generally liberal atmosphere. He reported that they had never had any problems expressing public affection as a gay couple in the city where they lived, but were much more vigilant when visiting family in a rural town elsewhere in the Midwest. When I asked if he ever held hands with his husband in the rural town he responded, "Never, never, never, never, never, never . . . No, never in a million years." Because Jason and his husband had what he described as fairly normative masculine presentations, they felt like they were relatively safe if they did not give any direct indication of their relationship or sexual identities as gay men.

Ken would also travel to a rural town, but in the West, to visit his partner's family and reported many of the same fears of homophobic violence. Ken and his partner, a cisgender woman, both identified as queer but were seen as a heterosexual couple by strangers for the most part. Although being seen as a man partnered with a woman provided him some sense of safety, he still had worries that he would face homophobic violence because other men might perceive his mannerisms and clothing as not appropriately masculine. He explained the difference between living in his large Western city and visiting the rural town:

> Here it's a city, and there are a lot of city people. . . . We're just more accustomed to differences, and we're ok with it and roll with it. I don't think about coming off as gay or worrying about that as much here as I do when I'm down in [the rural town]. And that's

more of a safety issue. Just feeling like I need to present a little bit better. I think in those places that being a gay dude in our society is still the worst thing to be perceived as.

When Ken felt a heightened sense of vulnerability to violence in the rural town he would adjust his clothing, voice, and mannerisms so that other men would not perceive him as gay. Ken and Jason's experiences navigating rural spaces highlight the assumptions about the heightened possibility for violence in rural versus urban places, but also reiterate that homophobic violence can be targeted at people who are perceived to be gay not only because of their sexual and romantic identities and practices, but also because their behavior or mannerisms are perceived as effeminate.

Although the fear of transphobic violence was not the most common everyday fear that trans men reported, this fear was heightened in rural places. More than half of the men interviewed brought up the story of Brandon Teena, a trans man who had been brutally raped and murdered in a small Nebraska town in 1993. Teena's story was much publicized at the time it happened and was immortalized in a documentary, *The Brandon Teena Story*, and the film *Boys Don't Cry*, for which Hilary Swank won an Oscar. This story seemed to work as a cautionary tale as trans men assessed their vulnerability to violence. Although most of the men did not fear transphobic violence because they were typically not perceived by other people as transgender, the prominence of Teena's story reinforced the idea that rural places and especially rural men were more prone to transphobic violence and that the cost of others knowing of their transgender status would be especially high there. Like the fear of homophobic violence, this perception of vulnerability affected how they presented themselves as men and pushed them toward more conforming practices, especially in rural places. This cautionary tale and the discourse of violent rural spaces also likely had the effect of partially blaming rural transgender and queer people for any violence they experience because they have remained in those supposedly more dangerous places. As Halberstam (2005) argues, a rural transgender person like Brandon Teena is seen by urban gay, lesbian, and transgender people as somehow immature and premodern

because he does not conform to the developmental narrative that a transgender identity should be accompanied by a move to a city. Thus, Teena's life and the repetition of his story becomes a warning that trans men's safety is particularly threatened in these supposedly more violent places and constitutes urban coastal cities, the supposed center of LGBT life, as more developed and safe. This narrative falls flat in a variety of ways, such as for black trans men based on their experiences of harassment by police in urban spaces.

VULNERABLE BODIES

Along with geographic context, particular bodily characteristics shaped trans men's perceptions of their vulnerability to violence from other men. The size and strength of their bodies seemed to influence how they believed they would fare in a physical confrontation with another man. In addition, the possibility of exposure of their bodies in particular contexts lead to heightened fears of transphobic violence. When they felt that they were vulnerable because of their bodies, this often made the possible consequences of a physical confrontation more worrisome. Badly losing such an altercation would not only mean physical injury but also diminish their masculinity.

Height and strength were the central bodily characteristics that shaped trans men's descriptions of their sense of vulnerability when encountering the possibility of physical violence from other men. Ken, who expressed his fear of homophobic violence in a rural town, went on to explain that he wanted to avoid conflict because his relative height and strength made him more vulnerable to the potential of violence when traveling to the small town. He said,

> When somebody is looking at you and calling you a faggot . . . given that I'm 5'2, and 145, when somebody is like 6' and 250, you get a little more concerned . . . I'm frequently the shortest person when I'm down there, frequently.

Ken's perceived stature relative to other men made him feel more vulnerable if a physical confrontation were to occur. It seems that Ken has the quite reasonable fear of the material consequences of physical violence from larger men, in the form of bruises, broken bones, and physical pain. It is also possible that being a victim of violence and not doing well in a fight against another man would discredit him as a man. Thus, avoiding a fight was potentially far better than losing a fight. Smaller men reported being "pushed around" by other men frequently in crowded public spaces, such as bars or concerts, which increased their general sense of vulnerability. Trans men who felt they were taller and stronger relative to other men reported increased confidence and safety because other men showed them respect by giving them space. Thus, their bodies seemed to shape both their interactions with other men and the consequences of potential violence in interactions, especially where they thought they might encounter more violent and intolerant men.

Although physical strength and height could ensure a sense of safety for some men, the health and strength of bodies can change and this change can sometimes occur suddenly. Chris said that he felt safe going backpacking alone in the wilderness because of his physical strength. At the same time, he felt quite vulnerable if he were to become sick on one of his trips and were to end up in the local rural hospital. Chris explained that he was worried that a physical exam would expose parts of his body and that medical personnel would realize he was transgender and react to that knowledge with extreme physical violence. Actually, it was in medical contexts that trans men in both regions reported the most frequent transphobic violence, from physical assault to other more subtle forms of violence. This was most likely the place where their bodies were exposed and they were already vulnerable because of illness and the need to seek care.

In sum, bodily differences can increase a sense of both vulnerability and safety. The perception of bodily vulnerability to violence is heightened in rural spaces, especially in regard to homophobic and transphobic violence. It seems that these bodily characteristics are central to understanding how men differently respond to the potential for violence from other men and how managing violence and potential victimization constitute normative masculinity. This sense of bodily vulnerability appears to heighten fear of any physical conflict. To be a victim would not only entail physical harm, but also diminish their achievement of normative masculinity.

CONCLUSION

This chapter argues that the relationship between normative masculinity and violence is not just about men perpetrating violence, but that this relationship also centrally involves men's management of their fear of and vulnerability to violence. Few of the men in this chapter had a brush with death like Thomas McBee, but they did encounter the "privilege of male violence" when they were recognized by others as men. Through examining the experiences of trans men, we can see that this violence is centrally organized around homophobia and the attendant policing, usually by other men, of men's expressions of femininity. Although individual men mapped their fears spatially according to their local context, most individuals saw rural spaces as inherently more dangerous, especially for the possibility of encountering highly violent homophobic and transphobic men. Vulnerability was mapped onto the body in multiple ways as it was also mapped spatially. Although trans men's new experiences of violence and perceptions of vulnerability more accurately reflect men's statistical patterns of victimization overall, the attendant discourses of fear likely also have the effect of shaping their lives even when they do not reflect experience.

The normative force that violence and fear of violence entails attempts to shore up the behaviors of all men and pushes toward ideals of heterosexuality, anti-femininity, and whiteness. The consequence of not fitting with the masculine, white, heterosexual ideal was to risk or actually experience violence, and one cannot necessarily blame men for wanting to avoid this. On the other hand, the discourse of fear can be a way to defend particular conforming behaviors. Regardless of the motivations, the effect is the same; the real or threatened violence from other men reinscribes a normative masculinity that is at least partly based on avoiding victimization and vulnerability.

To further understand the constitution of normative masculinity we must continue to look more closely at how men manage the threat of violence from other men along with how men perpetuate violence. How do these perceptions of vulnerability continually reproduce normalizing forces and power? How do these discourses of masculinity and vulnerability affect men who actually experience violence? This chapter demonstrates that violence stabilizes normative masculinity and we must look, too, for potential disruptions in these same processes.

As the experiences of transition and the new "privilege of male violence" demonstrate, trans men can have unique insights into the differences that men and women experience in regard to violence, fear, and perceptions of vulnerability. These experiences are likely similar to the experiences of other men because the strangers trans men interacted with did not have any idea that they were transgender in the first place. This is not to say that they did not have some fears that were specific to being transgender men, but I would argue that these specific fears of violence are men's fears. To argue otherwise would be to deny that these are men. We would not deny that other groups of men are men because they do not share some experience in common with all other men. As these trans men's stories demonstrate, a body that is assigned female at birth does not stop one from being seen and treated by others as a man. Thomas McBee had not yet transitioned to living as a man, nor had he even decided to, at the time of the robbery, but his assailant initially perceived him as one. This outward judgment of what we assume about one another's sex and gender is what most of our actions and interactions are based on anyway. Most studies of men and masculinity are based on a cisgender and essentialist bias that insists only bodies assigned as male can be men and what those bodies do is masculinity. Instead, this work points to the importance of including trans men among any diverse group of men in our hopes of better understanding both masculinity and the lives of men in general.

REFERENCES

Abelson, Miriam. 2014. "Dangerous Privilege: Trans Men, Masculinities, and Changing Perceptions of Safety." *Sociological Forum* 29 (3): 549–70.

Brownlow, Alec. 2005. "A Geography of Men's Fear." *Geoforum* 36 (5): 581–92.

Ferraro, Kenneth F. 1995. *Fear of Crime: Interpreting Victimization Risk*. Albany: State University of New York Press.

Ferraro, Kenneth. 1996. "Women's Fear of Victimization: Shadow of Sexual Assault?" *Social Forces* 75 (2): 667–90.

Grant, Jaime M., et al. 2011. *Injustice at Every Turn: A Report of the National Transgender Discrimination Survey*. Washington, DC: National Center for Transgender Equality and National Gay and Lesbian Task Force.

Halberstam, Judith. 2005. *In a Queer Time and Place : Transgender Bodies, Subcultural Lives*. New York: New York University Press.

Hollander, Jocelyn A. 2001. "Vulnerability and Dangerousness: The Construction of Gender through Conversation about Violence." *Gender & Society* 15 (1): 83–109.

Katz, Jackson. 2006. *The Macho Paradox: Why Some Men Hurt Women and How All Men Can Help*. March 2, 2006, edition. Naperville, IL: Sourcebooks.

Kimmel, Michael S. 1994. "Masculinity as Homophobia: Fear, Shame, and Silence in the Construction of Gender Identity." In *Theorizing Masculinities*, edited by Harry Brod and Michael Kaufman. Thousand Oaks, CA: Sage.

May, D., Rader, N., and Goodrum, S. 2010. "A Gendered Assessment of the 'Threat of Victimization': Examining Gender Differences in Fear of Crime, Perceived Risk, Avoidance, and Defensive Behaviors." *Criminal Justice Review* 35 (2): 159–82.

McBee, Thomas. "What I've Learned about Being a Man, from Being Born Female: One Fateful Night Held at Gunpoint That Sparked a Transition into Manhood." *Esquire*, September 24, 2014, http://www.esquire.com/blogs/news/thomas-mcbee-interview/.

Meyer, Doug. 2012. "An Intersectional Analysis of Lesbian, Gay, Bisexual, and Transgender (LGBT) People's Evaluations of Anti-Queer Violence." *Gender & Society* 26 (6): 849–73.

Pain, Rachel. 1997. "Whither Women's Fear? Perceptions of Sexual Violence in Public and Private Space." *International Review of Victimology* 4 (4): 297–312.

Reid, L. W., and Konrad, M. 2004. "The Gender Gap in Fear: Assessing the Interactive Effects of Gender and Perceived Risk on Fear of Crime." *Sociological Spectrum* 24 (4): 399–425.

Schafer, J. A., B. M. Huebner, and T. S. Bynum. 2006. "Fear of Crime and Criminal Victimization: Gender-Based Contrasts." *Journal of Criminal Justice* 34 (3): 285–301.

Schilt, Kristen. 2010. *Just One of the Guys? Transgender Men and the Persistence of Gender Inequality.* Chicago and London: University of Chicago Press.

Stanko, Elizabeth A. 1990. *Everyday Violence: How Women and Men Experience Sexual and Physical Danger.* London and Winchester, MA: Pandora and Unwin Hyman.

Stanko, Elizabeth A. 1995. "Women, Crime, and Fear." *The Annals of the American Academy of Political and Social Science* 539: 46–58.

Stanko, Elizabeth. A., and Kathy Hobdell. 1993. "Assault on Men: Masculinity and Male Victimization." *British Journal of Criminology* 33 (3): 400–15.

Valentine, David. 2007. *Imagining Transgender: An Ethnography of a Category.* Durham, NC: Duke University Press.

Westbrook, Laurel. 2008. "Vulnerable Subjecthood: The Risks and Benefits of the Struggle for Hate Crime Legislation." *Berkeley Journal of Sociology* 52 (3): 3–23.

NOTES

1. I use the terms "trans men", "transgender men," or just "men" to refer to the people who participated in this research project. Although some of the participants may not use these exact terms to describe themselves, they are less controversial than other terms. A portion of this research was funded by the Center for the Study of Women in Society and the Department of Sociology at the University of Oregon.

JANE WARD

31. DUDE-SEX: WHITE MASCULINITIES AND 'AUTHENTIC' HETEROSEXUAL AMONG DUDES WHO HAVE SEX WITH DUDES

"Closeted" men of color have increasingly become the focus of public health research and media exposés, with these accounts pointing to the likelihood that straight "men who have sex with men" (MSMs)[1] may explain rising rates of HIV infection among heterosexual women of color (Boykin, 2005; Denizet-Lewis, 2003). People of color—and particularly black men on the "down low" (DL) and Latino MSMs—are newly central figures in discussions regarding internalized homophobia, sexual repression, HIV/AIDS, the betrayal of unsuspecting wives and girlfriends, and the failure to come out of the closet (Boykin, 2005; Hill Collins, 2004; King, 2004; Denizet-Lewis, 2003; Mukherjea and Vidal-Ortiz, 2006). To make sense of the factors that would prevent men of color from being "honest" about their "real" lives and desires, analyses of MSMs have drawn heavily on theories of the closet and its racialized underpinnings (Boykin, 2005; Hill Collins, 2004; King, 2004). Black men on the DL, in particular, have been described as "a new subculture of gay men" for whom "masculinity that is so intertwined with hyper-heterosexuality renders an openly gay identity impossible" (Hill Collins, 2004: 207). Similarly, Latino MSMs have been implicitly characterized as closeted gay or bisexual men for whom cultural barriers, rigid ideas about gender, and strong ties to family and religion prevent public identification as gay or bisexual (Diaz, 1997).

Critics of these discourses have argued that the lack of discussion about white men on the DL has reinforced stereotypes about black male sexuality as dangerous and predatory, as well as provided "evidence" that African Americans are more homophobic than other racial groups (Boykin, 2005). Others have

shown that the down low has the all too familiar ingredients of moral panic: "concealed non-normative sexualities, a subaltern genre of expressive culture (Hip-Hop), a pandemic caused by a sexually transmitted agent, *innocent victims* (heterosexual women), and a population often accused of misbehavior (men of color)" (González, 2007: 27, emphasis in original). In sum, dominant narratives about the DL reveal a new set of fears about uncontrollable male bodies of color, or the volatile intersections or masculinity, race, and sexuality.

In addition to the racial components of down low rhetoric, the characterization of straight-identified MSMs as closeted also exemplifies the persistent tendency to view sex *acts* as meaningful and objective indictors of a true sexual selfhood and to gloss over larger questions about the gendered and racialized construction of heterosexual and homosexual categories (Foucault, 1978; Katz, 1996; Sedgwick, 1992). According to the logic of the closet, same-sex sexual practices among heterosexuals signify sexual repression, or a failure to be honest about who one *is*, and the sexual community or culture in which one belongs. The recent insistence that MSMs are actually closeted gay men constrained by racially specific or culturally-internal forms of homophobia has helped to solidify a narrow and essentialist conceptualization of homophobia. At the individual level, "internalized homophobia" is believed to arise from the unwillingness of MSMs to recognize and/or celebrate their essential nature, or "who they really are." At the cultural level, and akin to "culture of poverty" arguments used to pathologize African Americans, mainstream down low and MSM discourses imply that homophobia stems from essential, ethno-racial cultures of sexual repression.

This reading is an excerpt from Jane Ward's (2008) article in *Sexualities* 11 (2008): 414–34.

As I will argue, however, a more productive reading of homophobia views the disavowal of gay identity and culture as one of the constitutive elements of heterosexual subjectivity—or a primary means of expressing heterosexual selfhood in a sexually binary world. While down low discourse implies that same-sex sexuality reveals a homosexual selfhood and that homophobia is an expression of culture, this article explores the theoretical insights that emerge from a reversal of this logic, or from viewing gay and straight as cultural spheres, and homophobia as a subjectifying practice (or a struggle to construct heterosexual selfhood).

Based on examination of an online community in which white "str8"–identified men assert that sex with other white men *bolsters* their heterosexual masculinity, I highlight the heterosexual and racialized meanings that white MSMs attach to their same-sex behaviors. I argue that while some men who have sex with men prefer to do so within gay/queer cultural worlds, others (such as the "straight dudes" described here [. . .]) indicate a greater sense of belonging or cultural "fit" with heterosexual identity and heteroerotic culture. For the latter group, homophobia, or the need to strongly disidentify with gay men and gay culture, is less a symptom of the *repression* of a "true self," but rather an attempt to *express* a "true self"—or one's strong sense of identification with heteropatriarchal white masculinity—in the context of having sex with men.

More specifically, this study points to the role of whiteness—including white archetypes and images—in the process of establishing heterosexual "realness," or believable straight culture. In contrast with the media's recent efforts to locate tensions between sexual identity and practice within African American and Latino cultures, my findings suggest that whiteness is also a commonly used resource for bridging the gap between heterosexual identification and same-sex desire. Previous research has pointed to various institutional contexts in which straight-identified men have sex with men, such as "tearooms," prisons, and the military (Humphreys, 1978; Kaplan, 2003; Schifter, 1999). These studies have demonstrated how men leverage hyper-masculinity, socioeconomic success, and the "need" for quick and easy sex to preserve heterosexual identity and moral "righteousness" (to use Humphrey's term). Building upon this research, the present study considers how *race* (including racial identification) and *racialized culture* (including racialized images, clothing, language and "style") are also used to bolster claims to heterosexuality and to reframe sex between men as a heteromasculine and "not gay" act. Similar to the assertion of feminist theorists that gender is always an intersectional accomplishment—or a construction that takes forms in and through race, class, and sexuality (Bettie, 2002; Hill Collins, 2004; Hull et al., 1982)—I show that the appearance of "authentic" heterosexuality is also accomplished in interaction with race, socioeconomic class, and gender. [. . .]

RACE, CULTURE, AND THE SOCIAL CONSTRUCTION OF HETEROSEXUALITY

While other research has examined the historical relationship between racial ideologies and the invention of homosexuality (Ferguson, 2004; Somerville, 2000), limited attention has been given to the role of race in the routine and daily accomplishment of heterosexuality and homosexuality. In this [chapter], I argue that the ongoing construction of authentic or believable male heterosexuality is reliant upon racial codes that signify "normal" straight male bonding, "average" heterosexual masculinity, and lack of interest in gay culture. Whiteness—and more specifically the use of white masculine archetypes, for example, frat boys, surfers, skaters, jocks, and white "thugs"—can play a central role in the production of an authentic and desirable heterosexual culture distinct from gay male culture.

[. . .] I do not make claims about the "actual" sexual and racial identities of men who place advertisements for sex online, instead I am interested in the sexualized and racialized *cultures* these advertisements draw upon and reproduce. Indeed, a growing body of queer scholarship has pointed to the significance of *culture* in the construction and regulation of the heterosexual/homosexual binary. Following Foucault's assertion that "homosexuality threatens people as a 'way of life,' rather than a way of having sex," Halberstam (2005) has argued that "queer subjects" might be redefined as those who "live (deliberately, accidentally, or of necessity) during the hours when others sleep and in the spaces (physical, metaphysical, and economic) that others have abandoned," including, "ravers, club kids, HIV-positive barebackers, rent boys, sex workers, homeless people, drug dealers, and the unemployed" (2005: 10). Halberstam expands the boundaries of queerness to include subjects often not thought of as queer, and in a distinct but similarly motivated move, other queer scholars have "disidentified" with mainstream or "homonormative" lesbian and gay politics and its focus on monogamy, domesticity, and prosperity (Duggan, 2003; Muñoz, 1999). Queer, in each of these approaches, is less about sexual practices than about a "way of life" that defies the rules of normative, respectable adult citizenship. [. . .]

This [chapter] offers support for the argument that the lines between queerness and normativity are marked less by sexual practices and identities than by cultural practices and interpretive frames. In contrast with recent work that has expanded queer subjectivity or disavowed "normal" gays and lesbians, I take a different empirical approach by demonstrating how whiteness and masculinity interact to offer *heterosexual culture* to white men who have sex with men. [. . .]

METHOD: STUDYING DUDE-SEX

The "Casual Encounters" section of Craigslist–Los Angeles (craigslist.org) is an online community bulletin board in which predominantly white "str8 dudes" solicit sex with other white str8 dudes.[2] Exemplifying the arguments about culture described earlier, sex acts themselves are not meaningful indicators of sexual identification for str8 dudes on Craigslist. Instead, ads placed by str8 dudes suggest that it is willingness to identify with or consume "perverted" queer culture that makes others queer, and conversely, it is str8 dudes' mastery of "normal" heterosexual culture that makes them straight. [. . .]

For this study, I collected and analyzed all ads placed on Craigslist Los Angeles by "str8" self-identified men during May through July of 2006.[3] Of the resulting 125 "Casual Encounters" ads collected and analyzed, 71 percent made reference to race—either the racial identification of the person placing the ad or a specific racial preference for a sex partner. Among the ads that made reference to race, 86 percent were placed by men who either identified themselves as white, or included

a photo of themselves in which they appeared to be white (though I recognize that the latter is a flawed indicator of racial identity and that race itself is socially and historically constructed). [. . .] In order to capture all ads placed by straight-identified men seeking men, I searched for ads containing either the terms "DL" or "str8," the latter of which was more commonly used on Craigslist. In "Casual Encounters," self-identified white men placed approximately 85 percent of the ads, regardless of whether the term "str8" or "DL" was used. [. . .]

REGULAR DUDES, CASUAL ENCOUNTERS

Before describing how whiteness was deployed in Casual Encounters, I begin with a general description of str8 dudes' heteroerotic culture. In contrast with the logic that gay and straight are at opposite ends of a behavioral and biologically-determined binary, the str8 dudes who post on Craigslist construct "gay" as a chosen identity that is not particularly linked to who is having sex, or what sexual acts are involved. Instead, being gay is about *how* sex is done—the language that is used, the type of "porn" films that are watched, the beverages consumed, and the motivation that drives the sex itself. The following ads, representative of dozens of others, illustrate how str8 dudes lay claim to "straightness" while soliciting sex with other men:

Straight Dude Drunk and Horny . . . Any str8 bud wanna jack?—27. Here's the deal. Went out drinking and clubbing, thought I'd hook up with a chick, but didn't pan out. I'm buzzed, horny, checking out porn. Is there any other straight dude out there who would be into jacking while watching porn? . . . I'd rather hook up with a chick, but none of the CL [Craigslist] chicks ever work out.

What happened to the cool bi/str8 dude circle jerks?—33. What happened to a group of masc[uline] dudes just sitting around stroking, watching a game, drinking some brews, jerking, showing off, swapping college stories, maybe playing a drinking game and see what comes up?

Str8 guy wants to try BJ tonight—27. Ok, I'll make this short. I'm up late tonight. I have a girlfriend. But I'm at home by myself now. I watch porn and I like when the women suck on big cocks. I've been thinking about it, and I think I'd like to suck one. I'm not attracted to guys so I'd rather not look at you much. Just suck your cock. I have a Polaroid and would like to take a pic with cum on my face. But this is really only for tonight cuz I'm horny! . . . I am Caucasian and prefer Caucasian.

$300 Bucks Cash If You're STR8 & Goodlooking!!—27. Hey, are you str8, goodlooking and broke? Are you Under 30 and hella cool? Like watching porn and talking bout pussy? You're in luck. 300 bucks every time we hangout. Be under 30. Honestly STR8. I'm mostly str8, great looking chill bro.

Str8 jackoff in briefs outside male bonding edging stroke—34. I am a tall blond built packin' jockman with a big bulge in my jockeys. Dig hanging in just our briefs man to man in the hot sun workin' my bulge freely. . . . If you are into jackin' and being free to be a man, let's hang. If you have a pool or a yard to layout and jack freely smoke some 420 [marijuana] and just be men, hit me up. No gay sex, I am looking for legit male bonding, masturbating in the hot sun only.

Unlike in similar websites for gay men, women are a central part of str8 dudes' erotic discourse. As these ads illustrate, str8 dudes often describe sex between dudes as a less desirable, but "easy," alternative to sex with women, or suggest that dude-sex is a means of getting the kind of sex that all straight men want from women, but can only get from men—uncomplicated, emotionless, and guaranteed. Str8 dudes get drunk, watch heterosexual porn, talk about "pussy," and maintain a clear emotional boundary between each other that draws upon the model of adolescent friendship, or the presumably "harmless," "proto-sexual" circle jerk. References to being "chill bros" and "male bonding" help to reframe dude-sex as a kind of sex that bolsters, rather than threatens, the heterosexual masculinity of the participants. Only those who are "man enough" and "chill enough" will want dude-sex or be able to handle it.

In some cases, misogyny and references to violence against women are used to reinforce the link between dude-sex and heterosexual male bonding:

Whackin Off to Porn: STR8 porn. Gang bang. STR8, bi-curious masculine white guy lookin' for a masculine guy. Get into stroking bone with a bud, talkin' bout pussy and bangin' the bitch.

Any Straight/Bi Guys Want to Help Me Fuck My Blow-up Doll???: Come on guys . . .we can't always pick up the chick we want to bone right??? So let's get together and fuck the hell out of my hot blow-up doll. Her mouth, her pussy, and her ass all feel GREAT. Just be cool, uninhibited, horny, and ready to fuck this bitch. It's all good here . . . lates.

Such ads suggest that dude-sex is a sexual and often violent expression of heterosexual masculinity and heterosexual culture, distinct from gay male culture in which misogyny typically manifests as the invisibility, rather than the objectification, of women (Ward, 2000). Marilyn Frye (1983), in her analysis of drag queens, argues "What gay male affectation of femininity seems to be is a serious sport in which men may exercise their power and control over the feminine, much as in other sports. . . . But the mastery of the feminine is not feminine. It is masculine." I draw on Frye's analysis to suggest that while dude-sex makes use of and "masters" homosexual or non-normative sex practices, this deployment of non-normative sexuality in the service of "str8" culture is perhaps not best understood as "queer."

WHITE DUDES, RACE, AND CLASS

Str8 dudes draw on the imagery of male bonding and the symbols of straight male culture, including references to sports, beer, fraternity membership, smoking pot and being "chill," "buds," or "bros." Yet "dude speak" and "dude style" is not simply masculine and heterosexual, it is also racialized. Recent studies of black and Latino men on the down low have emphasized the importance of shared urban culture, and particularly hip hop, to the construction of down-low masculinity and sexuality (González, 2007). González explains that *culture* (and not public or politicized identity) is what is at stake for Latinos on the down low: "gay is not an option; Hip Hop is" (2007). Here I argue that *racial cultures* are also a central player in how white str8 dudes make sense of their str8 sexuality. In some cases, white dudes appropriate the symbols of black and Latino down-low masculinity; in other cases, they foreground symbols of white masculinity (surfers, frat guys, jocks and so on) or synthesize the former with the latter.

APPROPRIATING HIP HOP MASCULINITY: WHITE BROS AND THUGS ON THE DL

White str8 dudes—like a growing number of young white men in general—bolster their masculinity through the appropriation of terms and gestures used by black and Latino men, especially within rap lyrics and culture. Writers critical of the mainstreaming and white ownership of rap have pointed to the ways in which its consumption by white youth has bled into other forms of racial and cultural appropriation (Kitwana, 2005). [O]n Craigslist, str8 dudes [. . .] construct a masculine and heterosexual culture through a complex synthesis of white masculinity (e.g. surfer dudes) and masculinities of color (e.g. bros, thugs, and the DL). Str8 dudes commonly use phrases identified by African American studies scholars as "black slang," such as "sup?," "hit me up," and "thugged out" (Smitherman, 2000), such as in the following ads:

> 23 y/o white dude party in Hollywood—Hey guys, I'm partyin right now at home and have plenty of stuff to share. . . . I'm lookin to meet a cool str8 thugged out white dude around my age, who would wanna come over, kick back, watch a lil porn, smoke a lil, and stroke off together. I might even be down to deepthroat some cock so if you love getting awesome head you should definitely hit me back! [. . .]
>
> Str8 curious on the DL. Lookin' to chill—23. Sup? Just looking to chill with another str8/bi dude, into young or older bros type . . . to mess around, not into perverted shit. Also not into fatty, femm guys. If you're a guy, please be in shape. I'm sort of skinny, curious here and haven't really acted on it. Just regular sane dude. Discretion a must. Aiite, late.

In an effort to convey that the sexual encounter will be casual, meaningless, and embedded in heterosexual male culture, white str8 dudes rely upon "urban" slang derived from black culture to represent heterosexuality. However, as with many forms of cultural appropriation, the slang used by str8 dudes is fast becoming associated with whites, and white masculinity in particular. [. . .]

It may be most accurate to describe the racialized heterosexuality of str8 dudes as a kind of Eminem-inspired white working-class "thuggery," constructed through an in-your-face reclamation of "white trash" and homophobic, or anti-gay, sexuality. While some ads express desire for "average" working-class men (e.g. "carpenters, carpet layers, plumbers, construction workers, mechanics, truckers, cable guys, delivery guys, overall just a hard working guy as I am. NO GAYS sorry"), others eroticize aggressive "white trash" masculinity, such as in the following ad [. . .]:

> Str8 fuck a guy in his briefs, masc(uline) man to man fuck, hiv neg only. Hey fucks. I need to fuckin lay the pipe in some tight manhole today. I am hiv neg fuck with rubbers only. I want to have a hot packin guy in some tighty whities bent over and on all fours takin my dick like a champ. No fems or tweeking pnp ["party and play"] dudes. I hate that shit. Only 420 and a hot packin butt. Hit me up with your pix and your contact info.

Ads such as this amplify the appearance of heterosexuality through a synthesis of working-class culture, whiteness, and what is arguably the subtle appropriation of black masculinity through hip hop slang ("hit me up") and "thug" masculinity. Other ads produced similar images of "rough" white masculinity through reference to skinheads and other archetypes of white male rebellion historically rooted in white racist, sexist and homophobic violence—"lookin for str8, bi, surfr, sk8r, punk, military, truckers, skinhead, rough trade . . . I'll give you the best head ever, buddy."

Though being on the DL has been sensationalized in the media as a rejection of white gay culture specific to black men living "otherwise heterosexual lives" (Denizet-Lewis, 2003), a few white str8 dudes on Craigslist claimed DL identity as their own (though "str8" was used far more commonly):

> STR8 DUDES . . . White boy lookin for a NO CHAT suck . . . u lemme suck u . . .—29. [. . .] Love to deepthroat a hot str8 dude on the DL . . . bust ur nut and split. I'm a very goodlooking in shape white dude . . . totally on the DL. [. . .]

Black gay writer and activist Keith Boykin has argued that there is a racist stigma and double standard associated with the "down low." Referring to the white characters in the hit film *Brokeback Mountain*, Boykin contends,

> the reason why we don't say they're on the down low is simple—they're white. When white men engage in this behavior, we just call it what it is and move on. But when black men do it, then we have

to pathologize it into something evil called the "down low." (Boykin, blog on keithboykin.com, May, 2006)

Indeed, the stereotypical image of the DL is that of partnered, heterosexual, masculine black men having quick and deceitful sexual relations unconnected to mainstream gay culture. As such, the DL is a useful shorthand available to white str8 dudes wishing to affirm their own heterosexuality, as well as to invoke the perhaps fetishized imagery of deceitful, immoral, or "evil" sex [. . .].

SURFERS, SKATERS, AND FRAT GUYS: ARCHETYPES OF WHITE HETEROSEXUAL MASCULINITY

Archetypes of youthful, white, heterosexual masculinity are also popular among str8 dudes on Craigslist, who commonly include a list of desired "male types' in their ads. Many str8 dudes express an explicit preference for other white dudes, and this preference is strengthened by naming specific forms of hegemonic masculinity, such as jocks, skaters, surfers and frat dudes (Connell, 2005):

Any HOT White jocks lookin to get sucked off???—23. Hey guys, I'm just a chill good looking dude heading down to the area for a BBQ and I'm looking for any other HOT Str8 or bi white dudes looking to get sucked off. Just sit back and relax and get drained. I'm especially into sucking off hot jocks, skaters, surfers, and frat dudes. [. . .]

Seeking a MASCULINE JACK OFF BUD to STR8 PORN—29. Hot masculine white dude here . . . looking for another hot white dude to come by my place, and work out a hot load side by side. Straight Porn only. Prefer str8, surfer, etc. Not usually into gay dudes.

In such ads, the heterosexual culture of dude-sex is established by drawing upon available typologies of white heterosexual masculinity. Others make reference to specific white ethnicities, such as one ad seeking "blondes, Italian(s), Jewish types, fat dick heads, hairy, white and/or Latin dudes . . . suit and tie types." [. . .] Just as the appropriation of black and white working-class masculinities helps construct an authentic "heteroerotic" culture, so too does the image of a normative middle-class or professional whiteness

(i.e. dudes who go to college, participate in sports, wear suit and ties, and so on). In both cases, race and socioeconomic class play a central role in making heterosexuality legible in the context of men's sexual seduction of other men.

In addition to naming racialized archetypes, some ads include long and detailed accounts of the exact clothing, dialogue, sex acts, and erotic mood required to maintain the heteroeroticism of dude-sex. For instance, the following ad was placed by a "str8 guy" who "lives a very str8 life" seeking someone to enact a "role play" in exchange for $400. The ad included a much longer script from which I have excerpted only a small segment:

. . . You come to the hotel in loose shorts with no underwear on, a tank top and flip flops, and when you get there we just kick back and maybe have a few beers and shoot the shit to get to know each other a little bit and feel more comfortable, then we start talking about our girlfriends and girls that we have fucked before or the best blow jobs we have had, etc., the whole time acting like we are just good friends that are horny. I am kind of dumb and don't have a lot of experience with chicks and you want to teach me and help me learn more. You then tell me that you are getting really horny thinking about all the hot sex you have had and ask me if I have any porn we can watch. I put one on and as we watch the porn, you are constantly grabbing your dick and playing with it as it gets harder and harder . . . Then you sit down right next to me and you say, "dude, you gotta hear this story about this one chick that I made suck my dick until I blew my load in her," then you tell me the story about it. While you are telling me the story you act it out with me . . .

While whiteness is not explicitly named in the role-play, the script mirrors the white surfer/frat dude fetishism common in the "Casual Encounters" section of Craigslist–Los Angeles. [. . .] [S]ome of the ad's references—such as the "costume" of flip flops, shorts and a tank top—possibly hint at white surfer/frat masculinity, exemplifying the ways in which erotic fantasies may be implicitly or unintentionally racialized. Yet the glorification of surfers and frat dudes also illustrates the way in which the racialized construction of heterosexual and homosexual cultures are locally or regionally specific. [. . .]

Less Str8, More DL: Desiring Black Men?

In addition to self-identifying with the DL, a small number of white str8 dudes expressed desire for "no strings" sex with "hung" black men on the DL. [. . .] While many "white on white" ads implied sameness, reciprocity or egalitarianism (let's stroke together, watch porn together, "work out a hot load side by side" and so on), "white seeking black" ads typically emphasized difference, hierarchy, and service. The majority of such ads were placed by white men looking to perform "blow jobs" for big, muscular black men. Many of the ads in "Casual Encounters" mention the importance of being "hung," but ads seeking black men placed particular emphasis on the relationship between race and body size (e.g., "big BLACK cock," "nice big meaty black guys"):

> *Discreet White Deep Throat 4 DL Black—Size Matters—44.* Discreet 44 yr old white guy lookin' to service hot black guys on the DL. I'm hairy, good shape. I'm lookin' for very hung black guys who love to kick back, watch porn and get their cocks serviced. I really like to deep throat big BLACK cock. [. . .]
>
> *Looking to suck off big black men, on the DL—* White guy here looking to suck off big muscular black guys. I like them big, over 250lbs and muscular. No strings attached. Hoping to meet some men on the DL. Got my own place, it's private and discreet, no strings, no hassles, etc. Just want to suck off some nice big meaty black guys.

Ads placed by white guys seeking black men on the DL were less likely to focus on authenticating heterosexuality through reference to women, straight porn, and friendship (male bonding, "being buddies") and more likely to focus on "the DL" as pre-formulated code for impersonal sex across racial difference.

White submission and black dominance was also a central theme in these ads. In the following ad, an image is included that reverses the master/slave relationship (a dominant black male, and a shackled white male) and has likely been taken from BDSM-themed gay porn (see Image 1):

> *Muscled Guy Looking for Str8 or Bi to Service on the Down Low—*Meet me at the construction site. I will be there waiting for you [in the?] dark, service you and leave anonymous . . . Send pic must be hot like me.

Black Master White Slave

While race is not mentioned in the text of this ad, the figure of the dominant black male (and the submissive white male body) is used to represent the queerer—or less normal and natural—white fantasy of the down low. This and similar ads suggest that in the black–white encounter, black men are always dominant; they receive sexual service, but they don't provide it. Friendship, equity, and "normal and natural male bonding" are represented as either undesirable or impossible across racial lines. In some ads, class differences also pervade the encounter. [. . .] [T]he presence of (or desire for) race and class difference produces a darker, less natural and less straight encounter.

Because of its association with men of color and the closet (or hidden homosexuality), the term "DL" was less likely to be associated with authentic white heterosexuality in "Casual Encounters" ("str8" was preferred by white dudes) and was more likely to be used by men of color in the "Men Seeking Men" section of Craigslist. [. . .] [W]hite dudes uninterested in gay identification [might] be drawn to "Casual Encounters," given that its moniker makes no reference to gender identity (or identity at all), while "Men Seeking Men" makes gender identity primary.

While reference to the symbols of black masculinity and style helped in the production of authentic heterosexuality, reference to actual sexual contact with black men generally did not. Instead, cross-racial sex was permeated with difference and inequality, becoming itself somewhat queer. This finding mirrors the findings of the study more broadly—for straight-identified white men seeking men, maintaining a heteroerotic culture was largely reliant upon specifically white forms of heterosexual masculinity (including those that appropriate some elements of black culture).

DISCUSSION: DISAVOWING STR8 DUDES

Str8 dudes who seek sex with men draw upon a wide variety of conceptual resources to assert a heterosexual male identity, including the use of racialized archetypes and images intended to signify authentic heterosexuality. [. . .] This deployment of race to signify heterosexuality included both cross-racial identifications and the preservation of white racial boundaries. In some cases, white str8 dudes appropriated the symbols/language of black heterosexual masculinity to construct a culture of male bonding that is arguably recognizable as the antithesis of gay male culture. In other cases, white str8 dudes invoked the "DL" as a means of eroticizing deceitful and "evil"

sex or expressing desire for closeted black men looking to be "serviced."

However, most commonly, white str8 dudes drew on archetypes of white heterosexual masculinity to provide evidence of being an average, normal dude. [. . .] While being gay has often been stereotyped as a "white thing" (Muñoz, 1999), the figure of the "*straight* white man" symbolizes both financial and cultural power as well as the average man, the "everyman," the "regular dude." [. . .] [F]or white str8 dudes, whiteness played a key role in producing evidence of normal/average male heterosexuality. This may be because desire for the ostensibly deracialized (but white) "everyman" is less threatening than the desire for men of color, who are coded as both hypermasculine and hypersexual within US popular culture (Hill Collins, 2004).

However, despite the ways in which the emphasis on whiteness may be experienced as the absence of racial fetish, the erotic culture of "Casual Encounters" was rife with white fetishism. In addition to simply declaring oneself a white str8 dude, detailed descriptions of white male bodies, white male lifestyles ("looking for surfers, [and other] LA-types"), and white male bonding helped to create and maintain the heteroerotic culture of dude-sex. Surfers, for example, were a particularly desired type, not because of the importance of surfing skills or the desire to actually surf together, but more likely because of the white, hetero-masculine script associated with southern California surf lifestyle [. . .]. In sum, racial markers are not used only to identify one's physical "type," they also provide an entire cultural universe from which to draw heterosexual costumes, scripts, and countless other codes for heterosexual masculinity.

At a broader level, this and other studies indicate that racial categories are always already sexualized and that sexuality categories are always already raced (González, 2007; Muñoz-Laboy, 2004; Somerville, 2000). Though I have focused on the intersections of whiteness and heterosexuality, my aim is not to position whiteness simply as one of several possible and equivalent examples of the racialization of heterosexuality. Instead, the ads on Craigslist suggest that in a culture constituted by both a racial and sexual binary (white/other and heterosexual/other), whiteness and heterosexually become "natural" bedfellows. Both whiteness and heterosexuality simultaneously signify the "really, really normal, nothing out of the ordinary" subject. For the str8 dudes on Craigslist, it appears that the most average and normal of male heterosexualities is white heterosexuality, even when it engages in same-sex practices and appropriates black culture. In the context of white male bonding, black bodies disrupt the staging of normalcy and occupy a distinctly queerer space "down low." [. . .] Building on sociological analyses of hegemonic and marginalized masculinities (Connell, 2005), future research might also reveal the range and hierarchy of heterosexualities by conceptualizing white heterosexuality as "hegemonic" and heterosexualities of color as "marginalized."

In addition to highlighting the racialization of heterosexuality and heteroerotic culture, the ads placed by str8 dudes also confirm the importance of giving as much consideration to sexual *culture* as has been given to sexual practice. [. . .] In Casual Encounters, sex practices are not useful guides for delineating the boundaries of queer and non-queer, or establishing political alliances with queer stakeholders. While the white str8 dudes who post ads in Casual Encounters express their desire for sex with other men, their desire takes form within the context of heterosexual identification and heterosexual erotic culture [. . .].

To de-queer the sex described on Craigslist is to give up the epistemological pleasure of self-righteous knowing, owning, outing and naming. In the face of homophobia and heterosexism, honing one's "gaydar" and revealing that *we are everywhere* have been among few queer luxuries. Yet as others have argued (Halberstam, 2005; Duggan, 2003), political solidarity built primarily around sex acts misrecognizes what is most threatening, and subversive, about queerness. Queer *culture*—including a collective rejection of the rules associated with normal, adult, reproductive sexuality and (nonconsensual) heterosexual power relations—may better help scholars and activists determine the meaning of queer. [. . .] This complexity reveals the permeability of the categories "straight" and "queer," which signify not only the divide between normal and abnormal sexual practices but also the divide between normal and abnormal interpretive frames for understanding these practices. Str8 dudes

have abnormal sex, but they invest in ideologies of racial and sexual normalcy. [. . .] Rather than a symptom of repression, passivity, or lack of self-awareness, str8 dudes' rejection of queerness may be more accurately understood as agentic acts of identification with heterosexual culture.

This [chapter] has pointed to the value of viewing queer and straight as cultural spheres that people choose to inhabit in large part because they experience a cultural and political fit. [. . .] Redefining queer and nonqueer as cultural affiliations also implies that queer "rights" serve to protect not everyone who engages in same-sex sexuality, but all those who cannot or will not invest in hegemonic str8 culture—gender freaks, kids in gay–straight alliances, and all people.

REFERENCES

Bettie, Julie. 2002. *Women without Class: Girls, Race, and Identity.* Berkeley: University of California Press.

Boykin, Keith. 2005. *Beyond the Down Low: Sex, Lies, and Denial in Black America.* New York: Carroll & Graf.

Boykin, Keith. 2006. "The White Down Low." 23 May. Accessed May 5, 2008, from http://www .keithboykin.com/.

Connell, Raewyn. 2005. *Masculinities*, 2nd ed. Berkeley: University of California Press.

Craigslist.org. 2006. "Casual Encounters," ads posted by "str8" self-identified men, May through July 2006 (particular ads no longer available). Home page accessed April 2008, www.craigslist.org/.

Denizet-Lewis, Benoit. 2003. "Double Lives on the Down Low." *The New York Times Sunday Magazine* August 3. Accessed May 2008 from http://query. nytimes.com/gst/fullpage.html?res=9F0CE0D61 E3FF930A3575BC0A9659C8B63/.

Diaz, Rafael. 1997. *Latino Gay Men and HIV: Culture, Sexuality, and Risk Behavior.* New York: Routledge.

Duggan, Lisa. 2003. *The Twilight of Equality? Neoliberalism, Cultural Politics, and the Attack on Democracy.* New York: Beacon Press.

Ferguson, Roderick. 2004. *Aberrations in Black: Toward a Queer of Color Critique.* Minneapolis: University of Minnesota Press.

Foucault, Michel. 1978. *The History of Sexuality: An Introduction.* New York: Vintage Books.

Frye, Marilyn. 1983. "Lesbian Feminism and the Gay Rights Movement: Another View of Male Supremacy, Another Separatism." In *The Politics of Reality: Essays in Feminist Theory*, edited by Marilyn Frye, 128–51. New York: Crossing Press.

González, M. Alfredo. 2007. "Latinos on Da Down Low: The Limitations of Sexual Identity in Public Health." *Latino Studies* 5 (1): 25–52.

Halberstam, Judith. 2005. *In a Queer Time and Place: Transgender Bodies, Subcultural Lives*. New York: New York University Press.

Hill Collins, Patricia. 2004. *Black Sexual Politics: African Americans, Gender, and the New Racism*. New York: Routledge.

Hull, Gloria, Patricia Bell Scott, and Barbara Smith, eds. 1982. *All the Women Are White, All the Blacks Are Men, But Some of Us Are Brave: Black Women's Studies*. New York: Feminist Press.

Humphreys, Laud. 1978. *Tearoom Trade: Impersonal Sex in Public Places*, 2nd ed. Chicago: Aldine Transaction.

Kaplan, Danny. 2003. *Brothers and Others in Arms: The Making of Love and War in Israeli Combat Units*. New York: Harrington Park Press.

Katz, Jonathan. 1996. *The Invention of Heterosexuality*. New York: Plume.

King, J. K. 2004. *On the Down Low: A Journey Into the Lives of "Straight" Black Men Who Sleep with Men*. New York: Broadway.

Kitwana, Bakari. 2005. *Why White Kids Love Hip Hop: Wangstas, Wiggers, Wannabes, and the New Reality of Race in America*. New York: Basic Civitas Books.

Mukherjea, Ananya, and Salvador Vidal-Ortiz. 2006. "Studying HIV Risk in Vulnerable Communities: Methodological and Reporting Shortcomings in the Young Men's Study in New York City." *The Qualitative Report* 11 (2): 393–416.

Muñoz, Jose. 1999. *Disidentifications: Queers of Color and the Performance of Politics*. Minneapolis: University of Minnesota Press.

Muñoz-Laboy, Miguel. 2004. "Beyond 'MSM': Sexual Desire among Bisexually-Active Latino Men in New York City." *Sexualities* 7 (1): 55–80.

Schifter, Jacobo. 1999. *Macho Love: Sex behind Bars in Central America*. New York: Harrington Park Press.

Sedgwick, Eve Kosofsky. 1992. *Epistemology of the Closet*. Berkeley: University of California Press.

Smitherman, Geneva. 2000. *Black Talk: Words and Phrases from the Hood to the Amen Corner*. New York: Mariner Books.

Somerville, Siobhan. 2000. *Queering the Color Line: Race and the Invention of Homosexuality in American Culture*. Durham, NC: Duke University Press.

Urbandictionary.com. 1999–2008. Slang dictionary. Accessed April 2008 from http://www.urbandictionary.com/.

Ward, Jane. 2000. "Queer Sexism: Rethinking Gay Men and Masculinity." In *Gay Masculinities*, edited by Peter Nardi, 152–75. Thousand Oaks, CA: Sage.

NOTES

1. MSM is a term first adopted by epidemiologists to classify men who have sex with men, regardless of whether they identify as gay, bisexual, or heterosexual.

2. There is disagreement on the web regarding the meaning of the term "str8." In some online communities, "str8" functions simply as internet slang for "straight," and it has also been used as an abbreviation for "straight" in rap lyrics. However, others, such as contributors to "urbandictionary.com," argue that "str8" is used almost exclusively by gay and bisexual men "in the closet."

3. This study received approval from the University of California Internal Review Board for the use of human subjects. Though Craigslist is a public site, I have made every effort to protect the anonymity of the men whose personal ads I have used. Any specific identifying information (e.g. name of a small and specific neighborhood, physical descriptions, contact information) has been removed from the ads.

TRISTAN BRIDGES AND C. J. PASCOE

32. MASCULINITIES AND POST-HOMOPHOBIAS?

Two white, male, straight fans of Chick-fil-A, Skyler Stone and Mike Smith, found themselves disturbed by the company's public stance opposing same-sex marriage in 2012. The two men wanted to eat Chick-fil-A's delicious fast food, but did not want to compromise deeply held values about equality and civil rights for all. So they decided to stage a protest at their local Chick-fil-A. Theirs was not the usual protest featuring signs, urging boycotts, or presenting a list of demands. Instead, their protest consisted of showing exactly how far two straight guys were willing to go in support of both gay rights and the love of Chick-fil-A: they staged a kiss-in . . . with each other. While cameras rolled, these two handsome twenty-something heterosexual-identified men called their girlfriends to secure permission, washed their mouths with mouthwash, and asked gay men for kissing advice. Duly prepared, the pair walked up to a Chick-fil-A "take out" window, placed their order, and passionately embraced—kissing (with overdramatic use of tongue and leg movements) in full view of a gathered crowd and restaurant employees.

Stone and Smith are both comedians and played their protest for laughs. That a protest by two straight men in support of gay rights even happened, much less involved a same-sex kiss, however, signifies important social transformations underway. Indeed, the past decade has witnessed a sea change in gay rights, both in terms of visibility and in terms of response from heterosexual men to homosexuality. Take, for instance, the reaction to Jason Collins, a professional basketball player who came out after his first year playing in the NBA. While his story made front-page news, prominent basketball stars, politicians, and other public figures responded with support and praise. Similarly, straight men are publicly standing by their gay brethren, whether it be hip-hop artist Macklemore singing his support for marriage equality in his anthem "One Love" or straight male Canadian teenagers holding a school-wide "pink out" to protest homophobic bullying.

On first read, these changes seem to challenge understandings of homophobia as a central component of masculinity in the West (e.g., Kimmel 1994; Pascoe 2007). In her essay for this volume (Reading 10), Melanie Heath offers one way to more critically consider whether these practices are inconsistent with the enduring significance of homophobia. Heath refers to these practices as part of what she calls "soft-boiled" masculinity. Looking at the practices of evangelical Christian men, she argues that new masculine practices can sometimes work to conceal existing forms of inequality, but perhaps in new ways.[1]

In discussing the contemporary relationship between masculinity and homophobia, Heath's claims about the complexity of contemporary gender practices as both changing *and* reinscribing inequality in new ways is a useful starting point. In this essay we examine the contemporary relationship between masculinity and sexuality in three identity practices. In doing so we suggest that a useful way to think about the relationship between masculinity and sexuality is not to think of sexuality as inhered in male bodies (heterosexual or homosexual), but as *discursive practice*. That is, when we think of sexuality as located in particular homosexual or heterosexual bodies, it means that heterosexuals are the homophobic ones and that homophobia is being directed at gay men. Instead we argue that homophobia is best understood—as Connell (1995) suggests of masculinity—as multiple (e.g., Stein 2005). Homophobia is often discussed as a psychological or political disposition. But homophobias can also operate as complex forms of *gendered practice*.

The iterations of homophobia we address here do not necessitate the fear or hatred of gay men. Rather, they are contemporary forms of gender practice that recuperate existing relations of power and inequality among men and between men and women. A central mechanism of this "emergent homophobia" (Stein 2005) is what Pascoe (2005, 2007) refers to as "fag discourse." *Fag discourse* is a gendered and sexualized disciplinary practice, policing selves and others into acceptably masculine identities, dispositions, relations, and enactments. Within this framework, heterosexuality is not only about desire or identity, but also about gendered practice involving twin strategies: "repudiation" and "confirmation." Fag discourse is a gendered practice that simultaneously rejects a "fag" identity (repudiation) and enforces dominance over women (confirmation). In investigating practices of what Bridges (2014) refers to as sexual aesthetics (or the appearance of gayness or straightness), we complicate the face-value interpretation of changes in masculine practice as indicative of a transformation in gender and sexual relations. Although men's actions are often laudable and well intended, these new practices and performances often have the less visible consequence of shoring up particular masculine identities under the appearance of "open mindedness," progress, and change. What we are seeing is not necessarily a kinder, gentler form of masculinity, but a "soft-boiled" masculinity, discursively repackaged in light of feminist critique and challenge (e.g., Demetriou 2001; Bridges 2014; Bridges and Pascoe 2014). We argue that fag discourse, compulsive heterosexuality, and heterosexual men's comfort with and adoption of "gay aesthetics" are practices associated with emergent forms of homophobia. They illustrate the tenacity of gender *inequality* behind a façade of gender and sexual equality.

A POST-HOMOPHOBIA ERA?

The story about homophobia as a foundational element of contemporary manifestations of masculinity is a familiar one at this point. The argument may have emerged out of the fact that men have traditionally expressed more sexual prejudice than women on surveys (e.g., Herek 1986). As Michael Kimmel famously argued, "Homophobia is a central organizing principal of our cultural definition of manhood" (1994: 214). Similarly, Raewyn Connell (1995) situates "subordinated masculinities" as those against

which "hegemonic masculinity" is most powerfully defined. Gay masculinities, for Connell (1992, 1995), best illustrate contemporary configurations of subordinated masculinity. Homophobia is a central mechanism by which hegemonic masculinity is constituted and maintained (Connell 1992, 1995). Gay men, in other words, perform a constitutive role in shaping hegemonic masculinity.

This analysis makes intuitive sense. Popular examples of boys' and men's homophobia abound. Take, for example, the recent spate of stories about young men who have left this world by their own hands, unable to bear the homophobic bullying of which they were targets (Pascoe 2013). Indeed, homophobic epithets permeate popular culture—from the military, to Hollywood movies, to sporting events to schools. The phrase, "Hijack (sic) this Fags" was scrawled on the side of a bomb to be dropped on Afghanistan during 2001's Operation Enduring Freedom.[2] The "Bleacher Creatures" at Yankee baseball games regularly serenade fans of the opposing team by singing homophobic lyrics to the tune of the Village People's anthem "YMCA."[3] In 2012, a public school principal punished two young men for fighting by forcing them to sit and hold hands in front of the student body.[4] A brief glance at the online world reveals the prevalence of these sorts of epithets in mediated spaces as well. A project at the University of Alberta's Institute for Sexual Minority Studies and Service—www.NoHomophobes.com—has been tracking the use of the words "faggot," "dyke," "that's so gay," and "no homo" on the micro-blogging service Twitter since July 2012. By September 2014 the word "dyke" has been used almost 3 million times, "so gay" 8.2 million times, "no homo" 8.1 million, and "faggot" *more than 29 million* times. Given the role of homophobia in contemporary understandings of masculinity, the prevalence of a masculine homophobic insult on Twitter seems little accident.

Empirical studies show that these are not isolated incidents. Men continue to espouse higher levels of homophobic sentiment and behavior compared to women (Burn 2000; Falomir-Pichastor et al. 2009). Homophobic language and attitudes are disproportionately deployed by young men, and boys rate these insults much more seriously than do girls (Poteat and

Rivers 2010; Thurlow 2001). Men are also more likely to direct this homophobia at gay men, rather than lesbians (Herek 2002; Moskowitz et al. 2010). In fact, homophobic behavior, especially among young men, might even be considered *normative* behavior. These types of homophobic sentiments are tied to men's understandings of themselves as masculine. For instance, research shows that the more men express conformity to traditional masculine norms, the more they express negative attitudes toward gay men (Keiller 2010). Similarly, when men are told they are emasculated in experimental research, they are more likely to express homophobic attitudes (Willer et al. 2013).

Yet, evidence from popular culture such as the Chick-fil-A protest, openly gay professional athletes, or hip-hop songs evidencing straight male ally-ship seem to contradict some of these claims. If homophobia is so central to contemporary constructions of masculinity, these examples implicitly ask, why are straight, normatively masculine men kissing each other in public in support of gay rights? Recent survey research indicates that these examples illustrate a larger trend.

For instance, a 2014 report from the Pew Research Center indicated that support for gay marriage has reached an unprecedented level of 52 percent of Americans.[5] This is a dramatic and rapid rise from their 2003 survey indicating a level of support of 33 percent. Men still approve of gay marriage at lower rates than do women and older people at lower rates than younger people. But between 2003 and 2013, men between the ages of 18–49 changed the most in their approval of gay marriage, increasing their approval by 18 percentage points. Similarly, in 2010, Gallup reported that men were, for the first time since it has been measured, *more* likely than women to classify "gay/lesbian relations" as "morally acceptable."[6] Although we are not suggesting this is a tipping point, these changes—at least implicitly—question the continued centrality of homophobia to masculinity. If nothing else, they require explanation.

In this chapter we suggest a way to reconcile this seeming contradiction posed by these twin trends apparently happening side by side. Rather than suggesting that homophobia is *either* still a bedrock of masculinity *or* that it is in decline, we suggest that both of these trends are occurring. To understand how homophobia can *both* remain a normative foundation of contemporary Western masculinity *and* that men's homophobic attitudes can be drastically changing, we need to understand two issues. First, we need to understand sexuality as something that does not necessarily reside in particular bodies, but as gendered discursive practice. Second, we need to understand that there are multiple ways to measure and express homophobia; some may be declining, others remaining, and still others emerging. New forms of gender and sexual inequality materialize even as others are called into question. Indeed—as with masculinity—it is more appropriate to speak of "homophobias" than the singular homophobia.[7]

REFRAMING HOMOPHOBIA: REPUDIATION, CONFIRMATION, AND SEXUAL AESTHETICS

Think for a moment about the findings of the following study: in a survey of 111 Canadian undergraduate men, *none* of them answered affirmatively to the question "if you were to call a straight man a 'fag' or 'faggot' would you seriously be suggesting that you really and truly believe the man is gay?" (Brown and Alderson 2010). Yet, only 21 percent of them stated that they would *not* use a homophobic epithet to refer to another man (Brown and Alderson 2010). How can we make sense of this? One the one hand, the men in this study say they would use these terms to insult someone; on the other hand, they say this has nothing to do with a sexual identity. Brown and Alderson's study illustrates what others miss: when we only think of sexuality as inhering in particular bodies and identities, we miss the ways it operates to discursively construct masculinity as well. In other words, we have to think of sexuality as a form of gender policing, rather than solely as an identity, desire or practice. Below, we discuss three ways this happens—through "fag discourse," "compulsive heterosexuality," and straight men's strategic use of "gay aesthetics". Through examples drawn from different research projects, we suggest that these three phenomena exemplify the complex relations by which contemporary gender and sexual inequalities are challenged and reproduced (sometimes at the same time).

REPUDIATION: FAG DISCOURSE

One critically important aspect of the two young men who protested at Chick-fil-A is that they did so humorously.[8] Their protest was undertaken in ways that strategically ensured (throughout the protest) that no one could mistake them as *actually* gay. They signaled that they were explicitly not gay in a variety of ways: asking their girlfriends for permission to kiss (situating each of them within heterosexual relationships), asking gay men for advice (underscoring the fact that authentically straight men could not accomplish this without advice), cleaning their mouths out in ways that one usually would not for a kiss, and finally kissing in a manner that looked more like attacking each other than something erotic, passionate, tender, or loving. Their intentions merit celebration. On another level, however, Stone and Smith's protest accomplished something else: they made a big display of exactly how *straight* they are while making a joke about same-sex desire all in support of gay rights. How in the world could these men be making a homophobic joke while supporting gay rights? We suggest that answering this question means critically dissecting exactly what we mean by "homophobia" and how it works.

While researching contemporary understandings of masculinity among high schoolers in Northern California, Pascoe came to understand that for contemporary American boys, masculinity entails displaying power, competence, a lack of emotions, heterosexuality, and dominance. Said Kevin, one of her respondents, to be masculine is to be "tough." The ideal man is "strong" and "can't be too emotional," added Erik. Maleness does not confer masculinity on boys. Rather masculinity entailed repeatedly signaling power, competence, emotional stoicism, heterosexuality, and dominance. In Pascoe's research with teenage boys, she finds that this signaling appears in two ways: repudiation and confirmation. Repudiatory practices take the form of a *fag discourse* whereas confirmation practices take the form of *compulsive heterosexuality.*

Thinking of young men's gendered and sexual behavior as a fag discourse makes clear that the homophobia and homophobic language that is so central to shaping contemporary heterosexual masculine identities (Kehler 2007; Levy et al. 2012;

Pascoe 2007; Poteat et al. 2010) is not just about gay men. Rather, young men's homophobia is also a primary mechanism through which they socialize each other into normatively masculine behaviors, practices, attitudes, and dispositions (Pascoe 2007). A fag discourse consists of jokes, taunts, imitations, and threats on which young men rely to publicly signal their rejection of that which is considered "unmasculine." In other words, homophobic harassment has as much (if not more) to do with masculinity as it does with actual fear of gay men (Corbett 2001; Kimmel 1994). Homophobic insults are levied against boys who are not masculine, if only momentarily, *and* boys who identify (or are identified by others) as gay. Recent research has also documented the deployment of "no-homo" as having similar meanings (Brown 2011). Indeed, it is possible to rely on fag discourse with different terms (Fair 2011) or even without deploying a derogatory term at all (Bridges 2010).

Young men actively assert that "fag" is the ultimate insult for a boy. One respondent, Darnell, stated, "Since you were little boys you've been told, 'hey, don't be a little faggot.'" Another, Jeremy, emphasized that this insult essentially reduced a boy to nothing: "To call someone gay or fag is like the lowest thing you can call someone. Because that's like saying that you're nothing." Young men's daily lives often consist of interactions in which they frantically lob these epithets at one another and try to deflect them from themselves. Practices that seem to reflect basic homophobia such as imitating same-sex eroticism, calling someone queer, or mincing about with limp wrists are also about policing gendered identities and practices (see also Bridges 2010). Through making homophobic jokes, calling other boys gay, and imitating effeminate men, boys assure themselves and others of their masculinity.

Many young men explained their frequent use of insults like queer, gay, and fag by asserting, as Keith put it, "guys are just homophobic." However, analyzing their homophobic practices as a "fag discourse" shows that their behavior reflects not only a fear of same-sex desire, but also a specific fear of *men's* same-sex desire. Many reported that homophobic insults applied primarily to boys, not to girls. Whereas Jake asserted that he didn't like gay people, he quickly added, "Lesbians, okay, that's good!" Now, Jake is not situating lesbians as "good" because of some enlightened approach to sexuality, but because, as Ray said, "To see two hot chicks banging bodies in a bed, that's like every guy's fantasy right there. It's the truth. I've heard it so many times."

Furthermore, several boys strongly suggested that descriptors like fag, queer, and gay had little to do with actual sexual practices or desires. Much like the surveyed Canadian undergraduate men (Brown and Alderson 2010), Darnell claimed, "It doesn't have anything to do with being gay." Adding to this sentiment, J. L. said, "Fag, seriously, it has nothing to do with sexual preference at all. You could just be calling somebody an idiot, you know?" As David explained, "Being gay is just a lifestyle. It's someone you choose to sleep with. You can still throw a football around and be gay." David's final statement clarifies the distinction between popular understandings of these insults and young people's actual use of them. That is, they have to do with men's same-sex eroticism, but at their core they are best understood as discursive strategies that discipline gender practices and identities. In asserting the primacy of gender to the definition of these seemingly homophobic insults, young men reflect what Riki Wilchins (2003) calls the "Eminem exception." Eminem explains that his use of the term "faggot" does not refer to sexual orientation; rather, he claims that it simply means that they are weak and unmanly. Although it is not necessarily acceptable to be gay, if a man were gay *and* masculine—as in David's portrait of the football-throwing gay man—he does not deserve the insult.

Being subject to homophobic harassment has as much to do with failing at masculine tasks of competence, heterosexual prowess, or in any way revealing weakness as it does with sexual identity. Homophobic epithets such as "fag" have gendered meanings and sexual meanings. The insult is levied against boys who are not masculine (even momentarily) and boys who identify or are identified by others as gay. This sets up a very complicated daily ordeal in which boys continually strive to avoid being subject to the epithet but are constantly vulnerable to it.

This sort of homophobia appears frequently in boys' joking relationships. Sociologists have pointed

out that joking is central to men's relationships in general (Kehily and Nayak 1997; Lyman 1987). Through aggressive joking, boys cement friendship bonds with one another. Boys often draw laughs though imitating effeminate men or men's same-sex desire. Emir frequently imitated effeminate men who presumably sexually desired other men to draw laughs from students in his introductory drama class. One day his teacher, disturbed by noise outside the classroom, turned to close the door, saying, "We'll shut this unless anyone really wants to watch sweaty boys playing basketball." Emir lisped, "I wanna watch the boys play!" The rest of the class laughed at his imitation—collectively repudiating a gendered and sexual performance of masculinity. No one in the class thought Emir was actually gay, as he purposefully mocked both same-sex sexual desire and an effeminate gender identity and performance. Rather, this sort of ritual reminded other youth that *masculine* men do not desire other men, nor do they lisp or behave in other feminine ways. It also reminded them that those men who do behave in these ways merit laughter and social derision. Additionally, this is a powerful illustration of the ways that fag discourse is often at work even when no one explicitly uses the word "fag."

Because so many activities could render a boy vulnerable to these insults, perhaps it is little surprise that Ben asserted that one could be labeled for "anything, literally anything. Like you were trying to turn a wrench the wrong way, 'dude you're a fag.' Even if a piece of meat drops out of your sandwich, 'you fag!'" Although this research shows that there are a particular set of behaviors that might provoke the slur, it is no wonder that Ben felt this way. In that statement, he reveals the intensity and extent of the policing boys endure to avoid the epithet.

Indeed, examining fag discourse explains the humor contained in Smith and Stone's protest. Fag discourse can exist alongside support for civil rights for gay people. On the one hand, much like Emir, Stone and Smith are drawing laughs for their performance of same-sex desire. On the other, much like the other boys in Pascoe's study, they show how such homophobic jokes can also be divorced from actual dislike of gay men.

CONFIRMATION: COMPULSIVE HETEROSEXUALITY

Looking at young men's homophobia as a fag discourse—as a discursive engagement with masculinity—allows us to understand young men's practices of heterosexuality differently as well. They defend against the homophobic teasing and harassment of fag discourse by assuring others of their heterosexuality. In the same way that boys' homophobia is not specifically about sexual identity, compulsive heterosexuality is not only about expressing love, desire, and intimacy. "Compulsive heterosexuality" is about demonstrating a gendered and sexualized dominance over girls' bodies. In other words, the sort of gendered teasing in which boys engage takes a toll on girls as well as other boys; girls' bodies are physically and symbolically mobilized to shield young men from homophobic epithets.

Perhaps the most obvious example of compulsive heterosexuality is the process of and talk about "getting girls." Getting girls is such a hallmark of masculinity that students at River High laughed uproariously as two students lip-synced a Chris Tucker routine making fun of Michael Jackson for not being able to "get a girl." Indeed, young men suggest that "getting a girl" through having a girlfriend (and assumed sexual access to her body) is an important component of masculinity. For young men identified as feminine and teased for unmasculine practices, having a girlfriend functions as a form of symbolic protection against homophobic harassment. Justin, for instance, suggested that some boys have girlfriends "so they look like they're not losers or they're not gay." Because of the difficulty of avoiding all of the behaviors that might render one vulnerable to teasing, having a girlfriend helps to inure boys to accusations of the fag discourse.

Similarly, young men engaged in cross-gender touching to establish heterosexual reputations. Their physical interchanges may first appear to be harmless flirtation, but on closer inspection, the behaviors are integral in reinforcing young men's dominance over young women's bodies. The use of touch maintains social hierarchies (Henley 1977). Superiors touch subordinates, invade their space, and interrupt them

in ways subordinates do not interact with social superiors and these relationships are often gendered ones. Young people of both genders touch each other as part of daily interaction, communication, and flirtation. In many instances cross-sex touching was lightly flirtatious and reciprocal. But touching rituals ranged from playfully flirtatious to assault-like interactions. And even playful touching can also be understood as interactionally shoring up relations by which men dominate women's bodies. Young men might physically constrain girls under the guise of flirtation. For instance, Pascoe watched as one teen wrapped his arms around another and started to "freak" her, or grind his pelvis into hers, as she struggled to get away.[9] She watched as another young man wrapped his arms around a young woman's neck and hold her while his friend punched her in the stomach, albeit lightly, and she squealed until they stopped. Perhaps most dramatically, she watched as one young man jabbed a female classmate in the crotch with his drumstick as he yelled, "Get raped! Get raped!" Touching and constraining female bodies in these examples get translated as masculinity. Demonstrating dominance requires someone to (at least symbolically) be dominated.

Although people jokingly refer to young men's sex talk as "boys will be boys" or "locker room talk," this kind of sex talk is part of the process of constructing a masculine identity. Young men enact and naturalize their heterosexuality by asserting "guys are horndogs" or by claiming that it is "kind of impossible for a guy" to not "think of sex every two minutes." Thinking about young men's sexual performance in terms of compulsive heterosexuality shows that asserting that one is a "horndog" is actually a gendered performance. Young men's sex talk often takes the form of "mythic story telling" (Kehily and Nayak 1997) by which they tell larger-than-life tales about their sexual adventures, their bodies, and young women's bodies that do not reflect love, desire, or sensuality, but rather dominance over them. Pedro, for instance, laughed and acted out having sex with his girlfriend by leaning back up against the wall, legs and arms spread and head turning back and forth as he continued to say proudly, "I did her so hard when I was done she was bleeding. I tore her walls!" His friends surrounding him cheered in amazement. Violence frequently framed these young men's stories. At other times, young men shared stories about making girls bleed, fart, or defecate during sexual interactions. These stories are about sexual interactions, but have little to do with sex or intimacy. Rather, they are examples of how young men can manipulate young women's bodies. It does not matter whether they are true; what matters is that these young men enact discursive dominance through stories of heterosexual conquest.

To understand the role of sexuality in constructing and maintaining masculinity it is important to look at sexuality—and heterosexuality in particular—not as a set of desires, identities, or dispositions, but as discursive practice. In this way we can understand Stone and Smith's calls to their girlfriends to not actually be about respecting their girlfriends' wishes, but as a discursive practice that positioned their girlfriends as masculinity resources attending to their heterosexuality. Compulsive heterosexuality and fag discourse are twin practices through which young men reinforce linkages among sexuality, inequality, and gender.

STRAIGHT MEN AND GAY AESTHETICS

Importantly, Stone and Smith's protest at Chick-fil-A did not involve violence against women. Nor did they rely on derogatory homophobic terms. Arguably, however, they were engaging in a form of fag discourse, albeit unintentionally. They strategically framed their kiss, for instance, in a way that echoed Emir's temporary performance of a stereotype of gay masculinity. Certainly, Emir seemed not to have had a political motivation for his behavior in the classroom. As such, Stone and Smith's temporary performance of gay masculinity is different from Emir's in an important way. They were motivated to raise awareness about sexual inequality and to stand up against it. But, in doing so, like Emir, they had a complicated interactional task in front of them: they performed gay masculinity, but strategically framed that performance as "straight."

To fully appreciate this process as well as its relationship with gender and sexual inequality necessitates a discussion of what Bridges (2014) refers to as "sexual aesthetics." *Sexual aesthetics* refer to the cultural and stylistic distinctions utilized to delineate boundaries between gay and straight cultures and individuals. A wide variety of "things" can "count" as sexual aesthetics: interests, material objects, styles of bodily comportment, language, opinions, clothing, behaviors, and more. Sexual aesthetics are what allow us to put our sexual identities on display—even when we are not being "sexual." And sexual aesthetics (gay or straight) are deeply gendered. Indeed, it is not an exaggeration to say that sexual aesthetics are an integral component of gender performances. In fact, we often read gender transgressions as indicative of gay identities (or, perhaps more generally, "non-straight" identities) and gender conformity as indicative of straight identities. Yet, Stone and Smith, and some of Pascoe's heterosexual-identifying research participants, strategically rely on temporary transgressions that have the effect of shoring up (rather than calling into question) their *heterosexual* masculine identities. As Steve Seidman writes, "[M]ore and more Americans [are] becoming aware of homosexuality and skilled at reading signs of sexual identity" (2002: 56). Indeed, research suggests that young straight men are not only able to identify gay aesthetics, but also increasingly emboldened to accessorize their heterosexual identities with bits and pieces of gay culture (e.g., Demetriou 2001; Bridges 2010, 2014; Arxer 2011). There is, however, no necessary relationship between this process of cultural appropriation and gender or sexual equality.

For instance, in the pro-feminist group of men in Northern Virginia Bridges (2014) studied ethnographically for just over a year, it was common for men in the group to claim that they were "mistaken for gay" and to identify with aspects of gay culture in the process. Like Stone and Smith, one member of the group—Shane—claims to strategically mobilize a symbolic protest against sexual inequality: "I take it as an opportunity to help gay people. . . . I'll usually say something like, 'Because I'm stylish? Or because I'm nice to people? . . . What? Because I'm healthy and care about my clothes and the way I look?' You know? Like, 'Oh, because I have good taste in music?'" On the face of it, Shane is actively resisting heterosexism and attempting to emphatically illustrate to others that he is not homophobic. He may also be attempting to critique heteronormative configurations of masculinity if being "nice," "clean," "healthy," and "stylish" call men's (hetero)sexuality into question.

Yet, Shane is also relying on fag discourse—but he does so in a way that is qualitatively different from the young men in Pascoe's research. Fag discourse relies on clear boundaries between gay and straight. This is why boys and young men feel comfortable flirting with the boundary: their performances rely on and reproduce the belief that this boundary exists. And although Shane might appear to be calling the boundaries between "gay" and "straight" into question by illustrating that a straight man can look and act "gay" too, he also participates in (re)defining those behaviors, interests, and qualities as "gay" in the first place. When others in the group discussed having been mistaken for gay, it wasn't uncommon for them to joke about how to avoid a similar kind of mistake in the future. For instance, Ben, a school counselor in the group, shared that students mistake him for gay. He shared, "Maybe I'll put a car engine in [my office]. Or like hang some porn on my wall." Similarly, Jacob, a bank teller who loves to wear extremely colorful, fitted clothes, shared that his clothing has caused others to question his sexuality. In response, he joked, "Would it make you more comfortable if I looked like some oppressive Bible salesman, like telling women to get back in the kitchen?"

Shane, Ben, and Jacob are all doing something similar here. As feminist-identifying men, they strategically rely on gay aesthetics to discursively distance themselves from masculinities that have earned a bad reputation among feminists.[10] Their gendered performances and discussions often appear to be a sort of anti-fag discourse. That is, they wear being read as sexually illegible as a badge of honor rather than an insult. However, the ways Bridges's participants trade stories of having been "mistaken for gay" share a great deal of common ground with the "sex talk" Pascoe observed among high school boys. Whether the stories are objectively true misses the point. These stories are traded as a form of masculine capital, validating specific masculinities by implicitly "Othering" masculinities that fail to meet the criteria they interactionally define as worthy of status and respect. Thus, similar to Pascoe's participants, these men are

attempting to authenticate their masculinities. Like Stone and Smith's awkward protest at Chick-fil-A, these young men claim identities as "allies" or "feminists" that render any discussion of how their behavior might entail a gendered form of sexual inequality as impossible, or at the very least, unfair.

Yet, the pro-feminist men in Bridges's research transgress gender and sexual boundaries in ways that not only leave those boundaries intact, but also simultaneously symbolically reinforce them. One effect of this practice, for instance, was to discursively produce an understanding of gender and sexual inequality as one with "good guys" and "bad guys." In this way, mistaken-for-gay stories performed a bit of cultural work for these men, situating themselves as outside the very systems of inequality this group organizes to oppose. This is clearly a qualitatively different kind of cultural work than that performed by Pascoe's research participants. Problematically, however, a common set of consequences are associated with each: they strengthen symbolic boundaries separating "gay" from "straight." Whereas Pascoe's participants reiterate symbolic boundaries and hierarchies between gay and straight culture and people, Bridges's pro-feminist respondents who trade mistaken-for-gay stories do so in a way that attempts to symbolically invert sexual hierarchies for considerations of gay and straight aesthetics. Indeed, these men are not only claiming to be mistaken for gay, but also wear these instances as badges of honor. And although this is an important step in challenging inequality, the practice simultaneously obscures the fact that little is being done here to challenge inequalities between gay and straight *people*.

Thus, rather than calling this boundary into question, gender transgressions involving heterosexual men's strategic discussion of or reliance upon gay aesthetics to (often momentarily) perform gay masculinities or subjectively claim ownership over elements of gay culture. Yet, unlike Pascoe's participants, the young men in Bridges's (2014) research invoked fag discourse toward a different end. Although the repudiation and confirmation going on here is certainly a qualitatively different ilk than that associated with Pascoe's research, a set of common consequences unite young men's behavior and discursive strategies surrounding masculine identification and recognition in both studies.

CONCLUSION: MASCULINITIES AND EMERGENT HOMOPHOBIAS

In some ways, the cultural transformations we describe here can be interpreted as a sign of feminist progress—social change. We suggest, however, that rather than reading them as a *sign* of progress, they are better interpreted as a *consequence* of feminist progress. As Demetriou writes, "Patriarchy was in need of new legitimatory strategies and many men were asked to renegotiate their positions in patriarchal societies, their power, and the masculine identities" (2001: 349). As feminist critiques of normative masculinities have made their way into the mainstream, performances, discourses, ideologies, and practices that have historically upheld gender and sexual inequality have been put into the spotlight and publicly challenged. *Labeling* privilege, however, is not tantamount to *dismantling* privilege. Our research indicates a need to theorize homophobia—like masculinity—as multiple, as flexible (e.g., Johnson 2005). Powerful systems of inequality, like sexism and homophobia, are flexible and capable of adapting to new historical circumstances. Thus, sometimes, what might initially look like social *change* is actually *continuity*.

Our research supports Arlene Stein's (2005) analysis of what she refers to as "emergent homophobias." Stein suggests that it is not the case that new "variants of homophobia are supplanting earlier forms that focused on homosexual gender nonconformity. Rather, they may coexist alongside them, becoming more or less salient depending on the local context" (2005: 617). In other words, homophobia is not just about a simplistic fear of homosexuality (Bryant and Vidal-Ortiz 2008; Herek 2004; Plummer 1981); rather, homophobias can occupy a complex constellation of practices, ideologies, and discourses, some of which may even seem, on the surface, progressive. Whether emergent homophobias are "soft-boiled" or not, we must continue to focus not only on their form, but also on their associated consequences.

Emergent homophobias provide a language for understanding connections among fag discourse, compulsive heterosexuality, and straight men's engagement with gay aesthetics. Taken together, these are complex and often contradictory expressions of homophobia. Each, however, is connected by being tied to masculinity.[11] Pascoe's research found a form of homophobia among students that has as much to do with gender (and race) as it does with sexuality or fear of gay individuals. This is a *transformation* in gender and sexual inequality. Indeed, many students expressed, in earnest, that they would never direct "fag" maliciously at boys and young men identifying as gay. Rather, Pascoe argued that these boys' homophobia is best understood as a casual form of gender policing wherein they rely on and reproduce systems of gender and sexual inequality in interactions as a part of interactionally constructing their own gender identities vis-à-vis those of others (both young men and women) around them.

Bridges's participants too exhibit a transformation in masculinity. Historically, few heterosexual men have sought recognition as heterosexual men by associating themselves with gay culture. Yet this is precisely what Bridges's participants are doing. A superficial reading of these men's behavior might situate them as completely at odds with Pascoe's participants. Indeed, men in the group would have never used the term "fag" in any way other than to critique its use. Many men in the group used the term "the 'F' word" to refer to the epithet because many felt it was too offensive to say. At a more general level, just like Pascoe's participants, these men are attempting to demonstrate masculinity—attempting to prove they were "the right kind of man." It is a practical discourse enabling these men to gain symbolic distance from some of the more odious and publicly challenged elements of hegemonic masculinities. So, whereas Pascoe's respondents seem to be engaging in masculinity practices that might look familiar—homophobic and heterosexist behaviors—Bridges's respondents' identification with minority sexual identity practices and culture can obscure their participation in similar practices. The way in which men engage in masculinity projects and the role of homophobia in those projects is not always straightforward. This all suggests that emergent forms of masculinity and homophobia are best analyzed in terms of *both* their forms and their consequences. Whereas a great deal of research asks whether masculine practices are either challenging or reproducing inequality, our research illustrates that it is possible for gender and sexual inequality to be simultaneously challenged *and* reproduced.

REFERENCES

Arxer, Steven L. 2011. "Hybrid Masculine Power: Reconceptualizing the Relationship between Homosociality and Hegemonic Masculinity." *Humanity & Society* 35 (4): 390–422.

Bridges, Tristan. 2010. "Men Just Weren't Made to Do This: Performances of Drag at 'Walk a Mile in Her Shoes' Marches." *Gender & Society* 24 (1): 5–30.

Bridges, Tristan. 2014. "A Very 'Gay' Straight?: Hybrid Masculinities, Sexual Aesthetics, and the Changing Relationship between Masculinity and Homophobia." *Gender & Society* 28 (1): 58–82.

Bridges, Tristan, and C. J. Pascoe. 2014. "Hybrid Masculinities: New Directions in the Sociology of Men and Masculinities." *Sociology Compass* 8 (3): 246–258.

Brown, Joshua R. 2011. "No Homo." *Journal of Homosexuality* 58 (3): 299–314.

Brown, Tyler L., and Kevin G. Alderson. 2010. "Sexual Identity and Heterosexual Male Students' Usage of Homosexual Insults: An Exploratory Study." *Canadian Journal of Human Sexuality* 19 (1/2): 27–42.

Bryant, Karl, and Salvador Vidal-Ortiz. 2008. "Introduction to Retheorizing Homophobias." *Sexualities* 11 (4): 387–396.

Burn, Shawn Meghan. 2000. "Heterosexuals' Use of 'Fag' and 'Queer' to Deride One Another." *Journal of Homosexuality* 40 (2): 1–11.

Connell, Raewyn. 1992. "A Very Straight Gay: Masculinity, Homosexual Experience, and the Dynamics of Gender." *American Sociological Review* 57 (6): 735–751.

Connell, Raewyn. 1995. *Masculinities.* Berkeley: University of California Press.

Corbett, Ken. 2001. "Faggot = Loser." *Studies in Gender and Sexuality* 2 (1): 3–28.

Demetriou, Demetrakis. 2001. "Connell's Concept of Hegemonic Masculinity: A Critique." *Theory and Society* 30 (3): 337–61.

Donovan, Brian. 1998. "Political Consequences of Private Authority: Promise Keepers and the Transformation of Hegemonic Masculinity." *Theory and Society* 27 (6): 817–843.

Fair, Brian. 2011. "Constructing Masculinity through Penetration Discourse: The Intersection of Misogyny and Homophobia in High School Wrestling." *Men and Masculinities* 14 (4): 491–504.

Falomir-Pichastor, Juan Manuel, and Gabriel Mugny. 2009. "'I'm Not Gay . . . I'm a Real Man!': Heterosexual Men's Gender Self-Esteem and Sexual Prejudice." *Personality and Social Psychology Bulletin* 35 (9): 1233–43.

Heath, Melanie. 2003. "Soft-Boiled Masculinity: Renegotiating Gender and Racial Ideologies in the Promise Keepers Movement." *Gender & Society* 17 (3): 423–44.

Henley, Nancy. 1977. *Body Politics: Sex, Power and Nonverbal Communication.* New York: Prentice Hall.

Herek, Gregory M. 1986. "On Heterosexual Masculinity: Some Psychical Consequences of the Social Construction of Gender and Sexuality." *American Behavioral Scientist* 29 (5): 563–77.

Herek, Gregory M. 2002. "Gender Gaps in Public Opinion about Lesbians and Gay Men." *Public Opinion Quarterly* 66 (1): 40–66.

Herek, Gregory M. 2004. "Beyond 'Homophobia': Thinking about Sexual Prejudice and Stigma in the Twenty-First Century." *Sexuality Research & Social Policy* 1 (2): 6–24.

Johnson, Allan. 2005. *The Gender Knot*, rev. and updated ed. Philadelphia: Temple University Press.

Kehily, Mary Jane, and Anoop Nayak. 1997. "'Lads and Laughter': Humour and the Production of Heterosexual Hierarchies." *Gender and Education* 9 (1): 69–88.

Kehler, Michael D. 2007. "Hallway Fears and High School Friendships: The Complications of Young Men (Re)Negotiating Heterosexualized Identities." *Discourse: Studies in the Cultural Politics of Education* 28 (2): 259–77.

Keiller, Scott W. 2010. "Masculine Norms as Correlates of Heterosexual Men's Attitudes Toward Gay Men and Lesbian Women." *Psychology of Men & Masculinity* 11 (1): 38–52.

Kimmel, Michael. 1994. "Masculinity as Homophobia." In *Theorizing Masculinities*, edited by Harry Brod and Michael Kaufman, 119–41. Thousand Oaks, CA: Sage.

Levy, Nathaniel, Sandra Cortesi, Urs Gasser, Edward Crowley, Meredith Beaton, June Casey, and Caroline Nolan. 2012. *Bullying in a Networked Era: A Literature Review*. SSRN Scholarly Paper ID 2146877. Rochester, NY: Social Science Research Network. http://papers.ssrn.com/abstract=2146877/.

Lyman, Peter. 1987. "The Fraternal Bond as a Joking Relationship: A Case Study of the Role of Sexist Jokes in Male Group Bonding." In *Changing Men: New Directions in Research on Men and Masculinity*, edited by Michael Kimmel, 148–63. Newbury Park, CA: Sage.

Messner, Michael. 1993. "'Changing Men' and Feminist Politics in the United States." *Theory and Society* 22 (5): 723–37.

Messner, Michael A. 2007. "The Masculinity of the Governator: Muscle and Compassion in American Politics." *Gender & Society* 21 (4): 461–80.

Moskowitz, David A., Gerulf Rieger, and Michael E. Roloff. 2010. "Heterosexual Attitudes Toward Same-Sex Marriage." *Journal of Homosexuality* 57 (2): 325–36.

Pascoe, C. J. 2005. "'Dude, You're a Fag': Adolescent Masculinity and the Fag Discourse." *Sexualities* 8 (3): 329–46.

Pascoe, C. J. 2007. *"Dude, You're a Fag": Masculinity and Sexuality in High School*. Berkeley: University of California Press.

Pascoe, C. J. 2013. "Notes on a Sociology of Bullying: Young Men's Homophobia as Gender Socialization." *QED: A Journal in GLBTQ Worldmaking* 1: 87–103.

Plummer, Kenneth. 1981. *The Making of the Modern Homosexual*. London: Hutchinson.

Poteat, V. Paul, Michael S. Kimmel, and Riki Wilchins. 2010. "The Moderating Effects of Support for Violence: Beliefs on Masculine Norms, Aggression, and Homophobic Behavior During Adolescence." *Journal of Research on Adolescence* 21 (2): 434–47.

Poteat, V. Paul, and Ian Rivers. 2010. "The Use of Homophobic Language across Bullying Roles during Adolescence." *Journal of Applied Developmental Psychology* 31 (2): 166–72.

Ronen, Shelly. 2010. "Grinding on the Dance Floor: Gendered Scripts and Sexualized Dancing at College Parties." *Gender & Society* 24 (3): 355–77.

Seidman, Steven. 2002. *Beyond the Closet: The Transformation of Gay and Lesbian Life*. New York: Routledge.

Stein, Arlene. 2005. "Make Room for Daddy: Anxious Masculinity and Emergent Homophobias in Neopatriarchal Politics." *Gender & Society* 19 (5): 601–20.

Thurlow, Crispin. 2001. "Naming the 'Outsider Within': Homophobic Pejoratives and the Verbal Abuse of Lesbian, Gay and Bisexual High-School Pupils." *Journal of Adolescence* 24 (1): 25–38.

Wilchins, Riki. 2003. "Do You Believe in Fairies?" *The Advocate*, February 4.

Willer, Robb, Christabel L. Rogalin, Bridget Conlon, and Michael T. Wojnowicz. 2013. "Overdoing Gender: A Test of the Masculine Overcompensation Thesis." *American Journal of Sociology* 118 (4): 980–1022.

NOTES

1. See also Messner (1993, 2007), Donovan (1998), Demetriou (2001), Heath (2003), Stein (2005), Bridges (2014), and Bridges and Pascoe (2014) on related points.
2. http://la.indymedia.org/news/2001/10/12221.php/.
3. http://www.nydailynews.com/sports/baseball/yankees/bleacher-creatures-agree-stop-gay-chant-ymca-song-yankee-stadium-article-1.192948/.
4. http://nbclatino.com/2012/12/03/controversy-after-principal-makes-two-boys-hold-hands-in-public-after-fight/.
5. http://www.pewforum.org/2014/09/24/graphics-slideshow-changing-attitudes-on-gay-marriage/.
6. http://www.gallup.com/poll/135764/americans-acceptance-gay-relations-crosses-threshold.aspx/.
7. See the special issue of *Sexualities* 2008 11 (4) on "Retheorizing Homophobias" for more on this line of theorizing.

8. Humor and social protest are not incompatible. Yet, as Bridges's (2010) study of men's (mis)behavior in "Walk a Mile in Her Shoes" marches indicates, the uses of humor in social protest merit critical attention and reflection.

9. "Grinding" has been more systematically studied as well. For instance, Ronen's (2010) study of the gendered dynamics of grinding addresses the ways that the practice reproduces gendered interactions that privilege men's pleasure and sexual agency and afford them higher status than women.

10. See Bridges and Pascoe (2014) for a more thorough analysis of the diverse ways research has found that young, straight, white men are engaged in a diversity of practices we identify as "discursive distancing."

11. We connect the emergent homophobias addressed here with other emergent configurations of masculinity largely enacted by young, straight, white men with a larger issue in a separate article, referring to them as "hybrid masculinities" (see Bridges and Pascoe 2014). Much of the research on related social practices by contemporary young, white, heterosexual men has found that these changes more often shore up existing systems of power and inequality in new ways rather than dismantling them.

CONCLUSION

HISTORICIZING, MULTIPLYING, NAVIGATING, AND DISLOCATING
Looking to the Future of Gender Theory

In 2014, University of Missouri college football player Michael Sam made national head-lines when he came out, publicly identifying as gay. Activists and commentators praised the (generally) positive response from the public to his announcement. Some claimed that Sam's decision heralded a new day in sports—a day characterized by less homophobia or rigid expectations associated with toxic conceptualizations of masculinity. Several months after his announcement, cameras rolled during the much-anticipated National Football League (NFL) draft as Sam—accompanied by his boyfriend—received a call from the St. Louis Rams.[1] For the first time in history, an openly gay male player who came out *before* his involvement in the NFL was selected to play on an NFL team. To be sure, football is not just *any* sport. It is arguably among the *most* masculine of professional sports—the one most resistant to infiltration by women, the one exempted from Title IX requirements at the college level, and the one for which there is really no women's equivalent (unless one were to consider the largely misogynistic Lingerie Football League).

Sam's story, however, does not end with the draft pick itself. As Sam received the news, he promptly turned to embrace his boyfriend, celebrating his selection with a joyful kiss—a kiss that was televised nationwide. It hardly bears mentioning that men kissing is not a typical ESPN topic. This kiss, however, received extensive airtime on that particular day and over the days that followed. In some ways, the kiss rendered Sam's sexuality more real—at least for viewers. It is one thing for a player to identify as gay and let that identity remain largely theoretical in the mind of the observer. It is another to enact that identity, to show an audience what it actually looks like when a man (who defies homophobic ste-reotypes of gay men) lovingly embraces another man. In other words, Sam did not just identify as gay; he *did* gayness on national television.

Sam's selection and celebratory kiss prompted a landslide of reactions. Many were positive. President Obama congratulated Sam, as did his new teammates. The hashtag "#SamIAm" proliferated on all manner of social media as people proclaimed support and, for some, recognized Michael Sam as emblematic of their own struggles. Others, however,

425

responded with threats of boycotts and claims of damage to children and described the kiss as "horrible," "disgusting," "throwing it [homosexuality] in our faces," and more. Such responses indicate that it is one thing for a player to identify as gay, but clearly quite another to have men's same-sex eroticism displayed in any fashion.

Of course, players inducted into the NFL routinely kiss their spouses and partners when they receive the good news. Such embraces may often elicit public commentary about the "hotness" of the women *most* newly drafted NFL players are kissing, rather than disgust or fear. These kisses—and Sam's was no different in this way—are not passionate, sexual embraces; they are intimate, celebratory rituals. However, Sam's participation in this ritual seems to have tested the limits of American acceptance around issues of gender and sexuality (for more on these limits, see Doan et al. 2014). By not only identifying as gay, but also living his identity unapologetically (and in seeming contrast to myriad stereotypes of gay men as effeminate, unathletic, or white), we learned something about the distinction between sexual equality and what might better be understood as "sexual tolerance" (e.g., Seidman 2002). That kiss? The kiss was simply too much.

Sam's story illustrates the changing, contested, and conflicting understandings, interpretations, identifications, and practices of masculinity covered in this book. Indeed, the challenges illustrated in the twin reactions to Michael Sam's story are a powerful demonstration of just how complex gender identities and inequalities are to analyze. In some ways, Michael Sam's accomplishment is emblematic of incredible change (two men kissing on national television!). In other ways, however, the kiss and responses to it are better understood as continuity. That is, other than his sexual identity, for instance, Sam does not challenge heteronormative assumptions surrounding men or masculinity. Indeed, in many ways, Michael Sam is a contemporary masculine icon not so different from many others.

Sam's story provides us a way to think through the varied explorations of masculinity in this book and the complex ways gender identities and inequality are entangled. Sam's entry into the NFL is one small illustration of some powerful recent changes in gender and inequality in the United States. But to tell this story as *only* one of "progress" ignores the ways that the same systems of inequality that might have kept Sam out of the NFL a decade ago have not been eradicated. It is probably more accurate to say that they have changed form (as systems of inequality are wont to do). According to news reports, Sam's teammates seemed largely supportive of him. But his entry into the NFL was also mediated by those same systems of power and inequality that might have historically kept men who share his sexual identity out of the league altogether—a point dramatically made by the public reaction to the kiss he shared with his partner to celebrate his success in the draft.

Michael Sam's story illustrates intersections of power, inequality, race, class, violence, sexuality, and history. Sam's experience sheds light on the assumptions, strengths, and weaknesses of each of the four trajectories of exploring masculinities outlined in this book. Indeed, these different approaches would analyze the Michael Sam story in different ways, stressing different issues. This does not mean that one of these four approaches has the most "true" story. Rather, by emphasizing different aspects and relying on different theoretical frameworks, it is more accurate to say that the story of what a case like Michael Sam "means" can be told in more than one way. In other words, Michael Sam's struggles do not mean only one thing. Deciding what they mean requires that we consider how we ought to analyze that question in the first place. Below, we briefly consider how each of the exploratory trajectories we have outlined in this text might seek to make sense of Michael Sam.

HISTORICIZING: FROM "I AM A MAN" TO "#SAMIAM"

In the United States, the term "boy" has a difficult history within U.S. race relations. The term "boy" was used pejoratively by whites toward slaves and men of color in the United States. It was a small, but symbolic insult that stood in for a system of race relations whereby slaves and men of color were thought to be somehow "less than men" and, as such, not fully human. In the 1700s, abolitionists began to use the catchphrase, "Am I not a man and a brother?" to publicly challenge slavery and in promotion of justice and humanity for all.[2] On February 11, 1968, this history was resurrected during the Memphis Sanitation Strike in Tennessee. A total of 1,300 black sanitation workers declared their working conditions inhumane and walked off the job in protest. The strike that ensued became an issue around which many black people in Memphis collectively saw their struggle for equality—many of whom were living in poverty. The strike gained national attention. Indeed, Martin Luther King, Jr. went to Memphis to speak in March of 1968. The most striking visual from the strike that still resonates with viewers today involved pictures of men protesting, marching together, and holding signs that read "I Am a Man!" recalling abolitionist efforts two centuries earlier. "I Am a Man!" has become a rallying cry for civil rights movements asserting that all people be treated equally—a gendered rallying cry to be sure.

To understand the significance of Michael Sam utilizing a historicizing masculinities framework, we must historically situate Sam's struggle. Black men in the United States have a history of being understood as both emblematic of certain elements of masculinity and at the same time marginalized from the category altogether. The hashtag #SamIAm is a part of this difficult past.[3] Indeed, not unlike the fight Gayle Bederman analyzes in Reading 1 in this volume, Michael Sam's struggle is, simultaneously, about gender, race, class, sexuality, and more. A historicizing masculinities perspective would situate this issue historically, exploring the ways that Michael Sam is symbolic of a larger historical process through which masculinities are produced, contested, reworked, and negotiated.

MULTIPLYING: JUST HOW "HEGEMONIC" IS SAM'S MASCULINITY?

The multiplying masculinities approach emphasizes *relationships* between men and illuminates how these relationships are organized hierarchically. Importantly, this body of literature encourages scholars not to think of *masculinity* in the singular, but of *masculinities* in the plural. That said, this plurality is not neutral. Multiple and varied masculinities are shaped by inequality and power in a way that privileges hegemonic masculinity as a configuration of gender practice. Through attending to the way in which social power is conferred—but not conferred equally—through masculinity, this approach can help explore the ways in which some men benefit from gender inequality while they are simultaneously subordinated by race or class status.

In terms of Michael Sam's experience, this model may point out that Sam was concurrently positioned as enacting configurations of marginalized masculinity (in that he is a man of color) and subordinated masculinity (in that he is a gay man) but also benefited from the patriarchal dividend conferred upon all men (especially because of his participation in a hegemonically masculine enterprise like football). This helps to illustrate the fact that hegemonic masculinity, marginalized masculinity, and subordinated masculinity are configurations of practice—not static "types" of men. Indeed, Michael Sam might be understood within each of these configurations differently. As such, Sam's case also points to some of the limits in the ways that the multiplying masculinities approach is traditionally applied in that such an approach has a hard time reconciling these conflicting forms of masculinity associated with Sam—gay, African American, and athletic.

NAVIGATING: MICHAEL SAM AND THE MATRIX OF DOMINATION

Navigating masculinities approaches respond to some of the theoretical gaps left by the multiplying masculinities line of analysis. They actively embrace the intersectionality that positions Sam at the nexus of varied lines of inequality. He is a gay man of color who actively engages in athletic practices that underscore male dominance and the sexual objectification of women. From a navigating masculinities perspective, all of these identities, practices, and structural positions must be addressed simultaneously. They are not separate lines of scholarly inquiry or inequality—hegemonic, subordinated, and marginalized. Rather they intersect and each cannot be understood without the others. Indeed, hegemonic masculinity only exists through being propped up by marginalized and subordinated masculinities and emphasized femininity. This approach moves away from typologies of masculinity to examine the varied lines of inequality that constitute what we think of as "masculinity." How is it, in other words, that Sam's experience as a gay, male, African American athlete both constitutes and challenges masculinity? He represents both continuity and change in gender relations and systems of gender and sexual inequality. In this model, the category of masculinity itself is raced, classed, sexualized, gendered, and more. As such, what is considered masculine capital in one field may not be understood in precisely the same way in another.

DISLOCATING: DID MICHAEL SAM INADVERTENTLY EMASCULATE FOOTBALL?

A dislocating masculinities approach may widen the very lens with which one approaches a particular object of study. That is, rather than looking at Sam himself, a dislocating analysis may look at the sexualized environment of football itself—the context in which Sam is evaluated as masculine (or not). A dislocating approach emphasizes discursive constructions of reality in which gendered and sexualized meanings are embedded. We might begin here by examining how notions of heterosexuality and homoeroticism actually constitute the athletic field. Indeed, what may have been so upsetting about the Sam episode for some respondents was that he made explicit the implicit homoeroticism that is more often actively ignored in sports. That is, when same-sex touching and intimacies are contained in rule-bound heteronormative environments (such as sporting events), they are "safe." What Sam did, however, was to allow these sorts of interactions to escape the boundaries imposed by those rules. The same-sex touching so common on the athletic field (think of celebratory butt pats and full-body hugs) depends upon this containment. For this type of touching to escape a rule-bound environment calls into question the assumed heterosexuality of the players that allows this touching in the first place. As such, it can threaten to unravel the basis of sport itself—the containment of same-sex desire. A dislocating approach would use this discursive analysis to reveal the instability of the heteronormative framings of sport and show that the Sam case simply reveals the fragility of this framing and the contradictions therein.

LOOKING FORWARD

In the end, each of these separate lines of exploration is best understood as what sociologists refer to as an "ideal type." None is fully discrete from the others. Rather, each represents a genre of thinking about masculinity (and there is bound to be overlap). The goal of this text (and the previous exercise) is not to demonstrate that a particular approach is strongest, but to show the strengths of each and how each may answer a different set of questions about a given social phenomenon. This book offers a new way of making sense of how we make decisions about which trajectory of exploration best suits the issue with which we are concerned (and whether it might be possible to look at something from more than one perspective). As we demonstrate in this text, much is gained by widening the scope of what qualifies as "masculinities" scholarship.

The desire to organize these approaches and research really emerged out of necessity. Historically, different theoretical approaches have emerged to explain gender inequality: radical feminism, socialist feminism, liberal feminism, psychoanalytic feminism, and multiracial feminism as well as intersectional, structuralist, interactionist, and poststructuralist approaches (to name a few). Studies of men and masculinity became increasingly separate from this line of theorizing and, up until now, have never cohered into any sort of organized relationship in the way that scholarship on women and gender has. This book attempts to rectify that problem.

Thirty years ago, Tim Carrigan, Raewyn Connell, and John Lee in the seminal article, "A New Sociology of Masculinity" (1985), issued a challenge to scholars to bring theorizing about masculinity more closely in line with feminist theorizing. The language used to describe the two realms of study ("gender" versus "masculinity"), however, reveals the lack of response to this challenge. Indeed, it highlights the divergence and differential foci of the fields themselves. Men have masculinity, whereas women have gender. Gender scholars have never been so interested in femininity or femininities as masculinity scholars have in masculinities. In organizing this field by trajectories of exploration, we hope to enable a more explicit discussion of what is lost and gained by a "gender" focus versus a "masculinity" focus. The task of the next generation of scholars may be to bring these two fields into more explicit dialogue.

At present, the field of masculinity studies itself is simultaneously cohering and fracturing. Most evident in terms of its fracture is the breakdown of the hegemonic nature of hegemonic masculinities studies. As this volume has shown, a great deal of scholarly explorations of masculinities no longer take "hegemonic masculinity" as a starting point. When studies do not use Connell's theory (or her conceptualization of hegemonic masculinity) to frame their findings, however, they often are not recognized as a part of "masculinities studies." The field is also growing in directions not illustrated here. For instance, a growing field of scholarship addresses "masculine identity threat" (e.g., Munsch and Willer 2012; Willer et al. 2013). This approach actively measures the ways in which challenges to masculine identity result in negative consequences. Scholarship in this field has the potential to test the claims of some of the theoretical approaches covered in this book.

Although up until now the cannon has been built around a certain form of scholarship, we are hoping that this book will help to critically interrogate the boundaries around "masculinities studies." As we carefully document throughout this text, there is much to learn beyond our existing borders. Appreciating and acknowledging new kinds of dialogue and interdisciplinary veins of scholarship allow us to more fully explore masculinities, from identities and inequality to continuities and change.

REFERENCES

Carrigan, Tim, Raewyn Connell, and John Lee. 1985. "Toward a New Sociology of Masculinity." *Theory and Society* 14 (5): 551–604.

Doan, Long, Annalise Loehr, and Lisa R. Miller. 2014. "Formal Rights and Informal Privileges for Same-Sex Couples: Evidence from a National Survey Experiment." *American Sociological Review* 96 (6): 1172–95.

Munsch, Christin L., and Robb Willer. 2012. "The Role of Gender Identity Threat in Perceptions of Date Rape and Sexual Coercion." *Violence against Women* 18: 1125–46.

Seidman, Steven. 2002. *Beyond the Closet: The Transformation of Gay and Lesbian Life*. New York and London: Routledge.

Seuss, Dr. 1960. *Green Eggs and Ham*. New York: Random House.

Willer, Rob, Christabel L. Rogalin, Bridget Conlon, and Michael T. Wojnowicz. 2013. "Overdoing Gender: A Test of the Masculine Overcompensation Thesis." *American Journal of Sociology* 118 (4): 980–1022.

NOTES

1. Sam was initially drafted by the Rams in the seventh round of the 2014 NFL draft. At that point, Sam was the first openly gay player to be drafted in the NFL. Postdraft, the Rams did not elect to keep Sam and he was waived in the final round of cuts by the Rams in August of 2014. At that point, Sam was picked up by the Dallas Cowboys as a player on their practice squad. But on October 21, 2014, Sam was also cut from the Cowboys.

2. Sojourner Truth's "Ain't I a Woman" speech delivered at the Women's Convention in Akron, Ohio, in 1851 was connected with similar abolitionist discourses throughout U.S. history regarding citizenship and human rights. Truth symbolically labeled the abolitionist discourse as gendered—as a strategic discourse that relied on masculinity to make claims about civil rights and human dignity.

3. The hashtag may have been #SamIAm rather than #IAmSam because the latter was a hashtag for a movie starring Sean Penn. And some people were using #IAmSam as well. But, #SamIAm also achieves cultural currency as one of the opening lines in Dr. Seuss's *Green Eggs and Ham* (1960). This is significant because Dr. Seuss is a children's book author and illustrator with whom people all around the world are familiar. Thus, the hashtag might be read as a collective suggestion that Michael Sam's struggle ought to achieve similar cultural relevance.